Computer Communications and Netw

Series editor
A.J. Sammes
Centre for Forensic Computing
Cranfield University, Shrivenham Campus
Swindon, UK

The **Computer Communications and Networks** series is a range of textbooks, monographs and handbooks. It sets out to provide students, researchers, and nonspecialists alike with a sure grounding in current knowledge, together with comprehensible access to the latest developments in computer communications and networking.

Emphasis is placed on clear and explanatory styles that support a tutorial approach, so that even the most complex of topics is presented in a lucid and intelligible manner.

More information about this series at http://www.springer.com/series/4198

Joseph Migga Kizza

Guide to Computer Network Security

Fourth Edition

 Springer

Joseph Migga Kizza
University of Tennessee
Chattanooga, TN, USA

ISSN 1617-7975   ISSN 2197-8433   (electronic)
Computer Communications and Networks
ISBN 978-3-319-85706-0   ISBN 978-3-319-55606-2   (eBook)
DOI 10.1007/978-3-319-55606-2

This Springer imprint is published by Springer Nature
The registered company is Springer International Publishing AG
The registered company address is: Gewerbestrasse 11, 6330 Cham, Switzerland

Preface

It has been barely 3 years since our third edition came out, and we are again in need of a new and improved fourth edition. This quick turnaround of editions of a successful book like this is indicative of the rapidly changing technology landscape. We are excited by our growing number of users, and we are indeed indebted to them by continuously keeping a living promise we first made to our readers in the very first edition of maintaining the book materials as up to date as possible. In line with this promise, we have now embarked on this fourth edition. Since our first edition, we have been bringing to our growing ranks of users not only the concept of a changing computer network but also the correspondingly evolving repertoire of security tools, algorithms, and best practices, all mandated by the rapidly changing technology. The traditional computer network we introduced in the first edition with its nicely "demarcated" and heavily defended perimeter wall and well-guarded access points has been going into a transformation as a result of new technologies. Changes have occurred, as we pointed out in both the second and third editions, from within and outside the network, at the server, and most importantly at the boundaries resulting into a *virtualized and elastic network*, with rapid extensions at will, to meet the growing needs of users. These changes are driven by new technological developments and changing user demands and security needs. New developments in system resource virtualization, the evolving cloud computing models, and a growing and unpredictable mobile computing technology are creating new platforms that demand new extensions, usually on the fly and at will, thus making security of the traditional computer network more complex. Also, the rapidly emerging computing technology and the evolving and expanding reach of wireless technologies, broadening the last mile, are rapidly destroying the traditional computer network, the enterprise network, as mobile and home devices are slowly becoming essential parts of the enterprise and at the same time remaining in their traditional public commons, thus creating unpredictable and undefendable enterprise and home networks. When you think of a small mobile device now able to connect to a private enterprise network under BYOD policies and the same device able to be used as a home network device and that at the same time remains connected to networks in public commons, you start to get an image of the *anywhere and everywhere* computing network, a global sprawl of networks within networks, and indeed networks on demand. The ubiquitous nature of these *new* computing networks is creating new and uncharted territories with security night-mare quagmire. What is more worrying is that along with the sprawl, we are getting all types of characters joining amass in the new but rapidly changing technological "ecosystem," for the lack of a better word.

For these reasons, we need to remain vigilant with better, if not advanced, computer and information security protocols and best practices because the fre-quency of computing and mobile systems attacks and the vulnerability of these systems will likely not abet; rather, they are likely to increase. More efforts in developing adaptive and scalable security tools, protocols, and best practices and massive awareness, therefore, are needed to meet this growing challenge and bring the public to a level where they can be active and safe participants in the brave new world of computing.

This guide is a comprehensive volume touching not only on every major topic in computing and information security and assurance but also has gone beyond the security of computer networks as we used to know them, to embrace new and more agile mobile systems and new online social networks that are interweaving into our everyday fabric, if not already, and creating an overgrowing ecosystem of digital and associated social networks. We bring into our ongoing discussion on computer network security a broader view of the new ever-growing ecosystem of fixed, wireless, mobile, and online social networks. As with previous editions, it is intended to bring massive security awareness and education to the security realities of our time, a time when billions of people from the remotest place on earth to the most cosmopolitan world cities are using the smartest, smallest, and more powerful mobile devices loaded with the most fascinating and worrisome functionalities ever known to interconnect via a mesh of elastic computing networks in this ecosystem. We highlight security and privacy issues and concerns in public commons and private bedrooms as users around the globe intersect in this growing digital and social network ecosystem.

The volume is venturing into and exposing all sorts of known security problems, vulnerabilities, and dangers likely to be encountered by the users of these devices. In its own way, it is a pathfinder as it initiates a conversation toward developing better tools, algorithms, protocols, and best practices that will enhance the security of systems in the public commons, private and enterprise offices, and living rooms and bedrooms where these devices are used. It does this comprehensively in six parts and 26 chapters. Part I gives the reader an understanding of the working of and the security situation of the traditional computer networks. Part II builds on this knowledge and exposes the reader to the prevailing security situation based on a constant security threat. It surveys several security threats. Part III, the largest, forms the core of the guide and presents to the reader most of the tools, algorithms, best practices, and solutions that are currently in use. Part IV goes beyond the traditional computer network as we used to know it to cover new systems and technologies that have seamlessly and stealthily extended the boundaries of the traditional computer network. Systems and other emerging technologies including virtualization, cloud computing, and mobile systems are introduced and discussed. A new Part V ventures into wireless and other technologies creeping into the last mile creating a new security quagmire in the home computing environment and the growing home hotspots. Part VI, the last part, consists of projects.

What Is New in This Edition

There have been considerable changes in the contents of the book to bring it in line with the new developments we discussed above. In almost every chapter, new content has been added, and we have eliminated what looked as outdated and what seem to be repeated materials. Because of the required bedrock content in computer network theory and computer network security fundamentals essential to understand overall content and to gain from the book, the content in some chapters had not changed a great deal since the first edition. But of more interest to our readers and in recognition of the rapidly changing computer network ecosystem, a new chapter on the *Internet of Things (IoT)* has been added. The addition of this chapter has been driven by a number of burning security issues the advent of IoT has brought about to such an extent that some are calling it the old *Wild West* of security, a *security quagmire* that so far does not respect current and standard security protocols and best practices and whose security protocols are yet to be developed and best practices formalized. Throughout the text, the discussion is candid, intended to ignite students' interest and participation in class discussions of the issues and beyond.

Audience

As usual, in summary, the guide attempts to achieve the following objectives:

- Educate the public about computer security in the traditional computer network.
- Educate the public about the evolving computing ecosystem created by the eroding boundaries between the enterprise network, the home network, and the rapidly growing public commons-based social networks, all extending the functionalities of the traditional computer network.
- Alert the public to the magnitude of the vulnerabilities, weaknesses, and loopholes inherent in the traditional computer network and now resident in the new computing ecosystem.
- Bring to the public attention effective security tools, solutions and best practice, expert opinions on those solutions, and the possibility of ad hoc solutions.
- Look at the roles legislation, regulation, and enforcement play in securing the new computing ecosystem.
- Finally, initiate a debate on developing effective and comprehensive security algorithms, protocols, and best practices for new computing ecosystem.

Since the guide covers a wide variety of security topics, tools, algorithms, solutions, and best practices, it is intended to be both a teaching and a reference toolbox for those interested in learning about the security of the evolving computing ecosystem. Learn about available techniques to prevent attacks on these systems. The in-depth and thorough discussion and analysis of most of the security issues of the traditional computer network and the extending technologies and systems, together with the discussion of security algorithms and solutions given, make the guide a unique reference source of ideas for computer network and data security personnel, network security policy makers, and those reading for leisure. In addition, the guide provokes the reader by raising valid legislative, legal, social, technical, and ethical security issues, including the increasingly diminishing line between individual privacy and the need for collective and individual security in the new computing ecosystem.

The guide targets college students in computer science, information science, technology studies, library sciences, and engineering and to a lesser extent students in arts and sciences who are interested in information technology. In addition, students in information management sciences will find the guide particularly helpful. Practitioners, especially those working in data- and information-intensive areas, will likewise find the guide a good reference source. It will also be valuable to those interested in any aspect of information security and assurance and those simply wanting to become cyberspace literates.

Book Resources

There are two types of exercises at the end of each chapter: easy and quickly workable exercises whose responses can be easily spotted from the proceeding text and more thought-provoking advanced exercises whose responses may require research outside the content of this book. Also Chap. 25 is devoted to lab exercises. There are three types of lab exercises: weekly and biweekly assignments that can be done easily with either reading or using readily available software and hardware tools; slightly harder semester-long projects that may require extensive time, collaboration, and some research to finish them successfully; and hard open research projects that require a lot of thinking, take a lot of time, and require extensive research. Links are provided below for cryptographic and mobile security hands-on projects from two successful National Science Foundation (NSF)-funded workshops at the author's university:

- Teaching Cryptography Using Hands-On Labs and Case Studies—http://web2. utc.edu/~djy471/cryptography/crypto.htm
- Capacity Building Through Curriculum and Faculty Development on Mobile Security—http://www.utc.edu/faculty/li-yang/mobilesecurity.php

We have tried as much as possible, throughout the guide, to use open-source software tools. This has two consequences to it: one, it makes the guide affordable keeping in mind the escalating proprietary software prices, and two, it makes the content and related software tools last longer because the content and corresponding exercises and labs are not based on one particular proprietary software tool that can go out anytime.

Instructor Support Materials

As you consider using this book, you may need to know that we have developed materials to help you with your course. The help materials for both instructors and students cover the following areas:

- *Syllabus.* There is a suggested syllabus for the instructor, now part of the text.
- *Instructor PowerPoint slides.* These are detailed enough to help the instructor, especially those teaching the course for the first time.
- Answers to selected exercises at the end of each chapter.
- *Laboratory.* Since network security is a hands-on course, students need to spend a considerable amount of time on scheduled laboratory exercises. The last chapter of the book contains several laboratory exercises and projects. The book resource center contains several more and updates. Also as we stated above, links are also included at the author's Web site for cryptographic hands-on projects from two successful National Science Foundation (NSF)-funded workshops at the author's university.

These materials can be found at the publisher's Web site at http://www.springer. com/book/9783319556055 and at the author's Web site at http://www.utc.edu/ Faculty/Joseph-Kizza/.

Chattanooga, TN, USA   Joseph Migga Kizza
June, 2017

Contents

Part I

Introduction to Traditional Computer Network Security

Computer Network Fundamentals

1

1.1 Introduction

The basic ideas in all types of communication are that there must be three ingredients for the communication to be effective. First, there must be two entities, dubbed a sender and a receiver. These two must have something they need to share. Second, there must be a medium through which the sharable item is channeled. This is the transmission medium. Finally, there must be an agreed-on set of communication rules or protocols. These three apply to every category or structure of communication.

In this chapter, we will focus on these three components in a computer network. But what is a computer network? The reader should be aware that our use of a phrase *computer network*, from now on, will refer to the traditional computer network. A computer network is a distributed system consisting of loosely coupled computers and other devices. Any two of these devices, which we will from now on refer to as *network elements* or *transmitting elements* without loss of generality, can communicate with each other through a communication medium. In order for these connected devices to be considered a communicating network, there must be a set of communicating rules or protocols each device in the network must follow to communicate with another device in the network. The resulting combination consisting of hardware and software is a computer communication network or computer network in short. Figure 1.1 shows a computer network.

The hardware component is made of network elements consisting of a collection of nodes that include the end systems commonly called hosts and intermediate switching elements that include hubs, bridges, routers, and gateways that, without loss of generality, we will call network elements.

Network elements may own resources individually, that is, locally or globally. Network software consists of all application programs and network protocols that are used to synchronize, coordinate, and bring about the sharing and exchange of data among the network elements. Network software also makes the sharing of expensive resources in the network possible. Network elements, network software,

© Springer International Publishing AG 2017

J.M. Kizza, *Guide to Computer Network Security*, Computer Communications and Networks, DOI 10.1007/978-3-319-55606-2_1

Fig. 1.1 A computer network

and users all work together so that individual users can exchange messages and share resources on other systems that are not readily available locally. The network elements, together with their resources, may be of diverse hardware technologies, and the software may be as different as possible, but the whole combination must work together in unison.

Internetworking technology enables multiple, diverse underlying hardware technologies and different software regimes to interconnect heterogeneous networks and bring them to communicate smoothly. The smooth working of any computer communication network is achieved through the low-level mechanisms provided by the network elements and high-level communication facilities provided by the software running on the communicating elements. Before we discuss the working of these networks, let us first look at the different types of networks.

1.2   Computer Network Models

There are several configuration models that form a computer network. The most common of these are the centralized and distributed models. In a centralized model, several computers and devices are interconnected and can talk to each other. However, there is only one central computer, called the master, through which all correspondence must take place. Dependent computers, called surrogates, may have reduced local resources, such as memory, and sharable global resources are controlled by the master at the center. Unlike the centralized model, however, the distributed network consists of loosely coupled computers interconnected by a communication network consisting of connecting elements and communication channels. The computers themselves may own their resources locally or may request resources from a remote computer. These computers are known by a string of names, including host, client, or node. If a host has resources that other hosts need, then that host is known as a server. Communication and sharing of resources are not controlled by the central computer but are arranged between any two communicating elements in the network. Figures 1.2 and 1.3 show a centralized network model and a distributed network model, respectively.

Fig. 1.2 A centralized
network model

Fig. 1.3 A distributed
network model

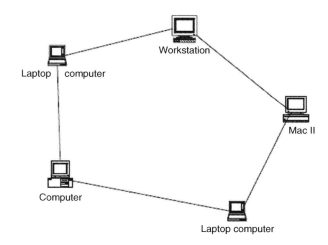

1.3   Computer Network Types

Computer networks come in different sizes. Each network is a cluster of network
elements and their resources. The size of the cluster determines the network type.
There are, in general, two main network types: the local area network (LAN) and
wide area network (WAN).

1.3.1   Local Area Networks (LANs)

A computer network with two or more computers or clusters of network and their
resources connected by a communication medium sharing communication
protocols and confined in a small geographic area, such as a building floor, a
building, or a few adjacent buildings, is called a local area network (LAN). The
advantage of a LAN is that all network elements are close together so the communication links maintain a higher speed of data movement. Also, because of the
proximity of the communicating elements, high-cost and high-quality

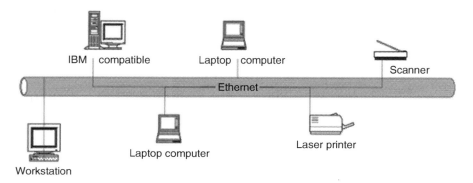

Fig. 1.4 A LAN

communicating elements can be used to deliver better service and high reliability. Figure 1.4 shows a LAN.

1.3.2   Wide Area Networks (WANs)

A wide area network (WAN), on the other hand, is a network made up of one or more clusters of network elements and their resources, but instead of being confined to a small area, the elements of the clusters or the clusters themselves are scattered over a wide geographic area as in a region of a country or across the whole country, several countries, or the entire globe like the Internet, for example. Some advantages of a WAN include distributing services to a wider community and availability of a wide array of both hardware and software resources that may not be available in a LAN. However, because of the large geographic areas covered by WANs, communication media are slow and often unreliable. Figure 1.5 shows a WAN.

1.3.3   Metropolitan Area Networks (MANs)

Between the LAN and WAN, there is also a middle network called the metropolitan area network (MAN) because it covers a slightly wider area than the LAN but not so wide to be considered a WAN. Civic networks that cover a city or part of a city are a good example of a MAN. MANs are rarely talked about because they are quiet often overshadowed by cousin LAN to the left and cousin WAN to the right.

1.4   Data Communication Media Technology

The performance of a network type depends greatly on the transmission technology and media used in the network. Let us look at these two.

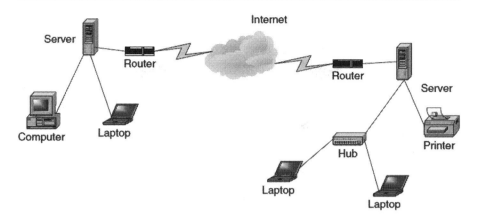

Fig. 1.5 A WAN

1.4.1   Transmission Technology

The media through which information has to be transmitted determine the signal to be used. Some media permit only analog signals. Some allow both analog and digital. Therefore, depending on the media type involved and other considerations, the input data can be represented as either *digital* or *analog* signal. In an analog format, data is sent as continuous electromagnetic waves on an interval representing things such as voice and video and propagated over a variety of media that may include copper wires, twisted coaxial pair or cable, fiber optics, or wireless. We will discuss these media soon. In a digital format, on the other hand, data is sent as a digital signal, a sequence of voltage pulses that can be represented as a stream of binary bits. Both analog and digital data can be propagated and many times represented as either analog or digital.

Transmission itself is the propagation and processing of data signals between network elements. The concept of representation of data for transmission, either as analog or digital signal, is called an *encoding scheme*. Encoded data is then transmitted over a suitable transmission medium that connects all network elements. There are two encoding schemes, *analog* and *digital*. Analog encoding propagates analog signals representing analog data such as sound waves and voice data. Digital encoding, on the other hand, propagates digital signals representing either an analog or a digital signal representing digital data of binary streams by two voltage levels. Since our interest in this book is in digital networks, we will focus on the encoding of digital data.

1.4.1.1 Analog Encoding of Digital Data
Recall that digital information is in the form of 1s or 0s. To send this information over some analog medium such as the telephone line, for example, which has limited bandwidth, digital data needs to be encoded using modulation and demodulation to produce analog signals. The encoding uses a continuous oscillating wave,

usually a sine wave, with a constant frequency signal called a *carrier* signal. The carrier has three modulation characteristics: *amplitude, frequency*, and *phase shift*. The scheme then uses a *modem*, a modulation-demodulation pair, to modulate and demodulate the data signal based on any one of the three carrier characteristics or a combination. The resulting wave is between a range of frequencies on both sides of the carrier as shown below [1]:

- *Amplitude* modulation represents each binary value by a different amplitude of the carrier frequency. The absence of or low carrier frequency may represent a 0 and any other frequency then represents a 1. But this is a rather inefficient modulation technique and is therefore used only at low frequencies up to 1200 bps in voice grade lines.
- *Frequency* modulation also represents the two binary values by two different frequencies close to the frequency of the underlying carrier. Higher frequencies represent a 1 and low frequencies represent a 0. The scheme is less susceptible to errors.
- *Phase shift* modulation changes the timing of the carrier wave, shifting the carrier phase to encode the data. A 1 is encoded as a change in phase by 180 degrees and a 0 may be encoded as a 0 change in phase of a carrier signal. This is the most efficient scheme of the three and it can reach a transmission rate of up to 9600 bps.

1.4.1.2 Digital Encoding of Digital Data

In this encoding scheme, which offers the most common and easiest way to transmit digital signals, two binary digits are used to represent two different voltages. Within a computer, these voltages are commonly 0 and 5 volts. Another procedure uses two representation codes: *nonreturn to zero level* (*NRZ-L*), in which negative voltage represents binary one and positive voltage represents binary zero, and *nonreturn to zero, invert on ones* (*NRZ-I*). See Figs. 1.6 and 1.7 for an example of these two codes. In NRZ-L, whenever a 1 occurs, a transition from one voltage level to another is used to signal the information. One problem with NRZ signaling techniques is the requirement of a perfect synchronization between the receiver and transmitter clocks. This is, however, reduced by sending a separate clock signal. There are yet other representations such as the Manchester and differential Manchester, which encode clock information along with the data.

One may wonder why go through the hassle of digital encoding and transmission. There are several advantages over its cousin, analog encoding. These include the following:

- Plummeting costs of digital circuitry
- More efficient integration of voice, video, text, and image
- Reduction of noise and other signal impairment because of the use of repeaters
- Capacity of channels is utilized best with digital techniques
- Better encryption and hence better security than in analog transmission

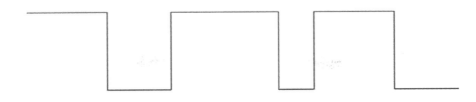

0000000000000001111111111000000000000000000000011111110000000000000000011111111 1

Fig. 1.6 NRZ-L N Nonreturn to zero level representation code

0000000000000001111100000000000000000001111111111111111111111000000000000

Fig. 1.7 NRZ-I Nonreturn to zero, invert on ones representation code

1.4.1.3 Multiplexing of Transmission Signals

Quite often during the transmission of data over a network medium, the volume of transmitted data may far exceed the capacity of the medium. Whenever this happens, it may be possible to make multiple signal carriers share a transmission medium. This is referred to as *multiplexing*. There are two ways in which multiplexing can be achieved: time-division multiplexing (TMD) and frequency-division multiplexing (FDM).

In FDM, all data channels are first converted to analog form. Since a number of signals can be carried on a carrier, each analog signal is then modulated by a separate and different carrier frequency, and this makes it possible to recover during the demultiplexing process. The frequencies are then bundled on the carrier. At the receiving end, the demultiplexer can select the desired carrier signal and use it to extract the data signal for that channel in such a way that the bandwidths do not overlap. FDM has an advantage of supporting full-duplex communication.

TDM, on the other hand, works by dividing the channel into time slots that are allocated to the data streams before they are transmitted. At both ends of the transmission, if the sender and receiver agree on the time-slot assignments, then the receiver can easily recover and reconstruct the original data streams. So multiple digital signals can be carried on one carrier by interleaving portions of each signal in time.

1.4.2 Transmission Media

As we have observed above, in any form of communication, there must be a medium through which the communication can take place. So network elements in a network need a medium in order to communicate. No network can function without a transmission medium because there would be no connection between the transmitting elements. The transmission medium plays a vital role in the performance of the network. In total, characteristic quality, dependability, and overall performance of a network depend heavily on its transmission medium. The transmission medium also determines a network's capacity in realizing the expected network traffic, reliability for the network's availability, size of the network in terms of the distance covered, and the transmission rate. Network transmission media can be either wired or wireless.

1.4.2.1 Wired Transmission Media

Wired transmission media are used in fixed networks physically connecting every network element. There are different types of physical media, the most common of which are copper wires, twisted pair, coaxial cables, and optical fibers.

Copper wires have been traditionally used in communication because of their low resistance to electrical currents that allows signals to travel even further. But copper wires suffer interference from electromagnetic energy in the environment, and because of this, they must always be insulated.

Twisted pair is a pair of wires consisting of insulated copper wire each wrapped around the other, forming frequent and numerous twists. Together, the twisted, insulated copper wires act as a full-duplex communication link. The twisting of the wires reduces the sensitivity of the cable to electromagnetic interference and also reduces the radiation of radio frequency noises that may interfere with nearby cables and electronic components. To increase the capacity of the transmitting medium, more than one pair of the twisted wires may be bundled together in a protective coating. Because twisted pairs were far less expensive, easy to install, and had a high quality of voice data, they were widely used in telephone networks. However, because they are poor in upward scalability in transmission rate, distance, and bandwidth in LANs, twisted pair technology has been abandoned in favor of other technologies. Figure 1.8 shows a twisted pair.

Coaxial cables are dual-conductor cables with a shared inner conductor in the core of the cable protected by an insulation layer and the outer conductor surrounding the insulation. These cables are called *coaxial* because they share the inner conductor. The inner core conductor is usually made of solid copper wire but at times can also be made up of stranded wire. The outer conductor commonly made of braided wires, but sometimes made of metallic foil or both, forms a protective tube around the inner conductor. This outer conductor is also further protected by another outer coating called the sheath. Figure 1.9 shows a coaxial cable. Coaxial cables are

Fig. 1.8 Coaxial cable

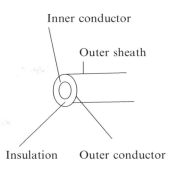

commonly used in television transmissions. Unlike twisted pairs, coaxial cables can be used over long distances. There are two types of coaxial cables: *thinnet*, a light and flexible cabling medium that is inexpensive and easy to install, and the *thicknet*, which is thicker and harder to break and can carry more signals through a longer distance than thinnet.

Optical fiber is a small medium made up of glass and plastics and conducts an optical ray. This is the most ideal cable for data transmission because it can accommodate extremely high bandwidths and has few problems with electromagnetic interference that coaxial cables suffer from. It can also support cabling for several kilometers. The two disadvantages of fiber-optic cables, however, are cost and installation difficulty. As shown in Fig. 1.10, a simple optical fiber has a central core made up of thin fibers of glass or plastics. The fibers are protected by a glass or plastic coating called a *cladding*. The cladding, though made up of the same materials as the core, has different properties that give it the capacity to reflect back the core rays that tangentially hit on it. The cladding itself is encased in a plastic jacket. The jacket protects the inner fiber from external abuses such as bending and abrasions. Optical fiber cables transmit data signals by first converting them into light signals. The transmitted light is emitted at the source from either a light-emitting diode (LED) or an injection laser diode (ILD). At the receiving end, the emitted rays are received by a photo detector that converts them back to the original form.

1.4.2.2 Wireless Communication

Wireless communication and wireless networks have evolved as a result of rapid development in communication technologies, computing, and people's need for mobility. Wireless networks fall in one of the following three categories depending on distance as follows:

- *Restricted Proximity Network*: This network involves local area networks (LANs) with a mixture of fixed and wireless devices.

Fig. 1.9 Optical fiber

Fig. 1.10 Twisted pair

- *Intermediate/Extended Network*: This wireless network is actually made up of two fixed LAN components joined together by a wireless component. The bridge may be connecting LANs in two nearby buildings or even further.
- *Mobile Network*: This is a fully wireless network connecting two network elements. One of these elements is usually a mobile unit that connects to the home network (fixed) using cellular or satellite technology.

These three types of wireless networks are connected using basic media such as infrared, laser beam, narrow-band and spread-spectrum radio, microwave, and satellite communication [2].

Infrared During an infrared transmission, one network element remotely emits and transmits pulses of infrared light that carry coded instructions to the receiving network element. As long as there is no object to stop the transmitted light, the receiver gets the instruction. Infrared is best used effectively in a small confined area, within 100 feet, for example, a television remote communicating with the television set. In a confined area such as this, infrared is relatively fast and can support high bandwidths of up to 10 Mbps.

High-Frequency Radio During a radio communication, high-frequency electro-magnetic radio waves or radio frequency commonly referred to as RF transmissions are generated by the transmitter and are picked up by the receiver. Because the range of radio frequency band is greater than that of infrared, mobile computing elements can communicate over a limited area without both transmitter and receiver being placed along a direct line of sight; the signal can bounce off light walls, buildings, and atmospheric objects. RF transmissions are very good for long distances when combined with satellites to refract the radio waves.

Microwave Microwaves are a higher-frequency version of radio waves but whose transmissions, unlike those of the radio, can be focused in a single direction. Microwave transmissions use a pair of parabolic antennas that produce and receive narrow, but highly directional signals. To be sensitive to signals, both the transmitting and receiving antennas must focus within a narrow area. Because of this, both the transmitting and receiving antennas must be carefully adjusted to align the transmitted signal to the receiver. Microwave communication has two forms: terrestrial, when it is near ground, and satellite microwave. The frequencies and technologies employed by these two forms are similar but with notably distinct differences.

Laser Laser light can be used to carry data for several thousand yards through air and optical fibers. But this is possible only if there are no obstacles in the line of sight. Lasers can be used in many of the same situations as microwaves, and like microwaves, laser beams must be refracted when used over long distances.

1.5   Network Topology

Computer networks, whether LANs, MANs, or WANs, are constructed based on a topology. There are several topologies including the following popular ones.

1.5.1   Mesh

A mesh topology allows multiple access links between network elements, unlike other types of topologies. The multiplicity of access links between the network elements offers an advantage in network reliability because whenever one network element fails, the network does not cease operations; it simply finds a bypass to the failed element and the network continues to function. Mesh topology is most often applied in MAN. Figure 1.11 shows a mesh network.

1.5.2   Tree

A more common type of network topology is the tree topology. In the tree topology, network elements are put in a hierarchical structure in which the most predominant element is called the *root* of the tree, and all other elements in the network share a child-parent relationship. As in ordinary, though inverted trees, there are no closed loops. So dealing with failures of network elements presents complications depending on the position of the failed element in the structure. For example, in a deeply rooted tree, if the root element fails, the network automatically ruptures and

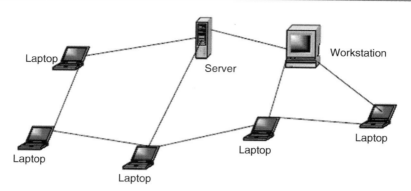

Fig. 1.11 Mesh network

splits into two parts. The two parts cannot communicate with each other. The functioning of the network as a unit is, therefore, fatally curtailed. Figure 1.12 shows a network using a tree topology.

1.5.3 Bus

A more popular topology, especially for LANs, is the bus topology. Elements in a network using a bus topology always share a bus and, therefore, have equal access to all LAN resources. Every network element has full-duplex connections to the transmitting medium which allows every element on the bus to send and receive data. Because each computing element is directly attached to the transmitting medium, a transmission from any one element propagates through the entire length of the medium in either direction and therefore can be received by all elements in the network. Because of this, precautions need to be taken to make sure that transmissions intended for one element can be received by that element and no other element. The network must also use a mechanism that handles disputes in case two or more elements try to transmit at the same time. The mechanism deals with the likely collision of signals and brings a quick recovery from such a collision. It is also necessary to create fairness in the network so that all other elements can transmit when they need to do so. See Fig. 1.13.

A collision control mechanism must also improve efficiency in the network using a bus topology by allowing only one element in the network to have control of the bus at any one time. This network element is then called the bus master, and other elements are considered to be its slaves. This requirement prevents collision from occurring in the network as elements in the network try to seize the bus at the same time. A bus topology is commonly used by LANs.

Fig. 1.12 Tree topology

Fig. 1.13 Bus topology

1.5.4   Star

Another very popular topology, especially in LAN technologies, is a star topology. A star topology is characterized by a central prominent node that connects to every other element in the network. So, all the elements in the network are connected to a central element. Every network element in a star topology is connected pairwise in a point-to-point manner through the central element, and communication between any pair of elements must go through this central element. The central element or node can either operate in a broadcast fashion, in which case information from one element is broadcast to all connected elements, or transmit as a switching device in which the incoming data is transmitted only to one element, the nearest element enroute to the destination. The biggest disadvantage to the star topology in networks is that the failure of the central element results in the failure of the entire network. Figure 1.14 shows a star topology.

Fig. 1.14 Star topology

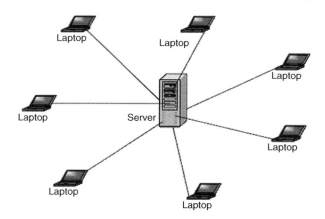

1.5.5   Ring

Finally another popular network topology is the ring topology. In this topology, each computing element in a network using a ring topology is directly connected to the transmitting medium via a unidirectional connection so that information put on the transmission medium can reach all computing elements in the network through a mechanism of taking turns in sending information around the ring. Figure 1.15 shows a ring topology network. The taking of turns in passing information is managed through a *token* system. A token is a system-wide piece of information that guarantees the current owner to be the bus master. As long as it owns the token, no other network element is allowed to transmit on the bus. When an element currently sending information and holding the token has finished, it passes the token downstream to its nearest neighbor. The token system is a good management system of collision and fairness.

There are variants of a ring topology collectively called *hub* hybrids combining either a star with a bus or a stretched star as shown in Fig. 1.16.

Although network topologies are important in LANs, the choice of a topology depends on a number of other factors, including the type of transmission medium, reliability of the network, the size of the network, and its anticipated future growth. Recently the most popular LAN topologies have been the bus, star, and ring topologies. The most popular bus- and star-based LAN topology is the Ethernet, and the most popular ring-based LAN topology is the token ring.

1.6   Network Connectivity and Protocols

In the early days of computing, computers were used as stand-alone machines, and all work that needed cross-computing was done manually. Files were moved on disks from computer to computer. There was, therefore, a need for cross-computing where more than one computer should talk to others and vice versa.

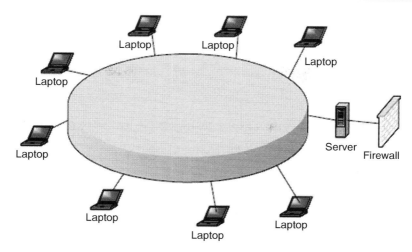

Fig. 1.15 Ring topology network

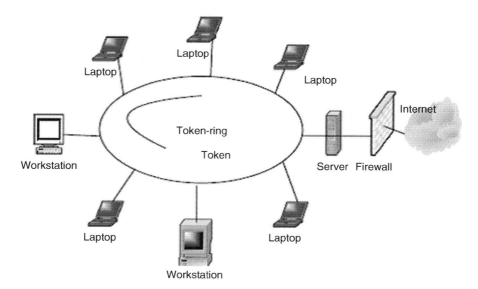

Fig. 1.16 Token ring hub

A new movement was, therefore, born. It was called the *open system movement*, which called for computer hardware and software manufacturers to come up with a way for this to happen. But to make this possible, standardization of equipment and software was needed. To help in this effort and streamline computer communication, the International Organization for Standardization (ISO) developed the Open Systems Interconnection (OSI) model. The OSI is an open architecture model that functions as the network communication protocol standard, although it is not the most widely used one. The Transmission Control Protocol/Internet Protocol (TCP/IP) model, a rival model to OSI, is the most widely used. Both OSI and TCP/IP models use two protocol stacks, one at the source element and the other at the destination element.

1.6.1 Open System Interconnection (OSI) Protocol Suite

The development of the OSI model was based on the secure premise that a communication task over a network can be broken into seven layers, where each layer represents a different portion of the task. Different layers of the protocol provide different services and ensure that each layer can communicate only with its own neighboring layers. That is, the protocols in each layer are based on the protocols of the previous layers.

Starting from the top of the protocol stack, tasks and information move down from the top layers until they reach the bottom layer where they are sent out over the network media from the source system to the destination. At the destination, the task or information rises back up through the layers until it reaches the top. Each layer is designed to accept work from the layer above it and to pass work down to the layer below it, and vice versa. To ease interlayer communication, the interfaces between the layers are standardized. However, each layer remains independent and can be designed independently, and each layer's functionality should not affect the functionalities of other layers above and below it.

Table 1.1 shows an OSI model consisting of seven layers and the descriptions of the services provided in each layer.

In peer-to-peer communication, the two communicating computers can initiate and receive tasks and data. The task and data initiated from each computer start from the top in the application layer of the protocol stack on each computer. The tasks and data then move down from the top layers until they reach the bottom layer, where they are sent out over the network media from the source system to the destination. At the destination, the task and data rise back up through the layers until the top. Each layer is designed to accept work from the layer above it and pass work down to the layer below it. As data passes from layer to layer of the sender machine, layer headers are appended to the data, causing the datagram to grow larger. Each layer header contains information for that layer's peer on the remote system. That information may indicate how to route the packet through the network or what should be done to the packet as it is handed back up the layers on the recipient computer.

Figure 1.17 shows a logical communication model between two peer computers using the OSI model. Table 1.2 shows the datagram with added header information as it moves through the layers. Although the development of the OSI model was intended to offer a standard for all other proprietary models, and it was as encompassing of all existing models as possible, it never really replaced many of those rival models it was intended to replace. In fact it is this "all-in-one" concept

Table 1.1 ISO protocol layers and corresponding services

Layer number	Protocol
7	Application
6	Presentation
5	Session
4	Transport
3	Network
2	Data link
1	Physical

Fig. 1.17 ISO logical peer communication model

that led to market failure because it became too complex. Its late arrival on the market also prevented its much anticipated interoperability across networks.

1.6.2   Transmission Control Protocol/Internet Protocol (TCP/IP) Model

Among the OSI rivals was the TCP/IP, which was far less complex and more historically established by the time the OSI came on the market. The TCP/IP model does not exactly match the OSI model. For example, it has two to three fewer levels than the seven layers of the OSI model. It was developed for the US Department of Defense Advanced Research Project Agency (DARPA); but over the years, it has seen a phenomenal growth in popularity, and it is now the de facto standard for the Internet and many intranets. It consists of two major protocols: the *Transmission Control Protocol* (TCP) and the *Internet Protocol* (IP), hence the TCP/IP designation. Table 1.3 shows the layers and protocols in each layer.

Since TCP/IP is the most widely used in most network protocol suites by the Internet and many intranets, let us focus on its layers here.

1.6.2.1 Application Layer

This layer, very similar to the application layer in the OSI model, provides the user interface with resources rich in application functions. It supports all network applications and includes many protocols on a data structure consisting of bit streams as shown in Fig. 1.18.

Table 1.2 OSI datagrams seen in each layer with header added

No header	Data	Application
H1	Data	Presentation
H2	Data	Session
H3	Data	Transport
H4	Data	Network
H5	Data	Data link
No header	Data	Physical

Table 1.3 TCP/IP layers

Layer	Delivery unit	Protocols
Application	Message	Handles all higher-level protocols including File Transfer Protocol (FTP), Name Server Protocol (NSP), Simple Mail Transfer Protocol (SMTP), Simple Network Management Protocol (SNMP), HTTP, remote file access (telnet), remote file server (NFS), name resolution (DNS), HTTP, TFTP, SNMP, DHCP, DNS, BOOTP
		Combines application, session, and presentation layers of the OSI model
		Handles all high-level protocols
Transport	Segment	Handles transport protocols including Transmission Control Protocol (TCP), User Datagram Protocol (UDP)
Network	Datagram	Contains the following protocols: Internet Protocol (IP), Internet Control Message Protocol (ICMP), Internet Group Management Protocol (IGMP)
		Supports transmitting source packets from any network on the internetwork and makes sure they arrive at the destination independent of the path and networks they took to reach there.
		Best path determination and packet switching occur at this layer.
Data link	Frame	Contains protocols that require IP packet to cross a physical link from one device to another directly connected device
		It included the following networks
		WAN – wide area network
		LAN – local area network
Physical	Bit stream	All network card drivers

Application header protocols	Bit stream

Fig. 1.18 Application layer data frame

1.6.2.2 Transport Layer

This layer, again similar to the OSI model session layer, is a slightly removed from the user and is hidden from the user. Its main purpose is to transport application layer messages that include application layer protocols in their headers between the host and the server. For the Internet network, the transport layer has two standard

Fig. 1.19 A TCP data
structure

$\longrightarrow$ 32 bits $\longleftarrow$

Source address	Destination address
Sequence number	Acknowledgement number
Other control information	
Data	

protocols: *Transmission Control Protocol* (TCP) and *User Datagram Protocol*
(UDP). TCP provides a connection-oriented service, and it guarantees the delivery
of all application layer packets to their destination. This guarantee is based on two
mechanisms: congestion control that throttles the transmission rate of the source
element when there is traffic congestion in the network and the flow control
mechanism that tries to match sender and receiver speeds to synchronize the flow
rate and reduce the packet drop rate. While TCP offers guarantees of delivery of the
application layer packets, UDP, on the other hand, offers no such guarantees. It
provides a nofrills connectionless service with just delivery and no
acknowledgements. But it is much more efficient and a protocol of choice for
real-time data such as streaming video and music. Transport layer delivers transport
layer packets and protocols to the network layer. Figure 1.19 shows the TCP data
structure, and Fig. 1.20 shows the UDP data structure.

1.6.2.3 Network Layer
This layer moves packets, now called datagrams, from router to router along the
path from a source host to the destination host. It supports a number of protocols
including the *Internet Protocol* (IP), *Internet Control Message Protocol* (ICMP),
and *Internet Group Management Protocol* (IGMP). The IP is the most widely used
network layer protocol. IP uses header information from the transport layer
protocols that include datagram source and destination port numbers from IP
addresses, and other TCP header and IP information, to move datagrams from
router to router through the network. Best routes are found in the network by using
routing algorithms. Figure 1.21 shows the IP datagram structure.

The standard IP address has been the so-called IPv4, a 32-bit addressing scheme.
But with the rapid growth of the Internet, there was fear of running out of addresses,
so IPv6, a new 64-bit addressing scheme, was created. The network layer conveys
the network layer protocols to the data link layer.

1.6.2.4 Data Link Layer
This layer provides the network with services that move packets from one packet
switch like a router to the next over connecting links. This layer also offers reliable
delivery of network layer packets over links. It is at the lowest level of communication, and it includes the *network interface card* (NIC) and *operating system*
(OS) protocols. The protocols in this layer include: Ethernet, asynchronous transfer
mode (ATM), and others such as frame relay. The data link-layer protocol unit, the
frame, may be moved over links from source to destination by different link-layer
protocols at different links along the way.

Fig. 1.20 A UDP data
structure

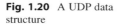

←	32 bits	→	
Source address		Destination address	
Other header control information		UDP Checksum	
	Data		

Fig. 1.21 An IP datagram
structure

Other header control information	Source port number	Destination port number	Data

1.6.2.5 Physical Layer

This layer is responsible for literally moving data link datagrams bit by bit over the links and between the network elements. The protocols here depend on and use the characteristics of the link medium and the signals on the medium.

1.7   Network Services

For a communication network to work effectively, data in the network must be able to move from one network element to another. This can only happen if the network services to move such data work. For data networks, these services fall into two categories:

- Connection services to facilitate the exchange of data between the two network-communicating end systems with as little data loss as possible and in as little time as possible
- Switching services to facilitate the movement of data from host to host across the length and width of the network mesh of hosts, hubs, bridges, routers, and gateways

1.7.1   Connection Services

How do we get the network-transmitting elements to exchange data over the network? Two types of connection services are used: the *connection-oriented* and *connectionless* services.

1.7.1.1 Connection-Oriented Services

With a connection-oriented service, before a client can send packets with real data to the server, there must be a *three-way handshake*. We will define this three-way handshake in later chapters. But the purpose of a three-way handshake is to establish a session before the actual communication can begin. Establishing a session before data is moved creates a path of virtual links between the end systems through a network and, therefore, guarantees the reservation and establishment of fixed communication channels and other resources needed for the exchange of data before any data is exchanged and as long as the channels are needed. For example, this happens whenever we place telephone calls; before we exchange words, the channels are reserved and established for the duration. Because this technique guarantees that data will arrive in the same order it was sent in, it is considered to be reliable. In short the service offers the following:

- Acknowledgments of all data exchanges between the end-systems
- Flow control in the network during the exchange
- Congestion control in the network during the exchange

Depending on the type of physical connections in place and the services required by the systems that are communicating, connection-oriented methods may be implemented in the data link layers or in the transport layers of the protocol stack, although the trend now is to implement it more at the transport layer. For example, TCP is a connection-oriented transport protocol in the transport layer. Other network technologies that are connection-oriented include the frame relay and ATMs.

1.7.1.2 Connectionless Service

In a connectionless service, there is no handshaking to establish a session between the communicating end systems, no flow control, and no congestion control in the network. This means that a client can start communicating with a server without warning or inquiry for readiness; it simply sends streams of packets, called datagrams, from its sending port to the server's connection port in single point-to-point transmissions with no relationship established between the packets and between the end systems. There are advantages and of course disadvantages to this type of connection service. In brief, the connection is faster because there is no handshaking which can sometimes be time consuming, and it offers periodic burst transfers with large quantities of data, and, in addition, it has simple protocol. However, this service offers minimum services and no safeguards and guarantees to the sender since there is no prior control information and no acknowledgment. In addition, the service does not have the reliability of the connection-oriented method and offers no error handling and no packet ordering; in addition, each packet self-identifies that leads to long headers, and finally, there is no predefined order in the arrival of packets.

Like the connection-oriented method, this service can operate both at the data link and transport layers. For example, UDP, a connectionless service, operates at the transport layer.

1.7.2   Network Switching Services

Before we discuss communication protocols, let us take a detour and briefly discuss data transfer by a switching element. This is a technique by which data is moved from host to host across the length and width of the network mesh of hosts, hubs, bridges, routers, and gateways. This technique is referred to as *data switching*. The type of data switching technique used by a network determines how messages are transmitted between the two communicating elements and across that network. There are two types of data switching techniques: *circuit switching* and *packet switching*.

1.7.2.1 Circuit Switching

In circuit switching networks, one must reserve all the resources before setting up a physical communication channel needed for communication. The physical connection, once established, is then used exclusively by the two end systems, usually subscribers, for the duration of the communication. The main feature of such a connection is that it provides a fixed data rate channel, and both subscribers must operate at this rate. For example, in a telephone communication network, a connected line is reserved between the two points before the users can start using the service. One issue of debate on circuit switching is the perceived waste of resources during the so-called silent periods when the connection is fully in force but not being used by the parties. This situation occurs when, for example, during a telephone network session, a telephone receiver is not hung up after use, leaving the connection still established. During this period, while no one is utilizing the session, the session line is still open.

1.7.2.2 Packet Switching

Packet switching networks, on the other hand, do not require any resources to be reserved before a communication session begins. These networks, however, require the sending host to assemble all data streams to be transmitted into packets. If a message is large, it is broken into several packets. Packet headers contain the source and the destination network addresses of the two communicating end systems. Then, each of the packets is sent on the communication links and across packet switches (routers). On receipt of each packet, the router inspects the destination address contained in the packet. Using its own routing table, each router then forwards the packet on the appropriate link at the maximum available bit rate. As each packet is received at each intermediate router, it is forwarded on the appropriate link interspersed with other packets being forwarded on that link. Each router checks the destination address, if it is the owner of the packet; it then reassembles the packets into the final message. Figure 1.22 shows the role of routers in packet switching networks.

Packet switches are considered to be store-and-forward transmitters, meaning that they must receive the entire packet before the packet is retransmitted or switched on to the next switch.

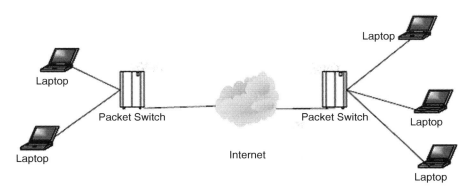

Fig. 1.22 Packet switching networks

Because there is no predefined route for these packets, there can be unpredictably long delays before the full message can be reassembled. In addition, the network may not dependably deliver all the packets to the intended destination. To ensure that the network has a reliably fast transit time, a fixed maximum length of time is allowed for each packet. Packet switching networks suffer from a few problems, including the following:

- The rate of transmission of a packet between two switching elements depends on the maximum rate of transmission of the link joining them and on the switches themselves.
- Momentary delays are always introduced whenever the switch is waiting for a full packet. The longer the packet, the longer the delay.
- Each switching element has a finite buffer for the packets. It is thus possible for a packet to arrive only to find the buffer full with other packets. Whenever this happens, the newly arrived packet is not stored but gets lost, a process called *packet dropping*. In peak times, servers may drop a large number of packets. Congestion control techniques use the rate of packet drop as one measure of traffic congestion in a network.

Packet switching networks are commonly referred to as *packet networks* for obvious reasons. They are also called *asynchronous* networks, and in such networks, packets are ideal because there is a sharing of the bandwidth, and of course, this avoids the hassle of making reservations for any anticipated transmission. There are two types of packet switching networks:

- *Virtual circuit network* in which a packet route is planned, and it becomes a logical connection before a packet is released.
- *Datagram network*, which is the focus of this book.

1.8   Network Connecting Devices

Before we discuss network connecting devices, let us revisit the network infrastructure. We have defined a network as a mesh of network elements, commonly referred to as network *nodes*, connected together by conducting media. These network nodes can be either at the ends of the mesh, in which case they are commonly known as clients or in the middle of the network as transmitting elements. In a small network such as a LAN, the nodes are connected together via special connecting and conducting devices that take network traffic from one node and pass it on to the next node. If the network is big *internetwork* (large networks of networks like WANs and LANs), these networks are connected to other special intermediate networking devices so that the Internet functions as a single large network.

Now let us look at network connecting devices and focus on two types of devices: those used in networks (small networks such as LANs) and those used in internetworks.

1.8.1   LAN Connecting Devices

Because LANs are small networks, connecting devices in LANs are less powerful with limited capabilities. There are hubs, repeaters, bridges, and switches.

1.8.1.1 A Hub

This is the simplest in the family of network connecting devices since it connects the LAN components with identical protocols. It takes in imports and retransmits them verbatim. It can be used to switch both digital and analog data. In each node, presetting must be done to prepare for the formatting of the incoming data. For example, if the incoming data is in digital format, the hub must pass it on as packets; however, if the incoming data is analog, then the hub passes as a signal. There are two types of hubs: simple and multiple port hubs, as shown in Figs. 1.23 and 1.24. Multiple port hubs may support more than one computer up to its number of ports and may be used to plan for the network expansion as more computers are added at a later time.

Network hubs are designed to work with network adapters and cables and can typically run at either 10 Mbps or 100 Mbps; some hubs can run at both speeds. To connect computers with differing speeds, it is better to use hubs that run at both speeds 10/100 Mbps.

1.8.1.2 A Repeater

A network repeater is a low-level local communication device at the physical layer of the network that receives network signals, amplifies them to restore them to full strength, and then retransmits them to another node in the network. Repeaters are used in a network for several purposes including countering the attenuation that occurs when signals travel long distances and extending the length of the LAN above the specified maximum. Since they work at the lowest network stack layer,

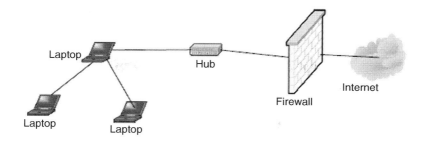

Fig. 1.23 A simple hub

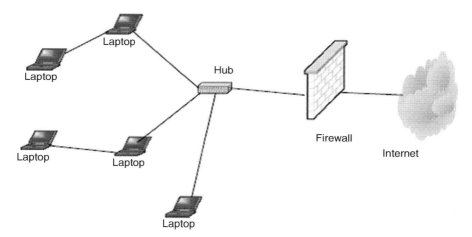

Fig. 1.24 Multi-ported hubs

they are less intelligent than their counterparts such as bridges, switches, routers, and gateways in the upper layers of the network stack. See Fig. 1.25.

1.8.1.3 A Bridge

A bridge is like a repeater but differs in that a repeater amplifies electrical signals because it is deployed at the physical layer; a bridge is deployed at the data link and therefore amplifies digital signals. It digitally copies frames. It permits frames from one part of a LAN or a different LAN with different technology to move to another part or another LAN. However, in filtering and isolating a frame from one network to another or another part of the same network, the bridge will not move a damaged frame from one end of the network to the other. As it filters the data packets, the bridge makes no modifications to the format and content of the incoming data. A bridge filters the frames to determine whether a frame should be forwarded or dropped. All "noise" (collisions, faulty wiring, power surges, etc.) packets are not transmitted.

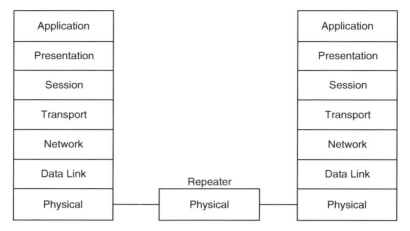

Fig. 1.25 A repeater in an OSI model

The bridge filters and forwards frames on the network using a dynamic bridge table. The bridge table, which is initially empty, maintains the LAN addresses for each computer in the LAN and the addresses of each bridge interface that connects the LAN to other LANs. Bridges, like hubs, can be either simple or multi-ported. Figure 1.26 shows a simple bridge, Fig. 1.27 shows a multi-ported bridge, and Fig. 1.28 shows the position of the bridge in an OSI protocol stack.

1.8.1.4 A Switch
A switch is a network device that connects segments of a network or two small networks such as Ethernet or token ring LANs. Like the bridge, it also filters and forwards frames on the network with the help of a dynamic table. This point-to-point approach allows the switch to connect multiple pairs of segments at a time, allowing more than one computer to transmit data at a time, thus giving them a high performance over their cousins, the bridges.

1.8.2   Internetworking Devices

Internetworking devices connect together smaller networks, like several LANs creating much larger networks such as the Internet. Let us look at two of these connectors: the router and the gateway.

1.8.2.1 Routers
Routers are general-purpose devices that interconnect two or more heterogeneous networks represented by IP subnets or unnumbered point-to-point lines. They are usually dedicated special-purpose computers with separate input and output interfaces for each connected network. They are implemented at the network

Fig. 1.26 Simple bridge

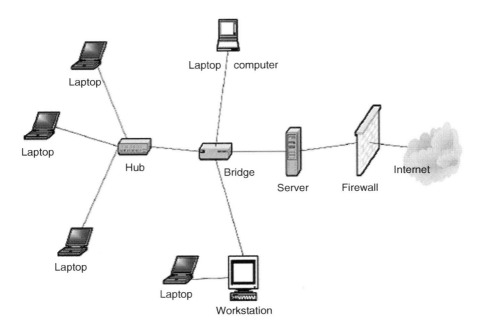

Fig. 1.27 Multi-ported bridge

layer in the protocol stack. Figure 1.29 shows the position of the router in the OSI protocol stack.

According to RFC 1812, a router performs the following functions [3]:

- Conforms to specific Internet protocols specified in the 1812 document, including the Internet Protocol (IP), Internet Control Message Protocol (ICMP), and others as necessary.

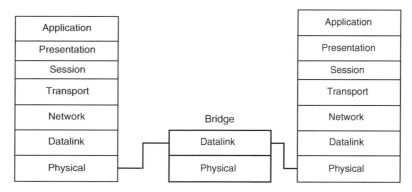

Fig. 1.28 Position of a bridge in an OSI protocol stack

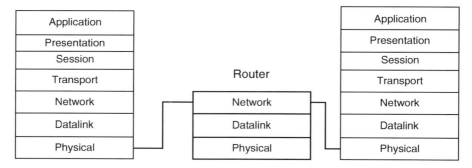

Fig. 1.29 Router in the OSI protocol stack

- Connects to two or more packet networks. For each connected network, the router must implement the functions required by that network because it is a member of that network. These functions typically include the following:
  - Encapsulating and decapsulating the IP datagrams with the connected network framing. For example, if the connected network is an Ethernet LAN, an Ethernet header and checksum must be attached.
  - Sending and receiving IP datagrams up to the maximum size supported by that network; this size is the network's maximum transmission unit or MTU.
  - Translating the IP destination address into an appropriate network-level address for the connected network. These are the Ethernet hardware address on the NIC, for Ethernet cards, if needed. Each network addresses the router as a member computer of its own network. This means that each router is a member of each network it connects to. It, therefore, has a network host address for that network and an interface address for each network it is connected to. Because of this rather strange characteristic, each router interface has its own address resolution protocol (ARP) module, its LAN address (network card address), and its own Internet Protocol (IP) address.
  - Responding to network flow control and error indications, if any.

- Receives and forwards Internet datagrams. Important issues in this process are buffer management, congestion control, and fairness. To do this the router must:
  - Recognize error conditions and generate ICMP error and information messages as required.
  - Drop datagrams whose time-to-live fields have reached zero.
  - Fragment datagrams when necessary to fit into the maximum transmission unit (MTU) of the next network.
- Chooses a next-hop destination for each IP datagram based on the information in its routing database.
- Usually supports an interior gateway protocol (IGP) to carry out distributed routing and reachability algorithms with the other routers in the same autonomous system. In addition, some routers will need to support an exterior gateway protocol (EGP) to exchange topological information with other autonomous systems.
- Provides network management and system support facilities, including loading, debugging, status reporting, exception reporting, and control.

Forwarding an IP datagram from one network across a router requires the router to choose the address and relevant interface of the next-hop router or for the final hop if it is the destination host. The next-hop router is always in the next network of which the router is also a member. The choice of the next-hop router, called *forwarding*, depends on the entries in the routing table within the router.

Routers are smarter than bridges in that the router with the use of a router table has some knowledge of possible routes a packet could take from its source to its destination. Once it finds the destination, it determines the best, fastest, and most efficient way of routing the package. The routing table, like in the bridge and switch, grows dynamically as activities in the network develop. On receipt of a packet, the router removes the packet headers and trailers and analyzes the IP header by determining the source and destination addresses and data type and noting the arrival time. It also updates the router table with new addresses if not already in the table. The IP header and arrival time information are entered in the routing table. If a router encounters an address it cannot understand, it drops the package. Let us explain the working of a router by an example using Fig. 1.30.

In Fig. 1.30, suppose host A in LAN1 tries to send a packet to host B in LAN2. Both host A and host B have two addresses: the LAN (host) address and the IP address. The translation between host LAN addresses and IP addresses is done by the ARP, and data is retrieved or built into the ARP table, similar to Table 1.4. Notice also that the router has two network interfaces: interface 1 for LAN1 and interface 2 for LAN2 for the connection to a larger network such as the Internet. Each interface has a LAN (host) address for the network the interface connects on and a corresponding IP address. As we will see later in the chapter, host A sends a packet to router 1 at time 10:01 that includes, among other things, both its addresses, message type, and destination IP address of host B. The packet is

Fig. 1.30 Working of a router

received at interface 1 of the router; the router reads the packet and builds row 1 of the routing table as shown in Table 1.5.

The router notices that the packet has to go to network 193.55.1.***, where *** are digits 0–9, and it has knowledge that this network is connected on interface 2. It forwards the packet to interface 2. Now, interface 2 with its own ARP may know host B. If it does, then it forwards the packet and updates the routing table with the inclusion of row 2. What happens when the ARP at the router interface 1 cannot determine the next network? That is, if it has no knowledge of the presence of network 193.55.1.***, it will then ask for help from a gateway. Let us now discuss how IP chooses a gateway to use when delivering a datagram to a remote network.

1.8.2.2 Gateways

Gateways are more versatile devices than routers. They perform protocol conversion between different types of networks, architectures, or applications and serve as translators and interpreters for network computers that communicate in different protocols and operate in dissimilar networks, for example, OSI and TCP/IP. Because the networks are different with different technologies, each network has its own routing algorithms, protocols, domain names servers, and network administration procedures and policies. Gateways perform all of the functions of a router and more. The gateway functionality that does the translation between different network technologies and algorithms is called a *protocol converter*. Figure 1.31 shows the position of a gateway in a network.

Gateways services include packet format and/or size conversion, protocol conversion, data translation, terminal emulation, and multiplexing. Since gateways perform a more complicated task of protocol conversion, they operate more slowly and handle fewer devices.

Table 1.4 ARP table for LAN1

IP address	LAN address	Time
127.0.0.5	16–73-AX-E4–01	10:00
127.76.1.12	07-1A-EB-17-F6	10:03

Table 1.5 Routing table for interface1

Address	Interface	Time
127.0.0.1	1	10:01
192.76.1.12	2	10:03

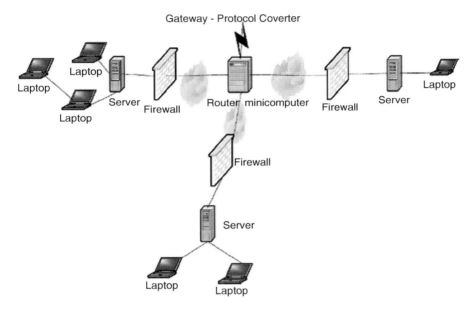

Fig. 1.31 Position of a gateway

Let us now see how a packet can be routed through a gateway or several gateways before it reaches its destination. We have seen that if a router gets a datagram, it checks the destination address and finds that it is not on the local network. It, therefore, sends it to the default gateway. The default gateway now searches its table for the destination address. In case the default gateway recognizes that the destination address is not on any of the networks it is connected to directly, it has to find yet another gateway to forward it through.

The routing information the server uses for this is in a *gateway routing table* linking networks to gateways that reach them. The table starts with the network entry 0.0.0.0, a catch-all entry, for default routes. All packets to an unknown network are sent through the default route. Table 1.6 shows the gateway routing table.

The choice between a router, a bridge, and a gateway is a balance between functionality and speed. Gateways, as we have indicated, perform a variety of

Table 1.6 A gateway routing table	Network	Gateway	Interface
	0.0.0.0	192.133.1.1	1
	127.123.0.1	198.24.0.1	2

functions; however, because of this variety of functions, gateways may become bottlenecks within a network because they are slow.

Routing tables may be built either manually for small LANs or by using software called *routing daemons* for larger networks.

1.9   Network Technologies

Earlier in this chapter, we indicated that computer networks are basically classified according to their sizes with the local area networks (LANs) covering smaller areas, and the bigger ones covering wider areas (WANs). In this last section of the chapter, let us look at a few network technologies in each one of these categories.

1.9.1   LAN Technologies

Recall our definition of a LAN at the beginning of this chapter. We defined a LAN to be a small data communication network that consists of a variety of machines that are all part of the network and cover a geographically small area such as one building or one floor. Also, a LAN is usually owned by an individual or a single entity such as an organization. According to IEEE 802.3 Committee on LAN Standardization, a LAN must be a moderately sized and geographically shared peer-to-peer communication network broadcasting information for all on the network to hear via a common physical medium on a point-to-point basis with no intermediate switching element required. Many common network technologies today fall into this category including the popular Ethernet, the widely used token ring/IEEE 805.2, and the *Fiber Distributed Data Interface* (FDDI).

1.9.1.1 Star-Based Ethernet (IEEE 802.3) LAN
Ethernet technology is the most widely used of all LAN technologies, and it has been standardized by the IEEE 802.3 Committee on Standards. The IEEE 802.3 standards define the *medium access control* (MAC) layer and the physical layer. The Ethernet MAC is a *carrier sense multiple access with collision detection* (CSMA/CD) system. With CSMA, any network node that wants to transmit must listen first to the medium to make sure that there is no other node already transmitting. This is called the carrier sensing of the medium. If there is already a node using the medium, then the element that was intending to transmit waits; otherwise, it transmits. In case two or more elements are trying to transmit at the same time, a collision will occur and the integrity of the data for all is compromised. However, the element may not know this. So it waits for an acknowledgment from the

receiving node. The waiting period varies, taking into account maximum round-trip propagation delay and other unexpected delays. If no acknowledgment is received during that time, the element then assumes that a collision has occurred, and the transmission was unsuccessful, and therefore it must retransmit. If more collisions were to happen, then the element must now double the delay time and so on. After a collision, when the two elements are in delay period, the medium may be idle and this may lead to inefficiency. To correct this situation, the elements, instead of just going into the delay mode, must continue to listen onto the medium as they transmit. In this case, they will not only be doing carrier sensing but also detecting a collision that leads to CSMA/CD. According to Stallings, the CSMA/CD scheme follows the following algorithm [1]:

- If the medium is idle, transmit.
- If the medium is busy, continue to listen until idle, and then transmit immediately.
- If collision is detected, transmit jamming signal for "collision warning" to all other network elements.
- After jamming the signal, wait random time units and attempt to transmit.

A number of Ethernet LANs are based on the IEEE 802.3 standards, including

- 10 BASE-X (where X = 2, 5, T and F; T = twisted pair and F = fiber optics)
- 100 BASE-T (where the T options include T4, TX, and FX)
- 1000 BASE-T (where T options include LX, SX, T, and CX)

The basic Ethernet transmission structure is a frame and it is shown in Fig. 1.32.

The source and destination fields contain 6-byte LAN addresses of the form xx-xx-xx-xx-xx-xx, where x is a hexadecimal integer. The error detection field is 4 bytes of bits used for error detection, usually using the *cyclic redundancy check* (CRC) algorithm, in which the source and destination elements synchronize the values of these bits.

1.9.1.2 Token Ring/IEEE 805.2

Token ring LANs based on IEEE 805.2 are also used widely in commercial and small industrial networks, although not as popular as Ethernet. The standard uses a frame called a token that circulates around the network so that all network nodes have equal access to it. As we have seen previously, token ring technology employs a mechanism that involves passing the token around the network so that all network elements have equal access to it.

Whenever a network element wants to transmit, it waits for the token on the ring to make its way to the element's connection point on the ring. When the token arrives at this point, the element grabs it and changes one bit of the token that becomes the start bit in the data frame the element will be transmitting. The element then inserts data, addressing information and other fields, and then releases the payload onto the ring. It then waits for the token to make a round and come back.

Other control headers	Destination address	Source address	Type	Data	Error detection (CRC)

Fig. 1.32 An Ethernet frame structure

The receiving host must recognize the destination MAC address within the frame as its own. Upon receipt, the host identifies the last field indicating the recognition of the MAC address as its own. The frame contents are then copied by the host, and the frame is put back in circulation. On reaching the network element that still owns the token, the element withdraws the token, and a new token is put on the ring for another network element that may need to transmit.

Because of its round-robin nature, the token ring technique gives each network element a fair chance of transmitting if it wants to. However, if the token ever gets lost, the network business is halted. Figure 1.33 shows the structure of a token data frame, and Fig. 1.16 shows the token ring structure.

Like Ethernet, the token ring has a variety of technologies based on the transmission rates.

1.9.1.3 Other LAN Technologies

In addition to those we have discussed earlier, several other LAN technologies are in use, including the following:

- Asynchronous transfer mode (ATM) with the goal of transporting real-time voice, video, text, e-mail, and graphic data. ATM offers a full array of network services that make it a rival of the Internet network.
- Fiber Distributed Data Interface (FDDI) is a dual-ring network that uses a token ring scheme with many similarities to the original token ring technology.
- AppleTalk, the popular Mac users' LAN.

1.9.2 WAN Technologies

As we defined it earlier, WANs are data networks like LANs, but they cover a wider geographic area. Because of their sizes, WANs traditionally provide fewer services to customers than LANs. Several networks fall into this category, including the *integrated services digital network* (ISDN), X.25, frame relay, and the popular Internet.

1.9.2.1 Integrated Services Digital Network (ISDN)

ISDN is a system of digital phone connections that allows data to be transmitted simultaneously across the world using end-to-end digital connectivity. It is a network that supports the transmission of video, voice, and data. Because the transmission of these varieties of data, including graphics, usually puts widely differing demands on the communication network, service integration for these

Start field	Access control	Source address	Destination address	Data	Ending field

Fig. 1.33 A token data frame

networks is an important advantage to make them more appealing. The ISDN standards specify that subscribers must be provided with

- *Basic Rate Interface (BRI)* services of two full-duplex 64-kbps B channels—the bearer channels and one full-duplex 16-kbps D channel—the data channel. One B channel is used for digital voice and the other for applications such as data transmission. The D channel is used for telemetry and for exchanging network control information. This rate is for individual users.
- *Primary Rate Interface (PRI)* services consisting of 23 64-kbps B channels and one 64-kbps D channel. This rate is for all large users.

BRI can be accessed only if the customer subscribes to an ISDN phone line and is within 18,000 feet (about 3.4 miles or 5.5 km) of the telephone company central office. Otherwise, expensive repeater devices are required that may include ISDN terminal adapters and ISDN routers.

1.9.2.2 X.25

X.25 is the *International Telecommunication Union* (ITU) protocol developed in 1993 to bring interoperability to a variety of many data communication wide area networks (WANs), known as *public networks*, owned by private companies, organizations, and governments agencies. By doing so, X.25 describes how data passes into and out of public data communications networks.

X.25 is a connection-oriented and packet-switched data network protocol with three levels corresponding to the bottom three layers of the OSI model as follows: the physical level corresponds to the OSI physical layer; the link level corresponds to OSI data link layer; and the packet level corresponds to the OSI network layer.

In full operation, the X.25 networks allow remote devices known as *data terminal equipment* (DTE) to communicate with each other across high-speed digital links, known as *data circuit-terminating equipment* (DCE), without the expense of individual leased lines. The communication is initiated by the user at a DTE setting up calls using standardized addresses. The calls are established over virtual circuits, which are logical connections between the originating and destination addresses.

On receipt, the called users can accept, clear, or redirect the call to a third party. The virtual connections we mentioned above are of the following two types [4]:

- *Switched virtual circuits (SVCs)*: SVCs are very much like telephone calls; a connection is established, data is transferred, and then the connection is released.

Each DTE on the network is given a unique DTE address that can be used much like a telephone number.

- *Permanent virtual circuits* (*PVCs*): A PVC is similar to a leased line in that the connection is always present. The logical connection is established permanently by the packet-switched network administration. Therefore, data may always be sent without any call setup.

Both of these circuits are used extensively, but since user equipment and network systems supported both X.25 PVCs and X.25 SVCs, most users prefer the SVCs since they enable the user devices to set up and tear down connections as required.

Because X.25 is a reliable data communications with a capability over a wide range of quality of transmission facilities, it provides advantages over other WAN technologies, for example,

- Unlike frame relay and ATM technologies that depend on the use of high-quality digital transmission facilities, X.25 can operate over either analog or digital facilities.
- In comparison with TCP/IP, one finds that TCP/IP has only end-to-end error checking and flow control, while X.25 is error checked from network element to network element.

X.25 networks are in use throughout the world by large organizations with widely dispersed and communication-intensive operations in sectors such as finance, insurance, transportation, utilities, and retail.

1.9.2.3 Other WAN Technologies

The following are other WAN technologies that we would like to discuss but cannot include because of space limitations:

- Frame relay is a packet-switched network with the ability to multiplex many logical data conversions over a single connection. It provides flexible efficient channel bandwidth using digital and fiber-optic transmission. It has many similar characteristics to X.25 network except in format and functionality.
- *Point-to-Point Protocol* (PPP) is the Internet standard for transmission of IP packets over serial lines. The point-to-point link provides a single, preestablished communications path from the ending element through a carrier network, such as a telephone company, to a remote network. These links can carry datagram or data-stream transmissions.
- *xDirect service line* (xDSL) is a technology that provides an inexpensive, yet very fast connection to the Internet.
- *Switched multi-megabit data service* (SMDS) is a connectionless service operating in the range of 1.5–100 Mbps; any SMDS station can send a frame to any other station on the same network.
- Asynchronous transfer mode (ATM) is already discussed as a LAN technology.

1.9.3   Wireless LANs

The rapid advances, miniaturization, and the popularity of wireless technology have opened a new component of LAN technology. The mobility and relocation of workers have forced companies to move into new wireless technologies with emphasis on wireless networks extending the local LAN into a wireless LAN. There are basically four types of wireless LANs [1]:

- LAN extension is a quick wireless extension to an existing LAN to accommodate new changes in space and mobile units.
- Cross-building interconnection establishes links across buildings between both wireless and wired LANs.
- Nomadic access establishes a link between a LAN and a mobile wireless communication device such as a laptop computer.
- Ad hoc networking is a peer-to-peer network temporarily set up to meet some immediate need. It usually consists of laptops, handheld PCs, and other communication devices.
- Personal area networks (PANs) that include the popular Bluetooth networks.

There are several wireless IEEE 802.11-based LAN types, including:

- Infrared
- Spread spectrum
- Narrowband microwave

Wireless technology is discussed in further detail in Chapter 17.

1.10   Conclusion

We have developed the theory of computer networks and discussed the topologies, standards, and technologies of these networks. Because we were limited by space, we could not discuss a number of interesting and widely used technologies both in LAN and WAN areas. However, our limited discussion of these technologies should give the reader an understanding and scope of the changes that are taking place in network technologies. We hope that the trend will keep the convergence of the LAN, WAN, and wireless technologies on track so that the alarming number of different technologies is reduced and basic international standards are established.

Exercises

1. What is a communication protocol?
2. Why do we need communication protocols?
3. List the major protocols discussed in this chapter.
4. In addition to ISO and TCP/IP, what are the other models?

5. Discuss two LAN technologies that are NOT Ethernet or token ring.
6. Why is Ethernet technology more appealing to users than the rest of the LAN technologies?
7. What do you think are the weak points of TCP/IP?
8. Discuss the pros and cons of four LAN technologies.
9. List four WAN technologies.
10. What technologies are found in MANs? Which of the technologies listed in 8 and 9 can be used in MANs?

Advanced Exercises

1. X.25 and TCP/IP are very similar but there are differences. Discuss these differences.
2. Discuss the reasons why ISDN failed to catch on as WAN technology.
3. Why is it difficult to establish permanent standards for a technology like WAN or LAN?
4. Many people see Bluetooth as a personal wireless network (PAN). Why is this so? What standard does Bluetooth use?
5. Some people think that Bluetooth is a magic technology that is going to change the world. Read about Bluetooth and discuss this assertion.
6. Discuss the future of wireless LANs.
7. What is a wireless WAN? What kind of technology can be used in it? Is this the wave of the future?
8. With the future in mind, compare and contrast ATMs and ISDN technologies.
9. Do you foresee a fusion between LAN, MAN, and WAN technologies in the future? Support your response.
10. Network technology is in transition. Discuss the direction of network technology.

References

1. Stallings W (2000) Local and metropolitan area network, 6th edn. Prentice Hall, Upper Saddle River
2. Comar DE (2000) Internetworking with TCP/IP: principles, protocols, and architecture, 4th edn. Prentice-Hall, Upper Saddle River
3. RFC (1812) Requirements for IP Version 4 Routers. http://www.cis.ohio-state.edu/cgi-bin/rfc/rfc1812.html#sec-2.2.3
4. Sangoma Technologies http://www.sangoma.com/x25.htm

Computer Network Security Fundamentals

2

2.1   Introduction

Before we talk about network security, we need to understand in general terms what security is. Security is a continuous process of protecting an object from unauthorized access. It is as state of being or feeling protected from harm. That object in that state may be a person, an organization such as a business, or property such as a computer system or a file. Security comes from secure which means, according to *Webster Dictionary*, a state of being free from care, anxiety, or fear [1].

An object can be in a *physical state* of security or a *theoretical state* of security. In a physical state, a facility is secure if it is protected by a barrier like a fence, has secure areas both inside and outside, and can resist penetration by intruders. This state of security can be guaranteed if the following four protection mechanisms are in place: deterrence, prevention, detection, and response [1, 2].

- *Deterrence* is usually the first line of defense against intruders who may try to gain access. It works by creating an atmosphere intended to frighten intruders. Sometimes this may involve warnings of severe consequences if security is breached.
- *Prevention* is the process of trying to stop intruders from gaining access to the resources of the system. Barriers include firewalls, demilitarized zones (DMZs), and the use of access items like keys, access cards, biometrics, and others to allow only authorized users to use and access a facility.
- *Detection* occurs when the intruder has succeeded or is in the process of gaining access to the system. Signals from the detection process include alerts to the existence of an intruder. Sometimes, these alerts can be real time or stored for further analysis by the security personnel.
- *Response* is an aftereffect mechanism that tries to respond to the failure of the first three mechanisms. It works by trying to stop and/or prevent future damage or access to a facility.

© Springer International Publishing AG 2017

J.M. Kizza, *Guide to Computer Network Security*, Computer Communications and Networks, DOI 10.1007/978-3-319-55606-2_2

The areas outside the protected system can be secured by wire and wall fencing, mounted noise or vibration sensors, security lighting, closed-circuit television (CCTV), buried seismic sensors, or different photoelectric and microwave systems [1]. Inside the system, security can be enhanced by using electronic barriers such as firewalls and passwords.

Digital barriers—commonly known as firewalls, discussed in detail in Chap. 12—can be used. Firewalls are hardware or software tools used to isolate the sensitive portions of an information system facility from the outside world and limit the potential damage by a malicious intruder.

A theoretical state of security, commonly known as pseudosecurity or security through obscurity (STO), is a false hope of security. Many believe that an object can be secured as long as nobody outside the core implementation group has knowledge about its existence. This security is often referred to as "bunk mentality" security. This is virtual security in the sense that it is not physically implemented like building walls, issuing passwords, or putting up a firewall, but it is effectively based solely on a philosophy. The philosophy itself relies on a need-to-know basis, implying that a person is not dangerous as long as that person doesn't have knowledge that could affect the security of the system like a network, for example. In real systems where this security philosophy is used, security is assured through a presumption that only those with responsibility and who are trustworthy can use the system and nobody else needs to know. So, in effect, the philosophy is based on the trust of those involved assuming that they will never leave. If they do, then that means the end of security for that system.

There are several examples where STO has been successfully used. These include Coca-Cola, KFC, and other companies that have, for generations, kept their secret recipes secure based on a few trusted employees. But the overall STO is a fallacy that has been used by many software producers when they hide their codes. Many times, STO hides system vulnerabilities and weaknesses. This was demonstrated vividly in Matt Blaze's 1994 discovery of a flaw in the Escrowed Encryption Standard (Clipper) that could be used to circumvent law-enforcement monitoring. Blaze's discovery allowed easier access to secure communication through the Clipper technology than was previously possible, without access to keys [3]. The belief that secrecy can make the system more secure is just a belief—a myth in fact. Unfortunately, the software industry still believes this myth.

Although its usefulness has declined as the computing environment has changed to large open systems, new networking programming, and network protocols, and as the computing power available to the average person has increased, the philosophy is in fact still favored by many agencies, including the military, many government agencies, and private businesses.

In either security state, many objects can be thought of as being secure if such a state, a condition, or a process is afforded to them. Because there are many of these objects, we are going to focus on the security of a few of these object models. These will be a computer, a computer network, and information.

2.1.1 Computer Security

This is a study, which is a branch of computer science, focusing on creating a secure environment for the use of computers. It is a focus on the "behavior of users," if you will, required and the protocols in order to create a secure environment for anyone using computers. This field, therefore, involves four areas of interest: the study of computer ethics, the development of both software and hardware protocols, and the development of best practices. It is a complex field of study involving detailed mathematical designs of cryptographic protocols. We are not focusing on this in this book.

2.1.2 Network Security

As we saw in Chap. 1, computer networks are distributed networks of computers that are either strongly connected meaning that they share a lot of resources from one central computer or loosely connected, meaning that they share only those resources that can make the network work. When we talk about computer network security, our focus object model has now changed. It is no longer one computer but a network. So computer network security is a broader study of computer security. It is still a branch of computer science, but a lot broader than that of computer security. It involves creating an environment in which a computer network, including all its resources, which are many; all the data in it both in storage and in transit; and all its users are secure. Because it is wider than computer security, this is a more complex field of study than computer security involving more detailed mathematical designs of cryptographic, communication, transport, and exchange protocols and best practices. This book focuses on this field of study.

2.1.3 Information Security

Information security is even a bigger field of study including computer and computer network security. This study is found in a variety of disciplines, including computer science, business management, information studies, and engineering. It involves the creation of a state in which information and data are secure. In this model, information or data is either in motion through the communication channels or in storage in databases on server. This, therefore, involves the study of not only more detailed mathematical designs of cryptographic, communication, transport, and exchange protocols and best practices but also the state of both data and information in motion. We are not discussing these in this book.

2.2   Securing the Computer Network

Creating security in the computer network model we are embarking on in this book means creating secure environments for a variety of resources. In this model, a resource is secure, based on the above definition, if that resource is protected from both internal and external unauthorized access. These resources, physical or not, are objects. Ensuring the security of an object means protecting the object from unauthorized access both from within the object and externally. In short, we protect objects. System objects are either tangible or nontangible. In a computer network model, the tangible objects are the hardware resources in the system, and the intangible object is the information and data in the system, both in transition and static in storage.

2.2.1   Hardware

Protecting hardware resources include protecting:

- End user objects that include the user interface hardware components such as all client system input components, including a keyboard, mouse, touchscreen, light pens, and others
- Network objects like firewalls, hubs, switches, routers, and gateways which are vulnerable to hackers
- Network communication channels to prevent eavesdroppers from intercepting network communications

2.2.2   Software

Protecting software resources includes protecting hardware-based software, operating systems, server protocols, browsers, application software, and intellectual property stored on network storage disks and databases. It also involves protecting client software such as investment portfolios, financial data, real estate records, images or pictures, and other personal files commonly stored on home and business computers.

2.3   Forms of Protection

Now, we know what model objects are or need to be protected. Let us briefly, keep details for later, survey ways and forms of protecting these objects. Prevention of unauthorized access to system resources is achieved through a number of services that include access control, authentication, confidentiality, integrity, and nonrepudiation.

2.3.1   Access Control

This is a service the system uses, together with a user pre-provided identification information such as a password, to determine who uses what of its services. Let us look at some forms of access control based on hardware and software.

2.3.1.1 Hardware Access Control Systems

Rapid advances in technology have resulted in efficient access control tools that are open and flexible, while at the same time ensuring reasonable precautions against risks. Access control tools falling in this category include the following:

- Access terminal: Terminal access points have become very sophisticated, and now they not only carry out user identification but also verify access rights, control access points, and communicate with host computers. These activities can be done in a variety of ways including fingerprint verification and real-time anti-break-in sensors. Network technology has made it possible for these units to be connected to a monitoring network or remain in a stand-alone off-line mode.
- Visual event monitoring: This is a combination of many technologies into one very useful and rapidly growing form of access control using a variety of real-time technologies including video and audio signals, aerial photographs, and Global Positioning System (GPS) technology to identify locations.
- Identification cards: Sometimes called proximity cards, these cards have become very common these days as a means of access control in buildings, financial institutions, and other restricted areas. The cards come in a variety of forms, including magnetic, bar coded, contact chip, and a combination of these.
- Biometric identification: This is perhaps the fastest growing form of control access tool today. Some of the most popular forms include fingerprint, iris, and voice recognition. However, fingerprint recognition offers a higher level of security.
- Video surveillance: This is a replacement of CCTV of yesteryear, and it is gaining popularity as an access control tool. With fast networking technologies and digital cameras, images can now be taken and analyzed very quickly and action taken in minutes.

2.3.1.2 Software Access Control Systems

Software access control falls into two types: point-of-access monitoring and remote monitoring. In *point of access* (POA), personal activities can be monitored by a PC-based application. The application can even be connected to a network or to a designated machine or machines. The application collects and stores access events and other events connected to the system operation and download access rights to access terminals.

In remote mode, the terminals can be linked in a variety of ways, including the use of modems, telephone lines, and all forms of wireless connections. Such terminals may, sometimes if needed, have an automatic calling at preset times if desired or have an attendant to report regularly.

2.3.2 Authentication

Authentication is a service used to identify a user. User identity, especially of remote users, is difficult because many users, especially those intending to cause harm, may masquerade as the legitimate users when they actually are not. This service provides a system with the capability to verify that a user is the very one he or she claims to be based on what the user is, knows, and has.

Physically, we can authenticate users or user surrogates based on checking one or more of the following user items [2]:

- Username (sometimes screen name).
- Password.
- *Retinal images*: The user looks into an electronic device that maps his or her eye retina image; the system then compares this map with a similar map stored on the system.
- *Fingerprints*: The user presses on or sometimes inserts a particular finger into a device that makes a copy of the user fingerprint and then compares it with a similar image on the system user file.
- *Physical location*: The physical location of the system initiating an entry request is checked to ensure that a request is actually originating from a known and authorized location. In networks, to check the authenticity of a client's location, a network or Internet Protocol (IP) address of the client machine is compared with the one on the system user file. This method is used mostly in addition to other security measures because it alone cannot guarantee security. If used alone, it provides access to the requested system to anybody who has access to the client machine.
- *Identity cards*: Increasingly, cards are being used as authenticating documents. Whoever is the carrier of the card gains access to the requested system. As is the case with physical location authentication, card authentication is usually used as a second-level authentication tool because whoever has access to the card automatically can gain access to the requested system.

2.3.3 Confidentiality

The confidentiality service protects system data and information from unauthorized disclosure. When data leave one extreme of a system such as a client's computer in a network, it ventures out into a nontrusting environment. So, the recipient of that data may not fully trust that no third party like a cryptanalysis or a man in the middle has eavesdropped on the data. This service uses encryption algorithms to ensure that nothing of the sort happened while the data was in the wild.

Encryption protects the communications channel from sniffers. *Sniffers* are programs written for and installed on the communication channels to eavesdrop on network traffic, examining all traffic on selected network segments. Sniffers are easy to write and install and difficult to detect. The encryption process uses an encryption algorithm and key to transform data at the source, called *plaintext*; turn it into an encrypted form called *ciphertext*, usually unintelligible form; and finally recover it at the sink. The encryption algorithm can either be *symmetric* or *asymmetric*. Symmetric encryption or secret key encryption, as it is usually called, uses a common key and the same cryptographic algorithm to scramble and unscramble the message. Asymmetric encryption commonly known as public key encryption uses two different keys: a public key known by all and a private key known by only the sender and the receiver. Both the sender and the receiver have a pair of these keys, one public and one private. To encrypt a message, a sender uses the receiver's public key which was published. Upon receipt, the recipient of the message decrypts it with his or her private key.

2.3.4 Integrity

The integrity service protects data against active threats such as those that may alter it. Just like data confidentiality, data in transition between the sending and receiving parties is susceptible to many threats from hackers, eavesdroppers, and cryptanalysts whose goal is to intercept the data and alter it based on their motives. This service, through encryption and *hashing algorithms*, ensures that the integrity of the transient data is intact. A hash function takes an input message M and creates a code from it. The code is commonly referred to as a hash or a message digest. A one-way hash function is used to create a signature of the message—just like a human fingerprint. The hash function is, therefore, used to provide the message's integrity and authenticity. The signature is then attached to the message before it is sent by the sender to the recipient.

2.3.5 Nonrepudiation

This is a security service that provides proof of origin and delivery of service and/or information. In real life, it is possible that the sender may deny the ownership of the exchanged digital data that originated from him or her. This service, through *digital signature* and encryption algorithms, ensures that digital data may not be repudiated by providing proof of origin that is difficult to deny. A digital signature is a cryptographic mechanism that is the electronic equivalent of a written signature to authenticate a piece of data as to the identity of the sender.

We have to be careful here because the term "nonrepudiation" has two meanings, one in the legal world and the other in the cryptotechnical world. Adrian McCullagh and Willian Caelli define "nonrepudiation" in a cryptotechnical way as follows [4]:

- In authentication, a service that provides proof of the integrity and origin of data, both in a forgery-proof relationship, which can be verified by any third party at any time

- In authentication, an authentication that with high assurance can be asserted to be genuine and that cannot subsequently be refuted

However, in the legal world, there is always a basis for repudiation. This basis, again according to Adrian McCullagh, can be as follows:

- The signature is a forgery.
- The signature is not a forgery, but was obtained via:
  - Unconscionable conduct by a party to a transaction
  - Fraud instigated by a third party
  - Undue influence exerted by a third party

We will use the cryptotechnical definition throughout the book. To achieve nonrepudiation, users and application environments require a *nonrepudiation service* to collect, maintain, and make available the irrefutable evidence. The best services for nonrepudiation are digital signatures and encryption. These services offer trust by generating unforgettable evidence of transactions that can be used for dispute resolution after the fact.

2.4   Security Standards

The computer network model also suffers from the standardization problem. Security protocols, solutions, and best practices that can secure the computer network model come in many different types and use different technologies resulting in incompatibility of interfaces (more in Chap. 16), less interoperability, and uniformity among the many system resources with differing technologies within the system and between systems. System managers, security chiefs, and experts, therefore, choose or prefer standards, if no de facto standard exists, that are based on service, industry, size, or mission. The type of service offered by an organization determines the types of security standards used. Like service, the nature of the industry an organization is in also determines the types of services offered by the system, which in turn determines the type of standards to adopt. The size of an organization also determines what type of standards to adopt. In relatively small establishments, the ease of implementation and running of the system influence the standards to be adopted. Finally, the mission of the establishment also determines the types of standards used. For example, government agencies have a mission that differs from that of a university. These two organizations, therefore, may choose different standards. We are, therefore, going to discuss security standards along these divisions. Before we do that, however, let us look at the bodies and organizations behind the formulation, development, and maintenance of these standards. These bodies fall into the following categories:

- International organizations such as the Internet Engineering Task Force (IETF), the Institute of Electrical and Electronics Engineers (IEEE), the International

Organization for Standardization (ISO), and the International Telecommunications Union (ITU)

- Multinational organizations like the European Committee for Standardization (CEN), Commission of European Union (CEU), and European Telecommunications Standards Institute (ETSI)
- National governmental organizations like the National Institute of Standards and Technology (NIST), American National Standards Institute (ANSI), and Canadian Standards Council (CSC)
- Sector-specific organizations such as the European Committee for Banking Standards (ECBS), European Computer Manufacturers Association (ECMA), and Institute of Electrical and Electronics Engineers (IEEE)
- Industry standards such as RSA, the Open Group (OSF + X/Open), Object Management Group (OMG), World Wide Web Consortium (W3C), and the Organization for the Advancement of Structured Information Standards (OASIS)
- Other sources of standards in security and cryptography

Each one of these organizations has a set of standards. Table 2.1 shows some of these standards. In the table, x is any digit between 0 and 9.

2.4.1 Security Standards Based on Type of Service/Industry

System and security managers and users may choose a security standard to use based on the type of industry they are in and what type of services that industry provides. Table 2.2 shows some of these services and the corresponding security standards that can be used for these services.

Let us now give some details of some of these standards.

2.4.1.1 Public Key Cryptography Standards (PKCS)

In order to provide a basis and a catalyst for interoperable security based on public key cryptographic techniques, the Public Key Cryptography Standards (PKCS) were established. These are recent security standards, first published in 1991 following discussions of a small group of early adopters of public key technology. Since their establishment, they have become the basis for many formal standards and are implemented widely.

In general, PKCS are security specifications produced by RSA Laboratories in cooperation with secure system developers worldwide for the purpose of accelerating the deployment of public key cryptography. In fact, worldwide contributions from the PKCS series have become part of many formal and de facto standards, including ANSI X9 documents, PKIX, SET, S/MIME, and SSL.

2.4.1.2 The Standards for Interoperable Secure MIME (S/MIME)

Secure/Multipurpose Internet Mail Extensions (S/MIME) is a specification for secure electronic messaging. It came to address a growing problem of e-mail

Table 2.1 Organizations and their standards

Organization	Standards
IETF	IPSec, XML-Signature XPath Filter 2, X.509, Kerberos, S/MIME, RFC 1108 US Department of Defense Security Options for the Internet Protocol, RFC 2196 Site Security Handbook, RFC 2222 Simple Authentication and Security Layer, RFC 2323 IETF Identification and Security Guidelines, RFC 2401 Security Architecture for the Internet Protocol, RFC 2411 IP Security Document Roadmap, RFC 2504 Users' Security Handbook, RFC 2828 Internet Security Glossary, RFC 3365 Strong Security Requirements for Internet Engineering Task Force Standard Protocols, RFC 3414 User-Based Security Model (USM) for version 3 of the Simple Network Management Protocol (SNMPv3), RFC 3631 Security Mechanisms for the Internet, RFC 3871 Operational Security Requirements for Large Internet Service Provider (ISP) IP Network Infrastructure, RFC 4033 DNS Security Introduction and Requirements, RFC 4251 The Secure Shell (SSH) Protocol Architecture, RFC 4301 Security Architecture for the Internet Protocol
ISO	ISO 7498-2:1989 Information processing systems—Open Systems Interconnection, ISO/IEC 979x, ISO/IEC 997, ISO/IEC 1011x, ISO/IEC 11xx, ISO/IEC DTR 13xxx, ISO/IEC DTR 14xxx
ITU	X.2xx, X.5xx, X.7xx, X.80x
ECBS	TR-40x
ECMA	ECMA-13x, ECMA-20x
NIST	X3 Information Processing, X9.xx Financial, X12.xx Electronic Data Exchange
IEEE	P1363 Standard Specifications for Public Key Cryptography, IEEE 802.xx, IEEE P802.11 g, Wireless LAN Medium Access Control (MAC) and Physical Layer (PHY) Specifications
RSA	PKCS #x—Public key cryptographic standard
W3C	XML Encryption, XML Signature, exXensible Key Management Specification (XKMS)

interception and forgery at the time of increasing digital communication. So, in 1995, several software vendors got together and created the S/MIME specification with the goal of making it easy to secure messages from prying eyes.

It works by building a security layer on top of the industry standard MIME protocol based on PKCS. The use of PKCS avails the user of S/MIME with immediate privacy, data integrity, and authentication of an e-mail package. This has given the standard a wide appeal, leading to S/MIME moving beyond just e-mail. Already vendor software warehouses, including Microsoft, Lotus, and Banyan, and other online electronic commerce services are using S/MIME.

2.4.1.3 Federal Information Processing Standards (FIPS)

Federal Information Processing Standards (FIPS) are National Institute of Standards and Technology (NIST)-approved standards for advanced encryption. These are US federal government standards and guidelines in a variety of areas in data processing. They are recommended by NIST to be used by the US government organizations and others in the private sector to protect sensitive information. They range from FIPS 31 issued in 1974 to current FIPS 198.

Table 2.2 Security standards based on services

Area of application	Service	Security standard
Internet security	Network authentication	Kerberos
	Secure TCP/IP communications over the Internet	IPsec
	Privacy-enhanced electronic mail	S/MIME, PGP
	Public Key Cryptography Standards	3DES, DSA, RSA, MD5, SHA-1, PKCS
	Secure Hypertext Transfer Protocol	S-HTTP
	Authentication of directory users	X.509/ISO/IEC 9594-8:2000
	Security protocol for privacy on Internet/transport security	SSL, TLS, SET
Digital signature and encryption	Advanced encryption standard/ PKI/ digital certificates, XML digital signatures	X.509, RSA BSAFE SecurXML-C, DES, AES, DSS/DSA, EESSI, ISO 9xxx, ISO, SHA/SHS, XML digital signatures (XML-DSIG), XML Encryption (XMLENC), XML Key Management Specification (XKMS)
Login and authentication	Authentication of user's right to use system or network resources.	SAML, Liberty Alliance, FIPS 112
Firewall and system security	Security of local, wide, and metropolitan area networks	Secure Data Exchange (SDE) protocol for IEEE 802, ISO/IEC 10164

2.4.1.4 Secure Sockets Layer (SSL)

SSL is an encryption standard for most Web transactions. In fact, it is becoming the most popular type of e-commerce encryption. Most conventional intranet and extranet applications would typically require a combination of security mechanisms that include

- Encryption
- Authentication
- Access control

SSL provides the encryption component implemented within the TCP/IP. Developed by Netscape Communications, SSL provides secure Web client and server communications, including encryption, authentication, and integrity checking for a TCP/IP connection.

2.4.1.5 Web Services Security Standards

In order for Web transactions such as e-commerce to really take off, customers will need to see an open architectural model backed up by a standards-based security framework. Security players, including standards organizations, must provide that open model and a framework that is interoperable, that is, as vendor neutral as possible, and able to resolve critical, often sensitive, issues related to security. The security framework must also include Web interoperability standards for access control, provisioning, biometrics, and digital rights.

To meet the challenges of Web security, two industry rival standards companies are developing new standards for XML digital signatures that include XML Encryption, XML Signature, and exXensible Key Management Specification (XKMS) by the World Wide Web Consortium (W3C), and BSAFE SecurXML-C software development kit (SDK) for implementing XML digital signatures by rival RSA Security. In addition, RSA also offers a Security Assertion Markup Language (SAML) specification, an XML framework for exchanging authentication, and authorization information. It is designed to enable secure single sign-on across portals within and across organizations.

2.4.2 Security Standards Based on Size/Implementation

If the network is small or it is a small organization such as a university, for example, security standards can be spelled out as either the organization's security policy or its best practices on the security of the system, including the physical security of equipment, system software, and application software:

- Physical security: This emphasizes the need for security of computers running the Web servers and how these machines should be kept physically secured in a locked area. Standards are also needed for backup storage media like tapes and removable disks.
- Operating systems: The emphasis here is on privileges and number of accounts, and security standards are set based on these. For example, the number of users with most privileged access like *root* in Unix or *Administrator* in NT should be kept to a minimum. Set standards for privileged users. Keep to a minimum the number of user accounts on the system. State the number of services offered to clients computers by the server, keeping them to a minimum. Set a standard for authentication such as user passwords and for applying security patches.
- System logs: Logs always contain sensitive information such as dates and times of user access. Logs containing sensitive information should be accessible only to authorized staff and should not be publicly accessible. Set a standard on who and when logs should be viewed and analyzed.
- Data security: Set a standard for dealing with files that contain sensitive data. For example, files containing sensitive data should be encrypted wherever possible using strong encryption or should be transferred as soon as possible and practical to a secured system not providing public services.

As an example, Table 2.3 shows how such standards may be set.

Table 2.3 Best security practices for a small organization

Application area	Security standards
Operating systems	Unix, Linux, Windows, etc.
Virus protection	Norton
E-mail	PGP, S/MIME
Firewalls	
Telnet and FTP terminal applications	SSH (secure shell)

2.4.3 Security Standards Based on Interests

In many cases, institutions and government agencies choose to pick a security standard based solely on the interest of the institution or the country. Table 2.4 below shows some security standards based on interest, and the subsections following the table also show security best practices and security standards based more on national interests.

2.4.3.1 British Standard 799 (BS 7799)

The BS 7799 standard outlines a code of practice for information security management that further helps to determine how to secure network systems. It puts forward a common framework that enables companies to develop, implement, and measure effective security management practice and provide confidence in intercompany trading. BS 7799 was first written in 1993, but it was not officially published until 1995, and it was published as an international standard BS ISO/IEC 17799:2000 in December 2000.

2.4.3.2 Orange Book

This is the US Department of Defense *Trusted Computer System Evaluation Criteria* (DOD-5200.28-STD) standard known as the *Orange Book*. For a long time, it has been the de facto standard for computer security used in government and industry, but as we will see in Chap. 15, other standards have now been developed to either supplement it or replace it. First published in 1983, its security levels are referred to as "Rainbow Series."

2.4.4 Security Best Practices

As you noticed from our discussion, there is a rich repertoire of standards security tools on the system and information security landscape because as technology evolves, the security situation becomes more complex and it grows more so every day. With these changes, however, some trends and approaches to security remain the same. One of these constants is having a sound strategy of dealing with the changing security landscape. Developing such a security strategy involves keeping an eye on the reality of the changing technology scene and rapidly increasing security threats. To keep abreast of all these changes, security experts and security

Table 2.4 Interest-based security standards

Area of application	Service	Security standard
Banking	Security within banking IT systems	ISO 8730, ISO 8732, ISO/TR 17944
Financial	Security of financial services	ANSI X9.x, ANSI X9.xx

managers must know how and what to protect and what controls to put in place and at what time. It takes security management, planning, policy development, and the design of security procedures. It's important to remember and definitely understand that there is no procedure, policy, or technology, however much you like it and trust it, that will ever be 100%, so it is important for a company preferably to have a designated security person, a security program officer, and chief security officer (CSO), under the chief information officer (CIO), and to be responsible for the security best practices. Here are some examples of best practices.

Commonly Accepted Security Practices and Regulations (CASPR) Developed by the CASPR Project, this effort aims to provide a set of best practices that can be universally applied to any organization regardless of industry, size or mission. Such best practices would, for example, come from the world's experts in information security. CASPR distills the knowledge into a series of papers and publishes them so they are freely available on the Internet to everyone. The project covers a wide area, including operating system and system security, network and telecommunication security, access control and authentication, infosecurity management, infosecurity auditing and assessment, infosecurity logging and monitoring, application security, application and system development, and investigations and forensics. In order to distribute their papers freely, the founders of CASPR use the open source movement as a guide, and they release the papers under the GNU Free Document License to make sure they and any derivatives remain freely available.

Control Objectives for Information and (Related) Technology (COBIT) Developed by IT auditors and made available through the Information Systems Audit and Control Association, COBIT provides a framework for assessing a security program. COBIT is an open standard for control of information technology. The IT Governance Institute has, together with the worldwide industry experts, analysts, and academics, developed new definitions for COBIT that consist of maturity models, critical success factors (CSFs), key goal indicators (KGIs), and key performance indicators (KPIs). COBIT was designed to help three distinct audiences [5]:

- Management who needs to balance risk and control investment in an often unpredictable IT environment

- Users who need to obtain assurance on the security and controls of the IT services upon which they depend to deliver their products and services to internal and external customers
- Auditors who can use it to substantiate their opinions and/or provide advice to management on internal controls

Operationally Critical Threat, Asset, and Vulnerability Evaluation (*OCTAVE*) by Carnegie Mellon's CERT Coordination Center: OCTAVE is an approach for self- directed information security risk evaluations that [6]:

- Puts organizations in charge
- Balances critical information assets, business needs, threats, and vulnerabilities
- Measures the organization against known or accepted good security practices
- Establishes an organization-wide protection strategy and information security risk mitigation plans

In short, it provides measures based on accepted best practices for evaluating security programs. It does this in three phases:

- It determines information assets that must be protected.
- It evaluates the technology infrastructure to determine if it can protect those assets and how vulnerable it is and defines the risks to critical assets.
- It uses good security practices and establishes an organization-wide protection strategy and mitigation plans for specific risks to critical assets.

General Best Practices—Matthew Putvinski, in his article *IT Security Series Part 1: Information Security Best Practices* [7], discusses under the following general categories:

- Chief information security officer or designate: Establish the need for a security designated officer to oversee security-related issues in the enterprise because the lack of a person responsible for security in any organization means the organization does not give information security priority.
- End user: The security guidelines here must be contained in the organization's security policy of what the organization's end users must and must not do as far as dealing with organization's information in general and computing services in particular. As we move into miniature mobile devices and if a policy is to use a bring-your-own-device (BYOD), specific data handling policies must be in place.
- Software updates and patches: Specific guidelines in the organization security policy book must specifically take a stance on how the organization will use software security patches and upgrades and the frequency of updates.
- Vendor management: If the organization is using software provided by third-party individuals or organizations as vendors, care must be taken to ensure that

any organization's confidential information provided to vendors to help identify a suitable software tool is well documented and indicated to whom.

- Physical security: This is squarely a security policy issue specifically spelling out the physical specification required to safeguard the organization's information and data. These include access to offices and digital equipment, when and where information is stored, and when and where information is destroyed. We will discuss more of this in the coming chapters.
- The following guidelines are also a security policy issues:
  - Data classification and retention
  - Password requirements and guidelines
  - Wireless networking
  - Mobile device usage and access
  - Employee awareness training
  - Incident response

Exercises

1. What is security and information security? What is the difference?
2. It has been stated that security is a continuous process; what are the states in this process?
3. What are the differences between symmetric and asymmetric key systems?
4. What is PKI? Why is it so important in information security?
5. What is the difference between authentication and nonrepudiation?
6. Why is there a dispute between digital nonrepudiation and legal nonrepudiation?
7. Virtual security seems to work in some systems. Why is this so? Can you apply it in a network environment? Support your response.
8. Security best practices are security guidelines and policies aimed at enhancing system security. Can they work without known and proven security mechanisms?
9. Does information confidentiality infer information integrity? Explain your response.
10. What are the best security mechanisms to ensure information confidentiality?

Advanced Exercises

1. In the chapter, we have classified security standards based on industry, size, and mission. What other classifications can you make and why?
2. Most of the encryption standards that are being used such as RSA and DES have not been formally proven to be safe. Why then do we take them to be secure—what evidence do we have?
3. IPsec provides security at the network layer. What other security mechanism is applicable at the network layer? Do network layer security solutions offer better security?

4. Discuss two security mechanisms applied at the application layer. Are they safer than those applied at the lower network layer? Support your response.
5. Are there security mechanisms applicable at transport layer? Is it safer?
6. Discuss the difficulties encountered in enforcing security best practices.
7. Some security experts do not believe in security policies. Do you? Why or why not?
8. Security standards are changing daily. Is it wise to pick a security standard then? Why or why not?
9. If you are an enterprise security chief, how would you go about choosing a security best practice? Is it good security policy to always use a best security practice? What are the benefits of using a best practice?
10. Why it is important to have a security plan despite the various views of security experts concerning its importance?

References

1. Kizza JM (2003) Social and ethical issues in the information age, 2nd edn. Springer, New York
2. Scherphier A. CS596 Client-server programming security. http://www.sdsu.edu/cs596/security. html
3. Mercuri R, Neumann P Security by obscurity. Commun ACM 46(11):160
4. McCullagh A, Caelli W Non-repudiation in the digital environment. http://www.firstmonday. dk/issues/issue5_8/mccullagh/index.html#author
5. CobiT a Practical Toolkit for IT Governance. http://www.ncc.co.uk/ncc/myitadviser/archive/ issue8/business_processes.cfm
6. OCTAVE: Information Security Risk Evaluation. http://www.cert.org/octave/
7. Putvinski M. IT security series part 1: information security best practices. http://www. corporatecomplianceinsights.com/information-security-best-practices

Part II
Security Issues and Challenges in the Traditional Computer Network

Security Threats and Threat Motives to Computer Networks

3

3.1 Introduction

In February, 2002, the Internet security watch group CERT Coordination Center first disclosed to the global audience that global networks, including the Internet, phone systems, and the electrical power grid, are vulnerable to attack because of weakness in programming in a small but key network component. The component, an Abstract Syntax Notation One, or ASN.1, is a communication protocol used widely in the Simple Network Management Protocol (SNMP).

There was widespread fear among government, networking manufacturers, security researchers, and IT executives because the component is vital in many communication grids, including national critical infrastructures such as parts of the Internet, phone systems, and the electrical power grid. These networks were vulnerable to disruptive buffer overflow and malformed packet attacks.

This example illustrates but one of many potential incidents that can cause widespread fear and panic among government, networking manufacturers, security researchers, and IT executives when they think of the consequences of what might happen to the global networks.

The number of threats is rising daily, yet the time window to deal with them is rapidly shrinking. Hacker tools are becoming more sophisticated and powerful. Currently, the average time between the point at which a vulnerability is announced and when it is actually deployed in the wild is getting shorter and shorter.

Traditionally, security has been defined as a process to prevent unauthorized access, use, alteration, theft, or physical damage to an object through maintaining high confidentiality and integrity of information about the object and making information about the object available whenever needed. However, there is a common fallacy, taken for granted by many, that a perfect state of security can be achieved; they are wrong. There is nothing like a secure state of any object, tangible or not, because no such object can ever be in a perfectly secure state and still be useful. An object is secure if the process can maintain its highest intrinsic value. Since the intrinsic value of an object depends on a number of factors, both internal and external

© Springer International Publishing AG 2017
J.M. Kizza, *Guide to Computer Network Security*, Computer Communications and Networks, DOI 10.1007/978-3-319-55606-2_3

to the object during a given time frame, an object is secure if the object assumes its maximum intrinsic value under all possible conditions. The process of security, therefore, strives to maintain the maximum intrinsic value of the object at all times.

Information is an object. Although it is an intangible object, its intrinsic value can be maintained in a high state, thus ensuring that it is secure. Since our focus in this book is on global computer network security, we will view the security of this global network as composed of two types of objects: the tangible objects such as the servers, clients, and communication channels and the intangible object such as information that is stored on servers and clients and that moves through the communication channels.

Ensuring the security of the global computer networks requires maintaining the highest intrinsic value of both the tangible objects and information—the intangible one. Because of both internal and external forces, it is not easy to maintain the highest level of the intrinsic value of an object. These forces constitute a *security threat* to the object. For the global computer network, the security threat is directed to the tangible and the intangible objects that make up the global infrastructure such as servers, clients, communication channels, files, and information.

The threat itself comes in many forms, including viruses, worms, distributed denial of services, and electronic bombs, and derives many motives, including revenge, personal gains, hate, and joy rides, to name but a few.

3.2   Sources of Security Threats

The security threat to computer systems springs from a number of factors that include:

Weaknesses in the network infrastructure and communication protocols that create an appetite and a challenge to the hacker mind

The rapid growth of cyberspace into a vital global communication and business network on which international commerce and business transactions are increasingly being performed and many national critical infrastructures are being connected

The growth of the hacker community whose members are usually experts at gaining unauthorized access into systems that run not only companies and governments but also critical national infrastructures

The vulnerability in operating system protocols whose services run the computers that run the communication network

The insider effect resulting from workers who steal and sell company databases and the mailing lists or even confidential business documents

Social engineering

Physical theft from within the organizations of things such as laptop and handheld computers with powerful communication technology and more potentially sensitive information

Security as a moving target

3.2.1   Design Philosophy

Although the design philosophy on which both the computer network infrastructure and communication protocols built have tremendously boosted was cyberspace development, the same design philosophy has been a constant source of the many ills plaguing cyberspace. The growth of the Internet and cyberspace in general was based on an *open architecture work in progress* philosophy. This philosophy attracted the brightest minds to get their hands dirty and contribute to the infrastructure and protocols. With many contributing their best ideas for free, the Internet grew in leaps and bounds. This philosophy also helped the spirit of individualism and adventurism, both of which have driven the growth of the computer industry and underscored the rapid and sometimes motivated growth of cyberspace.

Because the philosophy was not based on clear blueprints, new developments and additions came about as reactions to the shortfalls and changing needs of a developing infrastructure. The lack of a comprehensive blueprint and the demand-driven design and development of protocols are causing the ever present weak points and loopholes in the underlying computer network infrastructure and protocols.

In addition to the philosophy, the developers of the network infrastructure and protocols also followed a policy to create an interface that is as user-friendly, efficient, and transparent as possible so that all users of all education levels can use it unaware of the working of the networks and therefore are not concerned with the details.

The designers of the communication network infrastructure thought it was better this way if the system is to serve as many people as possible. Making the interface this easy and far removed from the details, though, has its own downside in that the user never cares about and pays very little attention to the security of the system.

Like a magnet, the policy has attracted all sorts of people who exploits the network's vulnerable and weak points in search of a challenge, adventurism, fun, and all forms of personal gratification.

3.2.2   Weaknesses in Network Infrastructure and Communication Protocols

Compounding the problems created by the design philosophy and policy is the weakness in the communication protocols. The Internet is a packet network that works by breaking the data to be transmitted into small individually addressed packets that are downloaded on the network's mesh of switching elements. Each individual packet finds its way through the network with no predetermined route, and the packets are reassembled to form the original message by the receiving element. To work successfully, packet networks need a strong trust relationship that must exist among the transmitting elements.

As packets are disassembled, transmitted, and reassembled, the security of each individual packet and the intermediary transmitting elements must be guaranteed. This is not always the case in the current protocols of cyberspace. There are areas where, through port scans, determined users have managed to intrude, penetrate, fool, and intercept the packets.

The two main communication protocols on each server in the network, UDP and TCP, use port numbers to identify higher-layer services. Each higher-layer service on a client uses a unique port number to request a service from the server, and each server uses a port number to identify the service needed by a client. The cardinal rule of a secure communication protocol in a server is never to leave any port open in the absence of a useful service. If no such service is offered, its port should never be open. Even if the service is offered by the server, its port should never be left open unless it is legitimately in use.

In the initial communication between a client and a server, the client addresses the server via a port number in a process called a *three-way handshake*. The three-way handshake, when successful, establishes a TCP virtual connection between the server and the client. This virtual connection is required before any communication between the two can begin. The process begins by a client/host sending a TCP segment with the synchronize (SYN) flag set; the server/host responds with a segment that has the acknowledge valid (ACK) and SYN flags set, and the first host responds with a segment that has only the ACK flag set. This exchange is shown in Fig. 3.1. The three-way handshake suffers from a *half-open* socket problem when the server trusts the client that originated the handshake and leaves its port door open for further communication from the client.

As long as the half-open port remains open, an intruder can enter the system because while one port remains open, the server can still entertain other three-way handshakes from other clients that want to communicate with it. Several half-open ports can lead to network security exploits including both TCP/IP and UDP protocols: Internet Protocol spoofing (IP spoofing), in which IP addresses of the source element in the data packets are altered and replaced with bogus addresses, and SYN flooding where the server is overwhelmed by spoofed packets sent to it.

In addition to the three-way handshake, ports are used widely in network communication. There are well-known ports used by processes that offer services. For example, ports 0 through 1023 are used widely by system processes and other highly privileged programs. This means that if access to these ports is compromised, the intruder can get access to the whole system. Intruders find open ports via port scans. The two examples below from G-Lock Software illustrate how a port scan can be made [1]:

- *TCP connect( ) scanning* is the most basic form of TCP scanning. An attacker's host is directed to issue a connect( ) system call to a list of selected ports on the target machine. If any of these ports is listening, connect( ) system call will succeed; otherwise, the port is unreachable and the service is unavailable.

Fig. 3.1 A three-way
handshake

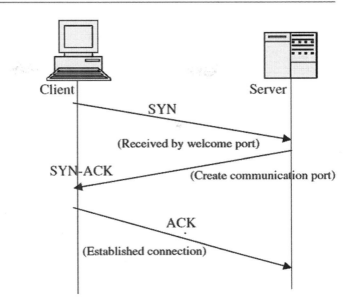

Client   Server

SYN

(Received by welcome port)

SYN-ACK

(Create communication port)

ACK

(Established connection)

- *UDP Internet Control Message Protocol (ICMP) port unreachable scanning* is
  one of the few UDP scans. Recall from Chap. 1 that UDP is a connectionless
  protocol; so, it is harder to scan than TCP because UDP ports are not required to
  respond to probes. Most implementations generate an ICMP port_unreachable
  error when an intruder sends a packet to a closed UDP port. When this response
  does not come, the intruder has found an active port.

In addition to port number weaknesses usually identifiable via port scans, both
TCP and UDP protocols suffer from other weaknesses.

Packet transmissions between network elements can be intercepted and their
contents altered such as in *initial sequence number attack*. Sequence numbers are
integer numbers assigned to each transmitted packet, indicating their order of
arrival at the receiving element. Upon receipt of the packets, the receiving element
acknowledges it in a two-way communication session during which both the
transmitting elements talk to each other simultaneously in full duplex.

In the initial sequence number attack, the attacker intercepts the communication
session between two or more communicating elements and then guesses the next
sequence number in a communication session. The intruder then slips the spoofed
IP addresses into the packets transmitted to the server. The server sends an
acknowledgment to the spoofed clients. Infrastructure vulnerability attacks also
include session attacks, packet sniffing, buffer overflow, and session hijacking.
These attacks are discussed in later chapters.

The infrastructure attacks we have discussed so far are of the penetration type
where the intruder physically enters the system infrastructure, either at the transmitting element or in the transmitting channel levels, and alters the content of

packets. In the next set of infrastructure attacks, a different approach of vulnerability exploitation is used. This is the distributed denial of services (DDoS).

The DDoS attacks are attacks that are generally classified as nuisance attacks in the sense that they simply interrupt the services of the system. System interruption can be as serious as destroying a computer's hard disk or as simple as using up all the available memory of the system. DDoS attacks come in many forms, but the most common are the following: smurfing, ICMP protocol, and ping of death attacks.

The "smurf" attack utilizes the broken down trust relationship created by IP spoofing. An offending element sends a large amount of spoofed ping packets containing the victim's IP address as the source address. Ping traffic, also called Protocol Overview Internet Control Message Protocol (ICMP) in the Internet community, is used to report out-of-band messages related to network operation or mis-operation such as a host or entire portion of the network being unreachable, owing to some type of failure. The pings are then directed to a large number of network subnets, a subnet being a small independent network such as a LAN. If all the subnets reply to the victim address, the victim element receives a high rate of requests from the spoofed addresses as a result, and the element begins buffering these packets. When the requests come at a rate exceeding the capacity of the queue, the element generates ICMP source quench messages meant to slow down the sending rate. These messages are then sent, supposedly, to the legitimate sender of the requests. If the sender is legitimate, it will heed the requests and slow down the rate of packet transmission. However, in cases of spoofed addresses, no action is taken because all sender addresses are bogus. The situation in the network can easily deteriorate further if each routing device itself takes part in smurfing.

We have outlined a small part of a list of several hundred types of known infrastructure vulnerabilities that are often used by hackers to either penetrate systems and destroy, alter, or introduce foreign data into the system or disable the system through port scanning and DDoS. Although for these known vulnerabilities, equipment manufacturers and software producers have done a considerable job of issuing patches as soon as a loophole or a vulnerability is known, quite often, as was demonstrated in the Code Red fiasco, not all network administrators adhere to the advisories issued to them.

Furthermore, new vulnerabilities are being discovered almost everyday either by hackers in an attempt to show their skills by exposing these vulnerabilities or by users of new hardware or software such as what happened with the Microsoft Windows IIS in the case of the Code Red worm. Also, the fact that most of these exploits use known vulnerabilities is indicative of our abilities in patching known vulnerabilities even if the solutions are provided.

3.2.3 Rapid Growth of Cyberspace

There is always a security problem in numbers. Since its beginning as ARPANET in the early 1960s, the Internet has experienced phenomenal growth, especially in the last 10 years. There was an explosion in the numbers of users, which in turn ignited an explosion in the number of connected computers.

Just less than 20 years ago in 1985, the Internet had fewer than 2000 computers connected, and the corresponding number of users was in the mere tens of thousands. However, by 2001, the figure has jumped to about 109 million hosts, according to Tony Rutkowski at the Center for Next Generation Internet, an Internet Software Consortium. This number represents a significant new benchmark for the number of Internet hosts. At a reported current annual growth rate of 51% over the past 2 years, this shows continued strong exponential growth, with an estimated growth of up to 1 billion hosts if the same growth rate is sustained [2].

This is a tremendous growth by all accounts. As it grew, it brought in more and more users with varying ethical standards, added more services, and created more responsibilities. By the turn of the century, many countries found their national critical infrastructures firmly intertwined in the global network. An interdependence between humans and computers and between nations on the global network has been created that has led to a critical need to protect the massive amount of information stored on these network computers. The ease of use of and access to the Internet and large quantities of personal, business, and military data stored on the Internet was slowly turning into a massive security threat not only to individuals and business interests but also to national defenses.

As more and more people enjoyed the potential of the Internet, more and more people with dubious motives were also drawn to the Internet because of its enormous wealth of everything they were looking for. Such individuals have posed a potential risk to the information content of the Internet, and such a security threat has to be dealt with.

Statistics from the security company Symantec show that Internet attack activity is currently growing by about 64% per year. The same statistics show that during the first 6 months of 2002, companies connected to the Internet were attacked, on average, 32 times per week compared to only 25 times per week in the last 6 months of 2001. Symantec reports between 400 and 500 new viruses every month and about 250 vulnerabilities in computer programs [3].

In fact, the rate at which the Internet is growing is becoming the greatest security threat ever. Security experts are locked in a deadly race with these malicious hackers that at the moment looks like a losing battle with the security community.

3.2.4   The Growth of the Hacker Community

Although other factors contributed significantly to the security threat, in the general public view, the number one contributor to the security threat of computer and telecommunication networks more than anything else is the growth of the hacker community. Hackers have managed to bring this threat into news headlines and people's living rooms through the ever-increasing and sometimes devastating attacks on computer and telecommunication systems using viruses, worms, DDoS, and other security attacks.

Table 3.1 Global hacker groups

0–9	I	R
The 414s	*Impact Team*	Red Hacker Alliance
A	Infonomicon	Redhack
AnonCoders	IPhone Dev Team	**S**
Anontune	Iranian Cyber Army	Securax
Anonymous (group)	Islamic State Hacking Division	Sofacy Group
Antisec Movement	Israeli Elite Force	Syrian Electronic Army
APT29	**L**	**T**
B	L0pht	Team Elite
Backtrace Security	Lazarus Group	TeaMp0isoN
C	Legion of Doom (hacking)	TeslaTeam
Chaos Computer Club	Level Seven (hacking group)	TESO (Austrian hacker group)
Croatian Revolution Hackers	Lizard Squad	The Shadow Brokers
Cult of the Dead Cow	LulzSec	The Shmoo Group
Cyber-collection	LulzRaft	The Unknowns
CyberBerkut	**M**	Titan Rain
Cyberwarfare in China	MalSec	**U**
D	Masters of Deception	UGNazi
Dark0de	Mazafaka (hacker group)	UXu
Decocidio	Milw0rm	**W**
Derp (hacker group)	Moonlight Maze	W00w00
Digital DawgPound	**N**	World of Hell
F	Network Crack Program Hacker (NCPH) Group	**X**
FinnSec Security	NullCrew	Xbox Underground
G	**O**	XDedic
Gay Nigger Association of America	Operation High Roller	**Y**
Genocide2600	Operation Sundevil	Yemen Cyber Army
Ghost Security	OurMine	
Global kOS	**P**	
GlobalHell	P.H.I.R.M.	
Goatse Security	Pakbugs	
H	Pangu Team	
HacDC	Phone Losers of America	
Hack Canada	Plover-NET	
HackBB	Port7Alliance	
Hacker Bible	Power Racing Series	
Hacker Dojo		
HackerspaceSG		
Hacktivismo		
Hackweiser		

(continued)

Table 3.1 (continued)

Harford Hackerspace		
Helith		
Hell (forum)		
Honker Union		
HubCityLabs		

Reference source: http://en.wikipedia.org/wiki/Category:Hacker_groups. Last modified on 2 June 2016, at 22:14

Until recently most hacker communities worked underground forming groups global like some in Table 3.1. Today, hackers are no longer considered as bad to computer networks as it used to be, and now hackers are being used by governments and organization to do the opposite of what they were supposed to be doing, defending national critical networks and hardening company networks. Increasingly, hacker groups and individuals are being used in clandestine campaigns of attacking other nations. So hacker groups and individuals are no longer as much under the cloud of suspicion as causing mayhem to computer networks, and many are now in the open. In fact hacker Web sites like www.hacker.org with messages like "The hacker explores the intersection of art and science in an insatiable quest to understand and shape the world around him. We guide you on this journey." are legitimately popping up everywhere.

However, for long, the general public, computer users, policy makers, parents, and law makers have watched in bewilderment and awe as the threat to their individual and national security has grown to alarming levels as the size of the global networks have grown and national critical infrastructures have become more and more integrated into this global network. In some cases, the fear from these attacks reached hysterical proportions, as demonstrated in the following major attacks that we have rightly called the big "bungs."

3.2.4.1 The Big "Bungs"

The Internet Worm
On November 2, 1988, Robert T. Morris, Jr., a computer science graduate student at Cornell University, using a computer at MIT, released what he thought was a benign experimental, self-replicating, and self-propagating program on the MIT computer network. Unfortunately, he did not debug the program well before running it. He soon realized his mistake when the program he thought was benign went out of control. The program started replicating itself and at the same time infecting more computers on the network at a faster rate than he had anticipated. There was a bug in his program. The program attacked many machines at MIT and very quickly went beyond the campus to infect other computers around the country. Unable to stop his own program from spreading, he sought a friend's help. He and his friend tried unsuccessfully to send an anonymous message from Harvard over

the network, instructing programmers how to kill the program—now a worm—and prevent its reinfection of other computers. The worm spread like wildfire to infect some 6000 networked computers, a whopping number in proportion to the 1988 size of the Internet, clogging government and university systems. In about 12 h, programmers in affected locations around the country succeeded in stopping the worm from spreading further. It was reported that Morris took advantage of a hole in the debug mode of the Unix *sendmail* program. Unix then was a popular operating system that was running thousands of computers on university campuses around the country. Sendmail runs on Unix to handle e-mail delivery.

Morris was apprehended a few days later; taken to court; sentenced to 3 years, probation, a $10,000 fine, and 400 h of community service; and dismissed from Cornell. Morris's worm came to be known as the Internet worm. The estimated cost of the Internet worm varies from $53,000 to as high as $96 million, although the exact figure will never be known [4].

Michelangelo Virus

The world first heard of the Michelangelo virus in 1991. The virus affected only PCs running MS-DOS 2.xx and higher versions. Although it overwhelmingly affected PCs running DOS, it also affected PCs running other operating systems such as Unix, OS/2, and Novell. It affected computers by infecting floppy disk boot sectors and hard disk master boot records. Once in the boot sectors of the bootable disk, the virus then installed itself in memory from where it would infect the partition table of any other disk on the computer, whether a floppy or a hard disk.

For several years, a rumor was rife, more so many believe, as a scare tactic by antivirus software manufactures that the virus is to be triggered on March 6 of every year to commemorate the birth date of the famous Italian painter. But in real terms, the actual impact of the virus was rare. However, because of the widespread publicity it received, the Michelangelo virus became one of the most disastrous viruses ever, with damages into millions of dollars.

Pathogen, Queeg, and Smeg Viruses

Between 1993 and April 1994, Christopher Pile, a 26-year-old resident of Devon in Britain, commonly known as the "Black Baron" in the hacker community, wrote three computer viruses, *Pathogen*, *Queeg*, and *Smeg*, all named after expressions used in the British sci-fi comedy "Red Dwarf." He used *Smeg* to camouflage both *Pathogen* and *Queeg*. The camouflage of the two programs prevented most known antivirus software from detecting the viruses. Pile wrote the *Smeg* in such a way that others could also write their own viruses and use *Smeg* to camouflage them. This meant that the *Smeg* could be used as a locomotive engine to spread all sorts of viruses. Because of this, Pile's viruses were extremely deadly at that time. Pile used a variety of ways to distribute his deadly software, usually through bulletin boards and freely downloadable Internet software used by thousands in cyberspace.

Pile was arrested on May 26, 1995. He was charged with 11 counts that included the creation and release of these viruses that caused modification and destruction of computer data and inciting others to create computer viruses. He pleaded guilty to 10 of the 11 counts and was sentenced to 18 months in prison.

Pile's case was in fact not the first one as far as creating and distributing computer viruses was concerned. In October 1992, three Cornell University students were each sentenced to several hundred hours of community service for creating and disseminating a computer virus. However, Pile's case was significant in that it was the first widely covered and published computer crime case that ended in a jail sentence [5].

Melissa Virus

On March 26, 1999, the global network of computers was greeted with a new virus named Melissa. Melissa was created by David Smith, a 29-year-old New Jersey computer programmer. It was later learned that he named the virus after a Florida stripper.

The Melissa virus was released from an "alt.sex" newsgroup using the America OnLine (AOL) account of Scott Steinmetz, whose username was "skyroket." However, Steinmetz, the owner of the AOL account who lived in the western US state of Washington, denied any knowledge of the virus, let alone knowing anybody else using his account. It looked like Smith hacked his account to disguise his tracks.

The virus, which spreads via a combination of Microsoft's Outlook and Word programs, takes advantage of Word documents to act as surrogates and the users' e-mail address book entries to propagate it. The virus then mailed itself to each entry in the address book in either the original Word document named "list.doc" or in a future Word document carrying it after the infection. It was estimated that Melissa affected more than 100,000 e-mail users and caused $80 million in damages during its rampage.

The Y2K Bug

From 1997 to December 31, 1999, the world was gripped by apprehension over one of the greatest myths and misnomers in the history. This was never a bug, a software bug as we know it, but a myth shrouded in the following story. Decades ago, because of memory storage restrictions and expanse of time, computer designers and programmers together made a business decision. They decided to represent the date field by two digits such as "89" and "93" instead of the usual four digits such as "1956." The purpose was noble, but the price was humongous.

The bug, therefore, is: On New Year's Eve of 1999, when world clocks were supposed to change over from 31/12/99 to 01/01/00 at 12:00 midnight, many computers, especially the older ones, were supposed not to know which year it was since it would be represented by "00." Many, of course, believed that computers would then assume anything from year "0000" to "1900," and this would be catastrophic.

Because the people who knew much were unconvinced about the bug, it was known by numerous names to suit the believer. Among the names were:

millennium bug, Y2K computer bug, Y2K, Y2K problem, Y2K crisis, Y2K bug, and many others.

The good news is that the year 2000 came and went with very few incidents of one of the most feared computer bug of our time.

The Goodtimes E-mail Virus

Yet another virus hoax, the *Goodtimes virus*, was humorous, but it ended up being a chain e-mail annoying everyone in its path because of the huge amount of "e-mail virus alerts" it generated. Its humor is embedded in the following prose: Goodtimes will re-write your hard drive. Not only that, but it will also scramble any disks that are even close to your computer. It will recalibrate your refrigerator's coolness setting so all your ice cream melts. It will demagnetize the strips on all your credit cards, make a mess of the tracking on your television, and use subspace field harmonics to scratch any CD you try to play.

It will give your ex-girlfriend your new phone number. It will mix Kool-Aid into your fish tank. It will drink all your beer and leave its socks out on the coffee table when company is coming over. It will put a dead kitten in the back pocket of your good suit pants and hide your car keys when you are running late for work.

Goodtimes will make you fall in love with a penguin. It will give you nightmares about circus midgets. It will pour sugar in your gas tank and shave off both your eyebrows while dating your current girlfriend behind your back and billing the dinner and hotel room to your Visa card.

It will seduce your grandmother. It does not matter if she is dead. Such is the power of Goodtimes; it reaches out beyond the grave to sully those things we hold most dear.

It moves your car randomly around parking lots so you can't find it. It will kick your dog. It will leave libidinous messages on your boss's voice mail in your voice! It is insidious and subtle. It is dangerous and terrifying to behold. It is also a rather interesting shade of mauve.

Goodtimes will give you Dutch Elm disease. It will leave the toilet seat up. It will make a batch of methamphetamine in your bathtub and then leave bacon cooking on the stove while it goes out to chase gradeschoolers with your new snowblower.

Distributed Denial of Service (DDoS)

February 7, 2000, a month after the Y2K bug scare and Goodtimes hoax, the world woke up to the real thing. This was not a hoax or a myth. On this day, a 16-year-old Canadian hacker nicknamed "Mafiaboy" launched his distributed denial-of-service (DDoS) attack. Using the Internet's infrastructure weaknesses and tools, he unleashed a barrage of remotely coordinated blitz of GB/s IP packet requests from selected, sometimes unsuspecting, victim servers which, in a coordinated fashion, bombarded and flooded and eventually overcame and knocked out Yahoo servers for a period of about 3 h. Within 2 days, while technicians at Yahoo and law enforcement agencies were struggling to identify the source of the

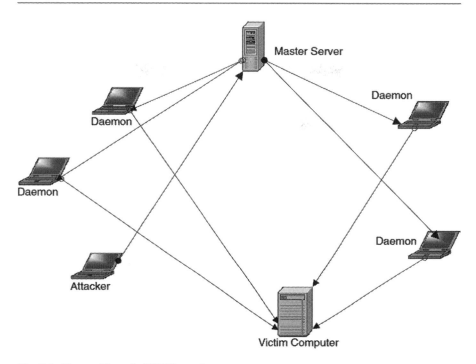

Fig. 3.2   The working of a DDOS attack

attacker, on February 9, 2000, Mafiaboy struck again, this time bombarding servers at eBay, Amazon, Buy.com, ZDNet, CNN, E*Trade, and MSN.

The DDoS attack employs a network consisting of a master computer responsible for directing the attacks, the "innocent" computers commonly known as "daemons" used by the master as intermediaries in the attack, and the victim computer—a selected computer to be attacked. Figure 3.2 shows how this works.

After the network has been selected, the hacker instructs the master node to further instruct each daemon in its network to send several authentication requests to the selected network nodes, filling up their request buffers. All requests have false return addresses; so, the victim nodes can't find the user when they try to send back the authentication approval. As the nodes wait for acknowledgments, sometimes even before they close the connections, they are again and again bombarded with more requests. When the rate of requests exceeds the speed at which the victim node can take requests, the nodes are overwhelmed and brought down.

The primary objective of a DDoS attack are multifaceted, including flooding a network to prevent legitimate network traffic from going through the network, disrupting network connections to prevent access to services between network nodes, preventing a particular individual network node from accessing either all network services or specified network services, and disrupting network services to either a specific part of the network or selected victim machines on the network.

The Canadian judge stated that although the act was done by an adolescent, the motivation of the attack was undeniable and had a criminal intent. He, therefore, sentenced the Mafiaboy, whose real name was withheld because he was under age, to serve 8 months in a youth detention center and 1 year of probation after his release from the detention center. He was also ordered to donate $250 to charity.

Love Bug Virus

On April 28, 2000, Onel de Guzman, a dropout from AMA computer college in Manila, Philippines, released a computer virus onto the global computer network. The virus was first uploaded to the global networks via a popular Internet Relay Chat program using Impact, an Internet ISP. It was then uploaded to Sky Internet's servers, another ISP in Manila, and it quickly spread to global networks, first in Asia and then Europe. In Asia, it hit a number of companies hard, including the Dow Jones Newswire and the *Asian Wall Street Journal*. In Europe, it left thousands of victims that included big companies and parliaments. In Denmark, it hit TV2 channel and the Danish parliament, and in Britain, the House of Commons fell victim too. Within 12 h of release, it was on the North American continent, where the US Senate computer system was among the victims [6].

It spread via Microsoft Outlook e-mail systems as surrogates. It used a rather sinister approach by tricking the user to open an e-mail presumably from someone the user knew (because the e-mail usually came from an address book of someone the user knew). The e-mail, as seen in Fig. 3.3, requests the user to check the attached "Love Letter." The attachment file was in fact a Visual Basic Script, which contained the virus payload. The virus then became harmful when the user opened the attachment. Once the file was opened, the virus copied itself to two critical system directories and then added triggers to the Windows registry to ensure that it ran every time the computer was rebooted. The virus then replicated itself, destroying system files including Web development such as ".js" and ".css" and multimedia files such as JPEG and MP3, searched for log-in names and passwords in the user's address book, and then mailed itself again [6].

de Guzman was tracked down within hours of the release of the virus. Security officials, using a caller ID of the phone number and ISP used by de Guzman, were led to an apartment in the poor part of Manila where de Guzman lived.

The virus devastated global computer networks, and it was estimated that it caused losses ranging between $7 billion and $20 billion [7].

Palm Virus

In August 2000, the actual palm virus was released under the name of Liberty Trojan horse, the first known malicious program targeting the Palm OS. The Liberty Trojan horse duped some people into downloading a program that erased data.

Another palm virus shortly followed Palm Liberty. On September 21, 2000, McAfee.com and F-Secure, two of the big antivirus companies, first discovered a really destructive palm virus they called Palm OS/Phage. When Palm OS/Phage is executed, the screen is filled with a dark gray box, and the application is terminated. The virus then replicates itself to other Palm OS applications.

Fig. 3.3 The love bug
monitor display

Wireless device viruses have not been widespread, thanks to the fact that the majority of Palm OS users do not download programs directly from the Web but via their desktop and then sync to their palm. Because of this, they have virus protection available to them at either their ISP's Internet gateway, at the desktop, or at their corporation.

The appearance of a Palm virus in cyberspace raises many concerns about the security of cyberspace because PDAs are difficult to check for viruses as they are not hooked up to a main corporate network. PDAs are moving as users move, making virus tracking and scanning difficult.

Anna Kournikova Virus

On February 12, 2001, global computer networks were hit again by a new virus, Anna Kournikova, named after the Russian tennis star. The virus was released by 20-year-old Dutchman Jan de Wit, commonly known in the hacker underworld community as "OnTheFly." The virus, like the I LOVE YOU virus before it, was a mass-mailing type. Written in Visual Basic scripting language, the virus spreads by mailing itself, disguised as a JPEG file named *Anna Kournikova*, through Microsoft Windows, Outlook, and other e-mail programs on the Internet.

The subject line of mail containing the virus bears the following: "Here ya have,;0)," "Here you are ;-)," or "here you go ;-)." Once opened, Visual Basic Script copies itself to a Windows directory as "AnnaKournikova.jpg.vbs." It then mails itself to all entries in the user's Microsoft Outlook e-mail address book. Figure 3.4 shows the Anna Kournikova monitor screen display.

Spreading at twice the speed of the notorious "I LOVE YOU" bug, Anna quickly circumvented the globe.

Fig. 3.4 Anna Kournikova
monitor display

Security experts believe Anna was of the type commonly referred to as a "virus creation kit," "a do-it-yourself program kit" that potentially makes everyone able to create a malicious code.

Code Red: "For One Moment Last Week, the Internet Stood Still."[1]

The Code Red worm was first released on July 12, 2001, from Foshan University in China, and it was detected the next day July 13 by senior security engineer Ken Eichman. However, when detected, it was not taken seriously until 4 days later when engineers at eEye Digital cracked the worm code and named it "Code Red" after staying awake with "Code Red"—labeled Mountain Dew [8]. By this time, the worm had started to spread, though slowly. Then on July 19, according to Rob Lemos, it is believed that someone modified the worm, fixing a problem with its random-number generator. The new worm started to spread like wildfire spreading, leaping from 15,000 infections that morning to almost 350,000 infections by 5 p.m. PDT [8].

The worm was able to infect computers because it used a security hole, discovered the month before, in computers using Microsoft's Internet Information Server (IIS) in the Windows NT4 and Windows 2000 Index Services. The hole, known as the Index Server ISAPI vulnerability, allowed the intruder to take control of a security vulnerability in these systems, resulting in one of several outcomes, including Web site defacement and installation of denial-of-service tools. The following Web defacement "*HELLO! Welcome to* http://www.worm.com*! Hacked By Chinese!*" usually resulted. The Web defacement was done by the worm

---

[1]Lemos, Rob. "Code Red: Virulent worm calls into doubt our ability to protect the Net," CNET News.com, July 27, 2001.

connecting to TCP port 80 on a randomly chosen host. If the connection was successful, the attacking host sent a crafted HTTP GET request to the victim, attempting to exploit a buffer overflow in the Indexing Service [9].

Because Code Red was self-propagating, the victim computer would then send the same exploit (HTTP GET request) to another set of randomly chosen hosts.

Although Microsoft issued a patch when the security hole was discovered, not many servers were patched before Code Red hit. Because of the large number of IIS servers on the Internet, Code Red found the going easy, and at its peak, it hit up to 300,000 servers. But Code Red did not do as much damage as feared; because of its own design flaw, the worm was quickly brought under control.

SQL Worm

On Saturday, January 25, 2003, the global communication network was hit by the SQL worm. The worm, which some refer to as the "SQL Slammer," spreads to computers that are running Microsoft SQL Server with a blank SQL administrator password. Once in the system, it copies files to the infected computer and changes the SQL administrator password to a string of four random characters.

The vulnerability exploited by the slammer warm preexisted in the Microsoft SQL Server 2000 and in fact was discovered 6 months prior to the attack. When the vulnerability was discovered, Microsoft offered a free patch to fix the problem; however, the word never got around to all users of the server software.

The worm spread rapidly in networks across Asia, Europe, and the United States and Canada, shutting down businesses and government systems. However, its effects were not very serious because of its own weaknesses that included its inability to affect secure servers and its ease of detection.

Hackers View 8 Million Visa/MasterCard, Discover, and American Express Accounts

On Monday, February 17, 2003, the two major credit card companies Visa and MasterCard reported a major infiltration into a third-party payment card processor by a hacker who gained access to more than 5 million Visa and MasterCard accounts throughout the United States. Card information exposed included card numbers and personal information that included social security numbers and credit limits.

The flood of the hacker victims increased by two on Tuesday, February 18, 2003, when both Discover Financial Services and American Express reported that they were also victims of the same hacker who breached the security system of a company that processes transactions on behalf of merchants.

While MasterCard and Visa had earlier reported that around 2.2 million and 3.4 million of their own cards were respectively affected, Discover Financial Services and American Express would not disclose how many accounts were involved. It is estimated, however, that the number of affected accounts in the security breach was as high as 8 million.

3.2.5   Vulnerability in Operating System Protocol

One area that offers the greatest security threat to global computer systems is the area of software errors, especially network operating systems errors. An operating system plays a vital role not only in the smooth running of the computer system in controlling and providing vital services, but by playing a crucial role in the security of the system in providing access to vital system resources. A vulnerable operating system can allow an attacker to take over a computer system and do anything that any authorized super user can do, such as changing files, installing and running software, or reformatting the hard drive.

Every OS comes with some security vulnerabilities. In fact many security vulnerabilities are OS specific. Hacker looks for OS-identifying information like file extensions for exploits.

3.2.6   The Invisible Security Threat: The Insider Effect

Quite often, news media reports show that in cases of violent crimes such as murder, one is more likely to be attacked by someone one does not know. However, real official police and court records show otherwise. This is also the case in network security. Research data from many reputable agencies consistently show that the greatest threat to security in any enterprise is the guy down the hall.

In 1997, the accounting firm Ernst & Young interviewed 4226 IT managers and professionals from around the world about the security of their networks. From the responses, 75% of the managers indicated that they believed authorized users and employees represent a threat to the security of their systems. Forty-two percent of the Ernst and Young respondents reported they had experienced external malicious attacks in the past year, while 43% reported malicious acts from employees [10].

The inside threat to organizational security comes from one of its own, the untrustworthy member of the organization. This "insider threat" is a person possibly who has privileged access to classified, sensitive, or propriety data and who uses this unique opportunity to remove information from the organization and transfer to unauthorized outsider users.

According to Jack Strauss, president and CEO of SafeCorp, a professional information security consultancy in Dayton, Ohio, company insiders intentionally or accidentally misusing information pose the greatest information security threat to today's Internet-centric businesses. Strauss believes that it is a mistake for company security chiefs to neglect to lock the backdoor to the building, to encrypt sensitive data on their laptops, or not to revoke access privileges when employees leave the company [11].

3.2.7 Social Engineering

Besides the security threat from the insiders themselves who knowingly and willingly are part of the security threat, the insider effect can also involve insiders unknowingly being part of the security threat through the power of *social engineering*. Social engineering consists of an array of methods an intruder such as a hacker, both from within or outside the organization, can use to gain system authorization through masquerading as an authorized user of the network. Social engineering can be carried out using a variety of methods, including physically impersonating an individual known to have access to the system, online, and telephone and even by writing. The infamous hacker Kevin Mitnick used social engineering extensively to break into some of the nation's most secure networks with a combination of his incredible solid computer hacking and social engineering skills to coax information, such as passwords, out of people.

3.2.8 Physical Theft

As the demand for information by businesses to stay competitive and nations to remain strong heats up, laptop computer and PDA theft is on the rise. There is a whole list of incidents involving laptop computer theft such as the reported disappearance of a laptop used to log incidents of covert nuclear proliferation from a sixth-floor room in the headquarters of the US State Department in January, 2000. In March of the same year, a British accountant working for the MI5, a British national spy agency, had his laptop computer snatched from between his legs while waiting for a train at London's Paddington Station. In December 1999, someone stole a laptop from the car of Bono, lead singer for the megaband U2; it contained months of crucial work on song lyrics. And according to the computer-insurance firm Safeware, some 319,000 laptops were stolen in 1999, at a total cost of more than $800 million for the hardware alone [12]. Thousands of company executive laptops and PDA disappear every year with years of company secrets.

3.3 Security Threat Motives

Although we have seen that security threats can originate from natural disasters and unintentional human activities, the bulk of cyberspace threats and then attacks originate from humans caused by illegal or criminal acts from either insiders or outsiders, recreational hackers, and criminals. The FBI's foreign counterintelligence mission has broadly categorized security threats based on terrorism; military espionage; economic espionage, targeting the National Information Infrastructure; vendetta and revenge; and hate [13].

3.3.1 Terrorism

Our increasing dependence on computers and computer communication has opened up the can of worms, we now know as electronic terrorism. Electronic terrorism is used to attack military installations, banking, and many other targets of interest based on politics, religion, and probably hate. Those who are using this new brand of terrorism are a new breed of hackers, who no longer hold the view of cracking systems as an intellectual exercise but as a way of gaining from the action. The "new" hacker is a cracker who knows and is aware of the value of information that he/she is trying to obtain or compromise. But cyberterrorism is not only about obtaining information; it is also about instilling fear and doubt and compromising the integrity of the data.

Some of these hackers have a mission, usually foreign power-sponsored or foreign power-coordinated that, according to the FBI, may result in violent acts, dangerous to human life, that are a violation of the criminal laws of the targeted nation or organization and are intended to intimidate or coerce people so as to influence the policy.

3.3.2 Military Espionage

For generations, countries have been competing for supremacy of one form or another. During the Cold War, countries competed for military spheres. After it ended, the espionage turf changed from military aim to gaining access to highly classified commercial information that would not only let them know what other countries are doing but also might give them either a military or commercial advantage without them spending a great deal of money on the effort. It is not surprising, therefore, that the spread of the Internet has given a boost and a new lease on life to a dying Cold War profession. Our high dependency on computers in the national military and commercial establishments has given espionage a new fertile ground. Electronic espionage has many advantages over its old-fashion, trench-coated, sun-glassed, and gloved Hitchcock-style cousin. For example, it is less expensive to implement; it can gain access into places that would be inaccessible to human spies; it saves embarrassment in case of failed or botched attempts; and it can be carried out at a place and time of choice.

3.3.3 Economic Espionage

The end of the Cold War was supposed to bring to an end-spirited and intensive military espionage. However, in the wake of the end of the Cold War, the United States, as a leading military, economic, and information superpower, found itself a constant target of another kind of espionage, economic espionage. In its pure form, economic espionage targets economic trade secrets which, according to the 1996 US Economic Espionage Act, are defined as all forms and types of financial, business, scientific, technical, economic, or engineering information and all types of intellectual property including patterns, plans, compilations, program devices, formulas, designs, prototypes, methods, techniques, processes, procedures, programs, and/or codes, whether tangible or not, stored or not, and compiled or not [14]. To enforce this act and prevent computer attacks targeting American commercial interests, US Federal Law authorizes law enforcement agencies to use wiretaps and other surveillance means to curb computer-supported information espionage.

3.3.4 Targeting the National Information Infrastructure

The threat may be foreign power sponsored or foreign power coordinated, directed at a target country, corporation, establishments, or persons. It may target specific facilities, personnel, information, or computer, cable, satellite, or telecommunication systems that are associated with the National Information Infrastructure.

Activities may include the following [15]:

- Denial or disruption of computer, cable, satellite, or telecommunication services
- Unauthorized monitoring of computer, cable, satellite, or telecommunication systems
- Unauthorized disclosure of proprietary or classified information stored within or communicated through computer, cable, satellite, or telecommunication systems
- Unauthorized modification or destruction of computer programming codes, computer network databases, stored information, or computer capabilities
- Manipulation of computer, cable, satellite, or telecommunication services resulting in fraud, financial loss, or other federal criminal violations

3.3.5 Vendetta/Revenge

There are many causes that lead to vendettas. The demonstrations at the last World Trade Organization (WTO) in Seattle, Washington, and subsequent demonstrations at the meetings in Washington, D.C., of both the World Bank and the International Monetary Fund are indicative of the growing discontent of the masses who are unhappy with big business, multinationals, big governments, and a million others. This discontent is driving a new breed of wild, rebellious, young people to hit back at systems that they see as not solving world problems and benefiting all of mankind. These mass computer attacks are increasingly being used as paybacks for what the attacker or attackers consider to be injustices done that need to be avenged. However, most vendetta attacks are for mundane reasons such as a promotion denied, a boyfriend or girlfriend taken, an ex-spouse given child custody, and other situations that may involve family and intimacy issues.

3.3.6   Hate (National Origin, Gender, and Race)

Hate as a motive of security threat originates from and is always based on an individual or individuals with a serious dislike of another person or group of persons based on a string of human attributes that may include national origin, gender, race, or mundane ones such as the manner of speech one uses. Then incensed, by one or all of these attributes, the attackers contemplate and threaten and sometimes carry out attacks of vengeance often rooted in ignorance.

3.3.7   Notoriety

Many, especially young, hackers try to break into a system to prove their competence and sometimes to show off to their friends that they are intelligent or superhuman in order to gain respect among their peers.

3.3.8   Greed

Many intruders into company systems do so to gain financially from their acts.

3.3.9   Ignorance

This takes many forms but quite often it happens when a novice in computer security stumbles on an exploit or vulnerability and without knowing or understanding it uses it to attack other systems.

3.4   Security Threat Management

Security threat management is a technique used to monitor an organization's critical security systems in real time to review reports from the monitoring sensors such as the intrusion detection systems, firewall, and other scanning sensors. These reviews help to reduce false positives from the sensors, develop quick response techniques for threat containment and assessment, correlate and escalate false positives across multiple sensors or platforms, and develop intuitive analytical, forensic, and management reports.

As the workplace gets more electronic and critical company information finds its way out of the manila envelopes and brown folders into online electronic databases, security management has become a full-time job for system administrators. While the number of dubious users is on the rise, the number of reported criminal incidents is skyrocketing, and the reported response time between a threat and a real attack is down to 20 min or less [15]. To secure company resources, security managers have to do real-time management. Real-time management requires access to real-time data from all network sensors.

Among the techniques used for security threat management are risk assessment and forensic analysis.

3.4.1   Risk Assessment

Even if there are several security threats all targeting the same resource, each threat will cause a different risk, and each will need a different risk assessment. Some will have low risk, while others will have the opposite. It is important for the response team to study the risks as sensor data come in and decide which threat to deal with first.

3.4.2   Forensic Analysis

Forensic analysis is done after a threat has been identified and contained. After containment, the response team can launch the forensic analysis tools to interact with the dynamic report displays that have come from the sensors during the duration of the threat or attack if the threat results in an attack. The data on which forensic analysis should be performed must be kept in a secure state to preserve the evidence. It must be stored and transferred, if this is needed, with the greatest care, and the analysis must be done with the utmost professionalism possible if the results of the forensic analysis are to stand in court.

3.5   Security Threat Correlation

As we have noted in the previous section, the interval time between the first occurrence of the threat and the start of the real attack has now been reduced about 20 min. This is putting enormous pressure on organizations' security teams to correspondingly reduce *the turnaround time,* the time between the start of an incident and the receipt of the first reports of the incident from the sensors. The shorter the turnaround time, the quicker the response to an incident in progress. In fact, if the incident is caught at an early start, an organization can be saved a great deal of damage.

Threat correlation, therefore, is the technique designed to reduce the turnaround time by monitoring all network sensor data and then use that data to quickly analyze and discriminate between real threats and false positives. In fact, threat correlation helps in:

- Reducing false positives because if we get the sensor data early enough, analyze it, and detect false positives, we can quickly re-tune the sensors so that future false positives are reduced.

- Reducing false negatives; similarly by getting early sensor reports, we can analyze it, study where false negatives are coming from, and re-tune the sensors to reveal more details.
- Verifying sensor performance and availability; by getting early reports, we can quickly check on all sensors to make sure that they are performing as needed.

3.5.1 Threat Information Quality

The quality of data coming from the sensor logs depends on several factors including:

- Collection—When data is collected, it must be analyzed. The collection techniques specify where the data is to be analyzed. To reduce on bandwidth and data compression problems, before data is transported to a central location for analysis, some analysis is usually done at the sensor, and then reports are brought to the central location. But this kind of distributed computation may not work well in all cases.
- Consolidation—Given that the goal of correlation is to pull data out of the sensors, analyze it, correlate it, and deliver timely and accurate reports to the response teams and also given the amount of data generated by the sensors and further the limitation to bandwidth, it is important to find good techniques to filter out relevant data and consolidate sensor data either through compression or aggregation so that analysis is done on only real and active threats.
- Correlation—Again given the goals of correlation, if the chosen technique of data collection is to use a central database, then a good data mining scheme must be used for appropriate queries on the database that will result in outputs that will realize the goals of correlation. However, many data mining techniques have problems.

3.6   Security Threat Awareness

Security threat awareness is meant to bring widespread and massive attention of the population to the security threat. Once people come to know of the threat, it is hoped that they will become more careful, more alert, and more responsible in what they do. They will also be more likely to follow security guidelines.

Exercises

1. Although we discussed several sources of security threats, we did not exhaust all. There are many such sources. Name and discuss five.
2. We pointed out that the design philosophy of the Internet infrastructure was partly to blame for the weaknesses and hence a source of security threats. Do

you think a different philosophy would have been better? Comment on your answer.

3. Give a detailed account of why the three-way handshake is a security threat.
4. In the chapter, we gave two examples of how a port scan can be a threat to security. Give three more examples of port scans that can lead to system security compromise.
5. Comment on the rapid growth of the Internet as a contributing factor to the security threat of cyberspace. What is the responsible factor in this growth? Is it people or the number of computers?
6. There seems to have been an increase in the number of reported virus and worm attacks on computer networks. Is this really a sign of an increase, more reporting, or more security awareness on the part of the individual? Comment on each of these factors.
7. Social engineering has been frequently cited as a source of network security threat. Discuss the different elements within social engineering that contribute to this assertion.
8. In the chapter, we gave just a few of the many motives for security threat. Discuss five more, giving details of why there are motives.
9. Outline and discuss the factors that influence threat information quality.
10. Discuss the role of data mining techniques in the quality of threat information.

Advanced Exercises

1. Research the effects of industrial espionage, and write a detailed account of a profile of a person who sells and buys industrial secrets. What type of industrial secrets is likely to be traded?
2. The main reasons behind the development of the National Strategy to Secure Cyberspace were the realization that we are increasingly dependent on the computer networks, the major components of the national critical infrastructure are dependent on computer networks, and our enemies have the capabilities to disrupt and affect any of the infrastructure components at will. Study the National Information Infrastructure and the weaknesses inherent in the system, and suggest ways to harden it.
3. Study and suggest the best ways to defend the national critical infrastructure from potential attackers.
4. We indicated in the text that the best ways to manage security threats is to do an extensive risk assessment and more forensic analysis. Discuss how reducing the turnaround time can assist you in both risk assessment and forensic analysis. What are the inputs into the forensic analysis model? What forensic tools are you likely to use? How do you suggest to deal with the evidence?
5. Do research on intrusion detection and firewall sensor false positives and false negatives. Write an executive report on the best ways to deal with both of these unwanted reports.

References

1. G-Lock Software TCP and UDP port scanning examples. http://www.glocksoft.com/tcpudpscan.htm
2. Rutkowski T Internet survey reaches 109 million host level. Center for next generation internet. http://www.ngi.org/trends/TrendsPR0102.txt
3. Battling the Net Security Threat, Saturday, 9 November, 2002, 08:15 GMT, http://news.bbc.co.uk/2/hi/technology/2386113.stm
4. Derived in part from a letter by Severo M. Ornstein. Commun ACM, June 1989 32(6)
5. Virus Writer Christopher Pile (Black Barron) Sent to Jail for 18 Months Wednesday 15 November 1995. http://www.gps.jussieu.fr/comp/VirusWriter.html
6. Hopper I Destructive 'I LOVE YOU' Computer virus strikes worldwide. CNN Interactive Technology. http://www.cnn.com/2000/TECH/computing/05/04/iloveyou/.
7. Former student: bug may have been spread accidentally. CNN Interactive. http:/www.cnn.com/2000/ASIANOWsoutheast/05/11/iloveyou.02/
8. National Security Threat List. http://rf-web.tamu.edu/security/SECGUIDE/T1threat/Nstl.htm
9. CERT® Advisory CA-2001–19 'Code Red' worm exploiting buffer overflow in IIS indexing service DLL. http://www.cert.org/advisories/CA-2001–19.html
10. Is IT safe? InfoTrac. Tennessee electronic library. HP Professional 1997, 1(12):14–20
11. Insider abuse of information is biggest security threat, SafeCop says. InfoTrac. Tennessee electronic library. Business Wire. November 10, 2000, p. 1
12. Hollows P Security threat correlation: the next battlefield. eSecurityPlanetcom. http://www.esecurityplanet.com/views/article.php/10752_1501001
13. Awareness of National Security Issues and Response [ANSIR]. FBI's Intelligence Resource Program. http://www.fas.org/irp/ops/ci/ansir.htm
14. Grosso A (2000) The economic espionage ACT: touring the minefields. Commun ACM 43 (8):15–18
15. ThreatManager ™ – the real-time security threat management suite. http://www.open.com/responsenetworks/products/threatmanager/threatmanager.htm?ISR1

Introduction to Computer Network Vulnerabilities

4.1 Definition

System vulnerabilities are weaknesses in the software or hardware on a server or a client that can be exploited by a determined intruder to gain access to or shut down a network. Donald Pipkin defines system vulnerability as a condition, a weakness of or an absence of security procedure, or technical, physical, or other controls that could be exploited by a threat [1].

Vulnerabilities exist not only in hardware and software that constitute a computer system but also in policies and procedures, especially security policies and procedures, that are used in a computer network system and in users and employees of the computer network systems. Since vulnerabilities can be found in so many areas in a network system, one can say that a security vulnerability is indeed anything in a computer network that has the potential to cause or be exploited for an advantage. Now that we know what vulnerabilities are, let us look at their possible sources.

4.2 Sources of Vulnerabilities

The frequency of attacks in the last several years and the speed and spread of these attacks indicate serious security vulnerability problems in our network systems. There is no definitive list of all possible sources of these system vulnerabilities. Many scholars and indeed many security incident reporting agencies, such as Bugtraq, the mailing list for vulnerabilities; CERT/CC, the US Computer Emergency Response Team; NTBugtraq, the mailing list for Windows security; RUS-CERT, the German Computer Emergency Response Team; and US DOE-CIAC, the US Department of Energy Computer Incident Advisory Capability, have called attention to not only one but multiple factors that contribute to these security problems and pose obstacles to the security solutions. Among the most frequently mentioned sources of security vulnerability problems in computer

© Springer International Publishing AG 2017
J.M. Kizza, *Guide to Computer Network Security*, Computer Communications and Networks, DOI 10.1007/978-3-319-55606-2_4

networks are design flaws, poor security management, incorrect implementation, Internet technology vulnerability, the nature of intruder activity, the difficulty of fixing vulnerable systems, the limits of effectiveness of reactive solutions, and social engineering [2].

4.2.1 Design Flaws

The two major components of a computer system, hardware and software, quite often have design flaws. Hardware systems are less susceptible to design flaws than their software counterparts owing to less complexity, which makes them easier to test; limited number of possible inputs and expected outcomes, again making it easy to test and verify; and the long history of hardware engineering. But even with all these factors backing up hardware engineering, because of complexity in the new computer systems, design flaws are still common.

But the biggest problems in system security vulnerability are due to software design flaws. A number of factors cause software design flaws, including overlooking security issues all together. However, three major factors contribute a great deal to software design flaws: human factors, software complexity, and trustworthy software sources [3].

4.2.1.1 Human Factors
In the human factor category, poor software performance can be a result of the following:

1. *Memory lapses and attentional failures*: For example, someone was supposed to have removed or added a line of code, tested, or verified, but did not because of simple forgetfulness.
2. *Rush to finish*: The result of pressure, most often from management, to get the product on the market either to cut development costs or to meet a client deadline can cause problems.
3. *Overconfidence and use of nonstandard or untested algorithms*: Before algorithms are fully tested by peers, they are put into the product line because they seem to have worked on a few test runs.
4. *Malice*: Software developers, like any other professionals, have malicious people in their ranks. Bugs, viruses, and worms have been known to be embedded and downloaded in software, as is the case with Trojan horse software, which boots itself at a timed location. As we will see in Sect. 8.4, malice has traditionally been used for vendetta, personal gain (especially monetary), and just irresponsible amusement. Although it is possible to safeguard against other types of human errors, it is very difficult to prevent malice.
5. *Complacency*: When either an individual or a software producer has significant experience in software development, it is easy to overlook certain testing and other error control measures in those parts of software that were tested

previously in a similar or related product, forgetting that no one software product can conform to all requirements in all environments.

4.2.1.2 Software Complexity

Both software professionals and nonprofessionals who use software know the differences between software programming and hardware engineering. In these differences underlie many of the causes of software failure and poor performance. Consider the following:

1. *Complexity*: Unlike hardwired programming in which it is easy to exhaust the possible outcomes on a given set of input sequences, in software programming a similar program may present billions of possible outcomes on the same input sequence. Therefore, in software programming, one can never be sure of all the possibilities on any given input sequence.
2. *Difficult testing*: There will never be a complete set of test programs to check software exhaustively for all bugs for a given input sequence.
3. *Ease of programming*: The fact that software programming is easy to learn encourages many people with little formal training and education in the field to start developing programs, but many are not knowledgeable about good programming practices or able to check for errors.
4. *Misunderstanding of basic design specifications*: This affects the subsequent design phases including coding, documenting, and testing. It also results in improper and ambiguous specifications of major components of the software and in ill-chosen and poorly defined internal program structures.

4.2.1.3 Trustworthy Software Sources

There are thousands of software sources for the millions of software products on the market today. However, if we were required to name well-known software producers, very few of us would succeed in naming more than a handful. Yet we buy software products every day without even ever minding their sources. Most importantly, we do not care about the quality of that software, the honesty of the anonymous programmer, and of course its reliability as long as it does what we want it to do.

Even if we want to trace the authorship of the software product, it is impossible because software companies are closed within months of their opening. Chances are when a software product is 2 years old, its producer is likely to be out of business. In addition to the difficulties in tracing the producers of software who go out of business as fast as they come in, there is also fear that such software may not even have been tested at all.

The growth of the Internet and the escalating costs of software production have led many small in-house software developers to use the marketplace as a giant testing laboratory through the use of beta testing, shareware, and freeware. Shareware and freeware have a high potential of bringing hostile code into trusted systems.

For some strange reason, the more popular the software product gets, the less it is tested. As software products make market inroads, their producers start thinking of producing new versions and releases with little to no testing of current versions. This leads to the growth of what is called a *common genesis* software product, where all its versions and releases are based on a common code. If such a code has not been fully tested, which is normally the case, then errors are carried through from version to version and from release to release.

In the last several years, we have witnessed the growth of the open-source movement. It has been praised as a novel idea to break the monopoly and price gauging by big software producers and most important as a timely solution to poor software testing. Those opposed to the movement have criticized it for being a source of untrusted and many times untested software. Despite the wails of the critics, major open-source products such as Linux operating system have turned out with few security flaws; still there are fears that hackers can look at the code and perhaps find a way to cause mischief or steal information.

There has been a rise recently in Trojan horses inserted into open-source code. In fact security experts are not recommending running readily available programs such as MD5 hashes to ensure that the code hasn't been altered. Using MD5 hashes and similar programs such as MD4, SHA, and SHA-1 continually compares codes generated by "healthy" software to hashes of programs in the field, thus exposing the Trojans. According to the recent CERT advisory, crackers are increasingly inserting Trojans into the source code for tcpdump, a utility that monitors network traffic, and libpcap, a packet capture library tool [4].

However, according to the recent study by the Aberdeen Group, open-source software now accounts for more than half of all security advisories published in the past year by the Computer Emergency Response Team (CERT). Also according to industry study reports, open-source software commonly used in Linux, Unix, and network routing equipment accounted for 16 of the 29 security advisories during the first 10 months of 2002, and there is an upswing in new virus and Trojan horse warnings for Unix, Linux, Mac OS X, and open-source software [4].

4.2.1.4 Software Reuse, Reengineering, and Outlived Design

New developments in software engineering are spearheading new developments such as software reuse and software reengineering. Software reuse is the integration and use of software assets from a previously developed system. It is the process in which old or updated software such as library, component, requirements and design documents, and design patterns is used along with new software.

Both software reengineering and reuse are hailed for cutting down on the escalating development and testing costs. They have brought efficiency by reducing time spent designing or coding, popularized standardization, and led to common "look-and-feel" between applications. They have made debugging easier through use of thoroughly tested designs and code.

However, both software techniques have the potential to introduce security flaws in systems. Among some of the security flaws that have been introduced into programming is first the mismatch where reused requirement specifications and designs may not completely match the real situation at hand and nonfunctional characteristics of code may not match those of the intended recipient. Second, when using object programming, it is important to remember that objects are defined with certain attributes, and any new application using objects defined in terms of the old ones will inherit all their attributes.

In Chap. 6, we will discuss the many security problems associated with script programming. Yet there is now momentum in script programming to bring more dynamism into Web programming. Scripting suffers from a list of problems including inadequate searching and/or browsing mechanisms before any interaction between the script code and the server or client software, side effects from software assets that are too large or too small for the projected interface, and undocumented interfaces.

4.2.2 Poor Security Management

Security management is both a technical and an administrative security process that involves security policies and controls that the organization decides to put in place to provide the required level of protection. In addition, it also involves security monitoring and evaluation of the effectiveness of those policies. The most effective way to meet these goals is to implement security risk assessment through a security policy and secure access to network resources through the use of firewalls and strong cryptography. These and others offer the security required for the different information systems in the organization in terms of integrity, confidentiality, and availability of that information. Security management by itself is a complex process; however, if it is not well organized, it can result in a security nightmare for the organization.

Poor security management is a result of little control over security implementation, administration, and monitoring. It is a failure in having solid control of the security situation of the organization when the security administrator does not know who is setting the organization's security policy, administering security compliance, and who manages system security configurations and is in charge of security event and incident handling.

In addition to the disarray in the security administration, implementation, and monitoring, a poor security administration team may even lack a plan for the wireless component of the network. As we will see in Chap. 17, the rapid growth of wireless communication has brought with it serious security problems. There are so many things that can go wrong with security if security administration is poor. Unless the organization has a solid security administration team with a sound security policy and secure security implementation, the organization's security may be compromised. An organization's system security is as good as its security policy and its access control policies and procedures and their implementation.

Good security management is made up of a number of implementable security components that include risk management, information security policies and procedures, standards, guidelines, information classification, security monitoring, and security education. These core components serve to protect the organization's resources:

- A risk analysis will identify these assets, discover the threats that put them at risk, and estimate the possible damage and potential loss a company could endure if any of these threats become real. The results of the risk analysis help management construct a budget with the necessary funds to protect the recognized assets from their identified threats and develop applicable security policies that provide direction for security activities. Security education takes this information to each and every employee.
- Security policies and procedures to create, implement, and enforce security issues that may include people and technology.
- Standards and guidelines to find ways, including automated solution for creating, updating, and tracking compliance of security policies across the organization.
- Information classification to manage the search, identification, and reduction of system vulnerabilities by establishing security configurations.
- Security monitoring to prevent and detect intrusions, consolidate event logs for future log and trend analysis, manage security events in real time, manage parameter security including multiple firewall reporting systems, and analyze security events enterprise-wide.
- Security education to bring security awareness to every employee of the organization and teach them their individual security responsibility.

4.2.3   Incorrect Implementation

Incorrect implantation very often is a result of incompatible interfaces. Two product modules can be deployed and work together only if they are compatible. That means that the module must be *additive*, that is, the environment of the interface needs to remain intact. An incompatible interface, on the other hand, means that the introduction of the module has changed the existing interface in such a way that existing references to the interface can fail or behave incorrectly.

This definition means that the things we do on the many system interfaces can result in incompatibility that results result in bad or incomplete implementation. For example, ordinary addition of a software or even an addition or removal of an argument to an existing software module may cause an imbalanced interface. This interface sensitivity tells us that it is possible because of interposition that the addition of a simple thing like a symbol or an additional condition can result in an incompatible interface, leading the new symbol or condition to conflict with all applications that have been without problems.

To put the interface concept into a wide system framework, consider a system-wide integration of both hardware and software components with differing technologies with no standards. No information system products, whether hardware or software, are based on a standard that the industry has to follow. Because of this, manufacturers and consumers must contend with the constant problems of system compatibility. Because of the vast number of variables in information systems, especially network systems, involving both hardware and software, it is not possible to test or verify all combinations of hardware and software. Consider, for example, that there are no standards in the software industry. Software systems involve different models based on platforms and manufacturer. Products are heterogeneous both semantically and syntactically.

When two or more software modules are to interface one another in the sense that one may feed into the other or one may use the outputs of the other, incompatibility conditions may result from such an interaction. Unless there are methodologies and algorithms for checking for interface compatibility, errors are transmitted from one module into another. For example, consider a typical interface created by a method call between software modules. Such an interface always makes assumptions about the environment having the necessary availability constraints that the accessibility of local methods to certain states of the module. If such availability constraints are not checked before the modules are allowed to pass parameters via method calls, errors may result.

Incompatibility in system interfaces may be caused by a variety of conditions usually created by things such as:

- Too much detail
- Not enough understanding of the underlying parameters
- Poor communication during design
- Selecting the software or hardware modules before understanding the receiving software
- Ignoring integration issues
- Error in manual entry

Many security problems result from the incorrect implementation of both hardware and software. In fact, system reliability in both software and hardware is based on correct implementation, as is the security of the system.

4.2.4   Internet Technology Vulnerability

In Sect. 4.2.1, we discussed design flaws in technology systems as one of the leading causes of system vulnerabilities. In fact we pointed out that systems are composed of software, hardware, and humanware. There are problems in each one of these components. Since the humanware component is influenced by the technology in the software and hardware, we will not discuss this any further.

The fact that computer and telecommunication technologies have developed at such an amazing and frightening speed and people have overwhelmingly embraced both of them has caused security experts to worry about the side effects of these booming technologies. There were reasons to worry. Internet technology has been and continues to be vulnerable. There have been reports of all sorts of loopholes, weaknesses, and gaping holes in both software and hardware technologies.

According to National Vulnerability Database (NVD), a US government repository of standards-based vulnerability management data using the Security Content Automation Protocol (SCAP), system vulnerabilities have been on the rise ever since system vulnerability data was first captured. The system vulnerability data captured by NVD enables automation of vulnerability management, security measurement, and compliance. NVD includes databases of security checklists, security-related software flaws, misconfigurations, product names, and impact metrics. Read more about NVD at https://nvd.nist.gov/home.cfm.

There is agreement among security experts that what is reported represents the tip of the iceberg. Many vulnerabilities are discovered and, for various reasons, are not reported.

Because these technologies are used by many who are not security experts (in fact the majority of users are not security literate), one can say that many vulnerabilities are observed and probably not reported because those who observe them do not have the knowledge to classify what has been observed as a vulnerability. Even if they do, they may not know how and where to report.

No one knows how many of these vulnerabilities are there in both software and hardware. The assumption is that there are thousands. As history has shown us, a few are always discovered every day by hackers. Although the list spans both hardware and software, the problem is more prevalent with software. In fact, software vulnerabilities can be put into four categories:

- Operating system vulnerabilities: Operating systems are the main sources of all reported system vulnerabilities. Going by the SysAdmin, Audit, Network, and Security (SANS) Institute, a cooperative research and education organization serving security professionals, auditors, system administrators, and network administrators, together with the Common Weakness Enumeration (CWE), a community-developed dictionary of weaknesses of software types, has been issuing lists annually: "CWE/SANS Top 25 Most Dangerous Software Errors." Popular operating systems cause many of the vulnerabilities. This is always so because hackers tend to take the easiest route by exploiting the best-known flaws with the most effective and widely known and available attack tools.
- Port-based vulnerabilities: Besides operating systems, network service ports take second place in sourcing system vulnerabilities. For system administrators, knowing the list of most vulnerable ports can go a long way to help enhance system security by blocking those known ports at the firewall. Such an operation, though not comprehensive, adds an extra layer of security to the network. In fact it is advisable that in addition to blocking and deny-everything filtering, security administrators should also monitor all ports including the blocked ones for intruders who entered the system by some other means. For the most common vulnerable port numbers, the reader is referred to the latest SANS at: https://www.sans.org/security-resources/idfaq/which-backdoors-live-on-which-ports/8/4.
- Application software-based errors.
- System protocol software such as client and server browser.

In addition to highlighting the need for system administrators to patch the most common vulnerabilities, we hope this will also help many organizations that lack the resources to train security personnel to have a choice of either focusing on the most current or the most persistent vulnerability. One would wonder why a vulnerability would remain among the most common year after year, while there are advisories on it and patches for it. The answer is not very farfetched, but simple: system administrators do not correct many of these flaws because they simply do not know which vulnerabilities are most dangerous; they are too busy to correct them all or they do not know how to correct them safely.

Although these vulnerabilities are cited, many of them year after year, as the most common vulnerabilities, there are traditionally thousands of vulnerabilities that hackers often use to attack systems. Because they are so numerous and new ones are being discovered every day, many system administrators may be overwhelmed, which may lead to loss of focus on the need to ensure that all systems are protected against the most common attacks.

Let us take stock of what we have said so far. Lots and lots of system vulnerabilities have been observed and documented by SANS and CWE in their series, "CWE/SANS Top 25 Most Dangerous Software Errors." However, there is a stubborn persistence of a number of vulnerabilities making the list year after year. This observation, together with the nature of software, as we have explored in Sect. 4.2.1, means it is possible that what has been observed so far is a very small fraction of a potential sea of vulnerabilities; many of them probably will never be discovered because software will ever be subjected to either unexpected input sequences or operated in unexpected environments.

Besides the inherently embedded vulnerabilities resulting from flawed designs, there are also vulnerabilities introduced in the operating environments as a result of incorrect implementations by operators. The products may not have weaknesses initially, but such weaknesses may be introduced as a result of bad or careless installations. For example, quite often products are shipped to customers with security features disabled, forcing the technology users to go through the difficult and error-prone process of properly enabling the security features by oneself.

4.2.5 Changing Nature of Hacker Technologies and Activities

It is ironic that as "useful" technology develops so does the "bad" technology. What we call useful technology is the development in all computer and telecommunication technologies that are driving the Internet, telecommunication, and the Web. "Bad" technology is the technology that system intruders are using to attack systems. Unfortunately these technologies are all developing in tandem. In fact, there are times when it looks like hacker technologies are developing faster than the rest of the technologies. One thing is clear, though: hacker technology is flourishing.

Although it used to take intelligence, determination, enthusiasm, and perseverance to become a hacker, it now requires a good search engine, time, a little bit of knowledge of what to do, and owning a computer. There are thousands of hacker Web sites with the latest in script technologies and hundreds of recipe books and sources on how to put together an impact virus or a worm and how to upload it.

The ease of availability of these hacker tools; the ability of hackers to disguise their identities and locations; the automation of attack technology which further distances the attacker from the attack; the fact that attackers can go unidentified, limiting the fear of prosecution; and the ease of hacker knowledge acquisition have put a new twist in the art of hacking, making it seem easy and hence attracting more and younger disciples.

Besides the ease of becoming a hacker and acquiring hacker tools, because of the Internet sprawl, hacker impact has become overwhelming, impressive, and more destructive in shorter times than ever before. Take, for example, recent virus incidents such as the "I Love You," "Code Red," "Slammer," and the "Blaster" worms' spread. These worms and viruses probably spread around the world much faster than the human cold virus and the dreaded severe acute respiratory syndrome (SARS).

What these incidents have demonstrated is that the *turnaround time*, the time a virus is first launched in the wild and the time it is first cited as affecting the system, is becoming incredibly shorter. Both the turnaround time and the speed at which the virus or a worm spreads reduce the *response time*, the time a security incident is first cited in the system and the time an effective response to the incident should have been initiated. When the response time is very short, security experts do not have enough time to respond to a security incident effectively. In a broader framework, when the turnaround time is very short, system security experts who develop patches do not have enough time to reverse engineer and analyze the attack in order to produce counter immunization codes. It has been and it is still the case in many security incidents for antivirus companies to take hours and sometime days, such as in the case of the Code Red virus, to come up with an effective cure. However, even after a patch is developed, it takes time before it is filtered down to the system managers. Meantime, the damage has already been done, and it is multiplying. Likewise, system administrators and users have little time to protect their systems.

4.2.6   Difficulty of Fixing Vulnerable Systems

In his testimony to the Subcommittee on Government Efficiency, Financial Management, and Intergovernmental Relations of the US House Committee on Government Reform, Richard D. Pethia, Director, CERT Centers, pointed out the difficulty in fixing known system vulnerabilities as one of the sources of system vulnerabilities. His concern was based on a number of factors, including the ever-rising number of system vulnerabilities and the ability of system administrators to cope with the number of patches issued for these vulnerabilities. As the number of vulnerabilities rises, system and network administrators face a difficult situation. They are challenged with keeping up with all the systems they have and all the patches released for those systems. Patches can be difficult to apply and might even have unexpected side effects as a result of compatibility issues [2].

Besides the problem of keeping abreast of the number of vulnerabilities and the corresponding patches, there are also logistic problems between the time at which a vendor releases a security patch and the time at which a system administrator fixes the vulnerable computer system. There are several factors affecting the quick fixing of patches. Sometimes, it is the logistics of the distribution of patches. Many vendors disseminate the patches on their Web sites; others send e-mail alerts. However, sometimes busy system administrators do not get around to these e-mails and security alerts until sometime after. Sometimes, it can be months or years before the patches are implemented on a majority of the vulnerable computers.

Many system administrators are facing the same chronic problems: the never-ending system maintenance, limited resources, and highly demanding management. Under these conditions, the ever-increasing security system complexity, increasing system vulnerabilities, and the fact that many administrators do not fully understand the security risks, system administrators neither give security a high enough priority nor assign adequate resources. Exacerbating the problem is the fact that the demand for skilled system administrators far exceeds the supply [2].

4.2.7 Limits of Effectiveness of Reactive Solutions

Going by daily reports of system attacks and hacks, the number of system attacks is steadily on the rise. However, a small percentage of all attacks is reported, indicating a serious and growing systems security problem. However, given that just a small percentage of all attacks is reported, this table indicates a serious growing system security problem. As we have pointed out earlier, hacker technology is becoming more readily available, easier to get and assemble, more complex, and their effects more far reaching. All these indicate that urgent action is needed to find an effective solution to this monstrous problem.

The security community, including scrupulous vendors, have come up with various solutions, some good and others not. In fact, in an unexpected reversal of fortunes, one of the new security problems is to find a "good" solution from among thousands of solutions and to find an "expert" security option from the many different views.

Are we reaching the limits of our efforts, as a community, to come up with a few good and effective solutions to this security problem? There are many signs to support an affirmative answer to this question. It is clear that we are reaching the limits of effectiveness of our reactive solutions. Richard D. Pethia gives the following reasons [2]:

- The number of vulnerabilities in commercial off-the-shelf software is now at the level that it is virtually impossible for any but the best resourced organizations to keep up with the vulnerability fixes.
- According to *World Internet Usage and Population Statistics*, (http://www. internetworldstats.com/stats.htm), with a 2016 global population of 7,340,093,980, there are currently 3,611,375,813 Internet users representing almost half of the global population at 49.2%. This represents a growth of 90.4% since 2000. This is a phenomenal growth and it continues to grow at a rapid pace. At any point in time, there are millions of connected computers and smart mobile devices that are vulnerable to one form of attack or another.
- Attack technology has now advanced to the point where it is easy for attackers to take advantage of these vulnerable machines and harness them together to launch high-powered attacks.
- Many attacks are now fully automated, thus reducing the turnaround time even further as they spread around cyberspace.
- The attack technology has become increasingly complex and in some cases intentionally stealthy, thus reducing the turnaround time and increasing the time it takes to discover and analyze the attack mechanisms in order to produce antidotes.
- Internet users have become increasingly dependent on the Internet and now use it for many critical applications so that a relatively minor attack has the potential to cause huge damages.

Without being overly pessimistic, these factors, taken together, indicate that there is a high probability that more attacks are likely and since they are getting more complex and attacking more computers, they are likely to cause significant devastating economic losses and service disruptions.

4.2.8   Social Engineering

According to John Palumbo, social engineering is an outside hacker's use of psychological tricks on legitimate users of a computer system in order to gain the information (usernames and passwords) one needs to gain access to the system [5].

Many have classified social engineering as a diversion, in the process of system attack, on people's intelligence to utilize two human weaknesses: first, no one wants to be considered ignorant and second is human trust. Ironically, these are two weaknesses that have made social engineering difficult to fight because no one wants to admit falling for it. This has made social engineering a critical system security hole.

Many hackers have and continue to use it to get into protected systems. Kevin Mitnick, the notorious hacker, used it successfully and was arguably one of the most ingenious hackers of our time; he was definitely very gifted with his ability to socially engineer just about anybody [5].

Hackers use many approaches to social engineering, including the following [6]:

- *Telephone.* This is the most classic approach, in which hackers call up a targeted individual in a position of authority or relevance and initiate a conversation with the goal of gradually pulling information out of the target. This is done mostly to help desks and main telephone switch boards. Caller ID cannot help because hackers can bypass it through tricks and the target truly believes that the hacker is actually calling from inside the corporation.
- *Online.* Hackers are harvesting a boom of vital information online from careless users. The reliance on and excessive use of the Internet have resulted in people having several online accounts. Currently an average user has about four to five accounts including one for home use, one for work, and an additional one or two for social or professional organizations. With many accounts, as probably any reader may concur, one is bound to forget some passwords, especially the least used ones. To overcome this problem, users mistakenly use one password on several accounts. Hackers know this, and they regularly target these individuals with clever baits such as telling them they won lotteries or were finalists in sweepstakes where computers select winners or they have won a specific number of prizes in a lotto, where they were computer selected. However, in order to get the award, the user must fill in an online form, usually Web-based, and this transmits the password to the hacker. Hackers have used hundreds of tricks on unsuspecting users in order for them to surrender their passwords.
- *Dumpster diving* is now a growing technique of information theft not only in social engineering but more so in identity theft. The technique, also known as trashing, involves an information thief scavenging through individual and company dumpsters for information. Large and critical information can be dug out of dumpsters and trash cans. Dumpster diving can recover from dumpsters and trash cans individual social security numbers, bank accounts, individual vital records, and a whole list of personal and work-related information that gives the hackers the exact keys they need to unlock the network.
- *In person* is the oldest of the information-stealing techniques that predates computers. It involves a person physically walking into an organization's offices and casually checking out note boards, trash diving into bathroom trash cans and company hallway dumpsters, and eating lunches together and initiating conversations with employees. In big companies, this can be done only on a few occasions before trusted friendships develop. From such friendships, information can be passed unconsciously.
- *Snail mail* is done in several ways and is not limited only to social engineering but has also been used in identity theft and a number of other crimes. It has been in the news recently because of identity theft. It is done in two ways: the hacker picks a victim and goes to the Post Office and puts in a change of address form to a new box number. This gives the hacker a way to intercept all snail mail of the victim. From the intercepted mail, the hacker can gather a great deal of information that may include the victim's bank and credit card account numbers and access control codes and pins by claiming to have forgotten his or her password or pin and requesting a reissue in the mail. In another form, the hacker drops a bogus survey in the victim's mailbox offering baits of cash award for completing

a "few simple" questions and mailing them in. The questions, in fact, request far more than simple information from an unsuspecting victim.

- *Impersonation* is also an old trick played on unsuspecting victims by criminals for a number of goodies. These days the goodies are information. Impersonation is generally acting out a victim's character role. It involves the hacker playing a role and passing himself or herself as the victim. In the role, the thief or hacker can then get into legitimate contacts that lead to the needed information. In large organizations with hundreds or thousands of employees scattered around the globe, it is very easy to impersonate a vice president or a chief operations officer. Since most employees always want to look good to their bosses, they will end up supplying the requested information to the imposter.

Overall, social engineering is a cheap but rather threatening security problem that is very difficult to deal with.

4.3 Vulnerability Assessment

Vulnerability assessment is a process that works on a system to identify, track, and manage the repair of vulnerabilities on the system. The assortment of items that are checked by this process in a system under review varies depending on the organization. It may include all desktops, servers, routers, and firewalls. Most vulnerability assessment services will provide system administrators with:

- Network mapping and system fingerprinting of all known vulnerabilities
- A complete vulnerability analysis and ranking of all exploitable weaknesses based on potential impact and likelihood of occurrence for all services on each host
- Prioritized list of misconfigurations

In addition, at the end of the process, a final report is always produced detailing the findings and the best way to go about overcoming such vulnerabilities. This report consists of prioritized recommendations for mitigating or eliminating weaknesses, and based on an organization's operational schedule, it also contains recommendations of further reassessments of the system within given time intervals or on a regular basis.

4.3.1 Vulnerability Assessment Services

Due to the massive growth of the number of companies and organizations owning their own networks, the growth of vulnerability monitoring technologies, the increase in network intrusions and attacks with viruses, and worldwide publicity of such attacks, there is a growing number of companies offering system vulnerability services. These services, targeting the internals and perimeter of the system,

Web-based applications, and providing a baseline to measure subsequent attacks against, include scanning, assessment and penetration testing, and application assessment.

4.3.1.1 Vulnerability Scanning

Vulnerability scanning services provide a comprehensive security review of the system, including both the perimeter and system internals. The aim of this kind of scanning is to spot critical vulnerabilities and gaps in the system's security practices. Comprehensive system scanning usually results in a number of both false positives and negatives. It is the job of the system administrator to find ways of dealing with these false positives and negatives. The final report produced after each scan consists of strategic advice and prioritized recommendations to ensure that critical holes are addressed first. System scanning can be scheduled, depending on the level of the requested scan, by the system user or the service provider, to run automatically and report by either automated or periodic e-mail to a designated user. The scans can also be stored on a secure server for future review.

4.3.1.2 Vulnerability Assessment and Penetration Testing

This phase of vulnerability assessment is a hands-on testing of a system for identified and unidentified vulnerabilities. All known hacking techniques and tools are tested during this phase to reproduce real-world attack scenarios. One of the outcomes of these real-life testings is that new and sometimes obscure vulnerabilities are found, processes and procedures of attack are identified, and sources and severity of vulnerabilities are categorized and prioritized based on the user-provided risks.

4.3.1.3 Application Assessment

As Web applications become more widespread and more entrenched into e-commerce and all other commercial and business areas, applications are slowly becoming the main interface between the user and the network. The increased demands on applications have resulted into new directions in automation and dynamism of these applications. As we saw in Chap. 6, scripting in Web applications, for example, has opened a new security paradigm in system administration. Many organizations have gotten sense of these dangers and are making substantial progress in protecting their systems from attacks via Web-based applications. Assessing the security of system applications is, therefore, becoming a special skills requirement needed to secure critical systems.

4.3.2   Advantages of Vulnerability Assessment Services

Vulnerability online services have many advantages for system administrators. They can, and actually always do, provide and develop signatures and updates for new vulnerabilities and automatically include them in the next scan. This eliminates the need for the system administrator to schedule periodic updates.

Reports from these services are very detailed not only on the vulnerabilities, sources of vulnerabilities, and existence of false positives, but they also focus on vulnerability identification and provide more information on system configuration that may not be readily available to system administrators. This information alone goes a long way in providing additional security awareness to security experts about additional avenues whereby systems may be attacked. The reports are then encrypted and stored in secure databases accessible only with the proper user credentials. This is because these reports contain critically vital data on the security of the system and they could, therefore, be a pot of gold for hackers if found. This additional care and awareness adds security to the system.

Probably, the best advantage to an overworked and many times resource-strapped system administrator is the automated and regularly scheduled scan of all network resources. They provide, in addition, a badly needed third-party "security eye," thus helping the administrator to provide an objective yet independent security evaluation of the system.

Exercises

1. What is a vulnerability? What do you understand by a system vulnerability?
2. Discuss four sources of system vulnerabilities.
3. What are the best ways to identify system vulnerabilities?
4. What is innovative misuse? What role does it play in the search for solutions to system vulnerability?
5. What is incomplete implementation? Is it possible to deal with incomplete implementation as a way of dealing with system vulnerabilities? In other words, is it possible to completely deal with incomplete implementation?
6. What is social engineering? Why is it such a big issue yet so cheap to perform? Is it possible to completely deal with it? Why or why not?
7. Some have described social engineering as being perpetuated by our internal fears. Discuss those fears.
8. What is the role of software security testing in the process of finding solutions to system vulnerabilities?
9. Some have sounded an apocalyptic voice as far as finding solutions to system vulnerabilities. Should we take them seriously? Support your response.
10. What is innovative misuse? What role does it play in the search for solutions to system vulnerabilities?

Advanced Exercises

1. Why are vulnerabilities difficult to predict?
2. Discuss the sources of system vulnerabilities.
3. Is it possible to locate all vulnerabilities in a network? In other words, can one make an authoritative list of those vulnerabilities? Defend your response.
4. Why are design flaws such a big issue in the study of vulnerability?

5. Part of the problem in design flaws involves issues associated with software verification and validation (V&V). What is the role of V&V in system vulnerability?

References

1. Pipkin D (2000) Information security: protecting the global enterprise. Prentice Hall PTR, Upper Saddle River
2. Pethia RD. Information technology—essential but vulnerable: how prepared are we for attacks? http://www.cert.org/congressional_testimony/Pethia_testimony_Sep26.html
3. Kizza JM (2003) Ethical and social issues in the information age, 2nd edn. Springer, New York
4. Hurley J, Hemmendinger E. Open source and Linux: 2002 poster children for security problems. http://www.aberdeen.com/ab_abstracts/2002/11/11020005.htm
5. Palumbo J. Social engineering: what is it, why is so little said about it and what can be done? SANS, http://www.sans.org/rr/social/social.php
6. Granger S. Social engineering fundamentals, part I: Hacker Tactics. http://www.securityfocus.com/infocus/1527

Cyber Crimes and Hackers

5

5.1 Introduction

The greatest threats to the security, privacy, and reliability of computer networks and other related information systems in general are cybercrimes committed by cybercriminals, but most importantly hackers. Judging by the damage caused by past cybercriminal and hacker attacks to computer networks in businesses, governments, and individuals, resulting in inconvenience and loss of productivity and credibility, one cannot fail to see that there is a growing community demand to software and hardware companies to create more secure products that can be used to identify threats and vulnerabilities, to fix problems, and to deliver security solutions.

The rise of the hacker factor; the unprecedented and phenomenal growth of the Internet; the latest developments in globalization, hardware miniaturization, and wireless and mobile technology; the mushrooming of connected computer networks; and the society's ever-growing appetite for and dependency on computers have all greatly increased the threats both the hacker and cybercrimes pose to the global communication and computer networks. Both these factors are creating serious social, ethical, legal, political, and cultural problems. These problems involve, among others, identity theft, hacking, electronic fraud, intellectual property theft, and national critical infrastructure attacks and are generating heated debates on finding effective ways to deal with them, if not stop them.

Industry and governments around the globe are responding to these threats through a variety of approaches and collaborations such as:

- Formation of organizations, such as the *Information Sharing and Analysis Centers* (ISACs).
- Getting together of industry portals and ISPs on how to deal with distributed denial-of-service attacks including the establishment of *Computer Emergency Response Teams* (CERTs).

© Springer International Publishing AG 2017
J.M. Kizza, *Guide to Computer Network Security*, Computer Communications and Networks, DOI 10.1007/978-3-319-55606-2_5

- Increasing the use of sophisticated tools and services by companies to deal with network vulnerabilities. Such tools include the formation of Private Sector Security Organizations (PSSOs) such as SecurityFocus, Bugtraq, and the International Chamber of Commerce's Cybercrime Unit.
- Setting up national strategies similar to the *US National Strategy to Secure Cyberspace*, an umbrella initiative of all initiatives from various sectors of the national critical infrastructure grid and the Council of Europe Convention on Cybercrimes.

5.2   Cybercrimes

According to the director of the US National Infrastructure Protection Center (NIPC), cybercrimes present the greatest danger to e-commerce and the general public in general [1]. The threat of crime using the Internet is real and growing, and it is likely to be the scourge of the twenty-first century. A *cybercrime* is a crime like any other crime, except that in this case, the illegal act must involve a connected computing system either as an object of a crime, an instrument used to commit a crime, or a repository of evidence related to a crime. Alternatively, one can define a cybercrime as an act of unauthorized intervention into the working of the telecommunication networks and/or the sanctioning of an authorized access to the resources of the computing elements in a network that leads to a threat to the system's infrastructure or life or that causes significant property loss.

Because of the variations in jurisdiction boundaries, cyber acts are defined as illegal in different ways depending on the communities in those boundaries. Communities define acts to be illegal if such acts fall within the domains of that community's commission of crimes that a legislature of a state or a nation has specified and approved. Both the International Convention of Cyber Crimes and the European Convention on Cyber Crimes have outlined the list of these crimes to include the following:

- Unlawful access to information
- Illegal interception of information
- Unlawful use of telecommunication equipment
- Forgery with use of computer measures
- Intrusions of the public switched and packet network
- Network integrity violations
- Privacy violations
- Industrial espionage
- Pirated computer software
- Fraud using a computing system
- Internet/e-mail abuse
- Using computers or computer technology to commit murder, terrorism, pornography, and hacking

5.2.1   Ways of Executing Cybercrimes

Because for any crime to be classified as a cybercrime, it must be committed with the help of a computing resource, as defined above, cybercrimes are executed in one of two ways: penetration and denial-of-service attacks.

5.2.1.1 Penetration

A penetration cyberattack is a successful unauthorized access to a protected system resource, or a successful unauthorized access to an automated system, or a successful act of bypassing the security mechanisms of a computing system [2]. A penetration cyberattack can also be defined as any attack that violates the integrity and confidentiality of a computing system's host.

However defined, a penetration cyberattack involves breaking into a computing system and using known security vulnerabilities to gain access to any cyberspace resource. With full penetration, an intruder has full access to all that computing system's resources. Full penetration, therefore, allows an intruder to alter data files, change data, plant viruses, or install damaging *Trojan* horse programs into the computing system. It is also possible for intruders, especially if the victim computer is on a computer network, to use it as a launching pad to attack other network resources. Penetration attacks can be local, where the intruder gains access to a computer on a LAN on which the program is run, or global on a WAN such as the Internet, where an attack can originate thousands of miles from the victim computer.

5.2.1.2 Distributed Denial of Service (DDoS)

A *denial of service* is an interruption of service resulting from system unavailability or destruction. It prevents any part of a target system from functioning as planned. This includes any action that causes unauthorized destruction, modification, or delay of service. Denial of service can also be caused by intentional degradation or blocking of computer or network resources [2]. These denial-of-service attacks, commonly known as *distributed denial-of-service* (DDoS) attacks, are a new form of cyberattacks. They target computers connected to the Internet. They are not penetration attacks, and, therefore, they do not change, alter, destroy, or modify system resources. However, they affect the system through diminishing the system's ability to function; hence, they are capable of degrading of the system's performance eventually bringing a system down without destroying its resources.

According to the *Economist* [3], the software tools used to carry out DDoS first came to light in the summer of 1999, and the first security specialist conference to discuss how to deal with them was held in November of the same year. Since then, there has been a growing trend in DDoS attacks mainly as a result of the growing number, sizes, and scope of computer networks which increase first an attacker's accessibility to networks and second the number of victims. But at the same time, as the victim base and sizes of computer networks have increased, there have been no to little efforts to implement spoof prevention filters or any other preventive action.

In particular, security managers have implemented little, if any, system protection against these attacks.

Like penetration electronic attacks (e-attacks), DDoS attacks can also be either local, where they can shut down LAN computers, or global, originating thousands of miles away on the Internet, as was the case in the Canadian-generated DDoS attacks. Attacks in this category include the following:

- IP spoofing is forging of an IP packet address. In particular, a source address in the IP packet is forged. Since network routers use packet destination address to route packets in the network, the only time a source address is used is by the destination host to respond back to the source host. So forging the source IP address causes the responses to be misdirected, thus creating problems in the network. Many network attacks are a result of IP spoofing.
- SYN flooding: In Chap. 3, we discussed a three-way handshake used by the TCP protocols to initiate a connection between two network elements. During the handshake, the port door is left half open. A SYN flooding attack is flooding the target system with so many connection requests coming from spoofed source addresses that the victim server cannot complete because of the bogus source addresses. In the process, all its memory gets hogged up, and the victim is thus overwhelmed by these requests and can be brought down.
- Smurf attack: In this attack, the intruder sends a large number of spoofed ICMP Echo requests to broadcast IP addresses. Hosts on the broadcast multicast IP network, say, respond to these bogus requests with reply ICMP Echo. This may significantly multiply the reply ICMP Echos to the hosts with spoofed addresses.
- Buffer overflow is an attack in which the attacker floods a carefully chosen field such as an address field with more characters than it can accommodate. These excessive characters, in malicious cases, are actually executable code, which the attacker can execute to cause havoc in the system, effectively giving the attacker control of the system. Because anyone with little knowledge of the system can use this kind of attack, buffer overflow has become one of the most serious classes of security threats.
- Ping of death: A system attacker sends IP packets that are larger than the 65,536 bytes allowed by the IP protocol. Many operating systems, including network operating systems, cannot handle these oversized packets; so, they freeze and eventually crash.
- Land.c attack: The land.c program sends TCP SYN packets whose source and destination IP addresses and port numbers are those of the victim's.
- Teardrop.c attack uses a program that causes fragmentation of a TCP packet. It exploits a reassembly and causes the victim system to crash or hang.
- Sequence number sniffing: In this attack, the intruder takes advantage of the predictability of sequence numbers used in TCP implementations. The attacker then uses a sniffed next sequence number to establish legitimacy.

5.2.1.3 Motives of DDoS Attack

DDoS attacks are not like penetration attacks where the intruders expect to gain from such attacks; they are simply a nuisance to the system. As we pointed out earlier, since these attacks do not penetrate systems, they do not affect the integrity of the resources other than deny access to them. This means that the intruders do not expect to get many material gains as would be expected from penetration attacks. So, because of this, most DDoS attacks are generated with very specific goals. Among them are:

- Preventing others from using a network connection with such attacks as *Smurf*, *UDP*, and *ping* flood attacks
- Preventing others from using a host or a service by severely impairing or disabling such a host or its IP stack with suck attacks as *land*, *teardrop*, *Bonk*, *Boink*, *SYN flooding*, and *ping of death*
- Notoriety for computer savvy individuals who want to prove their ability and competence in order to gain publicity

5.2.2 Cybercriminals

Who are the cybercriminals? They are ordinary users of cyberspace with a message. As the number of users swells, the number of criminals among them also increases at almost the same rate. A number of studies have identified the following groups as the most likely sources of cybercrimes [4]:

- *Insiders*: For a long time, system attacks were limited to in-house employee-generated attacks to systems and theft of company property. In fact, disgruntled insiders are a major source of computer crimes because they do not need a great deal of knowledge about the victim computer system. In many cases, such insiders use the system everyday. This allows them to gain unrestricted access to the computer system, thus causing damage to the system and/or data. The 1999 Computer Security Institute/FBI report notes that 55% of respondents reported malicious activity by insiders [5].
- *Hackers*: Hackers are actually computer enthusiasts who know a lot about computers and computer networks and use this knowledge with a criminal intent. Since the mid-1980s, computer network hacking has been on the rise mostly because of the widespread use of the Internet.
- *Criminal groups*: A number of cybercrimes are carried out by criminal groups for different motives ranging from settling scores to pure thievery. For example, such criminal groups with hacking abilities have broken into credit card companies to steal thousands of credit card numbers (see Chap. 3).
- *Disgruntled ex-employees*: Many studies have shown that disgruntled ex-employees also pose a serious threat to organizations as sources of cybercrimes targeting their former employers for a number of employee-employer issues that led to the separation. In some cases, ex-employees simply

use their knowledge of the system to attack the organization for purely financial gains.

• *Economic espionage spies*: The growth of cyberspace and e-commerce and the forces of globalization have created a new source of crime syndicates, the organized economic spies that plough the Internet looking for company secrets. As the price tag for original research skyrockets and competition in the market-place becomes global, companies around the globe are ready to pay any amount for stolen commercial, marketing, and industrial secrets.

5.3   Hackers

The word *hacker* has changed meaning over the years as technology changed. Currently, the word has two opposite meanings. One definition talks of a computer enthusiast as an individual who enjoys exploring the details of computers and how to stretch their capabilities, as opposed to most users who prefer to learn only the minimum necessary. The opposite definition talks of a malicious or inquisitive meddler who tries to discover information by poking around [2].

Before acquiring its current derogatory meaning, the term *hacking* used to mean expert writing and modification of computer programs. Hackers were considered people who were highly knowledgeable about computing; they were considered computer experts who could make the computer do all the wonders through programming. Today, however, hacking refers to a process of gaining unauthorized access into a computer system for a variety of purposes, including the stealing and altering of data and electronic demonstrations. For some time now, hacking as a political or social demonstration has been used during international crises. During a crisis period, hacking attacks and other Internet security breaches usually spike in part because of sentiments over the crisis. For example, during the two Iraq wars, there were elevated levels of hacker activities. According to the Atlanta-based Internet Security Systems, around the start of the first Iraq war, there was a sharp increase of about 37% from the fourth quarter of the year before, the largest quarterly spike the company has ever recorded [1].

5.3.1   History of Hacking

The history of hacking has taken as many twists and turns as the word hacking itself has. One can say that the history of hacking actually began with the invention of the telephone in 1876 by Alexander Graham Bell. For it was this one invention that made internetworking possible. There is agreement among computer historians that the term *hack* was born at MIT. According to Slatalla, in the 1960s, MIT geeks had an insatiable curiosity about how things worked. However, in those days of colossal mainframe computers, "it was very expensive to run those slow-moving hunks of metal; programmers had limited access to the dinosaurs. So, the smarter ones created what they called "hacks" – programming shortcuts – to complete computing tasks more quickly. Sometimes their shortcuts were more elegant than the original program" [6].

Although many early hack activities had motives, many took them to be either highly admirable acts by expert computer enthusiasts or elaborate practical jokes, including the first recorded hack activity in 1969 by Joe Engressia, commonly known as "The Whistler." Engressia, the grandfather of phone *phreaking*, was born blind and had a high pitch which he used to his advantage. He used to whistle into the phones and could whistle perfectly any tone he wanted. He discovered phreaking while listening to the error messages caused by his calling of unconnected numbers. While listening to these messages, he used to whistle into the phone and quite often got cut off. After getting cut off numerous times, he phoned AT&T to inquire why when he whistled a tune into the phone receiver he was cut off. He was surprised by an explanation on the working of the 2600-Hz tone by a phone company engineer. Joe learned how to phreak. It is said that phreakers across the world used to call Joe to tune their "blue boxes" [7].

By 1971 a Vietnam veteran, John Draper, commonly known as "Captain Crunch," took this practical whistling joke further and discovered that using a free toy whistle from a cereal box to carefully blow into the receiver of a telephone produces the precise tone of 2600 Hz needed to make free long-distance phone calls [8]. With this act, "phreaking," a cousin of hacking, was born and it entered our language. Three distinct terms began to emerge: hacker, cracker, and phreaker. Those who wanted the word hack to remain pure and innocent preferred to be called *hackers*; those who break into computer systems were called *crackers*; and those targeting phones came to be known as *phreakers*. Following Captain Crunch's instructions, Al Gilbertson (not his real name) created the famous little "blue box." Gilbertson's box was essentially a super telephone operator because it gave anyone who used it free access to any telephone exchange. In the late 1971, Ron Anderson published an article on the existence and working of this little blue box in *Esquire* magazine. Its publication created an explosive growth in the use of blue boxes and an initiation of a new class of kids into phreaking [9].

With the starting of a limited national computer network by ARPNET, in the 1970s, a limited form of a system of break-in from outsiders started appearing. Through the 1970s, a number of developments gave impetus to the hacking movement. The first of these developments was the first publication of the Youth International Party Line newsletter by activist Abbie Hoffman, in which he erroneously advocated for free phone calls by stating that phone calls are part of an unlimited reservoir and phreaking did not hurt anybody and therefore should be free. The newsletter, whose name was later changed to *TAP*, for Technical Assistance Program, by Hoffman's publishing partner, Al Bell, continued to publish complex technical details on how to make free calls [6].

The second was the creation of the bulletin boards. Throughout the seventies, the hacker movement, although becoming more active, remained splinted. This came to an end in 1978 when two guys from Chicago, Randy Seuss and Ward Christiansen, created the first personal-computer bulletin-board system (BBS).

The third development was the debut of the personal computer (PC). In 1981, when IBM joined the PC wars, a new front in hacking was opened. The PCs brought the computing power to more people because they were cheap, easy to program, and somehow more portable. On the back of the PC was the movie "WarGames" in 1983. The science fiction movie watched by millions glamorized and popularized hacking. The 1980s saw tremendous hacker activities with the formation of gang-like hacking groups. Notorious individuals devised hacking names such as Kevin Mitnick ("The Condor"), Lewis De Payne ("Roscoe"), Ian Murphy ("Captain Zap"), Bill Landreth ("The Cracker"), "Lex Luther" (founder of the Legion of Doom), Chris Goggans ("Erik Bloodaxe"), Mark Abene ("Phiber Optik"), Adam Grant ("The Urvile"), Franklin Darden ("The Leftist"), Robert Riggs ("The Prophet"), Loyd Blankenship ("The Mentor"), Todd Lawrence ("The Marauder"), Scott Chasin ("Doc Holiday"), Bruce Fancher ("Death Lord"), Patrick K. Kroupa ("Lord Digital"), James Salsman ("Karl Marx"), Steven G. Steinberg ("Frank Drake"), and "Professor Falken" [10].

The notorious hacking groups of the 1970s and 1980s included the "414- Club," the "Legion of Doom," the "Chaos Computer Club" based in Germany, "Nu Prometheus League," and the "Atlanta Three." All these groups were targeting either phone companies where they would get free phone calls or computer systems to steal credit card and individual user account numbers.

During this period, a number of hacker publications were founded including *The Hacker Quarterly* and *Hacker'zine*. In addition, bulletin boards were created, including "The Phoenix Fortress" and "Plovernet." These forums gave the hacker community a clearing house to share and trade hacking ideas.

Hacker activities became so worrisome that the FBI started active tracking and arrests, including the arrest, the first one, of Ian Murphy (Captain Zap) in 1981 followed by the arrest of Kevin Mitnick in the same year. It is also during this period that the hacker culture and activities went global with reported hacker attacks and activities from Australia, Germany, Argentina, and the United States. Ever since, we have been on a wild ride.

The first headline-making hacking incident that used a virus and got national and indeed global headlines took place in 1988 when a Cornell graduate student created a computer virus that crashed 6000 computers and effectively shut down the Internet for 2 days [11]. Robert Morris's action forced the US government to form the federal Computer Emergency Response Team (CERT) to investigate similar and related attacks on the nation's computer networks. The law enforcement agencies started to actively follow the comings and goings of the activities of the Internet and sometimes eavesdropped on communication networks traffic. This did not sit well with some activists, who formed the Electronic Frontier Foundation in 1990 to defend the rights of those investigated for alleged computer hacking.

The 1990s saw heightened hacking activities and serious computer network "near" meltdowns, including the 1991 expectation without incident of the "Michelangelo" virus that was expected to crash computers on March 6, 1992, the artist's 517th birthday. In 1995, the notorious, self-styled hacker Kevin Mitnick was first arrested by the FBI on charges of computer fraud that involved the stealing of thousands of credit card numbers. In the second half of the 1990s, hacking activities increased considerably, including the 1998 Solar Sunrise, a series of attacks targeting Pentagon computers that led the Pentagon to establish round-the-clock, online guard duty at major military computer sites, and a coordinated attacker on Pentagon computers by Ehud Tenebaum, an Israeli teenager known as "The Analyzer," and an American teen. The close of the twentieth century saw the heightened anxiety in the computing and computer user communities of both the millennium bug and the ever rising rate of computer network break-ins. So, in 1999, President Clinton announced a $1.46 billion initiative to improve government computer security. The plan would establish a network of intrusion detection monitors for certain federal agencies and encourage the private sector to do the same [8]. The year 2000 probably saw the most costly and most powerful computer network attacks that included the "Mellisa," the "Love Bug," the "Killer Resume," and a number of devastating DDoS attacks. The following year, 2001, the elusive "Code Red" virus was released. The future of viruses is as unpredictable as the kinds of viruses themselves.

The period since 1980 saw a rapid growth of hacking up to the present. As we observed in Sect. 5.3.2.4, until recently most hacker communities worked underground forming groups global like those listed in Table 3.1. Today, hackers are no longer considered as bad to computer networks as it used to be, and now hackers are being used by governments and organization to do the opposite of what they were supposed to be doing, defending national critical networks and hardening company networks. In fact hacker Web sites are growing.

5.3.2 Types of Hackers

There are several subsects of hackers based on hacking philosophies. The biggest subsects are crackers, hacktivists, and cyberterrorists.

5.3.2.1 Crackers
A cracker is one who breaks security on a system. Crackers are hardcore hackers characterized more as professional security breakers and thieves. The term was recently coined only in the mid-1980s by purist hackers who wanted to differentiate themselves from individuals with criminal motives whose sole purpose is to sneak through security systems. Purist hackers were concerned journalists were misusing the term "hacker." They were worried that the mass media failed to understand the distinction between computer enthusiasts and computer criminals, calling both hackers. The distinction has, however, failed; so, the two terms *hack* and *crack* are still being often used interchangeably.

Even though the public still does not see the difference between hackers and crackers, purist hackers are still arguing that there is a big difference between what they do and what crackers do. For example, they say cyberterrorists, cyber vandals, and all criminal hackers are not hackers but crackers by the above definition.

There is a movement now of reformed crackers who are turning their hacking knowledge into legitimate use, forming enterprises to work for and with cybersecurity companies and sometimes law enforcement agencies to find and patch potential security breaches before their former counterparts can take advantage of them.

5.3.2.2 Hacktivists

Hacktivism is a marriage between pure hacking and activism. Hacktivists are conscious hackers with a cause. They grew out of the old phreakers. Hacktivists carry out their activism in an electronic form in hope of highlighting what they consider noble causes such as institutional unethical or criminal actions and political and other causes. Hacktivism also includes acts of civil disobedience using cyberspace. The tactics used in hacktivism change with the time and the technology. Just as in the real world where activists use different approaches to get the message across, in cyberspace, hacktivists also use several approaches including automated e-mail bombs, Web defacing, virtual sit-ins, and computer viruses and worms [12].

Automated E-mail Bomb E-mail bombs are used for a number of mainly activist issues such as social and political, electronic, and civil demonstrations but can also be and have been used in a number of cases for coursing, revenge, and harassment of individuals or organizations. The method of approach here is to choose a selection of individuals or organizations and bombard them with thousands of automated e-mails, which usually results in jamming and clogging the recipient's mailbox. If several individuals are targeted on the same server, the bombardment may end up disabling the mail server. Political electronic demonstrations were used in a number of global conflicts including the Kosovo and Iraq wars. And economic and social demonstrations took place to electronically and physically picket the new world economic order as was represented by the World Bank and the International Monetary Fund (IMF) sitting in Seattle, Washington, and Washington DC in the United States and in Prague, Hungry, and Genoa, Italy.

Web Defacing The other attention getter for the hacktivist is Web defacing. It is a favorite form of hacktivism for nearly all causes, political, social, or economic. With this approach, the hacktivists penetrate into the Web server and replace the selected site's content and links with whatever they want the viewers to see. Some of this may be political, social, or economic messages. Another approach similar to Web defacing is to use the domain name service (DNS) to change the DNS server content so that the victim's domain name resolves to a carefully selected IP address of a site where the hackers have their content they want the viewers to see.

One contributing factor to Web defacing is the simplicity of doing it. There is detailed information for free on the Web outlining the bugs and vulnerabilities in both the Web software and Web server protocols. There is also information that details what exploits are needed to penetrate a Web server and deface a victim's Web site. Defacing technology has, like all other technologies, been developing fast. It used to be that a hacker who wanted to deface a Web site would, remotely or otherwise, break into the server that held the Web pages, gaining the access required to edit the Web page and then alter the page. Breaking into a Web server would be achieved through a remote exploit; for example, that would give the attacker access to the system. The hacktivist would then sniff connections between computers to access remote systems.

Newer scripts and Web server vulnerabilities now allow hackers to gain remote access to Web sites on Web servers without gaining prior access to the server. This is so because vulnerabilities and newer scripts utilize bugs that overwrite or append to the existing page without ever gaining a valid log-in and password combination or any other form of legitimate access. As such, the attacker can only overwrite or append to files on the system.

Since a wide variety of Web sites offer both hacking and security scripts and utilities required to commit these acts, it is only a matter of minutes before scripts are written and Web sites are selected and a victim is hit.

As an example, in November 2001, a Web defacing duo calling themselves Smoked Crew defaced *The New York Times* site. Smoked Crew had earlier hit the Web sites of big name technology giants such as Hewlett-Packard, Compaq Computer, Gateway, Intel, AltaVista, and Disney's Go.com [13].

On the political front, in April 2003, during the second Iraq war, hundred of sites were defaced by both antiwar and pro-war hackers and hacktivists; among them were a temporary defacement of the White House's Web site and an attempt to shut down British Prime Minister Tony Blair's official site. In addition to defacing of Web sites, at least nine viruses or "denial-of-service" attacks cropped up in the weeks leading to war [1].

Virtual Sit-ins A virtual sit-in or a blockade is the cousin of a physical sit-in or blockade. These are actions of civil concern about an issue, whether social, economic, or political. It is a way to call public attention to that issue. The process works through disruption of normal operation of a victim site and denying or preventing access to the site. This is done by the hacktivists generating thousands of digital messages directed at the site either directly or through surrogates. In many of these civil disobedience cases, demonstrating hacktivists set up many automated sites that generate automatic messages directed to the victim site. Although dated, let us look at two typical virtual sit-in incidents. On April 20, 2001, a group calling itself the *Electrohippies Collective* had a planned virtual sit-in of Web sites associated with the Free Trade Area of the Americas (FTAA) conference. The sit-in, which started at 00.00 UTC, was to object to the FTAA conference and the entire FTAA process by generating an electronic record of public pressure through the server logs of the organizations concerned. Figure 5.1 shows a logo an activist group against global warming may display.

On February 7, 2002, during the annual meeting of the World Economic Forum (WEF) in New York City, more than 160,000 demonstrators, organized by, among others, Ricardo Dominguez, cofounder of the Electronic Disturbance Theater (EDT), went online to stage a "virtual sit-in" at the WEF home page. Using

Fig. 5.1 A logo of an activist
group to stop global warming

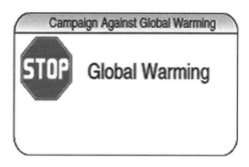

downloaded software tools that constantly reloaded the target Web sites, the
protestors replicated a denial-of-service attack on the site on the first day of the
conference, and by 10:00 AM of that day, the WEF site had collapsed and remained
down until late night of the next day [14].

5.3.2.3 Computer Viruses and Worms

Perhaps, the most widely used and easiest method of hacktivists is sending viruses
and worms. Both viruses and worms are forms of malicious code, although the
worm code may be less dangerous. Other differences include the fact that worms
are usually more autonomous and can spread on their own once delivered as
needed, while a virus can only propagate piggybacked on or embedded into another
code. We will give a more detailed discussion of both viruses and worms in
Chap. 14.

5.3.2.4 Cyberterrorists

Based on motives, cyberterrorists can be divided into two categories: the terrorists
and information warfare planners.

Terrorists The World Trade Center attack in 2001 brought home the realization
and the potential for a terrorist attack on not only organizations' digital infrastructure but also a potential for an attack on the national critical infrastructure.
Cyberterrorists who are terrorists have many motives, ranging from political,
economic, religious, to personal. Most often, the techniques of their terror are
through intimidation, coercion, or actual destruction of the target.

Information Warfare Planners This involves war planners to threaten attacking a
target by disrupting the target's essential services by electronically controlling and
manipulating information across computer networks or destroying the information
infrastructure.

5.3.3   Hacker Motives

Since the hacker world is closed to nonhackers and no hacker likes to discuss one's secrets with nonmembers of the hacker community, it is extremely difficult to accurately list all the hacker motives. From studies of attacked systems and some writing from former hackers who are willing to speak out, we learn quite a lot about this rather secretive community. For example, we have learned that hackers' motives can be put in two categories: those of the collective hacker community and those of individual members. As a group, hackers like to interact with others on bulletin boards, through electronic mail and in person. They are curious about new technologies and adventurous to control new technologies, and they have a desire and are willing to stimulate their intellect through learning from other hackers in order to be accepted in more prestigious hacker communities. Most important, they have a common dislike for and resistance to authority.

Most of these collective motives are reflected in the *hacker ethic*. According to Steven Levy, the hacker ethic has the following six tenets [1]:

- Access to computers and anything that might teach you something about the way the world works should be unlimited and total. Always yield to the hands-on imperative!
- All information should be free.
- Mistrust authority and promote decentralization.
- Hackers should be judged by their hacking, not bogus criteria such as degrees, age, race, or position.
- You can create art and beauty on a computer.
- Computers can change your life for the better.

Collective hacker motives can also be reflected in the following three additional principles ("*Doctor Crash*," 1986) [10]:

- Hackers reject the notion that "businesses" are the only groups entitled to access and use of modern technology.
- Hacking is a major weapon in the fight against encroaching computer technology.
- The high cost of computing equipment is beyond the means of most hackers, which results in the perception that hacking and phreaking are the only recourse to spreading computer literacy to the masses.

Apart from collective motives, individual hackers, just as any other computer system users, have their own personal motives that drive their actions. Among these are the following [15]:

Vendetta and/or Revenge Although a typical hacking incident is usually nonfinancial and is, according to hacker profiles, for recognition and fame, there are some incidents, especially from older hackers, that are for reasons that are only mundane, such as a promotion denied, a boyfriend or girlfriend taken, an ex-spouse given child custody, and other situations that may involve family and intimacy issues. These may result in hacker-generated attack targeting the individual or the company that is the cause of the displeasure. Also, social, political, and religious issues, especially issues of passion, can drive rebellions in people that usually lead to revenge cyberattacks. These mass computer attacks are also increasingly being used as paybacks for what the attacker or attackers consider to be injustices done that need to be avenged.

Jokes, Hoaxes, and Pranks Even though it is extremely unlikely that serious hackers can start cyberattacks just for jokes, hoaxes, or pranks, there are less serious ones who can and have done so. Hoaxes are scare alerts started by one or more malicious people and are passed on by innocent users who think that they are helping the community by spreading the warning. Most hoaxes are viruses and worms, although there are hoaxes that are computer-related folklore stories and urban legends or true stories sent out as text messages. Although many virus hoaxes are false scares, there are some that may have some truth about them, but that often become greatly exaggerated, such as "The Good Times" and "The Great Salmon." Virus hoaxes infect mailing lists, bulletin boards, and Usenet newsgroups. Worried system administrators sometimes contribute to this scare by posting dire warnings to their employees that become hoaxes themselves.

The most common hoax has been and still is that of the presence of a virus. Almost every few weeks, there is always a virus hoax of a virus, and the creator of such a hoax sometimes goes on to give remedies which, if one is not careful, results in removing vital computer systems' programs such as operating systems and boot programs. Pranks usually appear as scare messages, usually in the form of mass e-mails warning of serious problems on a certain issue. Innocent people usually read such e-mails and get worried. If it is a health issue, innocent people end up calling their physicians or going into hospitals because of a prank.

Jokes, on the other hand, are not very common for a number of reasons: first, it is difficult to create a good joke for a mass of people such as the numbers of people in cyberspace, and second, it is difficult to create a clear joke that many people will appreciate.

Terrorism Although cyberterrorism has been going on at a low level, very few people were concerned about it until after September 11, 2001, with the attack on the World Trade Center. Ever since, there has been a high degree of awareness, thanks to the Department of Homeland Security. We now realize that with globalization, we live in a networked world and that there is a growing dependence on computer networks. Our critical national infrastructure and large financial and business systems are interconnected and interdependent on each other. Targeting any point in the national network infrastructure may result in serious disruption of the working of these systems and may lead to a national disaster. The potential for electronic warfare is real and national defense, financial, transportation, water, and power grid systems are susceptible to an electronic attack unless and until the nation is prepared for it.

Political and Military Espionage   The growth of the global network of computers, with the dependence and intertwining of both commercial and defense-related business information systems, is creating fertile ground for both political and military espionage. Cyberspace is making the collection, evaluation, analysis, integration, and interpretation of information from around the globe easy and fast. Modern espionage focuses on military, policy, and decision-making information. For example, military superiority cannot be attained only with advanced and powerful weaponry unless one controls the information that brings about the interaction and coordination between the central control, ships, and aircrafts that launch the weapon and the guidance system on the weapon. Military information to run these kinds of weapons is as important as the weapons themselves. So, having such advanced weaponry comes with a heavy price of safeguarding the information on the development and working of such systems. Nations are investing heavily in acquiring military secrets for such weaponry and governments' policies issues. The increase in both political and military espionage has led to a boom in counterintelligence in which nations and private businesses are paying to train people that will counter the flow of information to the highest bidder.

Business Espionage   One of the effects of globalization and the interdependence of financial, marketing, and global commerce has been the rise in the efforts to steal and market business, commerce, and marketing information. As businesses become global and world markets become one global bazaar, the marketplace for business ideas and market strategies is becoming very highly competitive and intense. This high competition and the expense involved have led to an easier way out: business espionage. In fact, business information espionage is one of the most lucrative careers today. Cyber sleuths are targeting employees using a variety of techniques, including system break-ins, social engineering, sniffing, electronic surveillance of company executive electronic communications, and company employee chat rooms for information. Many companies now boast competitive or business intelligence units, sometimes disguised as marketing intelligence or research but actually doing business espionage. Likewise, business counterintelligence is also on the rise.

Hatred   The Internet communication medium is a paradox. It is the medium that has brought nations and races together. Yet it is the same medium that is being used to separate nations and races through hatred. The global communication networks have given a new medium to homegrown cottage industry of hate that used only to circulate through fliers and words of mouth. These hate groups have embraced the Internet and have gone global. Hackers who hate others based on a string of human attributes that may include national origin, gender, race, or mundane ones such as the manner of speech one uses can target carefully selected systems where the victim is and carry out attacks of vengeance often rooted in ignorance.

Personal Gain/Fame/Fun/Notoriety Serious hackers are usually profiled as reclusive. Sometimes, the need to get out of this isolation and to look and be normal and fit in drives them to try and accomplish feats that will bring them that sought after fame and notoriety, especially within their hacker communities. However, such fame and notoriety is often gained through feats of accomplishments of some challenging tasks. Such a task may be and quite often does involve breaking into a revered system.

Ignorance Although they are profiled as superintelligent with a great love for computers, they still fall victim to what many people fall victims to—ignorance. They make decisions with no or little information. They target the wrong system and the wrong person. At times also such acts usually occur as a result of individuals authorized or not, but ignorant of the workings of the system stumbling upon weaknesses or performing forbidden acts that result in system resource modification or destruction.

5.3.4 Hacking Topologies

We pointed out earlier that hackers are often computer enthusiasts with a very good understanding of the working of computers and computer networks. They use this knowledge to plan their system attacks. Seasoned hackers plan their attacks well in advance, and their attacks do not affect unmarked members of the system. To get to this kind of precision, they usually use specific attack patterns of topologies. Using these topologies, hackers can select to target one victim among a sea of network hosts, a subnet of a LAN, or a global network. The attack pattern, the topology, is affected by the following factors and network configuration:

- *Equipment availability*—This is more important if the victim is just one host. The underlying equipment to bring about an attack on only one host and not affect others must be available. Otherwise, an attack is not possible.
- *Internet access availability*—Similarly, it is imperative that a selected victim host or network be reachable. To be reachable, the host or subnet configuration must avail options for connecting to the Internet.
- *The environment of the network*—Depending on the environment where the victim host or subnet or full network is, care must be taken to isolate the target unit so that nothing else is affected.
- *Security regime*—It is essential for the hacker to determine what type of defenses is deployed around the victim unit. If the defenses are likely to present unusual obstacles, then a different topology that may make the attack a little easier may be selected.

The pattern chosen, therefore, is primarily based on the type of victim(s), motive, location, method of delivery, and a few other things. There are four of these patterns: one-to-one, one-to-many, many-to-many, and many-to-one [15].

5.3.4.1 One-to-One

These hacker attacks originate from one attacker and are targeted to a known victim. They are personalized attacks where the attacker knows the victim, and sometimes the victim may know the attacker. One-to-one attacks are characterized by the following motives:

- *Hate*: This is when the attacker causes physical, psychological, or financial damage to the victim because of the victim's race, nationality, gender, or any other social attributes. In most of these attacks, the victim is innocent.
- *Vendetta*: This is when the attacker believes he/she is the victim paying back for a wrong committed or an opportunity denied.
- *Personal gain*: This is when the attacker is driven by personal motives, usually financial gain. Such attacks include theft of personal information from the victim, for ransom, or for sale.
- *Joke*: This is when the attacker, without any malicious intentions, simply wants to send a joke to the victim. Most times, such jokes end up degrading and/or dehumanizing the victim.
- *Business espionage*: This is when the victim is usually a business competitor. Such attacks involve the stealing of business data, market plans, product blueprints, market analyses, and other data that have financial and business strategic and competitive advantages (Figs. 5.2 and 5.3).

5.3.4.2 One-to-Many

These attacks are fueled by anonymity. In most cases, the attacker does not know any of the victims. Moreover, in all cases, the attackers will, at least that is what they assume, remain anonymous to the victims. This topography has been the technique of choice in the last 2–3 years because it is one of the easiest to carry out. The motives that drive attackers to use this technique are as follows:

- *Hate*: There is hate when the attacker may specifically select a cross section of a type of people he or she wants to hurt and deliver the payload to the most visible location where such people have access. Examples of attacks using this technique include a number of e-mail attacks that have been sent to colleges and churches that are predominantly of one ethnic group.
- *Personal satisfaction* occurs when the hacker gets fun/satisfaction from other peoples' suffering. Examples include all the recent e-mail attacks such as the "Love Bug," "Killer Resume," and "Melissa."
- *Jokes/hoaxes* are involved when the attacker is playing jokes or wants to intimidate people.

5.3.4.3 Many-to-One

These attacks so far have been rare, but they have recently picked up momentum as the DDoS attacks have once again gained favor in the hacker community. In a

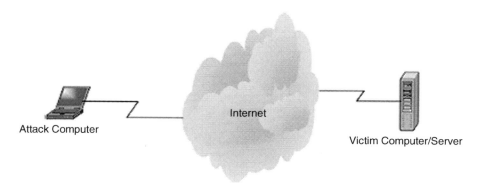

Fig. 5.2 Shows a one-to-one topology

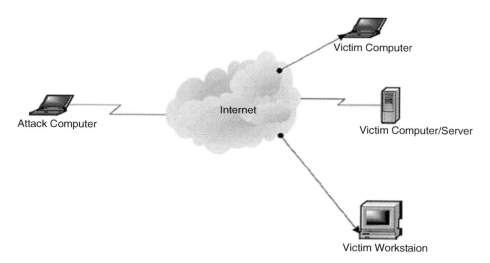

Fig. 5.3 Shows a one-to-many topology

many-to-one attack technique, the attacker starts the attack by using one host to spoof other hosts, the secondary victims, which are then used as the new source of an avalanche of attacks on a selected victim. These types of attacks need a high degree of coordination and, therefore, may require advanced planning and a good understanding of the infrastructure of the network. They also require a very well executed selection process in choosing the secondary victims and then eventually the final victim. Attacks in this category are driven by:

- *Personal vendetta*: There is personal vendetta when the attacker may want to create the maximum possible effect, usually damage, to the selected victim site.
- *Hate* is involved when the attacker may select a site for no other reasons than hate and bombard it in order to bring it down or destroy it.

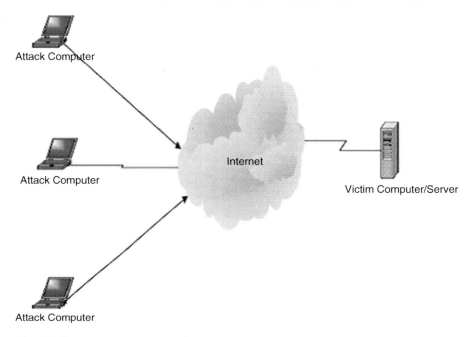

Fig. 5.4 Shows a many-to-one topology

- *Terrorism*: Attackers using this technique may also be driven by the need to inflict as much terror as possible. Terrorism may be related to or part of crimes like drug trafficking, theft where the aim is to destroy evidence after a successful attack, or even political terrorism.
- *Attention and fame*: In some extreme circumstances, what motivates this topography may be just a need for personal attention or fame. This may be the case if the targeted site is deemed to be a challenge or a hated site (Fig. 5.4).

5.3.4.4 Many-to-Many

As in the previous topography, attacks using this topography are rare; however, there has been an increase recently in reported attacks using this technique. For example, in some of the recent DDoS cases, there has been a select group of sites chosen by the attackers as secondary victims. These are then used to bombard another select group of victims. The numbers involved in each group many vary from a few to several thousands. As was the case in the previous many-to-one topography, attackers using this technique need a good understanding of the network infrastructure and a good and precise selection process to pick the secondary victims and eventually selecting the final pool of victims. Attacks utilizing this topology are mostly driven by a number of motives including:

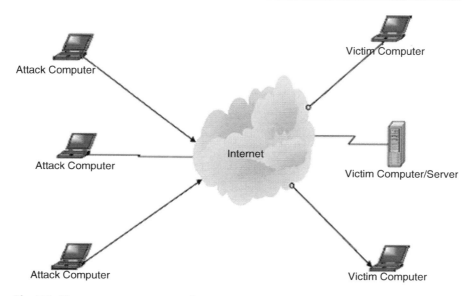

Fig. 5.5 Shows a many-to-many topology

- *Attention and fame* are sought when the attacker seeks publicity resulting from a successful attack.
- *Terrorism*: Terrorism is usually driven by a desire to destroy something; this may be a computer system or a site that may belong to financial institutions, public safety systems, or a defense and communication infrastructure. Terrorism has many faces including drug trafficking, political and financial terrorism, and the usual international terrorism driven by international politics.
- *Fun/hoax*: This type of attack technique may also be driven by personal gratification in getting famous and having fun (Fig. 5.5).

5.3.5 Hackers' Tools of System Exploitation

Earlier on, we discussed how hacking uses two types of attacking systems: DDoS and penetration. In the DDoS, there are a variety of ways of denying access to the system resources, and we have already discussed those. Let us now look at the most widely used methods in system penetration attacks. System penetration is the most widely used method of hacker attacks. Once in, a hacker has a wide variety of choices, including viruses, worms, and sniffers [15].

5.3.5.1 Viruses

Let us start by giving a brief description of a computer virus and defer a more detailed description of it until Chap. 14. A computer virus is a program that infects a chosen system resource such as a file and may even spread within the system and beyond. Hackers have used various types of viruses in the past as tools, including memory/resident, error-generating, program destroyers, system crushers, time theft, hardware destroyers, Trojans, time bombs, trapdoors, and hoaxes. Let us give a brief description of each and differ a more detailed study of each until Chap. 14.

Memory/Resident Virus This is more insidious, difficult to detect, fast spreading, and extremely difficult to eradicate and one of the most damaging computer viruses that hackers use to attack the central storage part of a computer system. Once in memory, the virus is able to attack any other program or data in the system. As we will see in Chap. 14, they are of two types: *transient*, the category that includes viruses that are active only when the inflicted program is executing, and *resident*, a brand that attaches itself, via a surrogate software, to a portion of memory and remains active long after the surrogate program has finished executing. Examples of memory resident viruses include all boot sector viruses such as the Israel virus [16].

Error-Generating Virus Hackers are fond of sending viruses that are difficult to discover and yet are fast moving. Such viruses are deployed in executable code. Every time the software is executed, errors are generated. The errors vary from "hard" logical errors, resulting in complete system shut down, to simple "soft" logical errors which may cause simple momentary blimps of the screen.

Data and Program Destroyers These are serious software destroyers that attach themselves to a software and then use it as a conduit or surrogate for growth, replication, and as a launch pad for later attacks to this and other programs and data. Once attached to a software, they attack any data or program that the software may come in contact with, sometimes altering the contents, deleting, or completely destroying those contents.

System Crusher Hackers use system crusher viruses to completely disable the system. This can be done in a number of ways. One way is to destroy the system programs such as operating system, compilers, loaders, linkers, and others. Another approach is to self-replicate until the system is overwhelmed and crashes.

Computer Time Theft Virus Hackers use this type of virus to steal system time either by first becoming a legitimate user of the system or by preventing other legitimate users from using the system by first creating a number of system interruptions. This effectively puts other programs scheduled to run into indefinite wait queues. The intruder then gains the highest priority, like a superuser with full access to all system resources. With this approach, system intrusion is very difficult to detect.

Hardware Destroyers Although not very common, these *killer viruses* are used by hackers to selectively destroy a system device by embedding the virus into device microinstructions or "mic" such as *bios* and device drivers. Once embedded into the mic, they may alter it in such ways that may cause the devices to move into positions that normally result in physical damage. For example, there are viruses that are known to lock up keyboards, disable mice, and cause disk read/write heads to move to nonexisting sectors on the disk, thus causing the disk to crash.

Trojans These are a class of viruses that hackers hide, just as in the Greek Trojan Horse legend, into trusted programs such as compilers, editors, and other commonly used programs.

Logic/Time Bombs Logic bombs are timed and commonly used type of virus to penetrate system, embedding themselves in the system's software and lying in wait until a trigger goes off. Trigger events can vary in type depending on the motive of the virus. Most triggers are timed events. There are various types of these viruses including Columbus Day, Valentine's Day, Jerusalem-D, and the Michelangelo, which was meant to activate on Michelangelo's 517 birthday anniversary.

Trapdoors Probably, these are some of the most used virus tools by hackers. They find their way into the system through weak points and loopholes that are found through system scans. Quite often, software manufacturers, during software development and testing, intentionally leave trapdoors in their products, usually undocumented, as secret entry points into the programs so that modification can be done on the programs at a later date. Trapdoors are also used by programmers as testing points. As is always the case, trapdoors can also be exploited by malicious people, including programmers themselves. In a trapdoor attack, an intruder may deposit virus-infected data file on a system instead of actually removing, copying, or destroying the existing data files.

Hoaxes Very common form of viruses, they most often do not originate from hackers but from system users. Though not physically harmful, hoaxes can be a disturbing type of nuisance to system users.

5.3.5.2 Worm
A worm is very similar to a virus. In fact, their differences are few. They are both automated attacks, both self-generate or replicate new copies as they spread, and both can damage any resource they attack. The main difference between them, however, is that while viruses always hide in software as surrogates, worms are stand-alone programs.

Hackers have been using worms as frequently as they have been using viruses to attack computer systems.

5.3.5.3 Sniffer

A sniffer is a software script that sniffs around the target system looking for passwords and other specific information that usually lead to identification of system exploits. Hackers use sniffers extensively for this purpose.

5.3.6   Types of Attacks

Whatever their motives, hackers have a variety of techniques in their arsenal to carry out their goals. Let us look at some of them here.

Social Engineering This involves fooling the victim for fun and profit. Social engineering depends on trusting that employees will fall for cheap hacker "tricks" such as calling or e-mailing them masquerading as a system administrator, for example, and getting their passwords which eventually lets in the intruder. Social engineering is very hard to protect against. The only way to prevent it is through employee education and employee awareness.

Impersonation This is stealing access rights of authorized users. There are many ways an attacker such as a hacker can impersonate a legitimate user. For example, a hacker can capture a user telnet session using a network sniffer such as TCPdump or nitsniff. The hacker can then later log-in as a legitimate user with the stolen log-in access rights of the victim.

Exploits This involves exploiting a hole in software or operating systems. As is usually the case, many software products are brought on the market either through a rush to finish or lack of testing, with gaping loopholes. Badly written software is very common even in large software projects such as operating systems. Hackers quite often scan network hosts for exploits and use them to enter systems.

Transitive Trust This exploits host-to-host or network-to-network trust. Either through client-server three-way handshake or server-to-server next-hop relationships, there is always a trust relationship between two network hosts during any transmission. This trust relationship is quite often compromised by hackers in a variety of ways. For example, an attacker can easily do an IP spoof or a sequence number attack between two transmitting elements and gets away with information that compromises the security of the two communicating elements.

Data Attacks Script programming has not only brought new dynamism into Web development, but it has also brought a danger of hostile code into systems through scripts. Current scripts can run on both the server, where they traditionally used to run, and also on the client. In doing so, scripts can allow an intruder to deposit hostile code into the system, including Trojans, worms, or viruses. We will discuss scripts in detail in the next chapter.

Infrastructure Weaknesses Some of the greatest network infrastructure weaknesses are found in the communication protocols. Many hackers, by virtue of their knowledge of the network infrastructure, take advantage of these loopholes and use them as gateways to attack systems. Many times, whenever a loophole is found in the protocols, patches are soon made available, but not many system administrators follow through with patching the security holes. Hackers start by scanning systems to find those unpatched holes. In fact, most of the system attacks from hackers use known vulnerabilities that should have been patched.

Denial of Service This is a favorite attack technique for many hackers, especially hacktivists. It consists of preventing the system from being used as planned through overwhelming the servers with traffic. The victim server is selected and then bombarded with packets with spoofed IP addresses. Many times, innocent hosts are forced to take part in the bombardment of the victim to increase the traffic on the victim until the victim is overwhelmed and eventually fails.

Active Wiretap In an active wiretap, messages are intercepted during transmission. When the interception happens, two things may take place: First, the data in the intercepted package may be compromised by the introduction of new data such as change of source or destination IP address or the change in the packet sequence numbers. Secondly, data may not be changed but copied to be used later such as in the scanning and sniffing of packets. In either case, the confidentiality of data is compromised, and the security of the network is put at risk.

5.4   Dealing with the Rising Tide of Cybercrimes

Most system attacks take place before even experienced security experts have advance knowledge of them. Most of the security solutions are best practices as we have so far seen, and we will continue to discuss them as either preventive or reactive. An effective plan must consist of three components: prevention, detection, and analysis and response.

5.4.1 Prevention

Prevention is probably the best system security policy, but only if we know what to prevent the systems from. It has been and it continues to be an uphill battle for the security community to be able to predict what type of attack will occur the next time around. Although prevention is the best approach to system security, the future of system security cannot and should not rely on the guesses of a few security people, who have and will continue to get it wrong sometimes. In the few bright spots in the protection of systems through prevention has been the fact that most of the attack signatures are repeat signatures. Although it is difficult and we are constantly chasing the hackers who are always ahead of us, we still need to do something. Among those possible approaches are the following:

- A security policy
- Risk management
- Perimeter security
- Encryption
- Legislation
- Self-regulation
- Mass education

We will discuss all these in detail in the chapters that follow.

5.4.2 Detection

In case prevention fails, the next best strategy should be early detection. Detecting cybercrimes before they occur constitutes a 24-h monitoring system to alert security personnel whenever something unusual (something with a non-normal pattern, different from the usual pattern of traffic in and around the system) occurs. Detection systems must continuously capture, analyze, and report on the daily happenings in and around the network. In capturing, analyzing, and reporting, several techniques are used, including intrusion detection, vulnerability scanning, virus detection, and other ad hoc methods. We will look at these in the coming chapters.

5.4.3 Recovery

Whether or not prevention or detection solutions were deployed on the system, if a security incident has occurred on a system, a recovery plan, as spelled out in the security plan, must be followed.

5.5 Conclusion

Dealing with rising cybercrimes in general and hacker activities in particular, in this fast-moving computer communication revolution in which everyone is likely to be affected, is a major challenge not only to the people in the security community but for all of us. We must devise means that will stop the growth, stop the spiral, and protect the systems from attacks. But this fight is already cut out for us, and it is tough in that we are chasing the enemy who seems, on many occasions, to know more than we do and is constantly ahead of us.

Preventing cybercrimes requires an enormous amount of effort and planning. The goal is to have advance information before an attack occurs. However, the challenge is to get this advance information. Also getting this information in advance does not help very much unless we can quickly analyze it and plan an appropriate response in time to prevent the systems from being adversely affected. In real life, however, there is no such thing as the luxury of advance information before an attack.

Exercises

1. Define the following terms:
   (i) Hacker
   (ii) Hacktivist
   (iii) Cracker
2. Why is hacking a big threat to system security?
3. What is the best way to deal with hacking?
4. Discuss the politics of dealing with hacktivism.
5. Following the history of hacking, can you say that hacking is getting under control? Why or why not?
6. What kind of legislation can be effective to prevent hacking?
7. List and discuss the types of hacker crimes.
8. Discuss the major sources of computer crimes.
9. Why is crime reporting so low in major industries?
10. Insider abuse is a major crime category. Discuss ways to solve it.

Advanced Exercises

1. Devise a plan to compute the cost of computer crime.
2. What major crimes would you include in the preceding study?
3. From your study, identify the most expensive attacks.
4. Devise techniques to study the problem of non-reporting. Estimate the costs associated with it.
5. Study the reporting patterns of computer crimes reporting by industry. Which industry reports best?

References

1. Cybercrime threat "real and growing" http://news.bbc.co.uk/2/hi/science/nature/978163.stm
2. Glossary of vulnerability testing terminology http://www.ee.oulu.fi/research/ouspg/sage/glossary/
3. Anatomy of an attack The Economist, February 19–25, 2000
4. Kizza JM (2003) Social and ethical issues in the information age, 2nd edn. Springer, New York
5. Louis J. Freeh. FBI Congressional Report on Cybercrime http://www.fbi.gov/congress00/cyber021600.htm
6. Michelle Slatalla. A brief history of hacking http://tlc.discovery.com/convergence/hackers/articles/history.html

7. Phone phreaking: the telecommunications underground http://telephonetribute.com/phonephreaking.html
8. "Timeline of Hacking" http://fyi.cnn.com/fyi/interactive/school.tools/timelines/1999/computer.hacking/frameset.exclude.html
9. Rosenbaum R. Secrets of the little blue box http://www.webcrunchers.com/crunch/esqart.html
10. The complete history of hacking http://www.wbglinks.net/pages/history/
11. Denning PJ (1990) Computers under attack: intruders, worms and viruses. ACM Press, New York
12. Denning, D. "*Activism, Hacktivism, and Cyberterrorisim: The Internet as a Tool or Influencing Foreign Policy* http://www.nautilus.og/info-policy/workshop/papers/denning.html
13. Lemos R. *Online vandals smoke New York Times site CNET* News.com. http://news.com.com/2009–1001–252754.html
14. Shachtman N. *Hacktivists Stage Virtual Sit-In at WEF Web site* AlterNet. http://www.alternet.org/story.html?StoryID=12374
15. Kizza JM (2001) Computer network security and cyber ethics. North Calorina, McFarland
16. Forchet K (1994) Computer security management. Boyd & Frasher Publishing

Scripting and Security in Computer Networks and Web Browsers

6

6.1   Introduction

The rapid growth of the Internet and its ability to offer services have made it the fastest-growing medium of communication today. Today's and tomorrow's business transactions involving financial data; product development and marketing; storage of sensitive company information; and the creation, dissemination, sharing, and storing of information are and will continue to be made online, most specifically on the Web. The automation and dynamic growth of an interactive Web has created a huge demand for a new type of Web programming to meet the growing demand of millions of Web services from users around the world. Some services and requests are tedious and others are complex, yet the rate of growth of the number of requests, the amount of services requested in terms of bandwidth, and the quality of information requested warrant a technology to automate the process. Script technology came in timely to the rescue. Scripting is a powerful automation technology on the Internet that makes the Web highly interactive.

Scripting technology is making the Web interactive and automated as Web servers accept inputs from users and respond to user inputs. While scripting is making the Internet and, in particular, the Web is alive and productive, it also introduces a huge security problem to an already security-burdened cyberspace. Hostile scripts embedded in Web pages, as well as HTML formatted e-mail, attachments, and applets introduce a new security paradigm in cyberspace security. In particular, security problems are introduced in two areas: at the server and at the client. Before we look at the security at both of these points, let us first understand the scripting standard.

© Springer International Publishing AG 2017
J.M. Kizza, *Guide to Computer Network Security*, Computer Communications and Networks, DOI 10.1007/978-3-319-55606-2_6

6.2   Scripting

A program script is a logical sequence of line commands which causes the computer to accomplish some task. Many times we refer to such code as *macros* or *batch files* because they can be executed without user interaction. A script language is a programming language through which you can write scripts. Scripts can be written in any programming language or a special language as long as they are surrogated by another program to interpret and execute them on the fly by a program unlike compiled programs which are run by the computer operating system.

Because scripts are usually small programs, written with a specific purpose in mind to perform tasks very quickly and easily, many times in constrained and embedded environments with abstracted performance and safety, unlike general-purpose programs written in general-purpose programming languages, scripts are not in most cases full-featured programs, but tend to be "glue" programs that hold together other pieces of software.

Therefore, scripting languages are not your general-purpose programming languages. Their syntax, features, library, etc. are focused more around accomplishing small tasks quickly. The scripts can be either application scripts, if they are executed by an application program surrogate like Microsoft spreadsheet, or command line scripts if they are executed from a command line like the Windows or Unix/Linux command line.

6.3   Scripting Languages

CGI scripts can be written in any programming language. Because of the need for quick execution of the scripts both at the server and in the client browsers and the need of not storing source code at the server, it is getting more and more convenient to use scripting languages that are interpretable instead of languages that are compiled like C and C++. The most common scripting languages include:

- JavaScript
- Perl
- Tcl/Tk
- Python
- VBA
- Windows Script Host
- Others including specific mobile device scripting languages

There are basically two categories of scripting languages, those whose scripts are on the server side of the client-server programming model and those whose scripts are on the client side.

6.3.1   Server-Side Scripting Languages

Ever since the debut of the World Wide Web and the development of HTML to specify and present information, there has been a realization that HTML documents are too static.

There was a need to put dynamism into HTTP so that the interaction between the client and the server would become dynamic. This problem was easy to solve because the hardware on which Web server software runs has processing power and many applications such as e-mail, database manipulation, or calendaring already installed and ripe for utilization [1]. The CGI concept was born.

Among the many sever-side scripting languages are ERL, PHP, ColdFusion, ASP, MySQL, Java servlets, and MivaScript.

6.3.1.1 Perl Scripts

Practical Extraction and Report Language (Perl) is an interpretable programming language that is also portable. It is used extensively in Web programming to make text processing interactive and dynamic. Developed in 1986 by Larry Wall, the language has become very popular. Although it is an interpreted language, unlike C and C++, Perl has many features and basic constructs and variables similar to C and C++. However, unlike C and C++, Perl has no pointers and defined data types.

One of the security advantages of Perl over C, say, is that Perl does not use pointers where a programmer can misuse a pointer and access unauthorized data. Perl also introduces a gateway into Internet programming between the client and the server. This gateway is a security gatekeeper scrutinizing all incoming data into the server to prevent malicious code and data into the server. Perl does this by denying programs written in Perl from writing to a variable, whereby this variable can corrupt other variables.

Perl also has a version called Taintperl that always checks data dependencies to prevent system commands from allowing untrusted data or code into the server.

6.3.1.2 PHP

PHP (Hypertext Preprocessor) is a widely used general-purpose scripting language that is especially suited for Web development and can be embedded into HTML. It is an open-source language suited for Web development, and this makes it very popular.

Just like Perl, PHP code is executed on the server, and the client just receives the results of running a PHP script on the server. With PHP, you can do just about anything other CGI program can do, such as collect form data, generate dynamic page content, or send and receive cookies.

6.3.2   Client-Side Scripting Languages

The World Wide Web (WWW) created the romance of representing portable information from a wide range of applications for a global audience. This was accomplished by the HyperText Markup Language (HTML), a simple markup language that revolutionized document representation on the Internet. But for a while, HTML documents were static. The scripting specifications were developed to extend HTML and make it more dynamic and interactive. Client-side scripting of HTML documents and objects embedded within HTML documents has been developed to bring dynamism and automation of user documents. Scripts including JavaScript and VBScript are being used widely to automate client processes.

For a long time, during the development of CGI programming, programmers noticed that much of what CGI does, such as maintaining a state, filling out forms, error checking, or performing numeric calculation, can be handled on the client's side. Quite often, the client computer has quite a bit of CPU power idle, while the server is being bombarded with hundreds or thousands of CGI requests for the mundane jobs above. The programmers saw it justifiable to shift the burden to the client, and this led to the birth of client-side scripting.

Among the many client-side scripting languages are DTML/CSS, Java, JavaScript, and VBScript.

6.3.2.1 JavaScripts

JavaScript is a programming that performs client-side scripting, making Web pages more interactive. Client-side scripting means that the code works only on the user's computer, not on the server side. It was developed by Sun Microsystems to bridge the gap between Web designers who needed a dynamic and interactive Web environment and Java programmers. It is an interpretable language like Perl. That means the interpreter in the browser is all that is needed for a JavaScript to be executed by the client and it will run. JavaScript's ability to run scripts on the client's browser makes the client able to run interactive Web scripts that do not need a server. This feature makes creating JavaScript scripts easy because they are simply embedded into any HTML code. It has, therefore, become the de facto standard for enhancing and adding functionality to Web pages.

This convenience, however, creates a security threat because when a browser can execute a JavaScript at any time, it means that hostile code can be injected into the script and the browser would run it from any client. This problem can be fixed only if browsers can let an executing script perform a limited number of commands. In addition, scripts run from a browser can introduce into the client systems programming errors in the coding of the script itself, which may lead to a security threat in the system itself.

6.3.2.2 VBScript

Based in part on the popularity of the Visual Basic programming language and on the need to have a scripting language to counter JavaScript, Microsoft developed VBScript (V and B for Visual Basic). VBScript has a syntax similar to the Visual Basic programming language syntax. Since VBScript is based on Microsoft Visual Basic and unlike JavaScript which can run in many browsers, VBScript interpreter is supported only in the Microsoft Internet Explorer.

6.4   Scripting in Computer Network

The use of scripting in computer network started when network administrators released that one of the best ways to tame the growing mountain of tasks required to have a well functioning network was to use scripting and take advantage of the automated natured of execution of scripts via surrogate programs. This cut down on the need for attention for many, sometimes repeated tasks, in the running of a system network.

According to Allen Rouse [2], scripting lets you automate various network administration tasks, such as those that are performed every day or even several times a day and those performed widely throughout the network like log-in scripts and modification to the registry scripts in a widely distributed network of servers. There are many functions in a daily administration of a network that are performed by scripts including [2]:

- Machine startup
- Machine shutdown
- User log-in and log-out
- Scripting basic TCP/IP networking on clients, including comparisons of GUI and command line tools to analogous scripting techniques
- Extending these scripting techniques to remote and multiple computers
- IP address allocation with DHCP and static IP addresses
- DNS client management
- WINS client management
- TCP/IP filtering, Internetwork Packet Exchange (IPX), and other network protocols
- Managing system time and network settings in the registry
- Addition of new clients to a network
- Client-server information exchange

With all these tasks taken over by scripting, you may notice the tremendous advantages scripting brings to the table for system administration in time savings, network consistence, and flexibility.

By every account, scripting is on the rise with the changing technologies. There is tremendous enthusiasm for growth in the four traditional areas of scripting that include:

- System administration
- Graphical user interface (GUI)
- Internet information exchange (CGI) and the growing popularity of the browser
- Application and component frameworks like ActiveX and others

We will focus on the Internet information exchange in this chapter.

6.4.1   Introduction to the Common Gateway Interface (CGI)

One of the most essential useful areas in network performance when scripting plays a vital role is in the network client-server information exchange. This is done via a *Common Gateway Interface* or *CGI*. CGI is a standard to specify a data format that servers, browsers, and programs must use in order to exchange information. A program written in any language that uses this standard to exchange data between a Web server and a client's browser is a *CGI script*. In other words, a CGI script is an external gateway program to interface with information servers such as HTTP or Web servers and client browsers. CGI scripts are great in that they allow the Web servers to be dynamic and interactive with the client browser as the server receives and accepts user inputs and responds to them in a measured and relevant way to satisfy the user. Without CGI, the information the users would get from an information server would not be packaged based on the request but based on how it is stored on the server.

CGI programs are of two types: those written in programming languages such as C/C++ and Fortran that can be compiled to produce an executable module stored on the server and scripts written in scripting languages such as PERL, Java, and Unix shell. For these CGI scripts, no associated source code needs to be stored by the information server as is the case in CGI programs. CGI scripts written in scripting languages are not compiled like those in nonscripting languages. Instead, they are text code which is interpreted by the interpreter on the information server or in the browser and run right away. The advantage to this is you can copy your script with little or no changes to any machine with the same interpreter and it will run. In addition, the scripts are easier to debug, modify, and maintain than a typical compiled program.

Both CGI programs and scripts, when executed at the information server, help organize information for both the server and the client. For example, the server may want to retrieve information entered by the visitors and use it to package a suitable output for the clients. In addition, GCI may be used to dynamically set field descriptions on a form and in real time inform the user on what data has been entered and yet to be entered. At the end, the form may even be returned to the user for proofreading before it is submitted.

CGI scripts go beyond dynamic form filling to automating a broad range of services in search engines and directories and taking on mundane jobs such as making download available, granting access rights to users, and order confirmation.

As we pointed out earlier, CGI scripts can be written in any programming language that an information server can execute. Many of these languages include script languages such as Perl, JavaScript, TCL, Applescript, Unix shell, VBScript, and nonscript languages such as C/C++, Fortran, and Visual Basic. There is dynamism in the languages themselves; so, we may have new languages in the near future.

6.4.1.1 CGI Scripts in a Three-Way Handshake

As we discussed in Chap. 3, the communication between a server and a client opens with the same etiquette we use when we meet a stranger. First, a trust relationship must be established before any requests are made. This can be done in a number of ways. Some people start with a formal "Hello, I'm... " and then "I need ..." upon which the stranger says "Hello, I'm ..." and then "Sure I can ...." Others carry it further to hugs, kisses, and all other ways people use to break the ice. If the stranger is ready for a request, then this information is passed back to you in a form of an acknowledgement to your first embrace. However, if the stranger is not ready to talk to you, there is usually no acknowledgment of your initial advances, and no further communication may follow until the stranger's acknowledgment comes through. At this point, the stranger puts out a welcome mat and leaves the door open for you to come in and start business. Now, it is up to the initiator of the communication to start full communication.

When computers are communicating, they follow these etiquette patterns and protocols, and we call this procedure a handshake. In fact, for computers it is called a three-way handshake. A three-way handshake starts with the client sending a packet, called a *SYN* (short for synchronization), which contains both the client and server addresses together with some initial information for introductions. Upon receipt of this packet by the server's welcome open door, called a *port*, the server creates a communication socket with the same port number such as the client requested through which future communication with the client will go. After creating the communication socket, the server puts the socket in queue and informs the client by sending an acknowledgment called a *SYN-ACK*. The server's commu-nication socket will remain open and in queue waiting for an ACK from the client and data packets thereafter. The socket door remains half-open until the server sends the client an ACK packet signaling full communication. During this time, however, the server can welcome many more clients that want to communicate, and communication sockets will be opened for each.

The CGI script is a server-side language that resides on the server side, and it receives the client's SYN request for a service. The script then executes and lets the server and client start to communicate directly. In this position, the script is able to dynamically receive and pass data between the client and server. The client browser has no idea that the server is executing a script. When the server receives the script's output, it then adds the necessary protocol data and sends the packet or packets back to the client's browser. Figure 6.1 shows the position of a CGI script in a three-way handshake.

The CGI scripts reside on the server side, in fact on the computer on which the server is, because a user on a client machine cannot execute the script in a browser on the server; one can view only the output of the script after it executes on the server and transmits the output using a browser on the client machine the user is on.

Fig. 6.1 The position of a
CGI script in a three-way
handshake

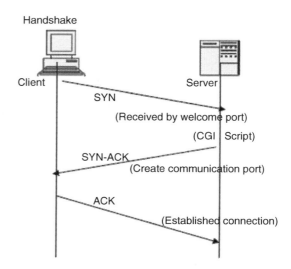

6.4.2   Server-Side Scripting: The CGI Interface

In the previous section, we stated that the CGI script is on the server side of the relationship between the client and the server. The scripts are stored on the server and are executed by the server to respond to the client demands. There is, therefore, an interface that separates the server and the script. This interface, as shown in Fig. 6.2, consists of information from the server supplied to the script that includes input variables extracted from an HTTP header from the client and information from the script back to the server. Output information from the server to the script and from the script to the server is passed through environment variables and through script command lines. Command line inputs instruct a script to do certain tasks such as search and query.

6.5   Computer Networks Scripts and Security

As we have pointed out above, by all accounts, scripting is on the rise with the changing technologies. There is tremendous enthusiasm for growth in the four traditional areas of scripting that include:

- System administration
- Graphical user interface (GUI)
- Internet information exchange (CGI) and the growing popularity of the browser
- Application and component frameworks like ActiveX and others

As scripting grows, so are will its associated security problems. Hackers are constantly developing and testing a repertoire of their own scripts that will compromise other scripts wherever they are on the Web, in the computer network system or

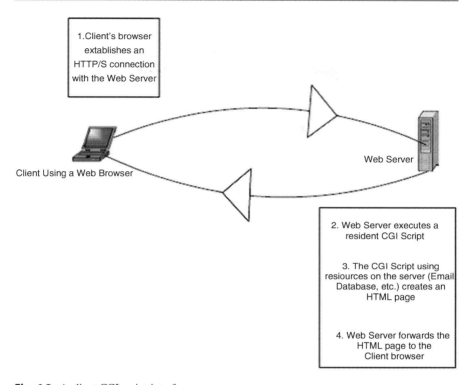

Fig. 6.2   A client CGI script interface

in applications. The most common of such hacker techniques today include Web cross-site scripting or XSS or CSS. Cross-site scripting allows attackers of Web sites to embed malicious scripts into dynamic unsuspecting Web and network scripts. Although this is a threat to most scripts, we will focus our script security discussion on the CGI scripts.

6.5.1   CGI Script Security

To an information server, the CGI script is like an open window to a private house where passersby can enter the house to request services. It is an open gateway that allows anyone anywhere to run an executable program on your server and even send their own programs to run on your server. An open window like this on a server is not the safest thing to have, and security issues are involved. But since CGI scripting is the fastest-growing component of the Internet, it is a problem we have to contend with and meet head on. CGI scripts present security problems to cyberspace in several ways including:

- *Program development*: During program development, CGI scripts are written in high-level programming language and compiled before being executed, or they are written in a scripting language and they are interpreted before they are executed. In either way, programming is more difficult than composing documents with HTML, for example. Because of the programming complexity and owing to lack of program development discipline, errors introduced into the program are difficult to find, especially in noncompiled scripts.
- *Transient nature of execution*: When CGI scripts come into the server, they run as separate processes from that of the host server. Although this is good because it isolates the server from most script errors, the imported scripts may introduce hostile code into the server.
- *Cross-pollination*: The hostile code introduced into the server by a transient script can propagate into other server applications and can even be retransmitted to other servers by a script bouncing off this server or originating from this server.
- *Resource guzzling*: Scripts that are resource intensive could cause a security problem to a server with limited resources.
- *Remote execution*: Since servers can send CGI scripts to execute on surrogate servers, both the sending and receiving servers are left open to hostile code usually transmitted by the script.

In all these situations, a security threat occurs when someone breaks into a script. Broken scripts are extremely dangerous.

Kris Jamsa gives the following security threats that can happen to a broken script [2]:

- Giving an attacker access to the system's password file for decryption.
- Mailing a map of the system which gives the attacker more time offline to analyze the system's vulnerabilities.
- Starting a log-in server on a high port and telneting in.
- Beginning a distributed denial-of-service attack against the server.
- Erasing or altering the server's log files.
- In addition to these others, the following security threats are also possible [3]:
  – Malicious code provided by one client for another client: this can happen, for example, in sites that host discussion groups where one client can embed malicious HTML tags in a message intended for another client. According to the Computer Emergency Response Team (CERT), an attacker might post a message like:
  Hello message board. This is a message.
  <SCRIPT>malicious code</SCRIPT>
  This is the end of my message.
  When a victim with scripts enabled in his or her browser reads this message, the malicious code may be executed unexpectedly. Many different scripting tags that can be embedded in this way include <SCRIPT>, <OBJECT>, <APPLET>, and <EMBED>.

   – Malicious code sent inadvertently by a client: When a client sends malicious
     data intended to be used only by itself. This occurs when the client relies on
     an untrustworthy source of information when submitting a request. To
     explain this case, CERT gives the following example. An attacker may
     construct a malicious link such as [3]:
     <A HREF = "http://example.com/comment.cgi?
     mycomment = <SCRIPT>malicious code</SCRIPT>">
     Click here </A>
     When an unsuspecting user clicks on this link, the URL sent to example.com
       includes the malicious code. If the Web server sends a page back to the
       user including the value of *mycomment*, the malicious code may be
       executed unexpectedly on the client.

All these security threats point at one security problem with scripts: they all let in
unsecured data.

6.5.1.1 Server-Side Script Security

A server-side script, whether compiled or interpreted, and its interpreter are
included in a Web server as a module or executed as a separate CGI binary. It
can access files, execute commands, and open network connections on the server.
These capabilities make server-side scripts a security threat because they make
anything run on the Web server unsecure by default. PHP is no exception to this
problem; it is just like Perl and C. For example, PHP, like other server-side scripts,
was designed to allow user-level access to the file system, but it is entirely possible
that a PHP script can allow a user to read system files such as /etc/passwd which
gives the user access to all passwords and the ability to modify network connections
and change device entries in /dev/ or COM1, configuration files /etc/ files, and .ini
files.

Since databases have become an integral part of daily computing in a networked
world and large databases are stored on network servers, they become easy prey to
hostile code. To retrieve or to store any information in a database, nowadays you
need to connect to the database, send a legitimate query, fetch the result, and close
the connection all using a query language, the Structured Query Language (SQL).
An attacker can create or alter SQL commands to inject hostile data and code, or to
override valuable ones, or even to execute dangerous system-level commands on
the database host.

6.5.2   JavaScript and VBScript Security

Recall that using all client-side scripts like JavaScript and VBScript that execute in
the browser can compromise the security of the user system. These scripts create
hidden frames on Web sites so that as a user navigates a Web site, the scripts
running in the browser can store information from the user for short-time use, just
like a cookie. The hidden frame is an area of the Web page that is invisible to the

user but remains in place for the script to use. Data stored in these hidden frames can be used by multiple Web pages during the user session or later. Also, when a user visits a Web site, the user may not be aware that there are scripts executing at the Web site. Hackers can use these loopholes to threaten the security of the user system.

There are several ways of dealing with these problems including:

- Limit browser functions and operations of the browser scripts so that the script, for example, cannot write on or read from the user's disk.
- Make it difficult for others to read the scripts.
- Put the script in an external file and reference the file only from the document that uses it.

6.5.3   Web Script Security

Our discussion of script security issues above has centered on CGI scripts stored and executed on the server. However, as the automation of the Web goes into overdrive, there are now thousands of Web scripts doing a variety of Web services from form filling to information gathering. Most of these scripts either transient or reside on Web servers. Because of their popularity and widespread use, most client and server Web browsers today have the capability to interpret scripts embedded in Web pages downloaded from a Web server. Such scripts may be written in a variety of scripting languages. In addition, most browsers are installed with the capability to run scripts enabled by default.

6.6   Dealing with the Script Security Problems

The love of Web automation is not likely to change soon, and the future of a dynamic Web is here to stay. In addition, more and more programs written for the Web are interacting with networked clients and servers, raising the fear of a possibility that clients and servers may be attacked by these programs using embedded scripts to gain unauthorized access.

It is, therefore, necessary to be aware of the following:

- Script command line statements: Scripting languages such as PERL, PHP, and the Bourne shell pass information needed to perform tasks through command line statements which are then executed by an interpreter. This can be very dangerous.
- Clients may use special characters in input strings to confuse other clients, servers, or scripts.
- Problems with server side include user-created documents in NCSA HTTPd that provide simple information, such as current date, the file's last modification date, and the size or last modification of other files, to clients on the fly. Sometimes this information can provide a powerful interface to CGI. In an unfortunate

situation, server-side scripts are a security risk because they let clients execute dangerous commands on the server.

We summarize the three concerns above in two good solutions: one is to use only the data from a CGI, only if it will not harm the system; and the second is to check all data into or out of the script to make sure that it is safe.

Exercises

1. How did CGI revolutionize Web programming?
2. What are the differences between client-side and server-side scripting? Is one better than the other?
3. In terms of security, is client-side scripting better than server-side scripting? Why or why not?
4. Suggest ways to improve script security threats.
5. Why was VBScript not very popular?
6. The biggest script security threat has always been the acceptance of untrusted data. What is the best way for scripts to accept data and preserve the trust?

Advance Exercises

1. The most common CGI function is to fill in forms; the processing script actually takes the data input by the Web surfer and sends it as e-mail to the form adminis- trator. Discuss the different ways such a process can fall victim to an attacker.
2. CGI is also used in discussions allowing users to talk to the customer and back. CGI helps in creating an ongoing dialog between multiple clients. Discuss the security implications of dialogs like this.
3. CGI is often used to manage extensive databases. Databases store sensitive information. Discuss security measures you can use to safeguard the databases.

References

1. Sol S. Server-side scripting. http://www.wdvl.com/Authoring/Scripting/WebWare/Server/
2. Rouse A. Understanding the role of scripting in network administration. http://www. techrepublic.com/article/understand-the-role-of-scripting-in-network-administration/

Additional References

1. The World Wide Web Security FAQ. http://www.w3.org/Security/Faq/wwwsf4.html
2. Jamsa K (2002) Hacker proof: the ultimate guide to network security, 2nd edn. Thomason Delmar Learning
3. CERT® Advisory CA-2000–02 Malicious HTML Tags Embedded in Client Web Requests. http://www.cert.org/advisories/CA-2000–02.html

Security Assessment, Analysis, and Assurance

7

7.1   Introduction

The rapid development in both computer and telecommunication technologies has resulted in massive interconnectivity and interoperability of systems. The world is getting more and more interconnected every day. Most major organization systems are interconnected to other systems through networks. The bigger the networks, the bigger the security problems involving the system resources on these networks. Many companies, businesses, and institutions whose systems work in coordination and collaboration with other systems as they share each other's resources and communicate with each other face a constant security threat to these systems, yet the collaboration must go on.

The risks and potential of someone intruding into these systems for sabotage, vandalism, and resource theft are high. For security assurance of networked systems, such risks must be assessed to determine the adequacy of existing security measures and safeguards and also to determine if improvement in the existing measures is needed. Such an assessment process consists of a comprehensive and continuous analysis of the security threat risk to the system that involves an auditing of the system, assessing the vulnerabilities of the system, and maintaining a creditable security policy and a vigorous regime for the installation of patches and security updates. In addition, there must also be a standard process to minimize the risks associated with nonstandard security implementations across shared infrastructures and end systems.

The process to achieve all these and more consists of several tasks including a system security policy, security requirements specification, identification of threat and threat analysis, vulnerability assessment, security certification, and the monitoring of vulnerabilities and auditing. The completion of these tasks marks a completion of a security milestone on the road to a system's security assurance. These tasks are shown in Table 7.1 below.

Security is a process. Security assurance is a continuous security state of the security process. The process, illustrated in Table 7.1 and depicted in Fig. 7.1, starts

© Springer International Publishing AG 2017   147
J.M. Kizza, *Guide to Computer Network Security*, Computer Communications and Networks, DOI 10.1007/978-3-319-55606-2_7

Table 7.1 System
security process

System security policy
Security requirements specification
Threat identification
Threat analysis
Vulnerability identification and assessment
Security certification
Security monitoring and auditing

with a thorough system security policy, whose components are used for system requirement specifications. The security requirement specifications are then used to identify threats to the system resources. An analysis of these identified threats per resource is then done. The vulnerabilities identified by the threats are then assessed, and if the security measures taken are good enough, they are then certified, along with the security staff.

After certification, the final component of the security process is the auditing and monitoring phase. This phase may reveal more security problems which require revisiting the security policy that makes the process start to repeat itself. That security cycle process is security assurance. The process of security assurance is shown in Fig. 7.1.

7.2   System Security Policy

To a system administrator, the security of the organization's system is very important. For any organization system, there must be somebody to say *no* when the *no* needs to be said. The *no* must be said because the administrator wants to limit the number of network computers, resources, and capabilities people have been using to ensure the security of the system. One way of doing this in fairness to all is through the implementation of a set of policies, procedures, and guidelines that tell all employees and business partners what constitutes acceptable and unacceptable use of the organization's computer system. The security policy also spells out what resources need to be protected and how organization can protect such resources. A security policy is a living set of policies and procedures that impact and potentially limit the freedoms and of course levels of individual security responsibilities of all users. Such a structure is essential to an organization's security. Having said that, however, let us qualify our last statement. There are as many opinions on the usefulness of security policies in the overall system security picture as there are security experts. However, security policies are still important in the security plan of a system. It is important for several reasons including:

- Firewall installations: If a functioning firewall is to be configured, its rule base must be based on a sound security policy.
- User discipline: All users in the organization who connect to a network such as the Internet, through a firewall, say, must conform to the security policy.

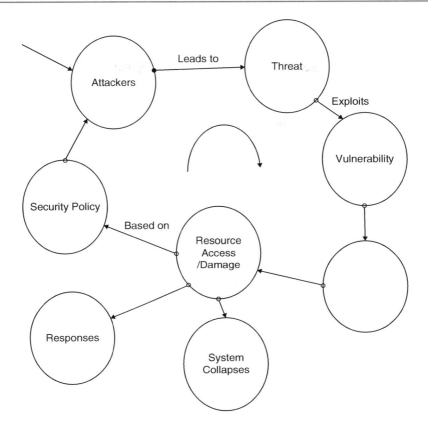

Fig. 7.1 System security assurance cycle

Without a strong security policy that every employee must conform to, the organization may suffer from data loss, employee time loss, and productivity loss all because employees may spend time fixing holes, repairing vulnerabilities, and recovering lost or compromised data among other things.

A security policy covers a wide variety of topics and serves several important purposes in the system security cycle. Constructing a security policy is like building a house; it needs a lot of different components that must fit together. The security policy is built in stages, and each stage adds value to the overall product, making it unique for the organization. To be successful, a security policy must:

- Have the backing of the organization top management.
- Involve everyone in the organization by explicitly stating the role everyone will play and the responsibilities of everyone in the security of the organization.
- Precisely describe a clear vision of a secure environment stating what needs to be protected and the reasons for it.
- Set priorities and costs of what needs to be protected.

- Be a good teaching tool for everyone in the organization about security and what needs to be protected, why, and how it is to be protected.
- Set boundaries on what constitutes appropriate and inappropriate behavior as far as security and privacy of the organization resources are concerned.
- Create a security clearing house and authority.
- Be flexible enough to adapt to new changes.
- Be consistently implemented throughout the organization.

To achieve these subgoals, a carefully chosen set of basic steps must be followed to construct a viable implementable and useful security policy.

According to Jasma, the core five steps are the following [1, 2]:

- Determine the resources that must be protected, and for each resource, draw a profile of its characteristics. Such resources should include physical, logical, network, and system assets. A table of these items ordered in importance should be developed.
- For each identified resource, determine from whom you must protect.
- For each identifiable resource, determine the type of threat and the likelihood of such a threat. For each threat, identify the security risk and construct an ordered table for these based on importance. Such risks may include:
  - Denial of service
  - Disclosure or modification of information
  - Unauthorized access
- For each identifiable resource, determine what measures will protect it the best and from whom.
- Develop a policy team consisting of at least one member from senior administration, legal staff, employees, member of IT department, and an editor or writer to help with drafting the policy.
- Determine what needs to be audited. Programs such as Tripwire perform audits on both Unix and Windows systems. Audit security events on servers and firewalls and also on selected network hosts. For example, the following logs can be audited:
  - Log files for all selected network hosts, including servers and firewalls
  - Object accesses
- Define acceptable use of system resources such as:
  - E-mail
  - News
  - Web
- Consider how to deal with each of the following:
  - Encryption
  - Password
  - Key creation and distributions
  - Wireless devices that connect on the organization's network

- Provide for remote access to accommodate workers on the road and those working from home and also business partners who may need to connect through a virtual private network (VPN).

From all this information, develop two structures, one describing the access rights of users to the resources identified and the other structure describing user responsibilities in ensuring security for a given resource. Finally, schedule a time to review these structures regularly.

7.3   Building a Security Policy

Several issues, including the security policy access matrix, need to be constructed first before others can fit in place. So let us start with that.

7.3.1   Security Policy Access Rights Matrix

The first consideration in building a security policy is to construct a security policy access rights matrix $M = \{S, R\}$ where $S = \{$set of all user groups, some groups may have one element$\}$ and $R = \{$set of system resources$\}$. For example $R = \{$network hosts, switches, routers, firewalls, access servers, databases, files, e-mail, Web site, remote access point, etc.$\}$. And $S = [\{$administrator$\}$, $\{$support technicians$\}$, $\{$Human Resource users$\}$, $\{$Marketing users$\}$, etc.$\}]$.

For each element rj of R, develop a set of policies Pj. For example, create policies for the following members of R:

- E-mail and Web access (SNMP, DNS, NTP, WWW, NNTP, SMTP)
- Hardware access (logon passwords/usernames)
- Databases (file access/data backup)
- Wireless devices (access point logon/authentication/access control)
- Laptops' use and connection to organization's network
- Remote access (telnet, FTP)

For each element si of S, develop a set of responsibilities Ni. For example, create responsibilities for the following members of S:

- Who distributes system resources access rights/remote access/wireless access?
- Who creates accounts/remote access accounts?
- Who talks to the press?
- Who calls law enforcement?
- Who informs management of incidents and at what level?
- Who releases and what data?
- Who follows on a detected security incident?

Fig. 7.2 Security policy
access rights matrix M

	Resource	R1	R2	R3
User				
S1		[s1,r1]	[s1,r2]	[s1,r3]
S2		[s2,r1]	[s2,r2]	[s2,r3]

Once all access rights and responsibilities have been assigned, the matrix M is fully filled, and the policy is now slowly taking shape. Up to this point, an entry in $M = \{[si, rj]\}$ means that user from group si can use any of the rights in group rj for the resource j. See Fig. 7.2.

A structure $L = \{S, R\}$, similar to M, for responsibilities can also be constructed. After constructing these two structures, the security policy is now taking shape, but it is far from done. Several other security issues need to be taken care of, including those described in the following sections [3]:

7.3.1.1 Logical Access Restriction to the System Resources

Logical access restriction to system resources involves the following:

- Restricting access to equipment and network segments using:
  - Preventive controls that uniquely identify every authorized user (via established access control mechanisms such as passwords) and deny others.
  - Detective controls that log and report activities of users, both authorized and intruders. This may employ the use of intrusion detection systems, system scans, and other activity loggers. The logs are reported to a responsible party for action.
- Creating boundaries between network segments:
  - To control the flow of traffic between different cabled segments such as subnets by using IP address filters to deny access of specific subnets by IP addresses from nontrusted hosts.
  - Permit or deny access based on subnet addresses, if possible.
- Selecting a suitable routing policy to determine how traffic is controlled between subnets.

7.3.1.2 Physical Security of Resources and Site Environment

Establish physical security of all system resources by:

- Safeguarding physical infrastructure including media and path of physical cabling. Make sure that intruders cannot eavesdrop between lines by using detectors such as time domain reflectometer for coaxial cable and optical splitter using an optical time domain reflectometer for fiber optics.
- Safeguarding site environment. Make sure it is as safe as you can make it from security threats due to:
  - Fire (prevention/protection/detection)
  - Water

- Electric power surges
- Temperature/humidity
- Natural disasters
- Magnetic fields

7.3.1.3 Cryptographic Restrictions

We have defined a computer and also a network system as consisting of hardware, software, and users. The security of an organization's network, therefore, does not stop only at securing software such as the application software like browsers on the network hosts. It also includes data in storage in the network, that is, at network servers, and also data in motion within the network.

Ensuring this kind of software and data requires strong cryptographic techniques. So an organization's security policy must include a consideration of cryptographic algorithms to ensure data integrity. The best way to ensure as best as possible that traffic on the network is valid is through the following:

- Supported services, such as firewalls, relying on the TCP, UDP, ICMP, and IP headers, and TCP and UDP source and destination port numbers of individual packets to allow or deny the packet.
- Authentication of all data traversing the network, including traffic specific to the operations of a secure network infrastructure such as updating of routing tables.
- Checksum to protect against the injection of spurious packets from an intruder, and in combination with sequence number techniques, protects against replay attacks.
- Software not related to work will not be used on any computer that is part of the network.
- All software images and operating systems should use a checksum verification scheme before installation to confirm their integrity between sending and receiving devices.
- Encryption of routing tables and all data that pose the greatest risk based on the outcome of the risk assessment procedure in which data is classified according to its security sensitivity. For example, in an enterprise, consider the following:
  - All data dealing with employee salary and benefits
  - All data on product development
  - All data on sales
- Also pay attention to the local network address translation (NAT)—a system used to help network administrators with large pools of hosts from renumbering them when they all come on the Internet.
- Encrypt the backups making sure that they will be decrypted when needed.

7.3.2   Policy and Procedures

No security policy is complete without a section on policy and procedures. In fact, several issues are covered under policy and procedures. Among the items in this section is a list of common attacks for technicians to be aware of education of users, equipment use, equipment acquisition, software standards and acquisition, and incident handling and reporting.

7.3.2.1 Common Attacks and Possible Deterrents

Some of the most common deterrents to common attacks include the following:

- Developing a policy to insulate internal hosts (hosts behind a firewall) from a list of common attacks.
- Developing a policy to safeguard Web servers, FTP servers, and e-mail servers, which of these are at most risk because even though they are behind a firewall, any host, even those inside the network, can misuse them. You are generally better of putting those exposed service providers on a *demilitarized zone* (DMZ) network.
- Installing a honey port.

The following list provides an example of some items in an infrastructure and data integrity security policy:

7.3.2.2 Staff

- Recruit employees for positions in the implementation and operation of the network infrastructure who are capable and whose background has been checked.
- Have all personnel involved in the implementation and supporting the network infrastructure must attend a security seminar for awareness.
- Instruct all employees concerned to store all backups in a dedicated locked area.

7.3.2.3 Equipment Certification

To be sure that quality equipments are used, make every effort to ensure that:

- All new equipment to be added to the infrastructure should adhere to specified security requirements.
- Each site of the infrastructure should decide which security features and functionalities are necessary to support the security policy.
- The following are good guidelines:
  - All infrastructure equipment must pass the acquisition certification process before purchase.
  - All new images and configurations must be modeled in a test facility before deployment.
  - All major scheduled network outages and interruptions of services must be announced to those who will be affected well ahead of time.
- Use of Portable Tools
  - Since use of portable tools such as laptops always pose some security risks, develop guidelines for the kinds of data allowed to reside on hard drives of portable tools and how that data should be protected.

7.3.2.4 Audit Trails and Legal Evidence

Prepare for possible legal action by:

- Keeping logs of traffic patterns and noting any deviations from normal behavior found. Such deviations are the first clues to security problems.
- Keeping the collected data locally to the resource until an event is finished, after which it may be taken, according to established means involving encryption, to a secure location.
- Securing audit data on location and in backups.

7.3.2.5 Privacy Concerns

There are two areas of concern with audit trail logs:

- Privacy issue of the data collected on users
- Knowledge of an intrusive behavior of others including employees of the organization

7.3.2.6 Security Awareness Training

The strength of a security policy lies in its emphasis on both employee and user training. The policy must stress that:

- Users of computers and computer networks must be made aware of the security ramifications caused by certain actions. The training should be provided to all personnel.
- Training should be focused and involve all types of security that are needed in the organization, the internal control techniques that will meet the security requirements of the organization, and how to maintain the security attained.
- Employees with network security responsibilities must be taught security techniques probably beyond those of the general public, methodologies for evaluating threats and vulnerabilities to be able to use them to defend the organization's security, the ability to select and implement security controls, and a thorough understanding of the importance of what is at risk if security is not maintained.
- Before connecting to a LAN to the organization's backbone, provide those responsible for the organization's security with documentation on network infrastructure layout, rules, and guidelines on controlled software downloads. Pay attention to the training given to those who will be in charge of issuing passwords.
- Social engineering.
- Train employees not to believe anyone who calls/e-mails them to do something that might compromise security.
- Before giving any information, employees must positively identify who they are dealing with.

7.3.2.7 Incident Handling

The security of an organization's network depends on what the security plan says should be done to handle a security incident. If the response is fast and effective, the losses may be none to minimum. However, if the response is bungled and slow, the losses may be heavy. Make sure that the security plan is clear and effective:

- Build an incident response team as a centralized core group, whose members are drawn from across the organization, who must be knowledgeable, and well rounded with a correct mix of technical, communication, and political skills. The team should be the main contact point in case of a security incident and responsible for keeping up-to-date with the latest threats and incidents, notifying others of the incident, assessing the damage and impact of the incident, finding out how to minimize the loss, avoid further exploitation of the same vulnerability, and making plans and efforts to recover from the incident.
- Detect incidents by looking for signs of a security breach in the usual suspects and beyond. Look for abnormal signs from accounting reports, focus on signs of data modification and deletion, check out complaints of poor system performance, pay attention to strange traffic patterns and unusual times of system use, and pick interest in large numbers of failed log-in attempts.
- Assess the damage by checking and analyzing all traffic logs for abnormal behavior, especially on network perimeter access points such as Internet access or dial-in access. Pay particular attention when verifying infrastructure device checksum or operating system checksum on critical servers to see whether operating system software has been compromised or if configuration changes in infrastructure devices such as servers have occurred to ensure that no one has tampered with them. Make sure to check the sensitive data to see whether it has been assessed or changed and traffic logs for unusually large traffic streams from a single source or streams going to a single destination, passwords on critical systems to ensure that they have not been modified, and any new or unknown devices on the network for abnormal activities.
- Report and alert.
  - Establish a systematic approach for reporting incidents and subsequently notifying affected areas.
  - Essential communication mechanisms include a monitored central phone, e-mail, pager, or other quick communication devices.
  - Establish clearly whom to alert first and who should be on the list of people to alert next.
  - Decide on how much information to give each member on the list.
  - Find ways to minimize negative exposure, especially where it requires working with agents to protect evidence.
- Respond to the incident to try to restore the system back to its pre-incident status. Sometimes it may require shutting down the system; if this is necessary, then do so but keep accurate documentation and a log book of all activities during the incident so that that data can be used later to analyze any causes and effects.
- Recover from an incident

- Make a postmortem analysis of what happened, how it happened, and what steps need to be taken to prevent similar incidents in the future.
- Develop a formal report with proper chronological sequence of events to be presented to management.
- Make sure not to overreact by turning your system into a fortress.

7.4   Security Requirements Specification

Security requirements specification derives directly from the security policy document. The specifications are details of the security characteristics of every individual and system resource involved. For details on individual users and system resources, see the security access matrix. These security requirements are established after a process of careful study of the proposed system that starts with a brainstorming session to establish and maintain a skeleton basis of a basket of core security requirements by all users. The brainstorming session is then followed by establishing a common understanding and agreement on the core requirements for all involved. For each requirement in the core, we then determine what we need and how far to go to acquire and maintain it, and finally for each core requirement, we estimate the time and cost for its implementation.

From the security policy access right matrix, two main entries in the matrix, the user and the resources, determine the security requirements specifications as follows [4]:

- For the user: Include username, location, and phone number of the responsible system owner and data/application owner. Also determine the range of security clearance levels, the set of formal access approvals, and the need-to-know of users of the system.
  - Personnel security levels: Set the range of security clearance levels, the set of formal access approvals, and the need-to-know of users of the system
- For the resources: Include the resource type, document any special physical protection requirements that are unique to the system, and brief description of a secure operating system environment in use. If the resource is data, then include the following also:
  - Classification level, top secret, secret, and confidential, and categories of data, restricted and formally restricted
  - Any special access programs for the data
  - Any special formal access approval necessary for access to the data
  - Any special handling instructions
  - Any need-to-know restrictions on users
  - Any sensitive classification or lack of

After the generation of the security requirements for each user and system resource in the security policy access matrix, a new security requirements matrix, Table 7.2, is drawn.

Table 7.2 Listing of system security requirements

System components (resources and content)	Security requirements
Network client	Sign-on and authentication of user
	Secure directory for user ID and passwords
	Secure client software
	Secure session manager to manage the session
Network server	Secure software to access the server
	Secure client software to access the server
Content/data	Data authentication
	Secure data on server
	Secure data on client

7.5   Threat Identification

To understand system threats and deal with them, we first need to be able to identify them. Threat identification is a process that defines and points out the source of the threat and categorizes it as either a person or an event. For each system component whose security requirements have been identified, as shown in Fig. 4.4, also identify the security threats to it. The security threats to any system component can be deliberate or nondeliberate. A threat is deliberate if the act is done with the intention to breach the security of an object. There are many types of threats under this category, as we saw in Chap. 3. Nondeliberate threats, however, are acts and situations that, although they have the potential to cause harm to an object, were not intended. As we saw in Chap. 3, the sources of threats are many and varied including human factors, natural disasters, and infrastructure failures.

7.5.1   Human Factors

Human factors are those acts that result from human perception and physical capabilities and may contribute increased risks to the system. Among such factors are the following [5]:

- Communication—Communication between system users and personnel may present risk challenges based on understanding of policies and user guidelines, terminology used by the system, and interpersonal communication skills, and languages.
- Human-machine interface—Many users may find a challenge in some of the system interfaces. How the individual using such interfaces handles and uses them may cause a security threat to the system. The problem is more so when there is a degree of automation in the interface.

- Data design, analysis, and interpretation—Whenever there is more than one person, there is always a chance of misinterpretation of data and designs. So if there is any system data that needs to be analyzed and interpreted, there is always a likelihood of someone misinterpreting it or using a wrong design.
- New tools and technologies—Whenever a system has tools and technologies that are new to users, there is always a risk in the use of those tools and technologies. Also long-term exposure to such tools may cause significant neuromusculoskeletal adaptation with significant consequences on their use.
- Workload and user capacity—Users in many systems become victims of the workload and job capacity; this may, if not adjusted, cause risk to systems. Attributes of the task such as event rate, noise, uncertainty, criticality, and complexity that affect human mental and physical behavior may have an effect on the effort required for users to complete their assigned tasks.
- Work environment—As many workers know, the work environment greatly affects the human mental and physical capacity in areas of perception, judgment, and endurance. The factors that affect the working environment include things such as lighting, noise, workstations, and spatial configuration.
- Training—Training of system personnel and also users creates a safer user environment than that of systems with untrained users and personnel. Trained users will know when and how certain equipment and technologies can be used safely.
- Performance—A safe system is a system where the users and personnel get maximum performance from the system and from the personnel. Efficient and successful completion of all critical tasks on the system hinges on the system personnel and users maintaining required physical, perceptual, and social capabilities.

7.5.2 Natural Disasters

There is a long list of natural acts that are sources of security threats. These include earthquakes, fires, floods, hurricanes, tornados, lightning, and many others. Although natural disasters cannot be anticipated, we can plan for them. There are several ways to plan for the natural disaster threats. These include creating up-to-date backups stored at different locations that can be quickly retrieved and set up and having a comprehensive recovery plan. Recovery plans should be implemented rapidly.

7.5.3 Infrastructure Failures

System infrastructures are composed of hardware, software, and humanware. Any of these may fail the system anytime without warning.

7.5.3.1 Hardware Failures

Because computers have been in use for a long time now, this gives us some digree of relief that computer hardware are getting more reliable than ever before. But still, hardware failures are common due to wear and tear and age. The operating environment also contributes greatly to hardware failures. For example, a hostile environment due to high temperatures and moisture and dust always results in hardware failures. There are several approaches to overcome hardware threats, including redundancy, where there is always a standby similar system to kick in whenever there is an unplanned stoppage of the functioning system. Another way of overcoming hardware failure threats is to have a monitoring system where two or more hardware units constantly monitor each other and report to others whenever one of them fails. In addition, advances in hardware technology have led to the development of self-healing hardware units whenever a system detects its component performance, and if one component shows signs of failure, the unit quickly disables the component and reroutes or reassigns the functions of the failing component and also reports the failing component to all others in the unit.

7.5.3.2 Software Failures

Probably the greatest security threat, when everything is considered, is from software. The history of computing is littered with examples of costly catastrophes of failed software projects and potential software failures and errors such as the millennium scare. Failure or poor performance of a software product can be attributed to a variety of causes, most notably human error, the nature of software itself, and the environment in which software is produced and used.

Both software professionals and nonprofessionals who use software know the differences between software programming and hardware engineering. It is in these differences that lie many of the causes of software failure and poor performance. Consider the following [6]:

- *Complexity*: Unlike hardwired programming in which it is easy to exhaust the possible outcomes on a given set of input sequences, in software programming a similar program may present billions of possible outcomes on the same input sequence. Therefore, in software programming, one can never be sure of all the possibilities on any given input sequence.
- *Difficult testing*: There will never be a complete set of test programs to check software exhaustively for all bugs for a given input sequence.
- *Ease of programming*: The fact that software programming is easy to learn encourages many people with little formal training and education in the field to start developing programs, but many are not knowledgeable about good programming practices or able to check for errors.
- *Misunderstanding of basic design specifications*: This affects the subsequent design phases including coding, documenting, and testing. It also results in improper and ambiguous specifications of major components of the software and in ill-chosen and poorly defined internal program structures.

- *Software evolution*: It is almost an accepted practice in software development that software products that grow out from one version or release to another are made by just additions of new features without an overhaul of the original version for errors and bugs. This is always a problem because there are many incompatibilities that can cause problems, including different programmers with different design styles from those of the original programmers; different software modules, usually newer, that may have differing interfaces; and different expectations and applications that may far exceed the capabilities of the original version. All these have led to major flaws in software that can be exploited and have been exploited by hackers.
- *Changing management styles*: Quite often organizations change management, and the new management comes in with a different focus and different agenda that may require changes that may affect the software used by the organization in order to accommodate the new changes. Because of time and cost considerations, many times the changes are made in-house. Introducing such changes into existing software may introduce new flaws and bugs or may reactivate existing but dormant errors.

7.5.3.3 Humanware Failures

The human component in the computer systems is considerable and plays a vital role in the security of the system. While inputs to and sometimes outputs from hardware components can be predicted, and also in many cases software bugs once found can be fixed and the problem forgiven, the human component in a computer system is so unpredictable and so unreliable that the inputs to the system from the human component may never be trusted, a major source of system threat. The human link in the computing system has been known to be a source of many malicious acts that directly affect the security of the system. Such malicious acts include hacking into systems and creating software that threaten the security of systems. In later chapters, we will talk more about these activities.

7.6   Threat Analysis

A working computer system with numerous resources is always a target of many security threats. A *threat* is the combination of an asset such as a system resource, a vulnerability, or an exploit that can be used by a hacker to gain access to the system. Although every system resource has value, there are those with more intrinsic value than others. Such resources, given a system vulnerability that can let in an intruder, attract system intruders more than their counterparts with limited intrinsic value. Security threat analysis is a technique used to identify these resources and to focus on them. In general, *system security threat analysis* is a process that involves ongoing testing and evaluation of the security of a system's resources to continuously and critically evaluate their security from the perspective of a malicious intruder and then use the information from these evaluations to increase the overall system's security.

The process of security threat analysis involves the following:

- Determining those resources with higher intrinsic value, prioritizing them, and focusing on that list as defense mechanisms are being considered.
- Documenting why the chosen resources need to be protected in the hierarchy they are put in.
- Determining who causes what threat to whose resources.
- Identifying known and plausible vulnerabilities for each identified resource in the system. Known vulnerabilities, of course, are much easier to deal with than vulnerabilities that are purely speculative.
- Identifying necessary security services/mechanisms to counter the vulnerability.
- Increasing the overall system security by focusing on identified resources.

7.6.1   Approaches to Security Threat Analysis

There are several approaches to security threat analysis, but we will consider two of them here: the simple threat analysis by calculating *annualized loss expectancies* (ALEs) and attack trees.

7.6.1.1 Threat Analysis by Annualized Loss Expectancies

Before we define annualized loss expectancies, let us define the terms from which ALE is derived. For a resource identified as having a high threat risk, the cost of replacing or restoring that resource if it is attacked is its *single-loss expectancy* cost. The security threat is a resource's vulnerability. So if the vulnerability is likely to occur a certain number of times (based on past occurrences), then the vulnerability's *expected annual rate of occurrence* (EAO) can be computed.

Then multiplying these two terms gives us the vulnerability's annualized loss expectancy as [7]

Annualized loss expectancy (ALE for a resource) = *single-loss expectancy* (cost) × (expected) *annual rate of occurrences.*

The reader is referred to a good example in Mich Bauer's paper: "Paranoid Penguin: Practical Threat Analysis and Risk Management." *Linux Journal,* Issue 93, March 2003.

7.6.1.2 Schneier's Attack Tree Method

Schneier approaches the calculation of risk analysis using a tree model he called an *attack tree.* An attack tree is a visual representation of possible attacks against a given target. The root of the attack forms the goal of the attack. The internal node from the leaves form the necessary subgoals an attacker must take in order to reach the goal, in this case the root.

The attack tree then grows as subgoals necessary to reach the root node are added depending on the attack goal. This step is repeated as necessary to achieve the level of detail and complexity with which you wish to examine the attack. If the attacker must pass through several subgoals in order to reach the goal, then the path in the tree from the leaves to the root is long and probably more complex.

Each leaf and corresponding subgoals are quantified with a cost estimate that may represent the cost of achieving that leaf's goal via the subgoals. The cheapest path in the tree from a leaf to the root determines the most likely attack path and probably the riskiest.

7.7 Vulnerability Identification and Assessment

A security vulnerability is a weakness in the system that may result in creating a security condition that may lead to a threat. The condition may be an absence of or inadequate security procedures and physical and security controls in the system. Although vulnerabilities are difficult to predict, no system is secure unless its vulnerabilities are known. Therefore, in order to protect a computer system, we need to be able to identify the vulnerabilities in the system and assess the dangers faced as a result of these vulnerabilities. No system can face any security threat unless it has a vulnerability from which a security incident may originate. However, it is extremely difficult to identify all system vulnerabilities before a security incident occurs. In fact, many system vulnerabilities are known only after a security incident has occurred. However, once one vulnerability has been identified, it is common to find it in many other components of the system. The search for system vulnerabilities should focus on system hardware, software, and also humanware as we have seen so far. In addition, system vulnerabilities also exist in system security policies and procedures.

7.7.1 Hardware

Although hardware may not be the main culprit in sourcing system vulnerabilities, it boasts a number of them originating mainly from design flows, imbedded programs, and assembling of systems. Modern computer and telecommunication systems carry an impressive amount of microprograms imbedded in the system. These programs control many functions in the hardware component.

However, hardware vulnerabilities are very difficult to identify, and even after they are identified, they are very difficult to fix for a number of reasons. One reason is cost; it may be very expensive to fix imbedded microprograms in a hardware component. Second, even if a vulnerability is inexpensive and easy to fix, the expertise to fix it may not be there. Third, it may be easy to fix, but the component required to fix it may not be compatible and interoperable with the bigger hardware. Fourth, even if it is cheap, easy to fix, and compatible enough, it may not be of priority because of the effort it takes to fix.

7.7.2 Software

Vulnerabilities in software can be found in a variety of areas in the system. In particular, vulnerabilities can be found in system software, application software, and control software.

7.7.2.1 System Software

System software includes most of the software used by the system to function. Among such software is the operating system that is at the core of the running of the computer system. In fact the vulnerabilities found in operating systems are the most serious vulnerabilities in computer systems. Most of the major operating systems have suffered from vulnerabilities, and intruders always target operating systems as they search for vulnerabilities. This is due to the complexity of the software used to develop operating systems and also the growing multitude of functions the operating system must perform. As we will discuss later, since the operating system controls all the major functions of the system, access to the system through the operating system gives the intruders unlimited access to the system. The more popular an operating system gets, the greater the number of attacks directed to it. All the recent operating systems such as Unix, Linux, Mac OS, Windows, and especially Windows NT have been major targets for intruders to exploit an ever-growing list of vulnerabilities that are found daily.

7.7.2.2 Application Software

Probably, the largest number of vulnerabilities is thought to be sourced from application software. There are several reasons for this. First, application software can be and indeed has been written by anybody with a minimum understanding of programming etiquettes. In fact, most of the application software on the market is written by people without formal training in software development. Second, most of the application software is never fully tested before it is uploaded on the market, making it a potential security threat. Finally, because software produced by independent producers is usually small and targeted, many system managers and security chiefs do not pay enough attention to the dangers produced by this type of software in terms of interface compatibility and interoperability. By ignoring such potential sources of system vulnerabilities, the system managers are exposing their systems to dangers of this software. Also security technologies are developing a lot faster than the rate at which independent software producers can include them in their software. In addition, since software is usually used for several years during that period, new developments in API and security tools tend to make the software more of a security threat. And as more reusable software becomes commonly used, more flaws in the libraries of such code are propagated into more user code. Unfortunately more and more software producers are outsourcing modules from independent sources, which adds to the flaws in software because the testing of these outsourced modules is not uniform.

7.7.2.3 Control Software

Among the control software are system and communication protocols and device drivers. Communication control protocols are at the core of digital and analog devices. Any weaknesses in these protocols expose the data in the communication channels of the network infrastructure. In fact, the open architecture policies of the major communication protocol models have been a major source of vulnerabilities in computer communication. Most of the recent attacks on the Internet and other communication networks have been a result of the vulnerabilities in these communication protocols. Once identified, these vulnerabilities have proven difficult to fix for a number of reasons. First, it has been expensive in some quarters to fix these vulnerabilities because of lack of expertise. Second, although patches have on many occasions been issued immediately after a vulnerability has been identified, in most cases, the patching of the vulnerability has not been at the rate the vulnerabilities have been discovered, leading to a situation where most of the current network attacks are using the same vulnerabilities that have been discovered, sometimes years back and patches issued. Third, because of the open nature of the communication protocols, and as new functional modules are added onto the existing infrastructure, the interoperability has been far from desirable.

7.7.3 Humanware

In Sect. 4.5.1, we discussed the human role in the security of computer systems. We want to add to that list the role social engineering plays in system security. Social engineering, as we saw in Chap. 3, is the ability of one to achieve one's stated goal, legally or otherwise, through the use of persuasion or misrepresentation. Because there are many ways of doing this, it is extremely difficult to prepare people not to fall for sweet talkers and masqueraders. Among the many approaches to social engineering are techniques that play on people's vulnerability to sympathy, empathy, admiration, and intimidation. Hackers and intruders using social engineering exploit people's politeness and willingness to help.

7.7.4 Policies, Procedures, and Practices

The starting point for organization security is a sound security policy and a set of security procedures. Policies are written descriptions of the security precautions that everyone using the system must follow. They have been called the building blocks of an organization's security. Procedures on the other hand are definitions spelling out how to implement the policies for a specific system or technology. Finally, practices are day-to-day operations to implement the procedures. Practices are implemented based on the environment, resources, and capabilities available at the site.

Many organizations do not have written policies or procedures or anything that is directly related to information security. In addition to security policies and procedures, security concerns can also be found in personnel policies and physical security procedures, for example, the protocols for accessing buildings and intellectual property statements.

The effectiveness of an organization's security policies and procedures must be measured against those in the same industry. Security policies and procedures are useless if they are applied to an industry where they are ineffective. When compared to a similar industry, weaknesses should be noted in quality, conformity, and comprehensiveness.

7.7.4.1 Quality

A policy or procedure has quality if it addresses all industry issues it is supposed to address. In addition to addressing all issues, policies and procedures are also tested on their applicability, that is, they are being specific enough in order to be effective. They are judged effective if they address all issues and protect system information.

7.7.4.2 Conformity

Conformity is a measure of the level of compliance based on the security policies and procedures. The measure includes how the policies or procedures are being interpreted, implemented, and followed. If the level is not good, then a security threat exists in the system. Besides measuring the level of compliancy, conformity also measures the effectiveness of the policies and procedures in all areas of the organization. A policy presents a security threat if it is not fully implemented or not implemented at all or not observed in certain parts of the organization.

7.7.4.3 Comprehensiveness

If the organization's security is required in a variety of forms such as physical and electronic, then the organization's security policy and procedures must effectively address all of them. In addition, all phases of security must be addressed including inspection, protection, detection, reaction, and reflection. If one phase is not effectively addressed or not addressed at all, then a security threat may exist in the system. Comprehensiveness also means that the policies and procedures must be widely and equitably applied to all parts of the system. And the policies and procedures must address all known sources of threats which may include physical, natural, or human.

7.8   Security Certification

Certification is the technical evaluation of the effectiveness of a system or an individual for security features. The defenses of a system are not dependent solely on secure technology in use, but they also depend on the effectiveness of staffing and training. A well-trained and proficient human component makes a good complement to the security of the system, and the system as a whole can withstand and react to intrusion and malicious code. Certification of a system or an individual attempts to achieve the following objectives that the system [5]:

- Employs a set of structured verification techniques and verification procedures during the system life cycle
- Demonstrates that the security controls of the system are implemented correctly and effectively
- Identifies risks to confidentiality, integrity, and availability of information and resources

7.8.1 Phases of a Certification Process

For the certification process to run smoothly, the following phases must be undertaken [5]:

- Developing a security plan to provide an overview of the system security requirements. The plan, as we have seen above, describes existing or planned security requirements and ways to meet them. In addition, the plan delineates responsibilities and expected behavior of individuals who access the system. The plan should be updated as frequently as possible.
- Testing and evaluation must be done, and it includes the verification and verification procedures to demonstrate that the implementation of the network meets the security requirements specified in the security plan.
- Risk assessment to determine threats and vulnerabilities in the system, propose and evaluate the effectiveness of various security controls, calculate trade-offs associated with the security controls, and determine the residual risk associated with a candidate set of security controls.
- Certification to evaluate and verify that the system has been implemented as described in the security policy and that the specified security controls are in place and operating properly. This provides an overview of the security status of the system and brings together all of the information necessary for the organization to make an informed and risk-conscious decision.

7.8.2 Benefits of Security Certification

In security, certification is important and has several benefits including:

- Consistency and comparability
- Availability of complete and reliable technical information leading to better understanding of complex systems and associated security risks and vulnerabilities

7.9   Security Monitoring and Auditing

Security monitoring is an essential step in security assurance for a system. To set up continuous security monitoring, controls are put in place to monitor whether a secure system environment is maintained. The security personnel and sometimes management then use these controls to determine whether any more steps need to be taken to secure the systems. The focus of the monitoring controls may depend on the system manager and what is deemed important for the system security, but in general control focuses on violation and exception reports that help the security personnel to determine quickly the status of security in the system and what needs to be done if the system is being or has been compromised.

Although monitoring decisions are made by the security administrator, what should be monitored and the amount of information logged are usually determined by either management or the security administrator. Also what should be included in the report and the details to be included to convey the best overall understanding of the security status of the system must be decided by the security administrator. It is not good, and in fact it is resource wasting to log too much information without being able to analyze it properly. Let us now focus on tools used to monitor, type of data gathered, and information analyzed from the data.

7.9.1   Monitoring Tools

There are several tools that can be used to monitor the performance of a system. The monitoring tool, once selected and installed, should be able to gather vital information on system statistics, analyze it, and display it graphically or otherwise. In more modern systems, especially in intrusion detection tools, the monitor can also be configured to alert system administrators when certain events occur. Most modern operating systems such as Microsoft Windows, Unix, Linux, Mac OS, and others have built-in performance monitors. In addition, there is a long list of independent security and system performance monitors that monitor, among other things, real-time performance monitoring and warehousing of event logs, real-time or delayed alerts to management, and customized performance reports that may include the history of the event and customized formats to allow quick legal proceedings and forensics analysis.

A variety of system monitoring tools are available, the majority of which fall into one of the following categories:

- System performance: This category includes most operating system performance loggers.
- Network security: This includes all IDS, firewalls, and other types of event loggers.
- Network performance and diagnosis: These are for monitoring all network performance activities.
- Networking links: To monitor the wiring in a network.

- Dynamic IP and DNS event logger.
- Remote control and file sharing applications event logger.
- File transfer tools.

7.9.2   Type of Data Gathered

Because of the large number of events that take place in a computer system, the choice of what event to monitor can be difficult. Most event loggers are preset to monitor events based on the set conditions. For example, for workstations and servers, the monitor observes system performance, including CPU performance, memory usage, disk usage, applications, system, security, DNS server, directory service, and File Replication Service. In addition, the monitor may also receive syslog messages from other computers, routers, and firewalls on a network. In a network environment, the logger may generate notifications that include e-mail, network popup, pager, syslog forwarding, or broadcast messages, to users or system administrator in real time following preset specified criteria. Further, the logger may support real-time registration of new logs, edit existing log registrations, and delete log registrations.

7.9.3   Analyzed Information

The purpose of a system monitoring tool is to capture vital system data, analyze it, and present it to the user in a timely manner and in a form in which it makes sense.

The logged data is then formatted and put into a form that the user can utilize. Several of these report formats are as follows:

- Alert is a critical security control that helps in reporting monitored system data in real time. Real time actually depends on a specified time frame. Time frames vary from, say, once a week to a few seconds. Once the alerts are selected and criteria to monitor are set, the alert tools track certain events and warn systems administrators when they occur.
- Chart is a graphic object that correlates performance to a selected object within a time frame. Most modern operating systems have Event Viewer that draws charts of the collected data.
- Log is the opposite of alerting in that it allows the system to capture data in a file and save it for later viewing and analysis. However, alerting generates a signal that it sends to the administrator based on the alert time intervals. Log information may also be used in a chart. Again most modern operating systems have log view tools.
- Report is a more detailed and inclusive form of system logs. Log reports provide statistics about the system's resources and how each of the selected system resource is being used and by whom. This information also includes how many processes are using each resource, who owns the process, and when he or she is using the resource. The timing of the generation of the report can be set, and the recipients of the report can also be listed.

7.9.4   Auditing

Auditing is another tool in the security assessment and assurance of a computer system and network. Unlike monitoring, auditing is more durable and not ongoing, and therefore, it is expensive and time-consuming. Like monitoring, auditing measures the system against a predefined set of criteria, noting any changes that occur. The criteria are chosen in such a way that changes should indicate possible security breaches.

A full and comprehensive audit should include the following steps:

- Review all aspects of the system's stated criteria.
- Review all threats identified.
- Choose a frequency of audits whether daily, weekly, or monthly.
- Review practices to ensure compliance to written guidelines.

7.10   Products and Services

A number of products and services are on the market for security assessment and audit. Hundreds of companies are competing for a market share with a multitude of products. These products fall under the following categories:

- Auditing tools
- Vulnerability assessment
- Penetration testing tools
- Forensic tools
- Log analysis tools
- Other assessment toolkits

Exercises

1. What is security assessment? Why is it important?
2. Discuss the necessary steps in analyzing the security state of an enterprise.
3. What is security assurance? How does it help in enterprise security?
4. What is security monitoring? Is it essential for enterprise security?
5. What is security auditing? Why is it necessary for system security?
6. What are the differences between security monitoring and auditing? Which is better?
7. What is risk? What is the purpose of calculating risk when analyzing security?
8. Give two ways in which risk can be calculated. Which is better?
9. What is social engineering? Why do security experts worry about social engineering? What is the best way to deal with social engineering?
10. Humanware is a cause of security threat. Discuss why this is so.

Advanced Exercises

1. Discuss any security surveillance system.
2. Discuss a good security auditing system.
3. Compare or discuss the differences between any two security systems.
4. Discuss human error or human factors as a major security threat.
5. What is the best way to deal with the security threat due to human factors?

References

1. Jamsa K (2002) Hacker proof: the ultimate guide to network security, 2nd edn. Onword Press, Albany
2. Holden G (2004) Guide to firewalls and network security: intrusion detection and VPNs. Delmar Thomson Learning, Boston
3. Kaeo M (1999) Designing network security: a practical guide to creating secure network infrastructure. Macmillan Technical Publishing, Indianapolis
4. Guidelines for the development of security plans for classified computer systems. http://cio.doe.gov/ITReform/sqse/download/secplngd.doc
5. Ross R. The development of standardized certification and accreditation guidelines and provider organizations. http://csrc.nist.gov/sec-cert/CA-workshop-fiac2002-bw.pdf
6. Kizza JM (2002) *Ethical and social issues in the information age*, 2nd edn. Springer, New York
7. Bauer M (2003) Paranoid penguin: practical threat analysis and risk management. Linux J 93:9

Additional References

1. Security architecture and patterns, KPMG. http://www.issa-oc.org/html/1
2. Threat analysis and vulnerability assessments. http://www.primatech.com/consulting/services/threat_analysis_and_vulnerability_assessments.htm

Part III

Dealing with Computer Network Security Challenges

Disaster Management

8

8.1   Introduction

Webster's Dictionary defines *disaster* as a sudden misfortune, a catastrophe that affects society [1]. It is the effect of a hazardous event caused by either man or nature. Man-made disasters are those disasters that involve a human element like intent, error, or negligence. Natural disasters are those caused by the forces of nature like hurricanes, tornados, and tsunamis. Disasters, natural or man-made, may cause great devastation to society and the environment. For example, the 2006 tsunami in Southeast Asia caused both huge human losses and environment destruction. The effects of a disaster may be short lived or long lasting. Most disasters, both man-made and natural, have long-lasting effects. To mitigate disaster effects on society and businesses, disaster management skills are needed.

In information technology, disaster situations are big security problems to the enterprise information systems that must be handled with skills just like other security problems we have discussed so far in this book. To understand how this is a very big security problem for a modern society, one has to understand the working of a modern business entity. Modern businesses have moved away from the typewriter and manila folders to desktops and large databases to process and store business day-to-day data and transactions. This growing use of computers in businesses, the ever-increasing speed of data transmission, and the forces of globalization all have forced businesses into a new digitized global corner that demands high-speed data access to meet the demands of the technology-savvy customers in a highly competitive global environment. In response, high-volume and high-speed databases have been set up.

For the business to remain competitive and probably ahead of the competitors, all business systems must remain online and in service 24/7. No modern business can afford a disaster to happen to its online systems. Failing to achieve that level of service would mean the failure of the business. Thousands of businesses close or lose millions of dollars every year depending on the level of attention they give to their online systems and failing to protect them against disasters like fire, power outage, theft, equipment failure, viruses, hackers, and human errors. No business

© Springer International Publishing AG 2017   175
J.M. Kizza, *Guide to Computer Network Security*, Computer Communications and Networks, DOI 10.1007/978-3-319-55606-2_8

can succeed in today's environment without plans to deal with disasters. The September 11, 2002 attack on New York financial district was an eye-opener to many businesses to be prepared for disasters. For a quick recovery of these enterprises, good disaster management principles are needed.

Also as company databases grew in size and complexity and the demand for their online fast access grew, the need for the protection of business-critical and irreplaceable company data is also growing in tandem. These developments are forcing business information system managers to focus on disaster prevention, response, and recovery. The importance of disaster planning and recovery can be born by the fact that 93% of the companies that did not have their data backed up properly when a disaster struck went out of business, according to DataSafe, Inc., one of the leading companies involved with data backup services [2].

The goal of chapter, therefore, is to treat disaster management as a major information systems' security problem and start a discussion of ways, tools, and best practices of dealing with disasters and mitigating their long-term effects on business information systems. We will break the discussion into three parts: disaster prevention, response, and recovery.

8.1.1 Categories of Disasters

Before we do that, however, let us look at the categories of disasters that can affect business information systems [3].

8.1.1.1 Natural Disasters: Due to Forces of Nature

- Tsunami
- Tornados
- Hurricanes (same as tsunami)
- Cyclone (same as tsunami)
- Flood
- Snowstorm
- Landslides
- Drought
- Earthquake
- Electrical storms
- Snowslides
- Fire

8.1.1.2 Human-Caused Disasters

- Terrorism
- Sabotage
- Theft

- Viruses
- Worms
- Hostile code
- War
- Theft
- Arson
- Loss of:
  - Power supply (both electric and gas). This can result in a large number of related failures like cooling system and machines.
  - Communications links.
  - Data.
- Cybercrime (many types)

8.2   Disaster Prevention

Disaster prevention is a proactive process consisting of a set of control strategies to ensure that a disaster does not happen. The controls may be people, mechanical, or digital sensing devices. Times and technology have improved both disaster prevention and recovery strategies. The elements of effective disaster prevention are the early detection of abnormal conditions and notification of persons capable of dealing with the pending crisis, for example, if you have a temperature detector to report on an air-conditioning failure as soon as the temperature starts to rise or a fire detector to gracefully power down all computing equipment before fire systems discharge. By detecting and treating minor problems early, major problems can be avoided.

Every system, big and small, needs a disaster prevention plan because the cost of not having one is overwhelming. According to Intra Computer, Inc., a disaster prevention and recovery company, in one of its surveys, 16% of those responding to the survey reported that a system-stopping event caused by environmental conditions occurred at least six times annually, and 12% of respondents put the minimum estimated dollar cost of each of these incidents at over $50,000 [4]. Also according to DataSafe, Inc. [2], thousands of businesses lose millions of dollars worth of information due to disasters like fire, power outage, theft, equipment failure, and even simple operator mistakes.

In past years, system disaster prevention depended entirely upon an on-site person's ability to detect and diagnose irregular conditions based on experience. This experience was based on one's knowledge and ability to analyze conditions created by unusual events such as high temperature, presence of smoke, water, and interruption in power to equipment that could lead to the likely corruption or destruction of the enterprise's information system's resources including active data files.

Technology has, however, through intelligent monitoring devices, helped and improved the process of disaster prevention. Monitoring devices nowadays are capable of quickly responding to unusual and irregular conditions caused by a disaster event. The monitoring devices, in case of an enterprise information system, monitor a variety of conditions from a given list. The list includes [4]:

- Temperature
- Humidity
- Water
- Smoke/fire
- Airflow
- AC power quality
- UPS AC/battery mode
- Personnel access security
- Halon triggering state
- State of in-place security/alarm systems
- Hidden conditions undetectable by security personnel
  - In air-conditioning ducts
  - Under raised floors
  - Inside computer chassis

During the monitoring process, if and when an event occurs that meets any one of the conditions being monitored, an immediate action is triggered. The choice of action taken is also predetermined by the system manager and is selected from a long list that includes [4]:

- Activating local or remote alarms indicators like sirens, bells, light signals, and synthesized voice.
- Taking over control of the affected resource to isolate it, cut it off from the supply line, or maintain the declining supply line. The supply line may be power, water, fuel, and a number of other things.
- Interfacing with existing or cutting off from existing security system as dictated by the event.
- Sending a signal to designated personnel. Among the designated personnel are [4]:
  - System users
  - Site managers
  - Security personnel
  - Maintenance personnel
  - Service bureaus and Alarm Co. central offices
  - Authorities at remote sites
- Gracefully degrading the system by terminating normal operations, closing and protecting data files, and disconnecting AC Power from protected equipment.

After one or more of the actions above have been taken, the system will then wait for a response. The response usually comes from the human component. Let us discuss this in the next section.

8.3   Disaster Response

As we pointed out earlier in this chapter, the rapid development in computer and information technology and the ever-growing society's dependence on computers and computer technology have created an environment where business-critical information, irreplaceable business data, and transactions are totally dependent and are stored on computer systems. This being the case makes a response to a disaster vital and of critical importance. Disaster response is a set strategies used to respond to both the short-term and long-term needs of the affected community. In dealing with business information system disasters, the strategies involve quick and timely response to the disaster prevention system (DPS) signals with directed action. The essential steps in disaster response include:

- Restoring services
- Identifying high-risk system resources

Six factors govern a quick disaster response. According to Walter Guerry Green [5]:

- Nature and extent of the destruction or risk in case the disaster occurs. This is based on either prior or a quick assessment of the situation.
- The environment of the disaster. The environment determines the kind of response needed. Take a quick inventory of what is in the room or rooms where the systems are. Make a note of how the chosen action to meet the needs is going to be carried out successfully.
- Make note of the available resources. The degree and effectiveness of the response to the disaster is going to depend on the available resources on the ground that can be used to increase and enhance the success rate of the chosen response.
- Time available to carry out the chosen response action. Time is so important in the operation that it determines how much action can be taken and how much effort is needed to control the disaster.
- Understanding of the effective policy. Every chosen action taken must fall within the jurisdiction of the company policy.

The degree of success in observing this success determines the effectives of the disaster recovery efforts.

8.4   Disaster Recovery

The value of a good disaster recovery plan is its ability to react to the threat shifty and efficiently. In order for this to happen, there must be an informed staff, disaster suppliers, and planned procedures. These three make up the disaster recovery plan. Every system manager must be aware and confident with the system's disaster recovery plan. The plan must not only be on the books and shelved but must be rehearsed several times a year. For example, since the September 11, 2001 attack on the World Trade Center, companies learned the value of off-site storage of data. And since then, rehearsed procedures for retrieving archived data media from off-site facilities are common. There are several other outsourced options to disaster recovery in addition to the in-house one we have so far discussed. These include maintenance contracts and services that offer from routine planned disaster testing to full extended warranty services, standby services that usually do only the storage and recovery of your data services and delivery very quickly, and distributed architectures that are companies that sell you the software that stores your data on their network and you can move it back and forth at a moment's notice. All these, when used effectively, help to continue business as usual in the hours during and immediately following a disaster.

8.4.1   Planning for a Disaster Recovery

Disaster recovery planning is a delicate process that must be handled with care. It involves risk assessment, developing, documenting, implementing, testing, and maintaining a disaster recovery plan [6]. For starters, the plan must be teamwork of several chosen people that form a committee—the Disaster Recovery Committee. The committee should include at least one person from management, information technology, record management, and building maintenance. This committee is in charge with deciding on the what, how, when, and who are needed to provide a good solid recovery that your company will be proud of. Such a plan must sustain critical business functions. The planning process, therefore, must start with steps that identify and document those functions and other key elements in the recovery process. According to [7], these steps include:

- Identifying and prioritizing the disaster
- Identifying and prioritizing business-critical systems and functions
- Identifying business-critical resources and performing impact analysis
- Developing a notification plan
- Developing a damage assessment plan
- Designating a disaster recovery site
- Developing a plan to recover critical functions at the disaster recovery site
- Identifying and documenting security controls
- Designating responsibilities

Because disasters do not happen at a particular time in a given month of a known year, they are unplanned and unpredictable. This makes disaster recovery planning an ongoing, dynamic process that continues throughout the information system's life cycle.

8.4.1.1 Disaster Recovery Committee

This committee is responsible for developing the disaster recovery plan. The committee must represent every function or unit of the business to ensure that all essential business information and resources are not left out. Before the committee starts its job, members must all be trained in disaster recovery. Each member of this committee is assigned responsibilities for key activities identified and duties outlined within their departments and as defined within the disaster recovery plan. The committee is also responsible for bringing awareness to the rest of the employees.

8.4.2 Procedures of Recovery

The procedures followed in disaster management and recovery are systematic steps taken in order to mitigate the damage due to the disaster. These steps are followed based on the rankings (above) of the nature of the disaster and the critical value of the items involved.

8.4.2.1 Identifying and Prioritizing the Disaster

These may be put in three levels: low, medium, and high:

- Low-level disasters may be local accidents like:
  - Human errors
  - High temperature in room
  - Server failure
- Medium-level disasters may be less local including:
  - Virus attack
  - Long power failures—may be a day long
  - Server crush (Web, mail)
- High-level disasters—this level includes the most devastating disasters like:
  - Earthquakes
  - Hurricanes
  - Big fire
  - Terrorism

8.4.2.2 Identifying Critical Resources

The ranking of critical assets may be based on the dollar amount spent on acquiring the item or on the utility of the item. Some examples of these critical assets include [2]:

- Servers, workstations, and peripherals
- Applications and data
- Media and output
- Telecommunication connections
- Physical infrastructure (e.g., electrical power, environmental controls)
- Personnel

Rank them in three levels:

- Low level—these include:
  - Printer paper, printer cartridges, and media
  - Pens, chairs, etc.
- Medium level—these include relatively costly items:
  - All peripherals
  - Switches
  - Workstations
  - Physical infrastructures
- High level—these include valued items and high ticket items like:
  - Servers
  - Disks (RAID)/application data
  - Workstations
  - Personnel

8.4.2.3 Developing a Notification Plan

This requires identifications of all those to be informed. This can also be done based on the previous levels of the disaster and the level of critical resources. This plan is represented into a matrix form below.

	Low-level disaster	Medium-level disaster	High-level disaster
Level 1—critical assets	System adm.	System adm.	System adm., management, law enforcement, the media
Level 2—critical assets	System adm.	System adm., management	System adm., management, law enforcement, the media
Level 3—critical assets	System adm.	System adm., management	System adm., management, law enforcement, the media

For each cell in the matrix, chose an acceptable method of transmitting the information to be transmitted. Determine how much information needs to be transmitted and when it should be transmitted. For each group of people to be informed, choose a representative person. For example, for management, who should be informed, the vice president for information or the chief executive officer?

Keep in mind that prompt notification can reduce the disaster's effects on the information system because it gives you time to take mitigating actions.

8.4.2.4 Training of Employees

Since disaster handling is a continuous process in the life cycle of an enterprise system, the training of employees about possible disasters and what each one has to do is desirable. However, the training of the select people on the Disaster Recovery Committee is critical. Plan ahead of time how this training is to be carried out.

There are several ways of doing this in a work environment depending on the number of people to be trained:

- Professional seminars for all those on the Disaster Recovery Committee
- Special in-house education programs for all those on the Disaster Recovery Committee, heads of departments, and everybody else

The choice of the type of training also requires to determine who will be conducting the training and who is responsible for the arranging the training. Somebody responsible for training could be somebody well trained to do that if available in-house or by using a vendor to come on the component premises or by sending people to vendor-designated sites.

8.4.2.5 Priorities for the Restoration of Essential Functions
One of the most critical and vital bit of information in disaster planning is to prioritize the order of critical resources as they come back online. Follow that order because it was chosen by the Disaster Recovery Committee for a reason.

8.5   Make Your Business Disaster Ready

In the introduction, we talked about the importance of a recovery plan for a business. In fact, the statistics we quoted indicate that almost 90% of all companies that did not have a disaster recovery plan did not survive are indicative of the importance of a business disaster recovery plan. Also in the introduction, we indicated that disaster planning is an ongoing process that never ends. This means that for your company to remain in business and remain competitive, the disaster recovery plan must be in place and must keep changing to meet the developing new technologies. Among the things to help you refresh your evolving business disaster plan are being disaster ready all the time; making periodic drills of checking the storage media to make sure that they are already ready for the big one to happen, for those working with databases, working with a base-function script for the capability of your interfaces; and always periodically doing a risk assessment for the disaster.

8.5.1   Always Be Ready for a Disaster

Because disasters can happen at any time and while some customers will under-stand, the majority will not wait for you to learn the tricks of handling a disaster.
They will move to your competitor. Do always be prepared for the big one by doing the following [3]:

- Periodically check and test your backup and recovery procedures thoroughly to ensure that you have the required backups to recover from various failures, that your procedures are clearly defined and documented, and that they can be executed smoothly and quickly by any qualified operator.

- Always secure, keep, and periodically check and review all system logs and transaction logs. This will help you to backtrack if you have to and to find anything you might have missed out.

8.5.2 Always Back Up Media

There is no better way to deal with a disaster than having a backup. We have been told since we were kids to keep a copy of everything important. You are doing the same thing here. In a computing system environment, also consider:

- A schedule to revisit the saved materials
- Whether to store at a location but in a different place or in a different location
- A chart of which data needs to be stored, where it is to be stored, and for how long

8.5.3 Risk Assessment

Risk assessment is a systematic process of evaluating a system's potential hazards and corresponding analysis of ways to mitigate damage if such hazards were to occur. One way of doing this is to use a matrix model consisting of all types of disasters that can happen to a system in a row and all the system resources that may be affected in each column. Each entry in the matrix cell is potential risks to the organization which could result to the resource in case of the disaster in that row occurring. This matrix model must have been done by the Disaster Planning Committee. There are tools on the market to help you achieve this, including COBRA [3].

8.6   Resources for Disaster Planning and Recovery

As businesses begin to see disasters as a huge security problem to the day-to-day running of the business, there is going to be a high demand for tools and services from vendors to manage disasters. These resources fallow into two categories: public agency-based and vendor-based resources. Also whether public- or private-based resources, these resources can be obtained quickly because they are local or they may take time because they are some distance off. Always start with local resources when you need them.

8.6.1 Local Disaster Resources

These resources can be freely obtained locally:

- Police
- Civil defense

- Fire department
- Ambulatory services

These resources can be obtained on the business premises:

- Paper
- Fire extinguisher
- Small capacity tapes and disks

These resources can be obtained from vendors (online or offline):

- Specialized computer equipment
- Specialized software tools like COBRA

Exercises

1. List as many of the emergency agencies in your community.
2. Of these listed in (1) above, which are dealing with information security?
3. We pointed out that the development of a good disaster recovery plan requires risk assessment. Design a matrix for the risk assessment of your security lab.
4. Using your security lab as your fictitious company, develop a disaster plan for the lab.
5. Study vendor tools in disaster recovery. Write about five of them, listing their merits and costs involved.
6. Study and develop a list of companies offering disaster recovery services in your area or state. Write about five, listing their merits and fees charged.
7. Based on your plan in (4) above, develop a rescue plan for the lab by developing a list of tools needed by the lab for disaster recovery, when needed.

Advanced Exercises: Case Studies

1. Check to see if your university has a disaster plan. Prepare a disaster plan for your university. Note that it should have the major headings as follows: (1) Introduction, (2) Emergency Procedures, (3) Response Plan, (4) Recovery Procedures, (5) Other Emergencies, and (6) Local Supplies.
2. Form a committee, whose size depends on the size of your college. Empower the committee to develop a disaster recovery plan for the college.
3. Consider the following company. HHR is a company involved with retail advertising. Major national chains use it to host their online catalogs. Every day, HHR gets about 5000 hits. It has four departments (Human Resources, Accounting, Advertising, IT), and employs about 2000 people nationally. The company is just getting started with disaster recovery and they have hired you to do it for them. Write a two-page document to the CEO of HHR selling your services.

4. Draw a plan of how you will go about setting up a Disaster Recovery Committee, indicating who will be in it and why. Also send a memo to the committee members telling them about the first organizing meeting, and list out the items to be discussed by the committee.
5. Develop a disaster recovery plan for HHR.

References

1. John Gage Allee (ed) (1998) Webster's dictionary. Literary Press, 1958
2. DataSafe, Inc., What is disaster planning? http://www.amarillodatasafe.com/abstracts.htm
3. The Disaster Recovery Guide (2002) http://www.disaster-recovery-guide.com/risk.htm
4. Intra Computer, Inc. Elements of an effective disaster prevention system. http://www.intracomp.com/page5.html
5. Walter Guerry Green (2001) Command and control of disaster operations, Universal Publishers, Inc/uPUBLISH.com
6. Erbschloe M (2003) Guide to disaster recovery. Course Technology, Boston
7. USAID. Disaster recovery planning procedures and guidelines. http://www.usaid.gov/policy/ads/500/545mal.pdf

Access Control and Authorization

9

9.1 Definitions

Access control is a process to determine "Who does what to what," based on a policy.

One of the system administrator's biggest problems, which can soon turn into a nightmare if it is not well handled, is controlling access of who gets in and out of the system and who uses what resources, when, and in what amounts. Access control is restricting this access to a system or system resources based on something other than the identity of the user. For example, we can allow or deny access to a system's resources based on the name or address of the machine requesting a document.

Access control is one of the major cornerstones of system security. It is essential to determine how access control protection can be provided to each of the system resources. To do this, a good access control and access protection policy is needed. According to Raymond Panko, such a policy has benefits including the following [1]:

- It focuses the organization's attention on security issues, and probably, this attention results in resource allocation toward system security.
- It helps in configuring appropriate security for each system resource based on role and importance in the system.
- It allows system auditing and testing.

As cyberspace expands and the forces of globalization push e-commerce to the forefront of business and commercial transactions, the need for secure transactions has propelled access control to a position among the top security requirements, which also include authorization and authentication. In this chapter, we are going to discuss access control and authorization; authentication will be discussed in the next chapter.

© Springer International Publishing AG 2017   187
J.M. Kizza, *Guide to Computer Network Security*, Computer Communications and Networks, DOI 10.1007/978-3-319-55606-2_9

9.2   Access Rights

To provide authorization, and later as we will see authentication, system administrators must manage a large number of system user accounts and permissions associated with those accounts. The permissions control user access to each system resource. So, user A who wants to access resource R must have permission to access that resource based on any one of the following modes: read, write, modify, update, append, and delete. Access control regimes and programs, through validation of passwords and access mode permissions, let system users get access to the needed system resources in a specified access mode.

Access control consists of four elements: subjects, objects, operations, and a reference monitor. In the normal operation, seen in Fig. 9.1, the subject, for example, a user, initiates an access request for a specified system resource, usually a passive object in the system such as a Web resource. The request goes to the reference monitor. The job of the reference monitor is to check on the hierarchy of rules that specify certain restrictions. A set of such rules is called an *access control list* (ACL). The access control hierarchy is based on the URL path for Web access or the file path for a file access such as in a directory. When a request for access is made, the monitor or server goes in turn through each ACL rule, continuing until it encounters a rule that prevents it from continuing and results in a request rejection or comes to the last rule for that resource, resulting into access right being granted.

Subjects are system users and groups of users, while objects are files and resources such as memory, printers, and scanners including computers in a network. An access operation comes in many forms including Web access, server access, memory access, and method calls. Whenever a subject requests to access an object, an access mode must be specified. There are two access modes: observe and alter. In the observe mode, the subject may only look at the content of the object; in the alter mode, the subject may change the content of the object. The observe mode is the typical read in which a client process may request a server to read from a file.

Access rights refer to the user's ability to access a system resource. There are four access rights: *execute, read, append,* and *write.* The user is cautioned not to confuse access rights and access modes. The difference lies in the fact that you can perform any access right within each access mode. Figure 9.2 shows how this can be done. Note that according to the last column in Fig. 9.2, there are X marks in both rows because in order to write, one must observe first before altering. This prevents the operating system from opening the file twice, one for the read and another for a write.

Access rights can be set individually on each system resource for each individual user and group. It is possible for a user to belong to a few groups and enjoy those groups' rights. However, user access rights always take precedence over group access rights regardless of where the group rights are applied. If there are inherited group access rights, they take precedence over user default access rights. A user has default rights when the user has no assigned individual or group rights from the root down to the folder in question. In the cascading of access rights application, user

Fig. 9.1 Access control
administration

Access request   Granted access request

Fig. 9.2 Access modes and
access rights (Ref. [2])

	execute	append	read	write
observe			X	X
alter		X		X

access rights that are closest to the resource being checked by the monitor take precedence over access rights assignments that are farther away.

We have so far discussed access rights to resources. The question that still remains to be answered is: Who sets these rights? The owner of the resource sets the access rights to the resource. In a global system, the operating systems own all system resources and therefore set the access rights to those resources. However, the operating system allows folders and file owners to set and revoke access rights.

9.2.1   Access Control Techniques and Technologies

Because a system, especially a network system, may have thousands of users and resources, the management of access rights for every user per every object may become complex. Several control techniques and technologies have been developed to deal with this problem; they include access control matrix, capability tables, access control lists, role-based access control, rule-based access control, restricted interfaces, and content-dependent access control.

Many of the techniques and technologies we are going to discuss below are new in response to the growth of cyberspace and the widespread use of networking. These new techniques and technologies have necessitated new approaches to system access control. For a long time, access control was used with user- or group-based access control lists, normally based in operating systems. However, with Web-based network applications, this approach is no longer flexible enough because it does not scale in the new environment. Thus, most Web-based systems employ newer techniques and technologies such as role-based and rule-based access control, where access rights are based on specific user attributes such as their role, rank, or organization unit.

9.2.1.1 Access Control Matrix
All the information needed for access control administration can be put into a matrix with rows representing the subjects or groups of subjects and columns representing the objects. The access that the subject or a group of subjects is

Fig. 9.3 Access matrix

Objects → Subjects/groups | V	R1	R2	R3	R4
A	W	R	R	W
B	R			
Group G1	W			
Group G2		W		
C				R

permitted to the object is shown in the body of the matrix. For example, in the matrix shown in Fig. 9.2, user A has permission to write in file R4. One feature of the access control matrix is its sparseness. Because the matrix is so sparse, storage consideration becomes an issue, and it is better to store the matrix as a list.

9.2.1.2 Access Control Lists
In the access control lists (ACLs), groups with access rights to an object are stored in association to the object. If you look at the access matrix shown in Fig. 9.2, each object has a list of access rights associated with it. In this case, each object is associated with all the access rights in the column. For example, the ACL for the matrix shown in Fig. 9.3 is shown in Fig. 9.4.

ACLs are very fitting for operating systems as they manage access to objects [2].

9.2.1.3 Access Control Capability
A capability specifies that "the subject may do operation O on object X."

Unlike the ACLs, where the storage of access rights between objects and subjects is based on columns in the access control matrix, capabilities access control storage is based on the rows. This means that every subject is given a capability, a forgery-proof token that specifies the subject's access rights [2].

From the access matrix shown in Fig. 9.3, we can construct a capability as shown in Fig. 9.5.

9.2.1.4 Role-Based Access Control
The changing size and technology of computer and communication networks are creating complex and challenging problems in the security management of these large networked systems. Such administration is not only becoming complex as technology changes and more people join the networks, it is also becoming extremely costly and prone to error when it is solely based on access control lists for each user on the system individually.

System security in role-based access control (RBAC) is based on roles assigned to each user in an organization. For example, one can take on a role as a chief executive officer, a chief information officer, or chief security officer. A user may

Fig. 9.4 Access control list (ACL)

Object	Access rights	Subjects
R1	W	A
	R	B
	W	Group G1
R2	R	A
	W	Group G2
R3	R	A
R4	R	A
	R	C

Subject	Object 1/Access	Object 2/Access	Object 3/Access	Object 4/Access
A	R1/W	R2/R	R3/R	R4/R
B	R1/R			
Group G1	R1/W			
Group G2		R2/W		
C				R4/R

Fig. 9.5 Access control capability lists

be assigned one or more roles, and each role is assigned one or more privileges that are permitted to users in that role. Access decisions are then based on the roles that individual users have as part of an organization. The process of defining roles should be based on a thorough analysis of how an organization operates and should include input from a wide spectrum of users in an organization.

Access rights are grouped by role name, and the use of resources is restricted to individuals authorized to assume the associated role. A good example to illustrate the role names and system users who may assume more than one role and play those roles while observing an organization's security policy is the following given in the NIST/ITL Bulletin, of December 1995. "Within a hospital system the role of doctor can include operations to perform diagnosis, prescribe medication, and order laboratory tests, and the role of researcher can be limited to gathering anonymous clinical information for studies" [3].

Accordingly, users are granted membership into roles based on their competencies and responsibilities in the organization. The types of operations that a user is permitted to perform in the role he or she assumes are based on that user's role. User roles are constantly changing as the user changes responsibilities and functions in the organizations, and these roles can be revoked. Role associations can be established when new operations are instituted, and old operations can be deleted as organizational functions change and evolve. This simplifies the administration and management of privileges; roles can be updated without updating the privileges for every user on an individual basis.

Like other types of access control, RBAC is also based on the concept of *least privilege* that requires identifying the user's job functions, determining the minimum set of privileges required to perform that function, and restricting the user to a domain with those privileges and nothing more. When a user is assigned a role, that user becomes associated with that role, which means that user can perform a certain and specific number of privileges in that role. Although the role may be associated with many privileges, individual users associated with that role may not be given more privileges than are necessary to perform their jobs.

Although this is a new technology, it is becoming very popular and attracting increasing attention, particularly for commercial applications, because of its potential for reducing the complexity and cost of security administration in large networked applications.

9.2.1.5 Rule-Based Access Control

Like other access control regimes, rule-based access control (RBAC), also known as *policy-based access control* (PBAC), is based on the least privilege concept. It is also based on policies that can be algorithmically expressed. RBAC is a multipart process, where one process assigns roles to users just like in the role-based access control techniques discussed above. The second process assigns privileges to the assigned roles based on a predefined policy. Another process is used to identify and authenticate the users allowed to access the resources.

It is based on a set of rules that determine users' access rights to resources within an organization's system. For example, organizations routinely set policies on the access to the organizations' Web sites on the organizations' intranet or Internet. Many organizations, for example, limit the scope and amount, sometimes the times, employees, based on their ranks and roles, can retrieve from the site. Such limits may be specified based on the number of documents that can be downloaded by an employee during a certain time period and on the limit of which part of the Web site such an employee can access.

The role of ACLs has been diminishing because ACLs are ineffective in enforcing policy. When using ACLs to enforce a policy, there is usually no distinction between the policy description and the enforcement mechanism (the policy is essentially defined by the set of ACLs associated with all the resources on the network). Having a policy being implicitly defined by a set of ACLs makes the management of the policy inefficient, error prone, and hardly scalable up to large enterprises with large numbers of employees and resources. In particular, every time an employee leaves a company or even just changes his/her role within the company, an exhaustive search of all ACLs must be performed on all servers, so that user privileges are modified accordingly.

In contrast with ACLs, policy-based access control makes a strict distinction between the formal statement of the policy and its enforcement. It makes rules explicit, and instead of concealing them in ACLs, it makes the policy easier to manage and modify. Its advantage is based on the fact that it administers the concept of least privilege justly because each user can be tied to a role which in turn can be tied to a well-defined list of privileges required for specific tasks in the role. In addition, the roles can be moved around easily and delegated without explicitly de-allocating a user's access privileges [4].

9.2.1.6 Restricted Interfaces

As the commercial Internet grows in popularity, more and more organizations and individuals are putting their data into organization and individual databases and restricting access to it. It is estimated that 88% of all cyberspace data is restricted data or what is called hidden data [5].

For the user to get access to restricted data, the user has to go via an interface. Any outside party access to restricted data requires a special access request, which many times requires filling in an online form. The interfaces restrict the amount and quality of data that can be retrieved based on filter and retrieval rules. In many cases, the restrictions and filters are instituted by content owners to protect the integrity and proprietary aspects of their data. The Web site itself and the browser must work in cooperation to overcome the over-restriction of some interfaces. Where this is impossible, hidden data is never retrievable.

9.2.1.7 Content-Dependent Access Control

In content-dependent access control, the decision is based on the value of the attribute of the object under consideration. Content-dependent access control is very expensive to administer because it involves a great deal of overhead resulting from the need to scan the resource when access is to be determined. The higher the level of granularity, the more expensive it gets. It is also extremely labor intensive.

9.2.1.8 Other Access Control Techniques and Technologies

Other access control techniques and technologies include those by the US Department of Defense (DoD) that include discretionary access control (DAC), mandatory access control (MAC), context-based access control (CBAC), view-based access control (VBAC), and user-based access control (UBAC).

DAC permits the granting and revoking of access control privileges to be left to the discretion of the individual users. A DAC mechanism departs a little bit from many traditional access control mechanisms where the users do not own the information to which they are allowed access. In DAC, users own the information and are allowed to grant or revoke access to any of the objects under their control.

Mandatory access control (MAC), according to DoD, is "a means of restricting access to objects based on the sensitivity (as represented by a label) of the information contained in the objects and the formal authorization (i.e., clearance) of subjects to access information of such sensitivity." [3].

Context-based access control (CBAC) makes a decision to allow access to a system resource based not only on who the user is, which resource it is, and its content but also on its history, which involves the sequence of events that preceded the access attempt.

View-based access control (VBAC), unlike other notions of access control which usually relate to tangible objects such as files, directories, and printers, takes the system resource itself as a collection of sub-resources, which are the views. This allows all users to access the same resource based on the view they have of the resource. It makes an assumption that the authentication of the source has been done by the authentication module.

User-based access control (UBAC), also known as identity-based access control (IBAC), is a technique that requires a system administrator to define permissions for each user based on the individual's needs. For a system with many users, this technique may become labor intensive because the administrator is supposed to know precisely what access each and every user needs and configure and update permissions.

9.3   Access Control Systems

In Sect. 2.3.1, we briefly discussed system access control as part of the survey of system security services. The discussion then was centered on both hardware and software access control regimes. Let us now look at these services in a more detailed form.

9.3.1   Physical Access Control

Although most accesses to an organization systems are expected to originate from remote sites and therefore access the system via the network access points, in a limited number of cases, system access can come from intruders physically gaining access to the system itself, where they can install password-cracking programs. Studies have shown that a great majority of system break-ins originate from inside the organization. Access to this group of users who have access to the physical premises of the system must be appropriate.

9.3.2   Access Cards

Cards as access control devices have been in use for sometime now. Access cards are perhaps the most widely used form of access control system worldwide. Initially, cards were used exclusively for visual identification of the bearer. However, with advanced digital technology, cards with magnetic strips and later with embedded microchips are now very common identification devices. Many companies require their employees to carry identity cards or identity badges with a photograph of the card holder or a magnetic strip for quick identification. Most hotels now have done away with metal keys in favor of magnet stripe keys. Access cards are used in most e-commerce transactions, payment systems, and in services such as health and education. These types of identification are also known as electronic keys.

Access control systems based on an embedded microprocessor, known as smart cards, have a number of advantages including the ability to do more advanced and sophisticated authentication because of the added processing power, storing large quantities of data, usually personal data, and smaller sizes. Smart cards also have exceptional reliability and extended life cycle because the chip is usually encased in tamper-resistant materials like stainless steel. The cards, in addition, may have built-in unique security identifier numbers called personal identification numbers (PINs) to prevent information falsification and imitations.

A cousin of the smart card is the proximity card. Proximity cards are modern, prestigious, and easy-to-use personal identifiers. Like magnetic and smart cards, proximity cards also have a great deal of embedded personal information. However, proximity cards have advantages the other cards do not have. They can be used in extreme conditions and still last long periods of time. They can also be read from a distance such as in parking lots where drivers can flash the card toward the reader while in a car and the reader still reads the card through the car window glass.

9.3.3 Electronic Surveillance

Electronic surveillance access control consists of a number of activity frame captures such as video recordings, system logs, keystroke and application monitors, screen-capture software commonly known as activity monitors, and network packet sniffers.

Video recordings capture the activities at selected access points. Increasingly these video cameras are now connected to computers and actually a Web, a process commonly now referred to as webcam surveillance. Webcam surveillance consists of a mounted video camera, sometimes very small and embedded into some object, camera software, and an Internet connection to form a closed-circuit monitoring system. Many of these cameras are now motion-activated, and they record video footage shot from vantage points at the selected points. For access control, the selected points are system access points. The video footage can be viewed live or stored for later viewing. These captures can also be broadcast over the Internet or transmitted to a dedicated location or sent by e-mail.

Keystroke monitors are software or hardware products that record every character typed on keyboards. Software-based keystroke monitors capture the signals that move between keyboard and computer as they are generated by all human-computer interaction activities that include the applications ran, chats, and e-mails sent and received. The captures are then sent live onto a closed-circuit recording system that stores them to a file for future review or sends them by e-mail to a remote location or user. Trojan horse spyware such as Back Orifice and Netbus are good examples of software-based monitoring tools [6].

Packet sniffers work at a network level to sniff at network packets as they move between nodes. Depending on the motives for setting them, they can motive all packets, selected packets, or node-originating and node-bound traffic. Based on the analysis, they can monitor e-mail messages, Web browser usage, node usage, traffic into a node, nature of traffic, and how often a user accesses a particular server, application, or network [6].

9.3.4 Biometrics

Biometric technology, based on human attributes, something you are, aims to confirm a person's identity by scanning a physical characteristic such as a fingerprint, voice, eye movement, facial recognition, and others. Biometrics came into use because we tend to forget something we have. We forget passwords, keys, and cards. Biometric has been and continues to be a catch-all and buzz word for all security control techniques that involve human attributes. It has probably been one of the oldest access control techniques. However, during the past several years and with heightened security, biometric technology has become increasingly popular. The technology, which can be used to permit access to a network or a building, has become an increasingly reliable, convenient, and cost-effective means of security.

Current technology has made biometric access control much more practical than it has ever been in the past. Now, a new generation of low-cost yet accurate fingerprint readers is available for most mobile applications so that screening stations can be put up in a few minutes. Although biometrics is one of those security control techniques that have been in use the longest, it does not have standards as yet. There is an array of services on the market for biometric devices to fit every form of security access control.

Technological advances have resulted in smaller, high-quality, more accurate, and more reliable devices. Improvements in biometrics are essential because bad biometric security can lull system and network administrators into a false sense of safety. In addition, it can also lock out a legitimate user and admit an intruder. So, care must be taken when procuring biometric devices.

Before a biometric technique can be used as an access control technique for the system, each user of the system first has his or her biometric data scanned by a biometric reader, processed to extract a few critical features, and then those few features stored in a database as the user's template. When a user requests access to a system resource and that user must be authenticated, the biometric readers verify customers' identities by scanning their physical attributes, such as fingerprints, again. A match is sought by checking them against prints of the same attributes previously registered and stored in the database.

One of the advantages that has made biometrics increasingly popular is that while other methods of access control such as authentication and encryption are crucial to network security and provide a secure way to exchange information, they are still expensive and difficult to design for a comprehensive security system. Other access control techniques such as passwords, while inexpensive to implement, are easy to forget and easy to guess by unauthorized people if they are simple and too complex to be of any use if they are complex.

9.3.4.1 Fingerprint Readers

Fingerprint recognition technology is perhaps one of the oldest biometric technologies. Fingerprint readers have been around for probably hundreds of years. These readers fall into two categories: mice with embedded sensors and stand-alone units. Mice are the latest 3D imaging developments and are threatening the stand-alone because they can play a dual role; they can be used on a desktop and also as network authentication stations. This is leading to the bundling of fingerprint recognition devices with smart cards or some other security token.

Although fingerprint technology is improving with current technology, making it possible to make a positive identification in a few seconds, fingerprint identification is susceptible to precision problems. Many fingerprints can result in false positives due to oil and skin problems on the subject's finger. Also, many of the latest fingerprint readers can be defeated by photos of fingerprints and 3D fingers from latent prints such as prints left on glass and other objects [1].

9.3.4.2 Voice Recognition

Although voice recognition technology is a biometric that is supposed to authenticate the user based on what the use is, voice imprint is based on something the user does, itself based on who the user is. Voice recognition has been around for years; however, its real-life application has been slow because of the difficulties in deployment. In order for voiceprint technology to work successfully, it needs to be deployed by first developing the front end to capture the input voice and connect it to the back-end systems which process the input and do the recognition.

The front end of the voiceprint authentication technology works much the same as other biometric technologies, by creating a digital representation of a person's voice using a set of sophisticated algorithms. Those attributes are stored in a database, part of the back end, which is prompted to make a match against the user's voice when the online system is accessed.

To set it up initially, each user is required to record and leave his or her voiceprint, which is stored in the system's database to be activated whenever the user requests access to the protected facility through a physical system input. The user is then prompted to speak into a computer's microphone to verify his or her identity.

Current systems use two servers to perform these functions. The first server runs the front-end system, and the second server then stores the database and does the processing for a recognition from the input server.

Voice recognition is not a safe authentication technique because it can be fooled by the types of recording.

9.3.4.3 Hand Geometry

Hand geometry is an authentication technology that uses the geometric shape of the hand to identify a user. The technique works by measuring and then analyzing the shape and physical features of a user's hand, such as finger length and width and palm width. Like fingerprints, this technique also uses a reader. To initiate the device, all users' hands are read and measured and the statistics are stored in a database for future recognition. To activate the system, the user places the palm of his or her hand on the surface of the reader. Readers usually have features that guide the user's hand on the surface. Once on the surface, the hand, guided by the guiding features, is properly aligned for the reader to read off the hand's attributes. The reader is hooked to a computer, usually a server, with an application that provides a live visual feedback of the top view and the side view of the hand. Hand features are then taken as the defining feature vector of the user's hand and are then compared with the user features stored in the database.

Although hand geometry is simple, human hands are not unique; therefore, individual hand features are not descriptive enough for proper identification. The technique must be used in conjunction with other methods of authentication.

9.3.4.4 Iris Scan

The human iris is the colored part of the human eye and is far more complex and probably more precise than a human fingerprint; thus, it is a good candidate for authentication. According to Panko, iris authentication is the gold standard of all biometric authentications [1]. Iris scan technology, unlike the retinal scan, does not have a long history. In fact, the idea of using iris patterns for personal identification was first mooted in 1936 by ophthalmologist Frank Burch. By the mid-1980s, the idea was still a science fiction appearing only in James Bond films. The technology came into full use in the 1990s [7].

Iris technology is an authentication technology that uses either regular or infrared light into the eye of the user to scan and analyze the features that exist in the colored tissue surrounding the pupil of the user's eye. Like the previous biometric technologies, iris technology also starts off by taking samples of the user eye features using a conventional closed-circuit digital (CCD) or video camera that can work through glasses and contacts. The camera scans the tissue around the pupils for analysis features. Close to 200 features can be extracted from this tissue surrounding the pupil and used in the analysis. The tissue gives the appearance of dividing the iris in a radial fashion. The most important of these characteristics in the tissue is the trabecular meshwork visible characteristic. Other extracted visible characteristics include rings, furrows, freckles, and the corona.

The first readings are stored in a database. Whenever a user wants access to a secure system, he or she looks in an iris reader. Modern iris readers can read a user's eye up to 2 ft away. Verification time is short and it is getting shorter. Currently it stands at about 5 s, although the user will need to look into the device only for a couple moments. Like in other eye scans, precautions must be taken to prevent a wrong person's eyes from fooling the system. This is done by varying the light shone into the eye and then pupil dilations are recorded.

The use of iris scans for authentication is becoming popular, although it is a young technology. Its potential application areas include law enforcement agencies and probably border patrol and airports. There is also potential use in the financial sector, especially in banking.

9.3.5 Event Monitoring

Event monitoring is a cousin of electronic monitoring in which the focus is on specific events of interest. Activities of interest can be monitored by video camera, webcam, digital or serial sensors, or a human eye. All products we discussed in Sects. 9.3.3 and 9.3.4.2 can be used to capture screenshots, monitor Internet activity, and report a computer's use, keystroke by keystroke, and human voice, including human movement. The activities recorded based on selected events can be stored, broadcast on the Internet, or sent by e-mail to a selected remote location or user.

9.4 Authorization

This is the determination of whether a user has permission to access, read, modify, insert, or delete certain data, or to execute certain programs. In particular, it is a set of access rights and access privileges granted to a user to benefit from a particular system resource. Authorization is also commonly referred to as access permissions, and it determines the privileges a user has on a system and what the user should be allowed to do to the resource. Access permissions are normally specified by a list of possibilities. For example, Unix allows the list {read, write, execute} as the list of possibilities for a user or group of users on a Unix file.

We have seen above that access control consists of defining an access policy for each system resource. The enforcement of each one of these access policies is what is called authorization. It is one thing to have a policy in place, but however good a policy is, without good enforcement, the policy serves no purpose. The implementation of mechanisms to control access to system resources is, therefore, a must for an effective access control regime.

The process of authorization itself has traditionally been composed of two separate processes: authentication, which we are going to discuss in the next chapter, and access control. To get a good picture, let us put them together. In brief, authentication deals with ascertaining that the user is who he or she claims he or she is. Access control then deals with a more refined problem of being able to find out "what a specific user can do to a certain resource." So authorization techniques such as the traditional centralized access control use ACL as a dominant mechanism to create user lists and user access rights to the requested resource. However, in more modern and distributed system environments, authorization takes a different approach from this. In fact, the traditional separation of authorization process into authentication and access control also does not apply [8].

As with access control, authorization has three components: a set of objects we will designate as O, a set of subjects designed as S, and a set of access permissions designated as S. The authorization rule is a function f that takes the triple (s, o, a), where $s \in S$, $o \in O$, $a \in A$ and maps then into a binary-value T, where $T = \{$true, false$\}$ as $f: S \times O \times A \rightarrow (True, False)$. When the value of the function f is true, this signals that the request for subject s to gain access to object o has been granted at authorization level a.

The modern authentication process is decentralized to allow more system independence and to give network services providers more control over system resource access. This is also the case in yet more distributed systems, since in such systems, it is hard and sometimes impossible to manage all users and resources in one central location. In addition, many servers actually do not need to know who the user is in order to provide services.

The capability mechanism so central in the traditional process, however, still plays a central role here, providing for decentralization of authorization through providing credentials to users or applications whenever it receives requests for resource access. Each user or application keeps a collection of capabilities, one for each resource they have access to, which they must present in order to use the requested resource. Since every resource maintains its own access control policy and complete proof of compliance between the policy and credentials collected from the user or application, the server receiving the request need not consult a centralized ACL for authorization [8].

9.4.1   Authorization Mechanisms

Authorization mechanisms, especially those in database management systems (DBMSs), can be classified into two main categories: discretionary and mandatory.

9.4.1.1 Discretionary Authorization

This is a mechanism that grants access privileges to users based on control policies that govern the access of subjects to objects using the subjects' identity and authorization rules, discussed in Sect. 9.3 above. These mechanisms are discretionary in that they allow subjects to grant other users authorization to access the data. They are highly flexible, making them suitable for a large variety of application domains.

However, the same characteristics that make them flexible also make them vulnerable to malicious attacks, such as Trojan horses embedded in application programs. The reason is that discretionary authorization models do not impose any control on how information is propagated, and once used, they have been accessed by users authorized to do so.

But in many practical situations, discretionary policies are preferred since they offer a better trade-off between security and applicability. For this reason, in this chapter, we focus on discretionary access control mechanisms. We refer the reader to [4] for details on mandatory access control mechanisms.

9.4.1.2 Mandatory Access Control

Mandatory policies, unlike the discretionary ones seen above, ensure a high degree of protection in that they prevent any illegal flow of information through the enforcement of multilevel security by classifying the data and users into various security classes. They are, therefore, suitable for contexts that require structured but graded levels of security such as the military. However, mandatory policies have the drawback of being too rigid in that they require a strict classification of subjects and objects in security levels and are therefore applicable only to very few environments [4].

9.5   Types of Authorization Systems

Before the creation of decentralized authorization systems, authorization was controlled from one central location. Operating system authorization, for example, was centrally controlled before the advent of network operating systems (NOSs). The birth of computer networks and therefore NOS created the decentralized authorization systems.

9.5.1   Centralized

Traditionally, every resource used to do its own local authorizations and maintained its own authorization database to associate authorizations to users. But this led to several implementation problems. For example, different resources and different software applied different rules to determine authorization for the same subject on an object. This led to the centralized authorization policy. In centralized authorization, only one central authorization unit grants and delegates access to system resources. This means that any process or program that needs access to any system resource has to request from the one omniscient central authority. Centralized authorization services allow you to set up generalized policies that control who gets access to resources across multiple platforms. For example, it is possible to set an authorization to a company's Web portal in such a way that authorization is based on either functions or titles. Those with such functions could control their organization's specially designated component of the portal, while others without functions access the general portal. This system is very easy and inexpensive to operate. A single database available to all applications gives a better more and consistent view of security. It also simplifies the process of adding, modifying, and deleting authorizations. All original operating systems have been using this authorization approach.

9.5.2   Decentralized

This differs from the centralized system in that the subjects own the objects they have created and are therefore responsible for their security, which is locally maintained. This means that each system resource maintains its own authorization process and maintains its own database of authorizations associated with all subjects authorized to access the resource. Each subject also possesses all possible rights to access every resource associated with it. Each subject may, however, delegate access rights to its objects to another subject. Because of these characteristics, decentralized authorization is found to be very flexible and easily adaptable to particular requirements of individual subjects. However, this access rights delegation may lead to the problem of cascading, and cyclic authorization may arise.

9.5.3   Implicit

In implicit authorization, the subject is authorized to use a requested system resource indirectly because the objects in the system are referenced in terms of other objects. That means that in order for a subject to access a requested object, the access must go through an access of a primary object. Using the mathematical set theoretical representation we presented earlier, in a given set of sets (s, o, a), a user s is implicitly given a type a authorization on all the objects of o. Take, for example, a request to use a Web page; the page may have links connected to other documents. The user who requests for authorization to use the Web has also indirect authorization to access all the pages linked to the authorized original page. This is, therefore, a level of authorization called granularity. We are going to discuss this later. Notice that a single authorization here enables a number of privileges.

9.5.4   Explicit

Explicit authorization is the opposite of the implicit. It explicitly stores all authorizations for all system objects whose access has been requested. Again in a mathematical representation seen earlier, for every request for access to object o from subject s that is grantable, the triple set (s, o, a) is stored. All others are not stored. Recall from the last chapter that one of the problems of access control was to store a large but sparse matrix of access rights. This technique of storing only authorized triples greatly reduces the storage requirements. However, although simple, the technique still stores authorizations whether needed or not, which wastes storage.

9.6   Authorization Principles

The prime object of authorization is system security achieved through the controlled access to the system resources. The authorization process, together with access control discussed earlier, through the use of authorization data structures, clearly defines who uses what system resources and what resources can and cannot be used. The authorization process, therefore, offers undeniable security to the system through the protection of its resources. System resources are protected through principles such as least privilege and separation of duties, which eventually results in increased accountability that leads to increased system security.

9.6.1   Least Privilege

The *principle of least privilege* requires that the subject be granted authorizations based on its needs. Least privilege principle is itself based on two other principles: *less rights* and *less risk*. The basic idea behind these principles is that security is improved if subjects using system resources are given no more privileges than the minimum they require to perform the tasks that they are intended to perform and in the minimum amount of time required to perform the tasks. The least privilege principle has the ability, if followed, to reduce the risks of unauthorized accesses to the system.

9.6.2   Separation of Duties

The principle of separation of duties breaks down the process of authorization into basic steps and requires that for every request for authorization from a subject to a system resource, each step be given different privileges. It requires that each different key step in a process requires different privileges for different individual subjects. This division of labor, not only in the authorization process of one individual request but also between individual subjects, stipulates not only that one subject should never be given a blanket authorization to do all the requested functions but also that no one individual request to an object should be granted blanket access rights to an object. This hierarchical or granular authorization distributes responsibilities and creates accountability because no one subject is responsible for large processes where responsibility and accountability may slack. For example, authorization to administer a Web server or an e-mail server can be granted to one person without granting him or her administrative rights to other parts of the organization system.

9.7   Authorization Granularity

We have used the concept of granularity in the last section without officially defining it. Let us do so here. Granularity in access authorization means the level of details an authorizing process requires to limit and separate privileges. Because a single authorization may enable a number of privileges or a privilege may require multiple authorizations, when requests come into the authorizing process from subjects requiring access to system resources, the authorizing authority must pay attention and separate these two authorization privileges. These two issues may complicate the authorization process. Granularity, therefore, should be defined on functions [9].

9.7.1 Fine-Grained Authorization

As we discussed above, granularity of authorizations should not be based on either authorization requests or on granted privileges but on functions performed. Fine-grained granularity defines very specific functions that individually define specific tasks. This means that each authorization request is broken up into small but specific tasks and each one of these tasks is assigned a function.

9.7.2 Coarse-Grained Authorization

Coarse-grained granularity is different from fine-grained granularity in that here only the basic ability to interact with resources is focused on. Then all lower detail tasks within the large functions are ignored. These abilities can be enforced by the operating system without concern for the applications. In fact, it is this type of authorization that is enforced by most operating systems. For example, most operating systems have the following abilities or functions: delete, modify, read, write, and create. Subject requests for access authorization must then be put into one of these major functions or abilities.

9.8 Web Access and Authorization

The growth of the Internet and e-commerce has made Web application the fastest-growing client-server application model and the mainstay of the Internet. Accordingly, Web servers have also become the main targets for intruder break-ins. So, controlling access to Web-based resources has naturally become an administrative nightmare.

The Web infrastructure supports a distributed authorizing structure based on node-naming structures, where each node is known by an URL and information to be retrieved from it is accessible through protocols such as HTTP. Under this structure, authorization is based on an access control list (ACL). In a distributed environment such as this, each server node needs to either know its potential clients or there must be an authorizing server that other servers must consult before request authorization. However, both of these approaches present problems for the Web authorization because the former approach presents a client administration problem when the client population changes at a fast rate. The latter approach presents a potential performance bottleneck as the processing of a node request depends on the performance and availability of the authorization server [10].

In a fully functioning distributed Web authorization process, a coordinated authorization approach is required that grants access not only to requested document but also to all other documents linked to it. But by this writing, this is not the case.

Whether using the present authorization model or those to come, every effort must be used to control access to Web servers and minimize unauthorized access to them. In addition to access control and authorization, here are the other tips for securing servers [11]:

- Web servers should not run any other services with the exception of a carefully configured anonymous FTP.
- Periodic security scans by a trusted third party should be scheduled to identify system security weaknesses.
- Minimize system risk by never running the Web server as "root" or "administrator." Server processes should be run from a new account with no other privileges on the machine.
- For shared file system such as AFS or NFS, give the Web server only "read only" access, or separately mount a "read only" data disk.

Exercises

1. Differentiate between access and authorization.
2. What are the benefits of authorization?
3. Why is it difficult to implement distributed authorization?
4. Discuss the merits and demerits of centralized and decentralized authorization.
5. Compare the authorization model used by the network operating systems (NOSs) to that used by the old stand-alone operating systems.
6. List and discuss the most common access privileges in a computing system.
7. Discuss the three components of a global access model.
8. Physical access to resources is essential and must be the most restricted. Why?
9. Discuss four access methods, giving the weaknesses of each.
10. Discuss the many ways in which access can be abused.

Advanced Exercises

1. Is it possible to implement full distributed authorization? What will be involved?
2. Web authorization is central to the security of all Web applications. What is the best way to safeguard all Web applications and at the same time make Web access reliable and fast?
3. Consider an environment where each server does its own authorization. If an access request is made to a document that has extended links and one of the link requests is denied, should the whole document request be denied? Why or why not?
4. Discuss the benefits and problems resulting from the "least privilege" principle often used in access control.
5. Discuss the concept of global privilege. Does it work well in a distributed authorization or centralized authorization?
6. With the principle of "least privilege," is it possible to have too much authorization? What happens when there is too much authorization?

References

1. Panko RR (2004) Corporate computer and network security. Prentice-Hall, Upper Saddle River
2. Gollman D (2000) Computer security. Wiley, New York
3. An Introduction to Role-based Access Control. NIST/ITL Bulletin, December, 1995. http:// csrc.nist.gov/rbac/NIST-ITL-RBAC-bulletin.html
4. Differentiating Between Access Control Terms. http://secinf.net/uplarticle/2/Access_Control_ WP.pdf
5. Byers S, Freire J, Silva C. Efficient acquisition of web data through restricted query interfaces. AT&T Labs-Research. http://www10.org/cdrom/posters/p1051/
6. Bannan K. Watching you, watching me PCs are turning informant. Whose side are they on? PC Magazine, July 1, 2002, http://www.pcmag.com/article2/0,4149,342208,00.asp
7. Iris scan. http://ctl.ncsc.dni.us/biomet%20web/BMIris.html
8. NASA World Wide Web Best Practices (2000–2001) Draft version 2.0. http://nasa-wbp.larc. nasa.gov/devel/4.0/4_4.html
9. Pipkin D (2000) Information security: protecting the global enterprise. Prentice-Hall, Upper Saddle River
10. Kahan J. A distributed authorization model for WWW. May, 1995. http://www.isoc.org/HMP/ PAPER/107/html/paper.html. Accessed on 5/6/2003
11. NASA. World wide web best practices 2000–2001 draft version 2.0. 8/20/2000. http://nasa-wbp.larc.nasa.gov/devel/4.0/4_4.html. 5/6/2003

Authentication

10

10.1 Definition

Authentication is the process of validating the identity of someone or something. It uses information provided to the authenticator to determine whether someone or something is in fact who or what it is declared to be. In private and public computing systems, for example, in computer networks, the process of authentication commonly involves someone, usually the user, using a password provided by the system administrator to *logon*. The user's possession of a password is meant to guarantee that the user is authentic. It means that at some previous time, the user requested, from the system administrator, and the administrator assigned and/or registered a self-selected password.

The user presents this password to the logon to prove that he or she knows something no one else could know.

Generally, authentication requires the presentation of credentials or items of value to really prove the claim of who you are. The items of value or credential are based on several unique factors that show something you know, something you have, or something you are [1]:

- *Something you know*: This may be something you mentally possess. This could be a password, a secret word known by the user and the authenticator. Although this is inexpensive administratively, it is prone to people's memory lapses and other weaknesses including secure storage of the password files by the system administrators. The user may use the same password on all system logons or may change it periodically, which is recommended. Examples using this factor include passwords, passphrases, and personal identification numbers (PINs).
- *Something you have*: This may be any form of issued or acquired self-identification such as:
  - SecurID
  - CryptoCard
  - ActivCard

© Springer International Publishing AG 2017
J.M. Kizza, *Guide to Computer Network Security*, Computer Communications
and Networks, DOI 10.1007/978-3-319-55606-2_10

– SafeWord
– Many other forms of cards and tags

This form is slightly safer than something you know because it is hard to abuse individual physical identifications. For example, it is harder to lose a smart card than to remember the card number.

- *Something you are*: This is a naturally acquired physical characteristic such as voice, fingerprint, iris pattern, and other biometrics discussed in Chap. 7. Although biometrics are very easy to use, this ease of use can be offset by the expenses of purchasing biometric readers. Examples of items used in this factor include fingerprints, retinal patterns, DNA patterns, and hand geometry.

In addition to the top three factors, another factor, though indirect, also plays a part in authentication:

- *Somewhere you are*: This usually is based on either physical or logical location of the user. The use, for example, may be on a terminal that can be used to access certain resources.

In general, authentication takes one of the following three forms [2]:

- *Basic authentication* involving a server. The server maintains a user file of either passwords and usernames or some other useful piece of authenticating information. This information is always examined before authorization is granted. This is the most common way computer network systems authenticate users. It has several weaknesses though, including forgetting and misplacing authenticating information such as passwords.
- *Challenge-response*, in which the server or any other authenticating system generates a challenge to the host requesting for authentication and expects a response. We will discuss challenge-response in Sect. 10.5.1.3.
- *Centralized authentication*, in which a central server authenticates users on the network and in addition also authorizes and audits them. These three processes are done based on server action. If the authentication process is successful, the client seeking authentication is then authorized to use the requested system resources. However, if the authentication process fails, the authorization is denied. The process of auditing is done by the server to record all information from these activities and store it for future use.

10.2 Multiple Factors and Effectiveness of Authentication

For an authentication mechanism to be considered effective, it must uniquely and in a forgery-proof manner identify an individual. The factors above do so in varying degrees depending on how they are combined. Each factor, if used alone to authenticate users, is effective enough to authenticate a user; however, these systems' authentication may be more vulnerable to compromise of the authenticator. For example, both factors "authentication by knowledge" and "authentication by ownership" in factors 1 and 2 above require a person to be associated with something by knowledge or acquisition.

Notice that the user is not required to be physically attached to the authentication information. Possession of something that is not physically attached to the user can result in that authentication information getting lost, stolen, or otherwise compromised. For example, information by knowledge can be duplicated through user negligence or somebody else learning it without the user knowing. It can also be acquired through possible guessing, repeated attempts, or through brute force by using automated mathematical exhaustive search techniques.

Similarly "authentication by ownership" suffers from a set of problems that make it not so effective. For example, although items in this category have their major strength in the difficulty of duplication, such objects also require more effort to guard from theft; they can be made using special equipment or procedures [3].

Although the third factor, "authentication by characteristic," is much stronger than the first two, it suffers from high costs incurred to acquire and build effective peripherals that can obtain a complete enough sample of a characteristic to entirely distinguish one individual from another. It requires readers with more advanced features and functions to read, analyze, and completely discriminate and distinguish one's physical features. Readers with these functions are often very expensive and require highly trained personnel and other operating expenses.

As the Internet becomes widely used in everyday transactions including e-commerce, a stronger form of authentication that differs from the traditional username password authentication is needed to safeguard system resources from the potentially hostile environment of the "bad" Internet. The "bad" Internet consists of wide array of "untrusted" public and private clients, including civic networks and public kiosks and cafes. In addition to these, it also includes commonly available software that allows an intruder to easily sniff, snoop, and steal network logon passwords as they are exchanged in the traditional authentication schemes.

To address this, an effective authentication scheme with multiple methods is preferred. Systems using two or more methods can result in greater system security.

This process of piggybacking authentication factors is one of the popular strategies now used widely for overcoming the limitations of a specific authentication factor by supplementing it with another factor. This technique of improving authentication assurance is referred to as *multifactor* authentication.

Although it is common to combine two or more authentication items from two or more factors as shown in Fig. 10.1, it is also possible to combine two or more items from the same authentication factor class. For example, one can combine an iris pattern and a fingerprint. There are generally two motives for taking this action [4]:

Fig. 10.1 Authentication
factor combinations

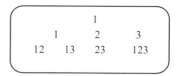

- The need to improve usability and accuracy. Combining items from different authenticating factors improves the accuracy of the authentication process. It may also lead to reduction in the false rejection rate of legitimate users.
- To improve the authentication process' integrity by reducing the effect of certain items in some factors that are prone to vulnerabilities that weaken it. The combining technique, therefore, reduces the risk of false negatives where, for example, an impersonating user can succeed in accessing the system.

The discussion above provides one very important element of authentication: that different mechanisms provide different levels of authentication effectiveness. Choosing the most effective authentication, therefore, depends on the technology used and also on the degree of *trust* placed on that technology. Generally, trust is a firm belief or confidence one has in someone or something. Trust is manifested in attributes such as honesty, reliability, integrity, justice, and others. Since authorization comes after approval of identity, that is, after authentication, a organizational framework spelling out an authorization policy based on authentication is a *trust model*. Organizations use trust model to create authentication groups. For example, a group of company executives may be put in a different authentication process than a group consisting of parking attendants. These authentication and authorization groupings are based on the company's trust model.

10.3   Authentication Elements

An authentication process as described above is based on five different elements: the person or group of people seeking authentication, distinguishing characteristics from that person or group presented for authentication, the authenticator, the authenticating mechanism to verify the presence of the authenticating characteristics, and the access control mechanism to accept or deny authentication.

10.3.1 Person or Group Seeking Authentication

These are usually users who seek access to a system either individually or as a group. If individually, they must be prepared to present to the authenticator evidence to support the claim that they are actually authorized to use the requested system resource. They may present any one of the basic factors discussed in Sect. 10.1. Similarly as a group, the group again must present to the authenticator evidence that any one member of the group is authorized to use the system based on a trust model.

10.3.2 Distinguishing Characteristics for Authentication

The second authentication element is the distinguishing characteristics from the user to the authenticator. In Sect. 10.1, we already discussed these characteristics and grouped them into four factors that include something you know, something you have, something you are, and a weaker one somewhere you are. In each of these factors, there are items that a user can present to the authenticator for authorization to use the system. Some of these items may not completely authenticate the user, and we have pointed out in Sect. 10.2 that a combination of items from different factors and trust may be used to strengthen the authentication and create better assurances.

10.3.3 The Authenticator

The job of the authenticator is to positively and sometimes automatically identify the user and indicate whether that user is authorized to access the requested system resource. The authenticator achieves application for authentication by prompting for user credentials when an authentication request is issued. The authenticator then collects the information and passes it over to the authentication mechanism.

The authenticator can be a user-designated server, a virtual private network (VPN), firewall, a local area network (LAN) server, an enterprise-wide dedicated server, independent authentication service, or some other form of global identity service. Whatever is being used as an authenticator must perform an authentication process that must result in some outcome value such as a token that is used in the authentication process to determine information about the authenticated user at a later time. A note of caution to the reader is that some authors call this token the authenticator. Because there is no standard on these tokens adhered to by all authenticating schemes, the format of the token varies from vendor to vendor.

10.3.4 The Authentication Mechanism

The authentication mechanism consists of three parts that work together to verify the presence of the authenticating characteristics provided by the user. The three parts are the input, the transportation system, and the verifier. They are linked with the appropriate technologies. An input component acts as the interface between the user and the authentication system. In a distributed environment, this could be a computer keyboard, card reader, video camera, telephone, or similar device. The captured user-identifying items need to be taken to a place where they are scrutinized, analyzed, and accepted or rejected. But in order for these items to reach this point, they have to be transported. The transport portion of the system is, therefore, responsible for passing data between the input component and the element that can confirm a person's identity. In modern-day authenticating systems, this information is transported over a network, where it can be protected by protocols like Kerberos or sent in plaintext [4].

The last component of the authentication system is the verification component, which is actually the access control mechanism in the next section.

10.3.5 Access Control Mechanism

We discussed access control and the working of the access control mechanism in Chap. 8. Let us briefly review the role of the access control mechanism in the authentication process. User-identifying and authenticating information is passed to access control from the transport component. Here, this information must be validated against the information in its database. The database may reside on a dedicated authentication server or may be stored in a file on a local medium. The access control mechanism then cross-checks the two pieces of information for a match. If a match is detected, the access control system then issues temporary credentials authorizing the user to access the desired system resource.

10.4   Types of Authentication

In Sect. 10.1, we identified three factors that are used in the positive authentication of a user. We also pointed out in the previous section that while these factors are in themselves good, there are items in some that suffer from vulnerabilities. Table 10.1 illustrates the shortcomings of user identity characteristics from the factors that suffer from these vulnerabilities.

From Table 10.1, one can put the factors into two categories: nonrepudiable and repudiable authentication. Other types of authentication include user, client, and session authentication.

Table 10.1 Authentication factors and their vulnerabilities[a]

Number	Factor	Examples	Vulnerabilities
1	What you know	Password, PIN	Can be forgotten, guessed, duplicated
2	What you have	Token, ID card, keys	Can be lost, stolen, duplicated
3	What you are	Iris, voiceprint, fingerprint	Nonrepudiable

[a]Ratha, Nalini K., Jonathan H. Connell and Ruud M. Bolle. "Secure Fingerprint-based Authentication for Lotus Notes." https://faculty.unlv.edu/thatcher/is485/readings/biometrics.pdf

10.4.1 Nonrepudiable Authentication

Nonrepudiable authentication involves all items in factor 3. Recall that factor 3 consists of items that involve some type of characteristics and whose proof of origin cannot be denied. The biometrics used in factor 3, which include iris patterns, retinal images, and hand geometry, have these characteristics. Biometrics can positively verify the identity of the individual. In our discussion of biometrics in Chap. 8, we pointed out that biometric characteristics cannot be forgotten, lost, stolen, guessed, or modified by an intruder. They, therefore, present a very reliable form of access control and authorization. It is also important to note that contemporary applications of biometric authorization are automated, which further eliminates human errors in verification. As technology improves and our understanding of the human anatomy increases, newer and more sensitive and accurate biometrics will be developed.

Next to biometrics as nonrepudiable authentication items are *undeniable and confirmer digital signatures*. These signatures, developed by Chaum and van Antwerpen, are signatures that cannot be verified without the help of a signer and cannot with non-negligible probability be denied by the signer. Signer legitimacy is established through a confirmation or denial protocol [5]. Many undeniable digital signatures are based on Rivest, Shamir, and Adleman (RSA) structure and technology, which give them provable security that makes the forgery of undeniable signatures as hard as forging standard RSA signatures.

Confirmer signatures [6, 7] are a type of undeniable signatures, where signatures may also be further verified by an entity called the confirmer designated by the signer.

Lastly, there are *chameleon signatures*, a type of undeniable signatures in which the validity of the content is based on the trust of the signer's commitment to the contents of the signed document. But in addition, they do not allow the recipient of the signature to disclose the contents of the signed information to any third party without the signer's consent [5].

10.4.2 Repudiable Authentication

In our discussion of authentication factors in Sect. 10.2, we pointed out that the first two factors, "what you know" and "what you have," are factors that can present problems to the authenticator because the information presented can be unreliable. It can be unreliable because such factors suffer from several well-known problems including the fact that possessions can be lost, forged, or easily duplicated. Also knowledge can be forgotten and taken together, and knowledge and possessions can be shared or stolen. Repudiation is, therefore, easy. Before the development of items in factor 3, in particular the biometrics, authorization, and authentication methods relied only on possessions and knowledge.

10.5   Authentication Methods

Different authentication methods are used based on different authentication algorithms. These authentication methods can be combined or used separately, depending on the level of functionality and security needed. Among such methods are password authentication, public key authentication, anonymous authentication, and remote and certificate-based authentication.

10.5.1 Password Authentication

The password authentication methods are the oldest and the easiest to implement. They are usually set up by default in many systems. Sometimes, these methods can be interactive using the newer keyboard-interactive authentication. Password authentication includes reusable passwords, one-time passwords, challenge-response passwords, and combined approach passwords.

10.5.1.1   Reusable Passwords

There are two types of authentication in reusable password authentication (user and client authentication):

- *User authentication*. This is the most commonly used type of authentication, and it is probably the most familiar to most users. It is always initiated by the user, who sends a request to the server for authentication and authorization for the use of a specified system resource. On receipt of the request, the server prompts the user for a username and password. On submission of these, the server checks for a match against copies in its database. Based on the match, authorization is granted.
- *Client authentication*. Normally, the user requests for authentication and then authorization by the server to use a system or a specified number of system resources. Authenticating users does not mean the user is free to use any system resource the user wants. Authentication must establish user authorization to use the requested resources in the amount requested and no more. This type of authentication is called client authentication. It establishes users' identities and controlled access to system resources.

Because these types of authentication are the most widely used authentication methods, they are the most abused. They are also very unreliable because users forget them, they write them down, they let others use them, and, most importantly, they are easy to guess because users choose simple passwords. They are also susceptible to cracking and snooping. In addition, they fall prey to today's powerful computers, which can crack them with brute force through exhaustive search.

10.5.1.2 One-Time Passwords

One-time password authentication is also known as session authentication. Unlike reusable passwords that can be used over extended periods of time, one-time passwords are used once and disposed of. They are randomly generated using powerful random number generators. This reduces the chances of their being guessed. In many cases they are encrypted and then issued to reduce their being intercepted if they are sent in the clear. There are several schemes of one-time passwords. The most common of these schemes are S/Key and token:

- *S/Key password* is a one-time password generation scheme defined in RFC 1760 and is based on MD4 and MD5 encryption algorithms. It was designed to fight against replay attacks where, for example, in a log-in session, an intruder eavesdrops on the network log-in session and gets the password and user ID for the legitimate user. Its protocol is based on a client-server model in which the client initiates the S/Key exchange by sending the first packet to which the server responds with an ACK and a sequence number. Refer to Chap. 1 for this. The client then responds to the server by generating a one-time password and passes it to the server for verification. The server verifies the password by passing it through a hash function and compares the hash digest to the stored value for a match.
- *Token password* is a password generation scheme that requires the use of a special card such as a smart card. According to Kaeo, the scheme is based on two schemes: challenge-response and time-synchronous [8]. We are going to discuss challenge-response in Sect. 10.5.1.3. In a time-synchronous scheme, an algorithm executes both in the token and on the server, and outputs are compared for a match. These numbers, however, change with time.

Although they are generally safer, one-time passwords have several difficulties including synchronization problems that may be caused by lapsed time between the time stamp in the password and the system time. Once these two times are out of phase, the password cannot be used. Also synchronization problems may arise when the one-time password is issued based on either a system or user. If it is based on the user, the user must be contacted before use to activate the password.

10.5.1.3 Challenge-Response Passwords

In Sect. 10.1, we briefly talked about challenge-response authentication as another form of relatively common form of authentication. Challenge-response, as a password authentication process, is a handshake authentication process in which the authenticator issues a challenge to the user seeking authentication. The user must provide a correct response in order to be authenticated. The challenge may take many forms depending on the system. In some systems, it is in the form of a message indicating "unauthorized access" and requesting a password. In other systems, it may be a simple request for a password, a number, a digest, or a nonce (a server-specified data string that may be uniquely generated each time a server generates a 401 server error). The person seeking authentication must respond to the system challenge. Nowadays, responses are by a one-way function using a password token, commonly referred to as *asynchronous tokens*. When the server receives the user response, it checks to be sure the password is correct. If so, the user is authenticated. If not or if for any other reason the network does not want to accept the password, the request is denied.

Challenge-response authentication is used mostly in distributed systems. Though becoming popular, challenge-response authentication is facing challenges as a result of weaknesses that include user interaction and trial-and-error attacks. The problem with user interaction involves the ability of the user to locate the challenge over usually clattered screens. The user then must quickly type in a response. If a longer than anticipated time elapses, the request may be denied. Based on the degree of security needed, sometimes the user has to remember the long response or sometimes is forced to write it down, and finally the user must transcribe the response and type it in. This is potentially error prone. Some vendors have tried to cushion the user from remembering and typing long strings by automating most of the process either by cut and paste of the challenge and responses or through a low-level automated process where the user response is limited to minimum yes/no responses.

In trial-and-error attacks, the intruders may respond to the challenge with a spirited barrage of trial responses hoping to hit the correct response. With powerful computers set to automatically generate responses in a given time frame, it is potentially possible for the intruder to hit on a correct response within the given time frame.

Also of interest is to remember that in its simplest form, challenge-responses that use passwords can be abused because passwords are comparatively easy to steal. And if transmitted in the clear, passwords can also be intercepted. However, this situation is slightly better in the nonce or digest authentication, the more sophisticated of the two forms of scheme, because the password is not sent in the clear over the network. It is encrypted which enhances security, although not fully hack-proof protection.

10.5.1.4 Combined Approach Authentication

Although basic authentication which uses either names or names and passwords is the most widely used authentication scheme, it is prudent not to rely on just basic authentication. Passwords are often transmitted in the clear from the user to the authentication agent, which leaves the passwords open to interception by hackers. To enhance the security of authentication, it is better sometimes to combine several schemes. One of the most secure authentication methods is to use a random challenge-response exchange using digital signatures. When the user attempts to make a connection, the authentication system, a server or a firewall, sends a random string back as a challenge. The random string is signed using the user's private key and sent back as a response. The authenticating server or firewall can then use the user's public key to verify that the user is indeed the holder of the associated private key [9].

10.5.2 Public Key Authentication

As we discussed in Sect. 2.3.2 and we will later see in the next chapter, the process of public key authentication requires each user of the scheme to first generate a pair of keys and store each in a file. Each key is usually between 1024 and 2048 bits in length. Public-private key pairs are typically created using a key generation utility. As we will discuss in the next chapter, the pair will consist of a user's public and private key pair. The server knows the user's public key because it is published widely. However, only the user has the private key.

Public key systems are used by authentication systems to enhance system security. The centralized authentication server, commonly known as the *access control server* (ACS), is in charge of authentication that uses public key systems. When a user tries to access an ACS, it looks up the user's public keys and uses it to send a challenge to the user. The server expects a response to the challenge where the user must use his or her private key. If the user then signs the response using his or her private key, he or she is authenticated as legitimate.

To enhance public key security, the private key never leaves the user's machine and, therefore, cannot be stolen or guessed like a password can. In addition, the private key has a *passphrase* associated with it; so even if the private key is stolen, the attacker must still guess the passphrase in order to gain access. The ACS is used in several authentication schemes including SSL, Kerberos, and MD5 authentication.

10.5.2.1 Secure Sockets Layer (SSL) Authentication

Secure Sockets Layer (SSL) is an industry standard protocol designed by Netscape Communications Corporation for securing network connections. SSL provides authentication, encryption, and data integrity using public key infrastructure (PKI). SSL authentication, being cryptographic-based, uses a public/private key pair that must be generated before the process can begin. Communicating elements acquire verification certificates from a *certificate authority* (CA).

> A certificate authority is a trusted third party, between any two communicating elements such as network servers, that certifies that the other two or more entities involved in the intercommunication, including individual users, databases, administrators, clients, servers, are who they say they are. The certificate authority certifies each user by verifying each user's identity and grants a certificate, signing it with the certificate authority's private key. Upon verification, the certificate authority then publishes its own certificate which includes its public key. Each network entity, server, database, and others gets a list of certificates from all the trusted CAs and it consults this list every time there is a communicating user entity that needs authentication. With the CA's issued certificate, the CA guarantees that anything digitally signed using that certificate is legal. As we will see in the next chapter, sometimes it is possible to also get a private key along with the certificate, if the user does not want to generate the corresponding private key from the certificate. As e-commerce picks up momentum, there is an increasing need for a number of creditable companies to sign up as CAs. And indeed many are signing up. If the trend continues, it is likely that the use of digital certificates issued and verified by a CA as part of a public key infrastructure (PKI) is likely to become a standard for future e-commerce.

These certificates are signed by calculating a checksum over the certificate and encrypting the checksum and other information using the private key of a signing certificate. User certificates can be created and signed by a signing certificate which can be used in the SSL protocol for authentication purposes. The following steps are needed for an SSL authentication [10]:

- The user initiates a connection to the server by using SSL.
- SSL performs the handshake between client and server.
- If the handshake is successful, the server verifies that the user has the appropriate authorization to access the resource.

The SSL handshake consists of the following steps [10]:

- The client and server establish which authenticating algorithm to use.
- The server sends its certificate to the client. The client verifies that the server's certificate was signed by a trusted CA. Similarly, if client authentication is required, the client sends its own certificate to the server. The server verifies that the client's certificate was signed by a trusted CA.
- The client and server exchange key material using public key cryptography (see more of this in the next chapter), and from this material, they each generate a session key. All subsequent communication between client and server is encrypted and decrypted by using this set of session keys and the negotiated cipher suite.

It is also possible to authenticate using a two-way SSL authentication, a form of mutual authentication. In two-way SSL authentication, both the client and server must present a certificate before the connection is established between them.

10.5.2.2 Kerberos Authentication

Kerberos is a network authentication protocol developed at the Massachusetts Institute of Technology (MIT) and designed to provide strong authentication for client/ server applications by using PKI technology. See RFC 1510 for more details on Kerberos. It was designed to authenticate users' requests to the server.

In his paper "The Moron's Guide to Kerberos," Brian Tung, using satire, compares the authentication by Kerberos to that of an individual using a driver's license issued by the Department of Motor Vehicles (DMV). He observes that in each case, personal identity consists of a name and an address and some other information, such as a birth date. In addition, there may be some restrictions on what the named person can do; for instance, he or she may be required to wear corrective lenses while driving. Finally, the identification has a limited lifetime, represented by the expiration date on the card.

He compares this real-life case to the working of Kerberos. Kerberos typically is used when a user on a network is attempting to make use of a network service and the service wants assurance that the user is who he says he is. To that end, just like a merchant would want you to present your driver's license issued by the DMV before he or she issues you with a ticket for the needed service, the Kerberos user gets a ticket that is issued by the Kerberos *authentication server* (AS). The service then examines the ticket to verify the identity of the user. If all checks out, then the user is issued an access ticket [11].

According to Barkley [12], there are five players involved in the Kerberos authentication process: the user, the client who acts on behalf of the user, the key distribution center, the ticket-granting service, and the server providing the requested service. The role of the key distribution center, as we will see in the coming chapter and also Chap. 16, is to play a trusted third party between the two communicating elements, the client and the server. The server, commonly known as the "Kerberos server," is actually the *key distribution center* or the KDC for short. The KDC implements the authentication service (AS) and the ticket-granting service (TGS).

When a user wants a service, the user provides the client with a password. The client then talks to the authentication service to get a *ticket-granting ticket*. This ticket is encrypted with the user's password or with a session key provided by the AS. The client then uses this ticket to talk to the ticket-granting service to verify the user's identity using the ticket-granting ticket. The TGS then issues a ticket for the desired service.

The ticket consists of the:

- Requested server name
- Client name
- Address of the client
- Time the ticket was issued
- Lifetime of the ticket
- Session key to be used between the client and the server
- Some other fields

The ticket is encrypted using the server's secret key and thus cannot be correctly decrypted by the user.

In addition to the ticket, the user must also present to the server an authenticator which consists of the:

- Client name
- Address
- Current time
- Some other fields

The authenticator is encrypted by the client using the session key shared with the server. The authenticator provides a time validation for the credentials.

A user seeking server authentication must then present to the server both the ticket and the authenticator. If the server can properly decrypt both the ticket, when it is presented by the client, and the client's authenticator encrypted using the session key contained in the ticket, the server can have confidence that the user is who he claims to be [12].

The KDC has a copy of every password and/or secret key associated with every user and server, and it issues ticket-granting tickets so users do not have to enter in their passwords every time they wish to connect to a kerberized service or keep a copy of their password around. If the ticket-granting ticket is compromised, an attacker can only masquerade as a user until the ticket expires [13].

Since the KDC stores all user and server secret keys and passwords, it must be well secured and must have stringent access control mechanism. If the secret key database is penetrated, a great deal of damage can occur.

10.5.2.3 MD5 for Authentication

In the previous chapter, we discussed MD5 as one of the standard encryption algorithms in use today. Beyond encryption, MD5 can be used in authentication. In fact, the authentication process using MD5 is very simple. Each user has a file containing a set of keys that are used as input into an MD5 hash. The information being supplied to the authenticating server, such as passwords, has its MD5 checksum calculated using these keys and is then transferred to the authenticating server along with the MD5 hash result. The authenticating server then gets user identity information such as password, obtains the user's set of keys from a key file, and then calculates the MD5 hash value. If the two are in agreement, authentication is successful [11].

10.5.3 Remote Authentication

Remote authentication is used to authenticate users who dial into the ACS from a remote host. This can be done in several ways, including using Secure Remote Procedure Call (RPC), dial-up, and Remote Authentication Dial-In User Service (RADIUS) authentication.

10.5.3.1 Secure RPC Authentication

There are many services, especially Internet services, in which the client may not want to identify itself to the server, and the server may not require any identification from the client. Services falling in this category, like the Network File System (NFS), require stronger security than the other services. Remote Procedure Call (RPC) authentication provides that degree of security. Since the RPC authentication subsystem package is open-ended, different forms and multiple types of authentication can be used by RPC including:

- NULL authentication
- Unix authentication
- Data Encryption Standard (DES) authentication
- DES authentication protocol
- Diffie-Hellman encryption

Servers providing the call services require that users be authenticated for every RPC call keys to servers and clients using any encryption standard.

10.5.3.2 Dial-In Authentication

As in remote calls, passwords are required in dial-in connections. Point-to-point protocol (PPP) is the most common of all dial-in connections, usually over serial lines or ISDN. An authentication process must precede any successful log-in. Dial-in authentication services authenticate the peer device, not the user of the device. There are several dial-in authentication mechanisms. PPP authentication mechanisms, for example, include the Password Authentication Protocol (PAP), the Challenge-Handshake Authentication Protocol (CHAP), and the Extensible Authentication Protocol (EAP) [8]:

- The PAP authentication protocol allows the peer to establish identity to the authenticator in a two-way handshake to establish the link. The link is used to send to the authenticator an initial packet containing the peer name and password. The authenticator responds with authenticate-ACK if everything checks out and the authentication process is complete. PAP is a simple authentication process that sends the peer authentication credentials to the authenticator in the clear, where they can be intercepted by the eavesdropper.
- The CHAP authentication protocol is employed periodically to verify any user who uses a three-way handshake. Like PAP, it uses the handshake to initialize a link. After establishing the link, CHAP requires the peer seeking authentication and the authenticator share a secret text that is never actually sent over the links. The secret is established through a challenge-response. The authenticator first sends a challenge consisting of an identifier, a random number, and a host name of the peer or user. The peer responds to the challenge by using a one-way hash to calculate a value; the secret is the input to the hash. The peer then sends to the authenticator an encrypted identification, the output of the hash, the random number, and the peer name or username. The authenticator verifies these by performing the same encryption and authenticates the peer, if everything checks out. It is possible for a relay attack on a CHAP authentication. So steps must be taken to safeguard the passing of the passwords.
- Extensible protocol supports multiple authentication mechanisms. Like all other PPP authentication mechanisms, a link is first established. The authenticator then first sends a request or requests, with a type field to indicate what is being requested, to the peer seeking authentication. The peer responds with a packet, with a type field, as requested. The authenticator then verifies the content of the packet and grants or denies authentication. EAP is more flexible as it provides a capability for new technologies to be tried.

10.5.3.3 Radius

Remote authentication Dial-in User Service (RADIUS) is a common user protocol that provides user dial-up to the ACS which does the user authentication. Because all information from the remote host travels in the clear, RADIUS is considered to be vulnerable to attacks and therefore not secure. We will discuss RADIUS in detail in Chap. 17.

10.5.4 Anonymous Authentication

Not all users who seek authentication to use system resources always want to use operations that modify entries or access protected attributes or entries that generally require client authentication. Clients who do not intend to perform any of these operations typically use anonymous authentication. Mostly these users are not indigenous users in a sense that they do not have membership to the system they want access to. In order to give them access to some system resources, for example, to a company Web site, these users, usually customers, are given access to the resources via a special "anonymous" account. System services that are used by many users who are not indigenous, such as the World Wide Web service or the FTP service, must include an anonymous account to process anonymous requests. For example, Windows Internet Information Services (IIS) creates the anonymous account for Web services, IUSR_ *machinename,* during its setup. By default, all Web client requests use this account, and clients are given access to Web content when they use it. You can enable both anonymous logon access and authenticated access at the same time [14].

10.5.5 Digital Signature-Based Authentication

Digital signature-based authentication is yet another authentication technique that does not require passwords and usernames. A *digital signature* is a cryptographic scheme used by the message recipient and any third party to verify the sender's identity and/or message on authenticity. It consists of an electronic signature that uses public key infrastructure (PKI) to verify the identity of the sender of a message or of the signer of a document. The scheme may include a number of algorithms and functions including the Digital Signature Algorithm (DSA), Elliptic Curve Digital Signature and Algorithm (ECDSA), account authority digital signature, authentication function, and signing function [6, 7].

The idea of a digital signature is basically the same as that of a handwritten signature, to authenticate the signer. It is used to authenticate the fact that what has been promised by a signature can't be taken back later. Like a paper signature, the digital signature creates a legal and psychological link between the signer of the message and the message.

As we will discuss in detail in the next chapter, since digital signatures use PKI, both a public key and a private key must be acquired in order to use the scheme. The private key is kept and used by the signer to sign documents. The person who verifies the document then uses the signer's corresponding public key to make sure the signer is who he or she claims to be. With keys, the user sends the authentication request to the ACS. Upon receipt of the request, the server uses its private key to decrypt the request. Again, as we will discuss in Chap. 10, both these keys are only mathematically related, so knowing the public key to verify the signer's signature does not require knowledge of the signer's private key. Many times, it is very difficult to compute one key from the knowledge of the other.

10.5.6 Wireless Authentication

Because of the growing use of wireless technology and its current low security, there is a growing need for wireless network authentication for mobile devices as they connect to fixed network as well as mobile networks. The IEEE 802.1X, through its Extensible Authentication Protocol (WEP), has built in authentication for mobile unit users. This authentication requires Wi-Fi mobile units to authenticate with network operating systems such as Windows XP.

10.6 Developing an Authentication Policy

Although in many organizations, the type of authentication used is not part of the security policy, which means that the rank and file of the users in the organization do not have a say in what authentication policy is used, it is becoming increasingly popular nowadays to involve as wide a spectrum of users as possible in as much detail of security as possible.

This means an early involvement of most users in the development of the authentication policy. Sometimes it even requires input from business and IT representative communities that do business with the organization. This is sometimes key to ensuring acceptance and compliance by those communities. Paul Brooke lists the following steps as necessary for a good authentication policy [15]:

- List and categorize the resources that need to be accessed, whether these resources are data or systems. Categorize them by their business sensitivity and criticality.
- Define the requirements for access to each of the above categories taking into account both the value of the resource in the category and the method of access (such as LAN, Internet, or dial-up). For example, as Brooke notes, common internal resources, such as e-mail or file and print systems, might require that the single-factor authentication included in the operating system is sufficient as long as the access is via the internal LAN.
- Set requirements for passwords and IDs. Every authentication policy should clearly state requirements for the following:
  - *ID format*: Authentication policies should strive to employ as universal an ID format as possible to make the management of IDs and passwords much easier.
  - *Complexity*: Whether to require nonalphabetic characters or not in the passwords.
  - *Length*: Stating the minimum and maximum password lengths.
  - *Aging*: Stating the frequency in changing passwords.
  - *Reuse*: How frequently a password can be reused.
  - *Administrative access*: Whether there will be special requirements for superuser passwords.

– *Defaults*: To allow default passwords for vendors and other special interest users.
– *Guest and shared accounts*: To decide if guest accounts will be used. If so, are there any special administration, password, or authentication requirements?
– *Storage*: Required storage for passwords. This is important for the storage of encrypted or hashed passwords.
– *Transmission*: To decide on the requirements for transmission of passwords; is clear-text transmission of passwords during authentication or is encryption required?
– *Replication*: To decide on the requirements for replication of password databases; how often must it occur, and are there any special requirements for transmission?
• Create and implement processes for the management of authentication systems.
• Communicate policies and procedures to all concerned in the organizations and outside it. The creation of policies and procedures has no value unless the community regulated by them is made aware. Compliance cannot be expected if people are not conscious of the requirements.

Exercises

1. Authentication is based on three factors. List the factors and discuss why each one determines which type of authentication to use.
2. Making an authentication policy must be a well-kept secret to ensure the security of the intended system. Why then is it so important that a security policy include an authentication policy that involves as many as possible? What kind of people must be left out?
3. In RPC authentication, why it is necessary that each client request that server services be authenticated by the authentication server?
4. The Kerberos authentication process actually involves two tickets. Explain the need for each ticket and why only one ticket cannot be used.
5. Discuss in detail the role played by each one of the five players in a Kerberos authentication process.
6. There are many compelling reasons why a system that must implement security to the maximum must give anonymous authentication to a class of users. Detail five of these reasons.
7. Does anonymous authentication compromise the security of systems for the advantages of a few services?
8. Discuss the role of certificate authentication in e-commerce.
9. Many predict that the future of e-commerce is pegged on the successful implementation of authentication. Discuss.
10. Discuss the role of public key authentication in the growth of e-commerce.

Advanced Exercises

1. Research and discuss the much talked about role of public key authentication in the future of e-commerce. Is the role of PKI in authentication exaggerated?
2. Study the dial-in authentication mechanisms. What mechanisms (discuss five) can be used in EAP?
3. Discuss the benefits of enhancement of basic authentication with a cryptographic scheme such as Kerberos, SSL, and others. Give specific examples.
4. Authentication using certificates, although considered safe, suffers from weaknesses. Discuss these weaknesses using specific examples.
5. Kerberos and SSL are additional layers to enhance authentication. Detail how these enhancements are achieved in both cases.

References

1. Pipkin DL (2000) Information security: protecting the global enterprise. Prentice Hall, Upper Saddle River
2. Holden G (2004) Guide to firewalls and network security: intrusion detection and VPNs. Thomason Learning, Boston
3. The Rainbow Books. National Computer Security Center, http://fas.org/irp/nsa/rainbow.htm
4. Marshall B. Consider your options for authentication. http://www.passwordresearch.com/files/TipsforAvoidingBadQuestions.pdf
5. Cryptography Research Group – Projects. http://www.research.ibm.com/security/projects.html
6. Galbraith S, Mao W Invisibility and anonymity of undeniable and consumer signatures. http://www-uk.hpl.hp.com/people/wm/papers/InAnRSA.pdf
7. Glossary of Terms. http://www.asuretee.com/developers/authentication-terms.shtm
8. Kaeo M (1999) Designing network security: a practical guide to creating a secure network infrastructure. Cisco Press, Indianapolis
9. Digital Signature Authentication. https://www.google.com/patents/US20080222049
10. Configuring SSL Authentication. Oracle advance security administrator's guide release 8.1.5. A677–01. http://www.csee.umbc.edu/help/oracle8/network.815/a67766/09_ssl.htm
11. Tung B. The Moron's Guide to Kerberos. http://www.isi.edu/~brian/security/kerberos.html
12. Barkley J. Robust authentication procedures. http://csrc.nist.gov/publications/nistpubs/800–7/node166.html
13. General Information on Kerberos. http://www.cmf.nrl.navy.mil/CCS/people/kenh/kerberos-faq.html#tgttgs
14. Winkelmeyer R. Explaining Certificate Authentication – 101 Style July 14. https://blog.winkelmeyer.com/2014/07/explaining-certificate-authentication-101-style/
15. Brooke P. Setting the stage for authentication network computing. http://www.networkcomputing.com/1211/1211ws22.html

Cryptography

11

11.1 Definition

So much has been said and so much has been gained; thousands of lives have been lost, and empires have fallen because a secret was not kept. Efforts to keep secrets have been made by humans probably since the beginning of humanity itself. Long ago, humans discovered the essence of secrecy. The art of keeping secrets resulted in victories in wars and in growth of mighty empires. Powerful rulers learned to keep secrets and pass information without interception; that was the beginning of cryptography. Although the basic concepts of cryptography predate the Greeks, the present word *cryptography*, used to describe the art of secret communication, comes from the Greek meaning "secret writing." From its rather simple beginnings, cryptography has grown in tandem with technology, and its importance has also similarly grown. Just as in its early days, good cryptographic prowess still wins wars.

As we get dragged more and more into the new information society, the kind of face-to-face and paper-traceable communication that characterized the nondigital communication before the information revolution, the kind of communication that guaranteed personal privacy and security, is increasingly becoming redefined into the new information society where faceless digital communication regimes are guaranteeing neither information and personal security nor personal privacy. Centuries old and trusted global transactions and commercial systems that guaranteed business exchange and payment systems are being eroded and replaced with difficult to trust and easily counterfeitable electronic systems. The technological and communication revolution has further resulted in massive global surveillance of millions of individuals and many times innocent ones by either their governments or private companies; the fight for personal privacy has never been any more fierce, and the integrity and confidentiality of data have become more urgent than ever before. The security and trust of digital transaction systems have become of critical importance as more and more organizations and businesses join

© Springer International Publishing AG 2017
J.M. Kizza, *Guide to Computer Network Security*, Computer Communications and Networks, DOI 10.1007/978-3-319-55606-2_11

Table 11.1 Modern cryptographic security services

Security services	Cryptographic mechanism to achieve the service
Confidentiality	Symmetric encryption
Authentication	Digital signatures and digital certificates
Integrity	Decryption of digital signature with a public key to obtain the message digest. The message is hashed to create a second digest. If the digests are identical, the message is authentic, and the signer's identity is proven
Nonrepudiation	Digital signatures of a hashed message then encrypting the result with the private key of the sender, thus binding the digital signature to the message being sent
Nonreplay	Encryption, hashing, and digital signature

the e-commerce train. The very future of global commerce is at stake in this new information society unless and until the security of e-commerce can be guaranteed.

Cryptography is being increasingly used to fight off this massive invasion of individual privacy and security, to guarantee data integrity and confidentiality, and to bring trust in global e-commerce. Cryptography has become the main tool for providing the needed digital security in the modern digital communication medium that far exceeds the kind of security that was offered by any medium before it. It guarantees authorization, authentication, integrity, confidentiality, and nonrepudiation in all communications and data exchanges in the new information society. Table 11.1 shows how cryptography guarantees these security services through five basic mechanisms that include symmetric and public key encryption, hashing, digital signatures, and certificates.

A cryptographic system consists of four essential components [1]:

- Plaintext—the original message to be sent
- Cryptographic system (cryptosystem) or a cipher—consisting of mathematical encryption and decryption algorithms
- Ciphertext—the result of applying an encryption algorithm to the original message before it is sent to the recipient
- Key—a string of bits used by the two mathematical algorithms in encrypting and decrypting processes

A cipher or a cryptosystem is a pair of invertible functions, one for encrypting or enciphering and the other for decrypting or deciphering. The word *cipher* has its origin in an Arabic word *sifr,* meaning *empty* or *zero.* The encryption process uses the cryptographic algorithm, known as the encryption algorithm, and a selected key to transform the plaintext data into an encrypted form called ciphertext, usually unintelligible form. The ciphertext can then be transmitted across the communication channels to the intended destination.

A cipher can either be a stream cipher or a block cipher. Stream ciphers rely on a key derivation function to generate a key stream. The key and an algorithm are then applied to each bit, one at a time. Even though stream ciphers are faster and smaller to implement, they have an important security gap. If the same key stream is used, certain types of attacks may cause the information to be revealed. Block ciphers, on the other hand, break a message up into chunks and combine a key with each chunk, for example, 64 or 128 bits of text. Since most modern ciphers are block ciphers, let us look at those in more details.

11.1.1 Block Ciphers

Block ciphers operate on combinations of blocks of plaintext and ciphertext. The block size is usually 64 bits, but operating on blocks of 64 bits (8 bytes) is not always useful and may be vulnerable to simple cryptanalysis attacks. This is so because the same plaintext always produces the same ciphertext. Such block encryption is especially vulnerable to replay attacks. To solve this problem, it is common to apply the ciphertext from the previous encrypted block to the next block in a sequence into a combination resulting into a final ciphertext stream. Also to prevent identical messages encrypted on the same day from producing identical ciphertext, an *initialization vector* derived from a *random number generator* is combined with the text in the first block and the key. This ensures that all subsequent blocks result in ciphertext that doesn't match that of the first encrypting.

Several block cipher combination modes of operation are in use today. The most common ones are described below [2]:

- Electronic Codebook (ECB) mode—this is the simplest block cipher mode of operation in which one block of plaintext always produces the same block of ciphertext. This weakness makes it easy for the cryptanalysts to break the code and easily decrypt that ciphertext block whenever it appears in a message. This vulnerability is greatest at the beginning and end of messages, where well-defined headers and footers contain common information about the sender, receiver, and date.
- Cipher Block Chaining (CBC) mode is a mode of operation for a block cipher that uses what is known as an initialization vector (IV) of a certain length. One of its key characteristics is that it uses a chaining mechanism that causes the decryption of a block of ciphertext to depend on all the preceding ciphertext blocks. As a result, the entire validity of all preceding blocks is contained in the immediately previous ciphertext block. A single bit error in a ciphertext block affects the decryption of all subsequent blocks. Rearrangement of the order of the ciphertext blocks causes decryption to become corrupted. Basically, in cipher block chaining, each plaintext block is XORed (exclusive ORed) with the immediately previous ciphertext block and then encrypted.
- Cipher Feedback (CFB) is similar to the previous CBC in that the following data is combined with previous data so that identical patterns in the plaintext result in different patterns in the ciphertext. However, the difference between CBC and CFB is that in CFB data is encrypted a byte at a time and each byte is encrypted along with the previous 7 bytes of ciphertext.

- Output Feedback (OFB) is a mode similar to the CFB in that it permits encryption of differing block sizes but has the key difference that the output of the encryption block function is the feedback, not the ciphertext. The XOR value of each plaintext block is created independently of both the plaintext and ciphertext. Also like CFB, OFB uses an initialization vector (IV) and changing the IV in the same plaintext block results in different ciphertext streams. It has no chaining dependencies. One problem with it is that the plaintext can be easily altered.

While cryptography is the art of keeping messages secret, *cryptanalysis* is the art of breaking cipher codes and retrieving the plaintext from the ciphertext without knowing the proper key. The process of cryptanalysis involves a cryptanalyst studying the ciphertext for patterns that can lead to the recovery of either the key or the plaintext. Ciphertexts can also be cracked by an intruder through the process of guessing the key.

This is an exhaustive trial-and-error technique which with patience or luck, whichever works first, may lead to the key. Although this seems to be difficult, with today's fast computers, this approach is becoming widely used by hackers than ever before.

The power of cryptography lies in the degree of difficulty in cracking the ciphertext back into plaintext after it has been transmitted through either protected or unprotected channels. The beauty of a strong encryption algorithm is that the ciphertext can be transmitted across naked channels without fear of interception and recovery of the original plaintext. The decryption process also uses a key and a decryption algorithm to recover the plaintext from the ciphertext. The hallmark of a good cryptographic system is that the security of the whole system does not depend on either the encryption or decryption algorithms but rather on the secrecy of the key. This means that the encryption algorithm may be known and used several times and by many people as long as the key is kept a secret. This further means that the best way to crack an encryption is to get hold of the key.

Key-based encryption algorithm can either be symmetric, also commonly known as conventional encryption, or asymmetric, also known as public key encryption. Symmetric algorithms are actually secret key based, where both the encryption and decryption algorithms use this same key for encryption and decryption. Asymmetric or public key algorithms, unlike symmetric ones, use a different key for encryption and decryption, and the decryption key cannot be derived from the encryption key.

11.2   Symmetric Encryption

Symmetric encryption or secret key encryption, as it is usually called, uses a common key and the same cryptographic algorithm to scramble and unscramble the message as shown in Figs. 11.1 and 11.2. The transmitted final ciphertext stream

Fig. 11.1 Symmetric encryption

Fig. 11.2 Encryption and decryption with symmetric cryptography

is usually a chained combination of blocks of the plaintext, the secret key, and the ciphertext.

The security of the transmitted data depends on the assumption that eavesdroppers and cryptanalysts with no knowledge of the key are unable to read the message. However, for a symmetric encryption scheme to work, the key must be shared between the sender and the receiver. The sharing is usually done through passing the key from the sender to the receiver. This presents a problem in many different ways, as we will see in Sect. 11.2.2. The question which arises is how to keep the key secure while being transported from the sender to the receiver.

Symmetric algorithms are faster than their counterparts, the public key algorithms.

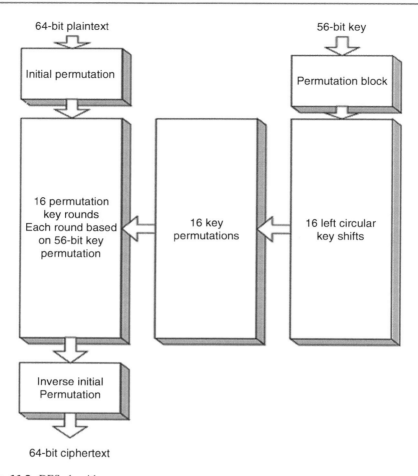

Fig. 11.3 DES algorithm

11.2.1 Symmetric Encryption Algorithms

The most widely used symmetric encryption method in the United States is the block ciphers Triple Data Encryption Standard (3DES). Triple DES developed from the original, and now cracked DES uses a 64-bit key consisting of 56 effective key bits and 8 parity bits. Triple DES encrypts the data in 8-byte chunks, passing it through 16 different iterations consisting of complex shifting, exclusive ORing, substitution, and expansion of the key along with the 64-bit data blocks. Figure 11.3 shows how Triple DES works.

Although 3DES is complicated and complex, and therefore secure, it suffers from several drawbacks including the length of its key fixed at 56 bits plus 8 bits of parity. The limited key length is making it possible for the ever-increasing speed of

Table 11.2 Symmetric
key algorithms

Algorithm	Strength	Features (key length)
3DES	Strong	64, 112, 168
AES	Strong	128, 192, 256
IDEA	Strong	64, 128
Blowfish	Weak	32–448
RC4	Weak	
RC5	Strong	32, 64, 128
BEST	Strong	
CAST-128	Strong	32, 128

See more of these algorithms at https://en.wikipedia.org/wiki/Symmetric-key_algorithm

newer computers to render it useless as it possible to compute all possible combinations in the range $0–2^{56} – 1$.

Because of this, the National Institute of Standards and Technology (NIST) has presented the Advanced Encryption Standard (AES), which is expected to replace DES. AES is Advanced Encryption Standard whose algorithm was decided to be Rijndael, developed by two Belgian researchers, Joan Daemen and Vincent Rijmen.

Several other symmetric encryption algorithms in use today include International Data Encryption Algorithm (IDEA), Blowfish, Rivest Cipher 4 (RC4), RC5, and CAST-128. See Table 11.2 for symmetric key algorithms.

11.2.2 Problems with Symmetric Encryption

As we pointed out earlier, symmetric encryption, although fast, suffers from several problems in the modern digital communication environment. These are a direct result of the nature of symmetric encryption. Perhaps the biggest problem is that a single key must be shared in pairs of each sender and receiver. In a distributed environment with large numbers of combination pairs involved in many-to-one communication topology, it is difficult for the one recipient to keep so many keys in order to support all communication.

In addition to the key distribution problem above, the size of the communication space presents problems. Because of the massive potential number of individuals who can carry on communication in a many-to-one, one-to-many, and many-to-many topologies supported by the Internet, for example, the secret key cryptography, if strictly used, requires billions of secret key pairs to be created, shared, and stored. This can be a nightmare! Large numbers of potential correspondents in the many-to-one, one-to-many, and many-to-many communication topologies may cause symmetric encryption to fail because of its requirement of prior relationships with the parties to establish the communication protocols like the setting up of and acquisition of the secret key.

Besides the problems discussed above and as a result of them, the following additional problems are also observable:

- The integrity of data can be compromised because the receiver cannot verify that the message has not been altered before receipt.
- It is possible for the sender to repudiate the message because there are no mechanisms for the receiver to make sure that the message has been sent by the claimed sender.
- The method does not give a way to ensure secrecy even if the encryption process is compromised.
- The secret key may not be changed frequently enough to ensure confidentiality.

11.3 Public Key Encryption

Since the symmetric encryption scheme suffered from all those problems we have just discussed above, there was a need for a more modern cryptographic scheme to address these flaws. The answers came from two people: Martin Hellman and Whitfield Diffie, who developed a method that seemed to solve at least the first two problems and probably all four by guaranteeing secure communication without the need for a secret key. Their scheme, consisting of mathematical algorithms, led to what is known as a *public key encryption* (PKE).

Public key encryption, commonly known asymmetric encryption, uses two different keys, a public key known to all and a private key known only to the sender and the receiver. Both the sender and the receiver own a pair of keys, one public and the other a closely guarded private one. To encrypt a message from sender A to receiver B, as shown in Fig. 11.4, both A and B must create their own pairs of keys. Then A and B publicize their public keys—anybody can acquire them. When A has to send a message M to B, A uses B's public key to encrypt M. On receipt of M, B then uses his or her private key to decrypt the message M. As long as only B, the recipient, has access to the private key, then A, the sender, is assured that only B, the recipient, can decrypt the message. This ensures data confidentiality. Data integrity is also ensured because for data to be modified by an attacker, it requires the attacker to have B's, the recipient's, private key. Data confidentiality and integrity in public key encryption are also guaranteed in Fig. 11.4.

As can be seen, ensuring data confidentiality and integrity does not prevent a third party, unknown to both communicating parties, from pretending to be A, the sender. This is possible because anyone can get A's, the sender's public key. This weakness must, therefore, be addressed, and the way to do so is through guaranteeing of sender nonrepudiation and user authentication. This is done as follows: after both A and B have created their own pairs of keys and exchanged the public key pair, A, the sender, then encrypts the message to be sent to B, the recipient, using the sender's private key. Upon receipt of the encrypted message, B, the recipient, then uses A's, the sender's public key to encrypt the message. The return route is also similar. This is illustrated in Fig. 11.5. Authentication of users is ensured because only the sender and recipient have access to their private keys. And

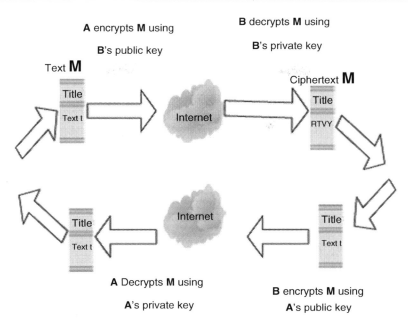

Fig. 11.4 Public key encryption with data integrity and confidentiality

unless their keys have been compromised, both cannot deny or repudiate sending the messages.

To ensure all four aspects of security, that is, data confidentiality and integrity and authentication and nonrepudiation of users, a double encryption is required as illustrated in Fig. 11.6.

The core of public key encryption is that no secret key is passed between two communicating parties. This means that this approach can support all communication topologies including one-to-one, one-to-many, many-to-many, and many-to-one, and along with it, several to thousands of people can communicate with one party without exchange of keys. This makes it suitable for Internet communication and electronic commerce applications. Its other advantage is that it solves the chronic repudiation problem experienced by symmetric encryption. This problem is solved, especially in large groups, by the use of digital signatures and certificates.

The various cryptographic algorithms used in this scheme rely on the degree of computational difficulty encountered as an attempt is made to recover the keys. These algorithms, as we will see in Sect. 11.4, should be labor intensive, and the amount and difficulty involved should, and actually always, increase with the key length. The longer the key, the more difficult and the longer it should take to guess the key, usually the private key.

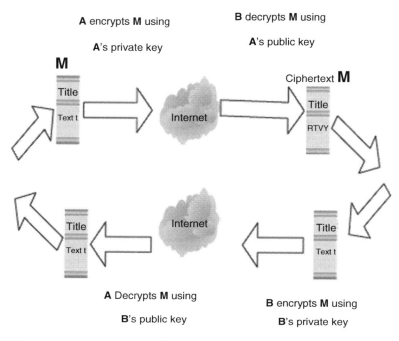

Fig. 11.5 Authentication and nonrepudiation

Fig. 11.6 Ensuring data confidentiality and integrity and user authentication and nonrepudiation

11.3.1 Public Key Encryption Algorithms

Various algorithms exist for public key encryption including RSA, DSA, PGP, and El Gamal. Table 11.3 shows the features of such algorithms.

Table 11.3 Public key algorithms

Algorithm	Strength	Features (key length)
RSA	Strong	768, 1024
ElGamal	Strong	768, 1024
DSA	Strong	512–1024
Diffie-Hellman	Strong	768, 1024

See more public key algorithms at https://en.wikipedia.org/wiki/Public-key_cryptography

11.3.2 Problems with Public Key Encryption

Although public key encryption seems to have solved the major chronic encryption problems of key exchange and message repudiation, it still has its own problems. The biggest problem for public key cryptographic scheme is speed. Public key algorithms are extremely slow compared to symmetric algorithms. This is because public key calculations take longer than symmetric key calculations since they involve the use of exponentiation of very large numbers which in turn take longer to compute. For example, the fastest public key cryptographic algorithm such as RSA is still far slower than any typical symmetric algorithm. This makes these algorithms and the public key scheme less desirable for use in cases of long messages.

In addition to speed, public key encryption algorithms have a potential to suffer from the *man-in-the-middle* attack. The man-in-the-middle attack is a well-known attack, especially in the network community where an attacker sniffs packets off a communication channel, modifies them, and inserts them back on to the channel. In case of an encryption channel attack, the intruder convinces one of the correspondents that the intruder is the legitimate communication partner.

11.3.3 Public Key Encryption Services

As it strives to solve the flaws that have plagued other encryption schemes, public key encryption scheme offers the following services:

- Secrecy which makes it extremely difficult for an intruder who is able to intercept the ciphertext to be able to determine its corresponding plaintext. See Fig. 11.4.
- Authenticity which makes it possible for the recipient to validate the source of a message. See Fig. 11.4.
- Integrity which makes it possible to ensure that the message sent cannot be modified in any way during transmission. See Fig. 11.5.
- Nonrepudiation which makes it possible to ensure that the sender of the message cannot later turn around and disown the transmitted message. See Fig. 11.5.

11.4 Enhancing Security: Combining Symmetric and Public Key Encryptions

As we noted in Sect. 11.2.2, symmetric algorithms, although faster than public key algorithms, are beset with a number of problems. Similarly public key encryption also suffers slowness and the potential of the "man-in-the-middle" attacker. To address these concerns and to preserve both efficiency and privacy of the communication channel and increase the performance of the system, a hybrid cryptosystem that uses the best of both and at the same time mitigating the worst in each system is widely used.

11.5 Key Management: Generation, Transportation, and Distribution

One would have thought that the development of advanced technologies would already have solved the chronic problem of exchanging a secret key between two communicating entities. However, one must seriously think that technology is created by humans and humans are part of any technology. But humans also naturally form the weakest links in any technology. They are very unpredictable in what they are likely to do and why they do what they do. Key exchange in cryptographic technologies would not have been a problem, but because of humans, it is.

In a small communication network based on a one-to-one communication topology, the key exchange probably would not be such a problem. However, in modern large networks that support many-to-one, many-to-many, and one-to-many communication topologies, the creation, distribution, and security of millions of keys boil down to a nightmare.

11.5.1 The Key Exchange Problem

In Sect. 11.2.2 we saw that although symmetric encryption is commonly used due to its historical position in the cryptography and its speed, it suffers from a serious problem of how to safely and secretly deliver a secret key from the sender to the recipient. This problem forms the basis for the *key exchange problem*. The *key exchange problem* involves [2] the following:

- Ensuring that keys are exchanged so that the sender and receiver can perform encryption and decryption
- Ensuring that an eavesdropper or outside party cannot break the code
- Ensuring the receiver that a message was encrypted by the sender

The strength of an encryption algorithm lies in its key distribution techniques. Poor key distribution techniques create an ideal environment for a man-in-the-middle attack. The key exchange problem, therefore, highlights the need for strong key distribution techniques. Even though the key exchange problem is more prominent in the symmetric encryption cryptographic methods, and it is basically solved by the public key cryptographic methods, some key exchange problems still remain in public key cryptographic methods. For example, symmetric key encryption requires the two communicating parties to have agreed upon their secret key ahead of time before communicating, and public key encryption suffers from the difficulty of securely obtaining the public key of the recipient. However, both of these problems can be solved using a trusted third party or an intermediary. For symmetric key cryptography, the trusted intermediary is called a *key distribution center* (KDC). For public key cryptography, the trusted and scalable intermediary is called a *certificate authority* (CA). See the side bar in Sect. 9.5.2.2 for a definition of a certificate authority.

Another method relies on users to distribute and track each other's keys and trust in an informal, distributed fashion. This has been popularized as a viable alternative by the PGP software which calls the model the *Web of trust* [2].

11.5.2 Key Distribution Centers (KDCs)

A key distribution center (KDC) is a single, trusted network entity with which all network-communicating elements must establish a shared secret key. It requires all communicating elements to have a shared secret key with which they can communicate with the KDC confidentially. However, this requirement still presents a problem of distributing this shared key. The KDC does not create or generate keys for the communicating elements; it only stores and distributes keys. The creation of keys must be done somewhere else. Diffie-Hellman is the commonly used algorithm to create secret keys, and it provides the way to distribute these keys between the two communicating parties. But since the Diffie-Hellman exchange suffers from the man-in-the-middle attacks, it is best used with a public key encryption algorithm to ensure authentication and integrity. Since all network-communicating elements confidentially share their secret keys with the KDC, it distributes these keys secretly to the corresponding partners in the communication upon request. Any network element that wants to communicate with any other element in the network using symmetric encryption schemes uses the KDC to obtain the shared keys needed for that communication. Figure 11.7 shows the working of the KDC.

Stallings [3] has a very good scenario which describes the working of the KDC, and he describes this working as follows. First both the message sender A and the message receiver B each must have a secret key they each share with the KDC. A initiates the communication process by sending a request to the KDC for a session key and B's secret key. The KDC responds to this request by sending a two-part packet to A. The first part to be sent to A consists of A's request to the KDC, B's secret key, and a session key. The second part, to be sent to B, consists of A's identity and a copy of the session key given to A. Since the packet is to be sent to A,

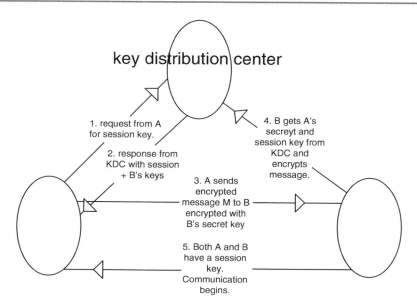

Fig. 11.7 The working of a KDC

it is encrypted by the secret key the KDC shares with A. When A receives the
packet, A then gets out B's secret key and encrypts the message together with B's
part of the packet with B's secret key and sends it to B. On receipt, B uses the secret
key B shares with the KDC to decrypt the package from A to recover the session
key. Now the session key has been distributed to both A and B. After a few
housekeeping and authentication handshake, communication can begin.

The KDC has several disadvantages including the following:

- The two network-communicating elements must belong to the same KDC.
- Security becomes a problem because a central authority having access to keys is
  vulnerable to penetration. Because of the concentration of trust, a single security
  breach on the KDC would compromise the entire system.
- In large networks that handle all communication topologies, the KDC then
  becomes a bottleneck since each pair of users needing a key must access a
  central node at least once. Also the failure of the central authority could disrupt
  the key distribution system [4].

In large networks with varying communication topologies where network-
communicating elements cannot belong to the same KDC, key distribution may
become a real problem. Such problems are solved by the Public Key Infrastructure
(PKI). We will discuss PKI in Sect. 11.6.

11.5.3 Public Key Management

Because there was a problem with both authenticity and integrity in the distribution of public keys, there was a need to find a solution to this problem. In fact, according to Stallings [3], there were two problems: the distribution of the public keys and the use of public key encryption to distribute the secret key. For the distribution of public keys, there were several solutions including the following:

- Public announcements where any user can broadcast their public keys or send them to selected individuals.
- Public directory which is maintained by a trusted authority. The directory is usually dynamic to accommodate additions and deletions.
- Certificate authority (CA) to distribute certificates to each communicating element. Each communicating element in a network or system communicates securely with the CA to register its public key with the CA. Since public keys are already in public arena, the registration may be done using a variety of techniques including the postal service.

11.5.3.1 Certificate Authority (CA)

The CA then certifies that a public key belongs to a particular entity. The entity may be a person or a server in a network. The certified public key, if one can safely trust the CA that certified the key, can then be used with confidence. Certifying a key by the CA actually binds that key to a particular network-communicating element which validates that element. In a wide area network such as the Internet, CAs are equivalent to the digital world's passport offices because they issue digital certificates and validate the holder's identity and authority. Just as the passport in the real world has embedded information about you, the certificate issued by the CAs has an individual's or an organization's public key along with other identifying information embedded in it and then cryptographically time-stamped, signed, and tamper-proof sealed. It can then be used to verify the integrity of the data within it and to validate this data whenever it is presented. A CA has the following roles [5]:

- It authenticates a communicating element to the other communicating parties that that element is what it says it is. However, one can trust the identity associated with a public key only to the extent that one can trust a CA and its identity verification techniques.
- Once the CA verifies the identity of the entity, the CA creates a *digital certificate* that binds the public key of the element to the identity. The certificate contains the public key and other identifying information about the owner of the public key (e.g., a human name or an IP address). The certificate is digitally signed by the CA.

Since CA verifies the validity of the communicating elements' certificates, it is in charge of enrolling, distributing, and revoking certificates. Because certificates are issued by many different CAs, much of the format of certificates has been defined to ensure validity, manageability, and consistence in the scheme.

To lessen the activities of the CA and therefore improve on the performance of the CA, users who acquire certificates become responsible for managing their own certificates. In doing so, any user who initiates a communication must provide his or her certificate and other identifying information such as a date and random number and send it to the recipient together with a request for the recipient's certificate. Upon receipt of these documents, the recipient sends his or her certificate. Each party then validates each other's certificate, and upon approval by either party, communication begins.

During the validation process, each user may periodically check the CA's lists of certificates which have become invalid before their expiration dates due to key compromise or administrative reasons. Since this may require online access to the CA's central facility, this may sometimes create a bottleneck.

11.5.3.2 Digital Certificates

A digital certificate is a digitally signed message used to attest to the validity of the public key of a communicating element. As we pointed out, digital certificates must adhere to a format. Most digital certificates follow the International Telecommunication Union (ITU-T) X.509 standard. According to RFC 1422, the X.509 digital certificate has the following fields as shown in Table 11.4 and in a sample in Fig. 11.8.

In modern communication, the use of certificates has become common and vital to the security of such communications. For example, in a network environment, in order to encrypt transmissions to your server, the client requires the server's public key. The integrity of that key is vital to the security of the subsequent sessions. If a third party, for example, were to intercept the communication and replace the legitimate key with his or her own public key, that man-in-the-middle could view all traffic or even modify the data in transit. Neither the client nor the server would detect the intrusion.

So to prevent this, the client demands from the server, and the server sends the public key in a certificate signed by a certificate authority. The client checks that digital signature. If the signature is valid, the client knows that the CA has certified that this is the server's authentic certificate, not a certificate forged by a man-in-the-middle. It is important that the CA be a *trusted* third party in order to provide meaningful authentication.

As we will see in Sect. 11.8, when we discuss digital signatures, digital signatures alone cannot authenticate any message and identify a user without a mechanism to authenticate the public key, a role played by the digital certificate. Similarly a digital certificate alone cannot authenticate a message or identify a user without a digital signature. So in order to get a full authentication of a message and identify the user, one needs both the digital signature and digital certificate, both of them working together.

Table 11.4 The ITU-T X.509 digital certificate format [6]

Field	Purpose
Version number	Most certificates use X.509 version 3
Serial number	Unique number set by a CA
Issuer	Name of the CA
Subject issued certificate	Name of a receiver of the certificate
Validity period	Period in which certificate will valid
Public key algorithm information of the subject of the certificate	Algorithm used to sign the certificate with digital signature
Digital signature of the issuing authority	Digital signature of the certificate signed by CA
Public key	Public key of the subject

Several companies now offer digital certificates—that means they are functioning as CAs. Among those are Verisign, American Express, Netscape, US Postal Service, and CyberTrust.

11.5.3.3 Using a Private Certificate Authority

If a business is running its own intranet, it is a security imperative that the security administrator chooses either a public CA or a private CA. It is also possible for the security administrator to create his or her own CA. If one decides to do this, then care must be taken in doing so. One should consider the following steps [7]:

- Consultation with a security expert before building is essential.
- Do all the CA work offline.
- Because it plays a crucial role in the security of the network, it is important that access, both physical and electronic, to the in-house CA must be highly restricted.
- Protect the CA from all types of surveillance.
- Require users to generate key pairs of adequate sizes, preferably 1024 bit.

If the decision is not to use an in-house CA, then it is important to be careful in choosing a good trusted CA.

11.5.4 Key Escrow

Key escrow is a scheme in which a copy of the secret key is entrusted to a third party. This is similar to entrusting a copy of the key to your house or car to a trusted friend. In itself, it is not a bad idea because you can genuinely lose the key or lock it inside the house or car. So in case of the loss of the main key, a copy can always be retrieved from the friend. For private arrangements such as this, the idea of a key escrow is great. However, in a public communication network like the Internet, the idea is not so good. Key escrow began because, as the Internet become more

```
Certificate:
    Data:
        Version: 3 (0x2)
        Serial Number: 1 (0x1)
        Signature Algorithm: md5WithRSAEncryption
        Issuer: C=ZA, ST=Western Cape, L=Cape Town, O=Thawte Consulting
cc,
                OU=Certification Services Division,
                CN=Thawte Server CA/emailAddress=server-certs@thawte.com
        Validity
            Not Before: Aug  1 00:00:00 1996 GMT
            Not After : Dec 31 23:59:59 2020 GMT
        Subject: C=ZA, ST=Western Cape, L=Cape Town, O=Thawte Consulting
cc,
                OU=Certification Services Division,
                CN=Thawte Server CA/emailAddress=server-
certs@thawte.com
        Subject Public Key Info:
            Public Key Algorithm: rsaEncryption
            RSA Public Key: (1024 bit)
                Modulus (1024 bit):
                    00:d3:a4:50:6e:c8:ff:56:6b:e6:cf:5d:b6:ea:0c:
                    68:75:47:a2:aa:c2:da:84:25:fc:a8:f4:47:51:da:
                    85:b5:20:74:94:86:1e:0f:75:c9:e9:08:61:f5:06:
                    6d:30:6e:15:19:02:e9:52:c0:62:db:4d:99:9e:e2:
                    6a:0c:44:38:cd:fe:be:e3:64:09:70:c5:fe:b1:6b:
                    29:b6:2f:49:c8:3b:d4:27:04:25:10:97:2f:e7:90:
                    6d:c0:28:42:99:d7:4c:43:de:c3:f5:21:6d:54:9f:
                    5d:c3:58:e1:c0:e4:d9:5b:b0:b8:dc:b4:7b:df:36:
                    3a:c2:b5:66:22:12:d6:87:0d
                Exponent: 65537 (0x10001)
        X509v3 extensions:
            X509v3 Basic Constraints: critical
                CA:TRUE
    Signature Algorithm: md5WithRSAEncryption
        07:fa:4c:69:5c:fb:95:cc:46:ee:85:83:4d:21:30:8e:ca:d9:
        a8:6f:49:1a:e6:da:51:e3:60:70:6c:84:61:11:a1:1a:c8:48:
        3e:59:43:7d:4f:95:3d:a1:8b:b7:0b:62:98:7a:75:8a:dd:88:
        4e:4e:9e:40:db:a8:cc:32:74:b9:6f:0d:c6:e3:b3:44:0b:d9:
        8a:6f:9a:29:9b:99:18:28:3b:d1:e3:40:28:9a:5a:3c:d5:b5:
        e7:20:1b:8b:ca:a4:ab:8d:e9:51:d9:e2:4c:2c:59:a9:da:b9:
        b2:75:1b:f6:42:f2:ef:c7:f2:18:f9:89:bc:a3:ff:8a:23:2e:
        70:47
```

Fig. 11.8 Sample X.509 certificates (Image source: http://en.wikipedia.org/wiki/X.509)

accessible, wrong characters and criminals joined in with vices such as money laundering, gambling pornography, and drugs. The US government, at least in public, found it necessary to rein in on organized crime on the Internet. The way to do it, as it was seen at that time, was through a key escrow program, and it was hence born.

Since it was first proposed by government, the key escrow program raised a heated debate between those who feel that the program of key escrow is putting individual privacy at risk and those who argue that law enforcement officials must be given the technological ability and sometimes advantage to fight organized crime on the Internet.

The key escrow debate was crystallized by the Clipper chip. The Clipper chip, funded by the U.S. government, was intended to protect private online and tele-communication communications, while at the same time permitting government agents to obtain the keys upon presentation of legal warrant. The government appointed two government agencies to act as the escrow bodies. These agencies were the NIST and the Treasury Department.

The opposition to the Clipper chip was so strong that government was forced to opt for its use to be voluntary.

11.6   Public Key Infrastructure (PKI)

We saw in Sect. 11.5.2 that in large networks with varying communication topologies where network-communicating elements cannot belong to the same KDC, key distribution becomes a real problem. These problems are solved when a Public Key Infrastructure (PKI) is used instead of KDCs to provide trusted and efficient key and certificate management. What then is this PKI? Merike Kaeo, quoting the Internet X.509 Public Key Infrastructure PKIX, defines public key infrastructure (PKI) as the set of hardware, software, people, policies, and procedures needed to create, manage, store, distribute, and revoke certificates based on public key cryptography [2]. PKI automate all these activities. PKI works best when there is a large mass of users. Under such circumstances, it creates and distributes digital certificates widely to many users in a trusted manner. It is made up of four major pieces: the certificates that represent the authentication token, the CA that holds the ultimate decision on subject authentication, the registration authority (RA) that accepts and processes certificate signing requests on behalf of end users, and the Lightweight Directory Access Protocol (LDAP) directories that hold publicly available certificate information [8].

11.6.1 Certificates

We defined certificates in Sect. 11.5.3.1 as the cryptographic proof that the public key they contain is indeed the one that corresponds to the identity stamped on the same certificate. The validation of the identity of the public key on the certificate is made by the CA that signs the certificate before it is issued to the user. Let us note here for emphasis that public keys are distributed through digital certificates. The X.509 v3 certificate format, as we noted in Sect. 11.5.3.2, has nine fields. The first seven make up the body of the certificate. Any change in these fields may cause the certificate to become invalid. If a certificate becomes invalid, the CA must revoke it. The CA then keeps and periodically updates the certificate revocation list (CRL). End users are, therefore, required to frequently check on the CRL.

11.6.2 Certificate Authority

CAs are vital in PKI technology to authoritatively associate a public key signature with an alleged identity by signing certificates that support the PKI. Although the CAs play an important role in the PKI technology, they must be kept offline and used only to issue certificates to a select number of smaller certification entities. These entities perform most of the day-to-day certificate creation and signature verification.

Since the CAs are offline and given their role in the PKI technology, there must be adequate security for the system on which they are stored so that their integrity is maintained. In addition, the medium containing the CA's secret key itself should be kept separate from the CA host in a highly secure location. Finally, all procedures that involve the handling of the CA private key should be performed by two or more operators to ensure accountability in the event of a discrepancy.

11.6.3 Registration Authority (RA)

The RAs accept and process certificate signing requests from users. Thus, they create the binding among public keys, certificate holders, and other attributes.

11.6.4 Lightweight Directory Access Protocols (LDAP)

These are repositories that store and make available certificates and certificate revocation lists (CRLs). Developed at the University of Michigan, the LDAP was meant to make the access to X.509 directories easier. Other ways of distributing digital certificates are by FTP and HTTP.

11.6.5 Role of Cryptography in Communication

From our discussion so far, you should by now have come to the conclusion that cryptography is a vital component in modern communication and that public key technology, in particular, is widely used and is becoming more and more acknowledged as one of the best ways to secure many applications in e-commerce, e-mail, and VPNs.

11.7 Hash Function

In the previous sections, we have seen how both symmetric and public key encryptions are used to ensure data confidentiality and integrity and also user authentication and nonrepudiation, especially when the two methods are combined. Another way to provide data integrity and authenticity is to use hash functions.

A hash function is a mathematical function that takes an input message M of a given length and creates a unique fixed-length output code. The code, usually a 128-bit or 160-bit stream, is commonly referred to as a hash or a *message digest*. A one-way hash function, a variant of the hash function, is used to create a signature or fingerprint of the message—just like a human fingerprint. On input of a message, the hash function compresses the bits of a message to a fixed-size hash value in a way that distributes the possible messages evenly among the possible hash values. Using the same hash function on the same message always results in the same message digest. Different messages always hash to different message digests.

A cryptographic hash function does this in a way that makes it extremely difficult to come up with two or more messages that would hash to a particular hash value. It is conjectured that the probability of coming up with two messages hashing on the same message digest is of the order of 2^{64} and that of coming up with any message hashing on a given message digest is of the order of 2^{128} [9].

In ensuring data integrity and authenticity, both the sender and the recipient perform the same hash computation using the same hash function on the message before the message is sent and after it has been received. If the two computations of the same hash function on the same message produce the same value, then the message has not been tampered with during transmission.

There are various standard hash functions of message digest length including the 160-bit (SHA-1 and MD5) and 128-bit streams (RSA, MD2, and MD4). Message digest hash algorithms MD2, MD4, and MD5 are credited to Ron Rivest, while Secure Hash Algorithm (SHA) was developed by the NIST. The most popular of these hash algorithms are SHA and MD5. Table 11.5 shows some more details of these algorithms.

11.8 Digital Signatures

While we use the hash functions to ensure the integrity and authenticity of the message, we need a technique to establish the authenticity and integrity of each message and each user so that we ensure the nonrepudiation of the users. This is achieved by the use of a digital signature.

A digital signature is defined as an encrypted message digest, by the private key of the sender, appended to a document to analogously authenticate it, just like the handwritten signature appended on a written document authenticates it. Just like in the handwritten form, a digital signature is used to confirm the identity of the sender and the integrity of the document. It establishes the nonrepudiation of the sender.

Digital signatures are formed using a combination of public key encryption and one-way secure hash function according to the following steps [10]:

- The sender of the message uses the message digest function to produce a message authentication code (MAC).

Table 11.5 Standard hash algorithms

Algorithm	Digest length (bits)	Features (key length)
SHA-1	160	512
MD5	160	512
HMAC-MD5	Version of MD5	512 (key version of MD5)
HMAC-SHA-1	Version of SHA-1	512 (key version of SHA-1)
PIPEND	160	128

See more hash algorithms at https://en.wikipedia.org/wiki/Secure_Hash_Algorithm

- This MAC is then encrypted using the private key and the public key encryption algorithm. This encrypted MAC is attached to the message as the digital signature.

The message is then sent to the receiver. Upon receipt of the message, the recipient then uses his or her public key to decrypt the digital signature. First, the recipient must verify that the message indeed came from the expected sender. This step verifies the sender's signature. It is done via the following steps [2]:

- The recipient separates the received message into two: the original document and the digital signature.
- Using the sender's public key, the recipient then decrypts the digital signature which results in the original MAC.
- The recipient then uses the original document and inputs it to the hash function to produce a new MAC.
- The new MAC is compared with the MAC from the sender for a match.

If these numbers compare, then the message was received unaltered, the data integrity is assured, and the authenticity of the sender is proven. See Fig. 11.9 for the working of a digital signature verification.

Because digital signatures are derived from the message as a digest which is then encrypted, they cannot be separated from the messages they are derived from and remain valid.

Since digital signatures are used to authenticate the messages and identify the senders of those messages, they can be used in a variety of areas where such double confirmation is needed. Anything that can be digitized can be digitally signed. This means that digital signatures can be used with any kind of message, whether it is encrypted or not, to establish the authenticity of the sender and that the message arrived intact. However, digital signatures cannot be used to provide the confidentiality of the message content.

Among the most common digital signature algorithms in use today are the Digital Signature Standard (DSS) proposed by NIST and based on the ElGamal public key algorithm and RSA. DSS is faster than RSA.

Although digital signatures are popular, they are not the only method of authenticating the validity of the sender and the integrity of the message. Because

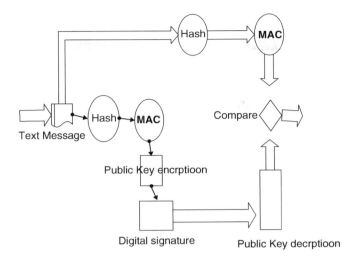

Fig. 11.9 Verifying a digital signature in message authentication

they are very complex, other less complex methods are also in use, especially in the network community. Such methods include the *cyclic redundancy checking* (CRC). In CRC, a digital message is repeatedly divided until a remainder is derived. The remainder, the divisor, along with the message is then transmitted to the recipient. Upon receipt, the recipient would execute the same division process looking for the same remainder. Where the remainder is the same, the recipient is assured that the message has not been tampered with during transmission.

Exercises

1. Discuss the basic components of cryptography.
2. Discuss the weaknesses of symmetric encryption.
3. Discuss the weaknesses of public key encryption.
4. Why is a hybrid cryptosystem preferred over symmetric and public key encryption systems?
5. Why is PKI so vital in modern communications?
6. Discuss the role of digital signatures in modern communication.
7. Some say that with the development of systems such as IPsec, the role the CAs play in modern communication will diminish and eventually cease. Comment on this statement.
8. In a modern communication network, what are the limitations of a tree-structured CA system? Why is it necessary?
9. Discuss the limitations of a KDC system in modern communication.
10. Discuss the future of PKI.

Advanced Exercises

1. Discuss the differences between digital certificates and digital signatures in authentication.
2. Discuss the role and function of a PKI.
3. Describe the sequence of steps a sender of a message takes when sending the message with a digital signature. What steps does the receiver of such a message take to recover the message?
4. Compare and contrast the problems and benefits of KDC and PKI.
5. Describe the message authentication process using:
   (a) Symmetric encryption
   (b) Public key encryption
   (c) Hash function

References

1. Stein LD (1998) Web security: a step-by-step reference guide. Addison-Wesley, Boston
2. Kaeo M (1999) Designing network security. Cisco Press, Indianapolis
3. Stallings W (1999) Cryptography and network security: principles and practice, 2nd edn. Prentice Hall, Upper Saddle River
4. Frame Technology. https://en.wikipedia.org/wiki/Frame_technology_(software_engineering)
5. Key Distribution and Certification. http://mscancer22.tripod.com/securityincomputernetworks/id6.html
6. Panko RR (2004) Corporate computer security. Prentice Hall, Upper Saddle River
7. Certificates and Certificate Authorities. https://en.wikipedia.org/wiki/Certificate_authority
8. Keeping PKI under lock and key. https://www.researchgate.net/publication/295995966_Keeping_PKI_under_lock_and_key
9. Message digests and digital signatures. http://www.diablotin.com/librairie/networking/puis/ch06_05.htm
10. Public key encryption and digital signature: how do they work? http://www.cgi.com/files/white-papers/cgi_whpr_35_pki_e.pdf

Firewalls

12

12.1 Definition

The rapid growth of the Internet has led to a corresponding growth of both users and activities in cyberspace. Unfortunately, not all these users and their activities are reputable; thus, the Internet has been increasingly, at least to many individuals and businesses, turning into a "bad Internet." Bad people are plowing the Internet with evil activities that include, among other things, intrusion into company and individual systems looking for company data and individual information that erodes privacy and security. There has, therefore, been a need to protect company systems, and now individual PCs, keeping them out of access from those "bad users" out on the "bad Internet." As companies build private networks and decide to connect them onto the Internet, network security becomes one of the most important concerns network system administrators face. In fact, these network administrators are facing threats from two fronts: the external Internet and the internal users within the company network. So network system administrators must be able to find ways to restrict access to the company network or sections of the network from both the "bad Internet" outside and from unscrupulous inside users.

Such security mechanisms are based on a *firewall*. A firewall is a hardware, a software, or a combination of both that monitors and filters traffic packets that attempt to either enter or leave the protected private network. It is a tool that separates a protected network or part of a network, and now increasingly a user PC, from an unprotected network—the "bad network" like the Internet. In many cases the "bad network" may even be part of the company network. By definition, a "firewall," is a tool that provides a filter of both incoming and outgoing packets. Most firewalls perform two basic security functions:

- Packet filtering based on *accept* or *deny* policy that is itself based on rules of the security policy.
- Application proxy gateways that provide services to the inside users and at the same time protect each individual host from the "bad" outside users.

© Springer International Publishing AG 2017
J.M. Kizza, *Guide to Computer Network Security*, Computer Communications and Networks, DOI 10.1007/978-3-319-55606-2_12

By denying a packet, the firewall actually drops the packet. In modern firewalls, the firewall logs are stored into log files, and the most urgent or dangerous ones are reported to the system administrator. This reporting is slowly becoming real time. We will discuss this shortly.

In its simplest form, a firewall can be implemented by any device or tool that connects a network or an individual PC to the Internet. For example, an Ethernet bridge or a modem that connects to the "bad network" can be set as a firewall. Most firewall products actually offer much more as they actively filter packets from and into the organization network according to certain established criteria based on the company security policy. Most organization firewalls are *bastion host*, although there are variations in the way this is set up. A bastion host is one computer on the organization network with bare essential services, designated and strongly fortified to withstand attacks. This computer is then placed in a location where it acts as a gateway or a choke point for all communication into or out of the organization network to the "bad network." This means that every computer behind the bastion host must access the "bad network" or networks through this bastion host. Figure 12.1 shows the position of a bastion host in an organization network.

For most organizations, a firewall is a network perimeter security, a first line of defense of the organization's network that is expected to police both network traffic inflow and outflow. This perimeter security defense varies with the perimeter of the network. For example, if the organization has an extranet, an extended network consisting of two or more LAN clusters, or the organization has a virtual private network (VPN) (see Sect. 17.4.2), then the perimeter of the organization's network is difficult to define. In this case, then each component of the network should have its own firewall. See Fig. 12.2.

As we pointed out earlier, the accept/deny policy used in firewalls is based on an organization's security policy. The security policies most commonly used by organizations vary ranging from completely disallowing some traffic to allowing some of the traffic or all the traffic. These policies are consolidated into two commonly used firewall security policies [1]:

- Deny-everything-not-specifically-allowed which sets the firewall in such a way that it denies all traffic and services except a few that are added as the organization needs develop.
- Allow-everything-not-specifically-denied which lets in all the traffic and services except those on the "forbidden" list which is developed as the organization's dislikes grow.

Based on these policies, the following design goals are derived:

- All traffic into and out of the protected network must pass through the firewall.
- Only authorized traffic, as defined by the organizational security policy, in and out of the protected network, will be allowed to pass.
- The firewall must be immune to penetration by use of a trusted system with secure operating system.

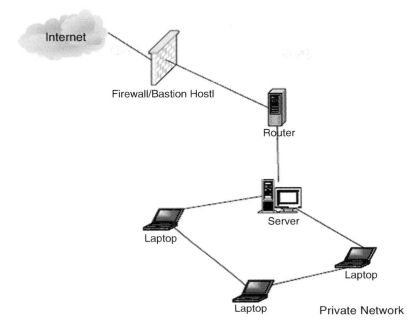

Fig. 12.1   Bastion host between a private network and the "bad network"

When these policies and goals are implemented in a firewall, then the firewall is supposed to [1]:

- Prevent intruders from entering and interfering with the operations of the organization's network. This is done through restricting which packets can enter the network based on IP addresses or port numbers.
- Prevent intruders from deleting or modifying information either stored or in motion within the organization's network.
- Prevent intruders from acquiring proprietary organization information.
- Prevent insiders from misusing the organization resources by restricting unauthorized access to system resources.
- Provide authentication, although care must be taken because additional services to the firewall may make it less efficient.
- Provide endpoints to the VPN.

Fig. 12.2 Firewalls in a changing parameter security

12.2   Types of Firewalls

Firewalls are used very widely to offer network security services. This has resulted in a large repertoire of firewalls. To understand the many different types of firewalls, we need only to look at the kind of security services firewalls offer at different layers of the TCP/IP stack.

As Table 12.1 shows, firewalls can be set up to offer security services to many TCP/IP layers. The many types of firewalls are classified based on the network layer it offers services in and the types of services offered.

The first type is the *packet inspection or filtering router*. This type of firewall uses a set of rules to determine whether to forward or block individual packets. A packet inspection router could be a simple machine with multiple network interfaces or a sophisticated one with multiple functionalities. The second type is the *application inspection or proxy server*. The proxy server is based on specific

Table 12.1 Firewall services based on network protocol layers

Layer	Firewall services
Application	Application-level gateways, encryption, SOCKS proxy server
Transport	Packet filtering (TCP, UDP, ICMP)
Network	NAT, IP filtering
Data link	MAC address filtering
Physical	May not be available

application daemons to provide authentication and to forward packets. The third type is the *authentication and virtual private networks* (VPN). A VPN is an encrypted link in a private network running on a public network. The fourth firewall type is the *small office or home* (SOHO) firewall, and the fifth is the network address translation (NAT).

12.2.1 Packet Inspection Firewalls

Packet filter firewalls, the first type of firewalls, are routers that inspect the contents of the source or destination addresses and ports of incoming or outgoing TCP, UDP, and ICMP packets being sent between networks and accept or reject the packet based on the specific packet policies set in the organization's security policy. Recall that a router is a machine that forwards packets between two or more networks. A packet inspection router, therefore, working at the network level, is programmed to compare each packet to a list of rules set from the organization's security policy, before deciding if it should be forwarded or not. Data is allowed to leave the system only if the firewall rules allow it.

To decide whether a packet should be passed on, delayed for further inspection, or dropped, the firewall looks through its set of rules for a rule that matches the contents of the packet's headers. If the rule matches, then the action to deny or allow is taken; otherwise, an alternate action of sending an ICMP message back to the originator is taken.

Two types of packet filtering are used during packet inspection: *static or stateless filtering* in which a packet is filtered in isolation of the context it is in, and *stateful filtering* in which a packet is filtered actually based on the context the packet is in. The trend now for most inspection firewalls is to use stateful filtering.

The *static or stateless filtering* is a full-duplex communication bastion server allowing two-way communication based on strict filtering rules. Each datagram entering the server either from the "bad" network outside the company network or from within the network is examined based on the preset filtering rules. The rules apply only to the information contained in the packet, and anything else like the state of the connection between the client and the server is ignored.

The *stateful filtering* is also a full-duplex communication bastion server. However, unlike the straight packet filtering firewall, this filters every datagram entering the server both from within and outside the network based on the context which requires a more complex set of criteria and restrictions. For each packet, the firewall examines the date and state of connection between the client and the server. Because this type of filtering pays attention to the data payload of each packet, it is, therefore, more useful and of course more complex. Examination of the data part of the packet makes it useful in detecting questionable data such as attachments and data from hosts not directly connected to the server. Requests from or to third-party hosts and server to server are strictly inspected against the rule base and logged by the firewall.

Whether static or stateful, the rules a filtering server follows are defined based on the organization's network security policy, and they are based on the following information in the packet [2, 3]:

- Source address: All outgoing packets must have a source address internal to the network. Inbound packets must never have source addresses that are internal.
- Destination address: Similarly, all outgoing packets must not have a destination address internal to the network. Any inbound packet must have a destination address that is internal to the network.
- TCP or UDP source and destination port number.
- ICMP message type.
- Payload data type.
- Connection initialization and datagram using TCP ACK bit.

As Table 12.1 shows, packet inspection based on IP addresses, port numbers, ACK, and sequence numbers, on TCP, UDP, and ICMP headers and on applications, may occur at any one of the following TCP/IP and ISO stack layers:

- The *link layer* provides physical addressing of devices on the same network. Firewalls operating on the link layer usually drop packets based on the *media access control* (MAC) addresses of communicating hosts.
- The *network layer* contains the *Internet protocol* (IP) headers that support addressing across networks. IP headers are inspected.
- The *transport layer* contains TCP, UDP, and ICMP headers and provides data flows between hosts. Most firewalls operate at the network and transport layer and inspect these headers.
- The *application layer* contains application-specific protocols like HTTP, FTP, and SET. Inspection of application-specific protocols can be computationally expensive because more data needs to be inspected.

Let us now look at the different ways of implementing the filtering firewall based on IP address, TCP/UDP port numbers, sequence numbers, and ACK filtering.

12.2.1.1 IP Address Filtering

IP address filtering rules are used to control traffic into and out of the network through the filtering of both source and destination IP addresses. Since in a stateless filter, no record is kept, the filter does not remember any packet that has passed

Table 12.2 Destination IP filtering

Application protocol	Source IP	Destination IP	Action
HTTP	Any	198.124.1.0	Allow
Telnet	Any	198.213.1.1	Deny
FTP	Any	198.142.0.2	Allow

Fig. 12.3 TCP, UDP, and port number filtering firewall

through it. This is a weakness that can be exploited by hackers to do IP spoofing. Table 12.2 shows rules that filter based on IP destination, and Fig. 12.3 shows a TCP, UDP, and port number filtering firewall.

12.2.1.2 TCP and UDP Port Filtering
Although IP address header filtering works very well, it may not give the system administrator enough flexibility to allow users from a trusted network to access specific services from a server located in the "bad network" and vice versa. For example, we may not want users from the "bad network" to telnet into any trusted network host, but the administrator may want to let them access the Web services

Table 12.3 Filtering rules
based on TCP and UDP
destination port numbers

Application	Protocol	Destination port number	Action
HTTP	TCP	80	Allow
SSL	UDP	443	Deny
Telnet	TCP	23	Allow

that are on the same or another machine. To leave a selective but restricted access to that machine, the administrator has to be able to set filters according to the TCP or UDP port numbers in conjunction with the IP address filters. Table 12.3 illustrates the filtering rules based on TCP and UDP ports number filtering.

Unfortunately, as Eric Hall [4] points out, there are a several problems with this approach. First, it is not easy to know what port numbers the servers that you are trying to access are running on. As Hall observes, modern-day servers such as HTTP and Gopher are completely configurable in this manner, allowing the user to run them on any port of choice. If this type of filtering is implemented, then the network users will not be able to access those sites that do not use the "standard" port numbers prescribed. In addition to not being able to pinpoint to a "standard" port number, there is also a potential of some of the incoming response packets coming from an intruder port 80.

12.2.1.3 Packet Filtering Based on Initial Sequence Numbers (ISNs) and Acknowledgment (ACK) Bits

A fundamental notion in the design and reliability of the TCP protocol is a sequence number. Every TCP connection begins with a three-way handshaking sequence that establishes specific parameters of the connection. The connection parameters include informing the other host of the sequence numbers to be used. The client initiates the three-way handshake connection request by not only setting the synchronization (SYN) flag but also indicating the *initial sequence number* (ISN) that it will start within addressing data bytes, the octets. This ISN is placed in the sequence number field.

Upon receipt of each octet, the server responds by setting the header flags SYN and ACK; it also sets its ISN in the sequence number field of the response, and it updates the sequence number of the next octet of data it expects from the client.

The acknowledgment is cumulative so that an acknowledgment of sequence number n indicates that all octets up to but not including n have been received. This mechanism is good for duplicate detection in the presence of retransmission that may be caused by replays. Generally, the numbering of octets within a packet is that the first data octet immediately following the header is the lowest numbered, and the following octets are numbered consecutively. For the connection to be maintained, every subsequent TCP packet in an exchange must have its octets' ACK bits set for the connection to be maintained. So the ACK bit indicates whether a packet is requesting a connection or a connection has been made. Packets with 0 in the ACK field are requesting for connections, while those with a 1 have ongoing connections. A firewall can be configured to allow packets with ACK bit 1 to access only specified ports and only in designated directions since hackers can

Table 12.4 Rules for filtering based on ACK field bit

Sequence number	IP Destination address	Port number	ACK	Action
15	198.123.0.1	80	0	Deny
16	198.024.1.1	80	1	Allow

insert a false ACK bit of 1 into a packet. This makes the host think that a connection is ongoing. Table 12.4 shows the rules to set the ACK field.

Access control can be implemented by monitoring these ACK bits. Using these ACK bits, one can limit the types of incoming data to only response packets. This means that a remote system or a hacker cannot initiate a TCP connection at all, but can only respond to packets that have been sent to it.

However, as Hall notes, this mechanism is not hacker proof since monitoring TCP packets for the ACK bit doesn't help at all with UDP packets, as they don't have any ACK bit. Also there are some TCP connections such as FTP that initiate connections. Such applications then cannot work across a firewall based on ACK bits.

12.2.1.4 Problems with Packet Filtering Firewalls

Although packet filtering, especially when it includes a combination of other preferences, can be effective, it, however, suffers from a variety of problems including the following:

- UDP port filtering: UDP was designed for unreliable transmissions that do not require or benefit from negotiated connections such as broadcasts, routing protocols, and advertise services. Because it is unreliable, it does not have an ACK bit; therefore, an administrator cannot filter it based on that. Also an administrator cannot control where the UDP packet was originated. One solution for UDP filtering is to deny all incoming UDP connections but allow all outgoing UDP packets. Of course, this policy may cause problems to some network users because there are some services that use UDP such as NFS, NTP, DNS, WINS, NetBIOS over TCP/IP, and NetWare/IP and client applications such as Archie and IRC. Such a solution may limit access to these services for those network users.
- Packet filter routers don't normally control other vulnerabilities such as SYN flood and other types of host flooding.
- Packet filtering does not control traffic on VPN.
- Filtering, especially on old firewalls, does not hide IP addresses of hosts on the network inside the filter but lets them go through as outgoing packets where an intruder can get them and target the hosts.
- They do not do any checking on the legitimacy of the protocols inside the packet.

12.2.2 Application Proxy Server: Filtering Based on Known Services

Instead of setting filtering based on IP addresses, port numbers, and sequence numbers, which may block some services from users within the protected network trying to access specific services, it is possible to filter traffic based on popular services in the organization. Define the filters so that only packets from well-known and popularly used services are allowed into the organization network, and reject any packets that are not from specific applications. Such firewall servers are known as *proxy servers*.

A proxy server, sometimes just an application firewall, is a machine server that sits between a client application and the server offering the services the client application may want. It behaves as a server to the client and as a client to the server, hence a proxy, providing a higher level of filtering than the packet filter server by examining individual application packet data streams. As each incoming data stream is examined, an appropriate application proxy, a program, similar to normal system daemons, is generated by the server for that particular application. The proxy inspects the data stream and makes a decision of either to forward, drop, or refer for further inspection. Each one of these special servers is called a *proxy server*. Because each application proxy is able to filter traffic based on an application, it is able to log and control all incoming and outgoing traffic and therefore offer a higher level of security and flexibility in accepting additional security functions like user-level authentication, end-to-end encryption, intelligent logging, information hiding, and access restriction based on service types [1].

A proxy firewall works by first intercepting a request from a host on the internal network and then passing it on to its destination, usually the Internet. But before passing it on, the proxy replaces the IP source address in the packet with its own IP address and then passes it on. On receipt of packet from an external network, the proxy inspects the packet, replaces its own IP destination address in the packet with that of the internal host, and passes it on to the internal host. The internal host does not suspect that the packet is from a proxy. Figure 12.4 shows a dual-homed proxy server. Modern proxy firewalls provide three basic operations [5]:

- Host IP address hiding: When the host inside the trusted network sends an application request to the firewall and the firewall allows the request through to the outside Internet, a sniffer just outside the firewall may sniff the packet, and it will reveal the source IP address. The host then may be a potential victim for attack. In IP address hiding, the firewall adds to the host packet its own IP header. So that the sniffer will only see the firewall's IP address. So application firewalls then hide source IP addresses of hosts in the trusted network.
- Header destruction: An automatic protection that some application firewalls use to destroy outgoing packet TCP, UDP, and IP headers and replace them with its own headers so that a sniffer outside the firewall will see only the firewall's IP address. In fact, this action stops all types of TCP, UDP, and IP header attacks.
- Protocol enforcement: Since it is common in packet inspection firewalls to allow packets through based on common port numbers, hackers have exploited this by

Fig. 12.4 A dual-homed proxy server

port spoofing where they hackers penetrate a protected network host using common used and easily allowed port numbers. With an application proxy firewall, this is not easy to do because each proxy acts as a server to each host, and since it deals with only one application, it is able to stop any port spoofing activities.

An example of a proxy server is a Web application firewall server. Popular Web applications are filtered based on their port numbers as below:

- HTTP (port 80)
- FTP (port 20 and 21)
- SSL (port 443)
- Gopher (port 70)
- Telnet (port 23)
- Mail (port 25)

For newer application firewall, the following proxies are also included: HTTP/ Secure HTTP, FTP, SSL, Gopher, email, telnet, and others. This works for both incoming and outgoing requests.

Proxy firewalls fall into two types: application and SOCKS proxies [7, 8].

12.2.2.1 Application Proxy

Application-level proxies automate the filtering and forwarding processes for the client. The client application initiates the process by contacting the firewall. The daemon proxy on the firewall picks up the request, processes it, and if it is acceptable, connects it to the server in the "bad network" (the outside world). If there is any response, it then waits and returns the data to the client application.

As we pointed out earlier, application level proxies offer a higher level of security because in handling all the communications, they can log every detail of the process, including all URLs visited and files downloaded. They can also be used as virus scans, where possible, and language filters for inappropriate content. At login, they can authenticate applications as well as users through a detailed authentication mechanism that includes a one-time password. Also since users do not have direct access to the server, it makes it harder for the intruder to install backdoors around the security system.

Traditional filter firewalls work at a network level to address network access control and block unauthorized network-level requests and access into the network. Because of the popularity of application level services such as e-mail and Web access, application proxy firewalls have become very popular to address application layer security by enforcing requests within application sessions. For example, a Web application firewall specifically protects the Web application communication Web protocol.

There are two models followed in designing an application firewall: a positive security model, which enforces positive behavior; and a negative security model, which blocks recognized attacks [6].

Positive Security Model

A positive security model enforces positive behavior by learning the application logic and then building a security policy of valid known requests as a user interacts with the application. The approach has the following steps [9]:

- The initial policy contains a list of valid starting conditions which the user's initial request must match before the user's session policy is created.
- The application firewall examines the requested services in detail. For example, if it is a Web page download, the page links and drop-down menus and form fields are examined before a policy of all allowable requests that can be made during the user's session is built.
- User requests are verified as valid before being passed to the server. Requests not recognized by the policy are blocked as invalid requests.
- The session policy is destroyed when the user session terminates. A new policy is created for each new session.

Negative Security Model

Unlike the positive model which creates a policy based on user behavior, a negative security model is based on a predefined database of "unacceptable" signatures. The approach again is as follows:

- Create a database of known attack signatures.
- Recognized attacks are blocked, and unknown requests (good or bad) are assumed to be valid and passed to the server for processing.
- All users share the same static policy.

Application firewalls work in real time to address security threats before they reach either the application server or the private network.

12.2.2.2 SOCKS Proxy

A SOCKS proxy is a circuit-level daemon server that has limited capabilities in a sense that it can only allow network packets that originate from non-prohibited sources without looking at the content of the packet itself. It does this by working like a switchboard operator who cross-wires connections through the system to another outside connection without minding the content of the connection, but pays attention only to the legality of the connection. Another way to describe SOCKS servers is to say that these are firewall servers that deal with applications that have protocol behaviors that cannot be filtered. Although they let through virtually all packets, they still provide core protection for application firewalls such as IP hiding and header destruction.

They are faster than application-level proxies because they do not open up the packets, and although they cannot provide for user authentication, they can record and trace the activities of each user as to where he or she is connected to. Figure 12.5 shows a proxy server.

12.2.3 Virtual Private Network (VPN) Firewalls

A VPN, as we will see in Chap. 17, is a cryptographic system including Point-to-Point Tunneling Protocol (PPTP), Layer 2 Tunneling Protocol (L2TP), and IPSec that carry Point-to-Point Protocol (PPP) frames across an Internet with multiple data links with added security. VPNs can be created using a single remote computer connecting on to a trusted network or connecting two corporate network sites. In either case and at both ends of the tunnels, a VPN server can also act as a firewall server. Most firewall servers, however, provide VPN protection which runs in parallel with other authentication and inspection regimes on the server. Each packet arriving at a firewall is then passed through an inspection and authentication module or a VPN module. See Fig. 12.6.

The advantages of a VPN over non-VPN connections like standard Internet connections are as follows:

• VPN technology encrypts its connections.
• Connections are limited to only machines with specified IP addresses.

12.2.4 Small Office or Home (SOHO) Firewalls

A SOHO firewall is a relatively small firewall that connects a few personal computers via a hub, a switch, a bridge, and even a router on one side and connecting to a broadband modem like DSL or cable on the other. See Fig. 12.7. The configuration can be in a small office or a home.

Fig. 12.5 A proxy firewall server

In a functioning network, every host is assigned an IP address. In a fixed network where these addresses are static, it is easy for a hacker to get hold of a host and use it to stage attacks on other hosts within and outside the network. To prevent this from happening, a NAT filter can be used. It hides all inside host TCP/IP information. A NAT firewall actually functions as a proxy server by hiding identities of all internal hosts and making requests on behalf of all internal hosts on the network. This means that to an outside host, all the internal hosts have one public IP address that of the NAT.

When the NAT receives a request from an internal host, it replaces the host's IP address with its own IP address. Inward bound packets all have the NAT's IP address as their destination address. Figure 12.8 shows the position of a NAT firewall.

12.3   Configuration and Implementation of a Firewall

There are actually two approaches to configuring a firewall to suit the needs of an organization. One approach is to start from nothing and make the necessary information gathering to establish the needs and requirements of the organization. This is a time-consuming approach and probably more expensive. The other approach is what many organizations do and takes a shortcut and installs a vendor firewall already loaded with features. The administrator then chooses the features that best meet the established needs and requirements of the organization.

Fig. 12.6 VPN connections and firewalls

Whether the organization is doing an in-house design of its own firewall or buying it off the shelf, the following issues must be addressed first [7]:

- Technical capacity: Whether large or small, organizations embarking on installation of firewalls need some form of technical capacity. Such capacity may be outsourced if it suits the organization.
- Security review: Before an organization can install a firewall, there must be security mechanisms based on a security policy to produce a prioritized list of security objectives.
- Auditing requirements: Based on the security policy, auditing frequency, and what must be in the audit, for example, the degree of logging needed and the

Fig. 12.7 A SOHO firewall

Fig. 12.8 A NAT firewall

details that are cost-effective and thorough. The details included guidelines for recordings, especially if the organization has plans of pursuing security incidents in courts of law.

- Filtering and performance requirements: Decide on the acceptable trade-off between security and performance for the organization. Then use this trade-off to set the level of filtering that meets that balance.
- Authentication: If authentication for outbound sessions is required, then install it and make sure that users are able to change their passwords.

- Remote access: If accepting remote access is to be allowed, include the requirements for authentication and encryption of those sessions. Also consider using VPN to encrypt the session. Many firewalls come with a VPN rolled in.
- Application and network requirements: Decide on the type of network traffic to be supported; whether network address translation (NAT), static routing, or dynamic routing are needed; and whether masquerading a block of internal addresses is sufficient instead of NAT. As Fennelly [10] puts it, a poor under-standing of the requirements can lead to implementing a complicated architec-ture that might not be necessary.
- Decide on the protocol for the firewall: Finally, the type of protocols and services (proxies) the firewall will work with must be decided on. The decision is actually based on the type of services that will be offered in the organization network.

12.4   The Demilitarized Zone (DMZ)

A DMZ is a segment of a network or a network between the protected network and the "bad external network." It is also commonly referred to as a service network. The purpose of a DMZ on an organization network is to provide some insulation and extra security to servers that provide the organization services for protocols such as HTTP/ SHTTP, FTP, DNS, and SMTP to the general public. There are different setups for these servers. One such setup is to make these servers actually bastion hosts so that there is a secure access to them from the internal protected network to allow limited access. Although there are restrictions on accesses from the outside network, such restrictions are not as restrained as those from within the protected network. This enables customers from the outside to access the organization's services on the DMZ servers.

Note that all machines in the DMZ area have a great degree of exposure from both external and internal users. Therefore, these machines have the greatest potential for attacks. This implies that these machines must be protected from both external and internal misuse. They are therefore fenced off by firewalls positioned on each side of the DMZ. See Fig. 12.9 for the positioning of DMZ servers.

According to Joseph M. Adams [8], the outer firewall should be a simple screening firewall just to block certain protocols, but let others through that are allowed in the DMZ. For example, it should allow protocols such as FTP, HTTP/ SHTTP, SMTP, and DNS while denying other selected protocols and address signatures. This selective restriction is important not only to machines in the DMZ but also to the internal protected network because once an intruder manages to penetrate the machines in the DMZ, it is that easy to enter the protected internal network. For example, if DMZ servers are not protected, then an intruder can easily penetrate them. The internal firewall, however, should be more restrictive in order to more protect the internal network from outsider intruders. It should deny even access to these protocols from entering the internal network.

Fig. 12.9 Placing of Web, DNS, FTP, and SMTP servers in the DMZ

Beyond the stated advantage of separating the heavily public accessed servers from the protected network, thus limiting the potential for outside intruders into the network, there are other DMZ advantages. According to Chuck Semeria [9], DMZs offer the following additional advantages to an organization:

- The main advantage for a DMZ is the creation of three layers of protection that segregate the protected network. So in order for an intruder to penetrate the protected network, he or she must crack three separate routers: the outside firewall router, the bastion firewall, and the inside firewall router devices.
- Since the outside router advertises the DMZ network only to the Internet, systems on the Internet do not have routes to the protected private network. This allows the network manager to ensure that the private network is "invisible" and that only selected systems on the DMZ are known to the Internet via routing table and DNS information exchanges.
- Since the inside router advertises the DMZ network only to the private network, systems on the private network do not have direct routes to the Internet. This guarantees that inside users must access the Internet via the proxy services residing on the bastion host.

- Since the DMZ network is a different network from the private network, a network address translation (NAT) can be installed on the bastion host to eliminate the need to renumber or resubnet the private network.

The DMZ also has disadvantages including the following:

- Depending on how much segregation is required, the complexity of DMZ may increase.
- The cost of maintaining a fully functional DMZ can also be high again depending on the number of functionalities and services offered in the DMZ.

12.4.1 Scalability and Increasing Security in a DMZ

Although the DMZ is a restricted access area that is meant to allow outside access to the limited and often selected resources of an organization, DMZ security is still a concern to system administrators. As we pointed out earlier, the penetration of the DMZ may very well result in the penetration of the protected internal network by the intruder, exploiting the trust relationships between the vulnerable host in the DMZ and those in the protected internal network.

According to Marcus Ranum and Matt Curtin [10], the security in the DMZ can be increased and the DMZ scaled by the creation of several "security zones." This can be done by having a number of different networks within the DMZ. Each zone could offer one or more services. For example, one zone could offer services such as mail, news, and host DNS. Another zone could handle the organization's Web needs.

Zoning the DMZ and putting hosts with similar levels of risk on networks linked to these zones in the DMZ helps to minimize the effect of intrusion into the network because if an intruder breaks into the Web server in one zone, he or she may not be able to break into other zones, thus reducing the risks.

12.5   Improving Security Through the Firewall

The firewall shown in Fig. 12.9 is sometimes referred to as a three-pronged firewall or a tri-homed firewall because it connects to three different networks: the external network that connects to the Internet, the DMZ screened subnet, and the internal protected network. Because it is three-pronged, it, therefore, requires three different network cards.

Because three-pronged firewalls use a single device and they use only a single set of rules, they are usually complex. Such a set of rules can be complex and lengthy. In addition, the firewall can be a weak point into the protected network since it provides only a single entry point into two networks: the DMZ network and the internal network. If it is breached, it opens up the internal network. Because of this, it is usually better for added security to use two firewalls as in Fig. 12.10.

Fig. 12.10 Two firewalls in a network with a DMZ

Other configurations of firewalls depend on the structure of the network. For example, in a setup with multiple networks, several firewalls may be used, one per network. Security in a protected network can further be improved by using encryption in the firewalls. Upon receipt of a request, the firewall encrypts the request and sends it on to the receiving firewall or server which decrypts it and offers the service.

Firewalls can also be equipped with intrusion detection systems (IDS). Many newer firewalls now have IDS software built into them. Some firewalls can be fenced by IDS sensors as shown in Fig. 12.11.

12.6   Firewall Forensics

Since port numbers are one of the keys used by most firewalls, let us start firewall forensics by looking at port numbers. A port number is an integer number between 1 and 65535 which identifies to the server what function a client computer wants to be performed. By port numbering, network hosts are able to distinguish one TCP and UDP service from another at a given IP address. This way, one server machine can provide many different services without conflicts among the incoming and outgoing data.

Fig. 12.11 Firewalls with IDS sensors

According to Robert Graham [11], port numbers are divided into three ranges:

- The *well-known ports* are those from 0 through 1023. These are tightly bound to services and usually traffic on these ports clearly indicates the protocol for that service. For example, port 80 virtually always indicates HTTP traffic.
- The *registered ports* are those from 1024 through 49151. These are loosely bound to services, which means that while there are numerous services bound to these ports, these ports are likewise used for many other purposes that have nothing to do with the official server.
- The *dynamic and/or private ports* are those from 49152 through 65535. In theory, no service should be assigned to these ports.

In reality, machines start assigning *dynamic ports* starting at 1024. There is also strangeness, such as Sun starting their RPC ports at 32768 [11].

Using port numbers and in a clear and concise document, Robert Graham explains what many of us see in firewall logs. His document is intended for both security experts and home users of personal firewalls. The full text of the article can be found here: http://www.robertgraham.com/pubs/firewall-seen.html. We encourage the reader to carefully read this document for a full understanding of and putting sense in what a firewalls outputs.

12.7   Firewall Services and Limitations

As technology improves, firewall services have widened far beyond old strict filtering to embrace services that were originally done by internal servers. For example, firewalls can scan for viruses and offer services such as FTP, DNS, and SMTP.

12.7.1 Firewall Services

The broad range of services offered by the firewall are based on the following access controls [4]:

- Service control: Where the firewall may filter traffic on the basis of IP addresses, TCP, UDP, port numbers, and DNS and FTP protocols in addition to providing proxy software that receives and interprets each service request before passing it on.
- Direction control: Where permission for traffic flow is determined from the direction of the requests.
- User control: Where access is granted based on which user is attempting to access the internal protected network, which may also be used on incoming traffic.
- Behavior control: In which access is granted based on how particular services are used, for example, filtering e-mail to eliminate spam.

12.7.2 Limitations of Firewalls

Given all the firewall popularity, firewalls are still taken as just the first line of defense of the protected network because they do not assure total security of the network. Firewalls suffer from limitations, and these limitations and other weaknesses have led to the development of other technologies. In fact, there is talk now that the development of IPSec technology is soon going to make firewall technology obsolete. We may have to wait and see. Some of the current firewall limitations are [11] as follows:

- Firewalls cannot protect against a threat that bypasses it, such as a dial-in using a mobile host.
- Firewalls do not provide data integrity because it is not possible, especially in large networks, to have the firewall examine each and every incoming and outgoing data packet for anything.
- Firewalls cannot ensure data confidentiality because, even though newer firewalls include encryption tools, it is not easy to use these tools. It can only work if the receiver of the packet also has the same firewall.
- Firewalls do not protect against internal threats.
- Firewalls cannot protect against transfer of virus-infected programs or files.

Exercises

1. Discuss the differences between a firewall and a packet filter.
2. Give reasons why firewalls do not give total security.
3. Discuss the advantages of using an application-level firewall over a network-level firewall.
4. Show how data protocols such as TCP, UDP, and ICMP can be implemented in a firewall and give the type of firewall best suited for each of these protocols.
5. What are circuit-level firewalls? How are they different from network-level firewalls?
6. Discuss the limitations of firewalls. How do modern firewalls differ from the old ones in dealing with these limitations?
7. How would you design a firewall that would let Internet-based users upload files to a protected internal network server?
8. Discuss the risks to the protected internal network as a result of a DMZ.
9. What is a bastion router? How different is it from a firewall?
10. Search and discuss as many services and protocols as possible offered by a modern firewall.

Advanced Exercises

1. Many companies now offer either trial or free personal firewalls. Using the following companies, search for a download, and install a personal firewall. *The companies are: Deerfield.com, McAfee, Network Ice, Symantec, Tiny Software, and Zone Labs.*
2. Design a security plan for a small (medium) company and use that plan to configure a firewall. Install the firewall—use some firewalls from #1 above.
3. Zoning the DMZ has resulted in streamlining and improving security in both the DMZ and the protected internal network. Consider how you would zone the DMZ that has servers for the following services and protocols: HTTP/SHTTP, FTP, ICMP, telnet, TCP, UDP, Whois, and finger. Install the clusters in the DMZ.
4. Research the differences between IPSec and firewalls. Why is it that some people are saying that IPSec will soon make firewalls obsolete?
5. Discuss the best ways of protecting an internal network using firewalls from the following attacks:
   - SMTP server hijacking
   - Bugs in operating systems
   - ICMP redirect bombs
   - Denial of service
   - Exploiting bugs in applications

References

1. Kizza JM (2002) Computer network security and cyber ethics. McFarland Publishers, Jefferson
2. Karose J, Ross K (2000) Computer networking: a top-down approach featuring the internet. Addison-Wesley, Boston
3. Holden G (2004) A guide to firewalls and network security: intrusion detection and VPNs. Clifton Paark, Thomson Learning
4. Hall E. Internet Firewall Essentials. http://www.windowsecurity.com/whitepapers/firewalls_and_VPN/Internet_Firewall_Essentials.html
5. Panko RR (2004) Corporate computer and network security. Prentice Hall, Upper Saddle River
6. SANS Institute. Web application firewalls. SANS Institute InfoSec Reading Room. https://www.sans.org/reading-room/whitepapers/application/web-application-firewalls-35817
7. Fennelly C. Building your firewall, Part 1. http://www.windowsecurity.com/whitepapers/firewalls_and_VPN/Building_your_firewall_Part_1.html
8. Adams JM. FTP server security strategy for the DMZ. https://www.giac.org/paper/gsec/805/ftp-server-security-strategy-dmz/101713
9. Semeria C. Internet firewalls and security. A technology overview. http://www.linuxsecurity.com/resource_files/firewalls/nsc/pdf/50061901.pdf
10. Ranum MJ, Curtin M. Internet firewalls: frequently asked questions. http://www.interhack.net/pubs/fwfaq/
11. Graham R. Firewall forensics (What am I seeing?). http://www.lysator.liu.se/~kjell-e/tekla/linux/security/firewall-seen.html

System Intrusion Detection and Prevention 13

13.1 Definition

The psychology and politics of ownership have historically dictated that individuals and groups tend to protect valuable resources. This grew out of the fact that once a resource has been judged to have value, no matter how much protection given to it, there is always a potential that the security provided for the resource will at some point fail. This notion has driven the concept of system security and defined the disciplines of computer and computer network security. Computer network security is made up of three principles: prevention, detection, and response. Although these three are fundamental ingredients of security, most resources have been devoted to detection and prevention because if we are able to detect all security threats and prevent them, then there is no need for response.

Intrusion detection is a technique of detecting unauthorized access to a computer system or a computer network. An intrusion into a system is an attempt by an outsider to the system to illegally gain access to the system. Intrusion prevention, on the other hand, is the art of preventing an unauthorized access of a system's resources. The two processes are related in a sense that while intrusion detection passively detects system intrusions, intrusion prevention actively filters network traffic to prevent intrusion attempts. For the rest of the chapter, let us focus on these two processes.

13.2 Intrusion Detection

The notion of intrusion detection in computer networks is a new phenomenon born, according to many, from a 1980 James Anderson's paper, "Computer Security Threat Monitoring and Surveillance." In that paper, Anderson noted that computer audit trails contained vital information that could be valuable in tracking misuse and understanding user behavior. The paper, therefore, introduced the concept of

© Springer International Publishing AG 2017   275
J.M. Kizza, *Guide to Computer Network Security*, Computer Communications
and Networks, DOI 10.1007/978-3-319-55606-2_13

"detecting" misuse and specific user events and has prompted the development of intrusion detection systems.

An *intrusion* is a deliberate unauthorized attempt, successful or not, to break into, access, manipulate, or misuse some valuable property and where the misuse may result into or render the property unreliable or unusable. The person who intrudes is an *intruder*.

Aurobindo Sundaram [1] divides intrusions into six types as follows:

- Attempted break-ins, which are detected by atypical behavior profiles or violations of security constraints. An intrusion detection system for this type is called anomaly-based IDS.
- Masquerade attacks, which are detected by atypical behavior profiles or violations of security constraints. These intrusions are also detected using anomaly-based IDS.
- Penetrations of the security control system, which are detected by monitoring for specific patterns of activity.
- Leakage, which is detected by atypical use of system resources.
- Denial of service, which is detected by atypical use of system resources.
- Malicious use, which is detected by atypical behavior profiles, violations of security constraints, or use of special privileges.

13.2.1 The System Intrusion Process

The intrusion process into a system includes a number of stages that start with the identification of the target, followed by reconnaissance that produces as much information about the target as possible. After enough information is collected about the target and weak points are mapped, the next job is to gain access into the system and finally the actual use of the resources of the system. Let us look at each one of these stages.

13.2.1.1 Reconnaissance

Reconnaissance is the process of gathering information about the target system and the details of its workings and weak points. Hackers rarely attack an organization network before they have gathered enough information about the targeted network. They gather information about the type of information used in the network, where it is stored, how it is stored, and the weak entry points to that information. They do the reconnaissance through system scanning for vulnerabilities.

Although vulnerability assessment is not intrusion, it is part of the intrusion process in that it proceeds the intrusion itself. Vulnerability assessment is an automated process in which a scanning program sends network traffic to all computers or selected computers in the network and expects receiving return traffic that will indicate whether those computers have known vulnerabilities. These vulnerabilities may include weaknesses in operating systems, application software, and protocols.

Through the years and as technology improved, vulnerability assessment itself has gone through several generations, including using code or script downloaded from the Internet or freely distributed that was compiled and executed for specific hardware or platforms.

Once they have identified the target system's vulnerability, then they just go in for a kill.

13.2.1.2 Physical Intrusion

Besides scanning the network for information that will eventually enable intruders to illegally enter an organization network, intruders also can enter an organization network masquerading as legitimate users. They do this through a number of ways ranging from acquiring special administrative privileges to low-privilege user accounts on the system. If the system doesn't have the latest security patches, it may not be difficult for the hacker to acquire these privileges. The intruder can also acquire remote access privileges.

13.2.1.3 Denial of Service

Denial-of-service (DoS) attacks are where the intruder attempts to crash a service (or the machine), overload network links, overload the CPU, or fill up the disk. The intruder is not trying to gain information, but to simply act as a vandal to prevent you from making use of your machine.

Common Denial-of-Service Attacks

- Ping of death sends an invalid fragment, which starts before the end of packet, but extends past the end of the packet.
- SYN flood sends a TCP SYN packet, which starts connections, very fast, leaving the victim waiting to complete a huge number of connections, causing it to run out of resources, and dropping legitimate connections.
- Land/Latierra sends a forged SYN packet with identical source/destination address/port so that the system goes into an infinite loop trying to complete the TCP connection.
- WinNuke sends an OOB/URG data on a TCP connection to port 139 (NetBIOS Session/SMB), which causes the Windows system to hang.

13.2.2 The Dangers of System Intrusions

The dangers of system intrusion manifests are many including the following:

- Loss of personal data that may be stored on a computer: Personal data loss means a lot and means different things to different people depending on the intrinsic value attached to the actual data lost or accessed. Most alarming in personal data loss is that the way digital information is lost is not the same as the loss of physical data. In physical data loss, you know that if it gets stolen, then somebody has it, so you may take precautions. For example, you may report to the police and call the credit card issuers. However, this is not the same with digital loss because in digital loss, you may even never know that your data was lost. The intruders may break into the system and copy your data and you never know. The damage, therefore, from digital personal data loss may be far greater.

- Compromised privacy: These days more and more people are keeping a lot more of their personal data online either through the use of credit or debit cards; in addition, most of the information about an individual is stored online by companies and government organizations. When a system storing this kind of data is compromised, a lot of individual data gets compromised. This is because a lot of personal data is kept on individuals by organizations. For example, a mortgage company can keep information on your financial credit rating, social security number, bank account numbers, and a lot more. Once such an organization's network is compromised, there is much information on individuals that is compromised, and the privacy of those individuals is compromised as well.
- Legal liability: If your organization network has personal information of the customer and it gets broken into, thus compromising personal information that you stored, you are potentially liable for damages caused by a hacker either breaking into your network or using your computers to break into other systems. For example, if a hacker does two- or three-level hacking using your network or a computer on your network, you can be held liable. A two-level hacking involves a hacker breaking into your network and using it to launch an attack on another network.

13.3   Intrusion Detection Systems (IDSs)

An *intrusion detection system* (*IDS*) is a system used to detect unauthorized intrusions into computer systems and networks. Intrusion detection as a technology is not new; it has been used for generations to defend valuable resources. Kings, emperors, and nobles who had wealth used it in rather an interesting way. They built castles and palaces on tops of mountains and sharp cliffs with observation towers to provide them with a clear overview of the lands below where they could detect any attempted intrusion ahead of time and defend themselves. Empires and kingdoms grew and collapsed based on how well intrusions from the enemies surrounding them could be detected. In fact, according to the Greek legend of the Trojan Horse, the people of Crete were defeated by the Greeks because the Greeks managed to penetrate the heavily guarded gates of the city walls.

Through the years, intrusion detection has been used by individuals and companies in a variety of ways including erecting ways and fences around valuable resources with sentry boxes to watch the activities surrounding the premises of the resource. Individuals have used dogs, flood lights, electronic fences, closed-circuit television, and other watchful gadgets to be able to detect intrusions.

As technology has developed, a whole new industry based on intrusion detection has sprung up. Security firms are cropping up everywhere to offer individual and property security—to be a watchful eye so that the property owner can sleep or take a vacation in peace. These new systems have been made to configure changes, compare user actions against known attack scenarios, and be able to predict changes in activities that indicate and can lead to suspicious activities.

In Sect. 13.2, we outlined six subdivisions of system intrusions. These six can now be put into three models of intrusion detection mechanisms: *anomaly-based* detection, *signature-based* detection, and *hybrid* detection. In anomaly-based detection, also known as behavior-based detection, the focus is to detect the behavior that is not normal or behavior that is not consistent with normal behavior. Theoretically, this type of detection requires a list of what is normal behavior. In most environments this is not possible, however. In real-life models, the list is determined from either historical or empirical data. However, neither historical nor empirical data represent all possible acceptable behavior. So a list has got to be continuously updated as new behavior patterns not on the list appear and are classified as acceptable or normal behavior. The danger with this model is to have unacceptable behavior included within the training data and later be accepted as normal behavior. Behavior-based intrusion detections, therefore, are also considered as rule-based detection because they use rules, usually developed by experts, to be able to determine unacceptable behavior.

In signature-based detection, also known as misuse-based detection, the focus is on the signature of known activities. This model also requires a list of all known unacceptable actions or misuse signatures. Since there are an infinite number of things that can be classified as misuse, it is not possible to put all these on the list and still keep it manageable. So only a limited number of things must be on the list. To do this and therefore be able to manage the list, we categorize the list into three broad activities:

- Unauthorized access
- Unauthorized modification
- Denial of service

Using these classifications, it is then possible to have a controlled list of misuse whose signatures can be determined. The problem with this model, though, is that it can detect only previously known attacks.

Because of the difficulties with both the anomaly-based and signature-based detections, a hybrid model is being developed. Much research is now focusing on this hybrid model [1].

13.3.1 Anomaly Detection

Anomaly based systems are "learning" systems in a sense that they work by continuously creating "norms" of activities. These norms are then later used to detect anomalies that might indicate an intrusion. Anomaly detection compares observed activity against expected normal usage profiles "leaned." The profiles may be developed for users, groups of users, applications, or system resource usage.

In anomaly detection, it is assumed that all intrusive activities are necessarily anomalous. This happens in real life too, where most "bad" activities are anomalous, and we can, therefore, be able to character profile the "bad elements" in society. The anomaly detection concept, therefore, will create, for every guarded system, a corresponding database of "normal" profiles. Any activity on the system is checked against these profiles and is deemed acceptable or not based on the presence of such activity in the profile database.

Typical areas of interest are threshold monitoring, user work profiling, group work profiling, resource profiling, executable profiling, static work profiling, adaptive work profiling, and adaptive rule-based profiling.

Anonymous behaviors are detected when the identification engine takes observed activities and compares them to the rule-based profiles for significant deviations. The profiles are commonly for individual users, groups of users, system resource usages, and a collection of others as discussed below [2]:

- Individual profile: A collection of common activities a user is expected to do and with little deviation from the expected norm. This may cover specific user events such as the time being longer than usual usage, recent changes in user work patterns, and significant or irregular user requests.
- Group profile: This is a profile that covers a group of users with a common work pattern, resource requests and usage, and historic activities. It is expected that each individual user in the group follows the group activity patterns.
- Resource profile: This includes the monitoring of the use patterns of the system resources such as applications, accounts, storage media, protocols, communications ports, and a list of many others the system manager may wish to include. It is expected, depending on the rule-based profile, that common uses will not deviate significantly from these rules.
- Other profiles: These include executable profiles that monitor how executable programs use the system resources. This, for example, may be used to monitor strange deviations of an executable program if it has an embedded Trojan worm or a trapdoor virus. In addition to executable profiles, there are also the following profiles: work profile which includes monitoring the ports, static profile whose job is to monitor other profiles periodically updating them so that those profiles cannot slowly expand to sneak in intruder behavior, and a variation of the work profile called the adaptive profile which monitors work profiles, automatically updating them to reflect recent upsurges in usage. Finally, there is also the adoptive rule-based profile which monitors historic usage patterns of all other profiles and uses them to make updates to the rule base [3].

Besides being embarrassing and time-consuming, the concept also has other problems. As pointed out by Sundaram [1], if we consider that the set of intrusive activities only intersects the set of anomalous activities instead of being exactly the same, then two problems arise:

- Anomalous activities that are not intrusive are classified as intrusive.
- Intrusive activities that are not anomalous result in false negatives, that is, events are not flagged intrusive, though they actually are.

Anomaly detection systems are also computationally expensive because of the overhead of keeping track of, and possibly updating, several system profile metrics.

13.3.2 Misuse Detection

Unlike anomaly detection where we labeled every intrusive activity anomalous, the misuse detection concept assumes that each intrusive activity is representable by a unique pattern or a *signature* so that slight variations of the same activity produce a new signature and therefore can also be detected. Misuse detection systems are, therefore, commonly known as *signature systems*. They work by looking for a specific signature on a system. Identification engines perform well by monitoring these patterns of known misuse of system resources. These patterns, once observed, are compared to those in the rule base that describe "bad" or "undesirable" usage of resources. To achieve this, a knowledge database and a rule engine must be developed to work together. Misuse pattern analysis is best done by expert systems, model-based reasoning, or neural networks.

Two major problems arise out of this concept:

- The system cannot detect unknown attacks with unmapped and unarchived signatures.
- The system cannot predict new attacks and will, therefore, be responding after an attack has occurred. This means that the system will never detect a new attack.

In a computer network environment, intrusion detection is based on the fact that software used in all cyber attacks often leave a *characteristic signature*. This signature is used by the detection system, and the information gathered is used to determine the nature of the attack. At each different level of network investigative work, there is a different technique of network traffic information gathering, analysis, and reporting. Intrusion detection operates on already gathered and processed network traffic data. It is usually taken that the anomalies noticed from the analysis of this data would lead to distinguishing between an intruder and a legitimate user of the network. The anomalies resulting from the traffic analyses are actually large and noticeable deviations from historical patterns of usage. Identification systems are supposed to identify three categories of users: legitimate users, legitimate users performing unauthorized activities, and of course intruders who have illegally acquired the required identification and authentication.

13.4   Types of Intrusion Detection Systems

Intrusion detection systems are also classified based on their monitoring scope. There are those that monitor only a small area and those that can monitor a wide area. Those that monitor a wide area are known as network-based intrusion detection, and those that have a limited scope are known as host-based detections.

13.4.1 Network-Based Intrusion Detection Systems (NIDSs)

Network-based intrusion detection systems have the whole network as the monitoring scope. They monitor the traffic on the network to detect intrusions. They are responsible for detecting anomalous, inappropriate, or other data that may be considered unauthorized and harmful occurring on a network. There are striking differences between NIDS and firewalls. Recall from Chap. 11 that firewalls are configured to allow or deny access to a particular service or host based on a set of rules. Only when the traffic matches an acceptable pattern is it permitted to proceed regardless of what the packet contains. An NIDS also captures and inspects every packet that is destined to the network regardless of whether it is permitted or not. If the packet signature based on the contents of the packet is not among the acceptable signatures, then an alert is generated.

There are several ways an NIDS may be run. It can either be run as an independent standalone machine where it promiscuously watches over all network traffic or it can just monitor itself as the target machine to watch over its own traffic. For example, in this mode, it can watch itself to see if somebody is attempting a SYN flood or a TCP port scan.

While NIDSs can be very effective in capturing all incoming network traffic, it is possible that an attacker can evade this detection by exploiting ambiguities in the traffic stream as seen by the NIDS. Mark Handley, Vern Paxson, and Christian Kreibich list the sources of these exploitable ambiguities as follows [4]:

- Many NIDSs do not have complete analysis capabilities to analyze a full range of behavior that can be exposed by the user and allowed by a particular protocol. The attacker can also evade the NIDS: even if the NIDS does perform analysis for the protocol.
- Since NIDSs are far removed from individual hosts, they do not have full knowledge of each host's protocol implementation. This knowledge is essential for the NIDS to be able to determine how the host may treat a given sequence of packets if different implementations interpret the same stream of packets in different ways.
- Again, since NIDSs do not have a full picture of the network topology between the NIDS and the hosts, the NIDS may be unable to determine whether a given packet will even be seen by the hosts.

IDS inside the firewall

Internet

Laptop

IDS Outside the firewall

Firewall

Server

Laptop

HOST-based IDS

Fig. 13.1 The architecture of a network-based intrusion detection system

13.4.1.1 Architecture of a Network-Based Intrusion Detection

An intrusion detection system consists of several parts that must work together to produce an alert. The functioning of these parts may be either sequential or sometimes parallel [5, 6]. The parts are shown in Fig. 13.1.

Network Tap/Load Balancer

The network tap, or the load balancer as it is also known, gathers data from the network and distributes it to all network sensors. It can be a software agent that runs from the sensor or hardware, such as a router. The load balancer or tap is an important component of the intrusion detection system because all traffic into the network goes through it, and it also prevents packet loss in high-bandwidth networks. Certain types of taps have limitations in selected environments such as switched networks. In networks where there are no load balancers, sensors must be placed in such a way that they are responsible for traffic entering the network in their respective subnetwork.

Network Sensor/Monitoring

The network sensor or monitor is a computer program that runs on dedicated machines or network devices on mission critical segments. In networks with a load balancer, the sensors receive traffic from the balancer. In other networks without a load balancer, the sensors receive live traffic from the network and separate it between suspicious and normal traffic. A sensor can be implemented as an agent on a mission critical destination machine in a network. They are either anomaly based or signature based. Promiscuous mode sensors, which are sensors that detect anything that seems like a possible attempt at intrusion, run on dedicated machines.

Analyzer
The analyzer determines the threat level based on the nature and threat of the suspicious traffic. It receives data from the sensors. The traffic is then classified as either safe or an attack. Several layers of monitoring may be done where the primary layer determines the threat severity; secondary layers then determine the scope, intent, and frequency of the threat.

Alert Notifier
It contacts the security officer responsible for handling incidents whenever a threat is severe enough according to the organization's security policy. Standard capabilities include on-screen alerts, audible alerts, paging, and e-mail. Most systems also provide SNMP so that an administrator can be notified. Frequent alerts for seemingly trivial threats must be avoided because they result in a high rate of false positives. It must also be noted that not reporting frequently enough because the sensors are set in such a way that they ignore a number of threats, many of them being real, result in false negatives which results in the intrusion detection system providing misleading sense of security.

Because the performance of the intrusion detection system depends on the balancing of both false positives and false negatives, it is important to use intrusion detection systems that are adjustable and can, therefore, offer balancing capabilities.

Command Console/Manager
The role of the command console or manager is to act as the central command authority for controlling the entire system. It can be used to manage threats by routing incoming network data to either a firewall or to the load balancer or straight to routers. It can be accessed remotely so the system may be controlled from any location. It is typically a dedicated machine with a set of tools for setting policy and processing collected alarms. On the console, there is an assessment manager, a target manager, and an alert manager. The console has its own detection engine and database of detected alerts, for scheduled operations and data mining.

Response Subsystem
The response subsystem provides the capabilities to take action based on threats to the target systems. These responses can be automatically generated or initiated by the system operator. Common responses include reconfiguring a router or a firewall and shutting down a connection.

Database
The database is the knowledge repository for all that the intrusion detection system has observed. This can include both behavioral and misuse statistics. These statistics are necessary to model historical behavior patterns that can be useful during

damage assessment or other investigative tasks. Useful information need not necessarily be indicative of misuse. The behavioral statistics help in developing the patterns for the individual, and the misuse statistics aid in detecting attempts at intrusion.

13.4.1.2 Placement of IDS Sensors

The position to place network IDS sensors actually depends on several factors, including the topology of the internal network to be protected, the kind of security policy the organization is following, and the types of security practices in effect. For example, you want to place sensors in places where intrusions are most likely to pass. These are the network "weak" points. However, it is normal practice to place IDS sensors in the following areas [6]:

- Inside the DMZ: We saw in Chap. 11 that the DMZ is perhaps the most ideal place to put any detection system because almost all attacks enter the protected internal network through the DMZ. IDS sensors are, therefore, commonly placed outside of the organization's network's first firewall in the DMZ. The IDS sensors in the DMZ can be enhanced by putting them into zoned areas. Another good location for IDS sensors is inside each firewall. This approach gives the sensors more protection, making them less vulnerable to coordinated attacks. In cases where the network perimeter does not use a DMZ, the ideal locations then may include any entry/exit points such as on both sides of the firewall, dial-up servers, and on links to any collaborative networks. These links tend to be low bandwidth (T1 speeds) and are usually the entry point of an external attack.
- Between the firewall and the Internet: This is a frequent area of unauthorized activity. This position allows the NIDS to "see" all Internet traffic as it comes into the network. This location, however, needs a good appliance and sensors that can withstand the high volume of traffic.
- Behind the network front firewall: This is a good position; however, most of the bad network traffic has already been stopped by the firewall. It handles all the bad traffic that manages to get through the firewall.
- Inside the network: Commonly placed in strategic points and used to "see" segments of the network. Network segments like these are usually the suspected weak areas of the network. The problem with this approach, however, is that the sensors may not be able to cover all the targets it is supposed to. Also it may cause the degradation of the network performance.

Figure 13.2 shows the various places where ID sensors can be deployed.

13.4.1.3 Advantages of Network-Based Intrusion Detection Systems

Although both NIDSs and HIDSs (Sect. 13.4.2) have different focuses, areas of deployment, and deployment requirements, using NIDS has the following advantages [7]:

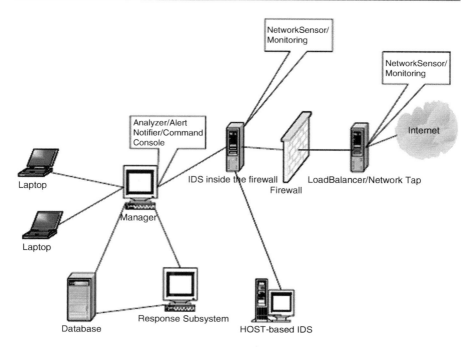

Fig. 13.2 The various places of placing the IDS sensors

- Ability to detect attacks that a host-based system would miss: Because NIDSs are on dedicated machines that are routinely protected, it is more difficult for an **attacker** to remove the evidence than it is with HIDSs which are near or at the attacker's desk. Also, since NIDSs use live network traffic and it is this traffic that is captured by NIDSs when there is an attack, this also makes it difficult for an attacker to remove evidence.
- Difficulty to remove evidence: Because NIDSs are on dedicated machines that are routinely protected, it is more difficult for an attack to remove the evidence than it is with HIDSs which are near or at the attacker's desk. Also, since NIDSs use live network traffic and it is this traffic that is captured by NIDSs when there is an attack, this also makes it difficult for an attacker to remove evidence.
- Real-time detection and response: Because the NIDSs are at the most opportune and strategic entry points in the network, they are able to detect foreign intrusions into the network in real time and report as quickly as possible to the administrator for a quick and appropriate response. Real-time notification, which many NIDSs have now, allows for a quick and appropriate response and can even let the administrators allow the intruder more time as they do more and targeted surveillance.
- Ability to detect unsuccessful attacks and malicious intent: Because the HIDSs are inside the protected internal network, they never come into contact with many types of attack since such attacks are many times stopped by the outside firewall. NIDSs, especially those in the DMZ, come across these attacks (those

that escape the first firewall) that are later rejected by the inner firewall and those targeting the DMZ services that have been let in by the outer firewall. Besides showing these attacks, NIDSs can also record the frequency of these attacks.

13.4.1.4 Disadvantages of NIDS

Although NIDSs are very well suited to monitor all the networks coming into the network, they have limitations [8]:

- Blind spots: Deployed at the borders of an organization network, NIDS are blind to the whole inside network. As sensors are placed in designated spots, especially in switched networks, NIDSs have blind spots—sometimes whole network segments they cannot see.
- Encrypted data: One of the major weaknesses of NIDS is on encrypted data. They have no capabilities to decrypt encrypted data. Although they can scan unencrypted parts of the packet such as headers, they are useless to the rest of the package.

13.4.2 Host-Based Intrusion Detection Systems (HIDS)

Recent studies have shown that the problem of organization information misuse is not confined only to the "bad" outsiders, but the problem is more rampant within organizations. To tackle this problem, security experts have turned to inspection of systems within an organization network. This local inspection of systems is called *host-based intrusion detection systems* (HIDS).

Host-based intrusion detection is the technique of detecting malicious activities on a single computer. A host-based intrusion detection system is, therefore, deployed on a single target computer, and it uses software that monitors operating system-specific logs, including system, event, and security logs on Windows systems and syslog in Unix environments to monitor sudden changes in these logs. When a change is detected in any of these files, the HIDS compares the new log entry with its configured attack signatures to see if there is a match. If a match is detected, then this signals the presence of an illegitimate activity.

Although HIDSs are deployable on a single computer, they can also be put on a remote host, or they can be deployed on a segment of a network to monitor a section of the segment. The data gathered, which sometimes can be overwhelming, is then compared with the rules in the organization's security policy. The biggest problem with HIDSs is that given the amount of data logs generated, the analysis of such raw data can put significant overhead not only on the processing power needed to analyze this data but also on the security staff needed to review the data.

Host sensors can also use user-level processes to check key system files and executables to periodically calculate their checksum and report changes in the checksum.

13.4.2.1 Advantages of Host-Based Intrusion Detection Systems

HIDSs are new kids on the intrusion detection block. They came into widespread in use in the early and mid-1980s when there was a realization after studies showed that a large number of illegal and illegitimate activities in organization networks actually originated from within the employees. Over the succeeding years as technology advanced, the HIDS technology has also advanced in tandem. More and more organizations are discovering the benefits of HIDSs on their overall security. Besides being faster than their cousins the NIDSs, because they are dealing with less traffic, they offer additional advantages including the following [7]:

- Ability to verify success or failure of an attack quickly: Because they log continuing events that have actually occurred, they have information that is more accurate and less prone to false positives than their cousins, the NIDSs. This information can accurately infer whether an attack was successful or not quickly, and a response can be started early. In this role, they complement the NIDSs, not as an early warning but as a verification system.
- Low-level monitoring: Because they monitor at a local host, they are able to "see" low-level local activities such as file accesses, changes to file permissions, attempts to install new executables or attempts to access privileged services, changes to key system files and executables, and attempts to overwrite vital system files or to install Trojan horses or backdoors. These low-level activities can be detected very quickly, and the reporting is quick and timely to give the administrator time for an appropriate response. Some of these low-level attacks are so small and far less intensive such that no NIDS can detect them.
- Near real-time detection and response: HIDSs have the ability to detect minute activities at the target hosts and report them to the administrator very quickly at a rate near real time. This is possible because the operating system can recognize the event before any IDS can, in which case, an intruder can be detected and stopped before substantial damage is done.
- Ability to deal with encrypted and switched environments: Large networks are routinely switch-chopped into many but smaller network segments. Each one of these smaller networks is then tagged with a NIDS. In a heavily switched network, it can be difficult to determine where to deploy a network-based IDS to achieve sufficient network coverage. This problem can be solved by the use of traffic mirroring and administrative ports on switches, but not as effective. HIDS provides this needed greater visibility into these switched environments by residing on as many critical hosts as needed. In addition, because the operating systems see incoming traffic after encryption has already been de-encrypted, HIDSs that monitor the operating systems can deal with these encryptions better than NIDSs, which sometimes may not even deal with them at all.
- Cost-effectiveness: Because no additional hardware is needed to install HIDS, there may be great organization savings. This compares favorably with the big costs of installing NIDS which require dedicated and expensive servers. In fact,

in large networks that are switch-chopped which require a large number of NIDSs per segment, this cost can add up.

13.4.2.2 Disadvantages of HIDS

Like their cousin the NIDS, HIDSs have limitations in what they can do. These limitations include the following [8]:

- Myopic viewpoint: Since they are deployed at a host, they have a very limited view of the network.
- Since they are close to users, they are more susceptible to illegal tampering.

13.4.3 The Hybrid Intrusion Detection System

We have noted in both Sects. 13.4.1 and 13.4.2 that there was a need for both NIDS and HIDS, each patrolling its own area of the network for unwanted and illegal network traffic. We have also noted the advantages of not using one over the other but of using one to complement the other. In fact, if anything, after reading Sects. 13.4.1.3 and 13.4.2.1, one comes out with an appreciation of how complementary these two intrusion detection systems are. Both bring to the security of the network their own strengths and weaknesses that nicely complement and augment the security of the network.

However, we also know and have noted in Sect. 13.4.1.4 that NIDSs have been historically unable to work successfully in switched and encrypted networks, and as we have also noted in Sect. 13.4.2.2, both HIDS and NIDS have not been successful in high-speed networks—networks whose speeds exceed 100 Mbps. This raises the question of a hybrid system that contains all the things that each system has and those that each system misses, a system with both components. Having both components provides greater flexibility in their deployment options.

Hybrids are new and need a great deal of support to gain on their two cousins. However, their success will depend to a great extent on how well the interface receives and distributes the incidents and integrates the reporting structure between the different types of sensors in the HIDS and NIDS spheres. Also the interface should be able to smartly and intelligently gather and report data from the network or systems being monitored.

The interface is so important and critical because it receives data, collects analysis from the respective component, coordinates and correlates the interpretation of this data, and reports it. It represents a complex and unified environment for tracking, reporting, and reviewing events.

13.5   The Changing Nature of IDS Tools

Although ID systems are assumed, though wrongly, by management and many in the network community that they protect network systems from outside intruders, recent studies have shown that the majority of system intrusions actually come from insiders. So newer IDS tools are focusing on this issue. Also, since the human mind is the most complicated and unpredictable machine ever, as new IDS tools are being built to counter systems intrusion, new attack patterns are being developed to take this human behavior unpredictability into account. To keep abreast of all these changes, ID systems must be changing constantly.

As all these changes are taking place, the primary focus of ID systems has been on a network as a unit where they collect network packet data by watching network packet traffic and then analyzing it based on network protocol patterns "norms," "normal" network traffic signatures, and network traffic anomalies built in the rule base. But since networks are getting larger, traffic heavier, and local networks more splintered, it is becoming more and more difficult for the ID system to "see" all traffic on a switched network such as an Ethernet. This has led to a new approach to looking closer at the host. So in general, ID systems fall into two categories: host based and network based.

13.6   Other Types of Intrusion Detection Systems

Although NIDS and HIDS and their hybrids are the most widely used tools in network intrusion detection, there are others that are less used but more targeting and therefore more specialized. Because many of these tools are so specialized, many are still not considered as being intrusion detection systems, but rather intrusion detection add-ons or tools.

13.6.1 System Integrity Verifiers (SIVs)

System integrity verifiers (SIVs) monitor critical files in a system, such as system files, to find whether an intruder has changed them. They can also detect other system components' data; for example, they detect when a normal user somehow acquires root/administrator level privileges. In addition, they also monitor system registries in order to find well-known signatures [9].

13.6.2 Log File Monitors (LFM)

Log file monitors (LFMs) first create a record of log files generated by network services. Then they monitor this record, just like NIDS, looking for system trends, tendencies, and patterns in the log files that would suggest that an intruder is attacking.

13.6.3 Honeypots

A *honeypot* is a system designed to look like something that an intruder can hack. They are built for many purposes, but the overriding one is to deceive attackers and learn about their tools and methods. Honeypots are also add-on/tools that are not strictly sniffer-based intrusion detection systems like HIDS and NIDS. However, they are good deception systems that protect the network in much the same way as HIDS and NIDS. Since the goal for a honeypot is to deceive intruders and learn from them without compromising the security of the network, then it is important to find a strategic place for the honeypot.

To many, the best location to achieve this goal is in the DMZ for those networks with DMZs or behind the network firewall if the private network does not have a DMZ. The firewall location is ideal because of the following [5]:

- Most firewalls log all traffic going through it; hence, this becomes a good way to track all activities of the intruders. By reviewing the firewall logs, we can determine how the intruders are probing the honeypot and what they are looking for.
- Most firewalls have some alerting capability, which means that with a few additions to the firewall rule base, we can get timely alerts. Since the honeypot is built in such a way that no one is supposed to connect to it, any packets sent to it are most likely from intruders probing the system. And if there is any outgoing traffic coming from the honeypot, then the honeypot is most likely compromised.
- The firewall can control incoming and outgoing traffic. This means that the intruders can find, probe, and exploit our honeypot, but they cannot compromise other systems.

So any firewall dedicated as a honeypot can do as long as it can control and log traffic going through it. If no firewall is used, then dedicate any machine either in the DMZ or behind a firewall for the purpose of logging all attempted accesses. Figure 13.3 shows the positioning of a honeypot.

Honeypots come in a variety of capabilities from the simplest monitoring one to two intruder activities to the most powerful monitoring many intruder activities. The simplest honeypot is a port monitor which is a simple socket-based program that opens up a listening port. The program can listen to any designed port. For example, *NukeNabbe*, for Windows, listens on ports typically scanned for by hackers. It then alerts the administrator whenever such designated ports are being scanned. The second type of honeypot is the deception system, which instead of listening quietly on a port, interacts with the intruder, responding to him or her as if it were a real server with that port number. Most deception systems implement only as much of the protocol machine as necessary to trap 90% of the attacks against the protocol [9]. The next type of honeypot is the multiprotocol deception system which offers most of the commonly hacked protocols in a single toolkit. Finally, there is a full system that goes beyond what the deception systems do to incorporate

Fig. 13.3 The positioning of a honeypot

the ability to alert the system administrator on any exceptional condition. Other more complex honeypots combine a full system with NIDSs to supplement the internal logging [9].

13.6.3.1 Advantages of Honeypots

Perhaps one would wonder why a system administrator would go through the pain of setting up, maintaining, and daily responding to honeypots. There are advantages to having honeypots on a network. They include the following [9]:

- Since NIDSs have difficulties distinguishing between hostile and nonhostile activities, honeypots are more suited to digging out hostile intrusions because isolated honeypots should not normally be accessed. So if they are accessed at all, such accesses are unwanted intrusions and they should be reported.
- A honeypot can attract would-be hackers into the trap by providing a banner that looks like a system that can easily be hacked.

13.7   Response to System Intrusion

A good intrusion detection system alert should produce a corresponding response. The type of response is relative to the type of attack. Some attacks do not require responses; others require a precautionary response. Yet others need a rapid and forceful response. For the most part, a good response must consist of preplanned defensive measures that include an incident response team and ways to collect IDS logs for future use and for evidence when needed.

13.7.1 Incident Response Team

An *incident response team* (IRT) is a primary and centralized group of dedicated people charged with the responsibility of being the first contact team whenever an incidence occurs. According to Keao [6], an IRT must have the following responsibilities:

- Keeping up-to-date with the latest threats and incidents
- Being the main point of contact for incident reporting
- Notifying others whenever an incident occurs
- Assessing the damage and impact of every incident
- Finding out how to avoid exploitation of the same vulnerability
- Recovering from the incident

In handling an incident, the team must carefully do the following:

- Prioritize the actions based on the organization's security policy but taking into account the following order:
  - Human life and people's safety
  - Most sensitive or classified data
  - Costly data and files
  - Preventing damage to systems
  - Minimizing the destruction to systems
- Assess incident damage: This is through doing a thorough check on all the following: system log statistics, infrastructure and operating system checksum, system configuration changes, changes in classified and sensitive data, traffic logs, and password files.
- Alert and report the incident to relevant parties: These may include law enforcement agencies, incident reporting centers, company executives, employees, and sometimes the public.
- Recovering from incident: This involves making a postmortem analysis of all that went on. This postmortem report should include steps to take in case of similar incidents in the future.

13.7.2 IDS Logs as Evidence

First and foremost, IDS logs can be kept as a way to protect the organization in case of legal proceedings. Some people tend to view IDS as a form of wiretap. If sensors to monitor the internal network are to be deployed, verify that there is a published policy explicitly stating that the use of the network is consent to monitoring.

13.8   Challenges to Intrusion Detection Systems

While IDS technology has come a long way and there is an exciting future for it as the marriage between it and artificial intelligence takes hold, it faces many challenges. Although there are IDS challenges in many areas, more serious challenges are faced in deploying IDSs in switched environments.

13.8.1 Deploying IDS in Switched Environments

There is a particularly hard challenge faced by organizations trying to deploy IDS in their networks. Network-based IDS sensors must be deployed in areas where they can "see" network traffic packets. However, in switched networks, this is not possible because by their very nature, sensors in switched networks are shielded from most of the network traffic. Sensors are allowed to "see" traffic only from specified components of the network.

One way to handle this situation has traditionally been to attach a network sensor to a mirror port on the switch. But port mirroring, in addition to putting an overhead on the port, gets unworkable when there is an increase in traffic on that port because overloading one port with traffic from other ports may cause the port to bulk and miss some traffic.

Several solutions have been used recently including the following [8]:

- Tapping: This involves deploying a line of passive taps that administrators can tap into to listen in on Ethernet connections; by sending "copies" of the frames to a second switch with dedicated IDS sensor, overloading a port can be avoided.
- By using standard Cisco access control lists (ACL) in a Cisco appliance that includes a Cisco Secure IDS, one can tag certain frames for inspection.
  Among other issues still limiting IDS technology are [2]:
- False alarms: Though the tools have come a long way and are slowly gaining acceptance as they gain widespread use, they still produce a significant number of both false positives and negatives.
- The technology is not yet ready to handle a large-scale attack. Because of its very nature, it has to literally scan every packet, every contact point, and every traffic pattern in the network. For larger networks and in a large-scale attack, it is not possible that the technology can be relied on to keep working with acceptable quality and grace.
- Unless there is a breakthrough today, the technology in its current state cannot handle very fast and large quantities of traffic efficiently.
- Probably the biggest challenge is the IDS's perceived and sometimes exaggerated capabilities. The technology, while good, is not the cure of all computer network ills that it is pumped up to be. It is just like any other good security tool.

13.9   Implementing an Intrusion Detection System

An effective IDS does not stand alone. It must be supported by a number of other systems. Among the things to consider, in addition to the IDS, in setting up a good IDS for the company network are the following [9]:

- Operating systems: A good operating system that has logging and auditing features. Most of the modern operating systems including Windows, Unix, and other variants of Unix have these features. These features can be used to monitor security critical resources.
- Services: All applications on servers such as Web servers, e-mail servers, and databases should include logging/auditing features as well.
- Firewalls: As we discussed in Chap. 11, a good firewall should have some network intrusion detection capabilities. Set those features.
- Network management platform: Whenever network management services such as OpenView are used, make sure that they do have tools to help in setting up alerts on suspicious activity.

13.10   Intrusion Prevention Systems (IPSs)

Although IDS have been one of the cornerstones of network security, they have covered only one component of the total network security picture. They have been and they are a passive component which only detects and reports without preventing. A promising new model of intrusion is developing and picking up momentum. It is the *intrusion prevention system* (IPS), which according to Andrew Yee [10] is to prevent attacks. Like their counterparts, the IDS, IPS fall into two categories: network based and host based.

13.10.1   Network-Based Intrusion Prevention Systems (NIPSs)

Because NIDSs are passively detecting intrusions into the network without preventing them from entering the networks, many organizations in recent times have been bundling up IDS and firewalls to create a model that can detect and then prevent.

The bundle works as follows. The IDS fronts the network with a firewall behind it. On the detection of an attack, the IDS then goes into the prevention mode by altering the firewall access control rules on the firewall. The action may result in the attack being blocked based on all the access control regimes administered by the firewall. The IDS can also affect prevention through the TCP resets; TCP utilizes the RST (reset) bit in the TCP header for resetting a TCP connection, usually sent as a response request to a nonexistent connection [10]. But this kind of bundling is both expensive and complex, especially to an untrained security team. The model suffers from *latency*—the time it takes for the IDS to either modify the firewall rules or issue a TCP reset command. This period of time is critical in the success of an attack.

To respond to this need, a new technology, the IPS, is making its way into the network security arena to address this latency issue. It does this by both the intrusion detection system in-line with the firewall. Like in NIDS, NIPS architecture varies from product to product, but there is a basic underlying structure to all. These include traffic normalizer, system service scanner, detection engine, and traffic shaper [10].

13.10.1.1 Traffic Normalizer

The normalizer is in the line of network traffic to intercept traffic, resolving the traffic that has abnormalities before it sends it on. As it normalizes traffic, it may come to a point where it will discard the packet that does not conform to the set security policy criteria like if the packet has a bad checksum. It also does further activities of the firewall, thus blocking traffic based on the criteria that would normally be put in a firewall. The normalizer also may hold packet fragments and reassemble them into a packet based on its knowledge of the target system. The knowledge of the target system is provided from a reference table built by the system service scanner.

13.10.1.2 The Detection Engine

The detection engine handles all pattern matching that is not handled by the normalizer. These are patterns that are not based on protocol states.

13.10.1.3 Traffic Shaper

Before traffic leaves the NIPS, it must go through the traffic shaper for classification and flow management. The shaper classifies traffic protocol, although this may change in the future to include classification based on user and applications.

13.10.1.4 NIPS Benefits

In his extensive and thorough article "Network Intrusions: From Detection to Prevention," Andre Lee gives the following NIPS benefits:

• Zero-latency prevention: Without the NIDS and firewall bundle, NIPSs reduce this latency drastically by providing the notification within one hardwired circuitry instead of two.
• Effective network hygiene: Since many attacks are recycle attacks whose signatures are known, NIPS remove these packets quickly, although it does not do much effective anomaly analysis that is done by the NIDS.
• Simplified management: Because the would-be bundle of a NIDS and firewall are all packaged into one hardware, it reduces storage space and of course overall management.

Although it has all these advantages, NIPSs suffer from a number of problems including the following [10]:

- Production readiness: This occurs because the technology is new and has not gotten the field testing it needs to prove effectiveness in every test.
- High availability: This occurs because it is in-line, and on the first contact with network traffic, it may not be able to withstand high traffic availability and tolerance needed by all first and head-on network devices.
- Detection effectiveness: It has not yet been tested for effectiveness of detection, and it does not ever stop everything, falling short like NIDS.

13.10.2 Host-Based Intrusion Prevention Systems (HIPSs)

Like its cousin, the NIDSs, NIPSs also have corresponding HIPS based on one host. Most HIPSs work by *sandboxing*, a process of restricting the definition of acceptable behavior rules used on HIPSs. HIPS prevention occurs at the agent residing at the host. The agent intercepts system calls or system messages by utilizing dynamic linked libraries (dll) substitution. The substitution is accomplished by injecting existing system dlls with vendor stub dlls that perform the interception. So function calls made to system dlls actually perform a jump to vendor stub code where then the bad calls are processed, evaluated, and dealt with. Most vendor stubs are kernel drivers that provide system interception at the kernel level because processes system calls can be intercepted easily.

13.10.2.1 HIPS Benefits
Again like their cousins the HIDS, HIPS have benefits that include the following [10]:

- Effective context-based prevention: HIPS are the only solution to prevention of attacks that require simulation context. HIPS agents reside on the protected host; they have complete context of the environment and are therefore more capable of dealing with such attacks.
- Effective against zero-day attacks: Since HIPS use sandboxing method to deal with attacks, they can define acceptable parameter application or operating system service behavior to enable the agent to prevent any malicious attack on the host.
  Although they have good benefits, HIPS also have disadvantages based on limitations that hamper their rapid adoption. Among these limitations are [10]:
- Deployment challenge: As we discussed in the HIDS, there are difficulties in deploying the remote agents on each and every host. These hosts need updating and are susceptible to tampering.
- Difficulty of effective sandbox configuration: It can be a challenge to define effective and nonrestrictive parameters on hosts.
- Lack of effective prevention: Because of the use of sandboxing, HIPS cannot use any standard prevention like signature prevention.

Table 13.1 Most current ID systems

(1) MetaFlows Security System *Vendor*: MetaFlows *What*: Cloud-based IDS/IPS/forensics managed security service Web site: http://www.metaflows.com	(14) AT&T Network-Based Firewall v3 *Vendor*: AT&T Corporation Web site: http://www.att.com
(2) IPS 5500 Model 75EC *Vendor*: Corero Network Security *What*: A stand-alone, purpose-built IPS Web site: http://www.toplayer.com	(15) AlertLogic Threat Manager v3.5.4 *Vendor*: AlertLogic Web site: http://www.alertlogic.com
(3) Sourcefire Next-Generation IPS *Vendor*: Sourcefire *What*: A distributed appliance-based offering modeled on the Snort detection engine Web site: http://www.sourcefire.com	(16) ZyWALL USG 200 *Vendor*: ZyXEL Communications Web site: http://www.zyxel.com
(4) NitroGuard IPS 4245 *Vendor*: NitroSecurity *What*: An intelligent packet filtering system that detects sophisticated network intrusion attempts and actively records and/or stops such attempts Web site: http://www.nitrosecurity.com	(17) Proventia IPS GX6116 *Vendor*: IBM-ISS Web site: http://www.iss.net/
(5) McAfee Network Security Platform *Vendor*: McAfee *What*: Provides threat protection for demanding networks Web site: http://www.mcafee.com	(18) NitroGuard IPS *Vendor*: NitroSecurity Web site: http://www.nitrosecurity. com/
(6) CounterSnipe APS *Vendor*: CounterSnipe Technologies *What*: Provides network-based intrusion prevention security Web site: http://www.countersnipe.com	(19) IPS 5500-150E v 5.12 *Vendor*: Corero Network Security Web site: http://info.corero.com/ ppc-casestudy-idc-liquid-web.html? gclid=CJir6P7a_ tICFUs7gQod9PcEDw Intrusion Detection Systems Reviews
(7) Snort *Vendor*: Open source Web site: http://www.snort.org	(20) Interceptor 1000 *Vendor*: Reflex Security Web site: http://www.reflexsecurity. com
(8) Symantec Managed IDS/IPS with Sourcefire *Vendor*: Symantec Web site: http://www.symantec.com	(21) IDS/IPS *Vendor*: SecurityMetrics Web site: http://securitymetrics.com/
(9) SecureWorks Managed IDS/IPS *Vendor*: SecureWorks Web site: http://www.secureworks.com	(22) DefensePro, Version 3.10 *Vendor*: RadWare Web site: http://www.radware.com
(10) Perimeter eSecurity Firewall and Intrusion Prevention *Vendor*: Perimeter eSecurity Web site: http://www.perimeterusa.com	(23) CounterSnipe Technologies Active Protection Software 3.0 *Vendor*: CounterSnipe Technologies Web site: http://www.countersnipe. com

(continued)

Table 13.1   (continued)

(11) Network Box v3.2 *Vendor*: Network Box USA, Inc. *Price*: from $2200 first year Web site: http://www.networkboxusa.com	(24) NetIQ Security Manager (IDS group test) *Vendor*: NetIQ Web site: http://www.netiq.com/products/sm
(12) BM Managed Protection Service *Vendor*: IBM ISS Web site: http://www.ibm.com	(25) NetScreen-IDP100 (IDS group test) *Vendor*: NetScreen Technologies Inc. Web site: http://www.netscreen.com
F-Secure Protection Service for Business v4 *Vendor*: F-Secure Web site: http://www.f-secureusa.com	(26) StealthWatch (IDS group test) *Vendor*: Lancope Web site: http://www.lancope.com
(13) Clone Systems Clone Guard Managed IDS/IPS *Vendor*: Clone Systems Web site: http://www.clone-systems.com	

Source: SC Magazine: http://www.scmagazine.com/intrusion-detection-systems/products/91/

13.11   Intrusion Detection Tools

Intrusion detection tools work best when used after vulnerability scans have been performed. They then stand watch. For the most current list of IDS systems, the reader is referred to SC Magazine at http://www.scmagazine.com/intrusion-detection-systems/products/91/.

Table 13.1 displays the most recent ID systems based on CS Magazine.

All network-based intrusion detection systems and tools can provide recon (reconnaissance) probes in addition to port and host scans. As monitoring tools, they give information on:

- Hundreds of thousands of network connections
- External break-in attempts
- Internal scans
- Misuse patterns of confidential data
- Unencrypted remote logins or a Web sessions
- Unusual or potentially troublesome observed network traffic

All this information is gathered by these tools monitoring network components and services that include the following:

- Servers for:
  - Mail
  - FTP
  - Web activities
- DNS, RADIUS, and others
- TCP/IP ports

- Routers, bridges, and other WAN connection
- Drive space
- Event log entries
- File modes and existence
- File contents

Exercises

1. Are IDSs similar to firewalls?
2. Why are system intrusions dangerous?
3. Discuss the best approaches to implementing an effective IDS.
4. Can system intrusions be stopped? Support your response.
5. For a system without a DMZ, where is the best area in the network to install a honeypot?
6. Why are honeypots important to a network? Discuss the disadvantages of having a honeypot in the network.
7. Discuss three approaches of acquiring information needed to penetrate a network.
8. Discuss ways a system administrator can reduce system scanning by hackers.
9. Discuss the benefits of system scanning.
10. Discuss as many effective ways of responding to a system intrusion as possible. What are the best? Most implementable? Most cost-effective?

Advanced Exercises

1. Snort is a software-based real-time network intrusion detection system developed by Martin Roesch. It is a good IDS that can be used to notify an administrator of a potential intrusion attempt. Download and install Snort and start using it.
2. The effectiveness of an IDS varies with the tools used. Research and develop a matrix of good and effective IDS tools.
3. If possible, discuss the best ways to combine a firewall and a honeypot. Implement this combination and comment on its effectiveness.
4. Intrusion detection hybrids are getting better. Research the products on the market and comment on them as far as their interfaces are concerned.
5. Discuss how exploits can be used to penetrate a network. Research and list ten different common exploits.

References

1. Sundaram A. An introduction to intrusion detection, ACM Digital Library. http://dl.acm.org/citation.cfm?id=332161
2. Kizza JM (2002) Computer network security and cyber ethics. McFarlans Publishers, Jefferson

3. Halme LR, Bauer KR (1995) AINT misbehaving: a taxonomy of anti-intrusion techniques. Proceedings of the 18th National Information Systems Security conference.
4. Handley M, Paxson V, Kreibich C. Network intrusion detection: evasion, traffic normalization, and end-to-end protocol semantics. ACM Digital Library. http://dl.acm.org/citation.cfm?id=1267621
5. Proctor P (2001) The practical intrusion detection handbook. Prentice Hall, Upper Saddle River
6. Innella P. The evolution of intrusion detection systems. Symantec-Connect. http://www.symantec.com/connect/articles/evolution-intrusion-detection-systems
7. Mullins M. Lock IT down: implementing an intrusion detection system on your network: how to implement a network intrusion detection system. Tech Republic. http://www.techrepublic.com/article/lock-it-down-implementing-an-intrusion-detection-system-on-your-network/
8. Internet Security Systems. Network- *vs* Host-based intrusion detection: a guide to intrusion detection technology. http://www.windowsecurity.com/archived/nvh_ids.html
9. Panko RR (2004) Corporate computer and network security. Prentice Hall, Upper Saddle River
10. Yee A (2003) Network intrusions: from detection to prevention. Int J Inform Assur Prof 8(1)

Computer and Network Forensics

14

14.1 Definition

The proliferation of computer technology, including wireless technology and tele-communication, the plummeting prices of these technologies, the miniaturization of computing and telecommunication devices, and the globalization forces have all together contributed to our ever-growing dependence on computer technology. This growing dependence has been a bonanza to computer criminals who have seen this as the best medium to carry out their missions. In fact, Richard Rubin [1] has called this new environment a tempting environment to cybercriminals, and he gives seven compelling reasons that cause such temptations. They are as follows:

- Speed. Both computer and telecommunication technology have greatly increased the speed of transmission of digital data, which means that one can violate common decency concerning transmission of such data speedily and not get caught in the act. Also, the act is over before one has time to analyze its consequences and one's guilt.
- Privacy and Anonymity. There is a human weakness that if no one is a witness to an act one has committed, then there is less to no guilt on the doer's part. Privacy and anonymity, both of which can be easily attained using this new technology, support this weakness enabling one to create what can be called "moral distancing" from one's actions.
- Nature of Medium. The nature of storage and transmission of digital information in the digital age is different in many aspects from that of the Gutenberg-print era. The electronic medium of the digital age permits one to steal information without actually removing it. This virtual ability to remove and leave the original "untouched" is a great temptation, creating an impression that nothing has been stolen.
- Aesthetic Attraction. Humanity is endowed with a competitive zeal to achieve far and beyond our limitations. So we naturally get an adrenaline high whenever we accomplish a feat that seems to break down the efforts of our opponents or

the walls of the unknown. It is this high that brings about a sense of accomplishment and creative pride whenever not so well-known creative individuals come up with elegant solutions to technological problems. This fascination and a sense of accomplishment create an exhilaration among criminals that mitigates the value and the importance of the information attacked and justifies the action itself.

- Increased Availability of Potential Victims. There is a sense of amusement and ease to know that with just a few key strokes, one's message and action can be seen and consequently felt over wide areas and by millions of people. This sense unfortunately can very easily turn into evil feelings as soon as one realizes the power he or she has over millions of invisible and unsuspecting people.
- International Scope. The global reach of cyberspace creates an appetite for greater monetary, economic, and political powers. The ability to cover the globe in a short time and to influence an entire global community can make a believer out of a nonbeliever.
- Enormous Powers. The international reach, the speed, and the distancing of one self from the act endow enormous powers to an individual which may lead to criminal activities.

There are reasons to believe Rubin because the rate of computer crime is on the rise. Fighting such rising crimes is a formidable task. It includes education, legislation, regulation, enforcement through policing, and forensics. In both computer forensics and network, the battle starts in the technical realms of investigative science that require the knowledge or skills to identify, track, and prosecute the cybercriminal. But before we discuss network forensics, which some call Internet forensics, let us start by looking at computer forensics. We will come back to network forensics in Sect. 14.3.

14.2 Computer Forensics

By definition, computer forensics is the application of forensic science techniques to computer-based material. This involves the extraction, documentation, examination, preservation, analysis, evaluation, and interpretation of computer-based material to provide relevant and valid information as evidence in civil, criminal, administrative, and other cases. In general, computer forensics investigates what can be retrieved from the computer's storage media such as hard disk and other disks. In Sect. 14.3, we will contrast it with network forensics. Because we are dealing with computer-based materials in computer forensic science, the focus is on the computer, first as a tool and as a victim of the crime. The computer as a tool in the crime is merely a role player, for example, as a communication tool, if the crime is committed using a computer network, or as a storage facility where the bounty is stored on the computer files. As a victim, the computer is now the target of the attack, and it becomes the focus of the forensic investigation. In either case, the computer is central to the investigations because nearly all forensic cases will involve extracting and investigating data that is retrieved from the disks of the computer, both fixed and movable, and all its parts.

14.2.1 History of Computer Forensics

The history of computer forensics is tied up in the history of forensic science. According to Hal Berghel [2], the art of forensic science is actually derived from forensic medicine, an already recognized medical specialty. Forensic medicine's focus was autopsy examination to establish the cause of death. Although computers were in full use by the 1970s, mainly in big organizations and businesses such as banks and insurance companies, crimes involving computers as tools and as victims were very rare. One of the first recorded computer crimes during that time period was based on "interest rounding." Interest rounding was a round-robin policy used by banks to fairly distribute truncated floating point interest on depositors' accounts. The banks would round a depositor's interest points to a full cent. Anything less than a cent would be moved to the next account in a round-robin fashion.

Programmers, however, saw this as a source of ill-gotten wealth. They established an account to which they moved this less than a cent interest. With big banks with many depositors, this would add up. Because these programmers, like all computer criminals of the time, were highly educated, all computer crimes of the period were "white-collar" crimes. Law enforcement agencies of the time did not know enough about these types of computer crimes. Even the tools to gather evidence were not available. In a few cases where tools were available, they were often homemade [3].

It was not until the mid-1980s that some computer forensic tools such as X-Tree Gold and Norton Disk Editor became available. With these tools, investigators were able to recognize file types and were able to extract data on DOS-based disks. The 1990s saw heightened activities in computer crime and forensic investigations. The decade also produced an assortment of fine forensic tools that included the Forensic Toolkit.

Although the development of computer forensics started slow, it has now evolved as technology developed to where we are today. The increasing use of computers by law enforcement investigators and prosecutors and, as noted earlier, the widespread and rampant increase in computer-related crimes have led to the development of computer forensics. The primary focus and methodology, although still embedded in the basic physical forensics, have been tracing and locating computer hardware, recovering hidden data from the digital storage media, identifying and recovering hidden data, decrypting files, decomposing data, cracking passwords, and bypassing normal operating system security controls and permissions [4].

14.2.2 Elements of Computer Forensics

There are three key elements in any forensic investigations: the material itself, its relevance to the case in question, and the validity of any observations/conclusions reached by the examiner. Since computer forensics is very similar to ordinary physical forensics, these elements remain the same in computer forensics.

14.2.2.1 The Material

In both roles the computer plays in forensic science, the cases we have given above, the materials involved are both electronic and physical. Physical material investigation falls within the realms of the traditional police investigations where files and manila envelopes and boxes are all examined. The electronic form data is a little trickier to deal with. It may be data that does exist in hard copy, such as e-mail text, e-mail headers, e-mail file attachments, electronic calendars, Web site log files, and browser information. It may be deleted documents that must be recovered and reconstructed because deleted data does not necessarily disappear. Even when the reference to the deleted file is removed from the computer's directory, the bits that make up the file often remain on the hard drive until they are overwritten by new data. Beside deleted data, data also may be encrypted or password protected, making it more difficult to get in its original form.

If the computer is the focus of the investigation, then information from all system components is part of the required data. For example, network nodes and stand-alone personal computer operating systems create a great deal of administrative, management, and control information that is vital in the investigation.

14.2.2.2 Relevance

Once the existence of the material has been established, the next important step is to make sure that the material is relevant. The relevancy of the material will depend on the requesting agency, nature of the request, and the type of the case in question. The requesting agencies are usually one of the following:

- The victim
- Government
- Insurance companies
- The courts
- Private business
- Law enforcement
- Private individuals

We will talk more about relevancy when we discuss analysis of evidence.

14.2.2.3 Validity

The question of validity of data is tied up with the relevance of data. It is also based on the process of authentication of data. We are going to discuss this next.

14.2.3 Investigative Procedures

Both computer and network forensics (Sect. 14.3) methodologies consist of three basic components that Kruse and Heiser [5] both call the three As of computer forensic investigations. These are as follows: acquiring the evidence, taking care to make sure that the integrity of the data is preserved, authenticating the validity of the extracted data—this involves making sure that the extracted data is as valid as the original—and analyzing the data while keeping its integrity.

14.2.3.1 Looking for Evidence
As Kruse puts it, when dealing with computer forensics, the only thing to be sure of is uncertainty. So the investigator should be prepared for difficulties in searching for bits of evidence data from a haystack. The evidence usually falls into the following categories:

- Impressions: This includes fingerprints, tool marks, footwear marks, and other types of impressions and marks.
- Bioforensics: This includes blood, body fluids, hair, nail scrapings, and blood stain patterns.
- Infoforensics: This includes binary data fixed in any medium such as on CDs, memory, and floppies.
- Trace evidence: This includes residues of things used in the committing of a crime like arson accelerant, paint, glass, and fibers.
- Material evidence: This includes physical materials such as folders, letters, and scraps of papers.

As you start, decide on what the focus of the investigation is. At the start, decide on:

- What you have to work with: This may include written and technical policies, permissions, billing statements, and system application and device logs.
- What you want to monitor: This includes employer and employee rights, Internet e-mail, and chat room tracking.

Deciding what to focus on requires the investigator to make a case assessment that identifies the case requirements. To do this, the investigator must establish the following [3]:

- Situation—gives the environment of the case
- Nature of the case—broadly states the nature of the case
- Specifics about the case—states out what the case is about
- Types of evidence to look for—stating physical and electronic data and the materials to be collected and examined
- Operating system in use at the time of the incident
- Known disk formats at the time of the incident
- Location of evidence both physical and electronic

Once this information is collected, the investigation may start creating the profile of the culprit. At this point, you need to decide whether to let the suspect systems identified above run for a normal day, run periodically, or be pulled altogether if such actions will help the evidence-gathering stage. Pulling the plug means that you will make copies of the computer content and work with the copies while keeping the original intact. Make sure that the system is disconnected and that all that may be affected by the disconnection such as volatile data is preserved before the disconnection. Make duplication and imaging of all the drives immediately, and ensure that the system remains in its "frozen" state without being used during the investigation.

One advantage of pulling the plug is to "freeze" the evidence and prevent it from being contaminated with either new use or modifications or alterations. Also freezing the system prevents errors committed after the reported incident and before a full investigation is completed. However, freezing the system may result in several problems, including the destruction of any evidence of any ongoing processes.

On the other hand, working with a live system has its share of problems. For example, the intruder may anticipate a "live" investigation that involves an investigator working with a system still in operation. If the intruder anticipates such action, then he or she may alter the evidence wherever the evidence is well ahead of the investigator, thus compromising the validity of the evidence.

Whether you use a "live" system or a "frozen" one, you must be careful in the use of the software, both investigative and system software. Be careful and weigh the benefits of using software found on the system or new software. A number of forensic investigators prefer not to use any software found on the system for fear of using compromised software. Instead they use new software on the copy system, including system software. Another variation used by some investigators is to verify the software found on the system and then use it after. Each of these methods has advantages and disadvantages, and one has to be careful to choose what best serves the particular situation under review.

14.2.3.2 Handling Evidence

The integrity of the evidence builds the validity of such evidence and consequently wins or loses a case under investigation because it is this evidence that is used in the case to establish the facts upon which the merits, or lack of, are based. It is, therefore, quite important and instructive that extreme care must be taken when handling forensic evidence. Data handling includes extraction and the establishment of a chain of custody. The chain of custody itself involves packaging, storage, and transportation. These three form the sequence of events along the way from the extraction point to the courtroom. This sequence of events is traceable if one answers the following questions:

- Who extracted the evidence and how?
- Who packaged it?
- Who stored it, how, and where?
- Who transported it?

The answers to these questions are derived from the following information [3]:

- Case:
  - Case number—a number assigned to the case to uniquely identify the case
  - Investigator—name of the investigator and company affiliation
  - Nature of the case—a brief description of the case
- Equipment involved:
  - For all computing equipment, carefully describe the equipment including the maker, vendor, model, and serial number.
- Evidence:
  - Location where it is recorded
  - Who recorded it
  - Time and date of recording

This information may be filled in a form called the *chain-of-evidence* form.

14.2.3.3 Evidence Recovery

The process of evidence extraction can be easy or complicated depending on the nature of the incident and the type of computer or network upon which the incident took place. The million dollar question in evidence extraction is: What do I extract and what do I leave behind? To answer this question, remember that if you are in an area extracting data and you remove what you think is sufficient evidence only to come back for more, you may find that what you left behind is of no value anymore, a big loss. So the rule of thumb is extract and collect as much as you can so that the return trip is never needed.

What are the candidates for evidence extraction? There are many, including hardware such as computers, printers, scanners, and network connectors such as modems, routers, and hubs. Software items include system programs and logs, application software, and special user software. Documentation such as scrap paper and anything printed within the vicinity are also candidates and so are materials such as backup tapes and disks, CDs, cassettes, floppy and hard disks, and all types of logs.

In fact, according to Sammes and Jenkinson [6], an investigator should start the job only when the following items are at hand:

- An adequate forensic toolkit which may be a complete forensic computer workstation
- A search kit
- Search and evidence forms and sketch plan sheets
- Evidence bag
- Still, digital, and video cameras
- Disk boxes
- Mobile phone
- Blank floppy disks
- A flashlight

- Bitstream imaging tool
- Evidence container

With these at hand, the investigator then starts to gather evidence by performing the following steps [3]:

- Arrange for interviews with all parties involved in the case. This gives the investigator a chance to collect more evidence and materials that might help the case.
- Fill out the evidence form.
- Copy the digital evidence disk by making a bitstream copy or bit-by-bit copy of the original disk. This type of disk copying is different from a simple disk copy which cannot copy deleted files or e-mail messages and cannot recover file fragments. Bitstream copying then creates a bitstream image. As we will see in Sect. 14.4, there are several tools on the market to do this. Digital evidence can be acquired in three ways:
  - Creating a bitstream of disk-to-image file of the disk. This is the most commonly used approach.
  - Making a bitstream disk to disk used in cases that a bit-by-bit imaging cannot be done due to errors.
  - Making a sparse data copy of a file or folder.

Always let the size of the disk, the duration you have to keep the disk, and the time you have for data acquisition determine which extraction method to use. For large original source disks, it may be necessary to compress the evidence or the copy. Computer forensics compress tools are of two types: *lossless* compression which does not discard data when it compresses a file and *lossy* compression which loses data but keeps the quality of the data upon recovery. Only lossless compression tools such as WinZip or PKZip are acceptable in computer forensics. Other lossless tools that compress large files include EnCase and SafeBack. Compressed data should always have MD5, SHA-1 hash, or cyclic redundancy check (CRC) done on the compressed data for security after storage and transportation.

For every item of the evidence extracted, assign a unique identification number. Also for each item, write a brief description of what you think it is and where it was recovered. You may also include the date and time it was extracted and by whom. It is also helpful, where possible, to keep a record of the evidence scene either by taking a picture or by video. In fact where possible, it is better to videotape the whole process including individual items. This creates an additional copy, a video copy, of the evidence. After all the evidence has been collected and identified and categorized, it must be stored in a good clean container that is clearly labeled and safely stored. It is important to store the evidence at the most secure place possible that is environmentally friendly to the media on which the evidence is stored. For example, the place must be clean and dry. If the evidence was videotaped, the video must be stored in an area where video recordings can last the longest. Where it requires seizure of items, care must be taken to make sure that evidence is not destroyed. If it requires dismantling the evidence object for easy moving and transportation, it is prudent that there be an identical reconstruction. Every electronic media item seized must be taken for examination.

When there is a need to deal with an unknown password, several approaches can be used. These include *second guessing*, use of *backdoors*, an undocumented key sequence that can be made available by manufacturers, and use of a *backup*.

And finally the investigator has to find a way of dealing with encrypted evidence. If the encrypting algorithm is weak, there are always ways and software to break such encryptions. However, if the algorithms are of a strong type, this may be a problem. These problems are likely to be encountered in encrypted e-mails, data files on hard drives, and hard disk partitions. Several products are available to deal with these situations [6]:

- For encrypted e-mails—use PGP.
- For encrypted hidden files—use Encrypted Magic Folders (http://www.pc-magic.com/des.htm).
- For hard drive encrypted files—use BestCrypt (http://www.jetico.com/encryption-bestcrypt/). Others are IDEA, Blowfish, DES, Triple DES, and CAST.

14.2.3.4 Preserving Evidence

There is no one standard way for securing evidence. Each piece of evidence, packing, and storage is taken on a case-by-case basis. Packaging the evidence is not enough to preserve its integrity. Extra storage measures must be taken to preserve the evidence for a long time if necessary. One of the challenges in preserving digital evidence is its ability to disappear so fast. In taking measures to preserve evidence, therefore, this fact must be taken into account. Evidence preservation starts at the evidence extraction stage by securing the evidence scene from onlookers and other interested parties. If possible, allow only those involved in the extraction to view it. Several techniques are used including the following:

- Catalogue and package evidence in a secure and strong antistatic, well-padded, and labeled evidence bag that can be secured by tape and zippers. Make sure that the packaging environment keeps the evidence uncontaminated by cold, hot, or wet conditions in the storage bag.
- Back up the original data including doing a disk imaging of all suspected media. Care must be taken especially when copying a disk to another disk; it is possible that the checksum of the destination disk always results in a different value than a checksum of the original disk. According to Symantec, the difference is due to differences in disk geometry between the source and destination disks [7]. Since Ghost, a Norton forensic product, does not create an exact duplicate of a disk but only recreates the partition information as needed and copies the contents of the files, investigators using Ghost for forensic duplication must be careful as it does not provide a true bit-to-bit copy of the original.
- Document and time-stamp, including the date, every and all steps performed in relation to the investigation, giving as many details as possible, however

insignificant the steps are. Note all network connections before and during the investigation.

- Implement a credible control access system to make sure that those handling the evidence are the only ones authorized to handle the evidence.
- Secure your data by encryptions, if possible. Encryption is very important in forensic science because it is used by both the investigator and the suspect. It is most commonly used by the suspect to hide content and by the investigator to ensure the confidentiality of the evidence. The integrity of the evidence is maintained when it has not been altered in any way. Encryption technology can also verify the integrity of the evidence at the point of use. Investigators must check to see that the encrypted system under examination has a key recovery system. It makes the job of the investigators ten times as more difficult if they encounter encrypted evidence. Data can become intercepted during transit.
- Preserve the evidence as much as possible by not adding or removing software, using only trusted tools, not using programs that use the evidence media.
- If possible validate and/or authenticate your data by using standards, such as Kerberos, and using digital certificates, biometrics, or timestamping. All these technologies are used in authentication, validation, and verification. The time when an object was signed always affects its trustworthiness because an expired or a revoked certificate is worthless. Timestamping is useful when collecting evidence because it provides incontestable proof that the digital evidence was in existence at a specific time and date and has not been changed since that date.

In addition to timestamping, the images of the hard drives and any volatile data saved before "freezing" the system, the following can also be time-stamped [5]:

- Ongoing collection of suspect activities including log files, sniffer outputs, and output from intrusion detection system
- Output from any reports or searches performed on a suspect machine, including all files and their associated access times
- Daily typed copies of investigator's notes

Note, however, that criminals can use all these same tools against investigators.

14.2.3.5 Transporting Evidence

Where it is necessary to transport the evidence either for safer security, more space, or to court, great care must be taken to safeguard the integrity of the evidence you have painstakingly collected and labored to keep safe and valid. Keep in mind that transportation pitfalls can be found across the transportation channel from the starting point all the way to the destination. Be aware that containers can be opened midway even from trusted individuals. So find the most secure, trusted, and verified way to transport the evidence. This may include constant and around-the-clock monitoring and frequent checks including signatures of all those handling the evidence along the way. The goal is to maintain a *chain of custody* to protect the integrity of the evidence and to make it difficult for anybody to deny the evidence because it was tempered with.

Since during transportation the integrity of data may be affected, it is important to use strong data hiding techniques such as encryptions, steganography, password-protected documents, and other ways. Data hiding, a form of steganography, embeds data into digital media for the purpose of identification and annotation. Several constraints, however, affect this process: the quantity of data to be hidden, the need for invariance of this data under conditions where a "host" signal is subject to distortions, and the degree to which the data must be immune to interception, modification, or removal by a third party [8].

One of the important goals of data hiding in digital media in general and computer forensics in particular is to provide assurance of content integrity. Therefore, to ensure content integrity, the hidden data must stay hidden in a host signal even if that signal is subjected to degrading manipulation such as filtering, resampling, cropping, or lossy data compression.

Since data can be compromised during transit, there are ways to test these changes. Among these are the use of parity bits, redundancy checks used by communication protocols, and checksums. Even though these work, unfortunately they can all fall prey to deliberate attempts by hackers using simple utilities that can render them all useless. To detect deliberate attempts at data during transmission, a better technique is a cryptographic form of checksum called a hash function. Applying a hash function to data results in a *hash value* or a *message digest*. A robust hash algorithm such as MD5 and SHA-1 can deliver a computationally infeasible test of data integrity. Hash algorithms are used by examiners in two ways: to positively verify that data has been altered by comparing digests taken before and after the incident and to verify that evidence have not been altered.

Another way to safeguard evidence in transition, if it has to be moved either as a digital medium carried by somebody or electronically transferred, is data compression. As we have seen in Sect. 14.2.3.4, data compression can be used to reduce the size of data objects such as files. Since compression is a weak form of encryption, a compressed file can be further encrypted for more security.

14.2.4 Analysis of Evidence

After dealing with the extraction of evidence, identification, storage, and transportation, there now remains the most important and most time-consuming part of computer and network forensic science, that of analysis. As Kruse et al. noted, the most important piece of advice in forensics is "don't take anything for granted." Forensic evidence analysis is painstakingly slow and should be thorough. The process of analyzing evidence done by investigators to identify patterns of activity, file signature anomalies, unusual behaviors, file transfers, and several other trends to either support or reject the case is the most crucial and time-consuming in forensic investigation and should depend on the nature of the investigation and amount of data extracted. For example, non-litigation cases may not involve as much care as the care needed for litigation ones because in litigation cases, there must be enough evidence of good quality to fend off the defense. According to Kruse, the following things should not be taken for granted [5]:

- Examine the shortcuts, Internet, recycle bins, and registry.
- Review the latest release of the system software with an eye on new methods of data hiding.
- Check every data tape, floppy disk, CD-ROM, DVD, and flash memory found during evidence extraction.
- Look in books, in manuals, under keyboards, on the monitor, and everywhere where people usually hide passwords and other pertinent information.
- Double-check the analysis.
- Reexamine every file and folder, log files, and print spooler.
- Recover any encrypted or archived file.

Once the evidence has been acquired and carefully preserved, then the analysis process begins. Make sure that all evidence is received at the examination center. All items must be in sealed evidence bags. An external examination of all items must be done before the internal examinations can begin. For disks and other recordable media, an imaging of each must be done. Currently tools to do this job include *DriveSpy*, *EnCase*, *CaptureIt*, *FTK Explorer*, and *dd* to name a few.

It is normal to start the hard drives with the following [9]:

- Hard drive physical analysis—seeking information of partitions, damaged sectors, and any data outside of the partitions
- Hard drive logical analysis—seeking information on active file metadata, context of information, file paths, file sizes, and file signatures
- Additional hard drive analysis—looking for active files, file system residues, erased files, electronic communications, and peripheral devices

After dealing with the hard drives, continue with other peripherals, documentation, and every other component that is relevant to the incident. The tools most used in this endeavor are discussed in Sect. 14.4. It is also important to note here that the amount of work done and sometimes the quality of the analysis done may depend on the platform you use. Forensic investigators are religiously devoted to their operating systems, but it is advisable to use whatever makes you comfortable.

The analysis itself should not be constrained; it should take any direction and any form. Specifically, it should focus on devices and on the storage media. Although we prefer the analysis to be loose and flowing, keeping close to the following guidelines is helpful [3]:

- Clearly know what you are looking for.
- Have a specific format for classifying data.
- Have and keep tools for data reconstruction.

- Request or demand for cooperation from agencies and departments, especially where you have to ask for help in evidence protection.
- Use only recently wiped media like disks as target media to store evidence. There are several tools to clean wipe a disk.
- Inventory the hardware and software on the suspect system because all may be part of the investigation.
- On the suspect system, remove the hard drive(s), noting the time and date in the system's CMOS.
- On the image disk:
  - List and check all directories, folders, and files.
  - Examine the contents of each. Where tools are needed to recover passwords and files, acquire such tools.
  - Note where every item found on the disk(s) was found and identify every executable, noting its function(s).

14.2.4.1 Data Hiding

While analyzing evidence data, it is very important to pay particular attention to data hiding. There are many ways data can be hidden in a file system including the following:

Deleted Files

Deleted files can be recovered manually using hex editor. When a file on a Windows platform is deleted, the first character of the directory entry is changed to a sigma character—hex value of E5. The operating system takes this sigma to indicate that the entry should not be displayed because the file has been deleted. The entry in the file allocation table (FAT) is also changed to zero, indicating unused sectors and therefore available to the operating system for allocation.

Similarly, MS-DOS does not remove data in clusters of files declared as deleted. It merely marks them as available for reallocation. It is, therefore, quite possible to recover a file that has been deleted, provided the clusters of the file have not been reused. DOS programs such as UNERASE and UNDELETE try to recover such files. But Norton Disk Editor is more effective.

Note that the operating system does not do anything to the data in these sectors until reallocating the sectors to another file. The data in the sectors are then overwritten. Before that, http://www.intergov.org/public_information/general_information/latest_web_stats.html data in these sectors can be reconstructed.

Hidden Files

Data hiding is one of the most challenging aspects of forensic analysis. With special software, it is possible to mark a partition "hidden" such that the operating system will no longer access it. Other hidden areas can be created by setting partition tables to start at head 0, sector 1 of a cylinder, and the first sector of the partition proper—the boot record—to start at head 1, sector 1 of the cylinder. The consequence of this is that there will invariably be a number of unused sectors at the beginning of each partition, between the partition table sector and the boot record sector [6].

In addition to these hidden areas, operating systems also hide files and filenames from users. Files and filenames, especially system files, are purposely hidden from users because we want the users not to be able to access those files from their regular display list. The filenames of system programs are usually hidden because average users do not have to know them and those who know them do not need to have them listed. When they need to see them, they can always list them.

Every operating system has a way of hiding and displaying hidden files. For example, Linux has a very simple way of "hiding" a file. Creating a file with an added period to the front of the filename which defines to Linux that the filename is "hidden" makes it hidden. To display Linux hidden files, add the **-a** flag (display all filenames) to the **ls** (list) command like "ls –a." This displays all of files in the current directory whether hidden or not. Similarly Unix does not display any files or directories that begin with the dot (.) character. Such files can be displayed by either the Show Hidden Files option or the -a switch of the ls command.

Because of these cases, it is, therefore, always prudent to assume that the candidate system has hidden files and data. Hidden data is always a clue for investigators to dig deeper. There are a number of ways to hide data including encryption; compression; codes; steganography; and using invisible names, obscure names, misleading names, and invisible names. We will discuss these throughout this chapter.

Slack Space

This is unused space in a disk cluster. Both DOS and Windows file systems use fixed-size clusters. During space allocation, even if the actual data being stored require less storage than the cluster size, an entire cluster is reserved for the file. Sometimes this leaves large swats of used space called *slack space*. When a file is copied, its slack space is not copied. It is not possible to eliminate all slack space without changing the partition size of the hard disk or without deleting or compressing many small files into a larger one. Short of eliminating these wasted spaces, it is good to have software tools to examine this slack space and find out how big it is and what is hidden in it. If this is not done, there is a risk of slack space containing remnants of hostile code or hidden confidential files.

Bad Blocks

A bad track is an area of the hard disk that is not reliable for data storage. It is possible to map a number of disk tracks as "bad tracks." These tracks are then put into a bad track table that lists any areas of the hard disk that should not be used. These "bad tracks" listed on the table are then aliased to good tracks. This makes the operating system avoid the areas of the disk that cannot be read or written. An area that has been marked as "bad" by the controller may well be good and could store hidden data. Or a good sector could be used to store incriminating data and then be marked as bad. A lot of data can be hidden this way in the bad sectors by the suspect. Never format a disk before you explore all the bad blocks because formatting a disk deletes any data that may be on the disk.

Steganography Utilities
Steganography is the art of hiding information in ways that prevent its detection. Steganography, an ancient craft, has seen a rebirth with the onset of computer technology with computer-based steganographic techniques that embed information in the form of text, binary files, or images by putting a message within a larger one in such a way that others cannot discern the presence or contents of the hidden message. The goal of steganography is to avoid drawing suspicion to the transmission of a hidden message. This is, therefore, a threat to forensic analysts as they now must consider a much broader scope of information for analysis and investigation. Steganalysis uses utilities that discover and render useless such covert messages.

Password-Cracking Software
This is software that once planted on a user's disk or finds its way to the password server tries to make any cryptosystems untrustworthy or useless by discovering weak algorithms, wrong implementation, or application of cryptalgorithms and human factor.

NTFS Streams
In NTFS (Windows NT File System), a file object is implemented as a series of streams. Streams are an NTFS mechanism allowing the association and linking of new data objects with a file. However, the NT NTFS has an undocumented feature that is referred to by different names, including alternate data streams, multiple data streams on the Microsoft TechNet CD, named data streams, and forked data streams. Whatever name it is called, this feature of NTFS is not viewable to ordinary NT tools. That means that data hidden in these streams are not viewable by GUI-based programs and Windows Explorer, for example. It is, however, easy to write in these streams using Windows Notepad. If this happens, however, then File Explorer has no mechanism to enumerate these additional streams. Therefore, they remain hidden to the observer. This is a security nightmare because these streams can be exploited by attackers for such things as denial-of-service and virus attacks. Also many network users can store data on an NT server that administrators are not aware of and cannot control.

Codes and Compression
There are two techniques combined here. Coding is a technique where characters of the data are systematically substituted by other characters. This technique can be used by system users to hide vital or malicious data. Data compression on the other hand is a way of reducing the size of data object like a file. This technique is also increasingly being used by suspects to hide data. Forensic investigators must find a way to decipher coded or compressed evidence. Uncompressing compressed data can reveal to investigators whether evidence is encrypted or not. To deal with all these, it is imperative that a forensic investigator acquires forensic tools that can decompress, decrypt, decode, and crack passwords and tools to uncover hidden data. We will survey these tools in Sect. 14.4.

Forensic analysis is done to positively identify the perpetrator and the method he or she is using or used to commit the act, to determine network vulnerabilities that allowed the perpetrator to gain access into the system, to conduct a damage assessment of the victimized network, and to preserve the evidence for judicial action, if it is necessary. These objectives which drive the analysis are similar in many ways to those set for physical forensics. So computer forensics examiners should and must develop the same level of standards and acceptable practices as those adhered to by physical investigators.

14.2.4.2 Operating System-Based Evidence Analysis

Most forensic analysis tools are developed for particular platforms. Indeed many forensic investigators prefer to work on specific platforms than on others. Let us briefly look at forensic analysis based on the following platforms:

Microsoft-Based File Systems (FAT8, FAT16, FAT 32, and VFAT)

Because most computer forensic tools so far are developed for Microsoft file systems, we will start with that. According to Bill Nelson et al., an investigator performing forensic analysis on a Microsoft file system must do the following [3]:

- Run an antivirus program scan for all files on the forensic workstation before connecting for a disk-to-disk bitstream imaging.
- Run an antivirus scan again after connecting the copied disk-to-disk bitstream image disk to all drives including the copied drive unless the copied volumes were imaged by EnCase or SaveSet.
- Examine fully the copied suspect disk noting all boot files in the root.
- Recover all deleted files, saving them to a specified secure location.
- Acquire evidence from FAT.
- Process and analyze all recovered evidence.

NTFS File System

Use tools such as DriveSpy to analyze evidence just like in FAT file systems.

Unix and Linux File Systems

Although forensic tools for Linux are still few, the recent surge in Linux use has led to the development of new tools, including some freeware such as the Coroner's Toolkit (TCT) and the Sleuth Kit (TSK). These tools and most GUI tools can also analyze Unix. These include EnCase, FTK, and iLook. Because most Unix and Linux systems are used as servers, investigators, according to Nelson et al., must use a live system. When dealing with live systems, the first task for the investigator is to preserve any data from all system activities that are stored in volatile memory. This saves the state of all running processes, including those running in the background. These activities include the following [3]:

- Console messages
- Running processes

- Network connections
- System memories
- Swap space

Macintosh File System
All system running Mac OS9X or later versions uses the same forensic tools such as Unix, Linux, and Windows. However, for older MAC systems, it is better to use tools like Expert Witness, EnCase, and iLook.

14.3   Network Forensics

In Sect. 14.2, we gave a definition for computer forensics that network forensics contrasts. Unlike computer forensics that retrieves information from the computer's disks, network forensics, in addition, retrieves information on which network ports were used to access the network. Dealing with network forensics, therefore, implies taking the problems of computer forensics and multiplying them one hundred times, a thousand times, and sometimes a million times over. Some of the things we do in computer forensics cannot be done in network forensics. For example, it is easy to take an image of a hard drive when we are dealing with one or two computers. However, when you are dealing with a network with five thousand nodes, it is not feasible. There are other differences. Network forensics, as Berghel observed, is different from computer forensics in several areas, although it grew out of it. And its primary objective, to apprehend the criminal, is the same. There are several differences that separate the two including the following:

- Unlike computer forensics where the investigator and the person being investigated, in many cases the criminals, are on two different levels with the investigator supposedly on a higher level of knowledge of the system, the network investigator and the adversary are at the same skills level.
- In many cases, the investigator and the adversary use the same tools: one to cause the incident and the other to investigate the incident. In fact, many of the network security tools on the market today, including NetScanTools Pro, Traceroute, and Port Probe, used to gain information on the network configurations, can be used by both the investigator and the criminal. As Berghel puts it, the difference between them is on the ethics level, not the skills level.
- While computer forensics, as we have seen in Sect. 14.3, deals with the extraction, preservation, identification, documentation, and analysis and it still follows well-defined procedures springing from law enforcement for acquiring, providing chain of custody, authenticating, and interpretation, network forensics on the other hand has nothing to investigate unless steps were in place (like packet filters, firewalls, and intrusion detection systems) prior to the incident.

However, even if network forensics does not have a lot to go after, there are established procedures to deal with both intrusive and nonintrusive incidents. For intrusive incidents, an analysis needs to be done.

14.3.1 Intrusion Analysis

Network intrusions can be difficult to detect let alone analyze. A port scan can take place without a quick detection, and more seriously a stealthy attack to a crucial system resource may be hidden by a simple innocent port scan. If an organization overlooks these simple incidents, it may lead to serious security problems. An intrusion analysis is essential to deal with these simple incidents and more serious ones like backdoors that can make reentry easy for an intruder, a program intentionally left behind to capture proprietary data for corporate espionage, or a program in waiting before launching a denial-of-service attack.

The biggest danger to network security is pretending that an intrusion will never occur. As we noted in Sect. 10.3, hackers are always ahead of the game; they intentionally leave benign or not easily detectable tools behind on systems that they want to eventually attack. Unless intrusion analysis is used, none of these may be detected. So the purpose of intrusion analysis is to seek answers to the following questions:

- Who gained entry?
- Where did they go?
- How did they do it?
- What did they do once into the network?
- When did it happen?
- Why the chosen network?
- Can it be prevented in the future?
- What do we learn from the incident?

Answers to these questions help us to learn exactly what happened, determine the intruder motives, prepare an appropriate response, and make sure it doesn't happen again. A thorough intrusion analysis requires a team of knowledgeable people who will analyze all network information to determine the location of evidence data. Such evidence data can reside in any one location of the network, including appliances and service files that are fundamental to the running of the network like [9]:

- Routers and firewalls.
- FTP and DNS server files.
- Intrusion detection systems monitor log files.
- System log files including security, system, remote access, and applications.
- Exchange servers.
- Servers' hard drives.

Intrusion analysis involves gathering and analyzing data from all these network points. It also consists of the following services [2]:

- Incident response plan
- Incident response
- Technical analysis of intrusion data
- Reverse engineering of attacker tools (reverse hacking)

All results of the analysis must be redirected to an external safe and secure place.

On systems such as Unix and Linux servers, the intrusion investigators must examine system log files to identify accounts used during the penetration. Investigators must also examine [3]:

- All running processes
- All network connections
- All deleted files
- All background processes
- File system
- Memory status
- Contents of each swap
- Backup media
- All files created or modified during the incident

These help the investigator to reconstruct the system in order to be able to determine what happened.

14.3.1.1 Incident Response Plan

The incident response plan should be based on one of the three philosophies: watch and warn, repair and report, and pursue and prosecute. In watch and warn, a monitoring and reporting system is set up to notify a responsible party when an incident occurs. This is usually a simple monitoring and reporting system with no actions taken beyond notifications. Some of these systems have now become real-time monitoring and reporting systems. The repair and report philosophy aims at bringing the system back to normal running as soon as possible. This is achieved through a quick identification of the intrusion, repairing all identified vulnerability, or blocking the attack and quickly reporting the incident to the responsible party. Finally, the pursue and prosecute philosophy involves monitoring for incidents, collection of evidence if an attack occurs, and reporting beyond technical staff that involves law enforcement and court charges.

The response plan should also outline the procedures to be taken and indicate the training needed. Under the procedures, everyone should know what he or she should do. The procedures should also indicate what level of priorities should receive the greatest level of attention. The response plan is important to an investigator because if the plan is good and it is followed, it should have documented the circumstances that may have caused the incident and what type of response was immediately taken. For example, were the machines "frozen"? When and by whom? What immediate information about the attack and the attacker was known, who knew about it, and what was done immediately? What procedures were taken to deal with remote systems and connections to public networks? Disconnecting from the network can isolate the systems and keep the attackers from entering or sometimes exiting the network. However, severing all connections may not only disrupt the services, but it may also destroy the evidence. Communication is important, and there should be one designated person to handle all communication, especially to the public. Finally response plan information also consists of documentation of the activities on the system and networks as well as system configuration information before the incident. It also consists of support information such as a list of contacts and their responses; documentation on the uses of tools and by whom is also included [10]. Since different circumstances require different responses, the investigator needs to know what response was taken and have all the documentation of whatever was done.

14.3.1.2 Incident Response

Incident response is part of the security plan that must be executed whenever an incident occurs. Two items are important to an investigator in the incident response. These are incident notification and incident containment. In incident notification, what the investigator wants to know are as follows: Who knew first and what were the first responses? Who was notified in the process and what were the responses? It is common that the first person to notice the incident always deals with it. Usually employees "see" the incident in progress first and inform the "Techs" that the machines are running "funny" or slow. Incident notification procedures need to be built into the operating incident plan. The work of the response team may also be of interest to the investigator. The response team should get clear and precise information, and it should consist of people with the knowledge and skills needed to handle security incidents. It is this expertise that the investigator needs to tap into. Finally, since the reporting procedures require management to know immediately, the investigator may be interested in that trail of information. Also the response team may have information, preliminary at first but may improve later, of the extent of the attack. Usually they know who was affected and what actions were taken on their machines and tools. Also note if law enforcement agencies were contacted and what type of information was given.

Incident containment is required to stop the incident if possible but more so to minimize the effects of the incident. Rapid response is critical in today's automated attacks that are able to scan systems, locate vulnerabilities, and penetrate them with lightning speed and with limited human intervention. Incident containment is important to the investigator because it contains efforts taken to deny access to the system and the number of affected systems. The containment plan consists of the following response items: determination of affected systems, denying the attacker access to systems, elimination of rogue processes, and regaining control [10]. The documentation in each of these should provide the investigator with a trove of good information. The investigators should be particularly interested in the plan's regaining of control because valuable evidence clues may be lost. To regain control means to bring the system back to the state it was in before the incident. The first effort in regaining control is to lock out the attacker. This is important because, when discovered, the attacker may try to destroy as much of the evidence as possible. Blocking the attacker's access may be achieved by blocking access at the firewall or a complete disconnection of the system. Actions that follow may include change of passwords, disabling of services, removal of backdoors, if those can be found, and monitoring of activities. In addition, if no further legal actions are required, the sanitation of the system may be required. However, if further legal recourse is anticipated, then this may be avoided for some time to allow the investigator to recover the evidence. After the evidence has been collected, then the rebuilding of the system involving the use of backups, applying security patches, and reloading of data begin. Since attacks can originate either from outside or internally, incident containment plans must be handled with care and secrecy in case the suspect is in the house.

14.3.1.3 Technical Analysis of the Intrusions

The most difficult, time-consuming, and technically challenging part of network forensics is the technical analysis of intrusions and intrusion data. Typically, unlike computer forensics where most of the evidence may reside on the victim machine, in network forensics, evidence does not reside on one hard drive or one machine; it may require to search many disks and many network computers. As we pointed out earlier, the investigator must have almost the same skills as the suspect and many times may use the same tools. In any case, as we discussed in Sect. 14.3.1, in any suspected incident occurring in a network environment, we may need to analyze the following network information to determine the location of pertinent information.

One of the most important and crucial source of logs on the Internet is the ISP. Since ISPs deal with lots of dial-up customers, each customer dialing in must be authenticated before a call is dynamically assigned an IP address by the Dynamic Host Configuration Protocol (DHCP) server. This IP address is associated with a DNS, thus allowing reverse lookup. The authentication is done by the Remote Authentication Dial-In User Service (RADIUS). However, RADIUS does not only authenticate calls, but it also maintains records that can be used to track down a suspect [5]. RADIUS information includes IP address assigned, connection time, telephone number used from a caller ID, and log-in name. ISPs maintain these logs for some time, sometimes up to a year, before purging them. However, investigators should not take this information as always valid. It can and it has been changed before. But as Kruse points out, the value of ISP information is to have the telephone number, date, and time of the incident. This can be followed by a subpoena.

Other good sources of investigator information are e-mail and new postings. Both these services offer good tracking attributes like:

- Store-and-forward architecture that moves messages of printable characters from network node to network node in a next-hop framework

- Human-readable message headers that contain the path between the sender and receiver

This information is useful to an investigator. For example, all e-mail servers have the ability to maintain a logging information. Let us look at this closely. E-mail programs, called clients, are based on application-level protocols. There are several of these protocols, including Post Office Protocol (POP), Internet Message Access Protocol (IMAP), Microsoft's Mail API (MAPI), and HTTP for Web-based mail. All outgoing e-mails use a different protocol called Simple Mail Transfer Protocol (SMTP). Unlike incoming protocols above used to receive e-mails, outgoing protocol SMTP does not require authentication. The SMTP at the client sends e-mail messages to the STMP at the mail server or at the ISP, which then relays e-mail messages to their destinations without any authentication. However, to give such e-mails some degree of trust, authentication protocols such as PGP or S/MIME (Secure/Multipurpose Internet Mail Extensions) are used on top of STMP. SMTP servers, however, maintain logging information which is more reliable than mail headers and may be useful to an investigator.

Another good source of information for forensic investigators is Usenet, a huge distributed news bulletin board consisting of thousands of news topics beautifully arranged. Throughout the news network are thousands of news servers running Network News Transfer Protocol (NNTP). In the header of each message news body, there is a path that forms the crest of the investigation. One can trace every NNTP host that the message has traversed in reverse chronological order. Also like mail servers, NNTP may or may not accept postings from nonmembers.

Finally, enormous amount of data can be gotten from monitoring systems like firewalls, intrusion detection systems, and operating system logs.

14.3.1.4 Reverse Hacking

Reverse engineering, commonly known as reverse hacking, is literally taking an offending package, breaking it up, and using it to try and trace the source of the attack. Antivirus writers have long used the technique by capturing the virus signature, usually a traffic package, breaking it up, and studying the patterns which then lead to an antivirus.

14.3.2 Damage Assessment

It has been difficult so far to effectively assess damage caused by system attacks. For the investigator, if the damage assessment report is available, it can provide a trove of badly needed information. It shows how widespread the damage was and who was affected and to what extent. Further it shows what data, system, services, and privileges were compromised. It is also from this report that the length of the incident can be established and the causes, vulnerability exploited, safeguards bypassed, and detection avoided. From this report, one can also be able to determine if the attack was manual or automated. If the source of the attack is indicated in the report, then one can use it to trace network connections which may lead to other directions of the investigation.

To achieve a detailed report of an intrusion detection, the investigator must carry out a postmortem of the system by analyzing and examining the following [3]:

- System registry, memory, and caches. To achieve this, the investigator can use dd for Linux and Unix systems.
- Network state to access computer network accesses and connections. Here netstat can be used.
- Current running processes to access the number of active processes. Use ps for both Unix and Linux.
- Data acquisition of all unencrypted data. This can be done using MD5 and SHA-1 on all files and directories. Then store this data in a secure place.

14.4 Forensic Tools

Let us end this chapter by looking at the tools of the trade for forensic investigators. Like a hunter, forensic investigators rely on their tools. They succeed or fail based on their tools. Because of this, it is important that the investigators make sure that their tools are not only trusted but also that they work before they start the job.

Always try the tools on something before they are fully deployed for work. Make sure that the tools do exactly what you want them to do.

Following Hal Berghel's observations on differentiating computer forensics from network forensics, we are going to split the tools into two. In Sect. 14.4.1, we will discuss tools used mainly in computer forensics, and in Sect. 14.4.2, we will look at those used in network forensics.

Having done that, however, we do not want to look naive as if we do not know that the two disciplines are actually intertwined. Network forensics, for all its knowledge level requirements and tools sharing between the suspects and investigators, is still very much anchored in computer forensics. Many of the tools, as we will see are, therefore, used in both areas without a thought.

In addition, despite the latest call for their separation, which in many areas is still academic, many still treat the two areas as one. In fact, much of the current writing on the market has yet to differentiate the two. However, efforts are on to try and differentiate the two for better services.

14.4.1 Computer Forensic Tools

In Sect. 14.3, we indicated that computer forensics, as an established science, has been in use for some time. As it grow, it developed major tasks that must be performed to complete the job. A forensic tool must have at least one of these functionalities. Many major forensic tools have all of the functionalities below:

- Acquisition—where the main task is making a copy of the original suspect medium with the intention of preserving the integrity of the evidence. Copying can be done in a number of ways including physical, logical, and remote. In doing the acquisition, care must be taken to understand the file formats and also to do a thorough job of preservation and validation.
- Validation and discrimination—these two issues are very important in digital forensics because the case is won or lost based on how well these two were performed. Validation is very important to preserve the integrity and reliability of the evidence. Discrimination is also important because it establishes the relevance of the evidence through search and sort.
- Extraction—is another critical task in forensic investigation because, through it, we recover the evidence which makes up the case. To extract evidence from an evidence medium, one can use any of the following tasks: data viewing, decrypting (when the evidence is found to be encrypted), decompressing (when the evidence was compressed), keyword search, and bookmarking.
- Reconstruction—is a process of recreating what happened during the crime process. It is important to note here that before any reconstruction is made, a copy or two of the original evidence medium must have been made. This reconstruction process requires a few subtasks including disk-to-disk copy, image-to-disk copy, partition-to-partition copy, and image-to-partition copy.
- Reporting—no digital forensic case is done until a final report is written. So this task involves generating a final report.

Forensic tools are either software based or hardware based [5].

14.4.1.1 Software-Based Forensic Tools
Most, if not all, major forensic tools have the capabilities to all these major tasks. Most of the current major tools are software based. Currently, the major commercial forensic tools are (Table 14.1):

- EnCase—by Guidance Software (http://www.guidancesoftware.com/)
- FTK (Forensic Toolkit)—by AccessData (http://accessdata.com/products/com puter-forensics/ftk)
- ProDiscover—by ProDiscover Forensics (http://www.techpathways.com/prodiscoverdft.htm)

14.4.1.2 Hardware-Based Forensic Tools
Although most forensic tools are software based, there is an ample supply of hardware-based forensic tools. Hardware tools are based on a workstation that can be stationary, portable, or lightweight. Lightweight workstations are based on laptops. The choice of the type of workstation an investigator uses is determined by the nature of the investigation and the environment of the incident location. There are fully configured turnkey workstations that can be bought, or the investigator can

Table 14.1   Functionalities of major forensic tools

	ProDiscover	FTK	EnCase
Acquisition	√	√	√
Validation and discrimination	√	√	√
Extraction	√	√	√
Reconstruction	√	√	√
Reporting	√	√	√

build his or her own. Hardware-based tools also include write blockers that allow investigators to remove and reconnect a disk drive on a system without having to shut the system down. These tools connect to the computer using FireWire, USB, or SCSI controllers.

14.4.2   Network Forensic Tools

Like in computer forensics, after collecting information as evidence, the next big decision is the analysis tools that are needed to analyze. This job is a lot easier if the system you are investigating was built up by you. Depending on the platform, you can start with *TCPdump* and the *strings* command. TCPdump will display individual packets or filter a few packets out of a large data set, and the string command gives a transcript of the information that passed over the network. Similarly *Snort* allows the investigator to define particular conditions that generate alarms or traps.

However, the job is not so easy if the investigator does not have any knowledge of the system. In this case, he or she is likely to depend on commercial tools. The forensic investigator's ability to analyze will always be limited by the capabilities of the system. Most commercial forensic tools perform continuous network monitoring based on observed data from internal and external sources. Monitoring examines the flow of packets into and out of every port in the network. With this blanket monitoring, it is possible to learn a lot about individual users and what they are doing and with whom. While analysis of individual traffic flows is essential to a complete understanding of network usage, with real-time monitoring on the way, network monitoring is going to require significant amounts of resources. One of the benefits of monitoring is the early warning intelligence-gathering technique sometimes called *recon probes*. A standard forensic tool such as TCPdump can provide the investigator with these probes. The probes can also come from other network monitoring tools such as firewalls and host-based and network-based intrusion detection systems.

Exercises

1. In your opinion, is computer forensics a viable tool in the fight against the cybercrime epidemic?
2. Discuss the difficulties faced by cybercrime investigators.

3. Differentiate between computer and network forensics.
4. Discuss the limitations of computer forensics in the fight against cybercrimes.
5. Many of the difficulties of collecting digital evidence stem from its ability to dry up so fast and the inability of investigators to move fast enough before the evidence disappears. Suggest ways investigators might use to solve this problem.
6. Handling forensic evidence in cybercrime situations must be done very carefully. Discuss the many pitfalls that an investigator must be aware of.
7. One of the methods used in extracting computer forensics evidence is to freeze the computer. While this is considered a good approach by many people, there are those who think it is a shoddy work. Discuss the merits and demerits of computer "freezing."
8. It is so much easier to extract evidence from a computer than from a network. Discuss the difficulties faced by investigators collecting evidence from a network.
9. Encryption can be used both ways: by the criminals to safeguard their data and by the investigators to safeguard their findings. Discuss the difficulties investigators face when dealing with encrypted evidence.
10. Discuss the many ways cybercriminals and other computer and network users may use to frustrate investigators.

Advanced Exercises

1. Hal Berghel meticulously distinguishes between computer forensics and network forensics by giving examples of the so-called "dual usage" network security tools. Study four such tools and demonstrate their "dual usage."
2. Discuss, by giving extensive examples, the claim put forward by Berghel that computer forensics investigators and network forensics investigators have similar levels of skills.
3. It has been stated on many occasions that "reverse hacking" is a good policy for network security. Define "reverse hacking" and discuss the stated opinion.
4. Study the new techniques of digital reconstruction and show how these new techniques are improving the fortunes of both computer and network forensics.
5. Discuss the future of both computer and network forensics in view of the observation that network forensics is but a small science soon to be forgotten.

References

1. Rubin R (1996) More distancing and the use of information: the seven temptations. In: Kizza JM (ed) Social and ethical effects of the computer revolution. McFarland & Company, Jefferson
2. "Intrusion Analysis." SANS. https://www.sans.org/curricula/intrusion-analysis
3. Nelson B, Amelia P, Frank E, Chris S (2004) Guide to computer forensics and investigations. Course Technologies, Boston

4. Berghel H. The discipline of internet forensics. Communications of the ACM, August 2003 46 (8)
5. Kruse W II, Jay GH (2002) Computer forensics: incident response essentials. Addison-Wesley, Reading
6. Sammes T, Brian J (2000) Forensic computing: a practitioner's guide. Springer, London
7. SymWise – Symantec Knowledge Base and MySymantec – Symantec Support. http://www.symantec.com/connect/articles/symwise-symantec-knowledgebase-and-mysymantec-symantec-support
8. Bender W, Gruhl D, Morimoto N, Lu A (1996) Techniques for data hiding. IBM Syst J 35 (3&4)
9. Wikipedia. Computer forensics. https://en.wikipedia.org/wiki/Computer_forensics
10. Pipkin DL (2000) Information security: protecting the global enterprise. Prentice Hall PTR, Upper Saddle River

Virus and Content Filtering

15

15.1 Definitions

As the size of global computer networks expands and the use of the Internet skyrockets, the security issues do manifest themselves not only in the security of computer networks but also in individual user security on individual PCs connected to the Internet either via an organization's gateway or an Internet service provider (ISP). The security of every user, therefore, is paramount whether the user is a member of an organization network or a user of a home PC via an independent ISP. In either case, the effort is focused on protecting not only the data but also the user.

The most effective way to protect such a user and the data is through content filtering. Content filtering is a process of removing unwanted, objectionable, and harmful content before it enters the user network or the user PC. The filtering process can be located in several locations including on a user's PC, on a server within an organization, as a service provided by an ISP, or by means of a third-party site that provides the basis of a closed community.

In their report to the Australian Government on Content Filtering, Paul Greenfield et al. [1] divide the process of content filtering into two approaches: inclusion filtering and exclusion filtering.

15.2 Scanning, Filtering, and Blocking

Scanning is a systematic process of sweeping through a collection of data looking for a specific pattern. In a network environment, the scanning process may involve a program that sweeps through thousands of IP addresses looking for a particular IP address string or a string that represents a vulnerability or a string that represents a vulnerable port number. Filtering, on the other hand, is a process of using a computer program to stop an Internet browser on a computer from being able to load certain Web pages based upon predetermined criteria such as IP addresses. Blocking, like filtering, is also a process of preventing certain types of information

© Springer International Publishing AG 2017

J.M. Kizza, *Guide to Computer Network Security*, Computer Communications and Networks, DOI 10.1007/978-3-319-55606-2_15

from being viewed on a computer's screen or stored on a computer's disk. In this section, we are going to look at these three processes and see how they are used in computer networks and personal computers as a way to enhance security.

15.2.1 Content Scanning

All Internet content inbound into and outbound from either an organization's network, an ISP gateway, or a user PC is always scanned before it is filtered. So scanning is very important in content filtering. Let us look at the ways scanning is done on the content of the Internet, either inbound or outbound. There are two forms of scanning: pattern-based and heuristic scanning.

15.2.1.1 Pattern-Based Scanning
In pattern-based scanning, all content coming into or leaving the network, an ISP gateway, or user PC is scanned and checked against a list of patterns, or definitions, supplied and kept up to date by the vendor. The technique involves simply comparing the contents, which can be done in several ways as we saw in Sect. 12.2.1. Nearly all antivirus software packages work this way. This approach can, however, be slow and resource intensive.

15.2.1.2 Heuristic Scanning
Heuristic scanning is done by looking at a section of code and determining what it is doing and then deciding whether the behavior exhibited by the code is unwanted, harmful like a virus, or otherwise malicious. This approach to scanning is complex because it involves modeling the behavior of code and comparing that abstract model to a rule set. The rule set is kept in a rule database on the machine and the database is updated by the vendor. Because of the checking and cross-checking, this approach takes more time, and it is also resource intensive, if not more than the previous one. Theoretically heuristics has several advantages over pattern-based scanning including better efficiency and accuracy. It can, potentially, detect viruses that haven't been written yet.

15.2.2 Inclusion Filtering

Inclusion filtering is based on the existence of an inclusion list. The inclusion list is a permitted access list—a "white list" probably vetted and compiled by a third party. Anything on this list is allowable. The list could be a list of URL for allowable Web sites, for example, it could be a list of allowable words, or it could be a list of allowable packet signatures for allowable packets. The nature of the list is determined by the security policy of the organization or a committee of a community. As Greenfield noted, this type of filtering can be 100% effective—assuming the person or organization that has compiled the white list shares the same set of values as the Internet user.

But the inclusion list approach, despite its effectiveness, has several drawbacks including the following:

- The difficulty to come up with a globally accepted set of criteria. This is a direct result of the nature of the Internet as a mosaic of a multitude of differing cultures, religions, and political affiliations. In this case, it is almost impossible to come up with a truly accepted global set of moral guidelines.
- The size of the inclusion list. As more and more acceptable items become available and qualify to be added on the list, there is a potential for the list to grow out of control.
- Difficulty of finding a central authority to manage the list. In fact, this is one of the most difficult aspects of the inclusion list approach to content filtering. For example, even though we have been suffering from virus attacks for years, there is no one authoritative list managed by a central authority that contains all the virus signatures that have ever been produced. There are currently highly inclusive lists managed by either private antivirus companies or publicly supported reporting agencies such as the Computer Emergency Reporting Team (CERT) Center.

15.2.3 Exclusion Filtering

Another approach to content filtering is the use of an exclusion list. This is the opposite of the inclusion list process we have discussed previously. An exclusion list is actually a "black list" of all unwanted, objectionable, and harmful content. The list may contain URLs of sites, words, signatures of packets, and patterns of words and phrases. This is a more common form of filtering than inclusion filtering because it deals with manageable lists. Also it does not pre-assume that everything is bad until proven otherwise.

However, it suffers from a list that may lack constant updates and a list that is not comprehensive enough. In fact, we see these weaknesses in the virus area. No one will ever have a fully exhaustive list of all known virus signatures, and antivirus companies are constantly ever updating their master lists of virus signatures.

15.2.4 Other Types of Content Filtering

In the previous two sections, we have discussed the two approaches to content filtering. In each one of these approaches, a list is produced. The list could be made up of URLs, words (keyword), phrases, packet signatures, profile, image analysis, and several other things. Let us now look at the details of content filtering based on these items [1].

15.2.4.1 URL Filtering

With this approach, content into or out of a network is filtered based on the URL. It is the most popular form of content filtering, especially in terms of denial of access to the targeted site. One of the advantages of URL filtering is its ability to discriminate and carefully choose a site but leave the IP address of the machine that hosts functioning and therefore providing other services to the network or PC.

Because of the low level of and fine-tuning involved in URL filtering, many details of the setup and format of the target are needed in order to be able to provide the required degree of effectiveness. In addition, because of the low-level details needed, when there are changes in the files in the URL, these changes must be correspondingly affected in the filter.

15.2.4.2 Keyword Filtering

Keyword filtering requires that all the inbound or outbound contents be scanned, and every syntactically correct word scanned is compared with words either on the inclusive white list or exclusive black list depending on the filtering regime used. Although it is the oldest and probably still popular, it suffers from several drawbacks including the following:

It is text based which means that it fails to check all other forms of data like images:

- It is syntactically based, meaning that it will block words with prefixes or suffixes that syntactically look like the forbidden words, ignoring the semantics of the surrounding text.

15.2.4.3 Packet Filtering

As we discussed in Chap. 1, network traffic moves between network nodes based on a packet, as an addressable unit, with two IP addresses: the source address and the destination address. Throughout this book we have discussed the different ways these addresses are used in transporting data. As we saw in Chap. 11, content is blocked based on these IP addresses. Because of this approach, if content is blocked or denied access based on IP addresses, this means that no content can come from or go to the machine whose address is in the block rules. This kind of blocking is indiscriminate because it blocks a machine based on its addresses, not content, which means that a machine may have other good services but they are all blocked. As we discussed in Sect. 11.2, packet filtering can also be done based on other contents of a packet such as port numbers and sequence numbers.

15.2.4.4 Profile Filtering

The use of artificial intelligence in content filtering is resulting into a new brand of content filters based on the characteristics of the text "seen" so far and the learning cycles "repeats" done to discriminate all further text from this source. However, because of the complexity of the process and the time involved and needed for the filters to "learn," this method, so far, has not gained popularity. In the preprocessing phase, it needs to fetch some parts of the document and scan it—either text based or content based—in order to "learn." This may take time.

15.2.4.5 Image Analysis Filtering

Ever since the debut of the World Wide Web with its multimedia content, Internet traffic in other formats different from text has been increasing. Audio and video contents are increasing daily. To accommodate these other formats and be able to filter based on them, new approaches had to be found. Among these approaches is the one based on analyzed images. Although new, this approach is already facing problems of preloading images for analysis, high bandwidth making it extremely slow, and syntactic filtering making it indiscriminate semantically.

15.2.5 Location of Content Filters

At the beginning of the chapter, we stated that there are four best locations to install content filters. These four locations include, first and foremost, the user's PC, at the ISP as the main gateway to and from the Internet to the user PC, at the organization server, and finally by the third-party machine. Let us briefly look at each one of these locations.

15.2.5.1 Filtering on the End User's Computer

At this location, the user is the master of his or her destiny. Using software installed on the user machine, the user can set blocking rules and blocking lists that are expressive of his or her likes and dislikes. Because this location makes the user the focus of the filtering, the user is also responsible for updating the blocking rules and lists. In addition, the user is responsible for providing the security needed to safeguard the blocking rules and lists from unauthorized modifications.

15.2.5.2 Filtering at the ISP's Computer

Unlike filtering at the user PC, filtering at the ISP removes the responsibility of managing the filtering rules from the user and lists and places it with the ISP. It also enhances the security of these items from unauthorized local changes. However, it removes a great deal of local control and the ability to affect minute details that express the user's needs.

Because this is a centralized filtering, it has several advantages over the others. First, it offers more security because the ISP can make more resources available than the user would. Second, the ISP can dedicate complete machines—called proxy servers—to do the filtering, thus freeing other machines and making the process faster. Finally, the ISP can have more detailed lists and databases of these lists than a user.

In Sect. 11.2.2, we discussed the use of proxy servers and filters as firewalls. So we have a basic understanding of the working of proxy servers. The proxy servers are installed in such a way that all traffic to and from the ISP must go through this proxy server to be able to access the Internet. A proxy filter can be configured to block a selected service.

15.2.5.3 Filtering by an Organization Server

To serve the interest of an organization, content filtering can also be done at a dedicated server at an organization. Just like at the ISP, the organization's system administrator can dedicate a server to filtering content into and out of the organization. All inbound and outbound traffic must go through the filters. Like ISP filtering, this is centralized filtering, and it offers a high degree of security because the filtering rules and lists are centrally controlled.

15.2.5.4 Filtering by a Third Party

For organizations and individuals that are unable to do their own filtering, the third-party approach offers a secure good alternative. Both inbound and outbound traffic on the user and organization gateways are channeled through the third-party filters. The third party may use proxy servers like the ISPs or just dedicated servers like organization servers. Third-party filters offer a high degree of security and a variety of filtering options.

15.3   Virus Filtering

Our discussion of viruses started in Chap. 3, where we introduced viruses as a threat to system security. We discussed the big virus incidents that have hit the Internet causing huge losses. In Sect. 5.3.5, we looked at viruses as hackers' tools. Although we did not specifically define the virus, we discussed several types of viruses and worms that hackers use to attack systems. Now we are ready to define a computer virus on our way to filtering it.

15.3.1 Viruses

A computer virus is a self-propagating computer program designed to alter or destroy a computer system resource. The term *virus* is derived from a Latin word *virus* which means poison. For generations, even before the birth of modern medicine, the term had remained mostly in medical circles, meaning a foreign agent injecting itself in a living body, feeding on it to grow and multiply. As it reproduces itself in the new environment, it spreads throughout the victim's body slowly, disabling the body's natural resistance to foreign objects, weakening the body's ability to perform needed life functions, and eventually causing serious, sometimes fatal, effects to the body.

Computer viruses also parallel the natural viruses. However, instead of using the living body, they use software (executable code) to attach themselves, grow, reproduce, and spread in the new environment. Executing the surrogate program starts them off, and they spread in the new environment, attacking major system resources that sometimes include the surrogate software itself, data, and sometimes hardware, weakening the capacity of these resources to perform the needed functions, and eventually bringing the system down.

The word virus was first assigned a nonbiological meaning in the 1972 science fiction stories about the G.O.D. machine that were compiled into a book *When Harlie Was One* by David Gerrold (Ballantine Books, First Edition, New York, NY, 1972). Later association of the term with a real-world computer program was by Fred Cohen and then a graduate student at the University of Southern California. Cohen wrote five programs, actually viruses, to run on a VAX 11/750 running Unix, not to alter or destroy any computer resources but for class demonstration. During the demonstration, each virus obtained full control of the system within an hour [2]. From that simple and harmless beginning, computer viruses have been on the rise. Computer viruses are so far the most prevalent, most devastating, and the most widely used form of computer system attack. And of all types of systems attacks, it is the fastest growing. As we reported in Chap. 2, Symantec reports that on the average there are between 400 and 500 new viruses per month [3]. The virus is, so far, the most popular form of computer system attack because of the following factors:

- Ease of generation. Considering all other types of system attacks, viruses are the easiest to generate because the majority of them are generated from computer code. The writing of computer code has been becoming easier every passing day because, first, programming languages are becoming easier to learn and develop programs; second, there are more readily available virus code floating around on the Internet; and finally, there is plenty of help for would-be virus developers in terms of material and physical support. Material support in form of how-to manuals and turn-key virus programs is readily available free on the Internet.
- Scope of reach. Because of the high degree of interconnection of global computers, the speed at which viruses are spread is getting faster and faster. The speed at which the "Code Red" virus spread from the Philippines through Asia to Europe to North America attests to this. Within a few days of release, Code Red had the global networks under its grip.
- Self-propagating nature of viruses. The new viruses now are far more dangerous than their counterparts several years ago. New viruses self-propagate, which gives them the ability to move fast and create more havoc faster. One of the reasons that the Code Red virus was able to move so fast was that it was self-propagating.
- Mutating viruses. The new viruses are not only self-propagating, which gives them speed, but they are also mutating which gives them a double punch of delaying quick eradication and consuming great resources and therefore destroying more in their wake, fulfilling the intended goals of the developers.
- Difficult to apprehend the developer. As the Code Red virus demonstrated, owing to legal and other limitations, it is getting more and more difficult to apprehend the culprits. This in itself is giving encouragement to would-be virus developers that they can really get way with impunity.

15.3.1.1 Virus Infection/Penetration

There are three ways viruses infect computer systems and are transmitted: boot sector, macro penetration, and parasites [4].

Boot Sector Penetration Although not very common nowadays, boot sectors are still being used somehow to incubate viruses. A boot sector is usually the first sector on every disk. In a boot disk, the sector contains a chunk of code that powers up a computer. In a nonbootable disk, the sector contains a file allocation table (FAT), which is automatically loaded first into the computer memory to create a roadmap of the type and contents of the disk for the computer to access the disk. Viruses imbedded in this sector are assured of automatic loading into the computer memory.

Macros Penetration Since macros are small language programs that can execute only after imbedding themselves into surrogate programs, their penetration is quite effective. The rising popularity in the use of script in Web programming is resulting in macro virus penetration as one of the fastest forms of virus transmission.

Parasites These are viruses that do not necessarily hide in the boot sector, nor use an incubator like the macros, but attach themselves to a healthy executable program and wait for any event where such a program is executed. These days, due to the spread of the Internet, this method of penetration is the most widely used and the most effective. Examples of parasite virus include Friday the 13th, Michelangelo, SoBig, and the Blaster viruses.

Once a computer attack is launched, most often a virus attack, the attacking agent scans the victim system looking for a healthy body for a surrogate. If it is found, the attacking agent tests to see if it has already been infected. Viruses do not like to infect themselves, hence wasting their energy. If an uninfected body is found, then the virus attaches itself to it to grow, multiply, and wait for a trigger event to start its mission. The mission itself has three components:

- To look further for more healthy environments for faster growth, thus spreading more
- To attach itself to any newly found body
- Once embedded, either to stay in the active mode ready to go at any trigger event or to lie dormant until a specific event occurs

15.3.1.2 Sources of Virus Infections

Computer viruses, just like biological viruses, have many infection sources. Again like biological viruses, these sources are infected first from first contact with either a newly released virus or a repeat virus. One interesting fact about computer virus attacks, again following their cousins the biological viruses, is that a majority of them are repeat attacks. So like in human medicine, a certain type of proven medications is routinely used to fight them off. Similarly with computer viruses, the same antivirus software is routinely used to fight many of the repeat viruses. Of late, however, even known viruses have been mutating, making antivirus companies work harder to find the code necessary to eliminate the mutating virus.

Of the known viruses, there are mainly four infection sources: movable computer disks such as floppies, zips, and tapes; Internet downloadable software such as beta software, shareware, and freeware; e-mail and e-mail attachments; and platform-free executable applets and scripts. It is important to note that just like biological viruses, infections are caused by coming in close contact with an infected body. Likewise in computer viruses, viruses are caught from close contact with infected bodies—system resources. So the most frequently infected bodies that can be sources of viruses are as follows [4]:

- Movable computer disks: Although movable computer disks like floppies, zips, and tapes used to be the most common way of sourcing and transmitting viruses, new Internet technologies have caused this to decline. Viruses sourced from movable computer disks are either boot viruses or disk viruses.
- Boot viruses: These viruses attack boot sectors on both hard and floppy disks. Disk sectors are small areas on a disk that the hardware reads in single chunks. For DOS formatted disks, sectors are commonly 512 bytes in length. Disk sectors, although invisible to normal programs, are vital for the correct operation of computer systems because they form chunks of data the computer uses. A boot sector is the first disk sector or first sector on disk or diskette that an operating system is aware of. It is called a boot sector because it contains an executable program the computer executes every time the computer is powered up. Because of its central role in the operations of computer systems, the boot sector is very vulnerable to virus attack, and viruses use it as a launching pad to attack other parts of the computer system. Viruses like this sector because from it, they can spread very fast from computer to computer, booting from that same disk. Boot viruses can also infect other disks left in the disk drive of an infected computer.
- Disk viruses: Whenever viruses do not use the boot sector, they embed themselves, as macros, in disk data or software. A macro is a small program embedded in another program and executes when that program, the surrogate program, executes. Macro viruses mostly infect data and document files, templates, spreadsheets, and database files.
- Internet downloadable software: Historically, it used to be that computer viruses were actually hand carried. People carried viruses on their floppy disks whenever they transferred these infected disks from one computer to the other. Those were the good old days before the Internet and the concept of downloads. The advent of the Internet created a new communication and virus transmission channel. In fact, the Internet is now the leading and fastest virus transmission channel there is. Internet downloads, bulletin boards, and shareware are the actual vehicles that carry the deadly virus across the seas in a blink of an eye.
- E-mail attachments: As recent mega virus attacks such as the "Code Red," "SoBig," and the "Blaster" have demonstrated, no computer connected to the

Internet is safe any longer. E-mail attachments are the fastest-growing virus transmission method today. With more than one half of all today's Internet traffic made up of e-mails and millions of e-mails being exchanged a day going through millions of other computers, the e-mail communication is the most potent channel of infecting computers with viruses. Incidentally straight-texted e-mails, these are e-mails without attachments, are free from viruses. Since attachment-free e-mails are pure texts, not executables, they cannot transport viruses. Viruses, as we have already seen, are executable programs or document macros that can be embedded into other executables or application documents.

- Platform-free executable applets and scripts: Dynamism has made Web application very popular these days. Web dynamism has been brought about by the birth of scripting languages such as Java, Pearl, and C/C++. As we discussed in Chap. 6, the Common Gateway Interface (CGI) scripts let developers create interactive Web scripts that process and respond to user inputs on both the client side and the server side. Both CGI scripts, which most often execute on the server side and JavaScript and VBScript that execute within the user's browser on the client side, create loopholes in both the server and the client to let in viruses. One way of doing this is through a hacker gaining access to a site and then changing or replacing the script file. The hacker can also lay a "man-in-the-middle" attack by breaking in a current session between the client browser and the server. By doing so, the hacker can then change the message the client is sending to the server script.

15.3.1.3 Types of Viruses

Just like living viruses, there are several types of digital (computer) viruses, and there are new brands almost every other day. We will give two classifications of computer viruses based on transmission and outcomes [4, 5].

Virus Classification Based on Transmission

- *Trojan horse viruses*: These viruses are labeled Trojan horse viruses because just like in the old myth in which the Greeks, as enemies of Troy, used a large wooden horse to hide in and enter the city of Troy, these viruses use the tricks these legendary Greeks used. During transmission, they hide into trusted common programs such as compilers, editors, and other commonly used programs. Once they are safely into the target program, they become alive whenever the program executes.
- *Polymorphic viruses*: These viruses are literally those that change form. Before a polymorphic virus replicates itself, it must change itself into some other form in order to avoid detection. This means that if the virus detector had known the signature for it, this signature then changes. Modern virus generators have learned to hide the virus signatures from antivirus software by encrypting the virus signatures and then transforming them. These mutations are giving virus hunters a really hard time. The most notorious mutating virus was the "Code

Red" virus which mutated into almost a different form every other day, throwing virus hunters off track.

- *Stealth virus*: Just like the polymorphic virus that uses mutation to distract its hunters from its track, a stealth virus makes modifications to the target files and the system's boot record, and then it hides these modifications. It hides these modifications by interjecting itself between the application programs the operating system must report to and the operating system itself. In this position, it receives the operating system reports and falsifies them as they are being sent to the programs. In this case, therefore, the programs and the antivirus detector would not be able to detect its presence. Once it is ready to strike then it does so. Jasma [5] gives two types of stealth viruses: the size stealth which injects itself into a program and then falsifies its size and the read stealth which intercepts requests to read infected boot records or files and provides falsified readings, thus making its presence unknown.
- *Retrovirus*: A retrovirus is an antivirus fighter. It works by attacking antivirus software on the target machine so that it can either disable it or bypass it. In fact, that is why it is sometimes called an *anti-antivirus* program. Other retroviruses focus on disabling the database of integrity information in the integrity checking software, another member of the antivirus family.
- *Multipartite virus*: This is a multifaceted virus that is able to attack the target computer from several fronts. It is able to attack the boot record and all boot sectors of disks including floppies, and it is also able to attack executable files. Because of this, it was nicknamed *multipartite*.
- *Armored virus*: Probably the name is fitting because this virus works in the target computer by first protecting itself so that it is more difficult to detect, trace, disassemble, or understand its signature. It gets the coat or armor by using an outer layer of protective coat that cannot easily be penetrated by antivirus software. Other forms of this virus work by not using a protective coat but by hiding from an antivirus software.
- *Companion virus*: This is a smarter virus that works by creating companions with executables. Then it piggybacks on the executable file and produces its own extension based on the executable file. By so doing, every time the executable software is launched, it always executes first.
- *Phage virus*: This virus parallels and is named after its biological counterpart that replaces an infected cell with itself. The computer counterpart also replaces the executable code with its own code. Because of its ability to do this, and just like its biological cousin, it is very destructive and dangerous. It destroys every executable program it comes into contact with.

Virus Classifications Based on Outcomes

- *Error-generating virus*: Error-generating viruses lunch themselves most often in executable software. Once embedded, they attack the software to cause the software to generate errors.

- *Data and program destroyers*: These are viruses that attach themselves to a software and then use it as a conduit or surrogate for growth, replication, and launch pad for later attacks and destruction to this and other programs and data.
- *System crusher*: These, as their name suggests, are the most deadly viruses. Once introduced in a computer system, they completely disable the system.
- *Computer time theft virus*: These viruses are not harmful in any way to system software and data. Users use them to steal system time.
- *Hardware destroyers*: While most viruses are known to alter or destroy data and programs, there are a few that literally attack and destroy system hardware. These viruses are commonly known as *killer viruses*. Many of these viruses work by attaching themselves to micro-instructions, or "mic," such as bios and device drivers.
- *Logic/time bombs*: Logic bombs are viruses that penetrate the system, embedding themselves in the system's software, using it as a conduit, and waiting to attack once a trigger goes off.

15.3.1.4 How Viruses Work

In Sects. 15.3.1.2 and 15.3.1.3, we discussed how computers get infected with viruses and how these viruses are transmitted. We pointed out that the viruses are usually contracted from an infected computer resource and then passed on. We discussed those most likely resources to be infected and from which viruses are passed on. We have also pointed out in other parts of this chapter that over time, the methods of virus transmission have actually multiplied. In the beginning, viruses used to be transmitted manually by users moving disks and other infected materials from one victim to another. Since the birth of the Internet, this method has, however, been relegated to the last position among the popular methods of virus transmission.

Let us look at how the Internet has transformed virus transmission by focusing on two types of viruses that form the biggest part of virus infection within the network environment. These are the macro virus and the file virus. Of the two, the macro viruses have the fastest-growing rate of infection in networks. This is a result of several factors including the following:

- Big software warehouses innocently intend to provide their users with the flexibility of expanding their off-the-shelf products capabilities and functionalities by including macro facilities in these products. For example, popular Microsoft products include these macros [5]. Using these macro facilities, able users can create their own macros to automate common tasks, for example. But as we saw in Sect. 15.3.1.1, these macros are becoming a vehicle for virus infection and transmission.
- Microprogramming languages are now built into popular applications. These microprogramming languages are getting more and more powerful and are now packing more features. They can be used to build macros to perform a variety of functions. For example, Microsoft *Visual Basic for Applications* (VBA) is such a language that is found in a number of Microsoft popular applications including

PowerPoint, Excel, and Word. Again as we pointed out in Sect. 15.3.1.1, this creates ready vehicles to carry viruses.

The problem with these macros is that they introduce loopholes in these popular Internet applications. For example, VBA can be used by hackers to define viral code within the applications. Other macros that are not built using programming and scripting languages are included in applications that can be used by hackers as easily. The fact that macros behave as executable code within the applications is very attractive to hackers to use it and introduce viral code into the computer and hence into the network.

Next to macros in applications software in network transmission capabilities are file viruses. File viruses may be any of the types we have already discussed that attack system or user files. File viruses present as much danger to a network as the macro viruses as long as the infected computer is attached to a network. Notice that we would have nothing to say if a computer is not attached to any network. In fact, the safest computers are disconnected computers in bankers.

15.3.1.5 Antivirus Technologies
There are four types of viruses that antivirus technologies are targeting. These are "in-the-wild" viruses that are active viruses detected daily on users' computers all over the world, macro viruses, polymorphic viruses, and standard viruses.

The "in-the-wild" viruses are collected and published annually in the *WildList* (a list of those viruses currently spreading throughout a diverse user population). Although it should not be taken as the list of "most common viruses," in recent times, the list has been used as the basis for in-the-wild virus testing and certification of antivirus products by a number of antivirus software-producing companies. Additionally, a virus collection based upon the *WildList* is being used by many antivirus product testers as the definitive guide to the viruses found in the real world and thus to standardize the naming of common viruses. For the archives and current list of the *WildList*, see *The WildList – (c)1993–2003 by Joe Wells* at http://www. wildlist.org.

The other three types of viruses—the macro viruses, polymorphic viruses, and standard viruses—have already been discussed in various parts of this chapter. Antivirus technologies are tested for their ability to detect all types of viruses in all these modes.

15.4   Content Filtering

As we noted in Sect. 11.2.1, content filtering takes place at two levels: at the application level where the filtering is based on URL which may, for example, result in blocking a selected Web page or an FTP site and filtering at the network level based on packet filtering which may require routers to examine the IP address of every incoming or outgoing traffic packet. The packets are first captured, and then their IP address both source and destination, port numbers, or sequence numbers are then compared with those on either the *black* or *white* list.

15.4.1 Application-Level Filtering

Recall in Sects. 11.2.1 and 15.2.4 that application-level filtering is based on several things that make up the blocking criteria, including URL, keyword, and pattern. Application filtering can also be located at a variety of areas including at the user's PC, at the network gateway, at a third party's server, and at an ISP. In each one of these locations, quite an effective filtering regime can be implemented successfully. We discussed that when applying application-level filtering either at the network or at the ISP, a dedicated proxy server may be used. The proxy then prevents inbound or outbound flow of content based on the filtering rules in the proxy. With each request from the user or client, the proxy server compares the clients' requests with a supplied "black list" of Web sites, FTP sites, or newsgroups. If the URL is on the black list, then effective or selective blocking is done by the proxy server. Besides blocking data flowing into or out of the network or user computer, the proxy also may store *(cache)* frequently accessed materials. However, the effectiveness of application-level blocking using proxy servers is limited as a result of the following technical and nontechnical factors [6].

15.4.1.1 Technical Issues

- *Use of translation services in requests can result in requested content from unwanted servers and sites:* If a user requests for content from a specified server or site, and if the requested content cannot be found at this site, the translation service operated by the request can generate requests to secondary sites for the content. In such cases then, the content returned may not be from the specified server unless secondary requests are specifically blocked.
- *The domain name server can be bypassed:* Since a user's request for a site access can be processed based on either a domain name or the IP address of the server, a black list that contains the domain names only without their corresponding IP addresses can, therefore, be bypassed. This usually results in several difficulties, including not processing requests whose IP addresses cannot be found on the black lists and doubling of the size of the black list if both domain names and equivalent IP addresses are used for every server on the list.
- *The reliability of the proxy server may be a problem:* The use of a single proxy server for all incoming and outgoing filtering may cause "bottleneck" problems that include reduced speed, some applications failing to work with specific servers, and loss of service should the server were to collapse.

15.4.1.2 Nontechnical Issues

- *ISPs problems:* ISPs involved into the filtering process may face several problems, including the added burden of financially setting up, maintaining, and administering the additional proxy servers, supporting and maintaining reluctant clients that are forced to use these servers, and meeting and playing a role of a moral arbiter for their clients, the role they may find difficult to please all their clients in. In addition to these problems, ISPs are also faced with the problems that include the creation or updating and hosting black lists that will satisfy all their clients or creating, updating, and distributing black lists in a secure manner to all their clients.
- *The costs of creating and maintaining a black list:* There is an associated high cost of creating and maintaining a black list. The associated costs are high because the black list creation, maintenance, and updates involve highly charged local politics and a high degree of understanding in order to meet the complex nature of the list that will meet the basic requirements that cover a mosaic of cultures, religions, and political views of the users. In addition to these costs, there are also the costs of security of the list. Black lists are high target objects and prime targets for hackers and intruders

15.4.2 Packet-Level Filtering and Blocking

In Chap. 2, we saw that every network packet has both source and destination IP addresses to enable the TCP protocol to transport the packet through the network successfully and to also report failures. In packet-level filtering and blocking, the filtering entity has a black list consisting of "forbidden" or "bad" IP addresses. The blocking and filtering processes then work by comparing all incoming and outgoing packet IP addresses against the IP addresses on the supplied black list. However, the effectiveness of packet-level blocking is limited by both technical and nontechnical problems [6].

15.4.2.1 Technical Issues

- *Packet-level blocking is indiscriminate:* Blocking based on an IP address of a victim server means that no one from within the protected network will be able to reach the server. This means that any service offered by that server will never be used by the users in the protected network or on the protected user computer. If the intent was to block one Web site, this approach ends up placing the whole server out of reach of all users in the protected server or the user PC. One approach to lessen the blow of packet-level filtering to the protected network or user PC is the use of port numbers that can selectively block or unblock the services on the victim server. However, this process can affect the performance of the proxy server.

- *Routers can easily be circumvented:* Schemes such as *tunneling,* where an IP packet is contained inside another IP packet, are commonly used, particularly in the implementation of virtual private networks for distributed organizations and the expansion of IPv4 to IPv6: one can very easily circumvent the inside victim IP address by enveloping it into a new IP address which is then used in the transfer of the encased packet. Upon arrival at the destination, the encased packet is then extracted by the receiver to recreate the original message. We will discuss tunneling in Sect. 16.4.2, 17.4.2
- *Blacklisted IP addresses are constantly changing:* It is very easy to determine that a server has been blacklisted just by looking at and comparing server accesses. Once it is determined that a server has been blacklisted, a determined owner can very easily change the IP address of the server. This has been done many times over. Because of this and other IP address changes due to new servers coming online and older ones being decommissioned, there is a serious need for black list updates. The costs associated with these constant changes can be high.
- *Use of nonstandard port numbers:* Although it is not very common, there are many applications that do not use standard port numbers. Use of such nonstandard port numbers may fool the server filter, and the blocked port number may go through the filter. This, in addition to other filtering issues, when implementing a firewall may complicate the firewall as well.

15.4.2.2 Nontechnical Issues

- *Increased operational costs and ISP administrative problems:* As we saw in the application-level blocking, there are significant cost increments associated with the creation, maintenance, and distribution of black lists. In addition, the ISPs are made to be moral arbiters and supervisors and must carefully navigate the cultural, religious, and political conflicts of their clients in order to maintain an acceptable blacklist.

15.4.3 Filtered Material

The list of filtered items varies from user to user, community to community, and organization to organization. It is almost impossible, due to conflicting religious, cultural, and political beliefs, to come up with a common morality upon which a list like a "black list" can be based. Lack of such a common basis has created a mosaic of spheres of interests based on religion, culture, and politics. This has caused groups in communities to come together and craft a list of objectionable materials that can be universally accepted. The list we give below is a collection of many objectionable materials that we have collected from a variety of sources. This list includes the following items [7, 6]:

- *Nudity* is defined differently in different cultures. However, in many cultures, it means the complete absence of clothing or exposure of certain living human body parts.
- *Mature content* is differently defined and lacks universal acceptance. However, in many cultures, it refers to material that has been publicly classified as bad and corrupting to minors. The material may be crude or vulgar language or gestures or actions.
- *Sex*: Verbal and graphic descriptions and depictions of all sexual acts and any erotic material as classified by a community based on their culture, religion, and politics.
- *Gambling*: There are many forms of gambling, again based on community standards. These forms include physical and online gambling and game batting.
- *Violence/profanity*: Physical display and depictions of all acts that cause or inflict physical and psychological human pain including murder, rape, and torture.
- *Gross depiction*: Any graphic images, descriptive or otherwise, that are crude, vulgar, and grossly deficient in civility and behavior.
- *Drug/drug culture and use*: Graphic images, descriptive or not, that advocate any form of illegal use of and encouraging usage of any recreational drugs, including tobacco and alcohol advertising.
- *Intolerance/discrimination*: Advocating prejudice and denigration of others' race, religion, gender, disability or handicap, and nationality.
- *Satanic or cult*: Satanic materials that include, among others, all graphic images descriptive or otherwise that contain sublime messages that may lead to devil worship, an affinity for evil, or wickedness.
- *Crime*: Encouragement of, use of tools for, or advice on carrying out universally criminal acts that include bomb making and hacking.
- *Tastelessness*: Excretory functions, tasteless humor, graphic images taken out of acceptable norms, and extreme forms of body modification, including cutting, branding, and genital piercing.
- *Terrorism/militant/extremists*: Graphic images in any form that advocate extremely aggressive and combatant behaviors or advocacy of lawlessness.

15.5 Spam

It may be difficult to define spam. Some people want to define it as unsolicited commercial e-mail. This may not fully define spam because there are times when we get wanted and indeed desired unsolicited e-mails and we feel happy to get them. Others define spam as automated commercial e-mail. But many e-mails that are unsolicited and sometimes automated are not commercial in nature. Take, for example, the many e-mails you get from actually worthy causes but unsolicited and sometimes annoying. So to cover all these bases and hit a balance, we define spam as *unsolicited automated e-mail*.

Because Internet use is more than 60% e-mail, spamming affects a large number of Internet users. There are several ways we can fight spam including the following:

- *Limit e-mail addresses posted in a public electronic place.* E-mail addresses usually posted at the bottom of personal Web pages are sure targets of spammers. Spammers have almost perfected a method of cruising the Internet hunting for and harvesting these addresses. If you must put personal e-mail on a personal Web page, find a way of disguising it. Also opt out of job, professional, and member directories that place member e-mail addresses online.
- *Refrain from filling out online forms that require e-mail addresses.* Always avoid, if you can, supplying e-mail addresses when filling any kind of forms, including online forms that ask for them. Supply e-mail addresses to forms only when replies are to be done online.
- *Use e-mail addresses that are* not *easy to guess.* Yes, passwords can be successfully guessed, and now spammers are also at it trying to guess e-mail addresses. The easiest way to do this is to start with sending mails to addresses with short stem personal fields on common ISPs such as AOL, Yahoo, and Hotmail, fields like tim@aol, tim26@aol, joe@hotmail, and so on.
- *Practice using multiple e-mail addresses.* Always use several e-mail addresses and use one address for strictly personal business. When filling forms for nonserious personal business and pleasure, use a different e-mail address. In fact, it is always easy to determine who sells your e-mail address this way. By noting which address was used on which form and to whom, one can also easily track what sites are causing spam. These days there are also one-time disposable e-mail addresses one can easily get and use with little effort.
- *Spam filtering.* Always using spam filters at either the network level or application level to block unwanted e-mails. In either case, the spam is prevented from reaching the user by the filter. We will discuss this more in Sect. 15.3. While this approach has its problems, as we will see, it can cut down tremendously the amount of spam a user receives. Many ISPs are now offering spam filters.
- *Spam laws.* The outcry caused by spamming has led many national and local governments to pass spam laws. In Europe, the European Union's digital privacy rules are passed and are in force; these rules require companies to get consent before sending e-mail, tracking personal data on the Web, or pinpointing callers' location via satellite-linked mobile phones. The same rules also limit companies' ability to use cookies and other approaches that gather user information [8]. In the United States, efforts are being made to enact spam laws both at federal and state levels.
    - Federal spam law: The Senate approved a do-not-spam list and ban on sending unsolicited commercial e-mail using a false return address or misleading subject line [8].
    - State spam laws. All states have some form of spam laws on the books.

The European Union, leading the pack of antispam legislators, has passed a digital privacy law that requires companies to seek users' consent before sending e-mails, tracking personal data on the Web, and pointing callers' location using satellite-linked cell phones unless it is done by the police or emergency services [9]. Other European countries have enacted spam laws with varying success, and these laws can be viewed at http://www.spamlaws.com/eu.html.

In the United States, the recently passed *Controlling the Assault of Non-Solicited Pornography and Marketing Act of 2003*, or the *CAN-SPAM Act of 2003*, tries to regulate interstate commerce by imposing limitations and penalties on the transmission of unsolicited commercial electronic mail via the Internet. In addition to the federal law, many states have much stronger antispam legislations.

In general, however good and strong antispam legislations are, it is extremely difficult and expensive to enforce.

Beside the United States, the EU, and European countries, several other countries outside Europe, including Australia, Canada, Japan, Russia, Brazil, and India, have or are in the process of enacted spam laws. This is an indication that there is a global movement to fight spam.

Exercises

1. What are the major differences between a boot virus and a macro virus? Which is more dangerous to a computer system?
2. List and briefly discuss three most common sources of virus infections.
3. In this chapter, we did not discuss the likely sources of computer viruses. Discuss four most likely sources of computer viruses.
4. Why is antivirus software always developed after the virus has stricken?
5. Describe the similarities between biological viruses and computer viruses.
6. What are the difficulties faced by a community that wants to filter the Internet content?
7. Describe how a virus is moved on the Internet.
8. Why it is that viruses are more dangerous on peer-to-peer networks than in client-server networks?
9. Study and discuss the virus infection rate in peer-to-peer network, client-server networks, and the Internet.
10. Why do macros have the highest infection rate in network virus transmission?

Advanced Exercises

1. Research and develop a comprehensive list of the currently known viruses.
2. Research, find, and study a virus code. Write an antivirus for that code.
3. Look at a popular application such as PowerPoint or Excel. Find and disable the micros. How do you enable them again?
4. Discuss and develop a policy for dealing with viruses.
5. What is a virus "in the wild?" Research and draw an estimate of all viruses in the wild. How do you justify your number?

References

1. Greenfield P, McCrea P, Ran S (1999) Access prevention techniques for internet content filtering. CSIRO, Commonwealth Scientific and Industrial Research Organization (Australia), Australia. National Office for the Information Economy
2. Forcht K (1994) Computer security management. Boyd & Fraser Publishing, Danvers
3. BBC News. Battling the Net Security Threat. http://news.bbc.co.uk/2/hi/technology/2386113.stm
4. Kizza JM (2002) Computer network security and cyber ethics. McFarland and Company, Jefferson
5. Jasma K (2002) Hacker proof: the ultimate guide to network security, 2nd edn. OnWord Press, Albany
6. CSIRO (1998) Blocking content on the internet: a technical perspective. CSIRO, Mathematical and Information Sciences
7. Kizza JM (1998) Civilizing the internet: global concerns and efforts towards regulation. Jefferson, McFarland & Company
8. The Associated Press. Anti-spam law goes into force in Europe. Chattanooga Times-Free Press. Saturday, November 1, 2003. C5
9. The Associated Press. Anti-spam law goes into force in Europe. Chattanooga Times Free Press. C5, Saturday, November 1, 2003

Standardization and Security Criteria: Security Evaluation of Computer Products

16

16.1 Introduction

The rapid growth of information technology (IT), our growing dependence on it, and the corresponding skyrocketing security problems arising from it have all created a high demand for comprehensive security mechanisms, and best practices mitigate these security problems. Solutions on two fronts are sought for. First well-implemented mechanisms and best practices are needed for fundamental security issues like cryptography, authentication, access control, and audit. Second, comprehensive security mechanisms are also needed for all security products so that consumers are assured of products and systems that meet their business security needs. The response to this high demand for security products has been an avalanche of products of all types, capabilities, varying price range, effectiveness, and quality. You name a product and you get a flood from vendors. As the marketplace for security products get saturated, competing product vendors and manufacturers started making all sorts of claims about their products in order to gain a market niche. In this kind of environment then, how can a customer shop for the right secure product, what security measures should be used, and how does one evaluate the security claims made by the vendors? Along the way, making a choice of a good effective security product for your system or business has become a new security problem we want to focus on in this chapter.

Buying computer products, even without the thousands of overzealous vendors and manufacturers fighting to make a buck, has never been easy because of the complexity of computer products to the ordinary person. One cannot always rely on the words of the manufacturers and those of the product vendors to ascertain the suitability and reliability of the products. This is currently the case in both computer hardware and software products. It is a new computer security problem all computer product buyers must grapple with and computer network managers must try to mitigate as they acquire new computer products.

There are several approaches to deal with this new security problem, but we will discuss two here: standardization and security evaluation of products. Since

© Springer International Publishing AG 2017
J.M. Kizza, *Guide to Computer Network Security*, Computer Communications and Networks, DOI 10.1007/978-3-319-55606-2_16

standardization leads into security evaluation, meaning that product security evaluation is done based on established standards, we will start with standardization.

16.2   Product Standardization

A standard is a document that establishes uniform engineering or technical specifications, criteria, methods, processes, or practices. Some standards are mandatory, while others are voluntary [1]. Standardization is then *a process* of agreeing on these standards. The process itself is governed by a Steering Committee that consists of representatives from the different engineering and technical areas with interests in the product whose standard is sought. The committee is responsible for drafting the standard legal and technical document, from product specifications, establishing processes by which the draft standards are reviewed and accepted by the interested community.

Theoretically, the process itself sounds easy and consists of several stages through which the product specifications must undergo. First, the specifications undergo a period of development and several iterations of review by the interested engineering or technical community, and the revisions are made based on members' experiences. These revisions are then adopted by the Steering Committee as draft standards. But as Bradner [2] observes, in practice, the process is more complicated, due to (1) the difficulty of creating specifications of high technical quality, (2) the need to consider the interests of all of the affected parties, (3) the importance of establishing widespread community consensus, and (4) the difficulty of evaluating the utility of a particular specification for the community.

In any case, the goals of this process are to create standards that [2]:

- Are technically excellent.
- Have prior implementation and testing.
- Are clear, concise, and easily understood documentation.
- Foster openness and fairness.

16.2.1   Need for Standardization of (Security) Products

Whenever a product is designed to be used by or on another product, the interfaces of the two products must agree to meet and talk to each other every time these two products are connected to each other. What this is saying is that *interface specification* is the protocol language these two products talk, enabling them to understand each other. If there are conflicts in the specification language, the two will never understand each other, and they will never communicate.

Products and indeed computer products are produced by many different companies with varying technical and financial capabilities based on different technical design philosophies. But however varied the product marketplace may be, the interface specifications for products meant to interconnect must be compatible.

Standardization reduces the conflicts in the interface specifications. In other words, standardization is needed to enforce conformity in the product interface specifications for those products that are meant to interconnect.

According to Rebecca T. Mercuri [3], standards provide a neutral ground in which methodologies are established that advance the interest of manufacturers as well as consumers while providing assurances of safety and reliability of the products. Currently, the computer industry has a large variety of standards covering every aspect of the industry.

Standards are used in setting up of product security testing procedures, the passing of which results in a certification of the product. However, as Mercuri notes, certification alone does not guarantee security. There are cases where it is only a sign of compliance. Because of this and other reasons, many of the major product security testing bodies and governments have a collection of standards that best test the security of a product. These standards are called *criteria*. Many of the criteria we are going to look at have several tiers or levels where each level is supposed to certify one or more requirements by the product.

16.2.2 Common Computer Product Standards

The rapid growth of computer technology has resulted into a mushrooming of standards organizations that have created thousands of computer-related standards for the certification of the thousands of computer products manufactured by hundreds of different manufacturers. Among the many standards organizations that developed the most common standards used by the computer industry today are shown in Table 16.1 [4].

16.3   Security Evaluations

Security evaluation of computer products by independent and impartial bodies creates and provides security assurance to the customers of the product. The job of the security evaluators is to provide an accurate assessment of the strength of the security mechanisms in the product and systems based upon a criterion [5]. Based on these evaluations, an acceptable level of confidence in the product or system is established for the customer.

The process of product security evaluation for certification consists of two components: the *criteria* against which the evaluations are performed and the *schemes* or methodologies which govern how and who can perform such security evaluations [5]. There are several criteria and methods used internationally, and we are going to discuss some in the following sections. The process of security evaluation, based on criteria, consists of a series of tests based on a set of levels where each level may test for a specific set of standards. The process itself starts by establishing the following [1]:

Table 16.1 Computer products and system-related standards organizations

Standards organization	Standards developed
American National Standards Institute (ANSI)	Has a lot of American and international standards. See http://webstore.ansi.org/sdo.aspx
British Standards Institute (BSI)	BS XXX: Year Title where XXX is the number of the standard (many)
Institute of Electrical and Electronic Engineers Standards Association (IEEE-SA)	Has thousands of standards. See http://www.ieee.org/web/publications/subscriptions/prod/standards_overview.html
International Organization for Standardization (ISO)	Has developed over 17,000 international standards on a variety of subjects with about 1100 new ISO standards that are published every year. http://www.iso.org/iso/iso_catalogue.htm
National Institute of Standards and Technology (NIST)	Supports over 1300 different Standards. See http://ts.nist.gov/MeasurementServices/ReferenceMaterials/PROGRAM_INFO.cfm
Organization for the Advancement of Structured Information Standards (OASIS)	Has a long list of standards. See http://www.oasisopen.org/specs/index.php
Underwriters Laboratories (UL)	Has developed more than 1000 standards for safety. See http://www.ul.com/info/standard.htm
World Wide Web Consortium (W3C)	W3C creates primarily Web standards and guidelines designed to ensure long-term growth for the Web. See http://www.w3.org/

- Purpose
- Criteria
- Structure/elements
- Outcome/benefit

16.3.1 Purpose of Security Evaluation

Based on the Orange Book, a security assessment of a computer product is done for [1]:

- Certification—To certify that a given product meets the stated security criteria and therefore is suitable for a stated application. Currently, there is a variety of security certifying bodies of various computer products. This independent evaluation provides the buyer of the product added confidence in the product.
- Accreditation—To decide whether a given computer product, usually certified, meets stated criteria for and is suitable to be used in a given application. Again, there are currently several firms that offer accreditations to students after they use and get examined for their proficiency in the use of a certified product.
- Evaluation—To assess whether the product meets the security requirements and criteria for the stated security properties as claimed.

Table 16.2 Common computer security products' standards

B	I
Blacker (security)	IEC 60870-6
BS 7799	IEEE 802.10
C	ISO 15292
Common Criteria	ISO/IEC 27002
Content Security Policy	ITSEC
CTCPEC	N
CVSS	NIST Cybersecurity Framework
Cyber Resilience Review	P
Cybersecurity standards	Pluggable authentication module
F	R
FIPS 140	Rainbow Series
FIPS 140-2	S
FIPS 140-3	S/MIME
FIPS 199	Security Content Automation Protocol
H	Standard of Good Practice
HTTP Strict Transport Security	T
	Trusted Computer System Evaluation Criteria

Source: Wikipedia. https://en.wikipedia.org/wiki/Category:Computer_security_standards

- Potential market benefit, if any for the product. If the product passes the certification, it may have a big market potential.

16.3.2 Security Evaluation Criteria

As we have discussed earlier, *security evaluation criteria* are a collection of security standards that define several degrees of rigor acceptable at each testing level of security in the certification of a computer product. The security of most computer products is evaluated based on the security standards in Table 16.2.

Security evaluation criteria also may define the formal requirements the product needs to meet at each assurance level. Each security evaluation criterion consists of several assurance levels with specific security categories in each level. See the Orange Book (TCSEC) criteria assurance levels in Sect. 16.3.3.

Before any product evaluation is done, the product evaluator must state the evaluation criteria to be used in the process in order to produce the desired result. By stating the evaluation criteria, the evaluator directly states the assurance levels and categories in each assurance level that the product must meet. The result of a product evaluation is the statement whether the product under review meets the stated assurance levels in each evaluation criteria category. The Trusted Computer System Evaluation Criteria widely used today all have their origin in and their assurance levels based on the Trusted Computer System Evaluation Criteria (TCSEC) in Sect. 16.3.3.

16.3.3 Basic Elements of an Evaluation

The structure of an effective evaluation process, whether product oriented or process oriented, must consider the following basic elements:

- *Functionality*: Because acceptance of a computer security product depends on what and how much it can do. If the product has limited utility and in fact if it does not have the needed functionalities, then it is of no value. So the number of functionalities the product has or can perform enhances the product's acceptability.
- *Effectiveness*: After assuring that the product has enough functionalities to meet the needs of the buyer, the next key question is always whether the product meets the effectiveness threshold set by the buyer in all functionality areas. If the product has all the needed functionalities, but these functionalities are not effective enough, then the product cannot guarantee the needed security, and therefore, the product is of no value to the buyer.
- *Assurance*: To give the buyer enough confidence in the product, the buyer must be given an assurance, a guarantee, that the product will meet nearly all, if not exceed, the minimum stated security requirements. Short of this kind of assurance, the product may not be of much value to the buyer.

16.3.4 Outcome/Benefits

The goal of any product producer and security evaluator is to have a product that gives the buyer the best outcome and benefits within a chosen standard or criteria. The product outcome may not come within a short time, but it is essential that eventually the buyers see the security benefits. Although the process to the outcome for both the evaluator and the buyer may be different, the goal must always be the same, a great product. For example, to the product evaluator, it is important to minimize the expenses on the evaluation process without cutting the stated value of the evaluation. That is to say that keeping costs down should not produce mediocre outcomes. However, to the buyer, the process of evaluation of a software product for security requirements must ultimately result in the best product ever in enhancing the security of the system where the product is going to be deployed. The process of evaluation is worth the money if the product resulting from it meets all buyer requirements and better if it exceeds them.

The evaluation process itself can be done using either a standard or criteria. The choice of what to use is usually determined by the size of the product. Mostly, small products are evaluated using standards, while big ones are evaluated using criteria. For example, a computer mouse I am using is evaluated and certified by the standards developed by the Underwriters Laboratories, Inc., and the mouse has an insignia UL in a circle. If you check your computer, you may notice that each component is probably certified by a different standard.

Let us now look at the evaluation process itself. The evaluation of a product can take one of the following directions [1]:

- Product oriented: This is an investigative process to thoroughly examine and test every state security criteria and determine to what extent the product meets these stated criteria in a variety of situations. Because covering all testable configurations may require an exhaustive testing of the product, which is unthinkable in software testing, for example, a variety of representative testing must be chosen. This, however, indicates that the testing of software products, especially in security, depends heavily on the situation the software product is deployed in. One has to pay special attention to the various topologies in which the product is tested in and whether those topologies are exhaustive enough for the product to be acceptable.
- Process oriented: This is an audit process that assesses the developmental process of the product and the documentation done along the way, looking for security loopholes and other security vulnerabilities. The goal is to assess how a product was developed without any reference to the product itself. Unlike product-oriented testing which tends to be very expensive and time-consuming, process-oriented testing is cheap and takes less time. However, it may not be the best approach in security testing because its outcomes are not very valuable and reliable. One has to evaluate each evaluation scheme on its own merit.

Whatever direction of evaluation is chosen, the product security evaluation processes can take the following steps [1]:

- *Proposal review*: Where the product is submitted by the vendor for consideration for a review. The market analysis of the product is performed by the evaluator [in the United States, it is usually the Trusted Product Evaluation Program (TREP) within the National Security Agency (NSA)] based on this proposal.
- *Technical assessment*: After the initial assessment, the product goes into the technical assessment (TA) stage where the design of the product is put under review. Documentation from the vendor is important at this stage.
- *Advice*: From the preliminary technical review, advise is provided to the vendor to aid the vendor in producing a product and supporting documentation that is capable of being evaluated against a chosen criterion.
- *Intensive preliminary technical review*: An independent assessment by the evaluator to determine if the product is ready for evaluation. This stage can be done as the vendor's site and evaluators become familiar with the product.
- *Evaluation* is a comprehensive technical analysis of every aspect of the product. Rigorous testing of every component of the product is done. At the end, if the product passes all the tests, it is awarded an Evaluated Products List (EPL) entry.
- *Rating maintenance phase* provides a mechanism for the vendor to maintain the criteria rating of the product. If security changes are needed to be made, the vendor makes them during this phase. At the end of the phase, a full approval of the product is recommended. The rating is then assigned to the product.

16.4   Major Security Evaluation Criteria

The best way product manufacturers and vendors can demonstrate to their customers the high level of security their products have is through a security evaluation criteria. Through security evaluation, independent but accredited organizations can provide assurance to product customers of the security of product. These evaluations, based on specified criteria, serve to establish an acceptable level of confidence for product customers. Consequently, there are two important components of product security evaluations: the *criteria* against which the evaluations are performed and the *schemes* or methodologies which govern how and by whom such evaluations can be officially performed [6].

There are now several broadly accepted security evaluation criteria to choose from. However, this is a recent phenomenon. Before that, there were small national criteria without widely used and accepted standard criteria. Every European country and the United States each had its own small criteria. But by the mid-1980s, the European countries abandoned their individual national criteria to form the combined Information Technology Security Evaluation Criteria (ITSEC) (see Sect. 16.3.4) to join the US TCSEC that had been in use since the 1960s. Following the merger, an international criteria board finally introduced a widely accepted International Organization for Standardization (ISO)-based Common Criteria (CC). Let us look at a number of these criteria over time.

16.4.1 Common Criteria (CC)

The Common Criteria (CC) is a joint effort between nations to develop a single framework of mutually recognized evaluation criteria. It is referred to as the Harmonized Criteria, a multinational successor to the TCSEC and ITSEC that combined the best aspects of ITSEC, TCSEC, CTCPEC (Canadian Criteria), and the US Federal Criteria (FC). It was internationally accepted and finalized as an ISO 15408 standard and has been embraced by most countries around the world as the de facto security evaluation criteria. Common Criteria version 2.3 (CC v2.3) consists of three parts:

- Introduction and general model
- Security functional requirements
- Security assurance requirements

Based on these parts, CC v2.3 awards successfully evaluated products' one of eight evaluation assurance level (EAL) ratings from EAL 0 (lowest) to EAL7 (highest). For more information on CC v2.3, see http://www.commoncriteriaportal.org/thecc.html.

16.4.2 FIPS

Information technology (IT) product manufacturers always claim that their products offer the desired security for whatever purpose. This claim is difficult to prove especially for smaller businesses. IT customers, including the government, in need of protecting sensitive data need to have a minimum level of assurance that a product will attain a certain level of required security. In addition to this, legislative restrictions may require certain types of technology, such as cryptography and access control, to be in all products used by either government or specific businesses. In this case, therefore, those products need to be tested and validated before they are acquired.

Under needs like these, the Information Technology Management Reform Act (Public Law 104–106) requires that the Secretary of Commerce approves standards and guidelines that are developed by the National Institute of Standards and Technology (NIST) for federal computer systems. NIST's standards and guidelines are issued as Federal Information Processing Standards (FIPS) for government-wide use. NIST develops FIPS when there are compelling federal government requirements such as for security and interoperability and there are no acceptable industry standards or solutions.

Under these standards and guidelines, products are validated against FIPS at ranging security levels from the lowest to the highest. The testing and validation of products against the FIPS criteria may be performed by NIST and CSE-approved and accredited certification laboratories. Level 2 is the highest level of validation pursued by software vendors, while level 4 is generally only attempted by hardware vendors. For more information, see http://www.itl.nist.gov/fipspubs/.

16.4.3 The Orange Book/TCSEC

Most of the security criteria and standards in product security evaluation have their basis in the *Trusted Computer System Evaluation Criteria* (TCSEC), the first collection of standards used to grade or rate the security of computer system products. The TCSEC has come to be a standard commonly referred to as "the Orange Book" because of its orange cover. The criteria were developed with three objectives in mind [7]:

- To provide users with a yardstick with which to assess the degree of trust that can be placed in computer systems for the secure processing of classified or other sensitive information
- To provide guidance to manufacturers as to what to build into their new, widely available trusted commercial products in order to satisfy trust requirements for sensitive applications
- To provide a basis for specifying security requirements in acquisition specifications

The criteria also address two types of requirements:

- Specific security feature requirements
- Assurance requirements

The criteria met these objectives and requirements through four broad hierarchical divisions of enhanced assurance levels. These divisions, as seen in Fig. 16.1, labeled D for minimum protect, C for discretionary protection or need-to-know protection, B for mandatory protection, and A for verified protection are detailed as follows [1, 7]:

- *Class D (Minimal Protection)*: A division containing one class reserved for systems that have been evaluated but that fail to meet the requirements for a higher evaluation class.
- *Class C*:
  - *C1 (Discretionary Security Protection (DSP))*: This is intended for systems in environments where cooperating users process data at the same level of integrity. Discretionary access control (DAC) based on individual users or groups of users enabled them to securely share access to objects between users and groups of users after user identification and authentication. This makes it impossible for other users from accidentally getting access to unauthorized data.
  - *C2: Controlled Access Protection (CAP)* is a system that makes users accountable for their actions. DAC is enforced at a higher granularity level than C1. Subjects with information of another subject must not get access rights to an object which makes users accountable for their actions through log-in and auditing procedures.
- *Class B*: The notion of a security-relevant portion of a system is called a Trusted Computing Base (TCB). A TCB that preserves the integrity of the sensitivity labels and uses them to enforce a set of mandatory access control rules is a major requirement in this division:
  - *B1 (Labeled Security Protection (LSP))*: This is intended for systems dealing with classified data. Each system has all the requirements in C2 and in addition has an informal requirement of the security policy model, data labels for subjects and objects whose integrity must be strictly guarded, and mandatory access control over all subjects and objects.
  - *B2 (Structured Protection (SP))*: To add security requirements to the design of the system, thus increasing security assurance. It also requires the TCB to be based on a security policy. The TCB interface must be well defined to be subjected to a more thorough testing and complete review. In addition, it strengthens authentication mechanism, trusted facility management provided, and configuration management imposed. Overall systems with B2 certification are supposed to be resistant to penetration.
  - *B3 (Security Domains (SD))*: To ensure a high resistance to penetration of systems. It requires a security administrator and an auditing mechanism to

Highest Protection	A1: Verified Design
Security Functionality and Assurance	B : Trusted Computing Base (TCB).
	B3: Security Domains (SD)
	B2: Structured Protection (SP)
	B1: Labeled Security Protection (LSP)
	C2: Controlled Access Protection (CAP)
	C1: Discretionary Security Protection (DSP)
	D: Minimal Protection
Lowest Protection	

Fig. 16.1 The TCSEC/Orange Book class levels

monitor the occurrence or accumulation of security-relevant events. Such events must always trigger an automatic warning. In addition, a trusted recovery must be in place.

Class A1 (Verified Protection) This division is characterized by the use of formal security verification methods to ensure that the mandatory and discretionary security controls employed in the system can effectively protect classified or other sensitive information stored or processed by the system. Extensive documentation is required to demonstrate that the TCB meets the security requirements in all aspects of design, development, and implementation.

Most evaluating programs in use today still use or refer to TCSEC. Among these programs are [3]:

- The Trusted Product Evaluation Program (TPEP). TPEP is a program with which the US Department of Defense's National Computer Security Center (NCSC) evaluates computer systems.
- The Trust Technology Assessment Program (TTAP). TTAP is a joint program of the US National Security Agency (NSA) and the National Institute of Standards and Technology (NIST). TTAP evaluates off-the-shelf products. It establishes, accredits, and oversees commercial evaluation laboratories focusing on products with features and assurances characterized by TCSEC B1 and lower level of trust (see Sect. 15.3.1 for details).
- The Rating Maintenance Phase (RAMP) Program was established to provide a mechanism to extend the previous TCSEC rating to a new version of a previously evaluated computer system product. RAMP seeks to reduce evaluation time and effort required to maintain a rating by using the personnel involved in the maintenance of the product to manage the change process and perform security analysis. Thus, the burden of proof for RAMP efforts lies with those responsible for system maintenance (i.e., the vendor or TEF) other than with an evaluation team.

- The Trusted Network Interpretation (TNI) of the TCSEC, also referred to as "The Red Book," is a restating of the requirements of the TCSEC in a network context.
- The Trusted Database Interpretation (TDI) of the TCSEC is similar to the Trusted Network Interpretation (TNI) in that it decomposes a system into smaller independent parts that can be easily evaluated. It differs from the TNI in that the paradigm for this decomposition is the evaluation of an application running on an already evaluated system. The reader is also referred to <http:// www.radium. ncsc.mil/tpep/library/rainbow/5200.28-STD.html#HDR4> for an extensive coverage of the standard criteria.

16.4.4 Information Technology Security Evaluation Criteria (ITSEC)

While the US Orange Book criteria were developed in 1967, the Europeans did not define unified valuation criteria well until the 1980s when the United Kingdom, Germany, France, and the Netherlands harmonized their national criteria into a European Information Technology Security Evaluation Criteria (ITSEC). Since then, they have been updated, and the current issue is version 1.2, published in 1991, followed 2 years later by its user manual, the IT Security Evaluation Manual (ITSEM), which specifies the methodology to be followed when carrying out ITSEC evaluations. ITSEC was developed because the Europeans thought that the Orange Book was too rigid. ITSEC was meant to provide a framework for security evaluations that would lead to accommodate new future security requirements. It puts much more emphasis on integrity and availability. For more information on ITSEC, see http://www.radium.ncsc.mil/tpep/library/non-US/ ITSEC-12.html.

16.4.5 The Trusted Network Interpretation (TNI): The Red Book

The Trusted Network Interpretation (TNI) of the TCSEC, also referred to as "The Red Book," is a restating of the requirements of the TCSEC in a network context. It attempted to address network security issues. It is seen by many as a link between the Red Book and new criteria that came after. Some of the shortfalls of the Orange Book that the Red Book tries to address include the distinction between two types of computer networks [7]:

- Networks of independent components with different jurisdictions and management policies
- Centralized networks with single accreditation authority and policy

While the Orange Book addresses only the first type, the second type presents many security problems that the Red Book tries to address. Including the evaluations of network systems, distributed or homogeneous, often made directly against the

TCSEC without reference to the TNI. TNI component ratings specify the evaluated class as well as which of the four basic security services the evaluated component provides. Read more about these difference in the paper "Network Security: Red Book vs. Orange Book Evaluation," by Rich Lee at https://support.novell.com/techcenter/tips/ant19960603.html.

16.5 Does Evaluation Mean Security?

As we noted in Sect. 16.4, the security evaluation of a product based on a criterion does not mean that the product is assured of security. No security evaluation of any product can guarantee such security. However, an evaluated product can demonstrate certain security mechanisms and features based on the security criteria used and demonstrate assurances that the product does have certain security parameters to counter many of the threats listed under the criteria.

The development of new security standards and criteria will no doubt continue to result in better ways of security evaluations and certification of computer products and will therefore enhance the computer systems' security. However, as Mercuri observes, product certification should not create a false sense of security.

Exercises

1. The US Federal Criteria drafted in the early 1990s were never approved. Study the criteria and give reasons why they were not developed.
2. One advantage of process-oriented security evaluation is that it is cheap. Find other reasons why it is popular. Why, despite its popularity, is it not reliable?
3. For small computer product buyers, it is not easy to apply and use these standard criteria. Study the criteria and suggest reasons why this is so.
4. Nearly all criteria were publicly developed; suggest reasons why? Is it possible for individuals to develop commercially accepted criteria?
5. There are evaluated computer products on the market. Find out how one finds out whether a computer product has a security evaluation.
6. If you have a computer product, how do you get it evaluated? Does the evaluation help a product in the marketplace? Why or why not?
7. Every country participating in the computer product security evaluation has a list of evaluated products. Find out how to find this list. Does the ISO keep a global list of evaluated products?
8. Why is the product rated as B2/B3/A1 better than that rated C2/B1, or is it?
9. Study the rating divisions of TCSEC and show how product ratings can be interpreted.
10. What does it mean to say that a product is CC or TCSEC compliant?

Advanced Exercises

1. Research and find out if there are any widely used computer product security evaluation criteria.
2. Using the product evaluation list for computer products, determine the ratings for the following products: DOS, Windows NT, 98, XP, Unix, and Linux.
3. Study the history of the development of computer product security evaluation and suggest the reasons that led to the development of ISO-based CC.
4. Study and give the effects of ISO on a criterion. Does ISO affiliation have any impact on the success of a criterion?
5. Does the rapid development of computer technology put any strain on the existing criteria for updates?
6. Study and compare TCSEC, ITSEC, and CC assurance levels.
7. Trace the evolution of the security evaluation criteria.
8. Discuss how standards influence the security evaluation criteria.

References

1. Wikipedia. http://en.wikipedia.org/wiki/Open_standard
2. Bradner S. FRC 2026: the internet standards process—revision 3. Network Working Group. https://tools.ietf.org/html/rfc2026
3. Mercuri R. Standards insecurity. Commun ACM, December 2003, 46(12) 21–25
4. Computer Security Evaluation FAQ, Version 2.1. http://www.faqs.org/faqs/computer-security/evaluations/
5. An Oracle White Paper. Computer security criteria: security evaluations and assessment, July 2001. http://otndnld.oracle.co.jp/deploy/security/pdf/en/seceval_wp.pdf
6. Oracle Technology Network. Security evaluations. http://www.oracle.com/technetwork/topics/security/security-evaluations-087427.html
7. Department of Defense Standards. Trusted computer system evaluation criteria. http://www.iwar.org.uk/comsec/resources/standards/rainbow/5200.28-STD.html

Computer Network Security Protocols

17

17.1 Introduction

The rapid growth of the Internet and corresponding Internet community has fueled a rapid growth of both individual and business communications leading to the growth of e-mail and e-commerce. In fact, studies now show that the majority of the Internet communication content is e-mail content. The direct result of this has been the growing concern and sometimes demand for security and privacy in electronic communication and e-commerce. Security and privacy are essential if individual communication is to continue and e-commerce is to thrive in cyberspace. The call for and desire for security and privacy has led to the advent of several proposals for security protocols and standards. Among these are Secure Socket Layer (SSL) and Transport Layer Security (TLS) protocols, secure IP (IPsec), Secure HTTP (S-HTTP), secure e-mail (PGP and S/MIME), DNDSEC, SSH, and others. Before we proceed with the discussion of these and others, we want to warn the reader of the need for a firm understanding of the network protocol stack; otherwise, go back and look over the material in Chap. 1 before continuing. To make sure that the reader understands the security of networks based on protocol stacks, we will consider these protocols in both the ISO and TCP/IP stacks. Figure 17.1 shows the relationships between the ISO and TCP/IP stacks.

We will discuss these protocols and standards within the framework of the network protocol stack as follows:

- Application-level security (for TCP/IP) and application and presentation (for ISO)—RADIUS, TACACS, PGP, S/MIME, S-HTTP, HTTPS, SET, SSH, and Kerberos
- Transport-level security (for TCP/IP) and session and transport (for ISO)—SSL and TLS
- Network-level security for both TCP/IP and ISO—PPTP, L2TP, IPsec, and VPNs

© Springer International Publishing AG 2017

J.M. Kizza, *Guide to Computer Network Security*, Computer Communications and Networks, DOI 10.1007/978-3-319-55606-2_17

Fig. 17.1 Relationships
between ISO and TCP/IP
Network Protocol stacks

TCP/IP	ISO
Application	Application
	Presentation
Transport	Session
	Transport
Network	Network
Physical	Data link
	Physical

- Physical link-level security (for TCP/IP) and data link and physical (for ISO)—packet filters, NAT, CHAP, and PAP

17.2   Application-Level Security

All the protocols in this section are application layer protocols, which means that they reside on both ends of the communication link. They are all communication protocols ranging from simple text to multimedia including graphics, video, audio, and so on. In the last 10 years, there has been almost an explosion in the use of electronic communication, both mail and multimedia content, that has resulted in booming e-commerce and almost unmanageable personal e-mails, much of it private or intended to be private anyway, especially e-mails. Along with this explosion, there has been a growing demand for confidentiality and authenticity of private communications. To meet these demands, several schemes have been developed to offer both confidentiality and authentication of these communications. We will give a brief description of each. These four protocols and the standards are shown in the application layer of the network stack in Fig. 17.2.

TCP/IP	ISO	Security Protocols
Application	Application Presentation	RADIUS, TACAS, PGP, S/MIME, S-HTTP, HTTPS, SET, SSH, and KERBEROS

Fig. 17.2 Application layer security protocols and standard

17.2.1 Remote Authentication Dial-In User Service (RADIUS)

RADIUS is a server for remote user authentication and accounting. It is one of the most, if not the most, widely used dial-up authentication protocols. During dial-up, it offers authentication and authorization for those intending to use the network. It is one of a class of Internet dial-in security protocols that include Password Authentication Protocol (PAP) and Challenge-Handshake Authentication Protocol (CHAP). Although it is mainly used by Internet service providers (ISPs) to provide authentication and accounting for remote users, it can be used also in private networks to centralize authentication and accounting services on the network for all dial-in connections for service. A number of organizations are having their employees work off-site, and many of these employees may require to dial-in for services. Vendors and contractors may need to dial-in for information and specifications. RADIUS is a good tool for all these types of off-site authentication and accounting.

Let us look at RADIUS's main components: authentication and accounting protocols.

17.2.1.1 Authentication Protocols

Upon contact with the RADIUS server, a user is authenticated from the data supplied by the user to the server either directly by answering the terminal server's log-in/password prompts or using PAP or CHAP protocols. The user's personal data can also be obtained from one of the following places [1]:

- *System database*: The user's log-in ID and password are stored in the password database on the server.
- *Internal database*: The user's log-in ID and password can also be encrypted by either MD5 or DES hash and then stored in the internal RADIUS database.
- *SQL authentication*: The user's details can also be stored in an SQL database.

17.2.1.2 Accounting Protocols

RADIUS has three built-in accounting schemes: Unix accounting, detailed accounting, and SQL accounting.

17.2.1.3 Key Features of RADIUS

RADIUS has several features including [2]:

- *Client/Server Model*: In client/server model, the client is responsible for passing user information to designated RADIUS servers and then acting on the response which is returned. RADIUS servers, on their part, are responsible for receiving user connection requests, authenticating the user, and then returning all configuration information necessary for the client to deliver service to the user.
- *Network Security*: All correspondence between the client and RADIUS server is authenticated through the use of a shared secret, which is never sent over the network. User passwords are sent encrypted between the client and RADIUS server.
- *Flexible Authentication Mechanisms*: The RADIUS server can support a variety of methods to authenticate a user. When it is provided with the username and the original password given by the user, it can support PPP PAP or CHAP, Unix log-in, and other authentication mechanisms.
- *Extensible Protocol*: RADIUS is a fully extensible system. It supports two extension languages: the built-in Rewrite language and Scheme. Based on RFC 2138, all transactions are comprised of variable length Attribute-Length-Value 3-tuples. New attribute values can be added without disturbing existing implementations of the protocol.

17.2.2 Terminal Access Controller Access Control System (TACACS+)

This protocol is commonly referred to as "tac-plus" is a commonly used method of authentication protocol. Developed by Cisco Systems, TACACS+ is a strong protocol for dial-up, and it offers the following [3]:

- Authentication—arbitrary length and content authentication exchange which allows many authentication mechanisms to be used with it.
- Authorization.
- Auditing—a recording of what a user has been doing and in TACACS+, it serves two purposes:
  - To account for services used
  - To audit for security services

TACACS+ has a "+" sign because Cisco has extended it several times and has derivatives that include the following:

- TACACS—the original TACACS, which offers combined authentication and authorization
- XTACACS, which separated authentication, authorization, and accounting
- TACACS+, which is XTACACS plus extensions of control and accounting attributes

17.2.3 Pretty Good Privacy (PGP)

The importance of sensitive communication cannot be underestimated. Sensitive information, whether in motion in communication channels or in storage, must be protected as much as possible. The best way, so far, to protect such information is to encrypt it. In fact, the security that the old snail mail offered was based on a seemingly protective mechanism similar to encryption when messages were wrapped and enclosed in envelopes. There was, therefore, more security during the days of snail mail because it took more time and effort for someone to open somebody's mail. First, one had to get access to it, which was no small task. Then, one had to steam the envelope in order to open it and seal it later so that it looks unopened after. There were more chances of being caught doing so. Well, electronic communication has made it easy to intercept and read messages in the clear.

So encryption of e-mails and any other forms of communication is vital for the security, confidentiality, and privacy of everyone. This is where PGP comes in and this is why PGP is so popular today. In fact, currently PGP is one of the popular encryption and digital signatures schemes in personal communication.

Pretty Good Privacy (PGP), developed by Phil Zimmermann, is a public key cryptosystem. As we saw in Chap. 9, in public key encryption, one key is kept secret and the other key is made public. Secure communication with the receiving party (with a secret key) is achieved by encrypting the message to be sent using the recipient's public key. This message then can be decrypted only using the recipient's secret key.

PGP works by creating a *circle of trust* among its users. In the circle of trust, users, starting with two, form a key ring of public key/name pairs kept by each user. Joining this "trust club" means trusting and using the keys on somebody's key ring. Unlike the standard PKI infrastructure, this circle of trust has a built-in weakness that can be penetrated by an intruder. However, since PGP can be used to sign messages, the presence of its digital signature is used to verify the authenticity of a document or file. This goes a long way in ensuring that an e-mail message or file just downloaded from the Internet is both secure and untampered with.

PGP is regarded as hard encryption, which is impossible to crack in the foreseeable future. Its strength is based on algorithms that have survived extensive public review and are already considered by many to be secure. Among these algorithms are RSA which PGP uses for encryption, DSS, and Diffie-Hellman for public key encryption; CAST-128, IDEA, and 3DES for conventional encryption; and SHA-1 for hashing. The actual operation of PGP is based on five services: authentication, confidentiality, compression, e-mail compatibility, and segmentation [4].

17.2.3.1 Authentication
PGP provides authentication via a digital signature scheme. The hash code (MAC) is created using a combination of SHA-1 and RSA to provide an effective digital signature. It can also create an alternative signature using DSS and SHA-1. The signatures are then attached to the message or file before sending. PGP, in addition,

supports unattached digital signatures. In this case, the signature may be sent separately from the message.

17.2.3.2 Confidentiality

PGP provides confidentiality by encrypting messages before transmission. PGP encrypts messages for transmission and storage using conventional encryption schemes such as CAST-128, IDEA, and 3DES. In each case, a 64-bit cipher feedback mode is used. As in all cases of encryption, there is always a problem of key distribution; so PGP uses a conventional key once. This means for each message to be sent, the sender mints a brand new 128-bit session key for the message. The session key is encrypted with RSA or Diffie-Hallman using the recipient's public key; the message is encrypted using CAST-128 or IDEA or 3DES together with the session key. The combo is transmitted to the recipient. Upon receipt, the receiver uses RSA with his or her private key to encrypt and recover the session key which is used to recover the message. See Fig. 17.8.

17.2.3.3 Compression

PGP compresses the message after applying the signature and before encryption. The idea is to save space.

17.2.3.4 E-mail Compatibility

As we have seen above, PGP encrypts a message together with the signature (if not sent separately) resulting into a stream of arbitrary 8-bit octets. But since many e-mail systems permit only use of blocks consisting of ASCII text, PGP accommodates this by converting the raw 8-bit binary streams into streams of printable ASCII characters using a radix-64 conversion scheme. On receipt, the block is converted back from radix-64 format to binary. If the message is encrypted, then a session key is recovered and used to decrypt the message. The result is then decompressed. If there is a signature, it has to be recovered by recovering the transmitted hash code and comparing it to the receiver's calculated hash before acceptance.

17.2.3.5 Segmentation

To accommodate e-mail size restrictions, PGP automatically segments e-mail messages that are too long. However, the segmentation is done after all the housekeeping is done on the message, just before transmitting it. So the session key and signature appear only once at the beginning of the first segment transmitted. At receipt, the receiving PGP strips off all e-mail headers and reassembles the original mail.

PGP's popularity and use have so far turned out to be less than anticipated because of two reasons: first, its development and commercial distribution after Zimmermann sold it to Network Associates, which later sold it to another company, did not do well; second, its open-source cousin, the OpenPGP, encountered market problems including the problem of ease of use. Both OpenPGP and commercial PGP are difficult to use because it is not built into many e-mail clients. This implies that any two communicating users who want to encrypt their e-mail using PGP have to manually download and install PGP, a challenge and an inconvenience to many users.

17.2.4 Secure/Multipurpose Internet Mail Extension (S/MIME)

Secure/Multipurpose Internet Mail Extension (S/MIME) extends the protocols of Multipurpose Internet Mail Extensions (MIME) by adding digital signatures and encryption to them. To understand S/MIME, let us first make a brief digression and look at MIME. MIME is a technical specification of communication protocols that describes the transfer of multimedia data including pictures, audio, and video. The MIME protocol messages are described in RFC 1521; a reader with further interest in MIME should consult RFC 1521. Because Web contents such as files consist of hyperlinks that are themselves linked onto other hyperlinks, any e-mail must describe this kind of interlinkage. That is what a MIME server does whenever a client requests for a Web document. When the Web server sends the requested file to the client's browser, it adds a MIME header to the document and transmits it [5]. This means, therefore, that such Internet e-mail messages consist of two parts: the header and the body.

Within the header, two types of information are included: *MIME type* and *subtype*. The MIME type describes the general file type of the transmitted content type such as image, text, audio, application, and others. The subtype carries the specific file type such as *jpeg* or gif, tiff, and so on. For further information on the structure of a MIME header, please refer to RFC 822. The body may be unstructured or it may be in MIME format which defines how the body of an e-mail message is structured. What is notable here is that MIME does not provide any security services.

S/MIME was then developed to add security services that have been missing. It adds two cryptographic elements: encryption and digital signatures [4].

17.2.4.1 Encryption
S/MIME supports three public key algorithms to encrypt session keys for transmission with the message. These include Diffie-Hallman as the preferred algorithm, RSA for both signature and session keys, and Triple DES.

17.2.4.2 Digital Signatures
To create a digital signature, S/MIME uses a hash function of either 160-bit SHA-1 or MD5 to create message digests. To encrypt the message digests to form a digital signature, it uses either DSS or RSA.

17.2.5 Secure HTTP (S-HTTP)

Secure HTTP (S-HTTP) extends the Hypertext Transfer Protocol (HTTP). When HTTP was developed, it was developed for a Web that was simple, that did not have dynamic graphics, and that did not require, at that time, hard encryption for end-to-end transactions that have since developed. As the Web became popular for businesses, users realized that current HTTP needed more cryptographic and graphic improvements if it were to remain the e-commerce backbone it had become.

Responding to this growing need for security, the Internet Engineering Task Force called for proposals that will develop Web protocols, probably based on current HTTP, to address these needs. In 1994, such protocol was developed by Enterprise Integration Technologies (EIT). IET's protocols were, indeed, extensions of the HTTP. S-HHTP extended HTTP by extending HTTP's instructions and added security facilities using encryptions and support for digital signatures. Each S-HTTP file is either encrypted, contains a digital certificate, or both. S-HTTP design provides for secure communications, primarily commercial transactions, between a HTTP client and a server. It does this through a wide variety of mechanisms to provide for confidentiality, authentication, and integrity while separating policy from mechanism. The system is not tied to any particular cryptographic system, key infrastructure, or cryptographic format [6].

HTTP messages contain two parts: the header and the body of the message. The header contains instructions to the recipients (browser and server) on how to process the message's body. For example, if the message body is of the type like MIME, Text, or HTML, instructions must be given to display this message accordingly. In the normal HTTP, for a client to retrieve information (text-based message) from a server, a client-based browser uses HTTP to send a request message to the server that specifies the desired resource. The server, in response, sends a message to the client that contains the requested message. During the transfer transaction, both the client browser and the server use the information contained in the HTTP header to negotiate formats they will use to transfer the requested information. Both the server and client browser may retain the connection as long as it is needed: otherwise, the browser may send message to the server to close it.

The S-HTTP extends this negotiation between the client browser and the server to include the negotiation for security matters. Hence, S-HTTP uses additional headers for message encryption, digital certificates, and authentication in the HTTP format which contains additional instructions on how to decrypt the message body. Tables 17.1 and 17.2 show header instructions for both HTTP and S-HTTP. The HTTP headers are encapsulated into the S-HTTP headers. The headers give a variety of options that can be chosen from as a client browser and the server negotiate for information exchange. All headers in S-HTTP are optional, except "Content Type" and "Content-Privacy-Domain."

To offer flexibility, during the negotiation between the client browser and the server, for the cryptographic enhancements to be used, the client and server must agree on four parts: property, value, direction, and strength. If agents are unable to

Table 17.1 S-HTTP headers

S-HTTP header	Purpose	Options
Content-Privacy-Domain	For compatibility with PEM-based secure HTTP	RSA's PKCS-7 (Public Key Cryptography Standard 7), "Cryptographic Message Syntax Standard," RFC-1421 style PEM, and PGP 2.6 format
Content-transfer-encoding	Explains how the content of the message is encoded	7, 8 bit
Content-type	Standard header	HTTP
Prearranged-Key-Info	Information about the keys used in the encapsulation	DEK (data exchange key) used to encrypt this message

Table 17.2 HTTP headers

HTTP header	Purpose	Options
Security scheme	Mandatory, specifies protocol name and version	S-HTTP/1.1
Encryption identity	Identity names the entity for which a message is encrypted. Permits return encryption under public key without others signing first	DN-1485 and Kerberos
Certificate info	Allows a sender to send a public key certificate in a message	PKCS-7, PEM
Key assign (exchange)	The message used for actual key exchanges	Krb-4, Krb-5 (Kerberos)
Nonces	Session identifiers, used to indicate the freshness of a session	

S-HTTP-Key-Exchange-Algorithms: *recv-required* = RSA, Kerb-5

discover a common set of algorithms, appropriate actions are then be taken. Adam Shastack [5] gives the following example as a negotiation line:

This means that messages *received* by this machine are *required* to use Kerberos 5 or RSA encryption to exchange keys. The choices for the *(recv-required)* modes are *(recv // orig)-(optional // required // refused)*. Where key length specifications are necessary in case of variable key length ciphers, this is then specifically referred to as cipher[length], or cipher[L1–L2], where length of key is length or, in the case of L1–L2, is between L1 and L2, inclusive [5].

Other headers in the S-HTTP negotiations could be [5, 6]:

- S-HTTP-Privacy-Domains
- S-HTTP-Certificate-Types
- S-HTTP-Key-Exchange-Algorithms
- S-HTTP-Signature-Algorithms
- S-HTTP-Message-Digest-Algorithms
- S-HTTP-Symmetric-Content-Algorithms
- S-HTTP-Symmetric-Header-Algorithms

- S-HTTP-Privacy-Enhancements
- Your-Key-Pattern

We refer a reader interested in more details of these negotiations to Adam Shastack's paper.

We had pointed out earlier that S-HTTP extends HTTP by adding message encryption, digital signature, and message and sender authentication. Let us see how these are incorporated into HTTP to get S-HTTP.

17.2.5.1 Cryptographic Algorithm for S-HTTP

S-HTTP uses a symmetric key cryptosystem in the negotiations that prearranges symmetric session keys and a challenge-response mechanism between communicating parties. Before the server can communicate with the client browser, both must agree upon an encryption key. Normally the process would go as follows: The client's browser would request the server for a page. Along with this request, the browser lists encryption schemes it supports and also includes its public key. Upon receipt of the request, the server responds to the client browser by sending a list of encryption schemes it also supports. The server may, in addition, send the browser a session key encrypted by the client's browser's public key, now that it has it. If the client's browser does not get a session key from the server, it then sends a message to the server encrypted with the server's public key. The message may contain a session key or a value the server can use to generate a session key for the communication.

Upon the receipt of the page/message from the server, the client's browser, if possible, matches the decryption schemes in the S-HTTP headers (recall this was part of the negotiations before the transfer), which include session keys, and then decrypts the message [6]. In HTTP transactions, once the page has been delivered to the client's browser, the server would disconnect. However, with S-HTTP, the connection remains until the client browser requests the server to do so. This is helpful because the client's browser encrypts each transmission with this session key.

Cryptographic technologies used by S-HTTP include Privacy-Enhanced Mail (PEM), Pretty Good Privacy (PGP), and Public Key Cryptography Standard 7 (PKGS-7). Although S-HTTP uses encryption facilities, non-S-HTTP browsers can still communicate with an S-HTTP server. This is made possible because S-HTTP does not require that the user preestablishes public keys in order to participate in a secure transaction. A request for secure transactions with an S-HTTP server must originate from the client browser. See Fig. 17.1.

Because a server can deal with multiple requests from client browsers, S-HTTP supports multiple encryptions by supporting two transfer mechanisms: one that uses public key exchange, usually referred to as *in-band*, and one that uses a third-party Public Key Authority (PKA) that provides session keys using public keys for both clients and servers.

17.2.5.2 Digital Signatures for S-HTTP

S-HTTP uses *SignedData* or *SignedAndEnvelopedData* signature enhancement of PKCS-7 [6]. S-HTTP allows both certificates from a certificate authority (CA) and a self-signed certificate (usually not verified by a third party). If the server requires a digital certificate from the client's browser, the browser must attach a certificate then.

17.2.5.3 Message and Sender Authentication in S-HTTP

S-HHTP uses an authentication scheme that produces a MAC. The MAC is actually a digital signature computed from a hash function on the document using a shared secret code.

17.2.6 Hypertext Transfer Protocol over Secure Socket Layer (HTTPS)

HTTPS is the use of Secure Sockets Layer (SSL) as a sub-layer under the regular HTTP in the application layer. It is also referred to as Hypertext Transfer Protocol over Secure Socket Layer (HTTPS) or HTTP over SSL, in short. HTTPS is a Web protocol developed by Netscape, and it is built into its browser to encrypt and decrypt user page requests as well as the pages that are returned by the Web server. HTTPS uses port 443 instead of HTTP port 80 in its interactions with the lower layer, TCP/IP. Probably to understand well how this works, the reader should first go over Sect. 17.3.1, where SSL is discussed.

17.2.7 Secure Electronic Transactions (SET)

SET is a cryptographic protocol developed by a group of companies that included Visa, Microsoft, IBM, RSA, Netscape, MasterCard, and others. It is a highly specialized system with complex specifications contained in three books with book one dealing with the business description, book two a programmer's guide, and book three giving the formal protocol description. Book one spells out the business requirements that include the following [4]:

- Confidentiality of payment and ordering information
- Integrity of all transmitted data
- Authentication of all cardholders
- Authenticating that a merchant can accept card transactions based on relationship with financial institution
- Ensuring the best security practices and protection of all legitimate parties in the transaction
- Creating protocols that neither depend on transport security mechanism nor prevent their use

- Facilitating and encouraging interoperability among software and network providers

Online credit and debit card activities that must meet those requirements may include one or more of the following: cardholder registration, merchant registration, purchase request, payment authorization, funds transfer, credits reversals, and debit cards. For each transaction, SET provides the following services: authentication, confidentiality, message integrity, and linkage [4, 7].

17.2.7.1 Authentication

Authentication is a service used to authenticate everyone in the transacting party that includes the customer, the merchant, the bank that issued the customer's card, and the merchant's bank, using X.509v3 digital signatures.

17.2.7.2 Confidentiality

Confidentiality is a result of encrypting all aspects of the transaction to prevent intruders from gaining access to any component of the transaction. SET uses DES for this.

17.2.7.3 Message Integrity

Again this is a result of encryption to prevent any kind of modification to the data such as personal data and payment instructions involved in the transaction. SET uses SHA-1 hash codes used in the digital signatures.

17.2.7.4 Linkage

Linkage allows the first party in the transaction to verify that the attachment is correct without reading the contents of the attachment. This helps a great deal in keeping the confidentiality of the contents.

SET uses public key encryption and signed certificates to establish the identity of everyone involved in the transaction and to allow every correspondence between them to be private.

The SET protocols involved in a transaction have several representations, but every one of those representations has the following basic facts: the actors and the purchase-authorization-payment control flow.

The actors involved in every transaction are as follows [4]:

- The buyer—usually the cardholder.
- The merchant—fellow with the merchandise the buyer is interested in.
- The merchant bank—the financial institution that handles the merchant's financial transactions.
- The customer bank—usually the bank that issues the card to the customer. This bank also authorizes electronic payments to the merchant account upon authorization of payment request from the customer. This bank may sometimes set up another entity and charge it with payment authorizations.

- Certificate authority (CA)—that issues X.509v3 certificates to the customer and merchant.

Purchase-authorization-payment control flow. This flow is initiated by the customer placing a purchase order to the merchant and is concluded by the customer bank sending a payment statement to the customer. The key cryptographic authentication element in SET is the *dual signature*. The dual signature links two messages (payment information and order information) intended for two different recipients, the merchant getting merchandise information and the customer bank getting payment information. The dual signature keeps the two bits of information separate letting the intended party see only the part they are authorized to see. The customer creates a dual signature by hashing the merchandise information and also payment information using SHA-1, concatenates the two, hashes them again, and encrypts the result using his or her private key before sending them to the merchant. For more details on dual signatures, the reader is referred to *Cryptography and Network Security: Principles and Practice,* Second Edition, by William Stallings. Let us now look at the purchase-authorization-payment control flow [4, 7].

- Customer initiates the transaction by sending to the merchant a purchase order and payment information together with a dual signature.
- The merchant, happy to receive an order from the customer, strips off the merchant information, verifies customer purchase order using his or her certificate key, and forwards the payment information to his or her bank.
- The merchant bank forwards the payment information from the customer to the customer bank.
- The customer bank, using the customer's certificate key, checks and authorizes the payments and informs the merchant's bank.
- The merchant's bank passes the authorization to the merchant, who releases the merchandise to the customer.
- The customer bank bills the customer.

17.2.8 Kerberos

Kerberos is a network authentication protocol. It is designed to allow users, clients, and servers authenticate themselves to each other. This mutual authentication is done using secret key cryptography. Using secret key encryption or, as it is commonly known, conventional encryption, a client can prove its identity to a server across an insecure network connection. Similarly, a server can also identify itself across the same insecure network connection. Communication between the client and the server can be secure after the client and server have used Kerberos to prove their identities. From this point on, subsequent communication between the two can be encrypted to ensure privacy and data integrity.

In his paper *The Moron's Guide to Kerberos, Version 1.2.2,* Brian Tung [7], in a simple but interesting example, likens the real-life self-authentication we always do with the presentation of driver licenses on demand to that of Kerberos.

Kerberos client/server authentication requirements are as follows [5]:

- Security—that Kerberos is strong enough to stop potential eavesdroppers from finding it to be a weak link.
- Reliability—that Kerberos is highly reliable, employing a distributed server architecture where one server is able to back up another. This means that Kerberos system is fail safe, meaning graceful degradation, if it happens.
- Transparency—that users are not aware that authentication is taking place beyond providing passwords.
- Scalability—that Kerberos systems accept and support new clients and servers.

To meet these requirements, Kerberos designers proposed a third-party-trusted authentication service to arbitrate between the client and server in their mutual authentication. Figure 17.3 shows the interaction between the three parties.

The actual Kerberos authentication process is rather complex, probably more complex than all the protocols we have seen so far in this chapter. So to help the reader grasp the concept, we are going to follow what many writers on Kerberos have done and go via an example and Fig. 17.3. And here we go [5]:

On a Kerberos network, suppose user A wants to access a document on server B. Both principals in the transaction do not trust each other. So the server must demand assurances that A is who he or she says he or she is. So just like in real life, when you are seeking a service from demands that you show proof of what you claim you are by pulling out a driver's license with a picture of you on it, Kerberos also demands proof. In Kerberos, however, A must present a *ticket* to B. The ticket is issued by a Kerberos *authentication server* (AS). Both A and B trust the AS. So A anticipating that B will demand proof works on it by digitally signing the request to access the document held by B with A's private key and encrypting the request with B's public key. A then sends the encrypted request to AS, the trusted server. Upon receipt of the request, AS verifies that it is A who sent the request by analyzing A's digital signature. It also checks A's access rights to the requested document. AS has those lists for all the servers in the Kerberos system. AS then mints a *ticket* that contains a session key and B's access information, uses A's public key to encrypt it, and sends it to A. In addition, AS mints a similar ticket for B which contains the same information as that of A. The ticket is transmitted to B. Now AS's job is almost done after connecting both A and B. They are now on their own. After the connection, both A and B compare their tickets for a match. If the tickets match, the AS has done its job, and A and B start communicating as A accesses the requested document on B. At the end of the session, B informs AS to recede the ticket for this session. Now if A wants to communicate with B again for whatever request, a new ticket for the session is needed.

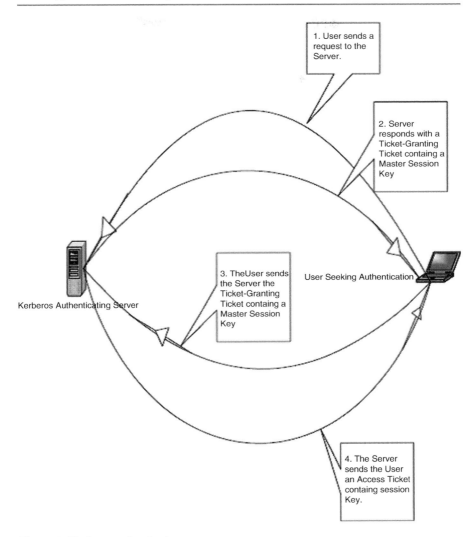

Fig. 17.3 Kerberos authentication system

17.2.8.1 Ticket-Granting Ticket

The Kerberos system may have more than one AS. While this method works well, it is not secure. This is so because the ticket stays in use for some time and is, therefore, susceptible to hacking. To tackle this problem, Kerberos systems use another approach that is more secure. This second approach uses the first approach as the basis. An authentication process goes as follows:

A, in need of accessing a document on server B, sends an access request text in the clear to AS for a *ticket-granting ticket*, which is a master ticket for the log-in process with B. AS, using a shared secret such as a password, verifies A and sends A a ticket-granting ticket. A then uses this ticket-granting ticket instead of A's public key to send to AS for a ticket for any resource from any server A wants. To send the ticket to A, the AS encrypts it with a master session key contained in the ticket-granting ticket.

When a company has distributed its computing by having Kerberos networks in two separate areas, there are ways to handle situations like this. One Kerberos system in one network can authenticate a user in another Kerberos network. Each Kerberos AS operates in a defined area of the network called a *realm*. To extend the Kerberos' authentication across realms, an inter-realm key is needed that allows clients authenticated by an AS in one realm to use that authentication in another realm. Realms sharing inter-realm keys can communicate.

Kerberos can run on top of an operating system. In fact it is a default protocol in Windows 2000 and later versions of Windows. In a nonnative environment, Kerberos must be "kerberized" by making server and client software make calls to Kerberos library.

17.3   Security in the Transport Layer

Unlike the last five protocols we have been discussing in the previous section, in this section we look at protocols that are a little deeper in the network infrastructure. They are at the level below the application layer. In fact they are at the transport layer. Although several protocols are found in this layer, we are only going to discuss two: Secure Socket Layer (SSL) and Transport Layer Security (TLS). Currently, however, these two are no longer considered as two separate protocols but one under the name SSL/TLS, after the SSL standardization was passed over to IETF, by the Netscape consortium, and Internet Engineering Task Force (IETF) renamed it TLS. Figure 17.3 shows the position of these protocols in the network protocol stack.

17.3.1 Secure Socket Layer (SSL)

SSL is a widely used general-purpose cryptographic system used in the two major Internet browsers: Netscape and Explorer. It was designed to provide an encrypted end-to-end data path between a client and a server regardless of platform or OS. Secure and authenticated services are provided through data encryption, server authentication, message integrity, and client authentication for a TCP connection through HTTP, LDAP, or POP3 application layers. It was originally developed by Netscape Communications, and it first appeared in a Netscape Navigator browser in 1994. The year 1994 was an interesting year for Internet security because during the same year, a rival security scheme to SSL, the S-HTTP, was launched. Both systems were designed for Web-based commerce. Both allow for the exchange of multiple messages between two processes and use similar cryptographic schemes such as digital envelopes, signed certificates, and message digest.

Fig. 17.4 Transport layer
security protocols and
standards

TCP/IP	ISO	Security Protocols
Transport	Session Transport	SSL and TLS

Although these two Web giants had much in common, there are some differences in design goals, implementation, and acceptance. First, S-HTTP was designed to work with only Web protocols. Because SSL is at a lower level in the network stack than S-HTTP, it can work in many other network protocols. Second, in terms of implementation, since SSL is again at a lower level than S-HTTP, it is implemented as a replacement for the sockets API to be used by applications requiring secure communications. On the other hand, S-HTTP has its data passed in named text fields in the HTTP header. Finally, in terms of distribution and acceptance, history has not been so good to S-HTTP. While SSL was released in a free mass circulating browser, the Netscape Navigator, S-HTTP was released in a much smaller and restricted NCSA Mosaic. This unfortunate choice doomed the fortunes of S-HTTP (Fig. 17.4).

17.3.1.1 SSL Objectives and Architecture

The stated SSL objectives were to secure and authenticate data paths between servers and clients. These objectives were to be achieved through several services that included data encryption, server and client authentication, and message integrity [8]:

- Data encryption—to protect data in transport between the client and the server from interception and could be read only by the intended recipient.
- Server and client authentication—the SSL protocol uses standard public key encryption to authenticate the communicating parties to each other.
- Message integrity—achieved through the use of session keys so that data cannot be either intentionally or unintentionally tampered with.

These services offer reliable end-to-end secure services to Internet TCP connections and are based on an SSL architecture consisting of two layers: the top layer, just below the application layer, that consists of three protocols, namely, the SSL Handshake protocol, the SSL Change Cipher Spec protocol, and the SSL Alert protocol. Below these protocols is the second SSL layer, the SSL Record Protocol layer, just above the TCP layer. See Fig. 17.5.

17.3.1.2 The SSL Handshake

Before any TCP connection between a client and a server, both running under SSL, is established, there must be almost a process similar to a three-way handshake we

Fig. 17.5 The SSL protocol stack

discussed in Sect. 3.2.2. This get-to-know-you process is similarly called the SSL handshake. During the handshake, the client and server perform the following tasks [9]:

- Establish a cipher suite to use between them.
- Provide mandatory server authentication through the server sending its certificate to the client to verify that the server's certificate was signed by a trusted CA.
- Provide optional client authentication, if required, through the client sending its own certificate to the server to verify that the client's certificate was signed by a trusted CA. The CA may not be the same CA who signed the client's certificate. CAs may come from a list of trusted CAs. The reason for making this step optional was a result of realization that since few customers are willing, know how, or care to get digital certificates, requiring them to do this would amount to locking a huge number of customers out of the system which would not make business sense. This, however, presents some weaknesses to the system.
- Exchange key information using public key cryptography, after mutual authentication, that leads to the client generating a session key (usually a random number) which, with the negotiated cipher, is used in all subsequent encryption or decryption. The customer encrypts the session key using the public key of the merchant server (from the merchant's certificate). The server recovers the session key by decrypting it using its private key. This symmetric key, which now both parties have, is used in all subsequent communication.

17.3.1.3 SSL Cipher Spec Protocol

The SSL Cipher Spec protocol consists of an exchange of a single message in a byte with a value of 1 being exchanged, using the SSL record protocol (see Sect. 17.3.1.4), between the server and client. The bit is exchanged to establish a pending session state to be copied into the current state, thus defining a new set of protocols as the new agreed on session state.

17.3.1.4 SSL Alert Protocol

The SSL Alert protocol, which also runs over the SSL Record protocol, is used by the two parties to convey session warning messages associated with data exchange and functioning of the protocol. The warnings are used to indicate session problems ranging from unknown certificate, revoked certificate, and expired certificate to fatal error messages that can cause immediate termination of the SSL connection. Each message in the alert protocol sits within two bytes, with the first byte taking a value of (1) for a warning and (2) for a fatal error. The second byte of the message contains one of the defined error codes that may occur during an SSL communication session [8]. For further working of these error codes, see [8].

17.3.1.5 SSL Record Protocol

The SSL record protocol provides SSL connections two services: confidentiality and message integrity [5]:

- *Confidentiality* is attained when the handshake protocol provides a shared secret key used in the conventional encryption of SSL messages.
- *Message integrity* is attained when the handshake defines a secret shared key used to form a message authentication code (MAC).

In providing these services, the SSL Record Protocol takes an application message to be transmitted and fragments the data that needs to be sent, compresses it, adds a MAC, encrypts it together with the MAC, adds an SSL header, and transmits it under the TCP protocol. The return trip undoes these steps. The received data is decrypted, verified, and decompressed before it is forwarded to higher layers. The record header that is added to each data portion contains two elementary pieces of information, namely, the length of the record and the length of the data block added to the original data. See Fig. 17.6.

The MAC, computed from a hash algorithm such as MD5 or SHA-1 as MAC = Hash function [secret key, primary data, padding, sequence number], is used to verify the integrity of the message included in the transmitted record. The verification is done by the receiving party computing its own value of the MAC and comparing it with that received. If the two values match, this means that data has not been modified during the transmission over the network.

SSL protocols are widely used in all Web applications and any other TCP connections. Although they are mostly used for Web applications, they are gaining ground in e-mail applications also.

Fig. 17.6 SSL record
protocol operation process

17.3.2 Transport Layer Security (TLS)

Transport Layer Security (TLS) is the result of the 1996 Internet Engineering Task Force's (IETF) attempt at standardization of a secure method to communicate over the Web. The 1999 outcome of that attempt was released as RFC 2246 spelling out a new protocol—the Transport Layer Security or TLS. TLS was charged with providing security and data integrity at the transport layer between two applications. TLS version 1.0 was an evolved SSL 3.0. So, as we pointed out earlier, TLS is the successor to SSL 3.0. Frequently, the new standard is referred to as SSL/TLS.

Since then, however, the following additional features have been added [8]:

- *Interoperability*—ability to exchange TLS parameters by either party, with no need for one party to know the other's TLS implementation details

Fig. 17.7 Network layer security protocols and standards

TCP/IP	ISO	Security Protocols
Network	Network	IPsec, VPN, PPTP and L2TP

- *Expandability*—to plan for future expansions and accommodation of new protocols

17.4 Security in the Network Layer

In the previous section, we discussed protocols in the transport part of the stack that are being used to address Internet communication security. In this section, we are going one layer down, to the network layer, and also look at the protocols and probably standards that address Internet communication security. In this layer, we will address IPsec and VPN technologies shown in Fig. 17.7.

17.4.1 Internet Protocol Security (IPsec)

IPsec is a suite of authentication and encryption protocols developed by the Internet Engineering Task Force (IETF) and designed to address the inherent lack of security for IP-based networks. IPsec, unlike other protocols we have discussed so far, is a very complex set of protocols described in a number of RFCs including RFC 2401 and 2411. It runs transparently to transport layer and application layer protocols which do not see it. Although it was designed to run in the new version of the Internet Protocol, IP version 6 (IPv6), it has also successfully run in the older IPv4. IPsec sets out to offer protection by providing the following services at the network layer:

- Access control—to prevent an unauthorized access to the resource.
- Connectionless integrity—to give an assurance that the traffic received has not been modified in any way.
- Confidentiality—to ensure that Internet traffic is not examined by nonauthorized parties. This requires all IP datagrams to have their data field, TCP, UDP, ICMP, or any other datagram data field segment encrypted.
- Authentication—particularly source authentication so that when a destination host receives an IP datagram, with a particular IP source address, it is possible to be sure that the IP datagram was indeed generated by the host with the source IP address. This prevents spoofed IP addresses.
- Replay protection—to guarantee that each packet exchanged between two parties is different.

Fig. 17.8 IPsec's AH
protocol protection

IPsec protocol achieves these two objectives by dividing the protocol suite into two main protocols: Authentication Header (AH) protocol and the Encapsulation Security Payload (ESP) protocol [10]. The AH protocol provides source authentication and data integrity but no confidentiality. The ESP protocol provides authentication, data integrity, and confidentiality. Any datagram from a source must be secured with either AH or ESP. Figures 17.8 and 17.9 show both IPsec's ESP and AH protections.

17.4.1.1 Authentication Header (AH)

AH protocol provides source authentication and data integrity but not confidentiality. This is done by a source that wants to send a datagram first establishing an SA, through which the source can send the datagram. A source datagram includes an AH inserted between the original IP datagram data and the IP header to shield the data field which is now encapsulated as a standard IP datagram. See Fig. 17.5. Upon receipt of the IP datagram, the destination host notices the AH and processes it using the AH protocol. Intermediate hosts such as routers, however, do their usual job of examining every datagram for the destination IP address and then forwarding it on.

17.4.1.2 Encapsulating Security Payload (ESP)

Unlike the AH protocol, ESP protocol provides source authentication, data integrity, and confidentiality. This has made ESP the most commonly used IPsec header. Similar to AH, ESP begins with the source host establishing an AS which it uses to send secure datagrams to the destination. Datagrams are secured by ESP by surrounding their original IP datagrams with a new header and trailer fields all encapsulated into a new IP datagram. See Fig. 17.6. Confidentiality is provided by DES_CBC encryption. Next to the ESP trailer field on the datagram is the ESP Authentication Data field.

17.4.1.3 Security Associations

In order to perform the security services that IPsec provides, IPsec must first get as much information as possible on the security arrangement of the two communicating hosts. Such security arrangements are called *security associations* (SAs). A security association is a unidirectional security arrangement defining a set of items

Fig. 17.9 IPsec's ESP protocol protection

and procedures that must be shared between the two communicating entities in order to protect the communication process.

Recall from Chap. 1 that in the usual network IP connections, the network layer IP is connectionless. However, with security associations, IPsec creates logical connection-oriented channels at the network layer. This logical connection-oriented channel is created by a security agreement established between the two hosts stating specific algorithms to be used by the sending party to ensure confidentiality (with ESP), authentication, message integrity, and anti-replay protection.

Since each AS establishes a unidirectional channel, for a full-duplex communication between two parties, two SAs must be established. An SA is defined by the following parameters [5, 11]:

- Security Parameter Index (SPI)—a 32-bit connection identifier of the SA. For each association between a source and destination host, there is one SPI that is used by all datagrams in the connection to provide information to the receiving device on how to process the incoming traffic.
- IP destination address—address of a destination host.
- A security protocol (AH or ESP)—to be used and specifying if traffic is to be provided with integrity and secrecy. The protocol also defines the key size, the key lifetime, and the cryptographic algorithms.
- Secret key—which defines the keys to be used.
- Encapsulation mode—defining how encapsulation headers are created and which parts of the header and user traffic are protected during the communication process.

Figure 17.10 shows the general concept of a security association.

17.4.1.4 Transport and Tunnel Modes

The security associations discussed above are implemented in two modes: transport and tunnel. This means that IPsec is operating in two modes. Let us look at these [5].

Fig. 17.10 A general concept of IPsec's security association

Transport Mode
Transport mode provides host-to-host protection to higher-layer protocols in the communication between two hosts in both IPv4 and IPv6. In IPv4, this area is the area beyond the IP address as shown in Fig. 17.11. In IPv6, the new extension to IPv4, the protection includes the upper protocols, the IP address, and any IPv6 header extensions as shown in Fig. 17.8. The IP addresses of the two IPsec hosts are in the clear because they are needed in routing the datagram through the network.

Tunnel Mode
Tunnel mode offers protection to the entire IP datagram both in AH and ESP between two IPsec gateways. This is possible because of the added new IP header in both IPv4 and IPv6 as shown in Fig. 17.12. Between the two gateways, the datagram is secure and the original IP address is also secure. However, beyond the gateways, the datagram may not be secure. Such protection is created when the first IPsec gateway encapsulates the datagram including its IP address into a new shield datagram with a new IP address of the receiving IPsec gateway. At the receiving gateway, the new datagram is unwrapped and brought back to the original datagram. This datagram, based on its original IP address, can be passed on further by the receiving gateway, but from this point on unprotected.

17.4.1.5 Other IPsec Issues
Any IPsec compliant system must support single DES, MD5, and SHA-1 as an absolute minimum; this ensures that a basic level of interworking is possible with two IPsec compliant units at each end of the link. Since IPsec sits between the network and transport layers, the best place for its implementation is mainly in hardware.

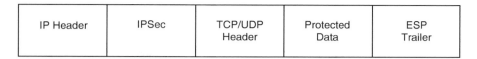

IP Header	IPSec	TCP/UDP Header	Protected Data	ESP Trailer

Fig. 17.11 IPsec's transport mode

IP Header	IPSec	IP Header	TCP/UDP Header	Protected Data	ESP Trailer

Fig. 17.12 IPsec's tunnel mode

17.4.2 Virtual Private Networks (VPN)

A VPN is a private data network that makes use of the public telecommunication infrastructure, such as the Internet, by adding security procedures over the unsecure communication channels. The security procedures that involve encryption are achieved through the use of a tunneling protocol. There are two types of VPNs: remote access which lets single users connect to the protected company network and site-to-site which supports connections between two protected company networks. In either mode, VPN technology gives a company the facilities of expensive private leased lines at much lower cost by using the shared public infrastructure like the Internet. See Fig. 17.13.

Figure 17.8 shows two components of a VPN [3]:

- Two terminators which are either software or hardware. These perform encryption, decryption, and authentication services. They also encapsulate the information.
- A tunnel—connecting the endpoints. The tunnel is a secure communication link between the endpoints and networks such as the Internet. In fact this tunnel is virtually created by the endpoints.

VPN technology must do the following activities:

- IP encapsulation—this involves enclosing TCP/IP data packets within another packet with an IP address of either a firewall or a server that acts as a VPN endpoint. This encapsulation of host IP address helps in hiding the host.
- Encryption—is done on the data part of the packet. Just like in SSL, the encryption can be done either in transport mode which encrypts its data at the time of generation or tunnel mode which encrypts and decrypts data during transmission encrypting both data and header.
- Authentication—involves creating an encryption domain which includes authenticating computers and data packets by use for public encryption.

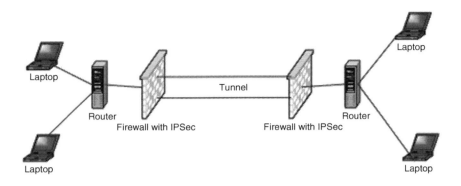

Fig. 17.13 Virtual private network (VPN) model

VPN technology is not new; phone companies have provided private shared resources for voice messages for over a decade. However, its extension to making it possible to have the same protected sharing of public resources for data is new. Today, VPNs are being used for both extranets and wide-area intranets. Probably owing to cost savings, the popularity of VPNs by companies has been phenomenal.

17.4.2.1 Types of VPNs

The security of VPN technologies falls into three types: trusted VPNs, secure VPNs, and hybrid VPNs.

Trusted VPNs

As we have noted above, before the Internet, VPN technology consisted of one or more circuits leased from a communications provider. Each leased circuit acted like a single wire in a network that was controlled by a customer who could use these leased circuits in the same way that he or she used physical cables in his or her local network. So this legacy VPN provided customer privacy to the extent that the communications provider assured the customer that no one else would use the same circuit. Although leased circuits ran through one or more communications switches, making them susceptible to security compromises, a customer trusted the VPN provider to safeguard his or her privacy and security by maintaining the integrity of the circuits. This security based on trust resulted into what is now called *trusted VPNs*.

Trusted VPN technology comes in many types. The most common of these types are what is referred to as *layer 2* and *layer 3* VPNs. Layer 2 VPNs include ATM circuits, frame relay circuits, and transport of layer 2 frames over Multiprotocol Layer Switching (MPLS). Layer 3 VPNs include MPLS with constrained distribution of routing information through Border Gateway Protocol (BGP) [11].

Because the security of trusted VPNs depends only on the goodwill of the provider, the provider must go an extra mile to assure the customers of the security responsibility requirements they must expect. Among these security requirements are the following [11]:

- *No one other than the trusted VPN provider can affect the creation or modification of a path in the VPN.* Since the whole trust and value of trusted VPN security rides on the sincerity of the provider, no one other than the provider can change any part of the VPN.
- *No one other than the trusted VPN provider can change data, inject data, or delete data on a path in the VPN.* To enhance the trust of the customer, a trusted VPN should secure not only a path but also the data that flows along that path. Since this path can be one of the shared paths by the customers of the provider, each customer's path itself must be specific to the VPN and no one other than the trusted provider can affect the data on that path.
- *The routing and addressing used in a trusted VPN must be established before the VPN is created.* The customer must know what is expected of the customer and what is expected of the service provider so that they can plan for maintaining the network that they are purchasing.

Secure VPNs

Since the Internet is a popular public communication medium for almost everything from private communication to businesses and the trusted VPN actually offers only virtual security, security concerns in VPN have become urgent. To address these concerns, vendors have started creating protocols that would allow traffic to be encrypted at the edge of one network or at the originating computer, moved over the Internet like any other data, and then decrypted when it reaches the corporate network or a receiving computer. This way it looks like encrypted traffic has traveled through a tunnel between the two networks. Between the source and the destination points, although the data is in the clear and even an attacker can see the traffic, still one cannot read it and one cannot change the traffic without the changes being seen by the receiving party and therefore rejected. Networks that are constructed using encryption are called *secure VPNs*.

Although secure VPNs are more secure than trusted VPNs, they too require assurance to the customer just like trusted VPNs. These requirements are as follows [11]:

- *All traffic on the secure VPN must be encrypted and authenticated.* In order for VPNs to be secure, there must be authentication and encryption. The data is encrypted at the sending network and decrypted at the receiving network.
- *The security properties of the VPN must be agreed to by all parties in the VPN.* Every tunnel in a secure VPN connects two endpoints who must agree on the security properties before the start of data transmission.
- *No one outside the VPN can affect the security properties of the VPN.* To make it difficult for an attacker, VPN security properties must not be changed by anyone outside the VPN.

Hybrid VPNs

Hybrid VPN is the newest type of VPN technologies that substitutes the Internet for the telephone system as the underlying structure for communications. The trusted VPN components of the new VPN still do not offer security, but they give customers a way to easily create network segments for wide area networks (WANs). On the other hand, the secure VPN components can be controlled from a single place and often come with guaranteed quality of service (QoS) from the provider.

Because of the inherited weaknesses from both components that make up this new hybrid VPN, a number of security requirements must be adhered to. Among the requirements is to clearly mark the address boundaries of the secure VPN within the trusted VPN because in hybrid VPNs, the secure VPN segments can run as subsets of the trusted VPN and vice versa. Under these circumstances, the hybrid VPN is secure only in the parts that are based on secure VPNs.

17.4.3 VPN Tunneling Technology, PPTP, and L2TP

Old VPN firewalls used to come loaded with software that constructed the tunnel. However, with new developments in tunneling technology, this is no longer the case. Let us now look at some different technologies that can be used to construct VPN tunnels:

- *IPsec with encryption* used in either tunnel or transport modes. Since IPsec cannot authenticate users, IPsec alone is not good in some host-to-network VPN [3]. However, this is usually overcome by supplementing IPsec with other authentication methods such as Kerberos. In combination with Internet Key Exchange (IKE) which provides a trusted public key exchange, IPsec is used to encrypt data between networks and between hosts and networks. According to Hoden, the sequence of events in the process of establishing an IPsec/IKE VPN connection goes as follows:
  - The host/gateway at one end of a VPN sends a request to the host/gateway at the other end to establish a VPN connection.
  - The remote host/gateway generates a random number and sends a copy of it to the requesting host/gateway.
  - The requesting host/gateway, using this random number, encrypts its pre-shared key it got from the IKE (shared with the remote host/gateway) and sends it back to the remote host/gateway.
  - The remote host/gateway also uses its random number and decrypts its pre-shared key and compares the two keys for a match. If there is a match with anyone of its keys on the key ring, then it decrypts the public key using this pre-shared key and sends the public key to the requesting host/gateway.
  - Finally, the requesting host/gateway uses the public key to establish the IPsec security association (SA) between the remote host/gateway and itself. This exchange establishes the VPN connection. See Fig. 17.14.

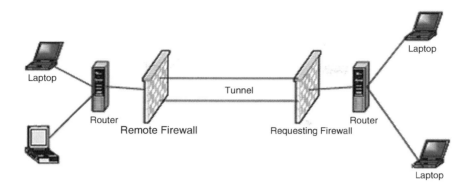

Protected Network A   Protected Network B

Fig. 17.14 Establishing a VPN using IPsec and IKE

- *Point-to-Point Tunneling Protocol (PPTP)*. This is a Microsoft-based dial-up protocol used by remote users seeking a VPN connection with a network. It is an older technology with limited use.
- *Layer 2 Tunneling Protocol* [**L2TP inside IPsec** (*see RFC 3193*)]. This is an extension of PPP, a dial-up technology. Unlike PPTP which uses Microsoft dial-up encryption, L2TP uses IPsec in providing secure authentication of remote access. L2TP protocol makes a host connect to a modem, and then it makes a PPP to the data packets to a host/gateway where it is unpacked and forwarded to the intended host.
- PPP over SSL and PPP over SSH. These are Unix-based protocols for constructing VPNs. Please note that PPP also tunnels Internet Protocol (IP) or other network layer 3 data between two directly connected nodes over a physical connection or over a direct link. Since IP and Transmission Control Protocol (TCP) do not support point-to-point connections, the use of PPP can enable them over Ethernet and other physical media (Fig. 17.15).

17.5 Security in the Physical Layer

17.5.1 Point-to-Point Protocol (PPP)

This is an old protocol because early Internet users used to dial into the Internet using a modem and PPP. It is a protocol limited to a single data link. Each call-in went directly to the remote access service (RAS) whose job was to authenticate the calls as they came in.

Fig. 17.15 Physical and data
link-layer security protocols
and standards

TCP/IP	ISO	Security Protocols
Physical	Data link Physical	PPP, Packet Filters, NAT, CHAP and PAP

A PPP communication begins with a handshake which involves a negotiation between the client and the RAS to settle the transmission and security issues before the transfer of data could begin. This negotiation is done using the Link Control Protocol (LCP). Since PPP does not require authentication, the negotiation may result in an agreement to authenticate or not to authenticate

17.5.1.1 PPP Authentication

If authentication is the choice, then several authentication protocols can be used. Among these are Password Authentication Protocol (PAP), Challenge-Handshake Authentication Protocol (CHAP), and Extensible Authentication Protocol (EAP) [12]:

- *Password Authentication Protocol (PAP)* requires the applicant to repeatedly send to the server authentication request messages, consisting of a username and password, until a response is received or the link is terminated. However, this information is sent in the clear.
- *Challenge-Handshake Authentication Protocol (CHAP)* works on a "shared secret" basis where the server sends to the client a challenge message and waits for a response from the client. Upon receipt of the challenge, the client adds on a secret message, hashes both, and sends the result back to the server. The server also adds a secret message to the challenge, hashes with an agreed-upon algorithm, and then compares the results. Authentication of the client results if there is a match. To harden the authentication process, the server periodically authenticates the client.
- *Extensible Authentication Protocol (EAP)* is open-ended, allowing users to select from among a list of authentication options.

17.5.1.2 PPP Confidentiality

During the negotiations, the client and server must agree on the encryption that must be used. IETF has recommended two such encryptions that include DES and 3DES.

17.5.2 Other Network Physical Layer Security Protocols Include [13]

(a) *Packet Filters*—A packet filter is designed to sit between the internal and external network. As packets enter or leave the network, they are compared to a set of rules. This determines if they are passed, rejected, or dropped. A router ACL is an example of a packet filter.

(b) *NAT* (network address translation) is a means of translating addresses. Most residential high-speed Internet users use NAT. It provides security as it hides the internal address from external networks.

(c) *CHAP* (Challenge-Handshake Authentication Protocol) is an authentication protocol that is used as an alternative to passing clear-text usernames and passwords. CHAP uses the MD5 hashing algorithm to encrypt passwords.

(d) *PAP* (Password Authentication Protocol)—this may not be the best security mechanism at the physical layer; however, it does provide some protection as it requires a user to present a username and password. Its Achilles heel is that it transmits this information in clear text.

Exercises

1. PGP has been a very successful secure communication protocol. Why is this so? What features brought it that success?
2. Discuss five benefits of IPsec as a security protocol.
3. Discuss the differences between the transport mode and the tunnel mode of IPsec. Is one mode better than the other? Under what conditions would you use one over the other?
4. Study the IPv4 and IPv6 and discuss the differences between them? By the mid-1990s, it was thought that IPv6 was destined to be a replacement of IPv4 in less than 5 years. What happened? Is there a future for IPv6?
5. Discuss the differences between RADIUS, as a remote authentication protocol, and Kerberos when using realms.
6. What are Kerberos authentication path? How do they solve the problem of remote authentication?
7. The Kerberos system has several bugs that pose potential security risks. Study the Kerberos ticketing service and discuss these bugs.
8. The Kerberos system is built on the principle that only a limited number of machines on any network can possibly be secure. Discuss the validity of this statement.
9. Investigate how Netscape Navigator and Internet Explorer implemented SSL technology.
10. Study both SSL and S-HTTP. Show that these two protocols have a lot in common. However, the two protocols have some differences. Discuss these differences. Discuss what caused the decline in the use of S-HTTP.

Advanced Exercises

1. X.509 is a good security protocol. Study X.509 and discuss how it differs from S-HTTP and IPsec.
2. SSL3.0 has been transformed into TLS 1.0. Study the TLS protocol specifications and show how all are met by SSL. There are some differences in the protocol specifications of the two. Describe these differences.
3. S/MIME and PGP are sister protocols; they share a lot. Study the two protocols and discuss the qualities they share. Also look at the differences between them. Why is PGP more successful? Or is it?
4. Study the SET protocols and one other payment system protocol such as Dig-Cash. What sets SET above the others? Is SET hacker proof? What problems does SET face that may prevent its becoming a standard as desired by Netscape?
5. Both S/MIME and PGP are on track for standardization by the IETF. In your judgment, which one of the twos likely to become the standard and why?

References

1. *Radius.* http://www.gnu.org/software/radius/radius.html#TOCintroduction
2. *RFC 2138.* http://www.faqs.org/rfcs/rfc2138.html
3. Hoden G (2004) Guide to firewalls and network security: intrision detection and VPNs. Thomson Delmar Learning, Clifton Park
4. Stallings W (1999) Cryptography and network security: principles and practice, 2nd edn. Prentice Hall, Upper Saddle River
5. Shastack A. An overview of S-HTTP. http://www.homeport.org/~adam/shttp.html
6. Jasma K (2002) Hacker proof: the ultimate guide to network security, 2nd edn. OnWord Press, Albany
7. Tung B. The Moron's Guide to Kerberos, Version 2.0. https://wpollock.com/AUnixSec/MoronsGuideToKerberos.htm
8. Onyszko T. Secure socket layer: authentication, access control and encryption. http://www.windowsecurity.com/articles-tutorials/authentication_and_encryption/Secure_Socket_Layer.html
9. *SSL Demystified: The SSL encryption method in IIS.* http://windowsitpro.com/security/ssl-demystified
10. Kurose J, Keith WR (2003) Computer networking: a top-down approach featuring the internet. Addison-Wesley, Reading.
11. VPN Consortium (2003) VPN technologies: definitions are requirements. http://www.hit.bme.hu/~jakab/edu/litr/VPN/vpn-technologies.pdf
12. Panko R (2004) Corporate computer and network security. Prentice Hall, Upper Saddle River
13. TechTarget. Security and the TCP/IP stack. http://searchnetworking.techtarget.com/tip/Security-and-the-TCP-IP-stack

Security in Wireless Networks and Devices

18

18.1 Introduction

It is not feasible to discuss security in wireless networks without a thorough understanding of the working of wireless devices and networks. In fact, as we first set out to teach the computer network infrastructure in Chap. 1 in order to teach network security, we are going, in the first parts of this chapter, to discuss the wireless network infrastructure. As was the case in Chap. 1, it is not easy to discuss a network infrastructure in a few paragraphs and expect a reader to feel comfortable enough to deal with the security issues based on the infrastructure. So, although we are promising the reader to be brief, our discussion of the wireless infrastructure may seem long to some readers and sometimes confusing to others. Bear with us as we dispose of the necessary theory for a good understanding of wireless security.

Wireless technology is a relatively new technology that started in 1946 as we will see later in the wireless evolution section. The rapid technological developments of the last 20 years have seen wireless technology as one of the fastest developing technologies of the communication industry. Because of its ability and potential to make us perform tasks while on the go and bring communication in areas where it would be impossible with the traditional wired communication, wireless technology has been embraced by millions. There are varying predictions all pointing to a phenomenal growth of the wireless technology and industry.

To meet these demands and expectations, comprehensive communication infrastructure based on several types of wireless network technologies has been developed. See Fig. 18.1. These technologies are based on the following IEEE standards shown in Table 18.1.

© Springer International Publishing AG 2017   397
J.M. Kizza, *Guide to Computer Network Security*, Computer Communications and Networks, DOI 10.1007/978-3-319-55606-2_18

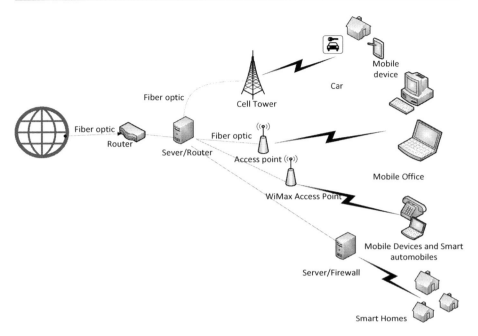

Fig. 18.1 A typical wireless broadband network

18.2   Types of Wireless Broadband Networks

Among the most popular of these networks, at the time of this writing, are shown in Table 18.1 and are discussed more in Chap. 24 as they play a significant role in home networking [1]:

All these different types of wireless networks offer some degree of *broadband* (the Internet connection speed) with varying speeds. The connection medium also varies starting with DSL, cable wireless, fiber, cellular, and others. The broader the broadband, the greater the capacity of information and data carried. A wireless network type is categorized by the technology used, the coverage area and the speed of the network connection.

18.2.1 Wireless Personal Area Networks (WPANs)

Wireless PANs or WPANs are small networks, based on IEEE standard 802.15.4 of 2005 and IrDa cable replacement for peripherals. See Table 18.1. As we will discuss in Chap. 24, they operate within a range of between 10 and 100 ms with a

Table 18.1 Wireless technology standards

Type	Wireless PAN	Wireless LAN	Wireless MAN	Mobile cellular (see Table 18.2)	Wireless WAM 4G (LTE)	5G (proposed—rollout by 2020)
Standard	IEEE 802.15	IEEE 802.11	IEEE 802.16	GSM, IS-95, UMTS, CDMA2000, LTE	IEEE 802.20/3GPP (3rd Generation Partnership Project) and is specified in its Release 8. GSM/UMTS networks and CDMA2000	IEEE 802.11ad.
Technology	Bluetooth	Wireless Fidelity (Wi-Fi)	WiMAX (Worldwide Interoperability for Microwave Access)	Global System for Mobile Communications (GSM), General Packet Radio Service (GPRS), cdmaOne, CDMA2000, Evolution-Data Optimized (EV-DO), Enhanced Data Rates for GSM Evolution (EDGE), Universal Mobile Telecommunications System (UMTS), Digital Enhanced Cordless Telecommunications (DECT), Digital AMPS (IS-136/TDMA), and Integrated Digital Enhanced Network (iDEN)	LTE (Long-Term Evolution)	
Coverage area	3–330 ft (10–100) meters	1/3 of a mile (500 meters)	Up to 70 miles	1/2 mile–25 miles	Over 70 miles	
Speed/s	250 kbit/s	50 Mbps	75 Mbp/s	50 MHz NMT, GSM 900 (900 MHz), GSM 1800 (1.8 GHz), UMTS,(2.1 GHz) GSM (800 MHz)	100 Mbps	1 Gb per second

Table 18.2 Cellular network standards

Cellular network standards		
0G (radio telephones)		MTS, MTA, MTB, MTC, IMTS, MTD, AMTS, OLT, Autoradiopuhelin
1G	AMPS family	AMPS (TIA/EIA/IS-3, ANSI/TIA/EIA-553) • N-AMPS (TIA/EIA/IS-91) • TACS • ETACS
	Other	NMT • Hicap • Mobitex • DataTAC
2G	GGSM/ 3GPP family	GSM • CSD
	3GPP2 family	cdmaOne (TIA/EIA/IS-95 and ANSI-J-STD 008)
	AMPS family	D-AMPS (IS-54 and IS-136)
	Other	CDPD • iDEN • PDC • PHS
2G transitional (2.5G, 2.75G)	GSM/ 3GPP family	HSCSD • GPRS • EDGE/EGPRS (UWC-136)
	3GPP2 family	CDMA2000 1X (TIA/EIA/IS-2000) • 1X Advanced
	Other	WiDEN
3G (IMT-2000)	3GPP family	UMTS (UTRAN) • WCDMA-FDD • WCDMA-TDD • UTRA-TDD LCR. (TD-SCDMA)
	3GPP2 family	CDMA2000 1xEV-DO Release 0 (TIA/IS-856)
3G transitional (3.5G, 3.75G, 3.9G)	3GPP family	HSPA • HSPA+ • LTE (E-UTRA)
	3GPP2 family	CDMA2000 1xEV-DO Revision A (TIA/EIA/IS-856-A) • EV-DO Revision B, (TIA/EIA/IS-856-B) • DO Advanced
	IEEE family	Mobile WiMAX (IEEE 802.16e) • Flash-OFDM • IEEE 802.20
4G (IMT-Advanced)	3GPP family	LTE-Advanced (E-UTRA)
	IEEE family	WiMAX-Advanced (IEEE 802.16m)
5G		It With full development, it is expected that 5G technology will have ultralow latency, high reliability, deep coverage, ultralow energy consumption, low complexity, high density, extreme capacity, extreme user mobility, and extreme data rates

From: http://en.wikipedia.org/wiki/Preferred_roaming_list

transfer rate of 250 kbit/s. WPANs focus on low-cost, low-speed ubiquitous communication between devices within the range. Devices using this standard, like mobile phones, computers, GPS receivers, digital cameras, and video game consoles, can exchange data and information using the network layers based on the OSI model, although only the lower layers, the physical and MAC layers, are defined in the standard. The most common of this technology are Bluetooth and radio-frequency identification (RFID). See more details of this in Chap. 24.

18.2.2 Wireless Local Area Networks (WLANs) (Wi-Fi)

As you will see in more details in Chap. 24, this type of wireless network technology is an extension of the WPAN technology, stretching the coverage range up to one third of a mile. The technology allows electronic devices to exchange data or connect to the Internet using 2.4 GHz UHF and 5 GHz SHF radio waves. Wi-Fi is probably the premier local area network (LAN) technology for high-speed Internet access for mobile devices like laptops, smartphones, tablets, and smart TV sets for video transfer. Wi-Fi technology is based on the IEEE 802.11 standard. We will see more of this in Chap. 24.

18.2.3 WiMAX LAN

WiMAX (Worldwide Interoperability for Microwave Access) is another limited area wireless communication technology based on IEEE 802.16 standard (2001) that includes IEEE 802.16d for fixed wireless and IEEE 802.16e for mobile wireless. Because of this, it functions in three modes—fixed, portable, and mobile. These modes help to extend the range of coverage that limited Wi-Fi technology functionalities. It provides high-speed, wide-area coverage of up to 40 miles, high-quality and high-capacity delivery with data rates reaching up to 75 megabits per second (Mb/s), and a number of wireless signaling options ranging anywhere from the 2 GHz range up to 66 GHz, with up to 1 Gbit/s for fixed stations. As we will see in Chap. 24, because of that range, WiMAX can be installed either by a service provider as base stations or as small receivers installed by clients to connect to the base station. The WiMAX base station then sends and receives data to and from a WiMAX-enabled router, which would then send the data to the different devices in the home LAN. WiMAX is based on the IEEE 802.16 standard.

WiMAX architecture allows multiple implementation options for a given functional entity and achieves interoperability among many functional entities as seen in Fig. 18.1. See also Fig. 18.2 for WiMAX deployment.

18.2.3.1 Overview and Evolution of WiMAX
Responding to the increasing demands for mobile broadband access to multimedia and Internet application and services, the IEEE Standards Board established the IEEE 802.16 Working Group (WS) in 1999. The specific goals for the WS were to interface standards for wireless metropolitan area networks (WMANs) as an extension of the successful WLAN or Wi-Fi. The interface standards developed focused on medium access control (MAC) and the physical layer (PHY). The initial versions

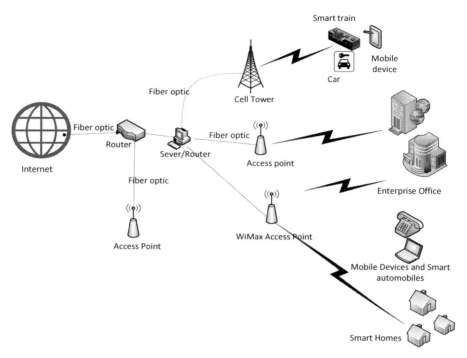

Fig. 18.2 Deployment of WiMAX

of the IEEE 802.16 a/d focused on fixed wireless applications. But later versions of
the 802.16-2005 (16e) included many functionalities to support enhanced quality of
service (QoS) and mobility. Those specifications made the WiMAX deployment
shown in Fig. 18.2 possible. The IEEE 802.16 Working Group is currently working
on the next-generation standards supporting LTE technology.

Current WiMAX networks can communicate from base stations (BSs) to end
user with non-line of sight (NLOS), whether it is mobile or fixed.

18.2.3.2 Protocol Layers of WiMAX

The IEEE 802.16 Working Group adopted for the IEEE 802.16 standard the Open
Systems Interconnection (OSI) as a reference model. Recall from Chap. 1 that the
OSI model protocols are implemented in layers. In fact, as you recall, there are
seven layers as shown in Fig. 18.3.

Although the IEEE 802.16 standard uses the OSI protocol stack with several
layers, the standard defines only two layers the PHY and the data link layer, which
is subdivided into two sub-layers. The data link layer is further subdivided into the
logical link layer and the medium access layer. WiMAX standard uses mostly
two-layered protocols, the MAC and PHY layers. The MAC layer is subdivided

Fig. 18.3 OSI layers implemented in the IEEE 802.16 standard

Application Layer
Presentation Layer
Session Layer
Transport Layer
Network Layer
Data Link Layer
Pysical Layer (PHY)

into three sub-layers, the convergence sub-layer, the common part sub-layer, and the security sub-layer as shown in Fig. 18.4.

The *MAC convergence sub-layer* (CS) maps the transport-layer-specific traffic to a MAC in a flexible way to efficiently carry any traffic type. This means that it adapts one or more transmission mediums, such as radio packet or circuit data transmission, to one or more alternative transmission formats such as ATM or IP data transmission. This is possible because it has two types of higher layers, the asynchronous transfer mode (ATM) and the packet to handle higher-layer protocols like IPv4 or IPv6. In addition, CS also handles the following action services [2]:

- Handling the quality of service (QoS) management mechanism
- Processing the higher-layer PDUs (information that is delivered as a unit among peer entities of a network and that may contain control information, such as address information, or user data), based on the classification
- An optional PHS (payload header suppression), the process of suppressing repetitive parts of payload headers at the sender and restoring these headers at the receiver
- Delivering CS PDUs to the appropriate MAC SAP (Service Access Point) (an identifying label for network endpoints used in Open Systems Interconnection (OSI) networking) and receiving CS PDUs from the peer entity

The *MAC common part sub-layer* (CPS) represents the core of the MAC protocol and is responsible for bandwidth allocation, connection establishment, and maintenance of the connection between the two sides. It receives data from the various CSs, through the MAC SAP, classified to particular MAC connections. It also includes many procedures of different types like frame construction, multiple access, bandwidth demands and allocation, scheduling, radio resource management, QoS management, etc. [2].

Fig. 18.4 The functional
OSI layers implemented in
the IEEE 802.16 standard

Data Link Layer

- Logical Link Control Layer (LLC)

- Medium Access Layer (MAC)

  o   Convergence sub-layer(CS)

  o   Common part sub-layer (CPS)

  o   Security sub-layer

Pysical Layer (PHY)

The *MAC security* layer provides authenticating and encrypting information including key exchange over the communication link in WiMAX. Let us now discuss this in further details.

18.2.3.3 WiMAX Security Protocols

In Fig. 18.2 we provided the differences between WiMAX and Wi-Fi. These differences, which indicate superior performance of WiMAX over Wi-Fi in delivering high-speed connectivity over long distances, are making WiMAX increasingly more attractive to Internet and telecommunication service providers. With the growing popularity of the technology driven by the increasing range of coverage and higher frequencies, as indicated in the list below and in Table 18.3, there was a need for a more robust security protocols to protect the users of the technology:

- 802.16.1-2001 (10–63 GHz, line of sight, up to 134 Mbit/s)
- 802.16.2 (minimizing interference between coexisting WMANs)
- 802.16a-2003 (2–11 Ghz, mesh, non-line of sight)
- 802.16b-2004 (5–6 Ghz)
- 802.16c (detailed system profiles)
- 802.16e-2005 (mobile wireless MAN)—called mobile WiMAX
- 802.16-2009-Current. Air interface for fixed and mobile broadband wireless access system
- 802.16m—in progress, data rates of 100 Mbit/s mobile and 1 Gbit/s fixed (4G)

To address this, the Working Group of the IEEE 802.16 designed several security protocols to safeguard and protect both users and providers. The evolving security architecture followed the following five components [3]:

- *Security associations*—a context to maintain the security state relevant to a connection between a base station (BS) and a subscriber station (SS)
- *Certificate profile*—X.509 to identify communication parties to each other

Table 18.3 WiMAX vs. Wi-Fi

Functionality	WiMAX	Wi-Fi
Application	Broadband Internet (multiuser—single tower connecting many users)	Wireless LAN, Internet
Range	50 km	100 m
Frequency range	2–11 GHz	2.4 GHz
Network type	MAN	LAN
Data range	70 Mbps	30–50 Mbps
Modulation	QAM	DSSS
Propagation	NLOS (non-line of sight)	LOS (line of sight)
Mobility	Yes	No

- *PKM authorization*—authorization protocol to distribute an authorization token to an authorized SS
- *Privacy and key management*—a protocol to rekey the security association (SA)
- *Encryption*—payload field encryption using Data Encryption Standard (DES) algorithm in the Cipher Block Chaining (CBC) mode of operation in 802.16d, DES-CBC, and Advanced Encryption Standard-Counter with Cipher Block Chaining-Message Authentication Code (AES-CCM) in 802.16e

Security associations, certificate profiles, PKI authorizations, and privacy key management are all used to form the standard's *authentication protocol*. For example, the X.509 certificate is used in authentication for uniquely identifying the subscribers and providers. An X.509 certificate offers security in two ways:

- By *verifying* a person's identity to make sure that the person really is who they say they are—*using the X.509 certificate*
- By sending the person who owns the *certificate-encrypted* data that only they can be able to decrypt and read—using Data Encryption Standard (DES) algorithm in the Cipher Block Chaining (CBC) mode of operation in 802.16d, DES-CBC, and Advanced Encryption Standard-Counter with Cipher Block Chaining-Message Authentication Code (AES-CCM) in 802.16e

X.509 certificate, however, was not enough for comprehensive authentication. For example, it was found that there was a flaw in the authentication mechanism of the original IEEE 802.16 standard's privacy and key management (PKM) protocol in that there was no requirement for base station (BS) or service provider authentication, thus making WiMAX networks based on the original IEEE 802.16 standard susceptible to man-in-the-middle attacks [4]. This weakness, however, has been addressed in the IEEE 802.16e, with addition of the Extensible Authentication Protocol (EAP) to the IEEE 802.16e.

Extensible Authentication Protocol (1999) (EAP) is an authentication framework used in network access authentication in dial-up, virtual private network

(VPN), 802.1X wireless, and 802.1X wired technologies using Network Policy Server (NPS), Routing and Remote Access Service (RRAS), or both. It consists of many authentication protocols including EAP-MD5, EAP-POTP, EAP-GTC, EAP-TLS, EAP-IKEv2, EAP-SIM, and EAP-AKA. Its commonly used protocols are EAP-TLS, EAP-SIM, EAP-AKA, LEAP, and EAP-TTLS.

EAP includes password-based authentication methods and more secure public key infrastructure certificate. It also includes Protected EAP (PEAP) and is extensible because it allows developers to create new authentication types that can plug into existing EAP deployment.

The Encryption Protocol
As Table 18.4 shows, the 802.16d used 3DES for authorization key (AK), DES for traffic encryption key (TEK), and the X.509 authentication certificate. It also employed Data Encryption Standard (DES) algorithm in the Cipher Block Chaining (CBC) encryption as part of its MAC protocol. However, neither the MAC header nor the packet cyclic redundancy check (CRC) is encrypted, thus leading to the 802.16d not providing for data authenticity.

With the 802.16e amendment, support for the Advanced Encryption Standard-Counter with Cipher Block Chaining-Message Authentication Code (AES-CCM) is available, providing strong support for confidentiality of data traffic. However, like in the standard 802.11 specification, management frames are not encrypted, thus allowing an attacker to collect information about subscribers in the area and other potentially sensitive network characteristics.

WiMAX Threats
Although WiMAX is secure, especially 802.16e, there are several potential attacks that can work around the present security protocols including [4]:

• Rogue base stations
• DoS attacks
• Man-in-the-middle attacks
• Network manipulation with spoofed management frames

This means that more work needs to be done to realize a more secure WiMAX standard.

The *physical layer* in all digital communications performs functions of encoding and decoding signals, preamble generation and removal, and bit transmission and reception. It encodes and decodes data and signals in such a way that the conversion fits the physical transmission medium characteristics such as copper, radio, or optical.

It also coordinates the transmission and reception of these physical signals on the medium between two or more communicating entities. In additional to coordinating transmission of data between physical entities, it also receives data for transmission from an upper layer and converts it into physical format suitable for transmission

Table 18.4 The security and functional evolvement of the IEEE 802.16 standard

Standard	Publication year	Range	Frequency	Goals	Security
802.16	2002		10–66 GHz	Original standard, line of sight, fixed-fixed point wireless	None
802.16a	2003		2–11 GHz	Added non-line of sight extension. Now supplanted by the 802.16d variant	None
802.16d	2004		2–11 GHz 10–66 GHz	Supports fixed and nomadic access in line of sight and non-line of sight environments	3DES for authorization key (AK), DES for traffic encryption key (TEK), X.509
802.16e	2006		2–6 GHz	Optimized for dynamic mobile radio channels, provides support for handoffs and roaming	AES-CCM Extensible Authentication Protocol (EAP)

through a network, such as frames and bursts. An upper layer provides the physical layer with the necessary data and control (e.g., maximum packet size) to allow conversion to a format suitable for transmission on a specific network type and transmission line.

WiMAX physical layer can operate in about five different specifications for licensed and unlicensed frequency bands as specified below [5]:

- SC—single-carrier modulation, to support line of sight (LOS) with high data rates.
- SCa—single-carrier air interface modulation.
- HUMAN—high-speed unlicensed metropolitan area network.
- OFDM (orthogonal frequency-division multiplexing)—for both line of sight (LOS) and non-line of sight (NLOS) in encoding digital data on multiple carrier frequencies. OFDM has developed into a popular scheme for wideband digital communication, whether wireless or over copper wires, used in applications such as digital television and audio broadcasting, DSL Internet access, wireless networks, powerline networks, and 4G mobile communications.
- OFDMA (orthogonal frequency-division multiple access) for both line of sight (LOS) and non-line of sight (NLOS) is a multiuser version of the popular orthogonal frequency-division multiplexing (OFDM) digital modulation scheme. Multiple access is achieved in OFDMA by assigning subsets of subcarriers to individual users as shown in the illustration below.

Any one out of these will be used in the system. For example, fixed WiMAX uses OFDM type of physical layer and mobile WiMAX uses OFDMA type.

18.2.4 4G (LTE) and 5G: Enhancing Mobile Broadband

The ushering in of 4G technology brought the enhanced capabilities of mobile devices to browse the Web, send text messages, make phone calls, and even download and upload large video files without any issues. The addition of LTE (Long-Term Evolution) standardization boasted 4G connectivity, and speed improved tremendously making 4G a far better wireless technology than the 3G technologies like WiMAX. The newest 5G wireless technology, building on 4G technology, has brought in an era of immersive experiences and hypermobile connectivity which promises to project to the next hypermobile wireless performance.

18.2.5 Mobile Cellular Network

A mobile cellular network is a radio network distributed over land through cells where each cell includes a fixed location transceiver known as base station (BS). These cells together provide radio coverage over larger geographic areas. User equipments (SS/MS for Subscriber Station/Mobile Station) such as mobile phones, laptops, and other mobile devices are able to communicate even if the devices are either fixed or moving through cells during transmission.

Cellular networks give subscribers advanced features over alternative solutions, including increased capacity, small battery power usage, a larger geographical coverage area, and reduced interference from other signals. The technologies in this category are cellular based having a broad coverage over large areas, such as cities or countries, and indeed worldwide via multiple satellite systems or antenna sites looked after by Internet service providers (ISPs).

18.2.5.1 Mobile Cellular Network Technologies
There are several and different cellular technologies as shown in Tables 18.1 and 18.2, including:

- Global System for Mobile Communications (GSM)
- General Packet Radio Service (GPRS)
- cdmaOne
- CDMA2000
- Evolution-Data Optimized (EV-DO)
- Enhanced Data Rates for GSM Evolution (EDGE)
- Universal Mobile Telecommunications System (UMTS)
- Digital Enhanced Cordless Telecommunications (DECT)
- Digital AMPS (IS-136/TDMA)
- Integrated Digital Enhanced Network (iDEN)

They include most evolving new generations of cellular technologies like CDPD and cellular 2G, 2.5G, 3G, and LTE or 4G. Because LTE is a newer technology, its communication protocols are based on Internet Protocol (IP). Because of this, it offers a variety of communication protocols that the older technologies could not offer including VoIP and other IP-based services. LTE can theoretically support downloads at 300 Mbps or more based on experimental trials. Finally, because it is a very new technology, it is only available in limited geographic areas, but it is growing after getting early support from telecommunication providers.

18.2.5.2 Mobile Cellular Communication Network Infrastructure

As we pointed out above, in its simplest form, wireless technology is based on a concept of a cell. That is why wireless communication is sometimes referred to as cellular communication. Cellular technology is the underlying technology for mobile telephones, personal communication systems, wireless Internet, and wireless Web applications. In fact, wireless telecommunication is one of the fastest-growing technologies in telecommunication today. Personal communications devices (PCD) are increasing in popularity as various wireless networks are growing.

The cell concept is based on the current cellular technology that transmits analog voice on dedicated bandwidth. This bandwidth is split into several segments permanently assigned to small geographical regions called cells. This has led to the tiling of the whole communication landscape with small cells of roughly 10 square miles or less depending on the density of cellular phones in the geographical cell. See Fig. 18.5. Each cell has, at its center, a communication tower called the base station (BS) which the communication devices use to send and receive data. See also Fig. 18.6. The BS receives and sends data usually via a satellite. Each BS operates two types of channels:

- The control channel which is used in the exchange when setting up and maintaining calls
- The traffic channel to carry voice/data

The satellite routes the data signal to a second communication unit, the Mobile Telephone Switching Office (MTSO). The MTSO, usually some distance off the origination cell, may connect to a land-based wired communication infrastructure for the wired receiver or to another MTSO or to a nearest BS for the wireless device receiver.

An enabled wireless device such as a cellular phone must be constantly in contact with the provider. This continuous contact with the provider is done through the cell device constantly listening to its provider's unique System Identification Code (SID) via the cell base stations. If the device moves from one cell to another, the current tower must hand over the device to the next tower and so on; so the continuous listening continues unabated. As long as the moving device is able to

Fig. 18.5 Tessellation of the cellular landscape with hexagon cell units

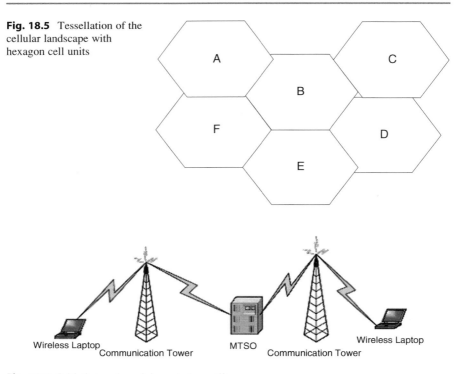

Fig. 18.6 Initiating and receiving wireless calls

listen to the SID, it is in the provider's service area, and it can, therefore, originate and transmit calls. In order to do this, however, the moving device must identify itself to the provider. This is done through its own unique SID assigned to the device by the provider. Every call originating from the mobile device must be checked against a database of valid device SIDs to make sure that the transmitting device is a legitimate device for the provider.

The mobile unit, usually a cell phone, may originate a call by selecting the strongest setup idle frequency channel from among its surrounding cells by examining information in the channel from the selected BS. Then using the reverse of this frequency channel, it sends the called number to the BS. The BS then sends the signal to the MTSO. As we saw earlier, the MTSO attempts to complete the connection by sending the signal, called a page call, to a select number of BSs via a land-based wired.

MTSO or another wireless MTSO, depending on the called number. The receiving BS broadcasts the page call on all its assigned channels. The receiving unit, if active, recognizes its number on the setup channel being monitored and responds to the nearest BS which sends the signal to its MTSO. The MTSO may backtrack the routes or select new ones to the call initiating MTSO which selects a channel and notifies the BS which notifies its calling unit. See Fig. 18.6 for details of this exchange.

During the call period, several things may happen including the following:

- Call block which happens when channel capacity is low due to high unit density in the cell. This means that at this moment all traffic channels are being used.
- Call termination when one of the two users hangs up.
- Call drop which happens when there is high interference in the communication channel or weak signals in the area of the mobile unit. Signal strength in an area must be regulated by the provider to make sure that the signal is not too weak for calls to be dropped or too strong to cause interference from signals from neighboring cells. Signal strength depends on a number of factors, including human-generated noise, nature, distance, and other signal propagation effects.
- Handoff when a BS changes assignment of a unit to another BS. This happens when the mobile unit is in motion such as in a moving car and the car moves from one cell unit to another adjacent cell unit.
- As customers use the allocated channels in a cell, traffic may build up, leading to sometimes serious frequency channel shortages in the cell to handle all the calls either originating or coming into the cell.
- The capacity of the communication channels within the cell is controlled by channel allocation rules. This capacity can be increased per cell by adding complexity and relaxing these channel allocation rules. Cell channel capacity can be expanded through [6].
- Cell splitting: By creating smaller geographical cells, better use can be made of the existing channels allocation. Usually cells have between 5 and 10 miles radius. Smaller cells may have about 2 miles radius. Attention must be paid for a minimum cell radius. It is possible to reach this minimum because as cells become smaller, power levels must be reduced to keep the signals within the cells, and also, there is an increase in the complexity resulting from more frequent handoffs as calls enter and leave the cells in higher numbers and high interferences due to smaller cells. Cell splitting can lead to microcelling, which is a concept of creating very small cells within the minimum limits called microcells which are small tessellations of a bigger cell and making BS antennas smaller and putting them on top of buildings and lamp posts. This happens often in large cities. Another version of microcelling is cell sectoring which also subdivides the original cell into small sectors and allocates a fixed number of frequency channels to each sector. The new sectors still share the BS but direction antennas face the BS to direct calls to and from the sector.
- Allocation of new channels: Once all free channels are used up, additional frequency channels may be added to meet the demand.
- Frequency borrowing: This calls for literally taking frequency channels from adjacent cells with redundant unused channels. Sometimes frequency channels from less congested adjacent cells can be dynamically allocated to congested cells.

Alternative multiple access architectures: The transition from analog to digital transmission is also significantly increasing capacity.

18.3   Development of Cellular Technology

In the United States, the development of wireless cellular communication began in 1946 when AT&T introduced the mobile telephone service (MTS).

However, this was preceded by the pre-cellular wireless communication that began in the early 1920s with the development of mobile radio systems using amplitude modulation (AM). Through the 1940s, their use became very popular, especially in police and other security and emergency communications. The channel capacity quickly became saturated as the number of users grew.

The actual cellular wireless communication started in 1946 when AT&T developed its first mobile communications service in St. Louis using a single powerful transmitter to radiate a frequency-modulated (FM) wave in an area with a radius of 50 miles. The popularity of this mode of communication forced the Federal Communications Commission (FCC) in 1950 to split the one 120-kHz channel that had been used into two equal 60-kHz channels to double capacity. This led to an unprecedented increase in the number of users so that by 1962 the technology had attracted up to 1.4 million users. Since then, the technology has gone through three generations.

18.3.1 First Generation

In the first generation, phones were very large and were based on analog technology. The most known technology of this era was based on a 1971 Bell Labs proposal to the FCC for a new analog cellular FM telecommunication system. The proposal gave rise to Advanced Mobile Phone Service (AMPS) cellular standard. Along with other cellular radio systems developed in other countries, all using FM for speech and frequency-division multiple access (FDMA) as the access technique, they formed the first generation of cellular technology. These systems became very popular, resulting in high levels of use. Although they are still in use today, their limited, uncoordinated, and independently chosen frequency band selections led to the development of the second-generation digital cellular technology.

18.3.2 Second Generation

Second-generation systems overcame most of the limitations of the first generation and improved on others. They offered higher-quality signals, greater capacity, better voice quality, and more efficient spectrum utilization through provision of several channels per cell and allowing dynamic sharing of these channels between users via multiplexing both TDMA and CDMA (seen in Chap. 1) and digital modulation techniques. Since they were backward compatible, they could use the same frequency range and signaling as their analog predecessors and therefore could receive and place calls on the first-generation analog network. In fact, 10% of the second-generation digital network is allocated to analog traffic. Also second-generation systems introduced encryption techniques, using digitized control and user traffic, to prevent unauthorized intrusions such as eavesdropping into the communication channels. The digitalization of traffic streams also led to the development and inclusion into the systems of error detection and correction mechanisms. These second-generation systems included the following [7]:

- *IS-54* (USA): Interim Standard-54 (1991) was designed to support large cities that had reached saturation within the analog system. It uses TDMA to increase capacity in the AMPS spectrum allocation.
- *IS-95* (USA): Interim Standard-95 (1994) operated in the dual mode (CDMA/AMPS) in the same spectrum allocation as AMPS. It is the most widely used second-generation CDMA.
- *GSM* (Europe): The Global System for Mobile Communications (GSM) (1990) is a pan-European, open digital standard accepted by the European Telecommunications Standards Institute (ETSI) and now very popular the world over. As an open standard, it allowed interoperability of mobile phones in all European countries. It has a greater capacity/voice quality than the previous analog standard.
- *PDC* (Japan): The Personal Digital Communications (PDC) (1991) is similar to IS-54 and also uses TDMA technology.
- *PHS* (Japan): The Personal Handyphone System (PHS) (1995) uses smaller cells, therefore leading to a dense network of antennas each with a range of 100–200 m, which allows lower power and less expensive handsets to be used. It also allows 32-kbit/s digital data transmission. Because of all these advantages and its compaction, it has been very successful in Japan.

With digital cellular systems, usage of phones increased, and as people became more mobile and new possibilities emerged for using the phones for data transfer such as uploading and downloading information from the Internet and sending video and audio data streams, a stage was set for a new generation that would require high-speed data transfer capabilities. But owing to unexpected problems, including higher development costs and a downturn in the global economy, the rollout of the third-generation (3G) cellular systems has proven to be slow.

18.3.3 Third Generation

In general, the third-generation cellular technology, known as (3G), was aiming to offer high-speed wireless communications to support multimedia, data, video, and voice using a single, unified standard incorporating the second-generation digital wireless architectures. The 3G standard was set to allow existing wireless infrastructure to continue to be employed after carrier transition as they offer increased capacities of at least 144 Kbps for full mobility, 384 Kbps for limited mobility in micro- and macro-cellular environments, and 2 Mbps for low mobility application

[8]. These goals could be achieved following these specific objectives: universality, bandwidth, flexibility, quality of service, and service richness [6, 7].

18.3.4 Fourth Generation (4G/LTE)

Like WiMAX, 4G/LTE (fourth generation/Long-Term Evolution) is a new and emerging technology for high-speed mobile broadband Internet service. Both WiMAX and LTE appear to have similar goals for enabling worldwide wireless data network connectivity for cell phones, laptops, and other computing devices. But wireless providers and industry vendors have not addressed them equally. Many prefer one over the other or both, depending on how these technologies benefit their businesses. It is so far likely that neither technology is expected to replace Wi-Fi home networks and hotspots.

In general, the fourth generation commonly known as 4G/LTE (fourth generation/Long-Term Evolution) is the next stage in mobile network development and provides users with much faster data speeds than 3G is able to. LTE was first proposed in Japan in 2004, the LTE standard was finalized in December 2008, and the first publicly available LTE service was launched in Europe in 2009 and North America in 2010. The LTE specification provides downlink peak rates of 300 Mbit/s, uplink peak rates of 75 Mbit/s, and QoS provisions permitting a transfer latency of less than 5 ms in the radio access network [5].

18.4   Other Features of Mobile Cellular Technology

Besides the evolution of the mobile cellular technology, a number of other features were also developing including the following.

18.4.1 Universality

Universality is one of the driving forces behind modern communication involving universal personal communications services (PCSs), personal communication networks (PSNs), and universal communications access. It requires achieving the following:

• A high degree of commonality of design worldwide
• Global compatibility of services within 3G wireless and fixed networks
• Service availability from multiple providers in any single coverage area
• Service reception on any terminal in any network based on a unique personal number
• Ability to economically provide service over a wide range of user densities and coverage areas

18.4.2 Flexibility

Flexibility requires:

- A framework for the continuing expansion of mobile network services and access to fixed network facilities
- A modular structure that will allow the system to start from a simple configuration and grow as needed in size and complexity
- Optimal spectrum usage for services, despite their differing demands for data rates, symmetry, channel quality, and delay
- Terminals that can adapt to varying demands for delay and transmission quality
- New charging mechanisms that allow tradeoffs of data vs. time
- Accommodation of a variety of terminals including the pocket-sized terminal

18.4.3 Quality of Service (QoS)

This requires quality comparable to that of a fixed network.

18.4.4 Service Richness

It involves:

- Integration of cellular, cordless, satellite, and paging systems
- Support for both packet and circuit-switched services (e.g., IP traffic and video conference)
- Support for multiple, simultaneous connections (e.g., Web browsing and voice)
- Availability of a range of voice and non-voice services
- Efficient use of the radio spectrum at an acceptable cost
- An *open architecture* to facilitate technological upgrades of different applications

When the International Telecommunication Union Radiocommunication (ITU-R) Standardization Sector, a body responsible for radio technology standardization, called for 3G proposals in 1998, responses to develop the standards came from the following national Standards Development Organizations (SDO): ETSI (Europe), ARIB (Japan), TIA and TIPI (USA), TTA (Korea), and one from China [8].

18.4.5 Mobile Cellular Security Protocol Stack

In Sect. 18.2.3.2 we discussed the protocol stack of WiMAX. We want to extend this discussion to broadly cover all cellular wireless communication networks that also include WiMAX.

18.4.5.1 Mobile Cellular Wireless Application Protocol (WAP)

The cellular wireless application protocol (WAP) stack was dictated by the mobility of users and their need to have access to information services, including the Internet and the Web. WAP works with all wireless technologies such as GSM, CDMA, and TDMA and is based on Internet technologies such as XML, HTML, IP, and HTTP. Although the technology is facing limitations dictated by the size of the devices, bandwidth, and speed, the technology has received wide acceptance in the mobile world. WAP technology includes the flowing facilities [6]:

- Programming facilities based on WWW programming model
- Wireless Markup Language (WML) similar to XML
- A wireless browser
- A wireless communications protocol stack—see Fig. 18.7
- A wireless telephony applications (WTA) framework
- A number of other protocols and modules

To understand the working of WAP, one has to understand the WAP programming model which is based on three elements: the client, the gateway, and the original server as depicted in Fig. 18.8.

In the WAP model, HTTP is placed and is used between the gateway and the original server to transfer content. The gateway component is actually a proxy server for the wireless domain.

It provides services that process, convert, and encode content from the Internet to a more compact format to fit on wireless devices. On a reverse service, it decodes and converts information from wireless devices that are compact to fit the Internet architecture infrastructure. See Fig. 18.9.

18.5   Security Vulnerabilities in Cellular Wireless Networks

In Chap. 19, we will discuss security in wireless sensor networks, a more specific type of wireless network. In this chapter, we are discussing security in a general wireless network. As the wireless revolution rages on and more and more organizations and individuals are adapting wireless technology for their communication needs, the technology itself and the speed are barely keeping pace with the demand. The Wi-Fi craze has been driven by the seemingly many Wi-Fi advantages over its cousin the fixed LAN. Such advantages include the following [9]:

- Affordability: Although Wi-Fi networks are still more expensive compared to their cousins the fixed LANs, yet given the advantage of mobility they offer and the plummeting prices for devices using wireless technology such as laptops and personal digital assistants, the technology has become more affordable, especially to large companies that need it more.
- The ease of network connections without having to "plug-in" and without using expensive network gurus for network setups.

Fig. 18.7 The WAP protocol stack

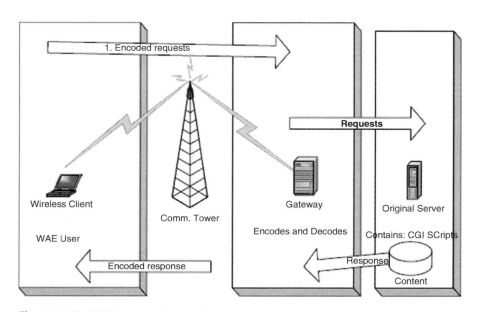

Fig. 18.8 The WAP programming model

Fig. 18.9 The WAP architecture infrastructure

- Increasing employee productivity by organizations and businesses by having employees remain productive even when on the road. End users, regardless of where they are either in the office facility or outside, are not very far from an untethered computing device.
- WLAN technology does not need licenses to use.

As newer standards such as the IEEE 802.11g are poised to deliver five times the speed of the current IEEE 80211b which currently is delivering about 11 Mbps of bandwidth, there is increasing concern and closer scrutiny regarding the security of wireless technology in general and WLANs in particular. WLANs need to not only provide users with the freedom and mobility which is so crucial for their popularity but also the privacy and security of all users and the information on these networks.

18.5.1 WLAN Security Concerns

As Russ Housley and William Arbaugh state in their paper "Security Problems in 802.11-Based Networks" [10], one of the goals of WLAN standard was to provide security and privacy that was "wired equivalent," and to meet these goals, the designers of the standard implemented several security mechanisms to provide confidentiality, authentication, and access control. The "wired equivalent" concept for the IEEE 802.11 WLAN standard was to define authentication and encryption based on the Wired Equivalent Privacy (WEP) algorithm. This WEP algorithm defines the use of a 40-bit secret key for authentication and encryption. But all these mechanisms failed to work fully as intended.

Attacks by hackers and others on the WLAN have been documented. Although sometimes exaggerated, there is a genuine security concern. Hackers armed with laptops, WLAN cards, and beam antennas are cruising the highways and city streets, industrial boulevards, and residential streets, sometimes called "war drives," accessing both public and private WLANs with impunity [11].

Wireless networks are inherently insecure. This problem is compounded by the untraceable hackers who use invisible links to victimize WLANs and the increasing number of fusions between LANs and WLANs, thus adding more access points (the weak points) to the perimeters of secure networks.

As a result, the WLAN found itself facing severe privacy and security problems including the following [10, 12, 13].

18.5.1.1 Identity in WLANs

Identity is a very important component of security mechanism. The WALN protocol contains a media access control (MAC) protocol layer in its protocol stack. The WLAN standard uses the MAC address of the WLAN card as its form of identity for both devices and users. Although in the early versions of the WLAN device drivers this MAC address was not changeable, in the newer open-source device drivers, this is changeable, creating a situation for malicious intruders to masquerade as valid users. In addition, WLAN uses a service set identifier (SSID) as a device identifier (name) in a network. As a configurable identification for a network device, it allows clients to communicate with the appropriate BS. With proper configuration, only clients configured with the same SSID as the BS can communicate with the BS. So SSIDs are shared passwords between BSs and clients. Each BS comes with a default SSID, but attackers can use these SSIDs to penetrate a BS. As we will see later, turning off SSID broadcasts cannot stop hackers from getting to these SSIDs.

18.5.1.2 Lack of Access Control Mechanism

The WLAN standard does not include any access control mechanism. To deal with this seemingly overlooked security loophole in the standard, many users and vendors have used a MAC address-based access control list (ACL), already discussed in Chap. 8. When ACL is used on MAC addresses, the lists consist of MAC addresses indicating what resources each specific MAC address is permitted to use. As we have indicated earlier, the MAC address can be changed by an intruder. So on interception of a valid MAC address by an intruder and subsequently changing and renaming his or her WLAN cards, he or she is now a legitimate client of the WLAN, and his or her MAC address now appears in the ACL. Another form of widely used access control is the "closed network" approach in which the client presents to the access point (AP), also common known as the base station, a secret known only to the AP and the client. For WLAN users, the secret is always the network name. But given the nature of WLAN broadcast, this name is broadcast in the clear and any eavesdropper or sniffer can get the network name.

18.5.1.3 Lack of Authentication Mechanism in 802.11

802.11 supports two authentication services: Open Systems and Shared Key. The type of authentication to be used is controlled by the Authentication Type parameter. The Open System type is a default null authentication algorithm consisting of a two-step process that starts with the access point demanding from the client an identity followed by authentication of almost every request from the client. With the Shared Key authentication type, a client is authenticated with a challenge and response. The present 802.11 requires the client to request for authentication using a secure channel that is independent of the standard. The WEP algorithm currently provides the WLAN standard with this encryption based on 40-bit and 104-bit secret keys. The clients request for authentication using these secret keys generated by WEP. The AP concatenates the secret key with a 14-bit quality known as an initialization vector (IV), producing a seed to the pseudorandom number generator. The random number generator produces a key sequence which is then combined with the message text and concatenated with the integrity check value (ICV). The comb {IV, message text, ICV} is put in an IEEE 802.11 data frame which is then sent to the client requesting authentication as the challenge. The client must then encrypt the challenge packet with the right key. If the client has the wrong key or no key at all, then authentication fails and the client cannot be allowed to associate with this access point [12]. However, several research outcomes have shown that this shared key authentication is flawed. It can be broken by a hacker who successfully detects both the clear text and the challenge from the station encrypted with WEP key. There is another type of WEP key that is not secure either. This key, called the "static" key, is a 40-bit or 128-bit key statically defined by the system administrator on an access point and all clients corresponding with this access point. The use of this type of key requires the administrator manually entering the key to all access points and all clients on the LAN. The key can be lost by a device. This causes a security problem. The administrator, in this case, must change all the keys.

18.5.1.4 Lack of a WEP Key Management Protocol

As we have noted above, the IEEE 802.11 WLAN standard does not have an encryption and authentication mechanism of its own. This mechanism is provided to the standard by the WEP. So the lack of a WEP key management protocol on the standard is another serious limitation of the security services offered by the standard. As noted by Arun Ayyagari and Tom Fout, the current IEEE 802.11 security options of using WEP for access control also do not scale well in large infrastructure network mode, in ad hoc, and network mode. The problem is compounded further by the lack of inter-access point protocol (IAPP) in a network with roaming stations and clients [12]. In addition to the above more structural problems, the WLAN also suffers from the following topographical problems:

- First, data is transmitted through WLANs through broadcasts of radio waves over the air. Because radio waves radiate in all directions and travel through walls that make ceilings and floors, transmitted data may be captured by anyone with a receiver in radio range of the access point. Using directional antennas, anyone who wants to eavesdrop on communications can do so. This further means that intruders can also inject into the WLAN foreign packets. Because of this, as we will see shortly, the access points have fallen prey to war-drivers, war-walkers, war-flyers, and war-chalkers [14].

- Second, WLAN introduced mobility in the traditional LANs. This means that the boundaries of WLANs are constantly changing as well as the APs of mobile-computing devices like laptops, personal assistants, and palms, as mobile nodes of the WLANs are everywhere. Perhaps the inability of a WLAN to control access to these APs by intruders is one of the greatest security threats to WLAN security. Let us give several examples to illustrate this.

Let us look at an extensive list of the security risks to the Wi-Fi. The majority of these security risks fall among the following five major categories:

- Insertion attacks
- Interception and monitoring wireless traffic
- Misconfiguration
- Jamming
- Client-to-client attacks

Most of these can be found at the Wireless LAN Security FAQ site at www.iss. net/WLAN-FAQ.php [15].

18.5.1.5 War-Driving, War-Walking, War-Flying, and War-Chalking

Based on the movie, "War Games," war-walking, war-driving, war-flying, and war-chalking all refer to the modes of transportation for going around and identifying various access points. As pointed out by Beyers et al. [14], war-walking, war-driving, and war-flying have resulted in identifying large numbers of wide open unsecure access points in both cities and countryside.

18.5.1.6 Insertion Attacks

These result from trusted employees or smart intruders placing unauthorized devices on the wireless network without going through a security process and review. There are several types of these including the following:

- Plug-in unauthorized clients, in which an attacker tries to connect a wireless client, typically a laptop or PDA, to a base station without authorization. Base stations can be configured to require a password before clients can access. If there is no password, an intruder can connect to the internal network by connecting a client to the base station.
- Plug-in unauthorized renegade base station, in which an internal employee adds his/her own wireless capabilities to the organization network by plugging a base station into the LAN.

18.5.1.7 Interception and Monitoring Wireless Traffic Attacks

This is a carryover from LANs. These intercepts and monitoring attacks are sniff and capture, session hijacking, broadcast monitoring, arpspoof monitoring, and hijacking. In arpspoof monitoring, an attacker using the arpspoof technique can trick the network into passing sensitive data from the backbone of the subnet and routing it through the attacker's wireless client. This provides the attacker both access to sensitive data that normally would not be sent over wireless and an opportunity to hijack TCP sessions. Further intercepts and monitoring attacks include hijacking SSL (Secure Socket Layer) and SSH (Secure Shell) connections. In addition, an attacker can also intercept wireless communication by using a base station clone (evil twin) by tricking legitimate wireless clients to connect to the attacker's honeypot network by placing an unauthorized base station with a stronger signal within close proximity of the wireless clients that mimics a legitimate base station. This may cause unaware users to attempt to log into the attacker's honeypot servers. With false log-in prompts, the user unknowingly can give away sensitive data such as passwords.

18.5.1.8 AP and Client Misconfigurations and Attack

Base stations out of the box from the factory are configured in the least secure mode or not configured at all. System administrators are left with the task of configuring them to their best needs. This is not always the case. Studies have shown that some system administrators configure base stations and others do not. In these studies, each vendor and system administrator had different implementation security risks. For example, each of the base station models came with default a server set IDs (SSIDs). Lucent, as one of the three base station manufacturers, has Secure Access mode which requires the SSID of both client and base station to match. By default, this security option is turned off at shipping. In the nonsecure access mode, clients can connect to the base station using the configured SSID, a blank SSID, and the SSID configured as "any." If not carefully configured, an attacker can use these default SSIDs to attempt to penetrate base stations that are still in their default configuration unless such base stations are configured right. Also, most base stations today are configured with SSID that acts as a single key or password that is shared with all connecting wireless clients. This server set ID suffers from the same problems as the original SSID.

Additionally, a base station SSID can be obtained by a brute-force dictionary attack by trying every possible password. Most companies and people configure most passwords to be simple to remember and therefore easy to guess. Once the intruder guesses the SSID, one can gain access through the base station. There are many other ways that SSIDs can be compromised ranging from disgruntled employees to social engineering methods.

18.5.1.9 SNMP Community Words

Many of the wireless base stations that deploy the Simple Network Management Protocol (SNMP) may fall victim to community word attacks. If the community word such as "public" is not properly configured, an intruder can read and potentially write sensitive information and data on the base station. If SNMP agents are enabled on the wireless clients, the same risk applies to them as well.

18.5.1.10 Client Side Security Risk

Clients connecting to the base station store sensitive information for authenticating and communicating to the base station. For example, Cisco client software stores the SSID in the Windows registry, and it stores the WEP key in the firmware. Lucent/Cabletron client software stores the SSID and WEP-encrypted information in the Windows registry as well. Finally 3Com client software also stores the SSID and WEP in the Windows registry. If the client is not properly configured, access to this information by a hacker is easy.

18.5.1.11 Risks Due to Installation

By default, all installations are optimized for the quickest configuration to enable users to successfully install out-of-the-box products.

18.5.1.12 Jamming

Jamming leading to denial-of-service attacks can also be carried out in wireless networks. For example, an attacker with the proper equipment and tools can easily flood the 2.4-GHz frequency so that the signal to noise drops so low that the wireless network ceases to function. Sometimes nonmalicious intents like the use of cordless phones, baby monitors, and other devices such as Bluetooth that operate on the 2.4-GHz frequency can disrupt a wireless network because there are so many in this band.

18.5.1.13 Client-to-Client Attacks

Two wireless clients can talk directly to each other bypassing the base station. Because of this, each client must protect itself from other clients. For example, when a wireless client such as a laptop or desktop is running TCP/IP services like a Web server or file sharing, communicating with an attacker is vulnerable to this attacker exploiting any misconfigurations or vulnerabilities on the client. Similarly, a wireless client can flood other wireless clients with bogus packets, creating a denial-of-service attack. Finally, a wireless client can infect other wireless clients; this threat is called a *hybrid threat*.

18.5.1.14 Parasitic Grids

Parasitic grids are actually self-styled free "metro" wireless networks that provide attackers and intruders completely untraceable anonymous access. Trying to locate and trace attackers using the parasitic grid becomes an impossible task, for example, something similar to *hotspots*, although hotspots are not maliciously used. Hotspots are Wi-Fi access point areas provided by businesses to give their customers access to the Internet. Hotspots are becoming very popular as more and more companies such as Starbucks, McDonalds, and start-ups to attract younger customers. They are also being deployed at airports, hotels, and restaurants for the same reasons.

18.5.2 Best Practices for Wi-Fi Security

Although the reliance of WLAN on SSID, open or shared key, static or MAC
authentication definitely offers some degree of security, there is more that needs to
be done to secure WLANs. Even though best security practices for WLANs are
meant to address unique security issues, specifically suited for wireless technology,
they must also fit within the existing organization security architecture. Any secure
WLAN solution must address the following issues, some of which we have
discussed in the preceding section [9]:

- 802.1X authentication standards
- WEP key management
- User and session authentication
- Access point authentication
- Detection of rogue access points
- Unicast key management
- Client session accounting records
- Mitigation of network attacks
- WLAN management
- Operating system support

In addition to addressing those issues, it must also include the following basic
and minimum set of routine but low-level steps [15]:

- Turn on basic WEP for all access points.
- Create a list of MAC addresses that are allowed to access the WLAN.
- Use dynamic encryption key exchange methods as implemented by various
  security vendors.
- Keep software and patches on all access points and clients updated.
- Create access point passwords that cannot be guessed easily.
- Change the SSID on the access point, and block the SSID broadcast feature.
- Minimize radio wave leakage outside the facility housing the WLAN through
  access point placement and antenna selection.
- For large organizations that value data, strong protection mechanisms must be
  put in place. Such mechanisms may include Kerberos or RADIUS, end-to-end
  encryption, password protection, user identification, virtual private
  networks (VPNs), Secure Socket Layer (SSL), and firewalls. All these are
  implementable.
- Change the default SSID and password protection drives and folders.

Realize, however, that these are basic and many things change. They just assure
you of minimum security.

Exercises

1. List the devices that can be used in a wireless network. How are they connected to form a wireless network?
2. Infrared devices exchange beams of light to communicate. Is this the method used in wireless communication? Explain how a communication link between two wireless devices is established.
3. Bluetooth devices communicate using radio waves. What are the differences between Bluetooth technology and 802.11? What are the weaknesses in Bluetooth technology compared to 802.11?
4. We have discussed at length the problems found in the 802.11 technology in assuring privacy and authentication. Suppose you are in charge of a LAN and you want to add a few access points to allow a limited use of wireless devices. How would you go about setting this network up?
5. Unlike infrared wireless devices, Bluetooth technology uses radio waves to communicate. What are the advantages of Bluetooth over these devices and also over 802.11 technology?
6. Study and discuss the reasons why WEP never realized its stated objectives. What are those objectives?
7. How does WPA, the new stopgap measure to plug the loopholes in WEP, go about solving the problems of WEP? Why is the technology considered a short-term technology? What long-term technology is being considered?
8. Study the security mechanisms in the new 802.11i and discuss how these mechanisms will solve the security problems of Wi-Fi.
9. One of the weakest points of WLAN is the access points. Discuss the most effective ways to close this weak point in the WLAN technology.
10. Many security experts have said that the biggest security problem in wireless technology is not to use security technology at all. Study this problem. Carry out a limited research and try to quantify the problem.
11. Looking at Table 18.4, WiMAX security has been going through rapid changes with the Working Group of the IEEE 802.16 designing several security protocols to safeguard and protect both users and providers. Have these changes improved security in WiMAX? Why or Why not?

Advanced Exercises

1. Some have likened the alphabet used in the 802.11 standard to an alphabet soup of confusion. Study the history of lettering in the 802.11 and how it is supposed to improve security. Does it work?
2. Suppose you are in charge of information security in a large organization where the value of data justifies strong protection in the hybrid network resulting from both LAN and WLAN. What are these additional security measures, and how would you go about implementing them?
3. Study and discuss how and in what type of wireless network or hybrid each one of the following methods enhances the security of the chosen network: RADIUS,

Kerberos, end-to-end encryption, password protection, user identification, virtual private network (VPN), Secure Socket Layer (SSL), and firewalls.

4. The IEEE 802.11 Task Group i (TGi) is developing new WLAN security protocols named TKIP and CCMP. CCMP is envisioned to supersede WEP and TKIP. Research and study these efforts and comment on the progress.

5. It has been given different names, based on the movie *War Games*. Some have called it war-driving, others war-walking. Whatever the name, AP scanning is becoming a hobby and a lucrative source of data from the high proliferation of wireless cards and mobile-computing devices. There is a serious moral and ethical dilemma associated with the "sport." Research and discuss such dilemma and propose solutions, if any.

6. We saw that LTE provides downlink peak of rates of 300 Mbit/s, uplink peak rates of 75 Mbit/s, and QoS provisions permitting a transfer latency of less than 5 ms in the radio access network. Why is LTE not currently addressed by all? What is preventing this?

References

1. Types of wireless Networks Computer Networking. *Notes.com*, http://computernetworkingnotes.com/wireless-networking-on-cisco-router/types-of-wireless-networks.html
2. Nuaymi L (2007) WiMAX-technology for broadband wireless access. ENST Bretagne/Wiley, Plouzané/Chichester
3. El-Gammal M. Overview of WiMAX security. https://courses.cs.washington.edu/courses/csep590/06wi/finalprojects/el-gammal.doc
4. Wright J (2006) WiMAX security issues. NetworkWorld|Dec 11 http://www.networkworld.com/article/2301883/network-securityimax-security-issues/network-security/wimax-security-issues.html
5. Wikipedia. https://en.wikipedia.org/wiki/LTE_(telecommunication)
6. Stallings W (2002) Wireless communication and networking. Prentice Hall, Upper Saddle River
7. Ritchie C, Sutton R, Taylor C, Warneke B (1999) The dynamics of standards creation in the global wireless telecommunications markets. http://courses.ischool.berkeley.edu/i224/s99/GroupD/project1/paper1.html
8. Nicopolitidis P, Papadimitriou GI, Obaidat MS, Pomportsis AS (2003) Third generation and beyond wireless systems: exploring the capabilities of increased data transmission rates. Commun ACM 46(8):120–124
9. Cisco Aironet Wireless LAN Security Overview (2006) http://www.cisco.com/c/en/us/products/collateral/wireless/aironet-1200-access-point/prod_brochure09186a00801f7d0b.html
10. Housely R, Arbaugh W (2003) Security problems in 802.11-based networks. Commun ACM 46(5):31
11. Keizer G (2003) WLAN security neglected, study shows. TechWeb News 27
12. Ayyagari A, Tom F (2001) Making IEEE 802.11 networks enterprise-ready. ResearchGate. https://www.researchgate.net/publication/250205039_Making_IEEE_80211_Networks_Enterprise-Ready
13. Klaus C (2001) WLAN security FAQ. http://www.ouah.org/wlan-security.html

14. Byers S, Dave K (2003) 802.11b access point mapping. Commun ACM 46(5):41–46
15. Cox J (2003) WLAN security: users face complex challenges. NetworkWorld. http://www. networkworld.com/article/2335565/network-security/wlan-security--users-face-complex- challenges.html

Security in Sensor Networks

19

19.1 Introduction

The rapid development of wireless technology in the last few years has created new interest in low-cost wireless sensor networks. Wireless sensor networks (WSNs) or just sensor networks are grids or networks made of spatially distributed autonomous but cooperating tiny devices called sensors, all of which have sensing capabilities that are used to detect, monitor, and track physical or environmental conditions, such as temperature, sound, vibration, pressure, motion, or pollutants, at different locations [1]. A sensor, similar to that in Fig. 19.1, is a small device that produces a measurable response to a change in a physical condition. Sensor nodes can be independently used to measure a physical quantity and to convert it into a signal that can be read by an observer or by an instrument [1]. The network may consist of just a few or thousands of tiny, mostly immobile, usually, randomly deployed nodes, covering a small or large geographic area. In many cases, sensor networks do not require predetermined positioning when they are randomly deployed making them viable for inaccessible terrains where they can quickly self-organize and form a network on the fly.

The use of sensors to monitor physical or environmental conditions is not new. Sensors have been used in both mechanical and electrical systems for a long time. However, what is new and exciting is that the new sensor nodes are now fitted with onboard tiny processors forming a new class of sensors that have the ability to partially process the collected data before sending it to the fusing node or base station. The sensor nodes now also have sophisticated protocols that help in reducing the costs of communications among sensors and can implement complex power saving modes of operations depending on the environment and the state of the network [2]. The accuracy of the data gathered has also greatly improved.

These recent advances have opened up the potential for WSN. According to David Culler et al. [3], wireless sensor networks could advance many scientific pursuits while providing a vehicle for enhancing various forms of productivity, including manufacturing, agriculture, construction, and transportation. In the

© Springer International Publishing AG 2017
J.M. Kizza, *Guide to Computer Network Security*, Computer Communications and Networks, DOI 10.1007/978-3-319-55606-2_19

Fig. 19.1 A wireless
sensor node

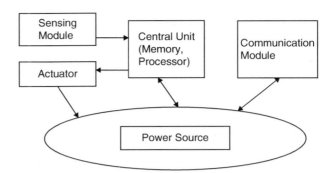

military, they are good for command and control, intelligence, and surveillance. In health, they are beneficial in monitoring patients, and in commercial application they can be used in managing inventory, monitoring production lines and product quality, and monitoring areas prone to disasters [4]. New technologies are creating more powerful and yet smaller devices. This miniaturization trend is leading us to ubiquitous computing capacities that are exponentially faster and cheaper with each passing day. With these developments, researchers are refocusing and developing techniques that use this miniaturization process to build radios and exceptionally small mechanical structures like sense fields and forces in physical environments that could only be imagined just a few years ago. Culler et al. believe that these inexpensive, low-power communication devices can be deployed throughout a physical space, providing dense sensing close to physical phenomena, processing and communicating this information, and coordinating actions with other nodes including a base station [3].

However, as wireless sensor networks with vast potential of applications unfold and their role in dealing with sensitive data increases, the security of these networks has become one of the most pressing issues in further development of these networks. This chapter gives a general discussion of the challenges and limitations of WSNs and how these challenges and limitations contribute to the security problems faced by the sensor network. We survey several interesting security approaches aimed at enhancing security, and we conclude by considering several potential future directions for security solutions.

19.2   The Growth of Sensor Networks

WSNs have evolved slowly from simple point-to-point networks with simple interface protocols providing for sensing and control information and analog signal providing a single dimension of measurement to the current large number and sophisticated wireless sensor node networks. The development of the microprocessor boasted the sensor node with increased onboard intelligence and processing capabilities, thus providing it with different computing capabilities. The sensor node is now a microprocessor chip with a sensor on board. The increased intelligence in the node and the development of digital standards such as RS-232, RS-422, and RS-485 gave impetus to the creation of numerous sensor networking schemes [5]. In addition, the popularization of the microcontrollers and the development of BITBUS, a field bus developed by Intel to interconnect stand-alone control units and terminals, thus making them able to interchange data telegrams, further improved the sensor node communication capabilities, thus bringing the dream of sensor networks closer [5].

Another outstanding development that further made the road to fully functioning sensor networks possible was the development of the Manufacturing Automation Protocol (MAP) by General Motors to reduce the cost of integrating various networking schemes into a plant-wide system. As Jay Warrior observes, this further resulted in the development of the Manufacturing Messaging Specification (MMS), a specification that made it possible for the networked nodes to exchange real-time data and supervisory control information [5]. With the development of other communication protocols that allowed simultaneous analog and digital communication for smart instruments, the sensor network, as we know it today, was born. Currently, there is a whole spectrum of different sensor network protocols for the many different types of sensor networks in use today.

19.3 Design Factors in Sensor Networks

Several factors influence the design philosophy of sensor networks. Among these factors are first whether the nodes are stationary or moving and whether the network is deterministic or self-organizing. Most sensor network applications use stationary nodes. However, there are a good number of applications that use mobile nodes. In this case, therefore, the network is bound to use more energy because of the need to track the moving node and the increase in bandwidth requirements for periodic reporting which increases traffic. In a deterministic topology, the positions of the nodes and the routes in the network are predetermined, and the nodes are manually placed. In a self-organizing topology, node positions are random, and the routes are also random and unreliable. Routing in these networks, therefore, becomes the main design concern. Also since self-organizing sensor networks demand a lot of energy, direct routing is not desirable, and multi-hop routing is more energy efficient. However, multi-hop routing requires considerable routing management techniques. In addition to routing and energy, other factors also influence the design philosophy of sensor networks [4]:

19.3.1 Routing

Communication in wireless sensor networks, like in traditional network communication, is based on a protocol stack with several layers as seen in Fig. 19.2. This stack also combines power and routing awareness, integrates data with networking protocols, communicates power efficiently through the wireless medium, and

Fig. 19.2 Sensor network protocol stack

promotes cooperation between nodes [4]. To achieve all these, the stack consists of five layers and three management planes, and these are physical layer, data link layer, network layer, transport layer, application layer, power management plane, mobility management plane, and task management plane. This stack is different from those of the traditional networks made of nonsensor nodes like the TCP/IP and the ISO's OSI.

- *Physical layer*—is responsible for several tasks including frequency selection, carrier frequency generation, signal detection, modulation, and data encryption.
- *Data link layer*—is responsible for a number of tasks including multiplexing of data streams, data frame detection, medium access, and error control.
- *Network layer*—is responsible for network routing. Routing in sensor networks, unlike in the traditional networks, is influenced by the following [4]:
  - Power efficiency as an important consideration
  - Sensor networks being mostly data centric
  - Data aggregation being useful only when it does not hinder the collaborative efforts of the sensor nodes
  - An ideal sensor network having attribute-based addressing and location awareness
- *Transport layer*—not yet in place. Because, unlike traditional networks, protocols like TCP where the end-to-end communication schemes are possible, here there is no global addressing. The development of global addressing schemes is still a challenge.
- *Application layer*—also not available. Although there are many application areas for sensor networks, application layer protocols are yet to be developed.

Based on the above discussion, therefore, sensor networks are largely still multi-hop wireless networks whose nodes can be either a host or a router, forwarding packets to other nodes in the network. In many sensor networks, the information collected from a large number of sensors is either lightly proceeded locally at the node or transmitted un-proceeded to the base station or other sensors using one of the three routing techniques: one-to-many, many-to-one, and one-to-one/point-to-point. However, the two most fundamental communication primitives are broadcast (one-to-many) and point-to-point (one-to-one).

Broadcast Communication   The broadcast packet routing technique is used extensively in wireless sensor networks due to the large number of sensor nodes in any wireless sensor network. Broadcasting, as a means of node communication, is highly desirable in this environment because of the limited signal range for each node. In the broadcast mode, the node that initiates the broadcast of a packet is referred to as the source or sender node and all others as receivers. The receivers of broadcast packet then forward the packet to their nearest adjacent neighbors which causes the packet to move throughout the network enabling all network nodes to eventually receive the broadcast packet.

Point-to-Point Communication   Though not common, point-to-point routing is still important for many applications in wireless sensor networks, including games based on wireless sensor networks and data-centric storage where nodes store information about the detected events using the geographic location as the key. Point-to-point routing can also be used to send data from the detection node to the storage node [6].

19.3.1.1 Routing Protocols
There are several routing protocols in use today for sensor networks, including data centric, hierarchical, and location based [7].

Data-Centric Routing   Because the sensor network may have thousands of nodes which are randomly deployed, it is inconceivable to have network-wide external addressing and network-layer-managed routing protocols found in traditional networks. In data-centric routing, the sink node, desiring data, sends out an attribute-based query to the surrounding nodes in the region. The attributes in the query specify the desired properties of the data. The sink then waits for the data [7]. If each node were to send out data to other nodes in the region, there would result a considerable redundancy of data and an inefficient use of scarce energy. For these reasons, data-centric routing techniques are more resource efficient. Common data-centric routing protocols include sensor protocols for information via negotiation (SPIN) and directed diffusion [7].

Hierarchical Routing   Hierarchical routing involves multi-hop communication and the aggregation and fusion of data within clusters of nodes in order to decrease the number of transmitted messages to the sink nodes which leads to conservation of energy. There are several hierarchical protocols in use today, including LEACH, PEGASIS, TEEN, and APTEEN [8].

Location-Based Routing   In location-based routing, each node maintains a location list consisting of location information for a number of nodes in a region of a sensor network. Each node periodically updates its location list by receiving information about locations and location lists of all its direct neighbors. It also, in turn, sends its location and location list to all its adjacent nodes. This keeps the location list of all nodes in the region current and up to date.

19.3.2 Power Consumption

Most sensor networks are entirely self-organizing and operate with extremely limited energy and computational resources. Because most nodes may be either in inaccessible environments, replenishing them with new power may be almost impossible. The life of a sensor node, therefore, may be in question, and it may not be able to transmit critical data when desired. The functionality of the network, therefore, depends on the consumption rate of energy by node units.

19.3.3 Fault Tolerance

If a sensor network is to face any one sensor node failure, we would like the network to be able to sustain all its functionalities. That is to say that the sensor network should be as reliable as possible and continue to function as much as possible in light of the failed node.

19.3.4 Scalability

We want to have a network such that the addition of more nodes to the network does not have any diverse effects to the functionality of the network.

19.3.5 Production Costs

Wireless sensor networks most often use large numbers of sensor nodes. The unit cost of each individual sensor node plays a crucial role in determining the overall costs of the entire sensor network. We would like a well-functioning network having a least per unit cost for individual nodes.

19.3.6 Nature of Hardware Deployed

A sensor node consists of four basic parts: the sensing unit, the processing unit, the transceiver unit, and the power unit. All these units must be packaged in a very small, matchbox-sized package. In addition, all these units and the overall sensor node must consume very low power.

19.3.7 Topology of Sensor Networks

Because a normal sensor network may contain thousands of sensor nodes deployed randomly throughout the field of observation, the wireless sensor network resulting may have uneven densities depending on how the nodes were deployed. Nodes can be deployed by dropping them from a plane, carefully placing them, or dropping by artillery. Also not every deployed sensor may work as expected. So the topology of the resulting network may determine the functionality of the wireless sensor network.

19.3.8 Transmission Media

In a wireless sensor network, the nodes are linked by a wireless medium. The medium could be by radio-like RF and Bluetooth, infrared, or optical waves. Both infrared and optical links require no obstructions like objects in the line of sight. The functionality of the network may depend on these media.

19.4   Security in Sensor Networks

Modern wireless sensor networks many times consist of hundreds to thousands of inexpensive wireless nodes, each with some computational power and sensing capability and usually operating in random unsupervised environments. The sensors in the network act as "sources" as they detect environmental events either continuously or intermittently whenever the occurrence of the event triggers the signal detection process. The data picketed up is either lightly processed locally by the node and then sent off or just sent off to the "sink" node or a base station. This kind of environment presents several security challenges.

19.4.1 Security Challenges

The most pressing of these challenges include the following:

19.4.1.1 Aggregation
Data aggregation in sensor networks is the process of gathering data from different sensor "source" nodes and expressing it in a summary form before it is sent off to a "sink" node or to a base station. There are two types of data aggregation: *in-stream* aggregation, which occurs over a single stream, generally over a time window, and *multi-stream* aggregation, which occurs across the values of multiple streams,

either at the same time or over a time window. Data aggregation is essential in sensor networks because as it combines data from different "source" nodes, it eliminates redundancy thus minimizing the number of transmissions and hence saving energy. In fact, significant energy gains are possible with data aggregation. The gains are greatest when the number of sources is large and when the sources are located relatively close to each other and far from the sink [9]. However, as sensor network applications expand to include increasingly sensitive measurements of everyday life, preserving data accuracy, efficiency, and privacy becomes an increasingly important concern as this is difficult to do with many current data aggregation techniques.

19.4.1.2 Node Capture/Node Deployment

Node compromise is a situation where a sensor node can be completely captured and manipulated by the adversary [10]. The conditions for node compromise are made possible as a result of sensor nodes in a wireless sensor network being randomly deployed many times in inaccessible or hostile environments. Usually these nodes are also unsupervised and unattended. In this kind of environments, nodes are undefendable and easy to compromise or totally captured by an adversary. There are several ways to capture a sensor node. One approach is the physical capture where an adversary can physically capture the node because of the node being in a hostile or unprotected environment. In another approach, software is used. Software-based capture occurs when an attacker uses software like a virus to capture a node.

19.4.1.3 Energy Consumption

Sensor networks are mostly and entirely self-organizing and operate with extremely limited energy and computational resources. Conservation of energy by sensor nodes results in minimizing their transmit power in order to maintain acceptable connectivity. This may prevent the network from maintaining the security solution like good cryptographic algorithms needed to protect critical data.

19.4.1.4 Large Numbers of Nodes/Communication Challenges

Because modern wireless sensor networks consist of hundreds to thousands of inexpensive wireless nodes, this large number of nodes presents a challenge of guaranteeing a secure, reliable, sometimes ad hoc communication among sensor nodes or groups of sensor nodes which sometimes can be mobile units. For example, since sensor nodes are typically battery driven, large numbers of them in a network make it a challenge to find and replace or recharge batteries.

19.4.2 Sensor Network Vulnerabilities and Attacks

Because of these limitations and the high dependency on the physical environment of deployment, sensor networks pose unique challenges that traditional security techniques like secrecy, authentication, privacy, cryptography, and robustness to

denial-of-service attacks used in traditional networks cannot be applied directly
[11]. This means that existing security mechanism fit for traditional networks
cannot be used wholesale in sensor networks. Yet there are no comprehensive
security mechanisms and best practices for sensor networks. One of the reasons
why traditional network security mechanisms and best practices fail with sensor
networks is because many of these security mechanisms and best practices are taken
and viewed as stand-alone. To achieve any semblance of desired security in a sensor
network, these security mechanisms and best practices must be a part of and be
embedded into every design aspect of the sensor network, including the communication protocols and deployment topologies. For example, we cannot talk about the
security of a sensor network if that network lacks secure routing protocols. Secure
routing protocols are essential security entities in sensor networks because a
compromised routing protocol compromises the network nodes and a single
compromised network sensor node completely compromises the entire network.
Current sensor network routing protocols suffer from many security vulnerabilities
as we will see shortly.

We have established that sensor networks have a number of issues that separate
them from traditional networks. Among these are the vulnerability of sensor nodes
to physical compromise, significant power and processing constraints, aggregation
of node outputs, and compromising individual nodes. Physical vulnerability
includes physical node access and compromise or local eavesdropping. Power
and processing constraints prevent sensor networks from running good security
encryptions. And aggregation of output may grossly obscure the effects of a
malicious attack from spreading throughout the network.

Sensor network adversaries target and exploit these weaknesses and other
network loopholes embedded within these limitations. Let us look at some of
these next.

19.4.2.1 Possible Attacks

There are several possible attack types, including *eavesdropping*, *disruption*,
hijacking, and *rushing* [12, 13]:

Eavesdropping Here, the attacker (eavesdropper) aims to determine the aggregate
data that is being *output* by either the node or the sensor network. The attacker
captures the message from the network traffic either by listening for some time to
the network traffic transmitted by the nodes or directly compromising the nodes.
There are two types of eavesdropping:

- *Passive*: The attacker's presence on the network remains unknown to the sensor
  nodes and uses only the broadcast medium to eavesdrop on all messages.
- *Active*: The attacker actively attempts to discern information by sending queries
  to sensors or aggregation points or by attacking sensor nodes.

Disruption The intent of the attacker here is to disrupt the sensor's working. It is
usually done in two ways:

- *Semantically*: where the attacker injects messages, corrupts data, or changes values in order to render the aggregated data corrupt or useless. Examples of this type of attacks includes the following [14]:
  - *Routing loop*: where an attacker injects malicious routing information that causes other nodes to form a routing loop causing all packets injected into this loop to go round in circles and eventually resulting into wasting precious communication and battery resources
  - *General DoS attacks*: where an attacker injects malicious information or alters the routing setup messages which end up preventing the routing protocol from functioning correctly
  - *Sybil attack*: where a malicious node influenced by an attacker creates multiple fake identities to perform desired attacks on the network
  - *Blackhole attack*: where a malicious node influenced by the attacker advertises a short distance to all destinations, thus attracting traffic destined to those destinations into the blackhole
  - *Wormhole attack*: where two nodes are caused to use an out-of-band channel to forward traffic between each other, enabling them to mount several other attacks along the way
- *Physically*: where the attacker tries to upsets sensor readings by directly manipulating the environment. For example, generating heat in the vicinity of sensors may result in erroneous values being reported.

Hijacking In this case, the attacker attempts to alter the aggregated output of an application on several network sensor nodes.

Rushing Attack According to YihChun Hu et al. [13], in an on-demand protocol, a node needing a route to a destination floods the network with ROUTE REQUEST packets in an attempt to find a route to the destination. To limit the overhead of this flood, each node typically forwards only one ROUTE REQUEST originating from any Route Discovery. In fact, all existing on-demand routing protocols, such as AODV, DSR, LAR, AODV, and others, only forward the REQUEST that arrives first from each Route Discovery. In the rushing attack, the attacker exploits this property of the operation of Route Discovery. The rushing attack is a very powerful attack that results in denial of service, and it is easy to perform by an attacker.

19.4.3 Securing Sensor Networks

The choice of a good security mechanism for wireless sensor networks depends on network application and environmental conditions. It also depends on other factors like sensor node processor performance, memory capacity, and energy. While in traditional networks, standard security requirements, such as availability, confidentiality, integrity, authentication, and nonrepudiation, are sufficient for security, in sensor networks, special security requirements such as message freshness, intrusion detection, and intrusion tolerance are necessary in addition.

19.4.3.1 Necessary Conditions for a Secure Sensor Network

Any security solution to sensor networks must preserve the confidentiality, integrity, authentication, and nonreplay of data within the network [14, 15].

Data Confidentiality Confidentiality of data in a sensor network is achievable only if those with access to network data are authorized to do so. Under no circumstances should sensor readings leak outside the network. The standard approach for preventing this from happening is to use encryption. This requires the use of a secret key that only intended receivers possess.

Data Integrity The integrity of data in any network means that data in that network is genuine, undiluted without authorization. This implies that data between the sender and the receiver is unaltered in transit by an adversary.

Data Authentication The process of authentication of both network data and users is very important in preserving network data integrity and preventing unauthorized access to the network. Without authenticating mechanisms in place, an attacker can easily access the network and inject dangerous messages without the receivers of the new altered data knowing and making sure that the data being used originates from a malicious source.

Data Freshness/Nonreplay Adrian Perrig et al. [15] define sensor network data freshness to mean recent data which for a sensor network would ensure that no adversary replayed old messages. There are two types of freshness: weak freshness, which provides partial message ordering but carries no delay information, and strong freshness, which provides a total order on a request-response pair and allows for delay estimation. Weak freshness is required by sensor measurements, while strong freshness is useful for time synchronization within the network [15].

These conditions are essential for the security of sensor networks. The problem that remains is how to ensure that these conditions hold throughout the wireless sensor network. This is still a big challenge and a problem for current research in sensor networks.

19.5   Security Mechanisms and Best Practices for Sensor Networks

We cannot ensure the confidentiality, integrity, authentication, and freshness of data in sensor networks without paying attention to the following issues particular to sensor networks:

- *Data aggregation.* Aggregation is generally consensus-based compromise, where missing readings from one or a few nodes may not significantly affect the overall system. Data aggregation is used in sensor networks to reduce energy consumption. With aggregation, however, raw data items from sensor nodes are invisible to the base station throwing in doubt the authenticity of the aggregated data. Without securing the data aggregation process, a compromised sensor node may forge an aggregation value and mislead the base station into trusting a false reading.

- *Antijamming.* Attackers can cause denial of service by jamming the base station or any other sensor node in the network. Attackers can also jam sensor radio frequencies. Protocols and services must be in place to stop this from happening.
- *Access control.* Access control is a process of granting the user the access right to the sensor network resources. It is essential to have an effective and efficient access control mechanisms, especially via a base station to authenticate user requests to get access to the network resources.
- *Key management.* Key management is crucial in supporting the basic security tenants like authentication and encryption in sensor networks. As the number of applications for sensor networks grows, an effective key management scheme is required.
- *Link-layer encryption.* Most widely used encryption schemes in sensor networks today involve the use of pre-distribution of key broadcasts by sensor nodes to thousands of sensors for pairwise exchange of information. But this scheme does not square well with known sensor network security problems like node compromise, low network connectivity, and a large communication overhead. However, a link-layer key management scheme can mitigate these problems and therefore be more efficient.
- *Data replication.* Data replication is the process of storing the same data on several sensor network nodes which created enough redundancy which in turn improves on reliability and availability and hence security.
- *Resilience to node capture.* One of the most challenging issues facing sensor networks is that of node capture. Online traditional networks can get high physical security; however, sensor networks are usually deployed in environments with limited physical security if any.

19.6   Trends in Sensor Network Security Research

Although we have outlined the difficulties in making a sensor network secure due to inherent limitations, it is, however, possible to design security protocols that are specific for a particular security issue. This is the direction that current sensor network security research is taking [15].

19.6.1 Cryptography

There are several cryptographic approaches being used to secure sensor networks. One of the first tasks in setting up a sensor network is to establish cryptographic system with secure keys for secure communication. It is important to be able to encrypt and authenticate messages sent between sensor nodes. However, doing this requires prior agreement between the communicating nodes on keys for performing encryption and authentication. Due to resource constraints in sensor nodes, including limited computational power, many key agreement schemes like trusted server, public key, and key pre-distribution used in traditional networks are just not applicable in sensor networks. Also pre-distribution of secret keys for all pairs of nodes is not viable due to the large amount of memory this requires when the network size is large. Although, over the years, efforts have been made to propose several approaches to do this, the inherent limited computational power of sensor nodes and the huge numbers of network nodes are making public key cryptographic primitives too expensive in terms of system overhead in key establishment [16]. Modern research has tried to handle the key establishment and management problem network wide by the use of a shared unique symmetric key between pairs of nodes. However, this also does not scale well as the number of nodes grows [16].

19.6.2 Key Management

Because of sensor node deployment and other sensor network limitations like limited computation capabilities, it is not possible to use key management as usually done in traditional networks where there may be a relationship in key sharing among members of the network. Because of these difficulties in sensor networks, if there were to be a single shared key, a compromise of just one node, may be through capture, would lay the entire network bare. A new framework of key exchange is needed. Eschenauer and Gligor [17] first proposed a framework of key exchange where a sensor randomly chooses m keys from the key pool with n keys before the deployment. After the node is deployed, it then contacts all its immediate neighbors to see if it shares any key with them. What must be noted in this solution is the noninvolvement of the base station in this key management framework. Several extensions of this framework have been developed including the following [18]:

- *The q-composite random key pre-distribution framework*—where two nodes share a common key hashed from q common keys. This approach adds more strength to the above approach. Because now an intruder would need to capture communication from more nodes in order to be able to compute a shared key.
- *Multi-key reinforcement framework*—where a message from a node is partitioned into several fragments and each fragment is routed through a separate secure path. Its advantages are balanced by its high overhead.
- *Random-pairwise framework*—where in the pre-deployment phase, N unique identities are generated for each network node. Each node identity is matched up with other m randomly selected distinct node identities, and a unique pairwise key is generated for each pair of nodes. The new key and the pair of node identities are stored on both key rings. After deployment, the nodes then broadcast their identities to their neighbors.

Other frameworks include a localized encryption and authentication protocol (LEAP) by Zhu et al. [19]. Under LEAP, it is observed that there are different types of messages in a sensor network. This leads to the use of four keys: individual, group, cluster, and pairwise key [18].

19.6.3 Confidentiality, Authentication, and Freshness

It is common knowledge to all security professionals that the use of strong cryptographic techniques strengthens the security of communication. In sensor networks, like in traditional networks, this is also the case. During authentication in sensor networks, the sending node, using a shared key with the receiving node, computes a Message Authentication Code (MAC) on the message about to be transmitted using a known hash function. The receiving node, upon receipt of the message, applies the shared key and the same hash function to the message to generate a new MAC. If this MAC agrees with the sender node's MAC, then the message has not been tempered with, and the receiving node knows that the message has been sent by the sending node since it is only this sending node that shares the key with the receiving node. Several studies including [15] SPINS have used this approach. SPINS has two building blocks: Secure Network Encryption Protocol (SNED) providing data confidentiality, a two-part data authentication, and data freshness and micro-Timed, Efficient, Streaming, Loss-tolerant Authentication (μTESLA) which provides authentication to node streaming broadcasts. In addition to SPINS, TinySec [20] which also supports message confidentiality, integrity, and authentication in wireless sensor networks also uses this approach. There are several other works on message confidentiality, authentication, and integrity, including that of Perrig et al. [15].

19.6.4 Resilience to Capture

While sensor networks, because of their size and deployment, are ideal for information gathering and environmental monitoring, node compromise poses a very serious security problem in these networks. While existing ad hoc security solutions can address a few security problems, on a limited number of nodes in a network, many of these solutions cannot scale up when the numbers of nodes in the network grows. Also when the node number is high and typically these nodes are unattended, they are prone to node compromise.

To overcome this problem, Yang et al. [20] have proposed a novel location-based key management solution through two techniques in which they bind symmetric secret keys to geographic locations and then assign those location-bound keys to sensor nodes based on the nodes' deployed locations. There are two approaches to this scheme: location-binding keys and location-based keys. In both of these approaches, the network terrain is divided into a grid where each cell on the grid is associated with multiple keys. Each node in a grid stores one key for each of its local neighboring cells and a few randomly selected remote cells. Any genuine real event must be validated by multiple keys bound to the specific location of that event. This requirement rules out any bogus event which might be a result of an attacker obtaining multiple keys from some compromised nodes because such event cannot combine all necessary keys to make the event genuine.

Exercises

1. Sensor networks are different from traditional networks. Discuss five reasons why.
2. Wireless sensor networks are different from wireless ad hoc networks. Discuss by giving reasons why this is so.
3. It is difficult to implement security mechanisms that are proven to work in traditional networks, even in wireless ad hoc networks in sensor networks. Why is this the case?
4. Discuss several ways to prevent node capture in sensor networks.
5. Encryption is very difficult to implement in sensor networks. However, there have been several papers exploring limited ways of doing this. Look for one or two papers, and discuss what approaches are being used.

Advanced Exercises

1. Since sensor networks are severely constrained by resources, can the deployment of sensor networks under a single administrative domain make it easier to secure these networks?
2. Based on question 1 above, can introducing redundancy or scaling the network help in creating secure sensor networks?
3. Again based on 1 above, is it possible to continue operating a sensor network with a selected number of sensors taken out? Is it possible to identify those nodes?
4. Devise ways (some cryptographic) of securing wireless communication links against eavesdropping, tampering, traffic analysis, and denial of service.
5. Is it possible to design an asymmetric encryption protocol with all computations based on the base station?

References

1. Wikipedia. http://en.wikipedia.org/wiki/Sensor
2. Seapahn M, Koushanfar F, Potkonjak M, Srivastava MB. Coverage problems in wireless Ad-hoc sensor networks. http://web.cs.ucla.edu/~miodrag/papers/Meguerdichian_Infocom_01.pdf
3. David C, Estrin D, Mani SM (2004) Overview of sensor networks. Computer 37:41–50
4. Akyildiz IF, Su W, Sankarasubramaniam Y, Cayirci A (2002) A survey on sensor networks. IEEE Commun Mag 40:102–114

5. Jay W. Smart sensor networks of the future. DA Systems. http://archives.sensorsmag.com/articles/0397/net_mar/main.shtml

6. Ortiz J, Moon D, Baker CR. Location service for point-to-point routing in wireless sensor networks. http://citeseerx.ist.psu.edu/viewdoc/download?doi=10.1.1.87.710&rep=rep1&type=pdf

7. Sure A, Iyengar SS, Cho E (2006) Ecoinformatics using wireless sensor networks: an overview. Ecolo Inform 1:287–293

8. Subramanian NVK. Survey on energy-aware routing and routing protocols for sensor networks. http://www.csee.umbc.edu/~younis/Publications/JAdHoc/SensNetRouting.pdf

9. Krishnamachari B, Estrin D, Wicker S. The impact of data aggregation in wireless sensor networks. ACM Digital Library. http://dl.acm.org/citation.cfm?id=708078

10. De P, Liu Y, Das SK (2006) Modeling node compromise spread in wireless sensor networks using epidemic theory. In: Proceedings of the 2006 international symposium on a world of wireless, mobile and multimedia networks (WoWMoM'06)

11. Stankovic JA. Research challenges for wireless sensor networks. http://doi.acm.org/10.1145/1121776.1121780

12. Anand M, Ives Z, Lee I (2005) Quantifying eavesdropping vulnerability in sensor networks, ACM international conference proceeding series. In: Proceedings of the 2nd international workshop on data management for sensor networks, vol 96

13. Hu YC, Perrig A, Johnson DB (2003) Rushing attacks and defense in wireless Ad Hoc network routing protocols. ACM Digital Library. http://dl.acm.org/citation.cfm?id=941317

14. Karlof C, Wagner D. Secure routing in wireless sensor networks: attacks and countermeasures. http://www.csee.umbc.edu/courses/graduate/CMSC691A/Spring04/papers/sensor-route.pdf

15. Perrig A, Szewczyk R, Wen V, Culler D, Tygar JD (2002) SPINS: security protocols for sensor networks. http://www.netsec.ethz.ch/publications/papers/mc2001.pdf

16. Perrig A, Stankovic J, Wagner D (2004) Security in wireless sensor networks. Commun ACM 47(6):53–57

17. Eschenauer L, Gligor VD (2002) A key-management scheme for distributed sensor networks. In: ACM conference on computer and communications security. ACM, New York

18. Sabbah E, Majeed A, Kyoung-Don K, Liu K, Abu-Ghazaleh N (2006) An application-driven perspective on wireless sensor network security. Q2SWinet'06, October 2, 2006

19. Zhu S, Setia S, Jajodia S (2003) LEAP: efficient security mechanisms for large-scale distributed sensor networks. In: The 10th ACM conference on computer and communication security (CCS '03), 2003

20. Karlof C, Sastry N, Wagner D (2004) TinySec: a link layer security architecture for wireless sensor networks. In: ACM SenSys, 2004

Other Efforts to Secure Data in Computer Networks and Beyond

20.1 Introduction

The rapid advances in computer technology, the plummeting prices of information processing and indexing devices, and the development of sprawling global networks have all made the generation, collection, processing, indexing, and storage of information easy. Massive information is created, processed, and moved around on a daily basis. The value of information has skyrocketed, and information has all of a sudden become a valuable asset for individuals, businesses, and nations. The security of nations has come to depend on computer networks that very few can defend effectively. Our own individual privacy and security have come to depend on the whims of the kid next door.

Protection of information, on which we have come to depend so much, has been a major challenge since the birth of the Internet. The widespread adoption of computer technology for business, organization, and government operations has made the problem of protecting critical personal, business, and national assets more urgent. When these assets are attacked, damaged, or threatened, our own individual, business, and more importantly national security is at stake.

The problem of protecting these assets is becoming a personal, business, and national priority that must involve everyone. Efforts and ways must be sought to this end. But getting this massive public involvement will require massive public efforts on several fronts including legislation, regulation, education, and activism. In this chapter, we examine these efforts.

20.2 Legislation

As the Internet Web grows, Internet activities increase, e-commerce booms, and globalization spreads wider, citizens of every nation infuriated by what they see as the "bad" Internet are putting enormous and growing pressures on their national legislatures and other lawmaking bodies to enact laws that would curb cyberspace

© Springer International Publishing AG 2017
J.M. Kizza, *Guide to Computer Network Security*, Computer Communications and Networks, DOI 10.1007/978-3-319-55606-2_20

activities in ways that they feel best serve their interests. The citizens' cause has been joined by special interest groups representing a variety of causes such as environmental protection, free speech, intellectual property rights, privacy, censorship, and security.

Already this has started happening in countries such as the United States, United Kingdom, Germany, France, China, and Singapore, and the list grows every passing day. In all these countries, laws, some good, many repressive, are being enacted to put limits on activities in cyberspace. The recent upsurge of illegal cyberspace activities such as the much publicized distributed denial of service and the headline-making e-mail attacks has fueled calls from around the world for legislative actions to be taken to stop such activities. Yet it is not clear and probably unlikely that such actions will at best stop and in the least arrest the escalating rate of illegal activities in cyberspace. Given the number of cyberspace legislations we presently have in place and the seemingly escalating illegal cyberspace incidents, it looks like the patchwork of legislation will not in any meaningful way put a stop to these malicious activities in the near future. If anything, such activities are likely to continue unabated unless and until long-term plans are in place. Such efforts and plans should include first and foremost ethical education.

Besides purely legislative processes which are more public, there are also private initiatives that work either in conjunction with public judicial systems and law enforcement agencies or work through workplace forces. Examples abound of large companies, especially high-technology companies such as software, telecommunications, and Internet providers coming together to lobby their national legislatures to enact laws to protect their interests. Such companies are also forming consortiums of some form or partnerships to create and implement private control techniques.

20.3   Regulation

As the debate between the freedom of speech advocates and children's rights crusaders heats up, governments around the world are being forced to revisit, amend, and legislate new policies, charters, statutes, and acts. As we will see in detail in the next section, this has been one of the most popular and, to politicians, the most visible means of dealing with the "runaway" cyberspace. Legislative efforts are being backed by judicial and law enforcement machinery. In almost every industrialized and many developing countries, large numbers of new regulations are being added to the books. Many outdated laws and acts are being revisited, retooled, and brought back in service.

20.4   Self-Regulation

There are several reasons why self-regulation as a technique of cyberspace policing is appealing to a good cross section of people around the globe. One reason, supported mostly by the free speech advocates, is to send a clear signal to governments around the world that the cyberspace and its users are willing to self-regulate, rather than have the heavy hand of government decide what is or is not acceptable to them.

Second, there is realization that although legislation and enforcement can go a long way in helping to curb cyber crimes, they are not going to perform the magic bullet that will eventually eradicate cyber crimes. It should be taken as one of a combination of measures that must be carried out together. Probably, one of the most effective prevention techniques is to give users enough autonomy to self-regulate themselves, each taking on the responsibility to the degree and level of control and regulation that best suits his or her needs and environment. This self-regulation cyberspace can be done through two approaches: hardware and software.

20.4.1 Hardware-Based Self-Regulation

There is a wide array of hardware tools to monitor and police cyberspace to a degree suited for each individual user of cyberspace. Among the tools are those individually set to control access, authorization, and authentication. Such hardware tools fall mainly in six areas, namely:

- *Prevention*: Prevention is intended to restrict access to information on the system resources such as disks on network hosts and network servers using technologies that permit only authorized people to the designated areas. Such technologies include, for example, firewalls.
- *Protection*: Protection is meant to routinely identify, evaluate, and update system security requirements to make them suitable, comprehensive, and effective.
- *Detection*: This involves deploying an early warning monitoring system for early discovery of security breaches both planned and in progress. This category includes all intrusion detection systems (IDS).
- *Limitation*: This is intended to cut the losses suffered in cases of failed security.
- *Reaction*: To analyze all possible security lapses and plan relevant remedial efforts for a better security system based on observed failures.
- *Recovery*: To recover what has been lost as quickly and efficiently as possible and update contingent recovery plans.

20.4.2 Software-Based Self-Regulation

Unlike hardware solutions which are few and very specialized, software solutions are many and varied in their approaches to cyberspace monitoring and control. They are also far less threatening and therefore more user-friendly because they are closer to the user. This means that they can either be installed by the user on the user's computer or by a network system administrator on a network server. If installed by the user, the user can set the parameters for the level of control needed. At a network level, whether using a firewall or specific software package, controls are set based on general user consensus. Software controls fall into three categories [1]:

- *Rating programs*: Rating programs rate cyberspace content based on a selected set of criteria. Among such criteria are violence, language, and sex content. Software rating labels enable cyberspace content providers to place voluntary labels on their products according to a set of criteria. However, these labels are not uniform for the whole industry; they depend on a rating company. There are many rating companies, including CyberPatrol, CYBERsitter, Net Nanny, and SurfWatch, all claiming to provide a simple yet effective rating system for Web sites to protect children and free speech of everyone who publishes in cyberspace. These labels are then used by the filtering program on the user's computer or server.
- *Filtering programs*: Filtering software blocks documents and Web sites that contain materials designated on a filter list, usually bad words and URLs. They always examine each Web document header looking for matching labels to those on the "bad" list. Filters are either client based, in which a filter is installed on a user's computer, or server based, in which they are centrally located and maintained. Server-based filters offer better security because they are not easy to tamper with. Even though filtering software has become very popular, it still has serious problems and drawbacks such as inaccuracies in labeling, restriction on unrated material, and just deliberate exclusion of certain Web sites by an individual or individuals.
- *Blocking*: As we discussed in Chap. 14, blocking software works by denying access to all except those on a "good" list. Blocking software works best only if all Web materials are rated. But as we all know, with hundreds of thousands of Web sites submitted every day, it is impossible to rate all materials on the Internet, at least at the moment.

20.5   Education

Perhaps one of the most viable tools to prevent and curb illegal cyberspace activities is through mass education. Mass education involves teaching as many people as possible the values of security, responsible use of computer technology, how to handle security incidents, how to recover from security incidents, how to deal with the evidence if legal actions are to be followed, and how to report security incidents. Although mass education is good, it has its problems including the length of time it takes to bear fruits. There are many people still not convinced that education alone can do the job. To these people, there is no time; if action is to be taken, then the time to do so is now. However, we are still convinced that the teaching of ethical use of computer technology, as long as it takes, always results in better security measures than what else we have discussed so far. For without ethics and moral values, whatever trap we make, one of us will eventually make a better trap. Without the teaching of morality and ethics, especially to the young, there is likely to be no break in the problems of computer and network security. Along these lines, therefore, education should be approached on two fronts: focused and mass education.

20.5.1 Focused Education

Focused education targets groups of the population, for example, children in schools, professionals, and certain religious and interest groups. For this purpose, focused education can be subdivided into formal education and occasional education.

Private companies are also conducting focused education. For example, there are a number of private companies conducting certification courses in security. These companies include Computer Science Institute (CSI), Cisco, Microsoft, SANS Institute, and others.

20.5.1.1 Formal Education
Formal education targets the whole length of the education spectrum from kindergarten through college. The focus and contact, however, should differ depending on the selected level. For example, in elementary education, while it is appropriate to educate children about the dangers of information misuse and computer ethics in general, the content and the delivery of that content are measured for that level. In high schools where there is more maturity and more exploratory minds, the content and the delivery system get more focused and more forceful. This approach changes in colleges because here the students are more focused on their majors, and the intended education should reflect this.

20.5.1.2 Occasional Education
Teaching morality, ethics, computer security, and responsible use of information and information technology should be lifelong processes just how teaching responsible use of a gun should be to a soldier. This responsibility should be and is usually passed on to the professions.

There are a variety of ways professions enforce this education to their members. For many traditional professions, this is done through introduction and enforcement of professional codes, guidelines, and cannons. Other professions supplement their codes with a requirement of in-service training sessions and refresher courses.

Quite a number of professions require licensing as a means of ensuring continuing education of its members. It is through these approaches of education that information security awareness and solutions should be channeled.

20.5.2 Mass Education

The purpose of mass education is to involve as many people as possible with limited resources and maximum effect. The methods to achieve this are usually through community involvement through community-based activities such as charity walks and other sports-related activities. Using an army of volunteers to organize local, regional, and national activities, the approach similar to that of common causes such as AIDS, cancer, and other life-threatening diseases, can bring quick and very effective awareness which leads to unprecedented education.

20.6   Reporting Centers

The recent skyrocketing rise in cyber crimes has prompted public authorities looking after the welfare of the general public to open up cyber crime reporting centers.

The purpose of these centers is to collect all relevant information on cyber attacks and make that information available to the general public. The centers also function as the first point of contact whenever one suspects or is electronically attacked. Centers also act as advice-giving centers for those who want to learn more about the measures that must be taken to prevent, detect, and recover from attacks, and in a limited capacity, these centers offer security education.

In the United States, there are several federally supported and private reporting centers, including NIST Computer Security Division:

Computer Security Resource Center (CSRC) (http://csrc.nist.gov/)
The Department of Homeland Security (DHS)'s National Cybersecurity and Communications Integration Center (NCCIC) (http://www.dhs.gov/national-cybersecurity-and-communications-integration-center)
The Center for Education and Research in Information Assurance and Security (https://www.cerias.purdue.edu/)
Carnegie Mellon Emergency Response Team (https://www.cert.org/about/)
The FedCIRC (http://ocio.os.doc.gov/ITPolicyandPrograms/IT_Security/DEV01_003675)
The National Infrastructure Protection Center (https://www.dhs.gov/national-infrastructure-coordinating-center)

These centers fall into two categories:

- Non-law enforcement to collect, index, and advise the population of all aspects of cyber attacks including prevention, detection, and survivability.
- Law enforcement centers to act as the nation's clearing house for computer crimes, linking up directly with other national and international Computer Emergency Response Teams to monitor and assess potential threats. In addition, law enforcement centers may provide training for local law enforcement officials and in cooperation with private industry and international law enforcement agencies.

20.7 Market Forces

The rapid rise in cyber crimes has also prompted collaboration between private industry and government agencies to work together to warn the public of the dangers of cyber crimes and outline steps to take to remove the vulnerabilities, thereby lessening chances of being attacked. Both major software and hardware manufacturers have been very active and prompt in posting, sending, and widely distributing advisories, vulnerability patches, and antivirus software whenever their products are hit. Cisco, a major Internet infrastructure network device manufacturer, for example, has been calling and e-mailing its customers worldwide, mainly Internet service providers (ISPs), notifying them of the possibilities of cyber attacks that target Cisco's products. It also informs its customers of software patches that could be used to resist or repair those attacks. It has also assisted in the dissemination of vital information to the general public through its Web sites concerning those attacks and how to prevent and recover from them.

On the software front, Microsoft, the most affected target in the software arena, has similarly been active in posting, calling, and e-mailing its customers with the vital and necessary information on how to prevent and recover from attacks targeting its products. Besides the private sector, public sector reporting centers have also been active in sending advisories of impending attacks and techniques to recover from attacks.

20.8 Activism

Beyond those awareness and mass education techniques discussed above, there are others widely used although less effective. They fall under the activism umbrella because they are organized and driven by the users. They include the following:

20.8.1 Advocacy

This is a mass education strategy that has been used since the beginning of humanity. Advocacy groups work with the public, corporations, and governments to enhance public education through awareness of the use. It is a blanket mass education campaign in which a message is passed through mass campaigns, magazines, and electronic publications, as well as support of public events and mass communication media like television, radio, and now the Internet.

Advocacy is intended to make people part of the intended message. For example, during the struggles for the voting rights in the United States, women's groups and minorities designed and carried out massive advocacy campaigns that were meant to involve all women who eventually became part of the movement. Similarly, in the minority voting rights struggles, the goal was to involve all minorities whose rights had been trodden upon. The purpose of advocacy is to consequently organize, build, and train so that there is a permanent and vibrant structure that people can be part of. By involving as many people as possible including the intended audience in the campaigns, the advocacy strategy brings awareness which leads to more pressure on lawmakers and everyone else responsible. The pressure brought about by mass awareness usually results in some form of action, most times the desired action.

20.8.2 Hotlines

Hotlines is a technique that makes the general public take the initiative to observe, notice, and report incidents. In fact, as we will see in the next chapter, the *National Strategy to Secure Cyberspace* (NSSC), in one of its priorities, advocates this very strategy to make the ordinary users get involved in not only their personal security but also that of their community and the nation as a whole. In many cases, the strategy is to set up hotline channels through which individuals who observe a computer security incident can report it to the selected reporting agency for action. Whenever a report is made, any technique that works can be applied. In many countries such agencies may include their ISPs and law enforcement agencies.

Exercises

1. Do you think education can protect cyberspace from criminal activities? Defend your response.
2. Looking at the array of education initiatives and different types of programs and the state of security in cyberspace, do you think education can advance/ improve system security?
3. The effects of education are not seen in a few years. In fact, education benefits may show 20–30 years later. However, security needs are for real and for now. Should we keep educating?
4. Choose three hardware solutions used in self-regulation and discuss how they are deployed and how they work.
5. Choose three software solutions based on self-regulation. Study the solutions and discuss how they work.
6. Study the various forms of activism. Comment on the effectiveness of each.

7. Software rating, although helpful in bringing awareness to concerned individuals, has not been successful. Discuss why.
8. Both blocking software and filtering software, although slightly more popular than rating software, suffer from a variety of problems. Discuss these problems and suggest solutions.
9. Given that worldwide a small percentage of people have college education, but, in some countries, more than half of the people use computers and get access to cyberspace, propose a way to get your education message to those people who may not have enough education to understand the computer lingo. Discuss how much of the computer lingo is a problem in mass education.
10. Information security awareness and education are effective if people do understand the lingo used. Computer technology has generated a basket of words that make it difficult for an average computer user to benefit fully from either vendor education or specialized education. Suggest ways to deal with the ever-expanding basket in computer and information security.

Advanced Exercises

1. Study five countries with strong laws on cyberspace activities, and comment on these laws' effectiveness.
2. One of the problems of cyberspace regulation is the hindrance to hot pursuit of cyber criminals. Hot pursuit laws prevent law enforcement officers from crossing jurisdictional boundaries without court permissions. However, digital evidence does not give you that much time to collect court permits. Discuss these problems and suggest ways to overcome them.
3. Study the big market players, both hardware and software, and discuss their efforts in bringing security awareness to their customers. Are they being noble or responding to pressure?
4. As a follow up to question #3 above, if there was more competition on the market, do you think there would be more security responsibility? Why or why not?
5. If possible, propose a unique education security solution that is not among those discussed. Give reasons why your solution might succeed where others have fallen short.

Reference

1. Committee to Study High Performance Computing and Communications (1995) Evolving the high performance computing and communications initiative to support the nation's information infrastructure. The National Academies Press, Washington, DC. http://www.nap.edu/readingroom/books/hpcc/contents.html

Part IV

The Emergence of the Digital and Social Network Ecosystem

The Elastic Extension of the Traditional Computer Network Through Virtualization, Cloud Computing and Mobile Technologies

Virtualization Technology and Security

21

21.1 Introduction

Virtualization is a process through which one can create something that is there in effect and performance but in reality not there—that is, virtual. It is a physical abstraction of the company's computing resources like storage, network servers, memory, and others. VMware.com, a software developer and a global leader in the virtualization market, defines virtualization as a process in which software creates virtual machines (VMs) including a virtual machine monitor called "hypervisor" that allocates hardware resources dynamically and transparently so that multiple operating systems, called "guest operating systems," can run concurrently on a single physical computer without even knowing it [1]. For example, using software virtualization, one can, using the existing underlying hardware and software resources like operating systems, create and run several independent virtual operating systems on top of one physical operating system using the existing hardware resources to execute independent system tasks. Hardware virtualization also takes the same concept where several servers or client machines can be created based on one underlying hardware. The virtualization concept has been with us for sometime.

The potential power of virtualization in substantially increasing the performance of computing systems such as hardware and software through division of the underlying physical computing resources into many equally powerful virtual machines has increased the popularity of the technology in the last 20 years, and this love continues today. According to the IDC, an IT research firm, 2012 ranking of chief information officer (CIO) priorities, virtualization and the server consolidation that it delivers were the top priority for chief information officers. Forty percent of CIOs picked virtualization and server consolidation, more than any other area of IT [2]. The rush to virtualization is driven by its resulting server consolidation creating savings to be invested in new IT initiatives such as cloud computing, mobility, data analytics, and use of social media for business purposes. This rapid growth is a reflection of the changing benefits of virtualization from being used only

© Springer International Publishing AG 2017
J.M. Kizza, *Guide to Computer Network Security*, Computer Communications and Networks, DOI 10.1007/978-3-319-55606-2_21

as a tactical tool to drive consolidation and higher system utilization to leveraging the mobility of virtual machines to improve management and operations of IT environments. The virtualization concept now includes a host of new use cases that range from high availability and disaster recovery to hosted clients and true utility computing.

21.2   History of Virtualization

The history of virtualization is as amazing as the concept itself. Since computers of the 1960s could do only one task at a time and depended on human operators, increasing system performance was bottlenecked at two points: at the submission stage and at the computation stage. One way to improve the submission stage was to use a batch, where jobs were submitted into a queue and the system picked them from there, thus reducing human intervention and errors. Batching improved some system performance but did not go far enough. This problem, together with creating backward compatibility for customers of older computing systems the ability to bring old functionalities of the old to the new, and thus keep customer royalty, led IBM to begin work on the S/360 mainframe system. The S/360 mainframe was capable of running legacy functionalities of nearly all IBM's older systems, although it was still a batch machine. In the following years, there was a growing need, especially in the research community like at Bell Labs and Massachusetts Institute of Technology (MIT), for a machine that was capable of running tasks of more than one simultaneous user. In response to this growing need for speedup, IBM responded with the CP-40 mainframe which later evolved into the CP-67 system, thought to be the first commercial mainframe to support virtualization. The CP-67 had a unique operating system combination consisting of CMS (Console Monitor System) piggybacked on a control program called rightly CP. The CP/CMS was a small single-user interactive operating system and CP, upon which CMS run, actually run on the mainframe to create the virtual machines which individually run their own copies of CMS. To each virtual machine running CMS, CP allocated parts of the underlying physical machine which formed the virtual machine [4].

When microprocessors made their debut into computing in the 1980s and beyond, creating an era of personal computers which led into desktops and small servers leading to computer networks of varying sizes which seemed to lower the costs of computing and improved system performance, virtualization technology took a back seat and was almost forgotten. The situation did not change until the mid-1990s when the cost of computing skyrocketed again in spite of large-scale distribution of computing by client-server models of computation. There was a growing need to revisit virtualization and rain in the rising costs of information technology.

In 1999, VMware introduced a new kind of virtualization technology which, instead of running on the mainframe, run on the x86 system. VMware virtualization technology was able to isolate the shared hardware infrastructure of the x86 architecture. Today, VMware is the global leader in x86 virtualization which offers desktop, server, and data center [3].

21.3 Virtualization Terminologies

For one to understand the virtualization process, one has to first understand the terminologies used and make up the process. There are several terminologies used specifically in the virtualization process, and they include *host CPU and guest CPU*, *host operating system* and *guest operating system*, *hypervisor*, and *emulation*.

21.3.1 Host CPU/Guest CPU

When a virtualization software is creating a new VM upon which the virtual OS runs, it creates a virtual CPU, known as a *guest CPU*, best on the time slices allowed on the underlying physical, now called a *host CPU* on the host machine. There is corresponding coordination and linkages between the host and guest CPUs. The guest CPU in the VM created is not aware of the host CPU or the host machine supporting it. It is also not aware of its sibling guest CPUs in the sibling VMs.

21.3.2 Host OS/Guest OS

During the virtualization process, the virtualization software creates complete VMs based on the underlying physical machine. These VMs have all the functionalities of the underlying physical/host machine. However, during the process, the virtualization software, for each VM created, may or may not create a new/guest operating system or make as a copy of the physical/host operating system. This new operating system, on each newly created VM, is a *guest operating system (guest OS)*, and the physical operating system running on the physical machine is the *host operating system (host OS)*. The guest operating system has no knowledge of the existence of either the host operating system or the sibling guest operating systems. All VMs are consistent with each other and the host VM in that each has the same resources, save the guest operating system, like the host machine. The only difference in consistency occurs in disk I/O operations. To solve this problem, there is a required mapping of the guest disk I/O operations with the physical disk I/O operations. For example, users of Windows VMs must interact with it over the network via Windows Terminal Services (RDP), and those using Unix/Linux VMs must interact with them via the network using SSH.

21.3.3 Hypervisor

A hypervisor, as a virtual machine manager, is a software program that allows multiple operating systems to share a single physical hardware host. In creating the virtual machine for each operating system, the hypervisor uses "slices" of the physical host machine's physical components like memory, processor, and other resources to anchor each guest operating system running the virtual machine created. The host physical machine's "slices" allocated to each virtual machine are managed by the hypervisor in amounts and time durations as needed by each operating system.

21.3.4 Emulation

An emulation is a process of making an exact copy of all the functionalities of an entity like a hardware resource of a computing system like a CPU and operating system, I/O devices and drivers, and others. Emulation software is an application software running on a host to emulate the host. Emulators can create guest OS. These emulated OS have no knowledge of the existence of either the host machine and its OS or its siblings. The problem with emulators as opposed to hypervisors is that emulators are slow.

21.4   Types of Computing System Virtualization

There are many types of virtualization including platform, network, storage, and application.

21.4.1 Platform Virtualization

Platform virtualization is the use of server hardware by the virtualization software to host multiple VMs as guest VMs. Each VM is a virtual environment with its operating system (the guest operating system), which may or may not be the same as the physical server's operating system (the host operating system), and emulates the whole physical infrastructure of a computing system including memory, and each VM is independent of other VMs sharing the physical server. Platform virtualization itself is subdivided into two types: workstation and server.

21.4.1.1 Workstation Virtualization
This is also referred to as *desktop virtualization*. It is the abstraction of the traditional workstation with its operating system, by moving it to a remote server system, accessed via a smart or dumb terminal. Desktop virtualization becomes popular to the business world because of its savings resulting from a reduction in desktop sprawl. Desktop virtualization has been around for decades starting in the

days of the timeshare systems. During those days, the technology was known by different names including terminal service computing that included dumb terminals, terminal emulators, and thin-client computing. It was also known as technology which allowed full exploitation of the true power and flexibility of a desktop or laptop computer by making it capable of running multiple operating systems simultaneously on a single processor. With the ability to emulate multiple fully operational "machines" on one computer, one can get the following benefits from that one computer [5]:

- Ability to run a variety of applications specific to individual operating systems not currently running on the physical machine.
- Ability to host legacy applications and overcome platform migration issues.
- Demonstrate multi-tier configurations on a single processor like running SQL Server database server running in one virtual machine, a Web server running on another virtual machine, and several other server-based applications all running on a single host desktop.
- Configure and test new software or patches in an isolated environment, thus reducing deployment risks and costs.
- Automate tasks for software development and testing.

21.4.1.2 Server Virtualization

Server virtualization is the process of having a physical server run a server-based virtualization software called a hypervisor to divide the physical server into multiple isolated virtual environments. Each virtual environment in a virtual machine, is homed on a virtual server, and has all the functionalities of the physical server it is homed on and runs a virtual operating system called a guest operating system. The virtual machines created are known by different names including virtual private servers, guest machines, instances, containers, or emulations.

According to [3], there are three popular approaches to server virtualization: the virtual machine model, the paravirtual machine model, and virtualization at the operating system (OS) layer.

The *virtual machine model* is based on a *host/guest* paradigm. Each guest runs on a virtual imitation of the physical hardware layer. This approach allows each guest operating system on each virtual machine to run without *modifications* to the resources of the underlying physical machine. It also allows the different virtual machines to run different guest operating systems. The guest operating systems has no knowledge of the host's operating system because they assume that they are running on the physical hardware. Each guest operating system access to the physical recourses of the host machine is managed by the hypervisor.

The paravirtual machine (PVM) model is also based on the *host/guest* paradigm. The two models are very much alike. The only difference though between the virtual machine and the paravirtual machine models lies in the fact that this time, the hypervisor can modify the guest operating system's code through a process called *porting*. With porting, the hypervisor can prioritize and utilize privileged system calls between the guest operating system and the physical processor.

Unlike the virtual machine and paravirtual machine models, the *OS-level* virtualization model is not based on the *host/guest* paradigm. In the OS-level model, the host runs a single OS kernel as its core and exports operating system functionality to each of the guests. Guests must use the *same* operating system as the host, although different distributions of the same system are allowed. This distributed architecture eliminates system calls between layers, which reduces CPU usage overhead. It also requires that each partition remain strictly isolated from its neighbors so that a failure or security breach in one partition isn't able to affect any of the other partitions. In this model, common binaries and libraries on the same physical machine can be shared, allowing an OS-level virtual server to host thousands of guests at the same time. Virtuozzo and Solaris Zones both use OS-level virtualization. Although we stated earlier that there are no modifications by the hypervisor of the characteristics of the underlying physical resources given to each virtual machine, there is in fact a limited modification by the hypervisor. The hypervisor actually modifies the guest operating system's code. This modification is called porting. Porting supports the hypervisor so it can utilize privileged system calls sparingly [10].

Whether workstation or server virtualization, platform virtualization is the more popular form of virtualization and it is growing fast. The table below lists a good number of platform virtual machine (VM) software packages, their host CPU, guest CPU, host operating systems, guest operating system, and type of license it carries [6]. Note licensing is classified as follows [9]:

- LGPL—GNU Lesser General Public License (formerly the GNU Library General Public License) is a free software license published by the Free Software Foundation (FSF). It was published in 1991 and adopted the version number 2 for parity with GPL version 2, renamed in 1997 as the GNU Lesser General Public License. It places *copyleft* (a general method for making a program (or other work) free, and requiring all modified and extended versions of the program to be free as well) restrictions on the program governed under it but does not apply these restrictions to other software that merely link with the program. It is primarily used for software libraries.
- GPL—The GNU General Public License (or simply GPL) is the most widely used free software license. Currently in version 3, the GPL is the first copyleft license for general use, which means that derived works can only be distributed under the same license terms.
- CDDL—Common Development and Distribution License (CDDL) is a free software license, produced by Sun Microsystems, based on the Mozilla Public License (MPL), version 1.1. Files licensed under the CDDL can be combined with files licensed under other licenses, whether open source or proprietary.
- BSD—BSD licenses are a family of permissive free software licenses. The original license was used for the Berkeley Software Distribution (BSD), a Unix-like operating system after which it is named.

Table 21.1 Platform virtualization software packages

Name	Responsible party	Host CPU	Guest CPU	Host OS(s)	Guest OS(s)	License
FreeBSD Jail	FreeBSD	Any running FreeBSD	Any running FreeBSD	FreeBSD	FreeBSD, Linux ABI	BSD
Hyper-V Server 2008 R2	Microsoft	x86-64 + hardware-assisted virtualization (Intel VT-x or AMD-V)	x86-64, x86 (up to eight physical CPUs)	Windows 2008 w/Hyper-V Role, Windows Hyper-V Server	Supported drivers for Windows 2000, Windows 2003, Windows 2008, Windows XP, Windows Vista, Linux (SUSE 10 released, more announced)	Proprietary
iCore Virtual Accounts	iCore Software	x86	x86	Windows XP	Windows XP	Proprietary
Integrity Virtual Machines	Hewlett-Packard	IA-64	IA-64	HP-UX	HP-UX, Windows, Linux (OpenVMS announced)	Proprietary
LynxSecure	LynuxWorks	x86, Intel VT-x, Intel VT-d	x86	No host OS	LynxOS, Linux, Windows	Proprietary
PikeOS	SYSGO AG	PowerPC, x86, ARM, MIPS, SPARC, SuperH	Same as host	PikeOS	PikeOS native, Linux, POSIX, AUTOSAR, ANDROID, RTEMS, OSEK, ARINC 653 APEX, ITRON	Proprietary
QuickTransit	Transitive Corp.	x86, x86-64, IA-64, POWER	MIPS, PowerPC, SPARC, x86	Linux, Mac OS X, Solaris	Linux, Mac OS X, Irix, Solaris	Proprietary

(continued)

Table 21.1 (continued)

Name	Responsible party	Host CPU	Guest CPU	Host OS(s)	Guest OS(s)	License
RTS Hypervisor	Real-Time Systems	x86	x86	No host OS	Windows 7, Windows XP, Windows Embedded, Windows CE, Linux, Android, VxWorks, OS-9, RTOS-32, QNX, RTEMS, T-Kernel, proprietary	Proprietary
Safe Virtual Machine, SVM	Altreonic, www.altreonic.com	Any	Any	OpenComRTOS or any other (RT)OS	N.A.	Binary, Open Technology License
Simics	Virtutech	x86, x86-64, SPARC v9	Alpha, ARM, IA-64, MIPS 32/64, MSP430, POWER, PowerPC 32/64, SPARC v8/v9, x86, x86-64, TI TMS320C64xx	Windows, Linux, Solaris	Depends on target machine, VxWorks, OSE, QNX, Linux, Solaris, Windows, FreeBSD, RTEMS, TinyOS, many others	Proprietary
Containers, or Zones	Sun Microsystems	x86, x86-64, SPARC (portable: not tied to hardware)	Same as host	Solaris 10, Solaris 11 Express, OpenSolaris 2009.06	Solaris (8, 9, 10, 11), Linux (BrandZ)	CDDL
Sun xVM Server	Sun Microsystems	x86-64, SPARC	Same as host	No host OS	Windows XP, 2003 Server (x86-64 only), Linux, Solaris	GPL version 3
Virtual PC 2007	Connectix	x86, x86-64	x86	Windows Vista (Business, Enterprise, Ultimate), XP Pro, XP Tablet PC Edition	DOS, Windows, OS/2, Linux (SUSE, Xubuntu), OpenSolaris (Belenix)	Proprietary

Virtual PC 7 for Mac	Connectix	PowerPC	x86	Mac OS X	Windows, OS/2, Linux	Proprietary
Virtual Server 2005 R2	Connectix	x86-64	x86	Windows 2003, XP	Windows NT, 2000, 2003, Linux (Red Hat, SUSE)	Proprietary
VirtualBox	Innotek, acquired by Oracle Corporation	x86, x86-64	x86, (x86-64 only on VirtualBox 2 and later with hardware virtualization)	Windows, Linux, Mac OS X x86, Solaris, FreeBSD, eComStation	DOS, Linux, Mac OS X Server,[6] FreeBSD, Haiku, OS/2, Solaris, Syllable, Windows	GPL version 2; full version with extra enterprise features is proprietary
VMware ESX Server	VMware	x86, x86-64	x86, x86-64	No host OS	Windows, Linux, Solaris, FreeBSD, OSx86 (as FreeBSD), virtual appliances, Netware, OS/2, SCO, BeOS, Darwin, others: runs arbitrary OS[7]	Proprietary
VMware ESXi	VMware	x86, x86-64	x86, x86-64	No host OS	Same as VMware ESX Server	Proprietary
VMware Fusion	VMware	x86, x86-64	x86, x86-64	Mac OS X x86	Same as VMware ESX Server	Proprietary
VMware Player 3.1	VMware	x86, x86-64	x86, x86-64	Windows, Linux	Same as VMware ESX Server	Proprietary, free of charge for personal noncommercial use[81]. [2]
VMware Server	VMware	x86, x86-64	x86, x86-64	Windows, Linux	Same as VMware ESX Server	Proprietary

(continued)

Table 21.1 (continued)

Name	Responsible party	Host CPU	Guest CPU	Host OS(s)	Guest OS(s)	License
VMware Workstation 7.1	VMware	x86, x86-64	x86, x86-64	Windows, Linux	Same as VMware ESX Server	Proprietary
Wind River hypervisor	Wind River	x86, PowerPC	Same as host	No host OS	Linux, VxWorks, unmodified guests (including MS Windows and RTOSs such as OSE, QNX, and others), bare metal virtual board	Proprietary
Windows Virtual PC	Connectix	x86, x86-64 with Intel VT-x or AMD-V	x86	Windows 7	Windows XP, Windows Vista, Windows 7, Windows Server 2003, Windows Server 2008	Proprietary
Xen	XenSource	x86, x86-64, IA-64	Same as host	NetBSD, Linux, Solaris	FreeBSD, NetBSD, Linux, Solaris, Windows XP and 2003 Server (needs vers. 3.0 and an Intel VT-x (Vanderpool) or AMD-V (Pacifica)-capable CPU), Plan 9	GPL
z LPARs	IBM	z/Architecture	z/Architecture	Integrated in firmware of System z mainframes	Linux on zSeries, z/OS, z/VSE, z/TPF, z/VM, MUSIC/SP, and predecessors	Integrated in firmware of System z mainframes

| PowerVM | IBM | POWER4, POWER5, POWER6, PowerPC 970 | POWER4/5/6, PowerPC 970, X86 (PowerVM Lx86) | No host OS | Linux PowerPC, x86; AIX, i5/OS, IBM i | Proprietary |
| z/VM | IBM | z/Architecture | z/Architecture, z/VM does not run on predecessor mainframes | No host OS, itself (single or multiple levels/versions deep, e.g., VM/ESA running in z/VM 4.4 in z/VM 5.2 in z/VM 5.1.) | Linux on zSeries, z/OS, z/VSE, z/TPF, z/VM, VM/CMS, MUSIC/SP, OpenSolaris for System z, predecessors | Proprietary |

Source and for a full list: Wikipedia. http://en.wikipedia.org/wiki/Comparison_of_platform_virtual_machines

- OPL—Open Publication License is a license open publications created by the Open Content Project, which now recommends [1] using one of the Creative Commons licenses.
- Proprietary—Proprietary software is computer software licensed under exclusive legal right of the copyright holder. The licensee is given the right to use the software under certain conditions, while restricted from other uses, such as modification, further distribution, or reverse engineering.
- Open Source—It is a philosophy which allows free redistribution, reuse, reengineering, and access to an end product's design and implementation details (Table 21.1).

What follows are some of the most popular platform virtualization software packages. A more extensive list can be found at http://en.wikipedia.org/wiki/Comparison_of_platform_virtual_machines.

21.4.2 Network Virtualization

Like storage virtualization, network virtualization pools the resources, like files, folders, storage, and I/O devices, of separate and different networks into one network. This in fact is a network abstraction which isolates network traffic from network physical elements like switches, network ports, routers, and others within those networks, replacing each physical element with virtual representations and being able to duplicate them. This is done by splitting up the available bandwidth into independent channels, within the system. This makes it easy for the network administrator to share and assign network resources out among local network users thus allowing each network user to access all of the pooled network resources from their computer. This perhaps is the greatest benefit for network virtualization. In addition, network virtualization improves the ability of a user to move data into and out of storage resources to meet their current demands.

There are two types of *network virtualization*, the external and internal. External network involves the creation of multiple networks or parts of networks into a single virtual entity using all physical network elements like cabling, network adapters, switches, routers, and so on. Internal virtualization on the other hand is the process of creating one or more logical networks by defining logical switches and network adapters within a virtualized server itself. Note that an internal virtual network can connect two or more virtual machines on a single server and allow data exchanges between the virtual machines via the virtual server without involving the underlying physical network infrastructure, thus creating a virtual system-wide sharing and other network functionality. This is creates a fast and more efficient communication between virtual machines in the network on the virtual server thus minimizing traffic on the physical network. Also it gives a network administrator flexibility to combine virtual network elements in any way to create a network of any size and scope for the organization or create multiple networks that will share the same physical network infrastructure. Although internal virtualization is fast and eases the job of a network administrator, it creates other problems including workload balancing and migration within the network.

For both external and internal network virtualization to work, it requires network virtualization software on each virtualized server as well as within switches and other network elements that support network virtualization. This integration between hardware and software elements must work well to support network virtualization. At the writing of this chapter, some of the best network virtualization software include Citrix; Vyatta; ConteXtream, Inc.; and others.

Finally, the concept network virtualization is not a new one. For years, we have been working with virtual private networks (VPNs), first by telephone companies before digital networks. With advent of digital network, security professionals have been using the concept VPN for years now. In addition to VPNs, there has also been the concept of virtual local area networks (VLANs), and virtual LAN (VLAN), a group of logically networked devices on one or more LANs configured so that they can communicate as if they were attached to the same wire, when in fact they are located on a number of different LAN segments, also represents a common variation of network virtualization.

21.4.3 Storage Virtualization

The process of pooling together of resources of many different network storage devices such as hard drives to create what looks like one big storage managed from a single console is referred to as *storage* virtualization. There are several advantages why storage virtualization is good for business. First it hides the complexity of having multiple storage devices in many and different networks into one and simplifying the interface and console operations. Second it reduces the costs of storage reducing the overall storage infrastructure problems. And finally it works well for backups. There are some drawbacks that tend to prevent some from utilizing the technology like being complex to implement therefore requiring external help sometimes.

21.4.4 Application Virtualization

In application virtualization, the software package allows the bytecode of an application package to be portably run on many different computer architectures and operating systems. The virtualization software package achieves this through the use of running an interpreter or just-in-time compilation of the application before it runs on the computer architecture of choice. An example of this is the Java machine virtualization.

21.5   The Benefits of Virtualization

As we discussed in Sect. 21.2, virtualization technology has had a long history. This history has been driven by developers longing for a technology that will come with handsome benefits that will yield a high return on investment. Virtualization technology fits that technology. It is a technology that has brought to the computing community the following benefits [6].

21.5.1 Reduction of Server Sprawl

For a growing business with intensive computing requirement, the demand for servers cannot be underestimated. With business growth, there is a corresponding growth in the number of servers in the business. This can be costly not only in terms of physical storage but also in management, monitoring, and maintenance. One of the best solutions to this problem is server virtualization. Server virtualizations allow the company to scale up the business server infrastructure without purchasing additional pieces of hardware and requiring more space to store them and less technical staff to maintain and manage them.

21.5.2 Conservation of Energy

With less physical servers at the business data center, there is likely to be far less power consumption, thus reducing the overall company IT costs.

21.5.3 Reduced IT Management Costs

Again with a reduced physical server count on the premises and the ability to manage all the virtual infrastructure via one or two consoles, there is corresponding reduction in the IT management requirements and therefore reduced IT management costs.

21.5.4 Better Disaster Recovery Management

The process of preparing for any disaster through routine server backups and recovery is made simpler and faster by the server virtualization because the virtual infrastructure essentially consists of software and files. So backing up of these is a lot easier and far less time-consuming than doing it on several individual machines. Moreover, hardware failures like hard disk failures do not affect virtual machines in the same way they would a physical machine.

21.5.5 Software Development Testing and Verification

If there is any software that is being either developed in-house or outsourced that will run on the business infrastructure, it is easier and cheaper to test it on the virtual infrastructure and verify its compatibility with the infrastructure and all other business processes before deploying it on a live system.

21.5.6 Isolation of Legacy Applications

With virtualization, there is no longer the drive to get rid of any useful software package just because it requires a legacy infrastructure or it is not compatible with newer software versions. Virtualization enables the creation of an isolated server environment where all these legacies can still gainfully function without retarding and constraining the company business.

21.5.7 Cross-Platform Support

Lastly but of great value is the platform flexibility that virtualization brings about that makes it easy to run software packages that would normally otherwise be run on only one specific platform, for example, to run a Windows-based software on a virtual machine running on a Mac physical machine and the other way round.

21.5.8 Minimizing Hardware Costs

One thing that causes more pain in African system management is first acquisition and upgrading of both hardware and software and maintaining these resources in good working conditions. When it comes to maintaining network equipment, this further creates a constant problem. For large institutions and businesses, the costs of keeping all servers and other hardware in top working conditions are always higher than in other parts of the world. Virtualization eases this burden of purchasing more hardware each time a new system is put in place. Why because one server can be used in place of several servers.

21.5.9 Faster Server Provisioning

It is always difficult to have a good estimate of how many servers may be needed especially during those times when there is unseasonal demand. Virtualization gives an answer to being always ready to meet the challenges of unseasonal demands by using its elastic capacity to provide system provisioning and deployment at a moment's notice.

21.5.10 Better Load Balancing

Each virtualization server runs a load balancer—a software that effectively spreads out network traffic among multiple systems, thus avoiding horrible network jams. Network traffic is easily dispersed to multiple systems, virtual or physical by the load balancer.

21.5.11 Reduce the Data Center Footprint

In addition to saving more on energy with smaller energy bills, server consolidation with virtualization will also reduce the overall footprint of the entire data center because data is now on fewer servers, requiring less networking gear, hence a smaller number of racks needed [2].

21.5.12 Increase Uptime

Most server virtualization platforms now offer a number of advanced features such as live migration, storage migration, fault tolerance, high availability, and distributed resource scheduling. These technologies give the virtual machines the ability to quickly recover from unplanned outages. In addition, modern virtualization software has the ability to quickly and easily move a virtual machine from one server to another. There will be more and better capabilities with newer virtualization software [2].

21.5.13 Isolate Applications

Virtualization technology has removed the old requirement of a "one app/one server." This requirement used to cause physical server sprawl, and increased costs, and underutilized servers. This also cuts down on server waste by more fully utilizing the physical server resources and by provisioning virtual machines with the exact amount of CPU, memory, and storage resources that it needs [2].

21.5.14 Extend the Life of Older Applications

Let's be honest—you probably have old legacy applications still running in your environment. These applications probably fit into one or more of these categories: It doesn't run on a modern operating system, it may not run on newer hardware, your IT team is afraid to touch it, and chances are good that the person or company who created it is no longer around to update it.

By virtualizing and encapsulating a legacy application and its environment, we can extend its life, maintain uptime, and finally get rid of that old and costly machines such an application used to run on, thus extending its life [2].

There are of course many other benefits, but we cannot discuss them all here.

21.6   Virtualization Infrastructure Security

To understand virtualization security problems and appreciate the efforts being made to protect any virtualized infrastructure, one has to remember that virtualization technology is based on software. So all security problems and vulnerabilities ever been encountered in any software product have the potential to be in a virtualized infrastructure. This opens up a very broad area of attach for those interested in securing virtualized infrastructures. To narrow the focus, it is important and probably more feasible to concentrate on specific major components of a virtualization infrastructure like the hypervisor, hosts, communication pathways, and probably users. These major focus points can be secured to the best of known security protocols and best practices. More specifically, the focus should be put on the understanding that all virtual infrastructures are based on physical port gateways so if we tighten security on those entry points, we can go a long way in securing the virtual infrastructure. So our first points of interest are those points where certain types of network traffic go within the physical network. We focus on these first because network traffic into and out of the virtual infra-structure goes through these points. The restriction of traffic into and out of the virtual infrastructure through a few of these designated points also offers additional security of the virtual resources from unauthorized users from outside of the virtual infrastructure access gateway ring. Security within the virtual infrastructure is also enhanced by the growing inclusion and migration into the virtual infrastructure of security components that were traditionally hardware-based firewall, VPN, and others, thus ensuring that virtual infrastructure customers can themselves extend the enforcement of security and compliance requirements of their physical network into the virtual environments.

Perhaps the greatest threat presented by virtualization to computer networks is the fact that using one physical computer, one can access many virtual infrastructures, a feat that is not so feasible in the physical networks. According to Gruman quoting Simard [7], "graphics cards and network cards today are really miniature computers that see everything in all the VMs." They could be used as spies across all the VMs, letting a single PC spy on multiple networks.

21.6.1 Hypervisor Security

In Sect. 21.3.3 we defined a virtualization hypervisor as a virtual machine manager software program that allows multiple operating systems to share a single physical hardware host. Besides its traditional role of creating and managing VMs, the hypervisor is also responsible for the security between the virtual machines. However, the security provided to the virtual infrastructure is not enough. One has to remember again that the hypervisor is still a software package that is prone to all software threats and vulnerabilities as usual.

21.6.2 Securing Communications Between Desktop and Virtual Infrastructure

This is an old problem with probably similar security threats and vulnerabilities and the same protocols and best practices with communications between two or more physical network infrastructures. In this particular case, we are focusing on the pathways between the desktop and the virtual infrastructure. Securing these pathways is essential in order to prevent eavesdropping, data leakage, and man-in-the-middle attacks. Best practices today for securing these pathways include SSH, SSL, and IPsec [8].

21.6.3 Security of Communication Between Virtual Machines

In a virtual infrastructure, every host has a virtual switch. This virtual switching component manages and directs all inter-VM traffic that go via the host. This virtual switch creates a potential threat to all virtual machines connected to this host. Although this is the case, standard protocols and best practices enjoyed in physical network router infrastructure for network monitoring and intrusion detection can still be deployed and successfully used in the virtual switching environment.

21.6.4 Threats and Vulnerabilities Originating from a VM

We have been talking only about threats and vulnerabilities that are pumped upstream from the workstations, the hypervisor, and the host machines into the virtual machines. There is also a high potential for threats and vulnerabilities originating from the individual virtual machines and spreading downstream to the hypervisor, the hosts, and the desktops. The good news is that most of these problems can be handled by current best practices including protocols and vendor patches.

Exercises

1. What is a virtual switching element?
2. Why should a small business opt to virtualize its computing resources?
3. In recent years, there has been a phenomenal growth in the business use of computing virtualization technology. What are the biggest challenges you see to the technology in its future growth?
4. Although there has been tremendous growth in the virtualization of computing resources, there are still many skeptics of the technology. List their concerns. Suggest ways to overcome those concerns.
5. Discuss the differences between desktop and server virtualization. Which one of the two is most likely to benefit a small business?
6. Discuss the differences between virtualization and emulation by giving examples.

Advanced Exercises

1. Discuss the connection between virtualization and cloud computing.
2. In the chapter we discussed the pros of virtualization, discuss the cons of virtualization.
3. Compare and contrast the two most popular virtualization software packages.
4. From the knowledge you have acquired in this chapter about virtualization, discuss the future of virtualization as a business model.
5. Compare and contrast the security concerns in a virtual network infrastructure and a physical network infrastructure.
6. Virtual PC from Microsoft Corp. is a free virtualization software that can start you going for a free VMs on Windows XP or Windows 2003 server. Download Virtual PC and create a few VMs on your Windows.
7. Sun xVM VirtualBox is also a free virtualization software. And it is open source best for small networks. Download Sun xVM and set up a couple of VMs.
8. Try out the following:
   (a) Citrix Xen
   (b) Linux KVM
9. QEMU is a free emulation software that runs on a limited number of architectures including x86 and x86-64. Try QUEM.

References

1. VMware.com
2. Mullins R (2012) Virtualization tops CIO priorities in 2012: IDC savings from server consolidation will go to new IT innovations, IDC says, InformationWeek. January 11, 2012. http://www.informationweek.com/news/storage/virtualization/232400150
3. http://www.infobarrel.com/History_of_Virtualization#ixzz1l9armMAL
4. History of virtualization http://www.everythingvm.com/content/history-virtualization
5. Workstation Virtualization Featuring VMware Workstation 7.0/7.1. http://mv4t.com/Virtualization_VMware-Workstation.php
6. Wikipedia: http://en.wikipedia.org/wiki/Comparison_of_platform_virtual_machines)
7. Gruman G (2008) Virtualization's secret security threats: virtualization can be both a blessing and a curse, serving up improved security while at the same time hiding dangers. InfoWorld, March 13, 2008, http://www.infoworld.com/d/security-central/virtualizations-secret-security-threats-159?page=0,0
8. Shackleford D (2010) An introduction to virtualization security, SANS – Tuesday, 9 March 2010. http://www.net-security.org/article.php?id=1397&p=2
9. Wikipedia. http://en.wikipedia.org/wiki
10. Kartheek. Virtualization technology. http://katireddykartheek.blogspot.com/

Cloud Computing Technology and Security 22

22.1 Introduction

Cloud computing as a technology is difficult to define because it is evolving without a clear start point and no clear prediction of its future course. Even though this is the case, one can say that it is a continuous evolution of a computer network technology going beyond the client-server technology. It is a technology extending the realms of a computer network creating an environment that offers scalability, better utilization of hardware, on-demand applications and storage, and lower costs over the long run through the creation of virtual servers cloned from existing instances each offering near instantaneous increase in performance, allowing companies to react quickly and dynamically to emerging demands. The "cloud" or "cloud solution," as the technology is commonly referred to, can either be hosted on-site by the company or off-site such as Microsoft's SkyDrive and Samsung's S-Cloud.

The cloud technology seems to be in flax; hence it may be one of the foundations of the next generation of computing. Keep watching! It may be in that in the next few years, a grid of a few cloud infrastructure may provide computing for millions of users. This is a broader view of cloud computing. Cloud computing technology consists of and rests on a number of sound, fundamental, and proven technologies including virtualization, service-oriented architectures, distributed computing, grid computing, broadband networks, Software as a Service, browser as a platform, free and open-source software, autonomic systems, Web application frameworks, and service-level agreements [1]. We will discuss many of these technologies in depth in this chapter.

First, let us start by trying to give a broad but specific view of the technology, what it is composed of, and how it works. We will start by a more specific definition given by the National Institute of Standards and Technology (NIST). According to NIST [1], cloud computing is a model for enabling ubiquitous, convenient, on-demand network access to a shared pool of configurable computing resources like networks, servers, storage, applications, and services that can be rapidly provisioned and released with minimal management effort or service provider

© Springer International Publishing AG 2017
J.M. Kizza, *Guide to Computer Network Security*, Computer Communications and Networks, DOI 10.1007/978-3-319-55606-2_22

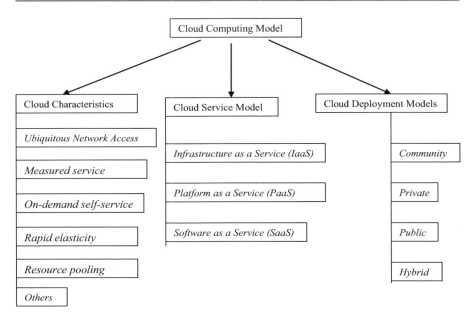

Fig. 22.1 Broad view of a cloud computing model

interaction. So for the remainder of this chapter, we are going to focus on this model of computing and discuss its benefits and security concerns. This computing model as shown in Fig. 22.1 is composed of a number of essential characteristics, three service models, and four deployment models.

22.2   Cloud Computing Infrastructure Characteristics

Traditionally data center computing models were mainly based on a client-server model architecture and design relying firmly on a three-tier architecture design that included access, distribution, and core switches connecting relatively few clients and meeting limited client needs compared to today's cloud service models. In most cases, each server was dedicated to either a single or limited applications and had IP addresses and media access control addresses. This static nature of the application environment worked well and lent itself to manual processes for server deployment or redeployment. According to both Jim Metzler and Steve Taylor of Network World [2], they primarily used a spanning tree protocol to avoid loops. But because of the dramatic advances in the previous years in virtualization technology, distributed computing, rapid improvements, and access to high-speed Internet have all dramatically changed the staid nature of the data center. Today's data center, providing cloud services, is but staid; it is bursting with activities and services with distinctly new characteristics that differentiate it from traditional cousin. For example, its services are now on demand, by the minute or the hour;

it is elastic, because users can have as much or as little of a service as they want at any given time; and the service is fully managed by the provider, that is, the consumer needs nothing but a personal computer and Internet access. Let us now briefly look at each one of these characteristics:

Ubiquitous Network Access

Like in the previous section on on-demand self-service, the advances and use of virtualization technology and the availability and access to high-speed Internet have also helped to change the nature of access to the computing services sought by customers and the increase in the number of services a customer can select from. With more choice also came the high specialization and quality of services that a customer can expert.

Measured Service

Because cloud services are flexible and on demand and are elastic, it is important, therefore, for these services to be metered. The concept of metered services allows customers to get what they want in the required amounts at the time they want the service. One of the most popular characteristics of cloud computing technology is measured or metered service for most, if not all, of the cloud services including storage, processing, bandwidth, and active user accounts. This pick-what-you-can-afford-to-pay-for principle based on metering results in an automatic control and optimization of cloud technology resource use based on the type of service, and these statistics can be reported as needed, thus providing transparency for both the provider and consumer.

On-Demand Self-Service

With the rapid and unprecedented use of virtualization technology and the availability and access to high-speed Internet, the traditional and all other models of acquisition of computing services that demanded perpetual ownership of software or computing hardware and long contracts with employees that helped to use the service and the need for redundancy and outsourcing of services all diminished and turned into a more flexible model where consumers of computing services were no longer restricted to having one of the rigid traditional models of either ownership, outsources, or boxed services. Now, a consumer is able to not only automatically provision any computing services and capabilities as needed but also to determine the time and how long to use the provisioned services.

Rapid Elasticity

Computing service elasticity means the ability to resize and dynamically scale the virtualized resources at hand such as servers, processors, operating systems, and others to meet the customer's on-demand needs. The provider must make sure that there are resources at hand that must meet elastic capabilities to ensure that end users' requests are continually and promptly met. Amazon's EC2 is a good example of a Web service interface that allows the customer to obtain and configure capacity with minimal effort.

Resource Pooling

Increased flexibility, access, and ease of use usually lead to high and varied demands of services from customers. To meet these new demands, providers usually respond by offering a variety of and polling of system resources and services. As noted in the NIST report, the provider's computing resources are pooled to serve multiple consumers using a multi-tenant model, with different physical and virtual resources dynamically assigned and reassigned according to consumer demand.

Others

There are other characteristics common to cloud computing beyond the five we have discussed above. Among these are:

- Massive scale —that the cloud offers the resources at a massive scale on demand.
- Virtualization—in fact this is the linchpin of the cloud technology. The cloud is possible because of virtualization of the fundamental functionalities of the physical machine.
- Free software—or near free software as needed from the cloud.
- Autonomic computing—in a sense that you scale computing resources at a time you want them on the fly.
- Multi-tenancy—because of cloud's massive-scale and easy access of those resources, cloud computing can accommodate a large number of users at a time.

22.3   Cloud Computing Service Models

Infrastructure as a Service (IaaS) The process of providing the customer with the ability and capability to manage and control, via a Web-based virtual server instance API, system resources such as starting, stopping, accessing, and configuring the virtual servers, operating systems, applications, storage, processing, and other fundamental computing resources is referred to as Infrastructure as a Service (IaaS). In doing all these, however, the consumer does not have access nor control of the underlying physical cloud infrastructure.

Platform as a Service (PaaS) This is a set of software and product development tools hosted on the provider's infrastructure and accessible to the customer via a Web-based virtual server instance API. Through this instance, the customer can create applications on the provider's platform over the Internet. Accessing the platform via the Web-based virtual instance API protects the resources because the customer cannot manage or control the underlying physical cloud infrastructure including network, servers, operating systems, or storage.

Software as a Service (SaaS)   Ever since the beginning of computing software, over the years, the key issue that has driven software development has been the issue of the cost of software. Trying to control the cost of software has resulted into software going through several models. The first model was the home-developed software where software users developed their own software based on their needs and they owned everything and were responsible for updates and management of it. The second model, the traditional software model, was based on packaged software where the customer acquired a more general-purpose software from the provider with a license held by the provider and the provider being responsible for the updates while the customer being responsible for its management. However, sometimes, software producers provide additional support services, the so-called premium support, usually for additional fees. Model three was the open-source model led by a free software movement starting around the late 1980s. By the late 1980s, free software turned into open source with the creation of the Open Source Initiative (OSI). Under the name "open-source" philosophy, some for-profit "free software" started to change the model from a purely free software to some form of payment for support of the updates of the software. The open-source software model transformed the cost of software remarkably. Model four consisted of software outsourcing.

The outsourcing model was in response to the escalating cost of software associated with software management. The component of software management in the overall cost of software was slowly surpassing all the costs of other components of software including licensing and updates. In model four, however, software is still licensed from the software company on a perpetual basis; support fees are still paid; however, the software producer takes on the responsibility of the management of that software.

Software model five is Software as a Service (SaaS). Under this model, there is a different way of purchasing. Under SaaS, there is the elimination of the upfront license fee. All software applications are retained by the provider, and the customer has access to all applications of choice from the provider via various client devices through either a thin client interface, such as a Web browser, a Web portal, or a virtual server instance API. The cloud user's responsibilities and actual activities in the use of and operations of the requested cloud services are limited to user-specific application configuration settings, leaving the management and control of the underlying cloud infrastructure including network, servers, operating systems, storage, or even individual application capabilities to the cloud provider.

Three Features of SaaS Applications
In particular, Software as a Service has the following features:

- Scalability—in that it can handle growing amounts of work in a graceful manner.
- Multi-tenancy—in that one application instance may be serving hundreds of companies. This is different from the client-server model from which the cloud computing model grows out of in which each customer is provisioned their own server running one instance.
- Metadata-driven configurability—customers can configure their application through metadata.

22.4   Cloud Computing Deployment Models

There are three cloud deployment models which are actually cloud types. These are the public, the private, and the hybrid models.

Public Clouds   The public clouds provide access to computing resources for the general public over the Internet allowing customers to self-provision resources typically via a Web service interface on a pay-as-you-go basis. One of the benefits of public clouds is to offer large pools of scalable resources on a temporary basis without the need for capital investment in infrastructure by the user.

Private Cloud   Unlike public clouds, private clouds give users immediate access to computing resources hosted within an organization's infrastructure and premises. Users, who are usually in some form of a relationship with the cloud owner, choose and scale collections of resources drawn from the private cloud, typically via Web service interface, just as with a public cloud. Also the private cloud is deployed within and uses the organization's existing resources and is always behind the organization's firewall subject to the organization's physical, electronic, and procedural security measures. In this case, therefore, private clouds offer a higher degree of security.

Hybrid Cloud   A hybrid cloud combines the computing resources of both the public and private clouds.

22.5   Virtualization and Cloud Computing

In this chapter, we are going to discuss virtualization in depth so here we are only defining the concept and showing its role in cloud computing. Virtualization is a process of creating something in effect and performance but not in reality—hence virtual. In computing, virtualization can be used on both software and hardware. In software, virtualization has been used in operating systems where the underlying operating systems create a number of virtual operating systems, not only clones of itself but even others, to run on the underlying machine and perform tasks at a higher performance level. In hardware, virtualization is being used to create new resources like servers, storage devices, and others. The potential power of virtualization in substantially increasing the performance of computing systems such as hardware and software through division of the underlying physical computing resources into many equally powerful virtual machines, thus scaling up the performance and creating elasticity of many computing system. With virtualization, computation and applications can be moved easily from physical to virtual machines. This transfer of computation and applications from one machine to another both physical and virtual is not truly a new idea. The client-server computing model is an example of this. But while in the client-server model, the applications running on the servers are managed by the service providers, in cloud computing model, computations and application may scale out to many other servers owned by the cloud provider. This is possible through the power of virtualization. Virtualization is a fundamental feature in cloud computing. Virtualization allows applications from different customers to run on different virtual machines, hence providing separation and protection.

22.6   Benefits of Cloud Computing

Cloud computing as a model of computing is very exciting and has tremendous benefits for those who dare to use it. It is not only exciting when you come to learn it, but it also has an array of benefits including but not limited to leveraging on a massive scale, homogeneity, virtualization, low-cost software, service orientation, and advanced security technologies.

Reduced Cost   For all cloud computing benefits to a company, perhaps the biggest benefit is cost savings. Whether it is a small-, medium-, or large-scale manufacturing business, there are essential cost benefits in using a cloud model for most of the company's computing needs. The biggest issue here is the fact that cloud computing is operated remotely off company premises except a few devices needed for accessing the cloud resources via a Web portal. This means that company personnel can do the same amount of work on fewer computers by having higher utilization, save on not housing data centers on premises, save on personnel for running the data center, and save on expenses that would normally be essential for running a data center on the premises. There is documentary evidence to support these views from industry experts. In the words of Greg Papadopoulos, CTO, Sun Microsystems [3], hosting providers bring "brutal efficiency" for utilization, power, security, service levels, and idea-to-deploy time. George Reese, founder of Valtira and enStratus, states that using cloud infrastructures saves 18–29% before considering that you no longer need to buy for peak capacity [3]. And according to Dan Farber, editor in chief, CNET News, we are at the beginning of the age of planetary computing where billions of people will be wirelessly interconnected, and the only way to achieve that kind of massive-scale usage is by massive-scale, *brutally efficient* cloud-based infrastructure [3]. And finally there are savings on power consumption since there are few computers on premises. Currently, servers are used at only 15% of their capacity in many companies, and 80% of enterprise software expenditure is on installation and maintenance of software. Use of cloud applications can reduce these costs from 50 to 90% [3].

Automatic Updates Our economy is now an online economy because most of, if not all, businesses are now online and depend on software applications for day-to-day services. Software is continuously changing, and as business functionalities change, software need to be changed or updated. The cost of software updates and management has always been on the rise, usually surpassing the cost of new software. For companies to stay competitive and in many cases afloat, they must be consistently updating and changing software. The business of software updates and software management and licensing is a big drain on company resources. So having automatic updates and management from the cloud provider can be a great relief to any company. But updates are not limited to only software. Also not worrying about hardware updates is cost effective for companies.

Green Benefits of Cloud Computing There has been a vigorous debate about cloud computing energy consumption, and this debate is continuing, pitting those claiming that cloud computing is gobbling up resources as large cloud and social networking sites need daily megawatts of power to feed insatiable computing needs and those who claim that the computing model is indeed saving power from millions of servers left idling daily and consuming more power. We will discuss this more in the coming sections. For now, we think that there are indeed savings in power consumption by cloud computing.

Remote Access With a Web portal access to the cloud, company employees may be able to work while they are on the road, at home, or in the office. This is of great benefit to the company so that there is no downtime because somebody is not in the office.

Disaster Relief Many companies live in constant fear of disasters occurring when they have company vital data stored on premises. No one likes to be a victim of large-scale catastrophes such as devastating hurricanes, earthquakes, fires, and of course terrorist attacks. Such misfortunes can create havoc to the companies' vital data and disrupt operations even if there were limited physical damage. Additionally, there are smaller disasters like computer crashes and power outages that can also wreak havoc on a company vital data. While this is possible, there are many companies, especially small ones, that may not even have any disaster recovery plan, and some who have it may not be able to execute it effectively. This fear can be overcome with investments in cloud technology. Company's vital backup data can be safely stored on secure data centers on the cloud instead of the company's server room.

Self-Service Provisioning Cloud computing allows users to deploy their own virtual sets of computing resources like servers, network, storage, and others, as needed without the delays, competency, and complications typically involved in physical resource acquisition, installation, and management. The cloud owners, irrespective of their physical location, not only can provide all the computing resources your organization needs but also have the necessary capacity needed to monitor, manage, and respond to the organization's daily and hour-by-hour infrastructure, software, and platform requirements.

Scalability Because of the minute-by-minute monitoring capability of cloud computing of an organization's computing needs and the ability to increase or reduce the required resources as the demand increases or decreases, cloud computing offers the best infrastructure, platform, and software scalability that cannot be matched in any owned computing facility.

Reliability and Fault Tolerance Because the cloud provider, with qualified professionals and experience, monitors the computing requirements of a client company and can easily scale to demand, cloud computing offers a high degree of reliability and fault tolerance.

Ease of Use To attract more customers, cloud providers must make the user interface as friendly as possible so that customers can scale into the cloud with least efforts.

Skills and Proficiency Some of the most sought-after assets from a cloud provider are profaneness, professionalism, and a vast skills set provided to the customers. Companies, especially small ones, would pay a high price to get an employee with the skills set, efficiency, proficiency, and experience found with cloud center staff.

Response Time Depending on the bandwidth at the company Web portal, cloud computing services normally have speed because the computing resources provided are modern and powerful to be able to accommodate large number of users.

Mobility Because of Web portal interface to the cloud, cloud computing essentially is a mobile computing platform, allowing the users to access their applications.

Increased Storage Storage is cloud computing's main function. Because of this, it is cheap and readily scalable to need.

Others Benefits Other benefits beyond those we discussed above include providing a high quality of service (QoS); providing a high-quality, well-defined, and stable industry standard API; and on-demand availability of computing resources based on "at hand" financial constraints.

Security We are going to discuss this more in the coming section, but cloud computing, because of its individual virtual machines created per use, has already a built-in security provision. In addition to these built-in provisions due to virtualization, the cloud model also offers a strong authentication regime at the browser interface gateway, a security mechanism that is individually and quickly set up and torn down as needed, and a strong validation and verification scheme that is expensive to deploy at an individual client-server model.

22.7   Cloud Computing, Power Consumption and Environmental Issues

As we briefly discussed in the last section, there is a heated debate ongoing pitting those claiming that cloud computing is gobbling up resources as large cloud and social networking sites need daily megawatts of power to feed insatiable computing needs and those who claim that the computing model is indeed saving power from millions of servers left idling daily and consuming more power. Let us not interject ourselves into the debate.

In the paper "Make IT Green: Cloud Computing and its Contribution to Climate Change" [4], Greenpeace called attention to the growing, power-hungry data center footprint, citing estimates that cloud computer sites could consume up to 622.6 billion kWh (kilowatts per hour) of power and also that the quintessential cloud computing devices like the smartphones including Apple iPad and the Androids offering online access to the cloud and social networks can contribute to a much larger carbon footprint of the information technology sector than previously estimated. Greenpeace has supporters in their camp, and these supporters are professionals adding weight to the debate. For example, in his paper "The Environmental Cost of Cloud Computing: Assessing Power Use and Impacts," Jonathan Koomey [5], professor of civil and environmental engineering at Stanford University, claims that by 2009, the cloud was responsible for 1–2% of the world's electricity use [6]. All major cloud providers including the Google, Facebook, Amazon, Yahoo, Microsoft, Apple, and others are involved in one way or the other in dealing with power producers to provide them with enormous amounts of power to run the data centers. For example, in 2010, Facebook signed an agreement with PacifiCorp, a utility provider in the northwest, to provide it with power for its Oregon data center. This did not go well with Greenpeace because PacifiCorp gets most of its energy from coal-fired power stations, the known largest source of greenhouse gas emissions in the United States.

In their climate projection for year 2020 report titled "SMART 2020: Enabling the Low Carbon Economy in the Information Age" [5], the Climate Group and the Global e-Sustainability Initiative (GeSI) noted the growth of 9.5% a year in ICT electricity consumption and GHG emissions by 2020. Projections like these are adding fuel to the debate about cloud computing technology and the environment [7].

The other side of the debate is no less vigorous. They are holding the view that because cloud computing technology makes companies share pooled resources and facilities, this is indeed helping to contain the expected degradation of the environment resulting from the projected, relentless, and viral growth of information technology device use as projected in the Climate Group and the Global e-Sustainability Initiative (GeSI) 2007 report titled "SMART 2020: Enabling the Low Carbon Economy in the Information Age" [5]. In that report it is projected that:

- PC ownership will quadruple between 2007 and 2020 to 4 billion devices, and emissions will double over the same period, with laptops overtaking desktops as the main source of global ICT emissions expected to reach 22% mark.
- Mobile phone ownership will almost double to nearly 5 billion accounts by 2020, but emissions will only grow by 4%.
- Broadband uptake will treble to almost 900 million accounts over the same period, with emissions doubling over the entire telecom infrastructure.

In the same report, the group makes a compelling case for ICT's significant potential to deliver climate and energy solutions, estimating that ICTs could cut 7.8 GtCO2 of global greenhouse gas emissions by 2020, a 15% reduction. We concur with this report in saying that new innovations in cloud computing technologies together with increased awareness and use of renewable energy can make cloud technology a greener technology and make it use less power.

22.8   Cloud Computing Security, Reliability, Availability, and Compliance Issues

The cloud computing model as we know it today did not start overnight. The process has taken years moving through seven software models beginning with in-house software, licensed software normally referred to as the traditional model, open source, outsourcing, hybrid, Software as a Service, and finally the Internet model, the last two being part of the cloud computing model. When one carefully examines the cloud servicing model, one does not fail to notice the backward compatibilities or the carryovers of many of the attributes that characterized software through all the models. While this brings the benefits of each one of those software models, also many, if not all, of the software complexity and security issues in those models were carried over into the cloud computing model. Because of this, our first thought was to discuss the security issues in the cloud computing model through the prism of these models. It is tempting, but we are going to follow a different path while keeping the reader rooted into the different software models. Security is and continues to be a top issue in the cloud computing model. The other three related issues are performance, compliance, and availability. We will discuss all four in this section, but since security is the number one issue, we will address it first.

We want to start the discussion of cloud computing security by paraphrasing Greg Papadopoulos, CTO of Sun Microsystems, who said that cloud users normally "trust" cloud service providers with their data like they trust banks with their money. This means that they expect the three issues of security, availability, and performance to be of little concern to them as they are with their banks [3]. To give a fair discussion of the security of anything, one has to focus on two things that are the actors and their roles in the process you are interested in securing and the application or data in play. The application or data is thought of in relation to the state it is in at anyone's time. For example, the states for both data and application can be are either in motion between the remote hosts and the service provider's hypervisors and servers or in the static state when it is stored at remote hosts, usually on the customer's premises or in the service provider's servers. The kind of security needed in either one of these two states is different.

22.8.1 Cloud Computing Actors, Their Roles, and Responsibilities

In the cloud computing model, the main players are the cloud provider, the customer who is the data owner and who seeks cloud services from the cloud provider, and the user who may or may not be the owner of the data stored in the cloud. The first two players have delegated responsibilities to all who work on their behalf. To fully understand these delegated responsibilities assigned to each one of these, we need to look at first the marginal security concerns resulting from the peripheral system access control that always result in the easiest breach of security for any system, usually through compromising user accounts via weak passwords. This problem is broad affecting both local and outsourced cloud solutions. Addressing this and all other administrative and user security concern requires companies offering and using cloud solutions to design an access control regime that covers and requires every user, local or remote, to abide by these access policies including the peripheral ones like the generation and storage of user passwords. Additionally, employees need to be informed of the danger of picking easy passwords and to understand the danger of writing a password down or divulging a password to anyone. Access control administration is so important that cloud providers spend large amounts of resources to design a strong assess control regimes. For example, let us look at the access control of the three major cloud providers, namely, Amazon Web Services (AWS), Microsoft Windows Azure, and Rackspace.

Amazon Web Services

With Amazon Web Services (AWS) EC2 and S3, one can remotely self-provision what they want seamlessly. This kind of easiness, while great, created a set of security problems unless there is a strong access control regime in place. For Amazon, the solution is through use of Amazon Identity and Access Management (IAM). This allows the account owner to create multiple accounts for other authorized users on a single amazon account. Then as usual, each user is assigned permissions on the main account, accessible via user ID and passwords based on the user's role and responsibility in the customer's company. Based on the traditional access control, fine-grained security can be attained for all service users.

Microsoft Windows Azure

Microsoft Azure on the other hand has several security modules including [8]:

- Azure Security Center—to prevent, detect, and respond to threats with increased visibility and control over the security of your Azure resources. This is done by:
  - Understand the cloud security state—Letting the user to get a central view of the security state of all Azure resources. This quickly lets the user make sure that all security controls are in place, and the user can quickly identify any resources needing attention.
  - Take control of cloud security—Using a security policy-driven monitoring of all security configurations to guide resource owners through the process of implementing their required controls.
  - Easily deploy integrated cloud security solutions—Rapidly enable a range of security solutions from Microsoft and its partners, including industry-leading firewalls and antimalware. Use streamlined provisioning to easily deploy security solutions.
  - Detect threats and respond fast—Staying ahead of current and emerging cloud threats requires an integrated, analytics-driven approach. By combining Microsoft global threat intelligence and expertise with insights into cloud security-related events across a customer Azure deployments, Azure Security Center helps the customer detect actual threats early, and it reduces false positives. Cloud security alerts offer insights into the attack campaign, including related events and impacted resources, and suggest ways to remediate issues and recover quickly.

Rackspace

In Rackspace, client authentication is done by the Cloud Authentication Service, also known as *Auth*. Auth allows each client needing authentication to obtain an authentication *token* and a list of regional service endpoints to the various services available in the cloud. Users must authenticate their credentials, but once authenticated they can create/delete containers and objects within that account. Since the Cloud Files system is designed to be used by many different customers, each user account is the user's portion of the Cloud Files system. Each client authentication is provided via a ReST (see below) interface which requires two headers, *X-Auth-User* and *X-Auth-Key* or *X-Auth-Token* with values for the *username* and *API access key*, respectively. Clients obtain this *token*, along with the Cloud Servers API URL, by first using the Rackspace Cloud Authentication Service [17].

Request: ReST
To authenticate, the client provides the following in x-headers:

- Username as *X-Auth-User x-header*
- API access key (from the Rackspace Cloud Control Panel in client Account API Access section) as *X-Auth-Key*

Response
Upon successful authentication, an HTTP status 204 is returned with the X-Storage-Url, X-CDN-Management-Url, and X-Auth-Token headers. Any 2xx response is a good response. For example, a 202 response means the request has been accepted. Also, additional x-headers may be returned. These additional headers are related to other Rackspace services and can be ignored. An HTTP status of 401 (unauthorized) is returned upon authentication failure. All subsequent container/object operations against Cloud Files should be made against the URI specified in X-Storage-Url or X-CDN-Management-Url and must include the X-Auth-Token header [17].

After these exchanges, the client is ready to use the cloud.

22.8.2 Security of Data and Applications in the Cloud

Let us next look at the security of data and applications in the cloud. To do this we need to focus first on the security and role of the hypervisor and then the servers on which user services are based. A hypervisor also called *virtual machine manager (VMM)* is one of the many hardware virtualization techniques allowing multiple operating systems, termed *guests*, to run concurrently on a host computer. The hypervisor is piggybacked on a kernel program, itself running on the core physical machine running as the physical server. The hypervisor presents to the guest operating systems a virtual operating platform and manages the execution of the guest operating systems. Multiple instances of a variety of operating systems may share the virtualized hardware resources. Hypervisors are very commonly installed on server hardware, with the function of running guest operating systems, that themselves act as servers. The security of the hypervisor therefore involves the security of the underlying kernel program and the underlying physical machine, the physical server, and the individual virtual operating systems and their anchoring virtual machines.

Hypervisor Security
The key feature of the cloud computing model is the concept of virtualization. We covered virtualization in the previous chapter. It is this virtualization that gives the cloud the near instant scalability and versatility that makes cloud computing so desirable a computing solution by companies and individuals. The core of virtualization in cloud computing is the easy process of minting of virtual machines on demand by the hypervisor. The hypervisor allocates resources to each virtual machine it creates, and it also handles the deletion of virtual machines. Since each virtual machine is initiated by an instance, the hypervisor is a bidirectional conduit into and out of every virtual machine. The compromise of either, therefore, creates a danger to the other. However, most hypervisors are constructed in such a way that

there is a separation between the environments of the sandboxes (the virtual machines) and the hypervisor. There is just one hypervisor, which services all virtual sandboxes, each running a guest operating system. The hypervisor runs as part of the native monolithic operating system, side by side with the device drivers, file system, and network stack, completely in kernel space. So, one of the biggest security concerns with a hypervisor is the establishment of covert channels by an intruder—"hyperjacking." If an intruder succeeds in establishing a covert channel, either by modifying file contents or through timing, it is possible for information to leak from one virtual machine instance to another [9].

Also since the hypervisor is the controller of all virtual machines, it, therefore, becomes the single point of failure in any cloud computing architecture. That is, if an intruder compromises a hypervisor, then the intruder has control of all the virtual machines the hypervisor has allocated. This means that the intruder can even create or destroy virtual machines at will. For example, the intruder can perform a denial-of-service attack, by bringing down the hypervisor which then brings down all virtual machines running on top of the hypervisor.

The processes of securing virtual hosts differ greatly from processes used to secure their physical counterparts. Securing virtual entities like a hypervisor, virtual operating systems, and corresponding virtual machines is more complex. To understand hypervisor security, let us first discuss the environment in which the hypervisor works. Recall that a hypervisor is part of a virtual computer system (VCS). In his 1973 thesis in the Division of Engineering and Applied Physics, Harvard University, Robert P. Goldberg defines a virtual computer system as a hardware-software duplicate of a real existing computer system in which a statistically dominant subset of the virtual processor's instructions execute directly on the host processor in native mode. He also gives two parts to this definition, the environment and implementation [10].

Environment   The virtual computer system must simulate a real existing computer system. Programs and operating systems which run on the real system must run on the virtual system with identical effect. Since the simulated machine may run at a different speed from the real one, timing-dependent processor and I/O code may not perform exactly as intended.

Implementation   Most instructions being executed must be processed directly by the host CPU without recourse to instruction by instruction interpretation. This guarantees that the virtual machine will run on the host with relative efficiency. It also compels the virtual machine to be similar or identical to the host and forbids tampering with the control store to add an entirely new order code.

In the environment of virtual machines, a hypervisor is needed to control all the sandboxes (virtual machines). Generally in practice, the underlying architecture of the hypervisor determines if there is a desired true separation between the sandboxes or not. Robert P. Goldberg classifies two types of hypervisor [11]:

Fig. 22.2 Type-1 hypervisor

Type-1 (Or Native, Bare Metal) Hypervisors run directly on the host's hardware to control the hardware and to manage guest operating systems. See Fig. 22.2. All guest operating systems then run on a level above the hypervisor. This model represents the classic implementation of virtual machine architectures. Modern hypervisors based on this model include Citrix XenServer, VMware ESX/ESXi, and Microsoft Hyper-V. The most common commercial hypervisors are based on a monolithic architecture below.

The underlying hypervisor services all virtual sandboxes, each running a guest operating system. The hypervisor runs as part of the native monolithic operating system, side by side with the device drivers, file system, and network stack, completely in kernel space.

Type-2 (Or Hosted) Hypervisors run just above a host operating system kernel such as Linux, Windows, and others as in Fig. 22.3. With the hypervisor layer as a distinct second software level, guest operating systems run at the third level above the hardware. The host operating system has direct access to the server's hardware like host CPU, memory, and I/O devices and is responsible for managing basic OS services. The hypervisor creates virtual machine environments and coordinates calls to CPU, memory, disk, network, and other resources through the host OS. Modern hypervisors based on this model include KVM and VirtualBox.

The discussion so far highlights the central role of the hypervisor in the operations of virtual machine systems, and it points to its central role in securing all virtual machine systems. Before we look at what can be done to secure it, let us ask ourselves what security breaches can happen to the hypervisor. There are

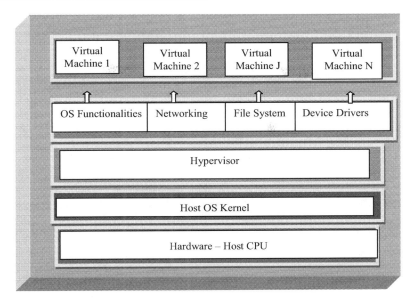

Fig. 22.3 Type-2 hypervisor

several of these security breaches most severe involving self-installation of both malware and rootkits masquerading as they are the hypervisor.

Hacking the Hypervisor

In his blog "Yes, Hypervisors Are Vulnerable," Neil MacDonald, vice president and a Gartner Fellow [12], observes the following about hypervisor and the vulnerabilities associated with it:

- The virtualization platform (hypervisor/VMM) is a software written by human beings and will contain vulnerabilities. Microsoft, VMware, Citrix, and others, all of them will and have had vulnerabilities.
- Some of these vulnerabilities will result in a breakdown in isolation that the virtualization platform was supposed to enforce.
- Bad guys will target this layer with attacks. The benefits of a compromise of this layer are simply too great.
- While there have been a few disclosed attacks, it is just a matter of time before a widespread publicly disclosed enterprise breach is tied back to a hypervisor vulnerability.

As we observed in Chap. 21, there has been a growing increase in the virtualization vulnerabilities. Published papers have so far shown that the security of hypervisors can be undermined. As far back as 2006, Samuel T. King, Peter M. Chen, Yi-Min Wang, Chad Verbowski, Helen J. Wang, and Jacob R. Lorch demonstrated in their paper, "SubVirt: Implementing malware with virtual machines," the use of type of malware, which they called a virtual machine-based rootkit (VMBR), installing a virtual machine monitor underneath an existing operating system and hoisting the original operating system into a virtual machine [14].

In fact in this study, the authors demonstrated a malware program that started to act as its own hypervisor under Windows. According to the IBM X-Force *2010 Mid-Year Trend and Risk Report*, which disclosed a 10-year virtualization vulnerability trend from 1999 through 2009, there were 373 reported vulnerabilities affecting virtualization solutions during the period with a steady growth trend starting around 2002 and peaking in 2008 to 100 and falling off by 12 percent in 2009. What do we learn from all these? We learn that the hypervisor layer of virtualization, playing the core role in the virtualization process, is very vulnerable to hacking because this is the weakest link in the data center. Therefore, attacks on hypervisor are on the rise. Data from the IBM X-Force *2010 Mid-Year Trend and Risk Report* show that every year since 2005, vulnerabilities in virtualization server products, the hypervisors, have overshadowed those in workstation products, an indication of the hackers' interest in the hypervisors. The report further shows that 35% of the server virtualization vulnerabilities are vulnerabilities that allow an attacker to "escape" from a guest virtual machine to affect other virtual machines or the hypervisor itself. Because, as Fig. 22.2 shows, the hypervisor in *type-1* environment is granted CPU privilege to access all system I/O resources and memory, this makes it a security threat to the whole cloud infrastructure. Just one vulnerability in the hypervisor itself could result in a hacker gaining access to the entire system, including all the guest operating systems. Because malware runs below the entire operating system, there is a growing threat of hackers using malware and rootkits to install themselves as a hypervisor below the operating system thus making them more difficult to detect. Once installed and operating below the main operating system, there is evidence that malware can intercept any operations of the operating system without the antivirus software detecting them, although there is a debate with some scholars disputing this. Since 2009, there have been efforts in producing kernel-mode anti-rootkit products, such as HooSafe from Microsoft and North Carolina State University and Rackspace's NoVirusThanks Anti-Rootkit [14].

In *type-2* hypervisor configuration (Fig. 22.3), the microkernel architecture is designed specifically to guarantee a robust separation of application partitions. This architecture puts the complex virtualization program in user space; thus every guest operating system uses its own instantiation of the virtualization program. In this case, therefore, there is a complete separation between the sandboxes (virtual boxes), thus reducing the risks exhibited in type-1 hypervisors.

An attack, therefore, on *type-2* hypervisors can bring down one virtual box, not more, and cannot bring down the cloud infrastructure as is the case in *type-1* hypervisors.

According to Samuel T. King et al., overall, virtual machine-based rootkits are hard to detect and remove because their state cannot be accessed by software running in the target system. Further, VMBRs support general-purpose malicious services by allowing such services to run in a separate operating system that is protected from the target system [13].

Securing Load Balancers

For every hypervisor, there is a load balancer, used to route traffic to different virtual machines to help spread traffic evenly across available machines. Load balancers in a hypervisor play a vital role of ensuring a fair distribution of available load to all virtual machines especially during high traffic and ensuring the full utilization of the cloud infrastructure. Elastic load balancers play a central in the cloud infrastructure along the following lines [14]:

- It listens to all traffic destined for the internal network and distributes incoming traffic across the cloud infrastructure.
- Automatically scales its request-handling capacity in response to incoming application traffic.
- It creates and manages security groups associated with each instance and provides additional networking and security options if and when needed.
- It can detect the health of the virtual machines, and if it detects unhealthy load-balanced virtual machine, it stops routing traffic to it and spreads the load across the remaining healthy virtual machines.
- It supports the ability to stick user sessions to specific virtual machines.
- It supports SSL termination at the load balancer, including offloading SSL decryption from application virtual machines, centralized management of SSL certificates, and encryption to backend virtual machines with optional public key authentication.
- It supports use of both the Internet Protocol version 4 and 6 (IPv4 and IPv6).

Due to the load balancer's ability to listen and process all traffic that is destined to the internal network of the cloud, it is a prime target for attackers. If a load balancer was compromised, an attacker could listen to traffic and may compromise secure traffic destined to outside the network. Additionally, if the load balancer is compromised along with a virtual machine, traffic could be directed to an unsecure internal server where further attacks are launched [15]. Because the load balancer is a single point in the cloud infrastructure, it is very vulnerable to denial-of-service attacks, if it is compromised. This can lead to cloud activity disruption.

What is the best way to secure the load balancer from attacks then? A load balancer is normally secured through proper configuration and monitoring of the balancer's logs. This is achieved through restriction of access to administration of the balancer itself by configuring the load balancer to only accept administrative access over a specific administrative network. This administrative network should be connected to the administrative only network. Limiting access over the administrator network greatly limits the number of users with access to the load balancer [16].

Virtual Operating System Security

Besides the hypervisor, the virtualization system also hosts virtual servers each running either a guest operating system or another hypervisor. And on the peripheral of the virtual machine system are the consoles and hosts. Through each one of these resources, the virtual machine system can be susceptible to security vulnerabilities. Let us briefly look at these since they were covered in more detail in the previous chapter.

Host Security

Through hosts like workstations, user gains access to the virtual machine system, hence to the cloud. Two problems are encountered here:

- Escape-to-hypervisor vulnerabilities—that allow intruders to penetrate the virtual machine from the host
- Escape-to-host vulnerabilities—that allow vulnerabilities in the virtual machine to move to the hosts

Guest Machines

Guest machines running guest operating system can also pose a security problem to the cloud. However, as we saw in the previous chapter, vulnerabilities in the guest virtual machines are confined to that machine, and they rarely affect other machines in the system.

22.8.3 Security of Data in Transition: Cloud Security Best Practices

With the vulnerabilities in the cloud we have discussed above, what is the best way to protect the user of the cloud? For a cloud customer, the key areas of concerns are virtualization technology security vulnerabilities that may be encountered during the use of the cloud that may affect the customer and unauthorized access to customer data and other resources stored or implemented in the cloud, whether the cloud provider uses strong enough encryption to safeguard customer data, secure access, and use of cloud applications and secure cloud management. Let us next discuss the best practices that try to address some of these concerns.

22.8.4 Service-Level Agreements (SLAs)

A service-level agreement (SLA) is a service contract between the provider of a service and the client defining the level of expected service in terms of security, availability, and performance. The cloud service-level agreements (SLAs) are a series of service contracts between cloud providers and clients to define the level(s) of service based on the types of services sought by the client because the effectiveness of these contracts depends on how well maximized and tailored these services are to the particular needs of each client. For example, the security of services sought by a client may depend on the tier of cloud offering the client is using. To see how involved and intricate these documents can be, take an example of security concerns. For IaaS, the security responsibilities are shared with the provider responsible for physical, environmental, and virtualization security, while the client takes care of the security in applications, operating system, and others. Now if we change the service model to SaaS, the provider is responsible for almost every aspect of security.

22.8.5 Data Encryption

The moment data leaves your endpoint Web-cloud access point in your location, it travels via a public network and stored in shared environment—the cloud. In a public or in a shared environment, data can be intercepted and infiltrated by intruders from within and outside the cloud and during transmission from man-in-the-middle cryptanalysis. To prevent these kinds of breaches, strong encryptions and authentications regimes are needed. Encryption to safeguard any kinds of data breaches required a strong access control and authentication to all Web-based cloud resource interface, encryption of all administrative access to the cloud hypervisor, and all access to applications and data.

22.8.6 Web Access Point Security

Most cloud access instances are Web based. Most security breaches to stored data originated from Web applications. There is therefore a need for strong security controls in the cloud APIs.

22.8.7 Compliance

Because most clouds are either public, community, or hybrids and clients using these clouds usually are in businesses that deal with personal data, cloud providers must observe a number of compliance regulations including FISMA, HIPAA, SOX, and SAS 70 II for clouds based in the United States and the Data Protection Directive for clouds based in the EU. In addition, providers accepting payments using credit card must comply with PCI DSS. Let us briefly look at these [16]:

The *Federal Information Security Management Act of 2002 (FISMA)* is a United States federal law enacted in 2002 as Title III of the E-Government Act of 2002 (Pub.L. 107–347, 116 Stat. 2899). The act recognized the importance of information security to the economic and national security interests of the United States. It requires federal agencies to develop, document, and implement an agency-wide program to provide information security for the information and information systems that support the operations and assets of the agency, including those provided or managed by another agency, contractor, or other source. So cloud providers intending to contract with or affiliate with any organization that provides services to the U.S. Federal government must adhere to FISMA.

The *Health Insurance Portability and Accountability Act of 1996* (HIPAA; Pub.L. 104–191, 110 Stat. 1936, enacted August 21, 1996) was enacted by the United States Congress 1996. It has two parts: Title I which protects health insurance coverage for workers and their families when they change or lose their jobs and Title II, also known as the Administrative Simplification (AS) provisions, requires the establishment of national standards for electronic health care transactions and national identifiers for providers, health insurance plans, and employers. The AS also address the security and privacy of health data. Cloud providers must abide by this provision.

Exercises

1. What is cloud computing?
2. Discuss the software models predating cloud computing.
3. Discuss the major models in cloud computing.
4. What are the benefits of cloud computing over Software as a Service (SaaS)?
5. Define and discuss Software as a Service (SaaS), Infrastructure as a Service (IaaS), and storage as a service.
6. Describe the seven business models of software.
7. Discuss the services that make up/describe cloud computing.
8. Discuss the differences between clouding computing and virtualization.
9. Discuss four business applications best suited for cloud computing.
10. To determine what business applications should go on the cloud, you need to estimate the return on investment for that application. What can you consider when computing ROI?
11. List and discuss three characteristics an application must have in order to be considered suited for the cloud.
12. What is MapReduce? Describe the structure and working of MapReduce.
13. What is Hadoop? Describe the three subprojects of Hadoop.
14. The structure and working of MapReduce are as follows:
    Structure
    – Map—for each input (Ki,Vi) produce zero or more output pairs (Km,Vm).
    – Combine—optional intermediate aggregation (less M->R data transfer).
    – Reduce—for input pair (Km, list(V1,V2... Vn)) produce zero or more output pairs (Kr,Vr).

Describe the functions in the dataflow of MapReduce that you need to write to make it usable.

Advanced Exercises
Cloud Computing Semester Projects

Research Guidelines
For these projects you can work either in groups or individually. Study the problems and use MapReduce/Hadoop, and try to find meaningful answers to the chosen problem through research and development.

Write a 20-double-spaced-page paper summarizing your research. The paper should be at a publishable level, meaning that it must have an abstract and must follow either IEEE or ACM scientific presentation guidelines. The paper must also be well referenced.

1. *Text Mining and Sentiment Analysis for Online Forums, Hotspot Detection, and Forecast*

Text sentiment analysis, or emotional polarity computation as it is commonly referred to also, has become a flourishing frontier in the text mining community. The research involves a careful study of online forums for hotspots, to detect and forecast options forming in these hotspots using sentiment analysis and text mining techniques and relevant tools.

Using MapReduce or Hadoop, split the chosen text into subtexts and analyze the emotional polarity of each subtext and to obtain a value for each subtext. Then try to group together the subtext to obtain value for the original text. Do this to as many texts as you can in the corpus or forum.

Then, use these analyzed pieces and a good and unsupervised text mining approach to group the forums into various clusters, with the center of each representing a hotspot forum within the current time span. The data sets used in your research should come from all social networks and the open Web.

Comment on whether your results demonstrate a good way of forecasting and whether it achieves highly consistent results. List ten top hotspot forums you found.

2. *Unlock the Power of the Mobile Cloud Through Development of New Powerful Cloud Mobile Hybrid Application Development*

Rapid advances and marriage between computing and telecommunication technologies have created an ubiquitous landscape of powerful smart mobile computing devices capable of and are progressively being used in a pay-as-you-go computing model, now called mobile cloud computing. This model of cloud computing is increasingly using a growing amount of big data, particularly in data-intensive domains. Define and develop a new class of cloud mobile hybrid (CMH) applications, collective applications that have a cloud-based back end and a mobile device front end that are capable of advancing and unlocking the huge potential of the mobile cloud landscape and its capabilities.

3. *Protect the Mobile Cloud Through Development of Applications*

Rapid advances and marriage between computing and telecommunication technologies have created an ubiquitous landscape of powerful smart mobile computing devices capable of and are progressively being used in a pay-as-you-go computing model, now called mobile cloud computing. This new model of cloud computing and the resulting mobile cloud landscape is currently highly unsecure from rogue application to unscrupulous users; it is a Wild West in there. Define and develop a new class of secure cloud mobile hybrid (CMH) applications.

4. *Opinion and Public Sentiment Setters and Leaders*

Rapid advances and marriage between computing and telecommunication technologies have created an ubiquitous landscape of powerful smart mobile computing devices capable of and are progressively being used as Internet-ready devices capable of and powerful enough to perform many of the Internet functionalities that are currently confined within the spheres of their big brothers, the PC and laptops. This hybrid new landscape is increasingly being used as trend and public opinion setters, thanks to Twitter, Facebook, and the like. Most opinion and trendsetting takes plan in social network groups or clusters. Use modern tools dealing with big data and text mining techniques to develop an analysis that identifies social groups for leaders, followers, and special hot topics and trends within the social networks. You can use your findings to comment on public options based on demographics of society.

5. *Real-Time Cloud Notifier*

Cloud Notify is a Web application that takes advantage of the cloud to provide management and notification services to users. Using Cloud Notify, users can create one or more topics and assign subscribers to those topics. Users can then send notifications either via text message or e-mail to the subscribers. The system should be able to bounce and inform the management console who is off and who has seen the message and the locations of those who have not seen the message. The system should be able to re-notify—two more times in a given period of time—and send a warning message to the management console.

References

1. Mell P, Grance T. The NIST definition of cloud computing, NIST special publication 800–145. http://nvlpubs.nist.gov/nistpubs/Legacy/SP/nistspecialpublication800-145.pdf
2. Metzler J, Taylor S. The data center network transition: wide area
3. Networking Alert. Network World, August 08, 2011. http://www.networkworld.com/newsletters/frame/2011/080811wan1.html?source=nww_rss
4. Mell P, Grance T. Effectively-and-securely-using-the-cloud-computing-paradigm. http://www.scribd.com/doc/13427395/
5. Greenpeace. Make IT Green: cloud computing and its contribution to climate change, Greenpeace, USA. http://www.greenpeace.org/international/Global/international/planet-2/report/2010/3/make-it-green-cloud-computing.pdf
6. Koomey J. The environmental cost of cloud computing: assessing power use and impacts. http://www.slideshare.net/gigaom/jonathan-koomey-the-environmental-cost-of-cloud-computing
7. Climate Group and the Global e-Sustainability Initiative (GeSI). SMART 2020: enabling the low carbon economy in the information age. http://gesi.org/article/43
8. Azure Security Center. https://azure.microsoft.com/en-us/services/security-center/
9. Larry Dignan Virtualization: what are the security risks? http://www.zdnet.com/article/virtualization-what-are-the-security-risks/
10. Bob Violino. Five cloud security trends experts see for 2011. http://www.csoonline.com/article/647128/five-cloud-security-trends-experts-seefor-2011

11. Goldberg RP (1973) Architectural principles for virtual computer systems. Harvard University, Cambridge, MA, pp 22–26
12. Wikipedia. http://en.wikipedia.org/wiki/Hypervisor
13. MacDonald N (2011) Yes, hypervisors are vulnerable, January 26, 2011. http://blogs.gartner.com/neil_macdonald/2011/01/26/yes-hypervisors-are-vulnerable/
14. King ST, Chen PM, Wang YM, Verbowski C, Wang HJ, Lorch JR (2006) SubVirt: implementing malware with virtual machines. http://web.eecs.umich.edu/~pmchen/papers/king06.pdf
15. Elastic Load Balancing, *AWS*. http://aws.amazon.com/elasticloadbalancing/
16. Global Information Assurance Certification Paper. https://www.giac.org/paper/gsna/119/ids-load-balancer-security-audit-administrators-perspective/103792
17. Wikipedia. http://en.wikipedia.org/wiki/Cloud_computing. Authenticate to the Rackspace Cloud. https://developer.rackspace.com/docs/cloud-files/v1/getting-started/authenticate/#authenticate-to-cloud

Mobile Systems and Corresponding Intractable Security Issues

23

23.1 Introduction

In the previous two chapters, 18 and 19, we dealt with wireless communication but restricted our discussion to sensor networks, wireless communication networks, and cellular networks. We discussed a good number of communication devices and their communication protocols. We also discussed the security problems and we propose solutions in some cases. What we did not do is actually put all these devices and technologies together to create the current phenomenal mobile communication devices, and the technology is currently driving computing and communication. We are going to do this in this chapter and more. The last two decades have witnessed a revolution of sorts in communication spearheaded by the rapidly evolving technologies in both software and hardware. A mobile communication system consists of two or more of the following devices, running specifically developed software to sustain, for a period of time, a wireless communication link between them: mobile telephone, broadly construed here to include devices based on code division multiple access (CDMA), time division multiple access (TDMA), Global System for Mobile Communications (GSM), and wireless personal digital assistant (WPDA) digital technologies and follow-ons, as well as satellite telephones and e-mail appliances. Mobile communication systems are revolutionizing the world today, shrinking the world to between two or more small handheld mobile devices. The rapid changes in communication technologies, the revolutionary changes in software, and the growth of large powerful communication network technologies all have eased communication and brought it to large swaths of the globe. The high-end competition between the mobile telecommunication operators resulting in plummeting device prices, the quickly developing smartphone technology, and the growing number of undersea cables and cheaper satellite technologies are bringing Internet access to almost every one of the global rural poor faster than many had anticipated.

© Springer International Publishing AG 2017   503
J.M. Kizza, *Guide to Computer Network Security*, Computer Communications and Networks, DOI 10.1007/978-3-319-55606-2_23

23.2   Current Major Mobile Operating Systems

Perhaps none has contributed more handsomely to the global digital communication revolution than the mobile operating system technology. The mobile operating system, commonly called the mobile OS, or just mOS, is an operating system that is specifically designed to run on mobile devices such as mobile phones, smartphones, PDAs, tablet computers, and other handheld devices. The mobile operating system is the software platform on top of which other programs, called application programs, can run on mobile devices. The mOS performs the same functionalities like its bigger brother that runs laptops and PCs. The differences, however, are in the size of memory that an ordinary and modern operating system will need to perform those functions. In the case of mOS, we are talking small sizes for everything. In additional to running in limited everything, modern mOSs must combine the required features of a personal computer with touch screen, cellular, Bluetooth, Wi-Fi, GPS navigation, camera, video camera, speech recognition, voice recorder, music player, near-field communication, personal digital assistant (PDA), and others.

Mobile operating systems are as crucial and central to the running and security of the mobile device as they are in the bigger less mobile devices like PCs and laptops. When it comes to security-related issues, the mobile device is as secure as its operating system. So every mobile device integrates as in its operating systems as much security as it can possibly carry without sacrificing speed, ease of use, and functionalities expected by the consumers. Since most mobile operating systems are similar in a number of ways to their older brothers, the operating systems in the PCs and laptops, which seem and continue to see a growing problems with security like backdoors, spyware, worms, Trojans, and a growing list of others, mOS developers and other application third parties should not wait and solve these security problems using a knee-jack reactions like was the case with PCs and laptop security. Probably quick preemptive measure could help safeguard the mobile device a lot faster.

At the writing of this chapter, the most popular mOSs are Google Android, Apple iOS, Research in Motion's BlackBerry OS, and Windows Phone OS. Of course there are many others. Table 23.1 shows some of the most popular mOS (as of September 2016).[1]

23.3   Security in the Mobile Ecosystems

As mobile devices, more importantly smart devices that can do almost everything a computer can do and more, become ubiquitous, the risk for using them is increasing. They are increasingly holding and storing more private data like personal and

---

[1]Wikipedia > Mobile Operating Systems. https://en.wikipedia.org/wiki/Mobile_operating_system#Tizen

Table 23.1 Major mobile operating systems (as of September 2016)

mOS	Owner	Properties	Mobile devices
Android	Google	Largest in market share. Based on the Linux kernel	Smartphones and tablets
iOS	Apple	Second largest in market share	Smartphones, tablets, in-vehicle infotainment (IVI) devices, and smart TV
BlackBerry OS 10	Research in Motion	Fourth largest in market share. Based on the QNX OS	Phones and tablets manufactured by Blackberry
Sailfish OS	Jolla—Finland	Linux-based operating systems. Partly open source and OS version releases are named after Finnish lakes adopt GPL	Smartphones, tablets, in-vehicle infotainment (IVI) devices
Firefox OS	Mozilla	Open source and is released under the Mozilla Public License. The OS is built on the Android Linux kernel, using Android drivers, but does not use any of the Java-like code of Android	Smartphones and tablets
Ubuntu Touch	Ubuntu	Open source and uses the GPL license	Smartphones and tablets
Tizen	Linux Foundation	Fourth largest in market share	Smartphones, tablets, in-vehicle infotainment (IVI) devices, and smart TV
Windows Phone 7, 8, 10	Microsoft	Closed source and proprietary. Integrated with Microsoft services such as OneDrive and Office, Xbox Music, Xbox Video, Xbox Live games and Bing	Smartphones as well as tablets with screen size under 8 inches

business, and they are roaming in public spaces on public networks with limited security and cryptographic protocols to protect the data. In fact the kind of security threats toward these devices is similar and probably more than that experienced by PCs and laptops in their heydays. The security threats to these mobile devices are comparable if not more than those facing servers in that these devices can remain on without user attention and are always connected to a network. Also because of the fact that these devices have the ability to roam on several networks, there is a wider sphere of attack beset by geographical, legal, and moral differences. Because of the high demand for global connectivity, especially in developing countries, service providers are responding with a zeal to consolidate networks and standardize communication protocols, thus making it easier for these devices to roam in large spaces and networks, creating fertile ground for attackers. The penetration trend of these smart mobile devices is not limited to faraway rural places, but more scaring is their rapid penetration on enterprise IT spaces where security is paramount for any device. This extension of smart devices into the enterprise IT spaces is a result of their popularity as they slowly eat away the enterprise laptop as the enterprise mobile device. This in turn is increasingly causing enterprise management to start focusing on their security issues. Although antivirus client applications have been available and security best practices have been in place for most high-level operating systems, this is not the case with small mobile devices. In his article, "New Security Flaws Detected in Mobile Devices," Byron Acohido [1] reports the two recent examinations by Cryptography Research, the company that did the research, of mobile devices that revealed gaping security flaws. In one study, Cryptography Research showed how it's possible to eavesdrop on any smartphone or tablet as it is being used to make a purchase, conduct online banking, or access a company's virtual private network. Also, McAfee, an antivirus software company and a division of Intel, showed ways to remotely hack into Apple iOS and steal secret keys and passwords and pilfer sensitive data, including call histories, e-mail, and text messages. What is more worrying is the reported fact that the device under attack would not in any way show that an attack is underway. Almost every mobile system user, security experts, and law enforcement officials are all anticipating that cyber gangs will accelerate attacks as consumers and companies begin to rely more heavily on mobile devices for shopping, banking, and working. So there is an urgent need for a broader array of security awareness of the community and actions by community to assist in providing all users the highest level of protection.

In its security report titled "Lookout Mobile Threat Report 2011," the Lookout Mobile Security, a smartphone security company [2], discusses security threats to mobile devices under four major areas: application, Web-based access, network, and physical environments. Major threats are encountered by mobile devices on a daily basis.

23.3.1 Application-Based Threats

For every mobile device, the biggest appealing feature is the ability to run thousands of applications (apps) to accomplish a variety of tasks. These applications are written by really unknown people with limited to no allegiance to anybody and taking no command from anyone. The applications archiving companies like the Apple Store really have any security standards for these applications and rely, if at all, check for security requirements. Do downloadable applications present the greatest security issues for any mobile device that is capable of downloading software? Application-based threats, therefore, generally fit into one or more of the following categories [2]:

- *Malware*—software designed with the intent to engage in malicious behavior on a device. As we will see later, malware can be used in a variety of ways including identity theft and stealing of personal information from a mobile device.
- *Spyware* is designed with the intent to collect or use data without a user's knowledge or approval. We will discuss this more later in Sect. 23.5.

- *Functionality features*—these are the device's normal functionality features that reveal or threaten an individual's privacy. These features include the GPS's location identification.
- *Vulnerable application* is a software that may have vulnerabilities that can be exploited for malicious purposes. Such software include the device's operating system.

23.3.2 Web-Based Threats

Mobile devices, once on, are continuously roaming in public spaces on public networks with limited security and cryptographic protocols to protect them. In many cases, they are often constantly connected to the Internet for normal Web-based services. Under such circumstances, they are exposed to Web-based threats such as [2]:

- *Phishing scams*—in this case intruders use Web-based services to launch attacks on those devices connected to the Web to acquire information such as usernames, passwords, and credit card details and other private data of the device owner by the intruder masquerading as a trustworthy friend in an electronic communication like e-mail and text.
- *Drive-by downloads*—these are like pop-ups written by scammers to automatically begin uploading treacherous application as soon as the device visits a Web page.
- *Other Web exploits*—anyone of the many Web exploits discussed in Sect. 23.5 below is possible. This is possible because scammers take advantage of vulnerabilities in a Web browser or software that can be launched via a Web browser to attack the mobile device.
- *Direct exploitation* is a threat to mobile browsers, some of them as code bases on mobile devices that malicious Web pages can target, including the browser itself and image viewers, Flash, PDF readers, and more [2].

23.3.3 Network Threats

As we stated above, once mobile devices are on, they immediately start looking for networks to connect on either cellular networks or the Internet. As we will see in Sect. 23.5 below, there are a number of threats that originate from these networks [2]:

- *Network exploits*—recall that mobile devices always network once on. Each one of these networks, including the Internet and Bluetooth, has their own exploits. See more of this discussion in Sect. 23.5 below.

23.3.4 Physical Threats

While all the different classes of threats we have discussed so far are based on the nature and the functionality of the mobile device itself, the physical threats are based on the size and the owner of the mobile device:

- *Lost or stolen devices*—the miniaturization of mobile devices while afford more convenience for the use, the small sizes make them more susceptible to theft and getting lost from the user. While there are ways to remote wipe the device, still very few users can think of it immediately giving enough time to the robbers to acquire the data on it. In fact there are more mobile devices prone to these kinds of threats than any other we have seen so far.

23.3.5 Operating System-Based Threats

The last major category of mobile devices is that category based on the device's operating system. As has been observed by many security experts, while the threats originating from the device's operating systems are many, there are so far two Windows opportunities: one is that we have learned a lot from operating system security and vulnerabilities from their bigger brothers the PC and the laptops, and the other is that so far the domain is still relatively safer than the domain of the PCs and laptops either because many would-be attackers have not yet acquired the script programming skills needed to develop and launch attacks or that since most attacks in the PC and laptop domains are repeat attacks supported by large archives of malware and viruses, the mobile device domain has yet to develop extensive archives of these malware and viruses. So far, it is lack of expertise that is still helping. Also most operating system threats are specific to the brand. So in our discussion, we will make specific mention of the brand whenever possible:

- KDataAtruct—This is a Windows Mobile (WM) operating system problem based on the vulnerability that in WM Microsoft placed all main system functions in one coredll.dll file so that developers do not have to include the code for functions in their own programs. They just call the coredll addresses of all the APIs it uses into memory space it is allocated. In so doing an address to the list of modules is provided so that the address of the coredll can be determined. From here, one can search through memory looking for the virtual address of the API wanted. This can open up the device for exploitation. This vulnerability is exploited by the virus WinCE.Duts.A.
- Pocket IE—another Windows vulnerability found in the small Internet Explorer, commonly known as Pocket IE (PIE), default Web browser for the WM Oss. The PIE has all the vulnerabilities found in the standard IE for the big brothers PC and laptops. See all these vulnerabilities in Sect. 23.5 below.
- Jailbreaking—is a process a user can alter the phone's operating system to gain full access (or root access) to the operating system and allow applications not officially vetted by the Apple's review policies. For example, JailbreakMe 3.0

for iOS devices is a nonmalicious Web page that exploits two vulnerabilities to jailbreak a device [3].

- DroidDream—is an Android malware that utilizes two exploits, Exploid and Rage Against The Cage to break out of the Android security sandbox, gain root control of the operating system, and install applications without user intervention [4].
- Update attacks—there is a growing problem of using application updates as an attack method in the Android Market. A malware writer first releases a legiti-mate application containing no malware. Once they have a large enough user base, the malware writer updates the application with a malicious version [2].
- Malvertising—is malicious advertising where an attacker lures victims into downloading malware, especially on the Android Market. They rely on the fact that developers commonly use in-app advertisements to gain more users, so people are used to downloading apps via advertisements [2].
- Other threats include flowed shell model (iOS), root account (iOS), static addressing (iOS), static systems (iOS), and reuse of code (iOS).

23.4   General Mobile Devices Attack Types

Most mobile system attacks are launched against specific mobile devices or operating systems or applications. Most of these attack techniques are carryovers from the computer and computer networks. So they are not generally new into the arsenal of attacks. Over the years, we have learned specific methodologies the attackers use to success in their quest. The most common attack chancels and techniques are [2, 5]:

Denial of Service (DDoS)
This technique is meant to cause system disruptions so that the device, the service, or the network on which the device operates cannot complete the operation under way.

Phone Hacking
This is a technique used to intercept phone calls or voicemail messages, either by accessing the voicemail or text messages of a mobile phone without the knowledge or consent of the phone's owner. You may recall the *News of The World* phone-hacking stories in the United Kingdom.

Mobile Malware/Virus
A mobile malware or virus is software that deliberately targets mobile phones or wireless-enabled PDAs.

Spyware
Spyware is a type of malware that automatically installs itself or in some cases is installed manually on computers so that it continuously or periodically collects information about a range or one event, user, or application without the owner's knowledge.

Exploit

An exploit is software code that takes advantage of a bug, glitch, or vulnerability in order to cause unintended or unanticipated consequences to occur on computer software, hardware, or something electronic.

Everything Blue

This is a collection of malwares and spywares that take advantage of Bluetooth technology. Just like in any other wireless network, Bluetooth, with its ability to automatically connect with other Bluetooth-enabled wireless devices, has a number of security problems that are exploited. Bluetooth is now basic feature of mobile devices. All mobile devices now all have this feature embedded in them. Before Bluetooth, infrared technology was used to transfer data and communication between any two wireless devices as long as they were within the line of sight. But infrared hindered meaningful mobility of the devices. So Bluetooth technology came in to solve that problem. Many Bluetooth offered the needed communication and mobility within the unlicensed band of radio waves without having to be in line of sight. Because of this, Bluetooth applications have emerged that allow peering of users with false security. Because this unlicensed radio band is under no regulation, it is more vulnerable to an array of security issues. Mobile devices operating within the Bluetooth range can be compromised easily as hackers can have easy access to data into these devices even commanding them to do anything the hacker wants. Without exhausting them all, let us look into the different categories of how hackers can infiltrate user's mobile devices using Bluetooth, and then we will discuss their mechanism briefly to make the end user aware of how vulnerable the user can be [6]:

- Bluejacking—this is similar to spamming but in Bluetooth by sending unsolicited messages to victim device which opens up communication between the paired devices. This can lead to the attacker gaining access to the victim device.
- Bluesnarfing—a form of Bluetooth hacking which can allow a hacker to gain access to the victim's device's contact list, text messages, e-mails, and other vital information. The hacker can even use brute force attack even if the device is invisible to guess the victims MAC address.
- Bluebugging—is the type of attack, like a Trojan horse, where the hacker uses sophisticated attack techniques to gain control of victim's mobile device. Once in control, the attacker can do anything with the mobile device.
- Bluetoothing—this is social engineering in Bluetooth where a hacker can use traditional social engineering tricks to masquerade as the legitimate user of the mobile device.
- BlueBumping—is an attack involving two mobile devices pairing up setting communication; the attacking device gets the victim to accept a connection for a trivial data exchange such as a picture and then uses that pairing to attack other services. While the connection is still open, the attacker requests for a link key regeneration which it uses later to gain access to the victim device and thus gets full access to any of the services on the victim device.
- BlueChopping—is an attack that targets Bluetooth piconet (an ad hoc Bluetooth network linking other Bluetooth devices. It allows one *master* device to

interconnect with many other active *slave* devices), for disruption by spoofing one of the participating piconet slaves leading to confusion of the master's internal state and thus disrupting the piconet.

- BlueDumping—is the act of sniffing a Bluetooth device's key exchange by forcing the Bluetooth victim mobile device to dump its stored link key. Before the sniff, the attacker needs to know the *BDADDR* of a set of paired devices. To get this, the attacker spoofs the address of one of the devices and connects to the other. Since the attacker has no link key, when the target device requests authentication, the attacker's device will respond with an "HCI_Link_Key_Request_Negative_Reply," which will, in some cases, cause the target device to delete its own link key and go into pairing mode [7].
- BlueSmucking—is a Bluetooth denial-of-service attack that knocks out some Bluetooth-enabled devices immediately. It is carried out using the old "ping of death" but transforms to work in Bluetooth. On the L2CAP (echo request) layer, there is the possibility to request an echo from another Bluetooth peer, to check connectivity, and to measure round-trip time on the established link. This is possible in Bluetooth because the **l2ping** in BlueZ utils allows the user to specify a packet length that is sent to the respective peer. This is done by means of the **-s** < **num** > option [7].
- BlueSniffing—is a Bluetooth version of war driving.

Phishing
Phishing in Bluetooth devices takes the same attempting techniques just like in their big brothers the PC and laptops in that it is intended to acquire information such as usernames, passwords, and credit card details and other private data of the device owner by the intruder masquerading as a trustworthy friend in an electronic communication like e-mail and text.

Smishing
Smishing is social engineering crime like phishing in that it uses the mobile devices and texts as baits to pull in the mobile device owner to divulge private and sometimes personal information.

Vishing
Vishing is another criminal practice in the social engineering class just like the last two. It mostly uses the mobile device phone features facilitated by Voice over IP (VoIP), to gain access to private personal and financial information from the public for the purpose of financial reward. The term is a combination of "voice" and phishing.

23.5   Mitigation of Mobile Devices Attacks

More and more people are now using some form of a data-carrying mobile device. The data on these devices is either personal or work related. Either way, this trend is growing. What is growing even faster and more worrying is the trend where a growing number of employers are increasingly using unmanaged personal devices to access sensitive enterprise resources and then connecting these devices to third-party services outside of the enterprise security controls. This potentially exposes the enterprise-sensitive data to possible attackers. This is creating a growing security headache for sometimes underfunded and overworked security staff. The enterprise security team has to deal with a plethora of different devices running different operating systems or different versions of an operating system. According to the report "Mobile Devices Expose Company Data To Severe Vulnerabilities" by Mobilisafe, a Seattle-based mobile risk management company and small and midsized business (SMB) are more affected by this growing move. The report found that [8]:

- SMBs are exposed to high-severity vulnerabilities from the increasing levels of mobile devices used to access and download company data.
- SMB IT managers cannot keep up with the rate of discovery of severe vulnerabilities these devices bring to their corporate network.
- SMB IT departments lack a standardized approach to mitigate the risks from different types of mobile devices, as they do with laptops, desktops, and servers.
- Even though they feel exposed to mobile device security risk, SMBs do not feel they have adequate tools to assess and mitigate these risks at a granular level.

So what needs to be done? There are several security protocols and best practices that can come in handy to situations like this. According to Michael Brandenberg quoting Clint Adams [9], the "holy trinity of mobile device management," there are three security components that must form the minimum security requirements for any mobile security management. These components are hardware encryption, remote wiping, and the ability to set a passcode policy. Therefore, those responsible for security in any enterprise that is intending to use mobile devices as one form of communication and corporate data access must pay attention to these three components of security. One good thing is that mobile device manufacturers and operating system developers have been paying increasing attention to these tenants at least the first two. Because of the rather large pool of mobile device makers and mobile operating system developers, the task of ensuring that these three security tenants are adhered to by all in the company can be daunting. To sort of lessen this task for a variety of companies and individuals, a new industry has sprung up. The mobile device management (MDM) system is a platform either from third-party or original mobile device manufacturers to support and help enterprises set up and enforce mobile security policies centrally. The mobile device management (MDM) software secures, monitors, manages, and supports mobile devices deployed across mobile operators, service providers, and enterprises. MDM functionality typically includes over-the-air distribution of applications, data, and configuration settings for all types of mobile devices, including mobile phones, smartphones, tablet computers, ruggedized mobile computers, mobile printers, mobile POS devices, and others [10].

23.5.1 Mobile Device Encryption

So it is important and probably a must that on either personal or business mobile devices where sensitive data is carried, such devices must be encrypted. Encrypting a mobile device is meant to protect such data as the power-on and screensaver password, the SIM card, passwords to open apps, or certain functions within apps such as logging into an e-commerce retailer account, confidential e-mail, instant messages, SMS messages, and confidential data and medical files [11].

There are two different ways mobile device encryption can be done, and these are application and hardware encryption.

Application Encryption
In securing mobile devices using applications, encryption protects the mobile device from attacks made on the host device, as well as across network connections end to end. There are many vendor solutions for this kind of encryption.

Hardware Encryption
Hardware encryption are encryption protocols embedded into the hardware by either the original mobile hardware manufacturer. For example, Research in Motion (RIM), the manufacturer of BlackBerry, is well known and indeed currently takes first place in hardware encryption of the BlackBerry phones. On the BlackBerry, RIM combines strong Advanced Encryption Standard (AES) and Triple Data Encryption Standard (Triple DES) encryption with a strong mobile device management platform to provide a strong security stance for enterprise BlackBerrys. Its BlackBerry Enterprise Server (BES) and the BlackBerry devices provide a strong solution that can deliver encryption, remote wipe, and passcode policy enforcement [12]. Similarly other mobile device manufacturers like Apple, Google, Microsoft, and others have corresponding embedded encryptions either in their device operating systems, embedded SIM cards, or movable encryption SIM cards.

23.5.2 Mobile Remote Wiping

To remotely wipe data from a mobile device is one of the security techniques in the mobile device security bag of tricks. It offers the security IT managers the basic mobile device management capabilities to remotely wipe data from lost mobile device. The remote wipe and other management features are both mobile device manufacturer and third-party developed. Many are cross-platform like the Google's Apps Premier and Education Edition which works for iPhones, Nokia E series devices, and Windows Mobile smartphones.

23.5.3 Mobile Passcode Policy

Because there is a plethora of different devices running different operating systems or different versions of an operating system, it is hard for the IT team to keep abreast of the many mobile device manufacturers and third-party vendor mobile security solutions. To cope with these problems, a security policy targeting the mobile devices in use is required.

A complete mobile security solution should include [13]:

- A firewall to secure the device from attacks and malicious code
- A VPN to allow flexible means to ensure secure communications for any wireless data traffic
- An authentication mechanism to ensure that unauthorized persons are not accessing the device if it is lost or stolen
- Data encryption on the device to ensure that information is not stolen, either physically or electronically
- Antivirus software to protect the device from viruses and malware

23.6   Users Role in Securing Mobile Devices

Although we are living in a time when mobile devices are inevitable to do without in day-to-day personal communication and personal access to data, users must be aware that there are risks to the convenience afforded by mobile devices. It is important to know that mobile computing devices can store large amounts of personal and sometimes sensitive data whose loss may cause problems to the owner or user. It is also important to know that it is easy to steal or lose that data. Furthermore, it is important to know that unless precautions are taken, an unauthorized person can gain access to the information stored on these mobile devices or gain access through these devices to other devices or data because these devices may provide access to other services that store or display nonpublic data. This access may be enabled because the mobile device contains passwords or security certificates and other information that may help to identify the device, its user, or its content. So our role as users is to be vigilant and security aware.

Exercises

1. Discuss the steps you would take to protect your mobile device.
2. Search the Internet to find a company's security policy for its mobile devices. Suggest what you would change in that security policy to enhance security.
3. Study three remote wiping solutions and compare them.
4. Comment on the reasons for the rapid growth of the Android operating system.
5. Recently Apple's iOS4 encryption was hacked by a Russian company. Discuss the weaknesses in the iOS4 disclosed by the Russian company.

Advanced Exercises

1. Study the mobile device management platforms and discuss the solutions it offered.
2. What does a typical MDM solution include?
3. List and discuss vendors of MDM.
4. Discuss the Windows Mobile security model, authentication services, Credential Manager, cryptography, and LASS application development and programming elements.
5. Discuss the IPhone Mobile Authentication system.

References

1. Acohido B. New security flaws detected in mobile devices, USA Today. http://www.enterprise-security-today.com/news/Mobile-Devices-Vulnerable-to-Attack/story.xhtml?story_id=0010003 FAI65, April 10, 2012 9:50AM
2. Lookout Mobile Threat Report, 2011. Lookout mobile security. https://www.mylookout.com/_downloads/lookout-mobile-threat-report-2011.pdf
3. Jean. Analysis of the jailbreakme v3 font exploit, Segeti ESEC Lab. http://esec-lab.sogeti.com/posts/2011/07/16/analysis-of-the-jailbreakme-v3-font-exploit.html
4. C-Skills (July23, 2010) http://c-skills.blogspot.com/search?q=exploid
5. Wikipe4dia. Mobile security. https://en.wikipedia.org/wiki/Mobile_security
6. Types Of Bluetooth Hacks And Its Security Issues, HubPages. http://hubpages.com/technology/Types-Of-Bluetooth-Hacks-And-Its-Security-Issues
7. Wikipedia. Bluetooth. https://en.wikipedia.org/wiki/Bluetooth#Security
8. Mobilifesafe. Mobile devices expose company data to severe vulnerabilities, PR Newswire. April 9, 2012. http://www.prnewswire.com/news-releases/mobilisafe-study-details-vulnerability-risk-to-company-data-for-smbs-146647805.html
9. Brandenberg M. Mobile device security overview. TechTarget. http://searchconsumerization.techtarget.com/tutorial/Mobile-device-security-overview
10. Wekipedia. http://en.wikipedia.org/wiki/Mobile_device_management
11. Adhikari R. Encryption on the Go, Part 1, TechNewsWorld. http://www.technewsworld.com/story/75245.html
12. http://trifinite.org/trifinite_stuff_bluedump.html
13. Komisky M. Mobile device security II: handheld operating systems, Bluefire. http://www.datamation.com/mowi/article.php/3575316/Mobile-Device-Security-II-Handheld-Operating-Systems.htm

Internet of Things (IoT): Growth, Challenges, and Security

24

24.1   Introduction

The Internet of things (IoT). What is it? Why is it exciting so many in the technology and innovation communities? The concept of the Internet of Things (IoT) was initially proposed by Kevin Ashton in 1998 [1], while he was working at P&G to launch a line of cosmetics for Oil of Olay. Because the father of IoT, as many call him, was bothered that this one shade of lipstick in his cosmetic line always seemed to be sold out in all his London, UK, local stores, he wanted to know where his lipstick was and what was happening to it. No one could tell him. When UK retailers experimenting with loyalty cards with a tiny "radio-enabled" chip, later called RFID, showed these to him, it gave him an idea of tracking his lipstick shade. He took the radio microchip out of the credit card and stuck it on his lipstick shade to see if a wireless network could pick up data on a card and tell him what shelf in the store the lipstick was on. By so doing, he started the forces that created the IoT. In about a decade, the simple idea and experiment have been extended to support pervasive connectivity and the integration of a variety of objects big and small creating an ecosystem of interconnected communication network whose devices or communication nodes are everyday electronic objects like mobile devices, entertainment devices in your home, fridges and temperature control devices, garage door openers, cloth and dish washers, and the list goes on and on. When network connectivity is achieved, it allows all these devices to talk to each other by sending and receiving data. This connectivity of things started long ago with the interconnection of computing devices to form the traditional computer network. Upon that a conceptual model of connectivity of all devices that can communicate and receive data forming a far wider communication network, the "Internet of Things," was born.

The conceptual model and now what is forming in reality has the potential to impact our lives in many unprecedented ways both good and bad, as most technologies are.

© Springer International Publishing AG 2017   517
J.M. Kizza, *Guide to Computer Network Security*, Computer Communications
and Networks, DOI 10.1007/978-3-319-55606-2_24

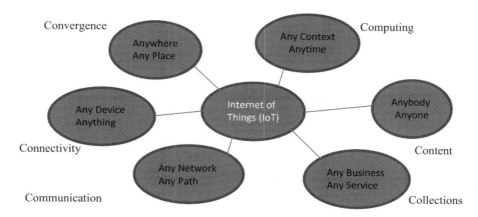

Fig. 24.1 Definition of Internet of Things (IoT) [3]

Jayavardhana Gubbia, Rajkumar Buyyab, Slaven Marusica, and Marimuthu Palaniswamia [2] have defined the Internet of Things as a smart environment that is made up of an interconnection of sensing and actuating devices providing the ability to share information across platforms through a unified framework, developing a common operating picture for enabling innovative applications. This smart environment is achieved by seamless ubiquitous sensing, data analytics, and information representation with cloud computing as the unifying framework. It is this ecosystem described by P. Guillemin and P. Friess in their paper "Internet of things strategic research roadmap," as part of the Cluster of European Research Projects [3] and represented in Fig. 24.1.

Jacob Morgan [4] also sees it an environmental ecosystem that "allows for virtually endless opportunities and connections to take place, many of which we can't even think of or fully understand the impact of today." Because it is going to affect our lives in every possible way, known and unknown in every sphere and dimension, it is in fact, as one scholar puts it, the new Industrial Revolution, again.

It's not hard to see how and why the IoT is such a hot topic today; it certainly opens the door to a lot of opportunities but also to many challenges. Security is a big issue that is oftentimes brought up. With billions of devices being connected together, what can people do to make sure that their information stays secure? Will someone be able to hack into your toaster and thereby get access to your entire network? The IoT also opens up companies all over the world to more security threats. Then we have the issue of privacy and data sharing. This is a hot-button topic even today, so one can only imagine how the conversation and concerns will escalate when we are talking about many billions of devices being connected. Another issue that many companies specifically are going to be faced with is around the massive amounts of data that all of these devices are going to produce. Companies need to figure out a way to store, track, analyze, and make sense of the vast amounts of data that will be generated.

24.2   Overview and Growth of Internet of Things

In their paper, "Internet of Things (IoT): A vision, architectural elements, and future directions," Jayavardhana Gubbia, Rajkumar Buyyab, Slaven Marusica, and Marimuthu Palaniswamia [2] state that the phrase "Internet of Things" was first coined by Kevin Ashton in 1999 in the context of supply chain management. Since then, it has involved to its present-day meaning. But all along the way, the core essence of making a computer device, which is a node in our IoT, sense information without the aid of human intervention remains the same. In its current meaning, each node of the IoT, may it be a sensor, an actuator, or a communicating device, is interconnected to other nodes in the mess that include the existing Internet, and all are able to intercommunicate, seamlessly passing and getting information to provide services for information transfer, analytics, applications, and communications using existing Internet Protocols. Several technologies have converged to create the Internet of Things technologies. These technologies include those which have led to ubiquitous sensing enabled by wireless sensor network (WSN) technologies and ubiquitous computing; miniature, mobile, and high-powered computing and communication devices; and the existing Internet Protocols to provide services for information transfer, analytics, applications, and communications.

In their paper, "The Internet of Things: A survey," Luigi Atzori, Antonio Iera, and Giacomo Morabito [5] argue that the Internet of Things can be realized in three paradigms—Internet-oriented (middleware), things-oriented (sensors), and semantic-oriented (knowledge). But according to Jayavardhana Gubbia et al., the usefulness of IoT can be unleashed only in an application domain where the three paradigms intersect.

With the expected continued growth of the Internet, there is unanimous expectation of an enormous growth of the Internet of Things in the next 5 years and beyond. Infographics [6] estimates that by 2018, there will be 42.1 billion items connected in the IoT.

John Greenough and Jonathan Camhi both of business intelligence (BI) [7] look IoT in terms of business growth predicting that IoT is the next Industrial Revolution or the Next Internet. On the future of IoT growth, they further predict the following:

- By 2020 there are likely to be 34 billion devices connected to the Internet, from 10 billion in 2015. IoT devices will account for 24 billion, while traditional computing devices (e.g., smartphones, tablets, smartwatches, etc.) will comprise 10 billion.
- Nearly $6 trillion will be spent on IoT solutions over the next 5 years.
- Businesses will be the top adopter of IoT solutions. They see three ways the IoT can improve their bottom line by (1) lowering operating costs, (2) increasing productivity, and (3) expanding to new markets or developing new product offerings.

- Governments are focused on increasing productivity, decreasing costs, and improving their citizens' quality of life. Governments will be the second largest adopters of IoT ecosystems.
- Consumers will lag behind businesses and governments in IoT adoption. Still, they will purchase a massive number of devices and invest a significant amount of money in IoT ecosystems.

24.3   Architecture and Networking of IoT

We defined the IoT in Sect. 24.1 as an interconnection of sensing, actuating, and communication digital devices providing the ability to share information across platforms through a unified framework, developing a common operating ecosystem (COE) for enabling innovative applications. For the IoT ecosystem to function and support intended applications and accommodate the heterogeneity of devices and applications in the ecosystem, the IoT had to adopt the open standards of TCP/IP suite. However, the open standards of TCP/IP suite were initially developed for the wired global Internet several decades ago, as the networking solution. But as we have outlined above in our discussion of IoT, there are fundamental differences between the traditional wired computer networks and the heterogeneous combination of wired and wireless device ecosystem. And as Wentao Shang, Yingdi Yu, and Ralph Droms [8] observe, those differences pose significant challenges in applying TCP/IP technologies to the IoT environment, and addressing these challenges will make a far-reaching impact on the IoT network architecture. To get a good understanding of the IoT architectures and networking, we need to first understand the underlying network topology supported by the heterogeneous technologies, devices, and standards. The networking technology standard currently being used in the IoT falls into three categories: (1) *point-to-point*, for example, an end device to a gateway; (2) *star*, with a gateway connected to several end devices by one hop links; and (3) a *mesh*, with one or more gateways connecting to several end devices one or more hop links away as demonstrated in Fig. 24.2.

Based on these three topologies, we can cascade end devices and gateways to get a real model of the IoT communication network architecture as shown in Fig. 24.3.

All IoT known technologies like Wi-Fi, Bluetooth, WiMax, ZigBee, Z-Wave, RFID, near-field communication (NFC), and others support this communication architecture.

24.3.1   Architecture and Protocol Stack of IoTs

As we will see in the coming Sect. 24.3.2, a typical TCP/IP IPv6 has a maximum transmission unit (MTU) size of 1500 bytes or higher and a near-infinite address space covering up to 2^{128} unique addresses, while IoT constrained low-energy links have very small MTUs averaging around 127 bytes. Even with the two IPv6 design specifications that include (a) IPv6 of 40-byte fixed length header with optional

Fig. 24.2 Current IoT topologies

Fig. 24.3 IoT communication network architecture

extension headers, which causes big protocol overheads for small packets, and (b) IPv6 specification requiring all IPv6-capable networks to support a minimum MTU size of 1280 bytes, typical IPv6 packets cannot be carried over the constrained IoT links. So a new 6LoWPAN protocol was defined to enable IPv6 packets to be carried on top of low-powered and lossy personal area networks (LLNs). A draft architecture for a gateway or middleware that provides interoperability between 6LoWPAN and external IPv6 networks has been defined. Other protocols have been defined to support the smooth transmission between IPv6 and low-powered IoT devices. These include [9]:

TCP/IP Protocol suite		IoT Protocol suite	
Application layer	HTTP/FTP/SMTP, etc	Application layer	CoAP
Transport layer	TCP/UDP	Transport layer	UDP
Network layer	IPv4/IPv6, RP, ICMP	Network layer	IPv6/6LoWPAN
Data Link layer	IEEE 802.3 Ethernet/802.11, Wireless LAN	Data Link layer	IEEE 802.15.4e
Physical layer	Ethernet (IEEE 802.3), Token Ring, RS-232, FDDI, and others	Physical layer	IEEE 802.15.4

Fig. 24.4 Comparative view of TCP/IP and IOT (IP Smart Objects) protocol suites

Constrained Application Protocol (CoAP)—this was developed by the IETF Constrained RESTful Environments (CoRE) workgroup. The protocol includes several HTTP functionalities although it has modified to work with low processing power and energy consumption constraints of IoT devices. Because CoAP is similar to HTTP, it also uses a universal resource identifier (URI) to identify resources and allow the resource to be affected using similar methods such as GET, PUT, POST, and DELETE.

Figure 24.4 gives a comparative view of TCP/IP and IOT (IP Smart Objects) protocol suites.

Another way of looking at the IoT protocols is via IoT device functionality. IoT devices must communicate with each other. This is referred to as D2D. An example for this is Web services and business applications. Data on data then must be collected and sent to the server infrastructure. This is referred to as D2S. An example for this is in all devices where there is a need for control plane. Finally the server infrastructure has to share device data, possibly providing it back to devices, to analyze programs, or to people. This is S2S. This includes all devices and intelligent systems. The protocols to do these services are [10]:

- MQTT: a protocol for collecting device data and communicating it to servers (D2S)
- XMPP: a protocol best for connecting devices to people, a special case of the D2S pattern, since people are connected to the servers
- DDS: a fast bus for integrating intelligent machines (D2D)
- AMQP: a queuing system designed to connect servers to each other (S2S)

Other IoT protocols include [11]:

- *Infrastructure* (e.g., 6LowPAN, IPv4/IPv6, RPL)
- *Identification* (e.g., EPC, uCode, IPv6, URIs)
- *Comms/transport* (e.g., Wi-Fi, Bluetooth, LPWAN)
- *Discovery* (e.g., Physical Web, mDNS, DNS-SD)
- *Data protocols* (e.g., MQTT, CoAP, AMQP, Websocket, Node)
- *Device management* (e.g., TR-069, OMA-DM)
- *Semantic* (e.g., JSON-LD, Web Thing Model)
- *Multilayer frameworks* (e.g., Alljoyn, IoTivity, Weave, HomeKit)

24.3.2 Challenges of Using TCP/IP Architecture over the IoT

As we just stated above, the IoT ecosystem of heterogeneous devices, wired, wireless, and restricted, using the traditional TCP/IP (though IPv6) meant for wired devices, presents a growing number of challenges in IoT networking that are likely to grow as the IoT ecosystem grows. Some of the issues causing these challenges are easy to see. Others are not. Most of the challenges are brought about by the IoT inherent heterogeneous low-battery-powered wireless devices, the multi-link subnet model, and the mesh network nature of the ecosystem that requires new scalable routing mechanisms. These challenges are thoroughly discussed by Wentao Shang, Yingdi Yu, and Ralph Droms in their paper "Challenges in IoT Networking via TCP/IP Architecture" as follows [8]:

1. *Maximum transmission unit (MTU) size*—While a typical TCP/IP IPv6 MTU has a minimum size of 1500 bytes or higher, the IoT constrained low-energy links have very small MTUs averaging around 127 bytes. Along with size, the IPv6 specification, of two design decisions that utilize either (a) IPv6 of 40-byte fixed length header with optional extension headers, which causes big protocol overheads for small packets, or (b) IPv6 specification requiring all IPv6-capable networks to support a minimum MTU size of 1280 bytes, is unrealistic for the IoT constrained links.
2. *Multi-link subnet model*—The current subnet model of both IPv4 and IPv6 considers two types of Layer-2 networks: multi-access link, where multiple nodes share the same access medium, and point-to-point link, where there are exactly two nodes on the same link. Both of them assume that the nodes in the same subnet can reach each other within one hop. However, the current IoT mesh network contains a collection of Layer-2 links joined together without any Layer-3 device, like routers, in between. This essentially creates a multi-link subnet model that is not anticipated by the original IP addressing architecture.
3. *Multicast efficiency*—A lot of IP-based protocols make heavy use of IP multicast (one-to-many or many-to-many where information is addressed to a group of destination computers simultaneously; see Sec. 5.3.4) to achieve one of the two functionalities: notifying all the members in a group and making a query without knowing exactly whom to ask. However, supporting multicast packet delivery is a big challenge for constrained IoT mesh networks. First, most wireless MAC

protocols disable link-layer ACK for multicast; consequently lost packets are not recovered at link layer. Second, multicast recipients may experience different data transmission rate due to the coexistence of multiple MAC protocols and/or the link-layer rate adaptation; therefore the sender has to transmit at the lowest common link speed among all receivers. Third, IoT nodes may switch to sleeping mode from time to time to conserve energy and thus may miss some multicast packets. Lastly, when nodes are connected through a mesh network, a multicast packet needs to be forwarded over multiple hops along many paths, potentially waking up many sleeping nodes and overloading the already-scarce network resource.

4. *Mesh network routing*—The topologies of typical IoT networks fall into three categories, as seen in Fig. 24.1: star topology, mesh (peer-to-peer), and point-to-point. The routing configuration is straightforward on a star and point-to-point networks where the hub node in a star topology and one of the two nodes in a point-to-point topology can act as the default gateway for the peripheral nodes. However, this limits the signal coverage of a single hub node in these two deployment topologies, making them unsuitable for applications that need wider coverage. The mesh topology, on the other hand, enables larger coverages by having the nodes relay the packets for each other. All mesh nodes cooperate in the distribution of data in the network. Mesh network routing can be supported at either the link layer or the network layer. The link-layer approach, called *mesh-under* in the IETF terminology [8], relies on Layer-2 forwarders to join multiple links into a single "one-IP-hop" subnet. The network-layer approach, called *route-over*, instead relies on IP routers to forward packets across multiple hops. IoT suffers from a *transport layer problem*. The Internet's TCP/IP architecture transport layer provides *congestion control and reliable delivery*, both of which are implemented by TCP, the dominant transport layer protocol on the Internet. TCP efficiently deliver a large bulk of data over a long-lived point-to-point connection without stringent latency requirement. It models the communication as a byte stream between sender and receiver and enforces reliable in-order delivery of every single byte in the stream. However, IoT applications usually face a variety of communication patterns which TCP cannot support efficiently. First, due to the energy constraints, devices may frequently go into sleep mode; thus it is infeasible to maintain a long-lived connection in IoT applications. Second, a lot of IoT communication involves only a small amount of data, making the overhead of establishing a connection unacceptable. Third, some applications may have low-latency requirement, which may not tolerate the delay caused by TCP handshaking.

5. *Resource discovery*—The resource-oriented communication model usually requires a resource discovery mechanism, whereby the applications can request or invoke operations on the resources. The solution for resource discovery in traditional IP networks is DNS-based Service Discovery (DNS-SD) [8]. However, this solution has several limitations in supporting IoT applications. First of all, DNS-SD aims to support service discovery, where the service usually refers to a running program. In contrast, the resources in the context of IoT cover a

broader scope: besides services, it may also refer to IoT devices, sensor data, etc. Therefore, the IoT resource discovery requires a more general approach to identify heterogeneous resources. For example, instead of using DNS records, CoAP adopts a URI-based naming scheme to identify the resources (like in HTTP). Based on that, the IETF core WG has developed CoRE-RD [26], a CoAP-based resource discovery mechanism that relies on less constrained resource directory (RD) servers to store the metainfo about the resources hosted on other devices. Secondly, traditional service discovery often relies on multicast when dedicated services such as DNS and CoRE-RD are not available in the local environment. For example, DNS-SD uses Multicast DNS (mDNS) [8] as the carrier of communications for service discovery and names resolution within the local network. However, link-local multicast has efficiency issues in IoT environments.

6. *Caching*—The TCP/IP communication model requires that both the client (resource requester) and the server (resource holder) are online at the same time. However, in IoT scenarios, the constrained devices may frequently go into sleeping mode for energy saving. Moreover, the dynamic and/or intermittent network environment usually makes it difficult to maintain stable connections between communicating parties. Consequently, the IoT applications often rely on caching and proxying to achieve efficient data dissemination. The selected proxy node can request the resources on behalf of the sleeping nodes and store the response data temporarily until the requesting nodes wake up. The cached contents can also be used to serve similar requests from other nodes who share the same proxy, which saves network bandwidth and reduces response latency. The resource origin server may also appoint some proxy nodes to handle the requests on its behalf (called reverse proxy) so that it can reduce the client traffic and may go offline when it needs to. While it is helpful, the application-level caching implemented by CoAP and HTTP has several limitations in the IoT environment. First, the clients need to explicitly choose a forward- or reverse-proxy node in order to utilize the content caching capability. Second, in dynamic network environments where the connectivity is intermittent, the preselected proxy point may become totally unreachable. When the network topology changes, the clients need to reconfigure or rediscover the proxies or otherwise stop using caches and proxies at all. Third, the caches and proxies break the end-to-end connections assumed by the current security protocols, making it even harder to protect the application data.

24.4   IoT Governance, Privacy, and Security Challenges

As we have pointed out throughout this chapter, an inherent characteristic of the IoT is its heterogeneity resulting from a plethora of things with different data communication capabilities like protocols and hardware, data rates, reliability, and others; computational, storage, and energy capabilities; diversity in the types and formats of data like audio, video, text, numeric, and streams; and IoT standards including device standards, standards to represent data, IEEE projects on IoT standards, ITU and ISO IoT standards, and others [12]. This diversity in devices, service, and protocols presents challenges unseen and unprecedented in the modern communication.

24.4.1 Governance and Privacy Concerns

As the IoT grows, it presents us with several challenges including global governance, individual privacy, ethics, and of course security. These are the most critical issues in the growth of IoT. As it grows, the IoT is expected to involve multiple stakeholders around the globe. It is important to understand that the meanings of and what defines these issues are differently understood and defined around the globe. So we will deal with the most widely accepted definitions and meanings here. Globally, governance is mostly understood to refer to the rules, processes, and behavior that affect the way in which powers are exercised, particularly as regards openness, participation, accountability, effectiveness, and coherence [13]. These five *principles of good governance* have been already applied to the Internet for specific aspects, and there are already organizations like IETF, ICANN, RIRs, ISOC, IEEE, IGF, and W3C, which are each responsible and dealing with every specific area [13]. But currently this is not the case with the IoT. What this is pointing to is that the governance of the current IoT possesses an array of problems for all those connected to the Internet, the most serious of which are security threats and attacks originating from and targeting both Internet-connected endpoints and data privacy risks posed by those same devices. Consider an IoT with 70 billion wireless-like standalone and embedded sensors and wired devices predicted in the next 3–5 years, all capturing, storing, and communicating data. A number of questions arise. For example, who owns that data? If those devices communicate with your mobile device in the public commons, who owns that data into and on your smart device? Where is the data exchanged with your device going to go? What is it going to be used for? From that point, if the data from or into your smart device is automatically combined with data from a smart passing car, what happens? Do others come to know about you? Do others come to spoof into your devices later? For those wearing medical devices that monitor their vital signs, what about their medical data? This raised a million security and privacy issues with no immediate answers. All these are happening because of lack of a central or at least coordinated distributed authority to harmonize governance of the IoT.

However, everything about the governance of IoT is not bad; there are promising efforts and initiatives in different places like North America and Europe that are developing policies and protocols that will eventually archive these governance goals.

24.4.2 Security Challenges

Security is critical to IoT applications due to their close interaction with the physical world. In Internet communication, based on TCP/IP, IP has the task of delivering packets from the source host to the destination host solely based on the IP addresses in the packet headers. For this purpose, IP defines packet structures that encapsulate the data to be delivered. It also defines addressing methods that are used to label the datagram with source and destination information. As a most widely used secure protocol in IP, TLS and its datagram variant DTLS are the main security protocols offering end-to-end secure communications between a server and client. TLS, with its two main constituent protocols, the handshake protocol, responsible for key exchange and authentication, and the record protocol, responsible for a secure channel for handling the delivery of data, makes the security of all IP-based communications a channel-based security. The secured-channel solutions, however, do not fit into the IoT environments for several reasons:

1. The first issue with *channel-based security* is the overhead of establishing a secure channel. Both TLS and DTLS require two or more rounds of security handshake to authenticate a channel and negotiate the security parameters, before the first application data is sent out. The second issue is that both ends of a channel have to maintain the states of the channel until it is closed. This may impose a high pressure on memory usage when a device needs to communicate with many peers simultaneously in a densely meshed network. Third, channel-based security does not guarantee the security of request-response once the application data get out of the channel. This is most troublesome when the *middleboxes*, like caches and proxies (see more details on this in Sect. 24.4.6), are deployed to cache the application data. The resource owners need to trust the middleboxes to enforce the access control policies correctly, while the resource requestors need to trust the middleboxes to provide authentic data without tampering. The limitations above highlight the need for a different security model for IoT applications.
2. *Insufficient authentication/authorization*—If recent attacks on the Internet, using smart house monitoring camera, resulting in distributed denial of service (DDS), are any evidence, the IoT with its growing mesh of heterogeneous devices, whose users and devices rely on weak and simple passwords and authorizations, is a growing security quagmire.
3. *Lack of transport encryption*—Most devices fail to encrypt data that are being transferred, even when the devices are using the Internet.
4. *Insecure Web/mobile interface*—Most of the billions of IoT-based devices connect on the Internet using bridging communication protocols and device management schemes that do not do an effective job. See more details in Sect. 24.3.2.

24.4.3 Autonomy

High heterogeneity and complexity and lack of dynamic and scalable management schemes in the IoT due to its plethora of sometimes constrained devices, with different data communication capabilities, create a challenge in the manual maintenance of a large number of devices, become inefficient, and demand the presence of intelligent and dynamic management schemes. According to Qazi Mamoon Ashraf and Mohamed Hadi Habaebi [14], strong autonomy in IoT can be realized by implementing self-managing systems. Self-management is the property of a system to achieve management and maintenance of its resources intrinsically and internally. It is achieved through levels of decision-making including access management, device management, as well as service management. This thus should lead to all devices in the IoT being aware of their owners' preferences and autonomously make decisions on behalf of their owners and at the same time cooperate with other devices on including securing network communication.

24.4.4 Computational Constraints

One of the characteristics of IoT is its heterogeneity and complexity as it connects to billions of sometimes constrained devices running different communication protocols and management schemes. Low-level devices on the fringes can be of limited power sometimes of less than 10 KBs of RAM, which are sometimes orders of magnitude lower than an ordinary desktop computer with GIGs of RAM. This presents data transfer, computation, and communication challenges. So in cases where high-demand computations cannot be handled by the low-power devices, a delegation of operations may be required.

24.4.5 Discovery

With the rapid growth of devices connected to the IoT, expected to hit 70 billion in the next few years, challenge for search and discovery for available services is increasingly becoming an impediment to the growth of IoT and will diminish future expected benefits of the IOT. Moreover, discovery methods currently being used in the Internet are not flexible to accommodate a growing regime of new services, and they are not capable of searching the heterogeneous devices running different discovery protocols. Therefore, we need new discovery technologies that are more expressive and able to evolve over time.

Discovery in the IoT is the process that enables application to access the IoT data without the need to know the actual source of data, sensor description, or location. According to Arkady Zaslavsky and Prem Prakash Jayaraman, the discovery process can be defined as two successive loops [12]:

- *Foraging loop*—Data sources are identified and assessed, where the relevant data is extracted and formatted into consumable form.
- *Sense-making loop*—The extracted data is analyzed and exploited to provide answers around a specific problem.

The challenge is then to develop a scalable framework (or architecture) along with protocols to provide complete capabilities, which work for all those who will use the IoT.

24.4.6 Trust Relationships

We have already seen and discussed the connectivity and heterogeneity of the IoT. We know that IoT connects to billions of devices with high connectivity complexities and challenges. IoT end devices play a variety of roles and perform many functions for the device owner. Some devices are wired; others are wireless. Some are low powered; others have access to full power. To enable communications with all these devices, there is a need for some degree of intelligence in these devices. The growth of embedded intelligence behavior in the end devices, as an extension of the device owner relationship, will increase and indeed become ubiquitous as the IoT plethora of things with different data communication capabilities grows. As the strong relationships and embedded intelligence between end devices and their owner grow, a citizen (user) relationship is created and introduced into the IoT. The "things" in an IoT are indeed the end devices. There are the new entities (new ontologies). Now these new entities are endowed with identity, connectivity, intelligence, and agency with and through which relationships.

These *human-IoT* relationships create a relationship-trust mesh in the IOT which result into a multitude of questions of a social, ethical, and legal nature. Questions are as follows [15]:

- What threats are caused by delegating fundamental aspects of humanness?
- How can we preserve the human capability to freely act and make choices in the IoT?

A lot more issues are and will continue to be raised as the IoT grows.

Exercises
From self-driving cars to factory robots, engineers are imagining new ways of connecting our world through IoT-enabled machines that integrate production processes.

1. In a short three-page paper, discuss how this is likely to happen.
2. Also using the same scenario above, cars, in say a four-way intersections, will be able to talk to each other and negotiate who goes first without involving the drive. What are the likely dangers of this?
3. With IoT, the toaster in your house will be able to wake you up to tell you that your sliced bread is just about ready. In man-machine interdependence so created, discuss our role, as humans.

4. Jack Williamson in *With Folded Hand* portrays a world ruled by robots, which seem benign but must follow and exist to discharge the Asimovian Prime Directive. The Prime Directive is "to serve and obey, and guard men from harm." In the story, robots replicate themselves and do all the jobs the man wants them to do until he realizes the mistake he make to create the robots in the first place. They just made him useless. Is the IoT likely to produce this utopia for humanity?

5. In this chapter, I call the IoT a security quagmire. Do you agree?

Advanced Exercises

1. What's the biggest risk associated with the IoT on society?
2. What factors would most influence and accelerate the benefits of the IoT?
3. Will IoT, including devices that make it, be secure? Perhaps this is the most difficult question to answer. Do you know why?
4. In any communication regime, privacy issues play a vital role. The IoT, as the future backbone of ubiquitous communication, how will privacy be assured? Or can it?
5. With the ubiquitous communication brought about by IoT, interoperability is critical. Can IoT architecture guarantee interoperability?

References

1. Maney K. Meet Kevin Ashton, father of the internet of things. http://www.newsweek.com/2015/03/06/meet-kevin-ashton-father-internet-things-308763.html
2. Gubbia J, Buyyab R, Marusica S, Palaniswamia M. Internet of Things (IoT): a vision, architectural elements, and future directions. Elsevier. http://www.sciencedirect.com/science/article/pii/S0167739X13000241
3. Guillemin P, Friess P. Internet of things strategic research roadmap. The Cluster of European Research Projects, Tech. Rep., September 2009. http://www.internet-of-things-research.eu/pdf/IoT_Cluster_Strategic_Research_Agenda_2009.pdf
4. Morgan J. A simple explanation of 'the internet of things'. http://www.forbes.com/sites/jacobmorgan/2014/05/13/simple-explanation-internet-things-that-anyone-can-understand/#5939c9768284
5. Atzori L, Iera A, Morabito G. The Internet of things: a survey. Computer Networks, Elsevier. http://ac.els-cdn.com/S1389128610001568/1-s2.0-S1389128610001568-main.pdf?_tid=1094eeaa-85ae-11e6-a405-00000aab0f01&acdnat=1475089513_ff39eabceaa7caece0fbe703937e25c1
6. Infographic: The growth of the internet of things. https://www.ncta.com/platform/industry-news/infographic-the-growth-of-the-internet-of-things/
7. Greenough J, Camhi J. Business intelligence. Here are IoT trends that will change the way businesses, governments, and consumers interact with the world, Aug. 29, 2016. http://www.businessinsider.com/top-internet-of-things-trends-2016-1?IR=T
8. Shang W, Yu Y, Droms R. Challenges in IoT networking via TCP/IP architecture. NDN Technical Report NDN-0038, 2016. http://named-data.net/techreports.html
9. Sutaria R, Govindachari R. Understanding the internet of things. http://electronicdesign.com/iot/understanding-internet-things#IoT
10. Schneider S. Understanding the protocols behind the internet of things. http://electronicdesign.com/iot/understanding-protocols-behind-internet-things

11. IoT Standards and Protocols.: http://www.postscapes.com/internet-of-things-protocols/
12. Zaslavsky A, Jayaraman PP (2015) The internet of things: discovery in the internet of things. Ubiquity 2015(October): 1–10
13. IERC. Internet of things IoT governance, privacy and security issues. European research cluster on the internet of things January, 2015. http://www.internet-of-things-research.eu/pdf/IERC_Position_Paper_IoT_Governance_Privacy_Security_Final.pdf
14. Ashiraf QM, Habaebi MH. Introducing autonomy in internet of things. http://www.wseas.us/e-library/conferences/2015/Malaysia/COMP/COMP-27.pdf
15. Kounelis I, Baldini G, Neisse R, Steri G, Tallacchini M, Pereira ÂG. Building trust in the human – Internet of things relationship. IEEEXplore. IEEE Technology and Society Magazine. Winter, 2014. http://ieeexplore.ieee.org/stamp/stamp.jsp?arnumber=6969184

Part V

Securing the Last Frontiers – The Home Front

Conquering the Last Frontier in the Digital Invasion: The Home Front

25

25.1 Introduction

As digital technology conquers new territory and there is ubiquitous use of technology, the last frontier has fallen in the digital invasion and the digital activity hub has come home. It is almost a paradox that as more technological activities have come home to make the lives of millions of people easier and more enjoyable, the threat to their core personal security is directly under attack. Since the early 1950s as digital technology become pervious, the main activity and locus of technological activities invaded the workplace first as the need for improvement in production become paramount. Millions of people took on the task of learning the new technologies as a way to prevent job losses as these new technologies entered the workplace to improve production and hence improve profitability. There were cries of "computers invading the workplace and eating jobs." After a while, we all got used to these new invaders and we became comfortable to work with the job skills they provided. Production skyrocketed and new jobs were created as old olds disappeared and the fear of job losses was overcome and confidence increased among young workers as they entered the workplace with ever-increasing new skills promising enormous fortunes. We saw new technology giants springing up every other day and making millions. With little fanfare and unknowingly, we become members of social networks as we linked up with colleagues and relatives and a million other people we never and we will never know.

We become the netizens and we become connected and linked to the world. We unknowingly became part of the foci of technology we carried in little ever powerful digital devices. Technology now had moved out of the workplace. We carried it whenever and wherever we went. We become unknowing carriers as we couldn't live without those devices. Noticing that as workers carried the little powerful gizmos, they remained productive, employers allowed us to bring the gizmos back to the workplace. Now technology was everywhere.

While all these activities and the silent digital crusade were going on, there is clear demarcation between the home and the workplace. The workplace was a place

© Springer International Publishing AG 2017
J.M. Kizza, *Guide to Computer Network Security*, Computer Communications and Networks, DOI 10.1007/978-3-319-55606-2_25

of production, of making a living, of discovery, and of personal development. The home on the other hand was a place of sanity, serenity, rest, and personal entertainment. The kind of technology that entered the home from was designed to do just that. For example, television, video, and audio technologies directed to the home front were meant to entertain—and they were stand-alone. Instead of becoming small like their production technologies, these homebound technologies became big to enhance realism in entertainment.

These divisions in the two technologies help up for a while. But in the early 2000s, things started to change; an invasion of sorts started to encroach on both technologies—the smartness and intelligence of digital devices whether big or small. Smartness in digital devices started to create a kind of relationship and courtship between the two divergent technologies. As the courtship grows, it started leading to a convergence of telecommunication, computing, and broadcasting technologies—a marriage that was unstoppable. The marriage took place without fanfare and the home front will never be the same. It became, in addition to entertainment, a production front.

More and more people are now working from home for convenience or otherwise. Employers are finding benefits for some kind of employees to work from home. More and more professions are discovering that working from home is more beneficial and profitable that the workplace outside the home. There is now a growing list of production activities that are better done home. In the following sections, we will discuss the enablers of home production.

25.2   The Changing Home Network and Hotspots

The growing and evolving entertainment technology in the home, the advent of the Internet, and the new monitoring home technologies have all turned the home place into the "new wild west" as far as the security and integrity of the home, including house data and individuals in the home, are concerned. Before we look at the data in the home, let us take a look at the way the home network has evolved over the years and the specific entry points into the home. There are several avenues that intruders and hackers can penetrate and access house data at will. Some of the most known of these avenues are:

25.2.1 Cable LAN

For a long time, homes used to have devices offering different functions like entertainment and communication, but these devices were never connected. As more digital devices started to enter the homes, there was a need to interconnect them with cables for easy use, better services, and experience. A central component to connect such devices was needed and it came to be the *router*. Using cables and wires, each house digital device plugs into a designated entry point into the router called a *port*. With this kind of cascading of home devices, a *local area network*

(LAN) is formed in the home, with the router as the central connecting device. A router can have several ports, called RJ45s, which can connect several devices in the house.

A router has two sets of ports, internal ports that connect all devices in the home onto a LAN and one special port, usually designated by a different color or with a word *Uplink*, known as the *wide-area network (WAN) port* [1]. This port, also known as the *Internet port*, connects the router, and hence the hone LAN, to an Internet source, such as a *broadband modem*. The WAN allows the router to connect to the Internet and share that connection with all the Ethernet-ready devices connected to it [1].

25.2.2 Wireless Home Networks

The development and the perverseness of wireless technology in the last few years have created great freedoms for and more mobility of users with mobile devices. This has also increased the use of mobile devices at home leading to the birth of wireless networks in homes. There are several types of wireless networks that can be found in homes:

25.2.2.1 Wireless Personal Area Network (WPANs)

These networks, based on IEEE standard 802.15.4 of 2004, interconnect home devices within a range of between 10 and 100 m with a transfer rate of 250 kbit/s. WPANs networks focus on low-cost, low-speed ubiquitous communication between devices within the range. Devices using this standard, like mobile phones, computers, GPS receivers, digital cameras, and video game consoles, can exchange data and information using the network layers based on the OSI model, although only the lower layers, the physical and MAC layers, are defined in the standard.

According Lou Frenzel [2], the 802.15.4 category is probably the largest standard for low-data-rate WPANs. It has many subcategories including the 802.15.4a/ 802.15.4c for China, 802.15.4d for Japan, 802.15.4e for industrial applications, 802.15.4f for active (battery powered) radio-frequency identification (RFID) uses, and 802.15.4g for smart utility networks for monitoring the smart grid. All of these special versions use the same base radio technology and protocol as defined in 802.15.4a/b.

The 802.15.4 standard defines the physical layer (PHY) and media access control (MAC) layer of the Open Systems Interconnection (OSI) model of network operation (Fig. 25.1). The PHY layer defines frequency, power, modulation, and other wireless conditions of the link. The MAC layer defines the format of the data handling. The remaining layers define other measures for handing the data and related protocol enhancements including the final application [2]. We will see more of these networks in Chap. 18.

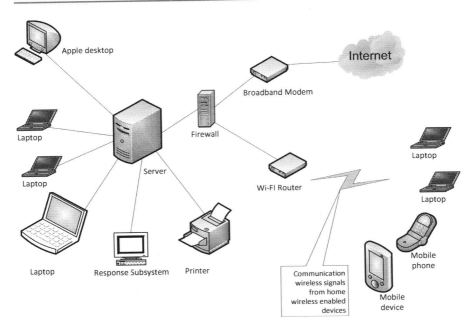

Fig. 25.1 The home LAN

25.2.2.2 Wireless Local Area Networks (WLAN (WI-FI))

This is another short-range, up to 500 m, local area wireless technology that allows an electronic device to exchange data or connect to the Internet using 2.4 GHz UHF and 5 GHz SHF radio waves. Wi-Fi is probably the premier local area network (LAN) technology for high-speed Internet access for mobile devices like laptops, smart phones, tablets, and smart TV sets for video transfer. Wi-Fi-enabled devices, like those we have given, can connect to the Internet when within range of a wireless router which connects to the *broadband modem (access point)*. A broadband modem is a device that bridges the Internet connection from a service provider to the LAN router or a computer, making the Internet available to the home devices [1]. With wireless technology, wireless-enabled devices can connect to one another in the same LAN or outside the LAN without being connected by cables as it used to be. See Fig. 25.1.

Although Wi-Fi ranges are limited, they can be extended with use of several overlapping coverage of access points to cover a large area as large as many square miles. Wi-Fi technology is increasingly being used in private homes, businesses, as well as in public spaces called hotspots usually set up by businesses or public authorities for free-of-charge use. Wi-Fi technology has been standardized as IEEE 802.11. We will see more of this in Chap. 18.

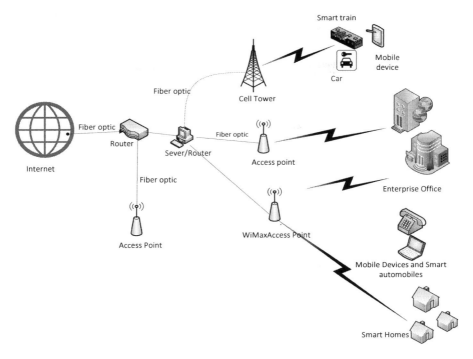

Fig. 25.2 WiMax coverage

25.2.2.3 WiMax LAN

WiMAX (Worldwide Interoperability for Microwave Access) is another limited area wireless communications technology based on IEEE 802–16 standard, designed to extend the range and functionalities of Wi-Fi technology. It provides data rates reaching up to 75 megabits per second (Mb/s) and a number of wireless signaling options ranging anywhere from the 2 GHz range up to 66 GHz, with up to 1 Gbit/s for fixed stations. It can also provide a service range of up to 10 miles. Because of that range, WiMAX can be installed either by a survive provider as base stations or as small receivers installed by clients to connect to the base station. The WiMAX base station then sends and receives data to and from a WiMAX-enabled router, which would then send the data to the different devices in the home LAN. It is possible to combine Wi-Fi with WiMAX by having the router send the data to the devices via Wi-Fi server. See Fig. 25.2.

As a step above DSL and cable modem, WiMAX protocol accommodates a whole range of data transmission protocols that both cable modems and DSL cannot, so far, like Voice Over Internet Protocol (VoIP). VoIP allows making local, long-distance, and even international calls through a broadband Internet connection possible. As we look forward, we will scale up city size *metropolitan area network* (MAN). See more in Chap. 18.

25.2.2.4 4G and LTE LAN

The last of the extension of the home LAN is the current 4G technology and its enhancement by LTE (Long-Term Evolution) LAN. The combo has created a wireless broadband technology designed to support roaming Internet access via cell phones and handheld devices. Nearly all devices running 4G and LTE technologies can also be part of the home inventory, and we will consider this technology as home-based technology to join the other three we have so far discussed. LTE, as a newer technology, its communication protocols are based on Internet Protocol (IP). Because of this, it offers a variety of communication protocols that the older technologies could not offer including VoIP- and other IP-based services. LTE can theoretically support downloads at 300 Mbps or more based on experimental trials. Finally, because it is still a new technology, it is only available in limited geographic areas, but it is growing after getting early support from telecommunications providers.

25.2.2.5 5G Wireless Technology

In Sect. 18.2.4 we briefly discussed 4G and associated LTE technology and the anticipated rollout of 5G technologies. These technologies are indeed enhancing mobile broadband, adding new exciting feature and increasing speed and footprint.

25.2.3 Types of Broadband Internet Connections

Doug Ngo [1] gives three types of broadband Internet connections as:

*   *Wired Internet (residential broadband)*: In this category, the home LAN is connected to the Internet via a physical cable such as a telephone line (DSL) or a cable line (cable), or a fiber optic line (FIOS). This is one of the good options for a home LAN because with it, there are no data caps or at least very high caps, so users don't need to worry about how much they download or upload.
*   *Satellite Internet (satellite broadband)*: With satellite broadband, the home LAN connection to the Internet is via a satellite disk, probably on the roof, which communicates with satellites to provide the LAN with Internet access. Although satellite Internet is slower and more expensive, it is a great, probably the only, option for remote areas with no cable, DSL, or FIOS services.
*   *Cellular Internet (wireless broadband)*: With this option, the LAN Internet connection is made possible via a cell phone signal to carry data and connect the supported device directly to the Internet. There are several cellular data standards, and starting with 3G, it's fast enough to be called "broadband." The latest standard, 4G LTE, offers the speed equivalent to that of a midrange residential broadband connection (somewhere between 5 Mbps and 20 Mbps download speed).

25.2.4 Smart Home Devices

For generation, the home has been a source of entertainment for the family and guest to the family. Throughout history, the family as an entertainment center has seen a growing number of gadgets to enhance entertainment. As technology started invading the home, it came via the entertainment devices. With changing technologies, the evolving entertainment menu, and the need to enhance the integrity and security of the family, a new role of technology in the home, beyond entertainment, of monitoring the home was born. This new role brought to the home a new breed of digital devices that will later turn into a security problem as we will soon discuss.

25.3 Data and Activities in the Home LAN

With the miniaturization of digital devices, there is a new breed of medical monitoring and wearable devices are in people's home. More and more people are wearing health supporting and monitoring devices that are actually connected or are able to connect to the Internet. There are now devices that are remotely regulating or delivering medicines to patients in their homes via the Internet. These kinds of devices are increasing. Also there are an increasing number and caliber of digital devices that are meant to monitor the integrity and security of the home letting the owner from afar know in real time or near real time, or through alerts, the status of the home. It used to be that the types of data that were most common in the home network were pictures, usually from family vacations and valued occasions of family like weddings and family get together, videos of family events, and various personal data files usually stored on the family computer hard drive. Given the changing nature and utility of the family network, although these data are still being stored in the family LAN, a lot more data types have come home too.

25.3.1 Work Data

The growth of work at home movement that started in the late 1980s has changed the home LAN, not only by bringing in new technologies but also bringing in the home enterprise data. Home workers routinely download and upload and consequently store enterprise data on the home LAN in their routine work. Also the new movement of bring your own device (BYOD) to the enterprise premises is creating avenues where employees are bringing enterprise data on their devices knowingly or otherwise. Mobile devices have a way of collecting and sometimes storing data either from the enterprise spaces or public commons.

25.3.2 Social Media Data

The increasing use of smart and more powerful mobile devices are increasing the amount of both personal and public data brought into the home LAN by these mobile devices from social media and from public commons.

25.3.3 Banking and Investment Data

Long lines in banks are numbered as more and more bank customers are running home to do their banking in the comfort of their homes. The banks themselves are encouraging this through advertising of online banking. Most people that do online banking do it either after work or on weekends, most at home. Doing any online banking activity on the home LAN transfers sensitive data back and forth between the family LAN and the banker servers. It is not only banking that invades the home LAN but also investment activities are not far behind. Again most people who have investments check invest and trade mostly after work or on weekends, again using the home LAN. Doing these activities, like in banking, a considerable amount of data is exchanged between the home LAN and the investment house servers. Some of this data and the trail of activities are stored in histories on the home LAN.

25.3.4 Health Devices

It has taken a while, but at last medical technology has become of age. In fact among all the sectors, the medical sector has seen the fastest growing and more promising technologies in the last several years. As providers, hospitals, and health insurance companies are fighting for consumer dollars, technology is coming in to the rescue. Health insurance providers in order to cut on long and expensive hospital stays are encouraging health providers to embrace and use technologies that enable patients to have operations and leave hospitals in a day or two. These patients and many other healthcare types are increasingly getting follow-up care at home. Medications, monitoring signals, and patient data information are usually and commonly uploaded on the family LAN, and many times this data stay stored either on the family LAN or LAN histories.

25.3.5 Home Monitoring and Security Devices

The growth in monitoring technology in the last few years has opened a flood gate in home monitoring. The usual movement sensor monitoring that home security providers like ADT used to offer is now archaic. All types of sensors are now packaged in minute, well-hidden devices that can be remotely controlled via the family LAN. We have already discussed the use of the family LAN to penetrate and take control of the family electronic devices through the electric meter. The marriage between the electric and cyber signals in the family LAN has made the remote control of most family devices and family electronic data a reality and has created a security quagmire in the home. No home, no home LAN is secure anymore.

25.4 Threats to the Home and Home LAN

As we pointed out before, the home front, as the last frontier of invasion to personal security and privacy, has become the "new wild west." What is more worrying is that the individuals in the home front, unlike their counterparts in the workplace, are less knowledgeable and far less prepared to deal with the intruders. In a way, they are helpless in a sense that they may not know what is or may happen to their home, data and home devices, and, more frightening, their personal lives because hackers can now use physical harm to individuals in the home. Even if they come to know, they may not be able to do anything to stop it. In "Hacking Home Automation Systems Through Your Power Lines," Kim Zetter [3] details how hackers can attack a home or even a business automation and security systems though power lines. Using this conduit, the hackers can, through remote commands, take control of a multitude of devices, such as lights, electronic locks, heating and air conditioning systems, and security alarms and cameras. The systems operate on Ethernet networks that communicate over the existing power lines in a home, sending signals back and forth to control devices. Beyond taking control of your devices, hackers can also introduce sniffers to the broadband power network through an electrical outlet and sniff the signals in the home to know what is going on in the home using already installed security and monitoring devices such motion sensors and image cameras.

What is worrying is that these cheap systems are running on open-source tools to conduct the hacks. Although most of the current tools are more successful on home systems running non-encrypted protocols, very soon, even systems supporting encryptions may be attacked as encryptions are increasingly being broken by hackers.

The tools and attacks to the home are varied and are on the increase. Attack types are also changing. With attackers now able to remotely enter the home, they are now able to reprogram the house devices to do things unimaginable including opening doors, jamming home security, and monitoring signals thus able to prevent security signals from ever reaching home security and monitoring companies, the police, and even the home owner.

As we have seen above, growth in medical and monitoring technologies are increasingly allowing an increasing number of patients to receiver care from their homes. With this kind of increasing potential attacks on home systems, the future of health home care is also in jeopardy.

Let us discuss a few of the major steps individuals can do to mitigate, if not stop, a home invasion by hackers for whatever reason. First, we will look at the most common threats to the home and home LAN.

25.4.1 Most Common Threats to Homes and Home LANs

The most common methods used by intruders to gain control of home computers are briefly described by CERT in "Home Network Security" [4]:

- Trojan horse programs—Trojan horse programs are social engineering programs sent by introducers and designed to make you trust them as they introduce access traps for easy access into the home LAN.
- Back door and remote administration programs—common on Windows computers, there are three tools used by intruders to gain remote access to the house LAN. The tools are BackOrifice, Netbus, and SubSeven. These tools allow access and control house LAN.
- Denial of service—this attack, common in the 1990s, causes digital devices on the home LAN to crash or to become so busy processing data that you are unable to use it.
- Mobile code (Java/JavaScript/ActiveX)—code from these Web programming languages is executed by most computer Web browser. This code can be used by intruders to gather or to run malicious code on any computer on the family LAN. Read more about this at http://www.cert.org/archive/pdf/activeX_report.pdf
- Cross-site scripting—this is malicious script moved around the Internet by computers visiting servers sitting these scripts. There are several ways a LAN computer can expose the family LAN to these types of code [4]:
  - Following links in Web pages, e-mail messages, or newsgroup postings without knowing what they link to
  - Using interactive forms on an untrustworthy site
  - Viewing online discussion groups, forums, or other dynamically generated pages where users can post text containing HTML tags
- E-mail spoofing—E-mail "spoofing" is a way to trick a user to believe an e-mail is coming from a specific source when it is actually coming from another. Spoofed e-mail can range from harmless pranks to social engineering ploys.
- E-mail-borne viruses—transporting and spreading viruses via e-mails. Most viruses are actually transported and spread using e-mails attachments.
- Hidden file extensions—Windows operating systems "file extension hiding," if not disabled, can be exploited by e-mail-borne viruses. So these file extension hiding options, whether in Windows systems or other products, which are usually defaults, must be disabled.
- Packet sniffing—these are programs deposited at strategic points of the Internet to capture data from information packets as they travel over the network. They can attach any designated network including the family LAN.

25.4.2 Actions to Safeguard the Family LAN

The most recommended steps a home owner and home LAN user can take are again CERT [4]:

- Consult your system support personnel if you work from home.
- Use virus protection software.
- Use a firewall.
- Don't open unknown e-mail attachments.
- Don't run programs of unknown origin.
- Disable hidden filename extensions.
- Keep all applications (including your operating system) patched.
- Turn off your computer or disconnect from the network when not in use.
- Disable Java, JavaScript, and ActiveX if possible.
- Disable scripting features in e-mail programs.
- Make regular backups of critical data.
- Make a boot disk in case your computer is damaged or compromised.

For more details of each one of these, the reader is referred to [4].

25.4.3 Using Encryption to Protect the Family LAN

The wireless family LAN has not only brought convenience in the use of home devices but has also brought ease of use and a far greater exposure and outreach of the family computer and other devices via the Internet. However, wireless technology has also brought more problems to the family with a wireless LAN. While wired home networks are confined by their connected wires, to send and receive data from specified points of the network, wireless networks, on the other hand, broadcast data in every direction to every device that happens to be listening, within a limited range [5]. Because of this, the security and integrity of the devices and the wireless LAN in the family is at risk. More directed steps, therefore, are called for to mitigate these risks.

As more advanced wireless communication technologies are developed, there is a need for stronger and more focused encryption protocols. Along the way, therefore, various wireless security protocols have been developed to protect home wireless networks. These wireless security protocols include WEP, WPA, and WPA2, each with their own strengths and weaknesses. These new wireless encryption protocols have improved the prevention of uninvited guests from connecting to the family LAN and have further helped to harden private data by encrypting it as it leaves and enters the family LAN. Lawrence C. Miller in "The Essentials of Setting Up a Wireless Network: Wireless Security Protocols: WEP, WPA, and WPA2" [5] discusses the three most popular protocols as follows [5]:

- *Wired Equivalent Privacy (WEP)*: The original encryption protocol developed for wireless networks. It was designed to provide the same level of security as wired networks, but WEP suffers from many well-known security flaws, it is difficult to configure, and it is easily broken.
- *Wi-Fi-Protected Access (WPA)*: To further harden the wireless network, a newer protocol, WPA, was developed as an interim security enhancement over WEP,

while the 802.11i wireless security standard was being developed. Most current WPA implementations use a pre-shared key (PSK), commonly referred to as *WPA Personal*, and the Temporal Key Integrity Protocol (TKIP, pronounced *tee-kip*) for encryption. *WPA Enterprise* uses an authentication server to generate keys or certificates.

- *Wi-Fi-Protected Access version 2 (WPA2)*: Based on the 802.11i wireless security standard, which was finalized in 2004. It enhanced WPA by introducing the use of the Advanced Encryption Standard (AES) for encryption. The security provided by AES is far superior to that of WPA. The US government uses it to encrypt information classified as top secret.

25.4.4 Protecting the Family LAN with Known Protocols

Although Wi-Fi LANs provide many benefits to a family using it, but as we pointed out earlier, WI-FI LANs broadcast data in every direction to every device that happens to be listening, within a limited range. Unprotected WI-FI LANs can result in unauthorized use and potential harm to the family LAN and those in the family. Family WI-FI LANs, therefore, need to be protected with the most efficient encryption protocols available to the user. In "Protecting Your Wireless Network," the US Federal Communications Commissions—Consumer Task Force [6] suggests the following security steps should be taken:

- *Turn encryption on*—Turn on the WI-FI LAN router's encryption setting right after installing the router. As the router comes out of the box, the encryption feature is usually disabled. Use "WPA2" the most current and most effective. When turning on WPA2, choose a longer password that utilizes a combination of letters, numbers, and symbols for better security.
- *Turn the firewall on*—In addition to turning on WPA2 at installation, also turn on the firewall to protect the LAN from harmful intrusions. Firewalls can be hardware based or software based. Wireless routers generally contain built-in firewalls, but are sometimes shipped with the firewall turned off. So it is important and recommended to check and see if the wireless router's firewall is turned on.
- *Change default passwords*—Most wireless routers come with preset passwords for administering the devices settings (this is different from the password used to access the wireless network itself). Unauthorized users may be familiar with the default passwords, so it is important to change the router device's password as soon as it is installed. Again, longer passwords made up of a combination of letters, numbers, and symbols are more secure.
- *Change the default name of the network*—A network's name is known as its "SSID" (service set identifier). When a computer with a wireless connection searches for and displays the wireless networks nearby, it lists each network that publicly broadcasts its SSID. Manufacturers usually give all of their wireless routers a default SSID, which is often the company's name. It is a good practice

to change the LAN's SSID. Never use personal information such as the names of family members.

- *Turn network name broadcasting off*—Wireless routers may broadcast the name of the network (the "SSID") to the general public. This feature is often useful for businesses and institutions offering free WI-FI to the public. For personal or family Wi-Fi networks, turn this feature off.
- *Use the MAC address filter*—Every device that can connect to a Wi-Fi network has a unique ID called the "physical address" or "MAC" (media access control) address. Wireless routers can screen the MAC addresses of all devices that connect to them, and users can set their wireless network to accept connections only from devices with MAC addresses that the router is set to recognize. In order to create another obstacle to unauthorized access, change the family LAN's router settings to activate its MAC address filter to include only the LAN authorized devices.

Exercises

1. Discuss why the home front is the last digital frontier of the digital invasion.
2. Discuss with evidence why the home front is the "new wild west" in personal privacy and security.
3. Why is the home LAN user in a more precarious state than an enterprise LAN user.
4. Discuss the growing hacker invasion and the pending potential threat to the home devices and home LAN security.
5. What are the security imperative of a home LAN user not knowing or ignoring putting security measures in the family LAN.
6. Based on your current knowledge, what must be done to stop or mitigate this pending Armageddon?
7. Do you think this is a mere small threat or a pending catastrophe?
8. How should the home LAN user be alerted or trained to meet the pending threat?
9. Given what you know, should working from home be discouraged?
10. Should corporations and businesses be responsible for the security of the family LAN for those working from home?

Advanced Exercises

1. Develop an application that can be used to run a security assessment of a family LAN.
2. Develop an application that can intercept and prevent a home-based medical device to be hacked in to save a life.
3. Develop an application that alerts a home LAN user of a penetration attempt and suggest quick remedies to mitigate prevent the intrusion.
4. Develop a series of remedies for a home LAN intrusion and develop applications for each.

5. Develop a menu of security applications for a family LAN capable of intercepting an intrusion into a family LAN and generating a corresponding alert.

References

1. Ngo D. CNET, Home networking explained, Part 4: Wi-Fi vs. Internet. http://www.cnet.com/how-to/home-networking-explained-part-4-wi-fi-vs-internet/
2. Frenzel L. What's the difference between IEEE 802.15.4 and ZigBee wireless? March 22, 2013, Electronic Design. http://electronicdesign.com/what-s-difference-between/what-s-difference-between-ieee-802154-and-zigbee-wireless
3. Zetter K. Hacking home automation systems through your power lines. Wired. http://www.wired.com/2011/08/hacking-home-automation/
4. CERT. Home network security. http://www.cert.org/historical/tech_tips/home_networks.cfm?#IV-A-1
5. Miller LC. The essentials of setting up a wireless network: wireless security protocols: WEP, WPA, and WPA2. Home Networking Do-It-Yourself For Dummies. http://www.dummies.com/how-to/content/wireless-security-protocols-wep-wpa-and-wpa2.html
6. Protecting your wireless network. Federal Communications Commissions – Consumer Task Force. http://www.fcc.gov/guides/protecting-your-wireless-network

Part VI

Hands-On Projects

Projects

26

26.1 Introduction

This is a special chapter dealing with security projects. We have arranged the projects in four parts. *Part 1* consists of current case study projects from two successful National Science Foundation (NSF) funded workshops at the authors university. *Part 2* consists of projects that can be done on a weekly or biweekly basis. *Part 3* consists of projects that can be done in a group or individually on a semi-semester or on a semester basis. Projects in *Part 4* may demand a great deal of work and may require extensive research to be done. Some of the projects in this part may fulfill a master's or even Ph.D. degree project requirements. We have tried as much as possible throughout these projects to encourage instructors and students to use open source as much as possible. This will decouple the content of the *Guide* from the rapidly changing proprietary software market.

26.2 Part 1: Case Studies

These links below are for Cryptographic and Mobile security hands-on projected and case studies from two successful National Science Foundation (NSF)-funded workshops at the author's university. They contain extensive hands-on labs and case studies for a variety of problems.

- Teaching Cryptography Using Hands-on Labs and Case Studies— http://web2. utc.edu/~djy471/cryptography/crypto.htm
- Capacity Building Through Curriculum and Faculty Development on Mobile Security—http://www.utc.edu/faculty/li-yang/mobilesecurity.php

As instructors using this Guide, I suggest that Part 1 should be the first port of call.

© Springer International Publishing AG 2017   551
J.M. Kizza, *Guide to Computer Network Security*, Computer Communications and Networks, DOI 10.1007/978-3-319-55606-2_26

26.3 Part 2: Weekly/Biweekly Laboratory Assignments

Projects in this part were drawn up with several objectives in mind. One is that students in a network security course must be exposed to hands-on experience as much as possible. However, we also believe that students, while getting hands-on experience, must also learn as much as they can about the field of security. Since no one can effectively cover in one course all areas of computer and network security, we must find a way to accomplish as much of this as possible without compromising the level needed in the few core areas covered by the course. Our second objective, therefore, is to cover as broad an area of both computer and network security issues as possible. We do this by sending the students out on a scavenger hunt and requiring them to study and learn as much as possible on their own.

For each of the selected areas the students must cover, they must write a paper. They doubly benefit, for not only do they learn about security in the broadest sense possible but they also learn to communicate, a crucial element in the security profession. Security professionals must investigate, analyze, and produce reports. By including report writing in the course on security, we accomplish, on the side, an important task.

Laboratory # 1

Exploratory (2 weeks)—to make students understand the environment and appreciate the field of network security

Study computer and network vulnerabilities and exploits (see Chaps. 4 and 7). In an essay of not less than three and not more than five double-spaced typed pages, discuss ten such exploits and/or vulnerabilities, paying attention to the following:

- Routing algorithm vulnerabilities: route and sequence number spoofing, instability, and resonance effects
- TCP/UDP vulnerabilities
- Denial of service
- ARP hazard: phantom sources, ARP explosions, and slow links
- Registry vulnerabilities
- Fragmentation vulnerabilities and remedies (ICMP echo overrun)

Laboratory # 2

Exploratory (2 weeks)—to make students aware of the availability of an array of solutions to secure the networks

Research and study the available software and hardware techniques to deter, if not eliminate, computer systems attacks. (See Part 3 of the text). Write a comparative discussion paper (minimum three and maximum five double-spaced pages) on five such techniques, paying attention to the following:

- Encryption techniques (DNSSEC, IPSec, PGP, S/MIME, S-HTTP, and HTTPS).
- Intrusion detection and prevention.
- Computer and network forensic techniques.
- Firewalls (DMZ).
- Secure network infrastructure services: DNS, NTP, and SNMP.
- Secure binding of multimedia streams: Secure RTP/Secure RPC.
- Access control and authentication: Secure RSVP.
- Mobile systems: WEP and WPA.
- Internet security models: IPv4/v6 encapsulation headers in IPSec.

Laboratory # 3

Exploratory (2 weeks)—to make students aware of the role and weaknesses of operating systems in network and data security

Research four major operating systems' vulnerabilities and write a five-page double-spaced paper on these vulnerabilities for each operating system.

Consider the following operating systems:

- Unix (and other varieties of Unix such as FreeBSD and OpenBSD)
- Linux
- Windows (NT, 2000, XP, etc.)
- OS/2
- Mac OS X
- Any mobile OS

Laboratory # 4

(1 week): A look at the security of Windows, Linux, and any mobile OS—to give students hands-on experience of handling security of the major operating systems today. A student picks one of these platforms and studies it for weaknesses and vulnerabilities and what is being done to harden it. A student then can make an oral presentation to the class on the findings.

Laboratory # 5

(1 week): Installation and maintenance of firewalls—to give students the experience of installing and maintaining a peripheral (fencing) security component of both small and large enterprise networks. There are plenty of open source and free firewalls. Also a number of companies on the Web offer a variety of firewalls both in software and ready configured hardware. Some of these companies offer free personal firewalls; others offer high-end but limited corporate firewalls you can download on a trial basis. Check out companies on the Web, and if you are not already using a firewall, download one for free or on a trial basis.

Install it and run it. Here is a list of some of the companies with good software firewalls:

- McAfee—www.mcafee.com (personal)
- Symantec—www.symantec.com (professional/personal)
- Sygate Personal Firewall—www.sygate.com
- Tiny Personal Firewall—www.tinysoftware.com
- ZoneAlarm Pro—www.zonelabs.com

Firewall policies: As you install your firewall, decide on the following:

- Whether you will let Internet users in your organization upload files to the network server
- What about letting them download?
- Will the network have a Web server? Will inside/outside people access the server?
- Will the site have telnet?

Laboratory # 6

(2 weeks): Research on key and certificate management to acquaint the students to the new and developing trends in key management: techniques that are leading to new security and customer confidence tools in e-commerce. In a three- to five-page double-spaced paper, discuss key management issues (Chaps. 10, 11, and 17). In particular, pay attention to:

- DNS certificates
- Key agreement protocols: STS protocol and IETF work orders
- Key distribution protocols: Kerberos, PGP, X.509, S/MIME, and IPSec
- SSL, SET, and digital payment systems
- One-time passwords: schemes based on S/KEY
- Session key management: blind-key cryptosystems (NTP)
- Secure access control and management: Secure SNMP
- Certificate authorities (CAs)

Laboratory # 7

(1 week): Network-based and host-based intrusion detection systems (IDS) and prevention. The laboratory is to give students practical experience in safeguarding a network, scanning for vulnerabilities and exploits, downloading and installation of scanning software, and scanning a small network. Options for scanning are *SATAN, LANguard Network Scanner* (Windows), and *Nmap*. For an IDS system, use *Snort*. See Part 2 for installation information.

Laboratory # 8

(1 week): Develop a security policy for an enterprise network to enable students to acquire the experience of starting from scratch and designing a functioning security system for an enterprise, an experience that is vital in the network security community. Write a three- to five-page double-spaced paper on the security policy you have just developed.

Laboratory # 9

Set up a functioning VPN. There are a variety of sources for materials on how to set up a VPN.

Laboratory # 10

Any project the instructor may find as having a culminating security experience

26.4   Part 3: Semester Projects

This part focuses on security tools that can make your network secure. We divide the tools into three parts: intrusion detection tools, network reconnaissance and scanning tools, and Web-based security protocols.

26.4.1 Intrusion Detection Systems

There are a number of free IDS that can be used for both network-based and host-based intrusion detection. Some of the most common are Snort and TCPdump.

26.4.1.1 Installing Snort (www.snort.org)

Snort is a free network analysis tool that can be used as a packet sniffer like TCPdump, a packet logger, or as a network intrusion detection system. Year after year, Snort has been excelling at traffic analysis and packet logging on IP networks (see more on network traffic analytics at http://www.smarter.com/se--qq-traffic%2Banalysis.html). Through protocol analysis, content searching, and various preprocessors, Snort detects thousands of worms, vulnerability exploit attempts, port scans, and other suspicious behaviors.

Developed in 1998 by Martin Roesch, it has been undergoing improvements. These improvements have made Snort highly portable, and now it can run on a variety of platforms including Linux, Solaris, BSD, IRIX, HP-UX, MacOS X, Win 32, and many more.

Also Snort is highly configurable allowing users, after installation, to create their own rules, from a flexible rule-based language to describe traffic for collecting or passing on, using a modular detection engine, and reconfigure its base functionality using its plug-in interface. For Web interface analysis of Snort alerts, see Basic Analysis and Security Engine (BASE) at http://base.secureideas.net/.

For this project, you need to:

- Take note of the operating system you are using.
- Choose the type of Snort to use based on your operating system.
- Download a free Snort Users' Manual.
- Download free Snort and install it.
- Analyze a Snort ASCII output.
- Read Snort rules and learn the different rules of handling Snort outputs.

Note: A Snort performance ASCII output has the following fields:

- Name of alert.
- *Time and date* (such as 06/05–12:04:54.7856231)—to mark the time the packet was sent. The last trailing floating number (.7856231) is a fraction of a second included to make the logging more accurate, given that within a second, many events can occur.
- *Source address* (192.163.0.115.15236)—IP source address. (.15236) is the port number. Using this string, it may be easy to deduce whether the traffic is originating from a client or server.
- (>)—direction of traffic.
- *Destination address* (192.168.1.05.www).
- *TCP options that can be set (port type, time to live, type of service, session ID, IP length, datagram length)*—they are set at the time a connection is made.
- *Don't fragment (DF)*.
- *S-Flags(P = PSH, R = RST, S = SYN, or F = FIN)*.
- *Sequence number* (5678344:5678346(2))—the first is the initial sequence number followed by the ending sequence number and (2) indicates the number of bytes transmitted.
- *Acknowledgment # (3456789)*.
- *Win (MSS)*—window size. MSS = maximum segment size. If the client sends packets bigger than the maximum window size, the server may drop them.
- *Hex payload* [56 78 34 90 6D 4F, ...].
- Human-readable format

26.4.1.2 Installation of *TCPdump* (http://www.tcpdump.org/)

TCPdump is a powerful command line network monitoring tool and packet analyzer and *libpcap*, a portable C/C++ library for network traffic capture. TCPdump was developed by the Department of Energy at Lawrence Livermore Laboratory and, as a freeware, is used extensively in intrusion detection.

To use TCPdump, do the following:

- Take note of the operating system you are using.
- Choose the type of Snort to use based on your operating system.

- Download and install TCPdump.
- Run a TCPdump trace.
- Analyze a TCPdump trace.

Note: In analyzing, consider each field of a TCPdump output. A normal TCPdump output has nine fields as follows:

- *Time* (such as 12:04:54.7856231) to mark the time the packet was sent. The last trailing floating number (.7856231) is a fraction of a second included to make the logging more accurate, given that within a second, many events can occur.
- *Interface* (ethX for Linux, hmeX for Solaris, and BSD-based systems, varied with platform)—interface being monitored.
- (>)—direction of traffic
- *Source address* (192.163.0.115.15236)—IP source address. (.15236) is the port number. Using this string, it may be easy to deduce whether the traffic is originating from a client or server.
- *Destination address* (192.168.1.05.www).
- *S-Flags(P = PSH, R = RST, S = SYN, or F = FIN)*.
- *Sequence number* (5678344:5678346(2))—the first is the initial sequence number followed by the ending sequence number and (2) indicates the number of bytes transmitted.
- *Win (MSS)*—window size. MSS = maximum segment size. If the client sends packets bigger than the maximum window size, the server may drop them.
- *TCP options that can be set*—they are set at the time a connection is made.
- *Don't fragment (DF)*—contains fragment information. If the size of the datagram exceeds the MTU (maximum transmission unit of an IP datagram), then fragmentation occurs.

Read more about TCPdump and the latest releases at http://www.tcpdump.org/.

26.4.1.3 Nping (http://nmap.org/nping/)

Nping is an open-source tool for network packet generation, response analysis, and response time measurement. Still in its infancy stages (Developed in 2009, as "Google Summer of Code"), Nping can generate network packets for a wide range of protocols, allowing users to have full control over protocol headers. While Nping can be used as a simple ping utility to detect active hosts, it can also be used as a raw packet generator for network stack stress testing, ARP poisoning, denial-of-service attacks, route tracing, etc. Nping's novel echo mode lets users see how packets change in transit between the source and destination hosts. Nping's features include:

- Custom TCP, UDP, ICMP, and ARP packet generation
- Support for multiple target host specification
- Support for multiple target port specification
- Unprivileged modes for non-root users

- Support for Ethernet frame generation
- Support for IPv6 (currently experimental)
- Runs on Linux, Mac OS, and MS Windows
- Route tracing capabilities
- Highly customizable
- Free and open source

26.4.2 Scanning Tools for System Vulnerabilities

26.4.2.1 Scans with Nmap (www.insecure.org)

Nmap for Network Mapper was created by Fyodor and is free under the GNU Public License (GPL). Nmap is a network-wide port scan and OS detection tool that audits the security of the network. Nmap traces are easily detected because it leaves a signature trail. Scans can be made more difficult by adding a few features such as stealth scanning and Xmas. For this exercise, do the following:

- Download Nmap and install it.
- Scan a selected network.
- Download additional features like Xman, SYN-FIN, and stealth scanning.
- Show how these help in creating a less detectable scanning tool.

26.5   The Following Tools Are Used to Enhance Security in Web Applications

26.5.1 Public Key Infrastructure

The aim of the project is to make students learn the basic concepts of a public key infrastructure (PKI) and its components. Get a free PKI tool from http://pki.winsite.com/, a WinSite specialty archive site. Among the activities to carry out in the project are the following:

- Identify trusted root certificate authorities.
- Design a certificate authority.
- Create a certification authority hierarchy.
- Manage a public key infrastructure.
- Configure certificate enrollment.
- Configure key archival and recovery.
- Configure trust between organizations.

26.5.1.1 Configuring E-Mail Security

In Chap. 17, we discussed at length the different ways of securing e-mail on the Internet. This project focuses on that. So read Chap. 17. The project will teach you how to implement secure e-mail messages in PGP. You will need to do the following:

- Go to http://www.pgpi.org/products/pgp/versions/freeware/ to pick up a PGP free version for your operating system.
- Install PGP on your computer:
  - Create your own keys.
  - Publicize your public key.
  - Import new PGP keys.
  - Encrypt a text message to send to a friend.
  - Decrypt a message from a friend encrypted with PGP.
  - Encrypt/decrypt a file with PGP.
  - Wipe a file with PGP.

26.6   Part 4: Research Projects

26.6.1 Consensus Defense

One of the weaknesses of the current global network is the lack of consensus within the network. When one node or system is attacked, that node or system has no way of making an emergency distress call to all other systems starting with the nearest neighbor so that others should get their defenses up for the eminent attack. This project is to design a system that can trigger an SOS message to the nearest neighbors to get their defenses up. The system should also include, where possible, all information the node being attacked can get about the attacking agent.

26.6.2 Specialized Security

Specialized security is vital to the defense of networks. A viable specialized security shell should be able to utilize any organization's specific attributes and peculiarities to achieve a desired level of security for that organization. This project is to design a security shell that can be used by any organization to put in its desired attributes and whatever peculiarities that organization may have in order to achieve its desired level of security.

26.6.3 Protecting an Extended Network

Enterprise network resources are routinely extended to users outside the organization, usually partner organizations and sometimes customers. This, of course, opens up huge security loopholes that must be plugged to secure network resources. We want to design an automated security system that can be used to screen external user access, mitigate risks, and automatically deal with, report, and recover from an incident, if one occurs.

26.6.4 Automated Vulnerability Reporting

Currently, reporting of system vulnerabilities and security incidents is still a manual job. It is the responsibility of the system administrator to scan and sort threats and incidents before reporting them to the national reporting centers. However, as we all know, this approach is both slow and is itself prone to errors (human and system). We are looking for an automated system that can capture, analyze, sort, and immediately and simultaneously report such incidents to both the system administrator and the national reporting center of choice.

26.6.5 Turn-Key Product for Network Security Testing

Most network attacks are perpetuated through network protocol loopholes. Additional weak points are also found in application software in the top most layers of the protocol stack. If security is to be tackled head on, attention should be focused on these two areas. This project is aimed at designing a turn-key product that a network administrator can use to comprehensively comb both the network protocol and the system application software for those sensitive loopholes. Once these weak points are identified, the administrator can then easily plug them.

26.6.6 The Role of Local Networks in the Defense of the National Critical Infrastructure

In the prevailing security realities of the time, local networks, as the building blocks of the national critical infrastructure, have become a focal point of efforts to defend the national infrastructure. While the federal government is responsible for managing threat intelligence and efforts to deter security threats on the national infrastructure, the defense of local networks is the responsibility of local authorities, civic leaders, and enterprise managers. One of the techniques to defend the thousands of local spheres of influence is the ability of these local units to be able to automatically separate themselves off the national grid in the event of a huge "bang" on the grid. This project is meant to design the technology that can be used by local networks to achieve this.

26.6.7 Enterprise VPN Security

The growth of Internet use in enterprise communication and the need for security assurance of enterprise information have led to the rapid growth and use of VPN technology. VPN technology has been a technology of choice for securing enterprise networks over public network infrastructure. Although emphasis has been put on the software side of VPN implementation which looks like a more logical thing, information in enterprise VPNs has not been secured to a desired level. This means that other aspects of VPN security need to be explored. Several aspects including implementation, policy, and enterprise organization, among many others, need to be researched. This project requires the researcher to look for ways of improving VPN security by critically examining these complementary security issues.

26.6.8 Perimeter Security

Although the perimeter of the traditional network has changed, it still remains the cornerstones of cyber system defense. We assume that all the things we want to protect should be enclosed within the perimeter. The perimeter, therefore, separates the "bad Internet" outside from the protected network. Firewalls have been built for this very purpose. Yet we still dream of a perfect security within the protected networks. Is it possible to design a penetration-proof perimeter defense?

26.6.9 Enterprise Security

Security threats to an enterprise originate from both within and outside the enterprise. While threats originating from outside can be dealt with to some extent, with a strong regime of perimeter defense, internal threats are more difficult to deal with. One way to deal with this elusive internal problem is to develop a strong and effective security policy. But many from the security community are saying that an effective security policy and strong enforcement of it are not enough. Security is still lacking. In this project, study, research, and devise additional ways to protect the enterprises against internal threats.

26.6.10 Password Security: Investigating the Weaknesses

One of the most widely used system access control security techniques is the use of passwords. However, it has been known that system access and authorization based on passwords alone are not safe. Passwords are at times cracked. But password access as a security technique remains the most economically affordable and widely used technique in many organizations because of its bottom line. For this project, research and devise ways to enhance the security of the password system access.

Index

© Springer International Publishing AG 2017
J.M. Kizza, *Guide to Computer Network Security*, Computer Communications
and Networks, DOI 10.1007/978-3-319-55606-2

Made in the USA
Middletown, DE
17 April 2021